issues
FACING
CHRISTIANS
TODAY

4th EDITION

issues
FACING
CHRISTIANS
TODAY

4th EDITION

JOHN
STOTT

FULLY REVISED and UPDATED by ROY MCCLOUGHRY,
with a NEW CHAPTER by JOHN WYATT

ZONDERVAN.com/
AUTHORTRACKER
follow your favorite authors

We want to hear from you. Please send your comments about this book to us in care of zreview@zondervan.com. Thank you.

Issues Facing Christians Today
Copyright © 1984, 1990, 1999, and 2006 by John Stott

Requests for information should be addressed to:
Zondervan, Grand Rapids, Michigan 49530

Library of Congress Cataloging-in-Publication Data

Stott, John R. W.
    Issues facing Christians today / John Stott. — 4th ed., fully rev. and updated / by Roy McCloughry ; with an additional chapter by John Wyatt.
        p.   cm.
    Rev. ed. of: Human rights & human wrongs.
    Includes bibliographical references and index.
    ISBN-10: 0-310-25269-5
    ISBN-13: 978-0-310-25269-6
    1. Christian sociology. 2. Church and social problems. 3. Evangelicalism. 4. Christian life. I. McCloughry, Roy. II. Wyatt, John. III. Stott, John R. W. Human rights & human wrongs. IV. Title.
    BT738.S77   2006
    261.8 — dc22   2006021647

Interior design by Beth Shagene

Printed in the United States of America

---

13 • 24 23 22 21 20 19 18 17 16 15

Abbreviations

The biblical text quoted is normally that of the New International Version, copyright © 1973, 1978, 1984 by International Bible Society. If another text is used, this is stated.

Arndt-Gingrich *A Greek-English Lexicon of the New Testament and Other Early Christian Literature*, by William F. Arndt and F. Wilbur Gingrich (University of Chicago Press and Cambridge University Press, 1957).

AV The Authorized (King James) Version of the Bible, 1611.

GNB The Good News Bible (The Bible Societies/Collins, 1976).

JB The Jerusalem Bible (Darton, Longman and Todd, 1966).

NASB The New American Standard Bible (Moody Press, Chicago, 1960).

NEB The New English Bible (Oxford University Press and Cambridge University Press, NT 1961, 2nd edition 1970; OT 1970).

NIV The New International Version of the Bible (Hodder & Stoughton, NT 1973; OT 1978; revised edition 1984).

RSV The Revised Standard Version of the Bible (HarperCollins, NT 1946, 2nd edition 1971; OT 1952).

Contents

PART ONE
CONTEXTUAL ISSUES

PART TWO
GLOBAL ISSUES

PART THREE
SOCIAL ISSUES

Preface to the First Edition (1984)

O ne of the most notable features of the worldwide evangelical movement during the last ten to fifteen years has been the recovery of our temporarily mislaid social conscience. For approximately fifty years (c. 1920–70) evangelical Christians were preoccupied with the task of defending the historic biblical faith against the attacks of theological liberalism, and reacting against its "social gospel". But now we are convinced that God has given us social as well as evangelistic responsibilities in his world. Yet the half-century of neglect has put us far behind in this area. We have a long way to catch up.

This book is my own contribution to the catching up process. Its source may be traced to 1978/9, when Michael Baughen, now Bishop of Chester, but then Rector of All Souls Church, invited me to preach a series of occasional sermons under the title "Issues Facing Britain Today". Several of these chapters began their life in the pulpit, and subsequently grew into lectures at the London Institute for Contemporary Christianity, whose raison d'être is to help people develop a Christian perspective on the complexities of the modern world.

I confess that several times in the course of writing I have been tempted to give up. I have felt now foolish and now presumptuous to attempt such an undertaking. For I am in no sense a specialist in moral theology or social ethics, and I have no particular expertise or experience in some of the fields into which I trespass. Moreover, each topic is complex, has attracted an extensive literature, only some of which I have been able to read, and is potentially divisive, even in a few cases explosive. Yet I have persevered, mainly because what I am venturing to offer the public is not a polished professional piece but the rough-hewn amateur work of an ordinary Christian who is struggling to think Christianly, that is, to apply the biblical revelation to the pressing issues of the day.

For this is my concern. I begin with a commitment to the Bible as "God's Word written", which is how it is described in the Anglican Articles and has been received by nearly all churches until comparatively recent times. Such is the basic presupposition of this book; it is not part of my present purpose to argue it. But we Christians have a second commitment, namely to the world in which God has placed us. And our two commitments often seem to be in conflict. Being a collection of documents which relate to particular and distant events, the Bible has an archaic feel. It seems incompatible with our Western culture, with its space probes and microprocessors. Like every other Christian I feel myself caught in the painful tension between these two worlds. They are centuries apart. Yet I have sought to resist the temptation to withdraw from either world by capitulation to the other.

Some Christians, anxious above all to be faithful to the revelation of God without compromise, ignore the challenges of the modern world and live in the past. Others, anxious to respond to the world around them, trim and twist God's revelation in their search for relevance. I have struggled to avoid both traps. For the Christian is at liberty to surrender neither to antiquity nor to modernity. Instead, I have sought with integrity to submit to the revelation of yesterday within the realities of today. It is not easy to combine loyalty to the past with sensitivity to the present. Yet this is our Christian calling: to live under the Word in the world.

Many people have helped me develop my thinking. I thank the "apostolic succession" of my study assistants – Roy McCloughry, Tom Cooper, Mark Labberton, Steve Ingraham and Bob Wismer – who have compiled bibliographies, assembled groups for the discussion of sermon topics, gathered information and checked references. Bob Wismer has been specially helpful in the final stages, reading the MS twice and making valuable suggestions. So has Frances Whitehead, my secretary for 28 years. She and Vivienne Curry typed the MS. Steve Andrews, my present study assistant, has been meticulous in proof correcting. I also thank friends who have read different chapters and given me the benefit of their comments – Oliver Barclay, Raymond Johnston, John Gladwin, Mark Stephens, Roy McCloughry, Myra Chave-Jones and my colleagues at the London Institute, Andrew Kirk (Associate Director) and Martyn Eden (Dean). I am particularly grateful to Jim Houston, founding Principal and now Chancellor of Regent College, Vancouver, whose vision of the need for Christians to have an integrated worldview has stimulated both my own thinking and the founding of the London Institute.

J S
JUNE 1984

Preface to the Second Edition (1990)

Six years have passed since the publication of *Issues Facing Christians Today* and in this brief period the world has witnessed many changes. Détente between the superpowers has dawned, and disarmament has begun. Freedom and democracy, undreamed of only a year ago, have taken root in Eastern Europe and the Soviet Union, even while brutal repression has trampled on these tender plants in China. Old debates (like the nuclear threat) have moved on, while new debates (like the AIDS epidemic) have arisen.

Hence the need for a second and revised edition of this book. The statistics on armaments, human rights violations, other religions, unemployment, divorce and abortion have all been brought up to date. It has been necessary to read and reflect on newly published books on almost every issue. A number of these have been written by evangelical authors, which is an encouraging sign of our developing social conscience. Another sign of this is the merger of the London Institute for Contemporary Christianity with the Shaftesbury Project for Christian Involvement in Society in order to form "Christian Impact", and so combine research, education and thought with action. Yet other signs are the stronger commitment to social action explicit in the Manila Manifesto, which was adopted at the conclusion of the second "Lausanne" Congress on World Evangelization (1989), and the "Salt and Light" project sponsored by the British Evangelical Alliance.

This second edition of *Issues Facing Christians Today* also incorporates new material on many topics – on the rapid growth of the green movement and its warnings about ozone layer depletion and the greenhouse effect; on the Brundtland Report, *Our Common Future*, and its concept of "sustainable development"; on the burden of debt borne by many nuclear families in the West and – to a crippling degree – by Third World countries; on three important Christian documents recently published in South Africa; on further thinking

11

by evangelical Christians about the role, ministry and leadership of women; on human fertilization and modern reproductive technologies; on the theological, moral, pastoral and educational aspects of AIDS; and of the effectiveness of Christian social protest and witness.

I express my cordial thanks to Toby Howarth and Todd Shy, my former and present study assistants, for painstakingly rereading the whole book and making numerous suggestions; to Martyn Eden, Elaine Storkey, Roy McCloughry, Maurice Hobbs, John Wyatt and Stephen Rand for perusing individual sections or chapters and proposing changes; to Lance Pierson for producing the study guide; and to Frances Whitehead for much retyping and some really skilful "scissors-and-paste" editing.

In conclusion, I feel the need to restate what I wrote in the Preface to the first edition, namely that *Issues* represents the struggles of a person who lays no claims to infallibility, who is anxious to go on increasing his Christian integrity over against the pressures of a largely secular society, and who, to that end, is continuously seeking fresh light from Scripture.

J S
JANUARY 1990

Preface to the Third Edition (1999)

Issues Facing Christians Today was first published in 1984, and its second, updated edition appeared in 1990. Since then eight more years have passed, and a third, revised edition is already overdue. It is extraordinary that in the topic of every chapter the debate has moved on, and in some cases the situation has changed significantly.

With the collapse of Euro-Marxism, following the demolition of the Berlin Wall, much of the map of Europe has had to be redrawn. The end of the Cold War has made possible some international disarmament treaties. The "Earth Summit" at Rio in 1992 both mirrored and stimulated growing public alarm over ozone layer depletion and global warming. New policies of development and proposals for debt cancellation have brought realistic hope to the poorest nations. The conciliatory leadership of President Mandela and the dismantling of apartheid shine brightly against the increase of racially motivated violence and the re-emergence of nationalism in Europe. Christians are also disturbed by the influences which undermine marriage and the family (especially cohabitation and same-sex partnerships) and which challenge the sanctity of human life (especially abortion and euthanasia).

Ten consultants, each a specialist in his own field, have been kind enough to read the chapter of their expertise and then to recommend changes to make, books to read and new issues to consider. I am most grateful for their criticisms and suggestions. They are (in alphabetical order) Sir Fred Catherwood, Martyn Eden, Dr David Green, Gary Haugen, Sir John Houghton, Roy McCloughry, Dr Alan Storkey, Pradip Sudra, Dr Neil Summerton and Professor John Wyatt.

I reserve my special gratitude for John Yates, my current study assistant. Not only has he given himself the chore of reading the book's second edition several times, made his own insightful suggestions, and updated the statistics, but he has also followed up our consultants' proposals, done some redrafting

13

himself and advised me which books and articles I needed to read and ponder myself. I cannot speak too highly of his conscientious work.

J S
Autumn 1998

Editor's Preface
to the Fourth Edition
(2006)

It has been a privilege to work on the fourth edition of this book, not only because of its influence on the Christian thinking of many people since the first edition in 1984, but also because of its influence on my own personal journey when I was a student in London listening to the sermons John Stott preached on these subjects. Then, as his first study assistant twenty-five years ago, I continued to be influenced by the development of his own thought on these issues. As someone called to reflect as a Christian on contemporary social, economic and political life, I found his own approach to be both illuminating and inspiring.

This has had more revision than previous editions. This was mostly because some of the chapters in the third edition referred to events or debates that were no longer as relevant as they once were. For instance, the Brandt report is no longer at the heart of the debate on global poverty; nor is the discussion of industrial relations as portrayed in previous editions as relevant as it once was to business life today. Some chapters have been left relatively untouched with only statistics being revised, since John felt that they still encapsulated what he had to say on the subject. The chapter "War and Peace", for instance, still contains a substantial theological reflection on nuclear war. Other chapters have had more extensive surgery to update them. However, both John and I are very aware that events are moving very fast in each of the areas described in this book. Like computers which are outdated as soon as they are taken out of their boxes, readers will find that some of the events which are discussed here have moved on since we went to print. Fortunately many who read this book will have access to the internet, which can update the material further.

Throughout the book a distinction has been made between setting the scene and John's own reflection and theological analysis. Whereas the former may have changed, the latter has not. Critics may say that the theological debate has moved on, and of course they would be right in that there are now, thankfully, many authoritative books and papers on each of these subjects, written by Christians, many of them evangelical. However, the reason for this fourth edition is that thousands of people still benefit from John's wisdom and reflection on these issues. His skilled handling of Scripture, together with its application to many contemporary problems, will be sought out for many years to come.

Throughout this book I have been careful not to allow my own prejudices and bias to show in the text, especially in those areas where John and I would express things differently. It is his book and not mine, and my hope is that readers will still recognize his distinctive voice as they read its pages. Those people who perceive a shift in John's stance on important issues in this book would be wrong. With the exception of a brief insertion in the chapter "Women, Men and God", John has not written anything new for this book, although he has read the new edition and made amendments where necessary. All changes come either from me or from some of those who have been kind enough to offer me their expertise, in all cases free of charge, which is very generous. They are Christopher Ash, Andrew Cornes, Mark Greene, Martin Hallet, Peter Harris, Mark Lovatt, Stephen Rand, Nick Riley, Trevor Stammers, Neil Summerton, Beverly Thomas and Scott Thomas. Mentioning them here should not be taken to mean that they agree with everything (or indeed anything!) written in their area of expertise.

I would like to thank three people especially. My friend John Wyatt was willing to take time from an extremely busy schedule to write an extra chapter for this edition on "The New Biotechnology" as well as giving advice on the chapter "Abortion and Euthanasia". I am very grateful to him. Also Matthew Smith, John's study assistant during this project, was extremely helpful, not only in updating statistics and other similar details but also in contributing to the "Business Relationships" chapter. He also wrote the Study Guide, which we hope will be helpful not only to individuals but also to those who wish to study the book in groups. My personal assistant, Kaja Ziesler, has also contributed a great deal to this book, not only in terms of research but also in writing drafts and offering her own advice. I accept responsibility for all errors of omission or commission!

This edition has taken much longer to complete than any of us involved in the project had imagined at its outset, and I am grateful to John for his own patience and graciousness. Zondervan has been very supportive throughout, and I would like to thank Amy Boucher-Pye, Maryl Darko and Angela Scheff in particular.

I hope that you enjoy this new edition and pray that it might continue to be used to inspire a new generation and challenge them to think Christianly about the world and take action to make it more pleasing to God.

ROY MCCLOUGHRY
WEST BRIDGFORD
SEPTEMBER 2005

A Note from John Stott

It is a thankless task to be invited to update somebody else's book! But Roy McCloughry has done it with considerable grace, skill and perseverance.

I asked Roy to take responsibility for the fourth edition of *Issues Facing Christians Today* because at my age (in my eighty-fifth year) I knew I couldn't, and because I had every confidence that he could.

I have not been disappointed. Although I have given Roy complete freedom, and his revision has been thorough and sometimes radical, it has been on the understanding that in the end the book would still be recognizably my own, which it is. In order to indicate this, in various places the first person singular ("I ...") and some personal anecdotes have been retained.

I am extremely grateful to Roy for the immense amount of time and energy which he has invested in the editorial work, and to all those who have assisted him, whom he has listed in his Preface, especially Matthew Smith, who was my study assistant at the time.

We send this fourth edition of *Issues* on its way with the prayerful hope that it will stimulate a new generation of readers to think Christianly about some of the big issues of our day.

JOHN STOTT
SEPTEMBER 2005

PART ONE

CONTEXTUAL
ISSUES

Our Changing World: Is Christian Involvement Necessary?

At the outset of the twenty-first century, we are faced with a bewildering array of challenges which fifty years ago we could never have imagined. On the one hand the pace of technological change has confirmed humanity's cleverness; on the other hand the persistence of global poverty remains a challenge to our sense of justice. We are increasingly interdependent globally and business opportunities abound, but rich and poor are as far apart as ever. We are addressed as consumers rather than as citizens in a material society of great sophistication but with little sense of purpose. The unintended consequences of our actions have caused environmental problems which seriously threaten our future together. Although the threat of nuclear war has receded, we are having to come to terms with the rise of global terrorism, the advent of the suicide bomber and the resurgence of violence which is religiously inspired. The breakdown of the family, particularly in the West, has laid heavy burdens on single parents, has threatened the cohesion of the community and in many cases has led to a sense of alienation amongst young people. We are confused about the nature of human identity, and this confusion can be seen both in the destruction of life through abortion and euthanasia and in our intention to create life through genetics and cloning.

Why get involved in such a world? It is extraordinary that we need to ask this question and that controversy should have blown up over the relationship between evangelism and social responsibility. All of these issues and many others affect both Christians and those with no religious faith. They challenge our sense of identity and purpose. They challenge us to apply Christian thinking to new issues which come upon us at a rapid rate. In the next chapter I will look at how Christians are called to develop a Christian mind, but in this chapter I

23

want to look at the call to become involved in this world. It is sadly still the case that some believe that Christians do not have social responsibility in this world but only a commission to evangelize those who have not heard the gospel. Yet it is evident that in his public ministry Jesus both "went about ... teaching ... and preaching" (Matthew 4:23; 9:35 RSV) and "went about doing good and healing" (Acts 10:38 RSV). In consequence, "evangelism and social concern have been intimately related to one another throughout the history of the Church ... Christian people have often engaged in both activities quite unselfconsciously, without feeling any need to define what they were doing or why."[1] Our God is a loving God who forgives those who turn to him in repentance, but he is also a God who desires justice and asks us, as his people, not only to live justly but to champion the cause of the poor and the powerless.

Why should Christians get involved? In the end there are only two possible attitudes which Christians can adopt towards the world. One is escape and the other engagement. (You could say that there is a third option, namely accommodation. But then Christians become indistinguishable from the world and on that account are no longer able to develop a distinctive attitude to it. They simply become part of it.) "Escape" means turning our backs on the world in rejection, washing our hands of it (though finding with Pontius Pilate that the responsibility does not come off in the wash), and steeling our hearts against its agonized cries for help. In contrast, "engagement" means turning our faces towards the world in compassion, getting our hands dirty, sore and worn in its service, and feeling deep within us the stirring of the love of God which cannot be contained.

Too many of us evangelicals either have been, or maybe still are, irresponsible escapists. Fellowship with each other in the church is much more congenial than service in an apathetic and even hostile environment outside. Of course we make occasional evangelistic raids into enemy territory (that is our evangelical speciality); but then we withdraw again, across the moat, into our Christian castle (the security of our own evangelical fellowship), pull up the drawbridge and even close our ears to the pleas of those who batter on the gate. As for social activity, we have tended to say it is largely a waste of time in view of the imminent return of the Lord. After all, when the house is on fire, what is the point of hanging new curtains or rearranging the furniture? The only thing that matters is to rescue the perishing. Thus we have tried to salve our conscience with a bogus theology.

THE HERITAGE
OF EVANGELICAL SOCIAL CONCERN[2]

Yet evangelicals have a remarkable history in terms of their commitment to social and economic justice, not least in eighteenth-century Europe and America. The Evangelical Revival, which stirred both continents, should not be thought of only in terms of the preaching of the gospel and the converting of sinners to Christ; it also led to widespread philanthropy, and profoundly affected society on both sides of the Atlantic. John Wesley remains the most striking instance. He is mainly remembered as the itinerant evangelist and open-air preacher, but the gospel he preached inspired people to take up social causes in the name of Christ. Historians have attributed to Wesley's influence rather than to any other the fact that Britain was spared the horrors of a bloody revolution like that in France.[3]

The change which came over Britain during this period was well documented in J. Wesley Bready's remarkable book *England: Before and After Wesley*, subtitled "The Evangelical Revival and Social Reform". His research forced him to conclude that "the true nursing-mother of the spirit and character values that have created and sustained Free Institutions throughout the English-speaking world", indeed "the moral watershed of Anglo-Saxon history", was "the much-neglected and oft-lampooned Evangelical Revival".[4] Bready described "the deep savagery of much of the eighteenth century",[5] which was characterized by:

> The wanton torture of animals for sport, the bestial drunkenness of the populace, the inhuman traffic in African negroes, the kidnapping of fellow-countrymen for exportation and sale as slaves, the mortality of parish children, the universal gambling obsession, the savagery of the prison system and penal code, the welter of immorality, the prostitution of the theatre, the growing prevalence of lawlessness, superstition and lewdness; the political bribery and corruption, the ecclesiastical arrogance and truculence, the shallow pretensions of Deism, the insincerity and debasement rampant in Church and State – such manifestations suggest that the British people were then perhaps as deeply degraded and debauched as any people in Christendom.[6]

Then things began to change. In the nineteenth century slavery and the slave trade were abolished, the prison system was humanized, conditions in

factories and mines were improved, education became available to the poor
and trades unions began.

> Whence, then, this pronounced humanity? – this passion for social justice,
> and sensitivity to human wrongs? There is but one answer commensurate
> with stubborn historical truth. It derived from a new social conscience.
> And if that social conscience, admittedly, was the offspring of more than
> one progenitor, it nonetheless was mothered and nurtured by the Evan-
> gelical Revival of vital, practical Christianity – a revival which illumined
> the central postulates of the New Testament ethic, which made real the
> Fatherhood of God and the Brotherhood of men, which pointed the prior-
> ity of personality over property, and which directed heart, soul and mind,
> towards the establishment of the Kingdom of Righteousness on earth.[7]

The Evangelical Revival "did more to transfigure the moral character of the
general populace, than any other movement British history can record".[8] For
Wesley was both a preacher of the gospel and a prophet of social righteousness.
He was "the man who restored to a nation its soul".[9]

The evangelical leaders of the next generation were committed with equal
enthusiasm to evangelism and social action. The most famous among them
were Granville Sharp, Thomas Clarkson, James Stephen, Zachary Macaulay,
Charles Grant, John Shore (Lord Teignmouth), Thomas Babington, Henry
Thornton and, of course, their guiding light, William Wilberforce. Because
several of them lived in Clapham, at that time a village three miles south of
London, and belonged to Clapham Parish Church, whose rector John Venn was
one of them, they came to be known as "the Clapham Sect", although in parliament and in the press they were mocked as "the Saints".

It was their concern over the plight of the African slaves which first brought
them together. Three days before his death in 1791, John Wesley wrote to Wilberforce to assure him that God had raised him up for his "glorious enterprise"
and to urge him not to be weary of well-doing. It is largely to the Clapham Sect
(under Wilberforce's leadership) that the credit belongs for the first settlement
of freed slaves in Sierra Leone (1787), the abolition of the trade (1807), the registration of slaves in the colonies (1820), which put an end to slave smuggling,
and finally their emancipation (1833). It is true that "the Saints" were wealthy
aristocrats, who shared some of the social blindspots of their time, but they
were extremely generous in their philanthropy and the range of their concerns
was extraordinary. In addition to the slavery question, they involved them-

selves in penal and parliamentary reform, popular education (Sunday schools, tracts and the *Christian Observer* newspaper), Britain's obligation to her colonies (especially India), the spread of the gospel (they were instrumental in the founding of both the Bible Society and the Church Missionary Society), and factory legislation. They also campaigned against duelling, gambling, drunkenness, immorality and cruel animal sports. Throughout they were directed and motivated by their strong evangelical faith. Ernest Marshall Howse has written of them:

> This group of Clapham friends gradually became knit together in an astonishing intimacy and solidarity. They planned and laboured like a committee that never was dissolved. At the Clapham mansions they congregated by common impulse in what they chose to call their "Cabinet Councils" wherein they discussed the wrongs and injustices which were a reproach to their country, and the battles which would need to be fought to establish righteousness. And thereafter, in Parliament and out, they moved as one body, delegating to each man the work he could do best, that the common principles might be maintained and their common purposes be realized.[10]

Reginald Coupland, in his biography of Wilberforce, justly commented: "It was, indeed, a unique phenomenon – this brotherhood of Christian politicians. There has never been anything like it since in British public life."[11]

Anthony Ashley Cooper was elected to the British parliament in 1826, aged twenty-five. First in the House of Commons, and then in the House of Lords as the seventh Earl of Shaftesbury, he concerned himself successively with the plight of lunatics, child workers in the factories and mills, "climbing boys" or chimney sweeps, women and children in the mines, and the children of the slums, more than 30,000 of whom in London were without a home, and more than a million of whom in the whole country were without schooling. His biographer Georgina Battiscombe, who is often sharply critical of him, nevertheless concludes her account of his life with this generous tribute: "No man has in fact ever done more to lessen the extent of human misery, or to add to the sum total of human happiness."[12] He himself felt able to claim that "most of the great philanthropic movements of the century have sprung from the Evangelicals".[13]

The same story can be told of the United States in the nineteenth century. Social involvement was both the child of evangelical religion and the twin sister of evangelism. This is clearly seen in Charles G. Finney, who is best known as the lawyer turned evangelist and author of *Lectures on Revivals of Religion* (1835). Through his preaching of the gospel large numbers were brought to faith in Christ. What is not so well known is that he was concerned for "reforms" as well as "revivals". He was convinced, as Donald W. Dayton has shown in his *Discovering an Evangelical Heritage*, both that the gospel "releases a mighty impulse toward social reform" and that the church's neglect of social reform grieved the Holy Spirit and hindered revival. It is astonishing to read Finney's statement in his twenty-third Lecture on Revival that "the great business of the Church is to reform the world ... The Church of Christ was originally organized to be a body of reformers. The very profession of Christianity implies the profession and virtually an oath to do all that can be done for the universal reformation of the world."[14]

It is hardly surprising to learn, therefore, that through Finney's evangelism God raised up "an army of young converts who became the troops of the reform movement of his age". In particular, "the anti-slavery forces ... were drawn largely from the converts of Finney's revivals."[15]

The nineteenth century is known also for the enormous expansion of Christian missions which it witnessed. It must not be imagined, however, that the missionaries concentrated exclusively on preaching, or indeed that their social concern was restricted to aid and relief, to the neglect of development and even socio-political activity. It is doubtful if these distinctions have ever been neatly drawn in practice. No, they took medicine and education, agricultural technique and other technologies as an expression of mission and compassion. They campaigned against injustice and oppression in the name of the gospel. Theirs was not a mission of words but of words and deeds.

"THE GREAT REVERSAL"

Then, however, something happened to challenge the evangelical commitment to social concern. This was especially apparent during the first thirty years of the twentieth century, and especially during the decade following World War I, when a major shift took place which the American historian Timothy L. Smith has termed "the Great Reversal", and which David O. Moberg investigates in his book with that title.[16]

The fight against liberalism

The first cause was the fight against theological liberalism which neglected the preaching of the gospel. Evangelicals felt they had their backs to the wall.[17] Understandably, they became preoccupied with the defence and proclamation of the gospel, for nobody else seemed to be championing historic biblical Christianity. This was the period (actually 1910 – 15) when the series of twelve small books entitled *The Fundamentals* was published in the United States, from which the term "fundamentalism" arose. When evangelicals were busy seeking to vindicate the fundamentals of the faith, they felt they had no time for social concerns.

The rejection of the "social gospel"

Secondly, evangelicals reacted against the so-called "social gospel" which theological liberals were developing at this time, in which the aim was to bring about a Christian society by social and political action. Theologians such as Walter Rauschenbusch, who was professor of church history at Rochester Seminary, New York, from 1897 to 1917, criticized capitalism and advocated a simple kind of "communism" or Christian socialism.[18] Firstly, he was in error in identifying the kingdom of God with "a reconstruction of society on a Christian basis".[19] Secondly, he implied that human beings can establish the divine kingdom by themselves (whereas Jesus always spoke of it as a gift of God). The kingdom of God is not Christianized society. It is the divine rule in the lives of those who acknowledge Christ. It has to be "received", "entered" or "inherited" by humble and penitent faith in him. God's new society is called to exhibit the ideals of his rule in the world and so to present the world with an alternative social reality. This social challenge of the gospel of the kingdom is quite different from the "social gospel". It is understandable (if regrettable) that, in reaction to him, evangelicals concentrated on evangelism and personal philanthropy, and steered clear of socio-political action.

The impact of war

The third reason for the evangelical neglect of social responsibility was the widespread disillusion and pessimism which followed World War I, because of its exposure of human evil. Earlier social programmes had failed. Human beings and human society appeared to be irreformable. Attempts at reform were useless. To be sure, because of the biblical doctrines of original sin and human depravity, evangelicals should not have been taken by surprise. But between the wars there was no evangelical leader to articulate the providence and common grace of God as grounds for persevering hope. Historic reformed Christianity was in eclipse.

The influence of premillennialism

Fourthly, there was the spread (especially through J. N. Darby's teaching and its popularization in the Scofield Bible) of the premillennial scheme. This portrays the present evil world as beyond improvement or redemption, and predicts instead that it will deteriorate steadily until the coming of Jesus, who will then set up his millennial reign on earth. If the world is getting worse, and if only Jesus at his coming will put it right, the argument runs, there seems no point in trying to reform it meanwhile. "Adopting political programs is like cleaning the staterooms on the Titanic after it has hit the iceberg ... It is far more important simply to preach the Gospel and to rescue souls for the next life."[20]

The rise of the middle classes

The fifth reason for evangelical alienation from social concern was probably the spread of Christianity among middle-class people, who tended to dilute it by identifying it with their own culture. We have to admit that many of us who place a high value on salvation are deeply conservative culturally and prefer to preserve the status quo rather than get involved in the "messy" business of social and political action. This is one of the reasons why many stereotype Christians as being preoccupied with their own salvation at the expense of the plight of the poor and powerless. Surely, if we are faithful to the Christian gospel, we must take action against injustice wherever we find it. Although I have been able earlier to mention some fine examples of social action in the eighteenth and nineteenth centuries, there have certainly been other situations in which the church has acquiesced in oppression and exploitation, and has taken no action against these evils, nor even protested against them.

This "Great Reversal" is explicable for these five reasons. We do not blame our evangelical forebears; in their place we would probably have reacted to contemporary pressures as they did. Not that all evangelicals mislaid their social conscience at the beginning of the twentieth century and between the wars. Some soldiered on, deeply involved in social as well as evangelical ministries, and thus retained this indispensable outworking of the gospel, without which evangelicalism loses part of its authenticity. But most turned away. Then during the 1960s, the decade of protest, when young people were rebelling against the materialism, superficiality and hypocrisy of the adult world they had inherited, the evangelical mainstream recovered its morale, and things began to change.

THE RECOVERY
OF EVANGELICAL SOCIAL CONCERN

Probably the first voice to recall the evangelical constituency to its social responsibilities was that of the American Christian scholar Carl F. H. Henry, the founding editor of *Christianity Today*, in his book *The Uneasy Conscience of Modern Fundamentalism* (1947). Not many seemed to listen, but gradually the message caught on. In 1966, at the conclusion of an American conference on world missions, the participants unanimously adopted the "Wheaton Declaration" which firmly bracketed "the primacy of preaching the gospel to every creature" and "a verbal witness to Jesus Christ" with "evangelical social action", and urged "all evangelicals to stand openly and firmly for racial equality, human freedom, and all forms of social justice throughout the world".

In Britain in the 1960s a number of evangelical leaders, most of whom were laymen in professional and business life, began to grapple with the social implications of the gospel. Among them were George Goyder, Fred Catherwood and Professor Norman Anderson. Then, at the first National Evangelical Anglican Congress at Keele University in 1967, Anglican evangelicals publicly repented of their tendency to withdraw from both the secular world and the wider church, concluding that "evangelism and compassionate service belong together in the mission of God".[21]

The turning point for the worldwide evangelical constituency was doubtless the International Congress on World Evangelization held in July 1974 at Lausanne, Switzerland. Some 2,700 participants gathered from more than 150 nations under the slogan "Let the Earth Hear His Voice", and at the conclusion of the congress endorsed the Lausanne Covenant. After three introductory sections on the purpose of God, the authority of the Bible and the uniqueness of Christ, its fourth is entitled "The Nature of Evangelism" and its fifth "Christian

Social Responsibility". The latter declares that "evangelism and socio-political involvement are both part of our Christian duty". But the two paragraphs stand side by side in the covenant, with no attempt to relate them, except for the statement in paragraph 6 that "in the church's mission of sacrificial service evangelism is primary".

During the years which followed the Lausanne Congress, there was a certain amount of tension within the evangelical movement, as some emphasized evangelism, others social activity, and all of us wondered how according to Scripture we should spell out the relationship between the two. So in June 1982, under the joint sponsorship of the Lausanne Committee and the World Evangelical Fellowship, the Consultation on the Relationship between Evangelism and Social Responsibility (CRESR) was held in Grand Rapids, and issued its report entitled "Evangelism and Social Responsibility: An Evangelical Commitment". Although of course we did not see eye to eye on every point, God led us to a remarkable degree of consensus. Social activity was said to be both a consequence of and a bridge to evangelism, and indeed the two were declared to be partners. Besides, they are united by the gospel. "For the gospel is the root, of which both evangelism and social responsibility are the fruits."[22]

Since then the commitment of evangelicals to social action has grown immeasurably. Many consultations have been held and statements issued on subjects as diverse as the environment, disability, war and peace and many aspects of economic and political life. New institutions have been born whose raison d'être is to facilitate Christian social action, and a large number of local churches now have projects which seek to apply Christian principles to social action. Many missionary agencies now espouse the concept of holistic mission, which brings evangelism and social action together. Throughout this book, projects, campaigns and organizations are mentioned or listed which are a witness to the recovery of evangelical social concern. Yet sadly in recent years there has also been a backlash against this rediscovery of our Christian social heritage. Some claim that we must focus only on the exposition of Scripture, and personal evangelism as social action is a distraction from these things. But this cannot be so. It is because we have a high view of Scripture and we read it carefully that we find that it does not separate out evangelism from social action and that the supreme example of this is the life and teaching of Jesus. He teaches us that we cannot separate love and justice: for what love desires, justice demands.

THE CHURCH AND POLITICS

In this context it is important to look carefully at the relationship between Christianity and politics, for it is often the case that social action will mean political action of some sort. Yet in the past, evangelicals have been extremely cautious about the relationship between Christianity and politics, believing that they don't mix. This belief was obviously not shared by the Clapham Sect!

In recent years, some of those who were most suspicious of political action have embraced it wholeheartedly. I am thinking here of the many conservative evangelicals in the United States who in the latter part of the twentieth century and the early part of the twenty-first century began to campaign and become vocal on ethical issues such as abortion, homosexuality, euthanasia and stem cell research, which they regarded as a threat from a secular liberalism which was antagonistic to the Christian gospel. They became known popularly as the "Moral Majority" and such was the power of their vote that it was thought they were a key factor in the re-election of President George W. Bush in 2004, not only because he was sympathetic to such beliefs but also because he professed a personal Christian faith. Others remained cautious about such a close identification of the Christian faith with one political stance, while groups who were focused on social justice also saw political action as an essential part of their commitment to Scripture.[23]

It is, therefore, extremely important to examine the relationship between Christianity and politics for two reasons. Firstly, to convince those who are overcautious that there is an appropriate involvement of Christians in politics and that this is part of our Christian calling. Secondly, to delineate the boundaries of that calling so that those who have become deeply involved in politics might appreciate the limits of that involvement and the dangers of politicizing the gospel.

Several different issues are involved in this controversy, and the waters of the debate are muddied by a failure to distinguish between them. The first is the definition of the word "politics". The second concerns the relationship between the social and the political, and why they cannot be kept apart. Thirdly, we need to consider the reasons why some people oppose the church's involvement in politics, and what it is they are trying to safeguard. Then fourthly, we need to examine the relationship between principles and programmes.

The definition of politics

Firstly, we must define our terms. The words "politics" and "political" may be given either a broad or a narrow definition. Broadly speaking, "politics" denotes the life of the city (*polis*) and the responsibilities of the citizen (*politēs*). It is concerned, therefore, with the whole of our life in human society. Politics is the art of living together in a community. According to its narrow definition, however, politics is the science of government. It is concerned with the development and adoption of specific policies with a view to their being enshrined in legislation. It is about gaining power for social change.

Once this distinction is clear, we may ask whether Jesus was involved in politics. In the latter and narrower sense, he clearly was not. He never formed a political party, adopted a political programme or organized a political protest. He took no steps to influence the policies of Caesar, Pilate or Herod. On the contrary, he renounced a political career. In the other and broader sense of the word, however, his whole ministry was political. For he had himself come into the world in order to share in the life of the human community, and he sent his followers into the world to do the same. Moreover, the kingdom of God he proclaimed and inaugurated was a radically new and different social organization, whose values and standards challenged those of the old and fallen community. In this way his teaching had "political" implications. It offered an alternative to the status quo. His kingship, moreover, was perceived as a challenge to Caesar's, and he was therefore accused of sedition.

It is irrelevant to state that Jesus and his apostles were not interested in politics, and that they neither required nor even commended political action, let alone engaged in it themselves. This is true. They did not. Yet although politics is about the business of the state, it is also about the gaining of power and the exercise of power. The fact that Jesus had a very different view of power was one of the reasons why he was feared by the politicians of his day and why political leaders saw him as attacking their government. It is not for nothing that Mary in the Magnificat said, "He has brought down rulers from their thrones but has lifted up the humble" (Luke 1:52). Although the teaching of Jesus was not overtly political, it subverted unjust political structures, challenged oppression and promised people that there was a new kingdom, characterized by justice, in which the truth rather than political promises set people free. The impact of this on social and political life was so profound that it is quite legitimate to talk of "the politics of Jesus".[24]

The outworking of this teaching took some time to have an impact. We have to remember that Christ's followers were a tiny, insignificant minority under the totalitarian regime of Rome. The legions were everywhere, and were under orders to suppress dissent, crush opposition and preserve the status quo. The question is: Would they have been politically active if they had had both the opportunity and the likelihood of success? I believe they would. For without appropriate political action some social needs simply cannot be met. The apostles did not demand the abolition of slavery. But are we not glad and proud that nineteenth-century Christians did? Their campaign was based on biblical teaching regarding human dignity, and was a legitimate extrapolation from it. The apostles did not build hospitals either, or require them to be built, but Christian hospitals are a legitimate extrapolation from Jesus' compassionate concern for the sick. Just so, political action (which is love seeking justice for the oppressed) is a legitimate extrapolation from the teaching and ministry of Jesus. As Archbishop Desmond Tutu has commented in his particularly colourful way, "I am puzzled which Bible people are reading when they suggest religion and politics don't mix."[25]

Social service and social action

Secondly, we need to consider the relation between the "social" and the "political", now using this word in its narrower sense. In its final chapter, the Grand Rapids report "Evangelism and Social Responsibility" addressed itself to this question. It distinguished between "social service" and "social action", and helpfully drew up the following table:

Social Service	Social Action
Relieving human need	Removing the causes of human need
Philanthropic activity	Political and economic activity
Seeking to minister to individuals and families	Seeking to transform the structures of society
Works of mercy	The quest for justice[26]

The report went on to delineate socio-political action in these terms: "It looks beyond persons to structures, beyond the rehabilitation of prison inmates to the reform of the prison system, beyond improving factory conditions to securing a more participatory role for the workers, beyond caring for the poor to improving – and when necessary transforming – the economic system (whatever it may be) and the political system (again, whatever it may be), until it facilitates their liberation from poverty and oppression."[27]

It seems clear, then, that genuine Christian social concern will embrace both social service and social action. It would be artificial to divorce them. Some cases of need cannot be relieved at all without political action (the harsh treatment of slaves could have been ameliorated, but not slavery itself; it had to be abolished). To go on relieving other needs, though necessary, may condone the situation which causes them. If travellers on the Jerusalem – Jericho road were habitually beaten up, and habitually cared for by "Good Samaritans", the need for better laws to eliminate armed robbery might well be overlooked. If road accidents keep occurring at a particular crossroads, it is not more ambulances that are needed but the installation of traffic lights to prevent accidents. It is always good to feed the hungry; it is better if possible to eradicate the causes of hunger. So if we truly love our neighbours, and want to serve them, our service may oblige us to take (or solicit) political action on their behalf.

The politicization of Christianity

Thirdly, we need to understand those who are hostile to the church being politically involved. There is, of course, a real danger of the politicization of the gospel, which is the identification of the Christian faith with a political programme. This is wrong for two reasons. The first is that it ignores the primary concern of the Christian faith, which is to love God – the "first and greatest" commandment. Loving our neighbours as ourselves is also important, and they belong together. The second reason is that in a fallen world, no one political programme can claim to be the expression of the will of God.

As Archbishop William Temple, probably the most socially concerned Archbishop of Canterbury in the twentieth century, put it, "Its assertion of Original Sin should make the Church intensely realistic and conspicuously free from Utopianism."[28] Certainly the evangelical Christians who gathered in Lausanne at the great International Congress on World Evangelization (1974) declared forthrightly in their covenant: "We . . . reject as a proud, self-confident dream the notion that man can ever build a Utopia on earth."[29]

We should also not forget that our call to social involvement must be integrated into our spiritual lives. We cannot, for instance, divorce social action or social service from prayer. One good example of this comes from the work of Mother Teresa of Calcutta.

> Many who visit Mother Teresa and her Missionaries of Charity are surprised that every lunchtime they leave their life-sustaining work in dispensaries and in the home for the dying. Why go back so soon? To pray. They have learnt that to work without prayer is to achieve only what is humanly possible, and their desire is to be involved in divine possibilities.[30]

The church should, therefore, not forget its primary calling to pray, worship, evangelize and call people to follow Christ. Politically, it also needs to be aware that even as it seeks the very best for human society and studies the Word of God in pursuit of a Christian mind, it cannot enshrine Christian thinking into a particular political programme. As we shall see, one of the virtues of democracy is that it leads us to humility and the necessity of listening to one another, especially when we disagree with one another and are seeking to find a way forward.

The relationship between principles and programmes

In 1942 William Temple emphasized the important distinction between principles and programmes in his well-known book *Christianity and the Social Order*.[31] "The Church is committed to the everlasting Gospel ... it must never commit itself to an ephemeral programme of detailed action."[32] Readers of Temple will know that he was very far from saying that religion and politics do not mix. His point was different, namely that "the Church is concerned with principles and not policy".[33] The reasons why he believed the church as a whole should refrain from "direct political action" by developing and advocating specific programmes could be summed up as "integrity" (the church lacks the necessary expertise, though some of her members may have it), "prudence" (she may prove to be mistaken and so be discredited) and "justice" (different Christians hold different opinions, and the church should not side with even a majority of its members against an equally loyal minority).

> So the Church is likely to be attacked from both sides if it does its duty. It will be told that it has become political when in fact it has been careful only to state principles and point to breaches of them; and it will be

told by advocates of particular policies that it is futile because it does not support these. If it is faithful to its commission it will ignore both sets of complaints and continue as far as it can to influence all agencies and permeate all parties.[34]

Of course, we need to recognize that individual Christians and even specialist Christian agencies will have expertise on policy issues and will speak out, campaign and conduct research on these issues. It may also be that a large number of Christians find themselves in agreement over a particular policy and unite in either supporting it or protesting against it. However, these are different from committing the church to a particular policy. Even if we agree with this clarification of roles and concede that not all Christians are responsible for working out policies, we still have to grapple with the principles, and these are by no means always easy to formulate.

THREE POLITICAL OPTIONS

What is necessary now is to take up the three possible attitudes to social change which we have been considering and give them a political twist, at the same time noting what view of human beings each presupposes.

Authoritarianism

Authoritarian governments impose their vision of the world on the people. They do not have the checks and balances of a constitution, bill of rights or free and fair elections. Authoritarian governments are obsessed with control and have a pessimistic view of human nature. They do not believe that trust is at the heart of civil society, but are suspicious of the consequences of human freedom and personal choice. Within human history, authoritarian government, whether it be fascist, communist or an expression of dictatorship as it can be found in some countries, does not believe in social discourse, as it does not believe that anything is to be learned from the people. Since people desire to have their human rights and wish to be free to choose how they live their lives, authoritarian government usually not only imposes its vision of society on the people but coerces the people into accepting that vision. This has led to violence and the suppression of human rights in many societies, not only of those who have resisted in the name of freedom but also of those groups who are not tolerated by the authoritarian regime. This, in the twentieth century, led in its most extreme form to Nazi concentration camps and the Gulag Archipelago of the former Soviet Union. Even if an autocracy were to be genuinely benevolent, it would demean its citizens because it did not trust them to have any share in decision-making.

Anarchism

At the other end of the spectrum comes anarchy. In this philosophy there is such optimism about the individual that law, government and indeed all authority are seen not only as superfluous but as a threat to human freedom. The Russian philosopher Bakunin was against any unequal distribution of power. He commented: "Do you want to make it impossible for anyone to oppress his fellow-man? Then make sure that no one shall possess power."[35] Writer Brian Morris has commented:

> The term anarchy comes from the Greek, and essentially means "no ruler". Anarchists are people who reject all forms of government or coercive authority, all forms of hierarchy and domination. They are therefore opposed to what the Mexican anarchist Flores Magon called the "sombre trinity" – state, capital and the church. Anarchists are thus opposed to both capitalism and to the state, as well as to all forms of religious authority. But anarchists also seek to establish or bring about by varying means, a condition of anarchy, that is, a decentralized society without coercive institutions, a society organized through a federation of voluntary associations.[36]

Although such a definition seems innocuous, anarchy has been associated with violence as well. Some anarchists have sought to bring about the fall of the state or of other institutions through violence, and in the popular imagination anarchy is more associated with chaos than social order. The problem is, then, that while authoritarianism has a pessimistic view of the human condition and denies people freedom and dignity, anarchy has a too-optimistic view of human nature, seemingly ignoring the fact that the human race is fallen and capable of great depravity. We now know that no Christian view of civil society can be expressed in a utopian dream, because people are not only created in the image of God but are fallen, and any society must come to terms with both of these elements of human nature. It is for this reason that we now turn to democracy.

Democracy

Democracy is the third option. It is the political expression of persuasion by argument. If authoritarianism, being pessimistic, imposes law arbitrarily, and anarchy, being optimistic, has an inadequate view of authority, then democracy, being realistic about human beings as both created and fallen, involves citizens in the framing of their own laws. At least this is the theory. In practice, it is easy for the media to manipulate the people and for corruption to interfere with the political process. And in every democracy there is the constant danger of trampling on minorities.

A number of political philosophies are consistent with democracy. Many forms of socialism see democracy at the heart of civil society, with social democracy seeing the provision of welfare as necessary for a just society. Here the aim is that society should be run for the good of all. In liberal democracy the focus is on freedom and the individual rather than on equality and the community. Economic markets are at the centre of the society and the role of the state is seen as secondary to individual choice. Social democracy and liberal democracy are perhaps the two most familiar models which we see in practice today. Yet two other models are worth mentioning. Libertarianism focuses entirely on the choices of individuals and confines the state to protecting individuals from coercion. In this view, providing help for those who are disadvantaged is to interfere with freedom. In some ways it is a more extreme form of liberalism. In communitarianism, the emphasis is on the community and tradition rather than the individual. It is an alternative to liberalism and libertarianism and points to the need to retain our shared moral values and institutions, such as the family, through which we discover our identity.

"The word 'democracy' and its derivatives apply to decision-procedures," writes John R. Lucas in his book *Democracy and Participation*. The word describes three aspects of the decision-making process. The first concerns who takes it. "A decision is democratically taken if the answer to the question 'who takes it?' is 'more or less everybody', in contrast to decisions taken only by those best qualified to take them, as in a meritocracy, or those taken by only one man, as in an autocracy or monarchy." Secondly, democracy describes how a decision is reached. "A decision is taken democratically if it is reached by discussion, criticism and compromise." Thirdly, democracy describes the spirit in which a decision is made, namely "being concerned with the interests of all, instead of only a faction or a party".[37]

So modern democracy has the best chance of reflecting the balanced biblical view of human beings, as we might expect in view of its roots in post-Reformation Christian Europe. It also gives Christians the opportunity to make a constructive contribution in a pluralistic society, by getting into the public debate (whether on disarmament or divorce, abortion or in vitro fertilization) and by seeking to influence public opinion until there is a public demand for legislation which would be more pleasing to God. For if democracy is government by consent, consent depends on consensus (or at least it does so when electoral procedures are truly democratic), and consensus arises out of a discussion in which the issues become clarified.

During the twentieth century the ideologies of fascism and communism were imposed on people by force. Both claimed to be able to reach an ideal state in which humanity could transcend its historical struggles. The result was misery, injustice and terror for millions of people. At the outset of the twenty-first century we have seen, with the collapse of Communism, a wave of democratization sweep over the former Soviet Union and the remarkable sight of elections in Iraq, formerly under the dictatorship of Saddam Hussein, even though Iraq is still fragile and chaotic.

What is so appealing about democracy? After all, it is a fragile way of organizing a society. It can be hijacked, corrupted and abused by the powerful. Yet, whatever our political colour may be, Christians tend to advocate democracy, which was popularly defined by Abraham Lincoln as "government of the people, by the people, for the people". Not that it is "perfect or all-wise", as Winston Churchill conceded in the House of Commons on 11 November 1947. "Indeed," he continued, "it has been said that democracy is the worst form of government – except for all those other forms that have been tried from time to time."

The fact is that it is the wisest and safest form of government yet devised. This is because it reflects the paradox of our humanness. On the one hand, it takes the creation seriously (that is, human dignity), because it refuses to govern human beings without their consent and insists instead on giving them a responsible share in the decision-making process. On the other hand, it takes the fall seriously (that is, human depravity), because it refuses to concentrate power in the hands of one person or a few people and insists instead on dispersing it, thus protecting human beings from their own pride and folly. Reinhold Niebuhr put it succinctly: "Man's capacity for justice makes democracy possible; but man's inclination to injustice makes democracy necessary."[38]

In talking about the importance of democracy, Catholic theologian Richard Neuhaus says:

> Democracy is the appropriate form of governance in a fallen creation in which no person or institution, including the church, can infallibly speak for God. Democracy is the necessary expression of humility in which all persons and institutions are held accountable to transcendent purposes imperfectly discerned . . . of course democracy is unsatisfactory. All orders short of the Kingdom of God are unsatisfactory. The discontents of democracy – its provisionality and incompleteness – are the signs of political health. The hunger for a truly satisfying way of putting the world in order is laudable. But that is a hunger for the Kingdom of God and it is dangerously misplaced when it is invested in the political arena.[39]

Christians should be careful not to "baptize" any political ideology (whether of the right, the left or the centre) as if it contained a monopoly of truth and goodness. At best a political ideology and its programme are only an approximation to the will and purpose of God. Those parties which explicitly label themselves as Christian need also to be aware of this. The fact is that Christians are to be found in most political parties and are able to defend their membership on conscientious Christian grounds. Thus, to indulge in a blunt oversimplification, both the main political ideologies in Western societies appeal to Christians for different reasons. Capitalism appeals because it encourages individual human initiative and enterprise, but also repels because it seems not to care that the weak succumb to the fierce competition it engenders. Socialism appeals, on the other hand, because it has great compassion for the poor and the weak, but also repels because it seems not to care that individual initiative and enterprise are smothered by the big government which it engenders. Each attracts because it emphasizes a truth about human beings, either the need to give free play to their creative abilities or the need to protect them from injustice. Each repels because it fails to take with equal seriousness the complementary truth. Both can be liberating. Both can also be oppressive. As economist and statesman J. K. Galbraith put it: "Under capitalism, man exploits man. Under communism, it's just the opposite." It is understandable that many Christians dream of a third option which overcomes the present confrontation and incorporates the best features of both.

    In democracy we are called to listen humbly to one another realizing that we do not have a monopoly of the truth, while pursuing the purposes of God for our society. Because human beings are fallen there is bound to be a gap between the divine ideal and the human reality, between what God has revealed and what humans find possible.

OUR CHRISTIAN POLITICAL RESPONSIBILITY

When faced with the complexities of modern life, Christians can be tempted to move to one of two extremes. Firstly, they can succumb to despair and even cynicism. They cite disagreements between Christians, a Bible which is out of date and issues which can only be understood by experts as the reasons why things are hopeless. They do not trust God to speak to us through the Scriptures and to lead us into the truth. Secondly, others can be naïve and simplistic. They want quick solutions and often see the issues in black and white rather than reflecting wisely on them in the light of Scripture. They may deny the problems, cite proof texts, rubbish those who disagree with them and do anything rather than grapple with the issues that face us in the light of Scripture. What is needed, then, as I shall discuss in the next chapter, is to develop a Christian mind and that means analysing the issues, reading the Scriptures, listening to others and taking action.

However, even when we have done our homework and discussed, debated and prayed together, we need to ask, "On whose shoulders does political responsibility rest?" Failure to ask and answer this question is one of the main reasons for the current confusion over Christian political involvement. We need to distinguish between Christian individuals, groups and churches. All individual Christians should be politically active in the sense that, as conscientious citizens, they will vote in elections, inform themselves about contemporary issues, share in the public debate, and perhaps write to a newspaper, lobby their member of parliament or congress or take part in a demonstration. Further, some individuals are called by God to give their lives to political service, in either local or national government. Christians who share particular moral and social concerns should be encouraged to form or join groups which will study issues at a deeper level and take appropriate action. In some cases these will be exclusively Christian groups; in others Christians will want to contribute their biblical perspective to mixed groups, whether in a political party, a trade union or a professional association.

Granted the propriety of political thought and action by Christian individuals and groups, however, should the church as a whole involve itself in politics?

Certainly the church must teach both the law and the gospel of God. This is the duty of the church's pastors, teachers and other leaders. And "when the church concludes that biblical faith or righteousness requires it to take a public stand on some issue, then it must obey God's Word and trust him with the consequences."[40] Whether we think the church should go beyond teaching and take corporate political action of some kind is likely to depend on whether we adhere to the Lutheran, Reformed or Anabaptist traditions within Protestantism in relation to church and state. At least we can agree that the church should not enter this field without the necessary expertise. But when church leaders do their homework thoroughly, and take time and trouble to study a topic together in order to reach a common Christian mind and recommend common Christian action, their informed and united stand is extremely influential.

Take the individual Christian first. In general terms, every Christian is called to be both a witness and a servant. For each of us is a follower of the Lord Jesus who both witnessed a good confession and said, "I am among you as a serving man". Thus *diakonia* (service) and *martyria* (witness) are inseparable twins. Yet different Christians are called to different specialist ministries, just as the Twelve were called to the ministry of the Word and prayer, while the Seven were called to take charge of the daily distribution to the widows (see Acts 6). The metaphor of the church as the body of Christ enforces the same lesson. Just as each member of the human body has a different function, so each member of the body of Christ has a different gift and so a different ministry. At the same time, whatever our specialist calling may be, emergencies will override it. The priest and the Levite in the parable of the good Samaritan could not excuse their shameful neglect of the man who had been assaulted and robbed by saying that their calling was to work in the temple. If we are called to a predominantly social ministry, we still have an obligation to witness. If we are called to a predominantly evangelistic ministry, we still cannot say that we have no social responsibilities.

As for the local church, the versatility of its outreach can be greatly increased if full use is made of all its members with their different gifts and callings. It is a very healthy thing for the local church's oversight or leadership to encourage people with similar concerns to coalesce into "special interest" groups or "study and action" groups. Some will have an evangelistic objective – house-to-house visitation, a music group, a world mission group, etc. Other groups will have a social concern – sick and welfare visiting, a housing association, community or race relations, the care of the natural environment, pro-life, anti-abortion campaigning, the needs of an ethnic minority, etc. Such specialist groups supplement one another. If an occasional opportunity is given to them to report back to the church membership as a whole, the representative nature of their work will be affirmed and they can receive valuable support from their parent body in terms of advice, encouragement, prayer and financial backing.

No one Christian could, or should try to, get involved in every kind of ministry. But each local church (at least of any size) can and should get involved in as many areas as possible, through its groups. The groups make it realistic for the church greatly to diversify its concern and action.[41] As we shall see in the next chapter, Christians need to have a thorough knowledge of the Scriptures in order to give them the theological foundations for Christian involvement. Christian reflection and Christian action cannot be separated.

I end this chapter with what may be a rather surprising reference to the Roman Catholic mass. The word "mass" is said to be derived from the final sentence of the old Latin rite, *Ite, missa est*. In polite English it might be rendered, "Now you are dismissed." In more blunt language it could be just, "Get out!" – out into the world which God made and godlike beings inhabit, the world into which Christ came and into which he now sends us. For that is where we belong. The world is the arena in which we are to live and love, witness and serve, suffer and die for Christ.

NOTES

1 "Evangelism and Social Responsibility: An Evangelical Commitment, The Grand Rapids Report", in John Stott (ed.), *Making Christ Known: Historic Mission Documents from the Lausanne Movement 1974–1989* (Carlisle: Paternoster, 1996; Grand Rapids: Eerdmans, 1997), p. 179.

2 The adjective "evangelical" is used in different ways by different people, but in this book it denotes those Christians who, as heirs of the Reformation, emphasize Scripture as having supreme authority in the church, and the cross of Christ as being the only ground of salvation.

3 G. M. Trevelyan endorsed the opinion of the French historian Elie Halevy that evangelical religion in England "was the chief influence that prevented our country from starting along the path of revolutionary violence", *English Social History* (London: Longmans Green, 1942), p. 477. See also W. E. H. Lecky, *A History of England in the Eighteenth Century, vol. VI* (London: Longmans Green, 1919), p. 376.

4 J. Wesley Bready, *England: Before and After Wesley* (London: Hodder & Stoughton, 1939), pp. 11, 14.

5 Ibid., p. 126.

6 Ibid., p. 405.

7 Ibid.

8 Ibid., p. 327.

9 Ibid., p. 316.

10 Ernest Marshall Howse, *Saints in Politics, The "Clapham Sect" and the growth of freedom* (London: George Allen & Unwin, 1953), p. 26. See also Kenneth Hylson-Smith, *Evangelicals in the Church of England 1734 – 1984* (Edinburgh: T. & T. Clark, 1989), chapter 5.

11 Howse, *Saints in Politics*, p. 27.

12 Georgina Battiscombe, *Shaftesbury: A Biography of the 7th Earl 1801 – 1885* (Bend, Ore.: Constable, 1974), p. 334.

13 Quoted by David O. Moberg in *The Great Reversal, Evangelism versus social concern* (1972; London: Scripture Union, 1973), p. 184. For an account of evangelical social work in Britain in the nineteenth century, see also Kathleen Heasman, *Evangelicals in Action* (London: Geoffrey Bles, 1962).

14 Donald W. Dayton, *Discovering an Evangelical Heritage* (New York: Harper & Row, 1976), pp. 15 – 24. See also Timothy L. Smith, *Revivalism and Social Reform: American Protestantism on the Eve of the Civil War* (1957; Baltimore: Johns Hopkins Univ. Press, 1980). Dr Smith begins his preface by saying that Thomas Paine, if he had visited New York in 1865, would have been amazed to discover that "the emancipating glory of the great awakenings had made Christian liberty, Christian equality and Christian fraternity the passion of the land" (p. 7).

15 From an article by Donald W. Dayton in *The Post-American* (March 1975).

16 Moberg, *The Great Reversal*. See also George Marsden, *Fundamentalism and American Culture* (Oxford: Oxford Univ. Press, 1980), pp. 85 – 93; Smith, *Revivalism and Social Reform*, p. 212. For a more concise, historical look at the period of "the Great Reversal" see James Davidson Hunter, *American Evangelicalism: Conservative Religion and the Quandary of Modernity* (New Brunswick, N.J.: Rutgers Univ. Press, 1983), pp. 23 – 34.

17 Michael Cassidy, *The Passing Summer: A South African Pilgrimage in the Politics of Love* (London: Hodder & Stoughton, 1989), pp. 253 – 4.

18 Ibid., pp. 391 – 400.

19 Ibid., p. 149.

20 George Marsden, "An Overview", in Michael Cromartie (ed.), *No Longer Exiles* (Washington, DC: Ethics and Public Policy Center, 1993), p. 14.

21 Philip Crowe (ed.), The National Evangelical Anglican Congress, Keele 67 (London: Falcon, 1967), para. 20.

22 Stott (ed.), *Making Christ Known*, p. 185.

23 See Jim Wallis, *God's Politics: Why the Right Gets It Wrong and the Left Doesn't Get It* (New York: HarperCollins, 2005).

24 On this, see Alan Storkey, *Jesus and Politics: Confronting the Powers* (Grand Rapids: Baker Academic, 2005).

25 Cited on *www.christian-aid.org.uk/worship/0210into/quotes.htm*.

26 Stott (ed.), *Making Christ Known*, p. 196.

27 Ibid., pp. 197 – 8.

28 William Temple, *Christianity and the Social Order* (London: Penguin, 1942), p. 29.

29 "The Lausanne Covenant", para. 15. See Stott (ed.), *Making Christ Known*, p. 49.

30 Jane Hatfield, *Creative Prayer*, Spirituality Series no. 7 (Cambridge: Grove Books, 1983).

31 Temple, *Christianity and the Social Order*, p. 54.

32 Ibid.

33 Ibid., p. 31.

34 Ibid., p. 59.

35 Mikhail Bakunin, *The Political Philosophy of Bakunin*, ed. G. P Maximoff (Rockland, Me.: The Free Press, 1965), p. 271.

36 Brian Morris, "Anthropology and Anarchism", pp. 35 – 41, in *Anarchy: A Journal of Desire Armed*, no. 45, p. 38.

37 John R. Lucas, *Democracy and Participation* (1975; Harmondsworth: Pelican, 1976), p. 10. Also recommended is Reinhold Niebuhr, *The Children of the Light and the Children of the Darkness* (London: Nisbet, 1945). He wrote it eighteen months before the end of World War II, in which he saw "bourgeois civilization" collapsing before the onslaught of Nazi barbarism. He subtitles his book "A vindication of democracy and a critique of its traditional defenders". His faith in democracy was not the blind optimism of liberals who, having no conception of original sin, held a "fatuous and superficial view of man" (p. 15). It was rather that democracy is the best way to resolve the tension between the individual and the community, self-interest and the common good, freedom and order.

38 Niebuhr, *The Children of the Light*, p. vi.

39 Richard Neuhaus, *The Naked Public Square: Religion and Democracy in America* (Grand Rapids: Eerdmans, 1984), pp. 116, 124 – 5.

40 Stott (ed.), *Making Christ Known*, p. 202.

41 CARE, Jubilee Trust, Tearfund and the Institute for Contemporary Christianity (among others) all sponsor groups which seek to blend Christian thought on specific issues, with action. See M. A. Eden and E. C. Lucas, *Being Transformed* (London: Marshall, 1988), especially Appendix 3; and Roy McCloughry, *The Eye of the Needle* (Leicester: InterVarsity Press, 1990).

Our Complex World: Is Christian Thinking Distinctive?

2

Although it is vital to be informed about the issues with which we are confronted and about which we wish to take action, it is important to be sure about the theological foundations of social involvement. As Christians we have to be convinced that we have a Christian worldview and this can only be attained if we have a thoroughly biblical understanding of the basic tenets of our faith. Only this will save us from both that naïve oversimplification and that sense of despair which I described in the last chapter. I suggest that there are five areas in which God is challenging us to have a fuller grasp of what the Bible is saying.

THE FIVE FOUNDATIONS

A fuller doctrine of God

To begin with, we need a fuller doctrine of God. We tend to forget that God is concerned for the whole of humankind and for the whole of human life in all its colour and complexity. These universals have important consequences for our thinking.

Firstly, the living God is the God of nature as well as of religion, of the "secular" as well as of the "sacred". In fact, Christians are always uncomfortable about this distinction. Everything is "sacred" in the sense that it belongs to God, and nothing is "secular" in the sense that God is excluded from it. God made the physical universe, sustains it and still pronounces it good (Genesis 1:31). Indeed, "everything God created is good, and nothing is to be rejected if it is received with thanksgiving" (1 Timothy 4:4). We should be more grateful than we usually are for the good gifts of a good Creator – for sex, marriage and the family, for the beauty and order of the natural world, for work and leisure, for friendships and the experience of interracial, intercultural community, and for music and other kinds of creative art which enrich the quality of human life. Our God is often too small because he is too religious. We imagine that he is chiefly interested in religion – in religious buildings (churches and chapels), religious activities (worship and ritual) and religious books (Bibles and prayer books). Of course he is concerned about these things, but only if they are related to the whole of life. According to the Old Testament prophets and the teaching of Jesus, God is very critical of "religion", if by that is meant religious services divorced from real life, loving service and the moral obedience of the heart. "Religion that God our Father accepts as pure and faultless is this: to look after orphans and widows in their distress and to keep oneself from being polluted by the world" (James 1:27). The only value of religious services is that they concentrate into an hour or so of public, vocal, congregational activity the devotion of our whole life. If they do not do this, if instead we say and sing things in church which have no corollary in our everyday life outside church, at home and work, they are worse than worthless; their hypocrisy is positively nauseating to God.

Secondly, the living God is the God of the nations as well as of his covenant people. We Christians sometimes make the mistake which Israel made in the Old Testament when they concentrated exclusively on the God of the covenant, who had chosen them out of all the nations to be the holy nation, and who had pledged himself to them, saying, "I will be your God and you will be my people." To be sure, this was a glorious truth. The notion of "covenant" is a major biblical theme; the biblical revelation is unintelligible without it. But it is a dangerous half-truth. When Israel overemphasized it, they diminished the living God. They reduced him to the status of a tribal deity, a petty godling. He became Yahweh the god of the Israelites, more or less on a par with Chemosh the god of the Moabites and Milcom the god of the Ammonites. They also forgot the other nations, or simply despised and rejected them.

But the Bible begins with the nations, not Israel; with Adam, not Abraham; with the creation, not the covenant. And when God chose Israel, he did not lose interest in the nations. Amos bravely gave voice to the word of the Lord: "Are not you Israelites the same to me as the Cushites [or Ethiopians]? . . . Did I not bring Israel up from Egypt, the Philistines from Caphtor [Crete] and the Arameans from Kir?" (Amos 9:7). Similarly, the arrogant emperor Nebuchadnezzar had to learn that "the Most High is sovereign over the kingdoms of men and gives them to anyone he wishes" (Daniel 4:32). He rules over the nations. Their destiny is under his control. Although Satan is called "the ruler of this world" and is de facto its usurper, God remains the ultimate governor of everything he has made. "From heaven the LORD looks down and sees all mankind; from his dwelling-place he watches all who live on earth – he who forms the hearts of all, who considers everything they do" (Psalm 33:13 – 15). More than that, he has promised that in blessing Abraham and his posterity he will bless all the families of the earth, and that one day he will restore what the fall has marred, and bring to perfection all that he has made.

Thirdly, the living God is the God of justice as well as of justification.[1] Of course he is the God of justification, the Saviour of sinners, "the compassionate and gracious God, slow to anger, abounding in love and faithfulness" (Exodus 34:6). But he is also concerned that our community life be characterized by justice.

> He upholds the cause of the oppressed
> and gives food to the hungry.
> The LORD sets prisoners free,
> the LORD gives sight to the blind,
> the LORD lifts up those who are bowed down,
> the LORD loves the righteous.
> The LORD watches over the alien
> and sustains the fatherless and the widow,
> but he frustrates the ways of the wicked.
>
> PSALM 146:7 – 9

This does not mean that he does all these things invariably, but rather that this is the kind of God he is.

Moreover, God's concern for justice, although he expects it particularly among his own people, extends beyond them to all people. Social compassion and justice mattered to him in the nations as well as in Israel. There is no clearer evidence of this than in the first two chapters of the prophecy of Amos. Before Amos rebuked Judah for rejecting God's law and turning to idolatry and Israel for crushing the poor and denying justice to the oppressed (2:4 – 8), he pronounced God's judgement on all the surrounding nations (1:3 – 2:3) – on Syria for savage cruelty, on Philistia for capturing whole communities and selling them into slavery, on Tyre for breaking a treaty of brotherhood, on Edom for pitiless hostility to Israel, on Ammon for atrocities in warfare, and on Moab for desecrating the bones of a neighbouring king.

Several of the prophetic books similarly contain a section of oracles about or against the nations. That God is the God of justice and desires justice in every nation and community is particularly evident from the book of Nahum, which is a prophecy against Nineveh, the capital and symbol of Assyria. Yahweh's denunciation of Assyria is not just because she was Israel's long-standing enemy (e.g., 1:9ff.; 2:2ff.), but because of her idolatry (1:14) and because she is a "city of blood, full of lies, full of plunder, never without victims" (3:1). Twice Yahweh says the terrible words, "I am against you" (2:13; 3:5), and the oracle ends with the rhetorical question (3:19): "Who has not felt your endless cruelty?"

It is clear from these Old Testament passages that God hates injustice and oppression everywhere, and that he loves and promotes justice everywhere. Indeed, wherever righteousness is to be found in our fallen world, it is due to the working of his grace. All human beings know this too. We have an inbuilt sense of justice, to which the child's expostulation "It isn't fair!" bears eloquent witness. It is solid evidence of Paul's teaching that God's moral law is written on the human heart (Romans 2:14 – 15). Both God's law and God's gospel are for our good.

Here, then, is the living God of the Bible. His concerns are all-embracing – not only the "sacred" but the "secular", not only religion but nature, not only his covenant people but all people, not only justification but social justice in every community, not only his gospel but his law. We must not attempt to narrow down his interests. Moreover, ours should be as broad as his.

A fuller doctrine of human beings

All our philanthropic work – that is, work inspired by love for human beings – depends on our evaluation of them. The higher our view of their worth, the more we shall want to serve them.

Secular humanists, who are sincere in describing themselves as dedicated to "the human case and the human cause",[2] sometimes appear more humane than Christians. But if we ask them why they are so committed to humankind, they are likely to reply with Julian Huxley that it is because of the human potential in the future aeons of evolution. "Thus the development of man's vast potential of realizable possibility," he wrote, "provides the prime motive for collective action."[3] The inadequacy of this as a basis for service is obvious. If the unimpeded progress of evolution were our chief concern, why should we care for the hardened criminal, the psychopath, the chronically sick, or the starving? Would it not be more prudent to put them to sleep like a well-loved dog, lest they hinder the evolutionary process? Compulsory euthanasia, not compassionate service, would be the logical deduction from the humanists' premise. The fact that they draw back from this abyss indicates that their heart is better than their head, and their philanthropy better than their philosophy.

Christian people have a sounder basis for serving their fellow human beings. It is not because of what they may become in the speculative future development of the race, but because of what they already are by divine creation. Human beings are godlike beings made in God's likeness and possessing unique capacities which distinguish them from the animal creation. True, human beings are fallen, and the divine image is defaced; but despite all contrary appearances it has not been destroyed (Genesis 9:6; James 3:9). It is this which accounts for their unique worth and which has always inspired Christian philanthropy.

These human but godlike creatures are not just souls (that we should be concerned exclusively for their eternal salvation), not just bodies (that we should care only for their food, clothing, shelter and health), nor just social beings (that we should become entirely preoccupied with their community problems). They are all three. A human being might be defined from a biblical perspective as "a body-soul-in-a-community". That is how God has made us. Therefore, if we truly love our neighbours, and because of their worth desire to serve them, we shall be concerned for their total welfare, the well-being of their soul, their body and their community. Our concern will lead to practical programmes of evangelism, relief and development. We shall not just prattle and plan and pray, like that country vicar to whom a homeless woman turned for help, and who (doubtless sincerely, and because he was busy and felt helpless) promised to pray for her. She later wrote this poem and handed it to a regional officer of Shelter.

> I was hungry,
>   and you formed a humanities group to discuss my hunger.
> I was imprisoned,
>   and you crept off quietly to your chapel and prayed for my release.
> I was naked,

and in your mind you debated the morality of my appearance.
I was sick,
     and you knelt and thanked God for your health.
I was homeless,
     and you preached to me of the spiritual shelter of the love of God.
I was lonely,
     and you left me alone to pray for me.
You seem so holy, so close to God
     but I am still very hungry – and lonely – and cold.

So many Christians have been involved in coming alongside the poor and powerless, the sick, addicted and imprisoned since the time of Christ, not only serving their immediate needs, but also seeking justice on their behalf. Why have they done it? Because of the Christian doctrine of man, male and female, all made in the image of God, though all also fallen. Because people matter. Because every man, woman and child has an intrinsic, inalienable value as a human being. Once we see this, we shall both set ourselves to liberate people from everything dehumanizing and count it a privilege to serve them, to do everything in our power to make human life more human.

A fuller doctrine of Christ

There have been many different reinterpretations and reconstructions of Jesus. Indeed, it is right that every generation of Christians should seek to understand and to present him in terms appropriate to their own age and culture. So we have had Jesus the ascetic, the sufferer, the monarch, the gentleman, the clown, the superstar, the capitalist, the socialist, the revolutionary, the guerrilla, the wonder drug. Several of these portraits are mutually contradictory, of course, and others have little or no historical warrant. We have now also had *The Da Vinci Code* with its fantastical portrayal of a married Jesus with a child.

We need, then, to recover an authentic picture of him whom the Lausanne Covenant calls "the historical, biblical Christ" (para. 4). We need to see him in his paradoxical fullness – his sufferings and glory, his servanthood and lordship, his lowly incarnation and cosmic reign. It is perhaps the incarnation which we evangelicals have tended to neglect most, in both its theological significance and its practical implications.

The Son of God did not stay in the safe immunity of his heaven. He emptied himself of his glory and humbled himself to serve. He became little, weak and vulnerable. He entered into our pain, our alienation and temptations. He not only proclaimed the good news of the kingdom of God, but demonstrated its arrival by healing the sick, feeding the hungry, forgiving the sinful, befriending the drop-out and raising the dead. He had not come to be served, he said, but to serve and to give his life as a ransom price for the release of others. So he allowed himself to become a victim of gross injustice in the courts, and as they crucified him he prayed for his enemies. Then in the awful God-forsaken darkness he bore our sins in his own innocent person.

Should this vision of Christ not affect our understanding of his commission, "As the Father has sent me, I am sending you" (John 20:21)? For if the Christian mission is to be modelled on Christ's mission, it will surely involve for us, as it did for him, an entering into other people's worlds. In evangelism it will mean entering their thought world, and the world of their tragedy and lostness, in order to share Christ with them where they are. In social activity it will mean a willingness to renounce the comfort and security of our own cultural background in order to give ourselves in service to people of another culture, whose needs we may never before have known or experienced. Incarnational mission, whether evangelistic or social or both, necessitates a costly identification with people in their actual situations. Jesus of Nazareth was moved with compassion by the sight of needy human beings, whether sick or bereaved, hungry, harassed or helpless; should his people's compassion not be aroused by the same sights?

Leonidas Proaño was formerly Roman Catholic Bishop of Riobamba, about a hundred miles south of Quito, Ecuador. Basing his thinking on the Bible, he was strongly committed to social justice in his country, not least for the Indians whose culture he wanted to see preserved against those who were threatening to erode and even destroy it. Although he refused to identify himself with Marxism, and was in fact not a Marxist, he was critical – indeed defiant – of the political and ecclesiastical systems in his country. He opposed feudalism and the oppressive power of the wealthy landowners. It is perhaps not surprising that he was threatened with assassination. At all events, after the overthrow and death in 1973 of President Salvador Allende of Chile, Bishop Proaño preached at a mass for Marxist students in Quito. He portrayed Jesus as the radical he was, the critic of the establishment, the champion of the downtrodden, the lover of the poor, who not only preached the gospel but also gave compassionate service to the needy. After the mass there was a question time, during which some students said, "If we had known this Jesus, we would never have become Marxists."

Which Jesus do we believe in? And which Jesus do we preach? Is it possible that in some parts of the church such a false Jesus ("another Jesus" – 2 Corinthians 11:4) is being presented to the young people, that we are repelling them from him and driving them into the arms of Karl Marx instead?

A fuller doctrine of salvation

There is a constant tendency in the church to trivialize the nature of salvation, as if it meant no more than a self-reformation, or the forgiveness of our sins, or a personal passport to paradise, or a private mystical experience without social or moral consequences. It is urgent that we rescue salvation from these caricatures and recover the doctrine in its biblical fullness. For salvation is a radical transformation in three phases, beginning at our conversion, continuing throughout our earthly life and brought to perfection when Christ comes. In particular, we must overcome the temptation to separate truths which belong together.

Firstly, we must not separate salvation from the kingdom of God. In the Bible these two expressions are virtual synonyms, alternative models to describe the same work of God. According to Isaiah 52:7, those who preach good news of peace are also those "who proclaim salvation, who say to Zion, 'Your God reigns!' " That is, where God reigns, he saves. Salvation is the blessing of his rule. Again, when Jesus said to his disciples, "How hard it is to enter the kingdom of God," it seems to have been natural for them to respond with the question, "Who then can be saved?" (Mark 10:24 – 6). They evidently equated entering the kingdom with being saved.

Once this identification has been made, salvation takes on a broader aspect. The kingdom of God is God's dynamic rule, breaking into human history through Jesus, confronting, combating and overcoming evil, spreading the wholeness of personal and communal well-being, taking possession of his people in total blessing and total demand. The church is meant to be the kingdom community, a model of what human community looks like when it comes under the rule of God, and a challenging alternative to secular society. Entering God's kingdom is entering the new age, long promised in the Old Testament, which is also the beginning of God's new creation. Now we look forward to the consummation of the kingdom when our bodies, our society and our universe will all be renewed, and sin, pain, futility, disease and death will all be eradicated. Salvation is a big concept; we have no liberty to reduce it.

Secondly, we must not separate Jesus the Saviour from Jesus the Lord. It is little short of incredible that some evangelists teach the possibility of accepting Jesus the Saviour, while postponing a surrender to him as Lord. God has exalted Jesus to his right hand and made him Lord. From that position of supreme power and executive authority he is able to bestow salvation and the gift of the Spirit. It is precisely because he is Lord that he can save. The affirmations "Jesus is Lord" and "Jesus is Saviour" are almost interchangeable. And his lordship extends far beyond the religious bit of our lives. It embraces the whole of our experience, public and private, home and work, church membership and civic duty, evangelistic and social responsibilities.

Thirdly, we must not separate faith from love. Evangelical Christians have always emphasized faith. *Sola fide*, "by faith alone", was one of the great watchwords of the Reformation, and rightly so. "Justification", or acceptance with God, is not by good works which we have done or could do; it is only by God's sheer unmerited favour ("grace"), on the sole ground of the atoning death of Jesus Christ, by simple trust in him alone. This central truth of the gospel cannot be compromised for anything. But, although justification is by faith alone, this faith cannot remain alone. If it is living and authentic, it will inevitably issue in good works, and if it does not, it is spurious. Jesus himself taught this in his "sheep and goats" description of judgement day. Our attitude to him, he said, will be revealed in, and so be judged by, our good works of love to the least of his brothers and sisters. The apostles all lay the same emphasis on the necessity of good works of love. James teaches it: "Faith by itself, if it is not accompanied by action, is dead . . . I will show you my faith by what I do" (2:17 – 18). So does John: "If anyone has material possessions and sees his brother in need but has not pity on him, how can the love of God be in him?" (1 John 3:17). And so does Paul. Christ died to create a new people who would be "eager to do what is good" (Titus 2:14). We have been re-created in Christ "to do good works, which God prepared in advance for us to do" (Ephesians 2:10). Again, "The only thing that counts is faith expressing itself through love . . . serve one another in love" (Galatians 5:6, 13). This, then, is the striking sequence – faith, love, service. True faith issues in love, and true love issues in service.

It is especially those of us who are called "evangelical" Christians who need to take this New Testament emphasis to heart. We have to beware of magnifying faith and knowledge at the expense of love. Paul did not. If he were able to "fathom all mysteries and all knowledge", he wrote, and if he had "a faith that can move mountains", yet had no love, he would be nothing (1 Corinthians 13:2). Saving faith and serving love belong together. Whenever one is absent, so is the other. Neither can exist in isolation.

A fuller doctrine of the church

Many people think of the church as a kind of club, rather like the local golf club, except that the common interest of its members happens to be God rather than golf. They are religious people who do religious things together. They pay their subscription and are entitled to the privileges of club membership. In that frame of mind they forget William Temple's perceptive phrase, "The church is the only cooperative society that exists for the benefit of its non-members."[4]

In place of the "club" model of the church, we need to recover the truth of the church's "double identity". On the one hand, the church is a "holy" people, called out of the world to belong to God. But on the other it is a "worldly" people, in the sense of renouncing "otherworldliness" and being sent back into the world to witness and to serve. This is what Dr Alec Vidler, following a lead of Dietrich Bonhoeffer's, has called the church's "holy worldliness".[5] Seldom in its long and chequered history has the church remembered or preserved its double identity. Sometimes, in a right emphasis on its "holiness", the church has wrongly withdrawn from the world and become insulated from it. At other times, in a right emphasis on its "worldliness" (i.e., its immersion in the life of the world), the church has wrongly become assimilated into the world's standards and values, and so become contaminated by them. Yet without the preservation of both parts of its identity, the church cannot engage in mission. Mission arises out of the biblical doctrine of the church in society. An unbalanced ecclesiology makes mission unbalanced too.

Jesus taught these truths himself, not only in his famous expression "in the world but not of it" (see John 17:11 – 19), but in his vivid metaphors of the salt and the light. "You are the salt of the earth," he said, and "You are the light of the world" (Matthew 5:13 – 16). He implied (as we shall see more fully in chapter 3) that the two communities, the new and the old, the church and the world, are as radically different from one another as light from darkness and salt from decay. He also implied that, if they were to do any good, the salt must soak into the meat, and the light must shine into the darkness. Just so, Christians must penetrate a society which has turned its back on God. Thus the double identity and responsibility of the church are plain.

In a similar way the apostle Peter describes the members of God's new people on the one hand as "aliens and strangers in the world" and on the other as needing to be conscientious citizens in it (1 Peter 2:11 – 17). We cannot be totally "world-affirming" (as if nothing in it were evil), nor totally "world-denying" (as if nothing in it were good); we need to be a bit of both, and we particularly need to be "world-challenging", recognizing its potentiality as God's world and seeking to conform its life increasingly to his lordship.

This vision of the church's influence on society is best described in terms of "reform" rather than "redemption". As A. N. Triton has expressed it, "Redemption is not an infection of social structures … It results in individuals restored to a right relationship to God. But that sets up horizontal shock waves in society from which all of us benefit. These benefits are in terms of reforming society according to God's law, and not redeeming it by the death of Christ."[6]

The effectiveness of the church depends on its combination of "holiness" and "worldliness". We shall return to these images later.

A CHRISTIAN MIND

With a clear and thorough grasp of these five foundations for social involvement, we are ready to take the next steps in developing a Christian mind, for it is this which is our goal. It is only such a mind which can think with Christian integrity about the problems of the contemporary world.

This proposal immediately provokes opposition, however, from those Christians who have assimilated the anti-intellectual mood of today's world. They do not want to be told to use their minds, they say. Some even declare that it is "unspiritual" to do so. In response, we draw attention to Paul's injunction to the Corinthians: "Stop thinking like children. In … your thinking be adults" (1 Corinthians 14:20). The fact is that a proper use of our minds is wonderfully beneficial. (1) It glorifies God, because he has made us rational beings in his own image and has given us in Scripture a rational revelation which he intends us to study. (2) It enriches us, because every aspect of our Christian discipleship (e.g., our worship, faith and obedience) depends for its maturing on our reflection, respectively, upon God's glory, faithfulness and will. (3) It strengthens our witness in the world, because we are called like the apostles not only to "preach" the gospel, but also to "defend" and "argue" it and so "persuade" people of its truth (e.g., Acts 17:2f.; 19:8; 2 Corinthians 5:11; Philippians 1:7).

Towards the beginning of Romans 12 Paul uses the expression "the renewing of your mind". He has just issued his famous appeal to his Roman readers that, in gratitude for God's mercies, they should present their bodies to him as a "living sacrifice" and as their "spiritual worship". Now he goes on to explain how it is possible for God's people to serve him in the world. He sets before us an alternative. One way is to "be conformed" to this world or "age", to its standards (or lack of them), its values (largely materialistic) and its goals (self-centred and godless). These are the characteristics of Western culture. Moreover, the prevailing culture (like the prevailing wind) is not easy to stand up against. It is easier to take the line of least resistance and bow down before it, like "reeds swayed by the wind". Contemporary secularism is strong and subtle; the pressures to conform are great.

Paul exhorts us, however, not to be conformed to the world, but instead to "be transformed" by the renewing of our mind with a view to discerning God's pleasing and perfect will. Here, then, is the apostle's assumption both that Christians have or should have a renewed mind, and that our renewed mind will have a radical effect on our lives, since it will enable us to discern and approve God's will, and so transform our behaviour. The sequence is compelling. If we want to live straight, we have to think straight. If we want to think straight, we have to have renewed minds. Once our minds are renewed, we shall become preoccupied not with the way of the world, but with the will of God, which will change us.

Christian conversion means total renewal. The fall led to total depravity – a doctrine rejected, I suspect, only by those who misunderstand it. It has never meant that every human being is as depraved as he could possibly be, but rather that every part of our humanness, including our mind, has become distorted by the fall. So redemption involves total renewal (meaning not that we are now as good as we could be, but that every part of us, including our mind, has been renewed). The contrast is clear. Our old outlook led to conformity to the crowd; our new outlook has led us into moral nonconformity, out of concern for the will of God. Our fallen mind followed the way of the world; our renewed mind is engrossed with the will of God, as revealed in the Word of God. Between the two lies repentance, *metanoia*, a complete change of mind or outlook.

Paul writes not only of a "renewed mind" but also of "the mind of Christ". He exhorts the Philippians: "Let this mind be in you, which was also in Christ

Jesus" (2:5 AV). That is, as we study the teaching and example of Jesus, and consciously put our minds under the yoke of his authority (Matthew 11:29), we begin to think as he thought. His mind is gradually formed within us by the Holy Spirit, who is the Spirit of Christ. We see things his way, from his perspective. Our outlook becomes aligned to his. We almost dare to say what the apostle could say: "We have the mind of Christ" (1 Corinthians 2:16).

"The renewed mind." "The mind of Christ." "A Christian perspective." "The Christian mind." It was Harry Blamires who popularized this fourth expression in his book of that title, which since its publication in 1963 has had widespread influence. By a "Christian mind" he was referring not to a mind occupied with specifically "religious" topics, but to a mind which could think about even the most "secular" topics "Christianly" – that is, from a Christian perspective. It is not the mind of a schizoid Christian who "hops in and out of his Christian mentality as the topic of conversation changes from the Bible to the day's newspaper".[7] No, the Christian mind, he writes, is "a mind trained, informed, equipped to handle data of secular controversy within a framework of reference which is constructed of Christian presuppositions".[8] Blamires laments the contemporary loss of Christian thinking even among church leaders: "The Christian mind has succumbed to the secular drift with a degree of weakness and nervelessness unmatched in Christian history."[9] Having deplored its loss, Harry Blamires sets about canvassing for its recovery. He wants to witness the rise of the kind of Christian thinker who "challenges current prejudices ... disturbs the complacent ... obstructs the busy pragmatists ... questions the very foundations of all about him, and ... is a nuisance".[10]

Mr Blamires then goes on to list what he sees as the six essential "marks" of a Christian mind: (1) "its supernatural orientation" (it looks beyond time to eternity, beyond earth to heaven and hell, and meanwhile inhabits a world fashioned, sustained and "worried over" by God); (2) "its awareness of evil" (original sin perverting even the noblest things into instruments of "hungry vanity"); (3) "its conception of truth" (the givenness of divine revelation which cannot be compromised); (4) "its acceptance of authority" (what God has revealed requires from us "not an egalitarian attachment, but a bending submission"); (5) "its concern for the person" (a recognition of the value of human personality over against servitude to the machine); and (6) "its sacramental cast" (e.g., recognizing sexual love as "one of God's most efficient instruments" for the opening of man's heart to reality).

THE FOURFOLD FRAMEWORK

I have personally found it yet more helpful to adopt the framework provided by Scripture as a whole. The truly Christian mind has repented of "proof-texting" (the notion that we can settle every doctrinal and ethical issue by quoting a single, isolated text, whereas God has given us a comprehensive revelation), and instead saturates itself in the fullness of Scripture. In particular, it has absorbed the fourfold scheme of biblical history. The Bible divides human history into epochs, which are marked not by the rise and fall of empires, dynasties or civilizations, but by four major events: the creation, the fall, the redemption and the consummation.

Creation

Firstly, the creation. It is absolutely foundational to the Christian faith (and, therefore, to the Christian mind) that in the beginning, when time began, God made the universe out of nothing. He went on to make the planet earth, its land and seas and all their creatures. Finally, as the climax of his creative activity, he made man, male and female, in his own image. The godlikeness of humankind emerges as the story unfolds: Men and women are rational and moral beings (able to understand and respond to God's commands), responsible beings (exercising dominion over nature), social beings (with a capacity to love and be loved), and spiritual beings (finding their highest fulfilment in knowing and worshipping their Creator). Indeed, the Creator and his human creatures are depicted as walking and talking together in the garden. All this was the godlikeness which gave Adam and Eve their unique worth and dignity.

Fall

Next, the fall. They listened to Satan's lies, instead of God's truth. In consequence of their disobedience they were driven out of the garden. No greater tragedy has befallen human beings than this, that though made by God like God and for God, they now live without God. All our human alienation, disorientation and sense of meaninglessness stem ultimately from this. In addition, our relationships with each other have become skewed. Sexual equality was upset: "Your husband . . . will rule over you" (Genesis 3:16). Pain came to haunt the threshold of motherhood. Cain's jealous hatred of his brother erupted into murder. Even nature was put out of joint. The ground was cursed because of man, the cultivation of the soil became an uphill struggle, and creative work degenerated into drudgery. Over the centuries men and women have slipped from the responsible stewardship of the environment entrusted to them, and have cut down the forests, created deserts and dustbowls, polluted rivers and seas, and fouled the atmosphere with poisons. "Original sin" means that our inherited human nature is now twisted with a disastrous self-centredness. Evil is an ingrained, pervasive reality. Although our godlikeness has not been destroyed, it has been seriously distorted. We no longer love God with all our being, but are hostile to him and under his just condemnation.

Redemption

Thirdly, the redemption. Instead of abandoning or destroying his rebellious creatures, as they deserved, God planned to redeem them. No sooner had they sinned than God promised that the woman's seed would crush the serpent's head (Genesis 3:15), which we recognize as the first prediction of the coming Saviour. God's redemptive purpose began to take clearer shape when he called Abraham and entered into a solemn covenant with him, promising to bless both him and through his posterity all the families of the earth – another promise which we know has been fulfilled in Christ and his worldwide community. God renewed his covenant, this time with Israel, at Mount Sinai, and kept promising through the prophets that there was more, much more, to come in the days of the messianic kingdom. Then in the fullness of time the Messiah came. With him the new age dawned, the kingdom of God broke in, the end began. Now today, through the death, resurrection and Spirit-gift of Jesus, God is fulfilling his promise of redemption and is remaking marred humankind, saving individuals and incorporating them into his new, reconciled community.

Consummation

Fourth will come the consummation. One day, when the good news of the kingdom has been proclaimed throughout the whole world (Matthew 24:14), Jesus Christ will appear in great magnificence. He will raise the dead, judge the world, regenerate the universe and bring God's kingdom to its perfection. From it all pain, decay, sin, sorrow and death will be banished, and in it God will be glorified for ever. Meanwhile, we are living in between times, between kingdom come and kingdom coming, between the "now" and the "then" of redemption, between the "already" and the "not yet".

Here, then, are four events which correspond to four realities – namely the creation ("the good"), the fall ("the evil"), the redemption ("the new") and the consummation ("the perfect"). This fourfold biblical reality enables Christians to survey the historical landscape within its proper horizons. It supplies the true perspective from which to view the unfolding process between two eternities, the vision of God working out his purpose. It gives us a framework into which to fit everything, a way of integrating our understanding, the possibility of thinking straight, even about the most complex issues.

The four events or epochs we have been thinking about, especially when grasped in relation to one another, teach major truths about God, human beings and society which give direction to our Christian thinking.

THREE APPLICATIONS

The reality of God

First, let us look at the reality of God. The fourfold biblical scheme is essentially God-centred; its four stages are disclosed from his point of view. Even the fall, though an act of human disobedience, is presented in the context of divine commandments, sanctions and judgement. Thus it is God who creates, judges, redeems and perfects. The initiative is his from beginning to end. In consequence, there is a cluster of popular attitudes which are fundamentally incompatible with Christian faith: e.g., the concept of blind evolutionary development; the assertion of human autonomy in art, science and education, and the declarations that history is random, life is absurd and everything is meaningless. The Christian mind comes into direct collision with these notions precisely because they are "secular" – that is, because they leave no room for God. It insists that human beings can be defined only in relation to God, that without God they have ceased to be truly human. For we are creatures who depend on our Creator, sinners who are accountable to him and under his judgement, waifs and strays who are lost apart from his redemption.

This God-centredness is basic to the Christian mind. The Christian mind is a godly mind. More than that, it understands "goodness" above all in terms of "godliness". It cannot describe as "good" a person who is "ungodly". This is the clear testimony of the Bible's Wisdom Literature. The five books of Wisdom (Job, Psalms, Proverbs, Ecclesiastes and the Song of Songs) all focus, in different ways and with different emphases, on what it means to be human, and on how suffering, evil, oppression and love fit into our humanness. The book of Ecclesiastes is best known for its pessimistic refrain, "Vanity of vanities! All is vanity" (NASB), well translated by the NIV as "meaningless, meaningless, utterly meaningless". It demonstrates the folly and futility of a human life circumscribed by time and space. If life is restricted to the average brief lifespan, overshadowed by pain and injustice, and culminates for everybody in the same fate, death; if it is also restricted by the dimensions of space to human experiences "under the sun", with no ultimate reference point beyond the sun – then indeed life is as profitless as "a chasing after wind". Only God, Creator and Judge, Beginning and End, by adding to human life the missing dimensions of transcendence and eternity, can give it meaning, and so turn folly into wisdom.

Over against the pessimism of Ecclesiastes we read the oft-repeated maxim of the Wisdom Literature, namely, "The fear of the Lord – that is wisdom [or its "beginning" or "principle"], and to shun evil is understanding" (Job 28:28; cf. Psalm 111:10; Proverbs 1:7; 9:10; Ecclesiastes 12:13). Here are the two major realities of human experience, God and evil. They are not equal realities, for Christians are not dualists, but they dominate life on earth. The one (God) brings human fulfilment, even ecstasy; the other (evil) human alienation, even despair. Wisdom consists in adopting a right attitude to both: loving God and hating evil, "fearing" God with the worship which acknowledges his infinite worth, and "shunning" evil in the holiness which despises it for its worthlessness. It is because God has made us spiritual and moral beings that religion and ethics, godliness and goodness, are fundamental to authentic humanness. Hence the tragedy of "secularism", the closed worldview which denies God and even glories in the spiritual vacuum it creates. T. S. Eliot was right to call it a "waste land", and Theodore Roszak in *Where the Wasteland Ends* to characterize it as a desert of the spirit. "For what science can measure is only a portion of what man can know. Our knowing reaches out to embrace the sacred." Without transcendence "the person shrivels".[11] Secularism not only dethrones God; it destroys human beings.

If, because of the reality of God, the Christian mind is a godly mind, it is also a humble mind. This is another consistent theme of Scripture. When Nebuchadnezzar strutted like a peacock round the flat rooftop of his Babylonian palace claiming for himself instead of God the kingdom, the power and the glory, he went mad. Only when he acknowledged the rule of God and worshipped him were his reason and his kingdom simultaneously restored to him. Daniel pointed out the moral: "Those who walk in pride he is able to humble"

(Daniel 4:28 – 37). It is a sobering story. If pride and madness go together, so do humility and sanity.

Jesus' contemporaries must have been dumbfounded when he told adults that they had to become like children if they wanted to enter God's kingdom, and (even worse) that greatness in the kingdom would be measured by child-like humility. We are too familiar with this teaching; it has lost its power to shock or stun. Yet Jesus not only taught it; he exhibited it. He emptied himself and humbled himself. So now, Paul adds, "Let this mind be in you which was in him". The medieval moralists were right to see pride as the worst of the "seven deadly sins" and as the root of the others. There is nothing so obscene as pride, nothing so attractive as humility.

Probably at no point does the Christian mind clash more violently with the secular mind than in its insistence on humility and its implacable hostility to pride. The wisdom of the world despises humility. Western culture has imbibed more than it knows of the power philosophy of Nietzsche. The world's model, like Nietzsche's, is the "superman"; the model of Jesus remains the little child.

Thus the reality of God (as Creator, Lord, Redeemer, Father, Judge) gives to the Christian mind its first and most fundamental characteristic. Christians refuse to honour anything which dishonours God. We learn to evaluate everything in terms of the glory it gives to, or withholds from, God. That is why, to the Christian mind, wisdom is the fear of God and the pre-eminent virtue is humility.

The human enigma

I turn now from God to man, from the unalloyed splendour which character-izes whatever is "divine" to the painful ambiguity which attaches to everything "human". We have already seen that the biblical understanding of humankind takes equal account of the creation and the fall. It is this that constitutes "the paradox of our humanness". We human beings have both a unique dignity as creatures made in God's image and a unique depravity as sinners under his judgement. The former gives us hope; the latter places a limit on our expecta-tions. Our Christian critique of the secular mind is that it tends to be either too naïvely optimistic or too negatively pessimistic in its estimates of the human condition, whereas the Christian mind, firmly rooted in biblical realism, both celebrates the glory and deplores the shame of our human being. We can behave like God in whose image we were made, only to descend to the level of the beasts. We are able to think, choose, create, love and worship, but also to refuse to think, to choose evil, to destroy, to hate, and to worship ourselves. We build churches and drop bombs. We develop intensive care units for the critically ill and use the same technology to torture political enemies who presume to disagree with us. This is "humanity", a strange, bewildering paradox, dust of earth and breath of God, shame and glory. So, as the Christian mind applies itself to human life on earth, to our personal, social and political affairs, it seeks to remember what paradoxical creatures we are – noble and ignoble, rational and irrational, loving and selfish, godlike and bestial.

The possibility of social change

A third sphere to which it may be helpful to apply the Bible's fourfold scheme is that of the possibility of social change. What expectation should we cherish that society can be improved? On this issue Christians of different traditions are to be found along a broad spectrum.

"Liberal" Christians have tended to be social activists. Because of their almost boundless confidence in human achievement, they dream dreams of building Utopia (sometimes mistakenly identified as "the kingdom of God") on earth.

"Evangelical" Christians, on the other hand, have tended – at least earlier in the twentieth century – to be social quietists. Because of their gloomy view of human depravity, they lack confidence in human beings (at least until they have been born again). They, therefore, consider social action a waste of time and social transformation all but impossible.

I have deliberately expressed both positions in their more extreme forms. Stated thus, the polarization fails to hold together the two parts of the human paradox.

Because human beings are made in the image of God, and the divine image (though marred) has not been wholly lost, they retain some perception of the just and compassionate society which would please him, and some desire to bring it about. On the whole, all humankind still prefers peace to war, justice to oppression, harmony to discord, order to chaos. So social change is possible, and indeed has happened. In many parts of the world we can see rising standards of hygiene and health care, a greater respect for women and children, the increasing availability of education, a clearer recognition of human rights, a growing concern to conserve the natural environment, and better conditions in mines, factories and prisons. Much of this has been due (directly or indirectly) to Christian influence, although by no means have all social reformers been committed Christians. But whenever God's people have been effective as salt and light in the community, there has been less social decay and more social uplift. In the United States, for example, after the early nineteenth-century awakening associated with Charles G. Finney, "born-again Christians were in the forefront of every major social reform in America ... They spear-headed the abolitionist movement, the temperance movement, the peace movement, and the early feminist movement."[12]

Because human beings are fallen, however, and inherit a twist of self-centredness, we shall never succeed in building a perfect society. Improvement – yes; perfect justice – no. Utopian dreams are unrealistic; they belong to the world of fantasy. All human plans, though launched with great hopes, have to some degree disappointed the planners, for they have foundered on the rock of human selfishness. Christians have usually remembered this. It is socialists who have tended to be too optimistic about human achievement. Professor C. E. M. Joad is a good example. Having been brought up on the confessions and collects of the Church of England's 1662 Book of Common Prayer, he began by believing in the inherent sinfulness of human beings. But later he discarded this notion in favour of their "infinite perfectibility", until World War II shattered this illusion and convinced him again that "evil is endemic in man". He wrote candidly in his book *Recovery of Belief*: "It is because we rejected the doctrine of original sin that we on the Left were always being disappointed; disappointed by the refusal of people to be reasonable, by the subservience of intellect to emotion, by the failure of true Socialism to arrive ... above all, by the recurrent fact of war."[13]

How, then, can we sum up an attitude to the possibility of social change which reflects "neither the easy optimism of the humanist, nor the dark pessimism of the cynic, but the radical realism of the Bible"?[14] How can we do equal justice to the truths of the creation, the fall, the redemption and the consummation? I suggest that the biblical balance is well expressed by Paul in 1 Thessalonians 1:9 – 10, where he describes the results of conversion from idols to God as being "to serve the living and true God, and to wait for his Son from heaven". The combination of "serving" and "waiting" is striking, since the former is actively getting busy for Christ on earth, while the latter is passively looking for him to come from heaven. We must serve, but there are limits to what we can achieve. We must wait, but have no liberty to do so in idleness. Thus "working" and "waiting" go together. The need to wait for Christ from heaven will rescue us from the presumption which thinks we can do everything; the need to work for Christ on earth will rescue us from the pessimism which thinks we can do nothing. Only a Christian mind which has developed a biblical perspective can enable us to preserve the balance.

I began this chapter by admitting the complexity of the problems of personal and social ethics which confront us today. Neat, cut-and-dried solutions are usually impossible. Simplistic shortcuts, which ignore the real issues, are unhelpful. At the same time, it is not Christian to give up in despair.

We need to remember for our encouragement that God has given us four gifts.

THE FOUR GIFTS

Our minds

His first gift is a mind with which to think. He has made us rational, intelligent creatures. He still forbids us to behave like horses and mules which lack understanding, and tells us in our thinking to be not babies but adults (Psalm 32:9; 1 Corinthians 14:20).

The Bible

Secondly, he has given us the Bible and its witness to Christ, in order to direct and control our thinking. As we absorb its teaching, our thoughts will increasingly conform to his. This is not because we memorize a lot of proof texts, which we trot out at appropriate moments, each text labelled to answer its own question. It is rather that we have grasped the great themes and principles of Scripture and the fourfold framework which we have been considering in this chapter.

The Holy Spirit

God's third gift is the Holy Spirit, the Spirit of truth, who opens up the Scriptures to us and illumines our minds so that we can understand and apply them.

The Christian community

Fourthly, God has given us the Christian community as the context in which to do our thinking. Its heterogeneity is the best safeguard against blinkered vision. The church has members of both sexes and of all ages, temperaments, experiences and cultures. Each local church should reflect this colourful diversity. With rich insights contributed to the interpretation of Scripture from different backgrounds, it will be hard to maintain our prejudices.

With these four gifts, used in concert – a mind, a textbook, a Teacher and a school – it should be possible for us to develop an increasingly Christian mind and to learn to think straight.

In the rest of this book these issues are present either explicitly or implicitly in every chapter. Whether the subject is the political process, which I have already mentioned or issues to do with sexuality, war or the environment, the Christian mind is distinctive in approach, humble in attitude and godly in character.

NOTES

1 I think it was Dr Carl Henry who coined this phrase. See his autobiography, *Confessions of a Theologian* (Waco: Word, 1986), p. 257.

2 H. J. Blackham, *Humanism* (Harmondsworth: Penguin, 1968). He writes: "Humanism is the human case and the human cause, an age-old conviction about the human case ... which will induce men and women ... to espouse the human cause with head and heart and with two hands", (p. 9).

3 Sir Julian Huxley (ed.), *The Humanist Frame* (London: George Allen & Unwin, 1961), p. 47.

4 Quoted by Charles Smyth in *Cyril Forster Garbett* (London: Hodder & Stoughton, 1959), p. 106.

5 A. R. Vidler, *Essays in Liberality* (London: SCM, 1957), pp. 95 – 112. Dr Vidler contrasted it with "unholy worldliness", which is "to conform uncritically and complacently to the standards and fashions that prevail" (p. 96).

6 A. N. Triton, *Whose World?* (Leicester: InterVarsity Press, 1970), pp. 35 – 36.

7 Harry Blamires, *The Christian Mind* (London: SPCK, 1963), p. 70.

8 Ibid., p. 43.

9 Ibid., p. 3.

10 Ibid., p. 50.

11 Theodore Roszak, *Where the Wasteland Ends: Politics and Transcendence in Post-Industrial Society* (1972; New York: Anchor, 1973), pp. xxi, 67.

12 Tom Sine, *The Mustard Seed Conspiracy* (Waco: Word, 1981), p. 70.

13 C. E. M. Joad, *The Recovery of Belief* (London: Faber & Faber, 1952), p. 82.

14 J. S. Whale, *Christian Doctrine* (1941; London: Fontana, 1957), p. 41.

Our Plural World: Is Christian Witness Influential?

3

We accept that we should get involved, and we struggle to think Christianly about the issues. In consequence, we develop some quite strong convictions, but others do not share them. Indeed, Western Christians find themselves increasingly out of step with a post-Christian society. So how can we hope to influence our country into a return to Christian values, in its laws, its institutions and its culture? Should Christians attempt to impose their views on a nation which has turned its back on God?

COMING TO TERMS WITH PLURALISM

In Europe and America, and in those Commonwealth countries which inherited the "Christian civilization" of the West, we certainly have to come to terms with the new "pluralism", meaning a society composed of different groups, some of them ethnic and religious groups, who do not share a Christian worldview. Pluralism is due largely to three factors.

The process of secularization

The first is the process of secularization, seen as the diminishing influence of the church on both people and institutions. Although in the 2001 population census in the UK 72% of the population described themselves as Christian, this was a decline from 76% in 1980. One indicator of the pattern of decline can be seen in the percentage that UK church membership is of the total population. In 1990 one person in nine in the population was a church member; by 2020 it will be just one person in fourteen.[1] Over the period 1990 – 2040, if current trends prove to be accurate, Sunday attendance in the UK is set to more than halve.

So whatever happens to the number of buildings in which worship takes place or the number of ministers of whatever kind who are present, the numbers of people attending church will be significantly reduced. It is also significant to note that these declining numbers are part of a larger pattern of decline that has been in place since World War II.

While overall church membership has continued to decline in recent years, the statistics are not as depressing as they may seem at first glance. Many evangelical and charismatic churches are experiencing periods of growth, and there is a renewed interest in church-planting as well as an exploration of new ways of being church, which has been in part stimulated by the current crisis. When the trends to 2040 are considered, it can be seen that in several denominations larger churches are growing. This is true for the Anglicans, Christian Brethren, Fellowship of Independent Evangelical Churches and the charismatic New Churches. The word "larger" in each case is relative to the particular denomination, but the very large churches are growing – though more likely in church attendance than in church membership. However, with overall church membership reducing, this can only mean that the membership of smaller churches is declining while membership of larger churches is increasing.[2] In particular, the proportion of evangelicals is growing both in the developed world and in the Majority World. It is also happening in the UK among both institutional and free churches.

It is important to remember that when the state of the church is analysed within a global perspective, we see that in many countries the church is growing at a rapid rate. In much of the Majority World many are joining the church. Even in countries such as China, where the church is persecuted, it is expanding.

An increase in religious alternatives

Alongside the Christian decline has gone an increase in religious alternatives. The second cause of pluralism is the liberal immigration policy of the immediate post-war years. As a result, most Western countries now include in their populations sizeable ethnic groups from Africa, Asia, the Middle East and the Caribbean. This makes possible for all of us a rich experience of cultural diversity. But it also leads to religious competition and to consequent demands for recognition of other religions in those countries' educational systems, laws and institutions.

In recent years in the UK, this has led to a concern about the influence of religious groups on mainstream culture. As tension between Islamicists and the West has increased, this tension has sometimes been projected onto Muslims worshipping peacefully in our society. It is important to respect the right of Muslims and members of other religions to worship freely, yet it is also important to have the right to debate and disagree with one another about the way we live together and organize our society. In Canada, more specifically in the state of Ontario, some forms of arbitration can be conducted according to the principles of the faith community to which people belong rather than by state regulation. In other words, it is possible for a divorce, for instance, to be carried out in accordance with Jewish or Muslim law rather than secular law. This has been the case for some time, and there is now a debate as to whether it should continue. Opposition to this comes from those groups who believe that the status of women is undermined when divorce takes place under shariah law. So, while respecting the views of those who belong to other religions, we must be careful to be aware of their influence on the society in which we live, as we also invite them to debate with us about the way we live and the positions we hold. What we cannot do is seek to impose our worldview on other religious groups even though we are aware that we disagree with them. However, we must never succumb to stereotyping or conspiracy theories, blaming religious groups for what we perceive as the spiritual decline of the nation when the causes lie elsewhere.

Elsewhere in the world, even if Christians represent a substantial minority, the predominant culture is either Hindu or Buddhist, Jewish or Islamic, Marxist or secular. So here too, usually in a more acute form, Christians are faced with the same dilemma. In many issues they believe they know the will of God. They also believe it is their Christian duty to pray and work for God's will to be done. Should they hope to impose their Christian convictions on those people who are not Christians? If it is possible, is it desirable? Even if they could, should they try?

The development of a postmodern imagination

Our world, particularly the West, has shifted on its axis and has in many respects moved from being modern to postmodern. The old certainties and convictions that humanity had the answers to life's problems have given way to a new sense of uncertainty and even anxiety as we realize that many of our actions have produced unintentional consequences which have been disastrous – not least in the area of the environment. We also live in a post-traditional society where institutions such as marriage have become one choice among many. Pluralism is not, then, just an expression of the number of ethnic or religious groups in a society. It also involves the fragmentation of all kinds of beliefs due to the breakdown of shared values and the distrust of any kind of authority, particularly political and religious authority. The so-called "metanarratives" – the big stories which purported to explain all of life, Christianity among them – have now fragmented, and truth is seen as personal rather than public, subjective rather than objective. The idea that each person has a different view of truth, but that no one person has the right to challenge another as to the veracity of that belief, is at the heart of the postmodern worldview.

In such a society Christianity cannot back down on its essential claim that God has revealed the truth through Christ and that this truth is what the late Francis Schaeffer used to call "true truth". God's revelation in Christ is at the heart of the gospel. It is non-negotiable. At the same time we have to realize that our postmodern society provides creative challenges for Christian witness which are very positive. We cannot go back to the evangelistic methods of the 1950s; we must rethink the way we conduct mission for the twenty-first century. How can we best witness to Christ in a pluralistic society which views truth as relative? This question is at the heart of dozens of new creative experiments in what it means to reach out to people who distrust the church and are indifferent to its message. This is not the time to succumb to despair because of the challenge of church decline, or to be defensive in a multicultural society. This is a time to regain what theologian Lesslie Newbigin called "a proper confidence" in the gospel (neither imposing it on others nor being timid in holding to its truths) and make a stand in the middle of a community which is built on shifting sand.

So pluralism is mainly due to three factors: the decline of the institutional church, the rise of religious alternatives and the fragmentation of the nature of belief. What are we to do about this?

THREE RESPONSES TO PLURALISM

The two commonest responses to this question represent opposite extremes. One is "imposition", the crusading attempt to coerce people by legislation to accept the Christian way. The other is "laissez-faire", the defeatist decision to leave people alone and not interfere or try to influence them in any way. We need to look carefully at these alternatives, with some historical examples, before we shall be ready for a third and better option.

Imposition

Here are Christians with a commendable zeal for God. They believe in revelation and care deeply about God's revealed truth and will. They long to see society reflecting it. So the desire to achieve this end by force is an understandable temptation. One example of this is the Inquisition, which started in 1252 and lasted for 300 years. During this time the Roman Catholic Church sought out those who were thought of as heretics and, using torture and other coercive means, tried to get them to confess and if they would not do so brought them to trial and then death, often at the stake. Today, of course, we are ashamed of such methods, as they are incompatible with the Christian faith. I have already talked about the incompatibility of any authoritarian regime with Christianity, and this is yet another example of that.

But then the policy of imposition is impossible to those who hold a biblical doctrine of human beings. God made male and female to be responsible beings. He told them to be fruitful (to exercise their powers of procreation), to subdue the earth and rule its creatures, to work and to rest, and to obey him ("you may ... you must not..."). These injunctions would be meaningless if God had not endowed humankind with two unique gifts – conscience (to discern between alternatives) and freedom (to choose between them). The rest of the Bible confirms this. It is assumed throughout that human beings are moral beings, who are accountable for their actions. They know the moral law, since it is "written on their hearts" (Romans 2:14 – 15), and are exhorted to obedience and warned of the penalties of disobedience. But they are never coerced. No compulsion is ever used – only persuasion by argument: " 'Come now, let us reason together,' says the Lord" (Isaiah 1:18).

You cannot force people to believe what they do not believe or practise what they do not want to practise. Similarly, to imagine today that we can force Christian convictions and standards on Europe (for example) is totally unrealistic. It is a foolish, nostalgic desire for a Christendom which has long since vanished.

Laissez-faire

The opposite to imposition, I suggest, is laissez-faire. The term was originally used in the eighteenth century of free trade economists, and the concept was important in nineteenth-century economic debate and political policy. It was a principled belief in the necessity of non-interference by government.

In our postmodern age, there is a confusion between tolerance and laissez-faire to such an extent that it is sometimes believed that to disagree with somebody is to be intolerant of them. It is certainly the case that all worldviews are seen to be equal and that, therefore, no perspective has the right to see itself as more authoritative than another. However, as I have already mentioned, if Christians believe that God has revealed the truth in Jesus Christ, then taking this position is not an option. What has happened is that true tolerance, which respects the views of others while disagreeing with them, has become a false or empty tolerance, which does not bother to engage and amounts to indifference. It is also important to point out that on many occasions those who are meant to be tolerant of all other perspectives find themselves being extremely intolerant of Christian perspectives, thus giving the game away.

Christians should be tolerant of the views of others and show respect towards them. They should also be socially tolerant in the sense that they should want to see political and religious minorities accepted in the community and protected by law, just as the Christian minority in a country which is not Christian expects to be legally free to profess, practise and propagate the gospel. But how can we Christians be intellectually tolerant of opinions we know to be false or actions we know to be evil? What kind of unprincipled indulgence is this? God is not indifferent to questions of social justice, so how can the church be? To remain silent and inactive when error or evil is being canvassed has very serious consequences, for the Christian option has then gone by default. Is it not at least partly because Christians have failed to raise their voices for Jesus Christ that our country has slipped its Christian moorings and drifted away from them?

The gravest modern example of Christian laissez-faire is the failure of German churches to speak out against the Nazis' treatment of the Jews, thoroughly documented by Richard Gutteridge in his book *Open Thy Mouth for the Dumb*.[3] After World War I there were several attempts to give a theological foundation for the Aryan views associated with the National Socialist Movement, citing the need to remain pure and separate from the links of Christianity with Judaism. Only a few brave voices (like those of Karl Barth and Paul Tillich) were raised in protest. Meanwhile, the "Faith Movement of German Christians", under the patronage of the Nazi Party, affirmed the Aryan race.

After Hitler came to power in 1933, a law was passed to purge the civil service of officials of non-Aryan descent and, incredible as it may seem, the racially compromised "German Christians" wanted to apply this "Aryan Clause" to the church. Several synods adopted it, against the opposition of men like Martin Niemöller, Walter Künneth, Hans Lilje and Dietrich Bonhoeffer. Yet "the Evangelical Church never spoke out officially against the Aryan legislation in general." Bonhoeffer was deeply upset by the church's silence and frequently quoted Proverbs 31:8: "Open thy mouth for the dumb." [4]

In the terrible pogrom of November 1938, tens of thousands of Jews suffered horribly at the hands of Hitler and his followers. The general public was aghast, and some church leaders protested. But both the Evangelical Church and the Catholic Church kept almost completely silent. It was not until 1943, two years after the onset of Hitler's "Final Solution", that a conference of Lutheran Church leaders resolved to attack the Reich government for its anti-Jewish atrocities. Barth called this failure to denounce anti-Semitism "the sin against the Holy Ghost" and a "rejection of the grace of God".[5] Some other church officials were equally bold, and paid dearly for their courage. But when Evangelical Church leaders met soon after the end of the war and issued their "Stuttgart Declaration", they had to acknowledge: "It is our self-indictment that we have not made a more courageous confession."[6] Of course church leaders had to take their share of the blame, but there was also no expression of righteous indignation by ordinary decent Christian folk. Such widespread condemnation would have had to be taken seriously by the Nazi leadership.

The story Richard Gutteridge tells speaks for itself. It needs no additional comment from me. The complicity of the "German Christians", who failed to develop a biblical critique of the Nazis' blatant racism, should be enough to outlaw laissez-faire for ever. Could they not have prevented the Holocaust?

Persuasion

Better than the extremes of imposition and laissez-faire is the strategy of persuasion by argument. This is the way the Christian mind advocates, for it arises naturally from the biblical doctrines of God and human beings.

The nature of God

The living God of the biblical revelation, who created and sustains the universe, intended the human beings he made to live in loving community. He loves all people whatever their condition and desires them to be saved. We too are to love others. We are to respect men and women made in God's image, seek justice, hate injustice, care for the needy, guard the dignity of work, recognize the necessity of rest, maintain the sanctity of marriage, be zealous for the honour of Jesus Christ and long that every knee will do homage to him and every tongue confess him. Why? Because all these are God's concerns. How can we acquiesce in things which passionately displease him, or affect nonchalance about things to which he is strongly committed? The policy of laissez-faire is inconceivable to Christians who hold a biblical doctrine of God.

Respect for conscience

A basic ground for this is that the human conscience must be treated with the greatest respect. Paul expresses his personal determination "to keep my conscience clear before God and man" (Acts 24:16). He also has much to say about other people's consciences. They may be "strong" (well educated and free) or "weak" (overscrupulous and full of qualms), but whatever the condition of a person's conscience, even when it is mistaken, it is to be respected. Weak consciences need to be strengthened and deceiving consciences enlightened, but there must be no bullying of consciences. Only in the most extreme circumstances should people be induced to act against their consciences. In general, consciences are to be educated, not violated. This principle, which arises out of the Christian doctrine of human beings, should affect our social behaviour and institutions. It is the reason why Christians oppose autocracy and favour democracy. Autocracy crushes consciences; democracy (at least in theory) respects them, since democratic governments derive "their just powers from the consent of the governed" (as the American Declaration of Independence states).[7] Once laws have been promulgated, however, all citizens (in a democracy as in an autocracy) are under constraint to obey them. They may not do as they please. Yet in matters of great moment (e.g., conscription in time of war) a civilized government will allow "conscientious objection". This provision is also the product of Christian thinking.

So both the biblical doctrine of God and that of human beings guide our behaviour in a pluralistic society, the former ruling out laissez-faire and the latter ruling out imposition. Because God is who he is, we cannot be indifferent when his truth and law are flouted, but because human beings are who they are, we cannot try to impose them by force.

What, then, should Christians do? We should seek to educate the public conscience to know and desire the will of God. The church should seek to be the conscience of the nation. If we cannot impose God's will by legislation, neither can we convince people of it merely by biblical quotation. Both these approaches are examples of "authority from above", which people resent and resist. More effective is "authority from below", the intrinsic truth and value of a thing which is self-evident and, therefore, self-authenticating. (Not that the two are incompatible; God's authority is essentially both.) This principle applies equally in evangelism and social action.

In evangelism we should neither try to force people to believe the gospel, nor remain silent as if we were indifferent to their response, nor rely exclusively on the dogmatic proclamation of biblical texts (vital as authoritative biblical exposition is), but rather, like the apostles, we should reason with people from both nature and Scripture, commending God's gospel to them by rational arguments.

In social action, similarly, we should neither try to impose Christian standards by force on an unwilling public, nor remain silent and inactive before the contemporary landslide, nor rely exclusively on the dogmatic assertion of biblical values, but rather reason with people about the benefits of Christian morality, commending God's law to them by rational arguments. We believe that God's laws are both good in themselves and universal in their application because, far from being arbitrary, they fit the human beings God has made. This was God's claim for his laws from the beginning. He gave them, he said, "For your own good" (Deuteronomy 10:13), and pleaded with the people to obey them "so that it might go well with them and their children for ever" (Deuteronomy 5:29). There was thus an essential correspondence between what was "good and right in the eyes of the LORD" and what was "well with them" (Deuteronomy 12:28). The "good" and the "well" coincided. We believe, moreover, that everybody has an inkling that this is so – but because they may be either unable or unwilling to acknowledge it, we have to deploy arguments to demonstrate that God's laws are for the well-being both of individuals and of society.

We, therefore, need a doctrinal apologetic in evangelism (arguing the truth of the gospel) and an ethical apologetic in social action (arguing the goodness of the moral law). Apologists of both kinds are wanted urgently in today's church and world.

In many senses this book provides a set of examples of persuasion by argument. I hope that whatever the subject you find yourself discussing, or whatever the campaign you find yourself organizing, you will find the following chapters provide you with that blend of biblical insight and social analysis that is needed for us to be informed Christians and enter into today's debates with confidence.

FRAGMENTATION AND ALIENATION

When we see pluralism as an expression of difference, we realize that we need true tolerance, respect and a commitment to persuasion. But a society which is losing its shared values also experiences pluralism as fragmentation and eventually alienation. It is certainly true in Britain today, as in many other countries, that certain groups, especially minority groups, feel alienated from the mainstream. This is true, for instance, of young Muslim men in the urban centres of the UK and indeed of many young people who feel sidelined. It is often true of those who are unemployed for a long time, or of many people with disabilities who feel that they are regarded as consumers of the community's resources rather than contributors to its life. Although people may not use the word itself, they may feel that they cannot relate to society any longer and that they are powerless to change their situation.

In spite of my attempted theological defence of democratic theory, and my plea that Christians should take advantage of the democratic process and join in the public debate, I have to admit that democracy does not always cure alienation, for many are disillusioned with its realities. It is this gulf between theory and practice which lies at the heart of John R. Lucas's book *Democracy and Participation*, from which I quoted earlier. People exercise their democratic right to vote and, to be sure, "the vote constitutes a form of minimal participation".[8] Thereafter, however, "democracy becomes an autocracy, in which all decisions save one are taken by the autocrat, and the only decision left to the people is the occasional choice of autocrat". So he renames democracy an "elective autocracy", because it "enables people to participate in government only to a derisory extent". It also "makes the government singularly insensitive to the wishes of the governed and the requirements of justice".[9] Again, "although elective autocracy has its democratic aspect, it is deeply undemocratic as regards the way and the spirit in which decisions are taken ... It is non-participatory".[10] Without doubt, this disenchantment with the actual workings of democracy is widespread. Christians should share with others the concern to broaden the context of public debate, until parliamentary discussions "reverberate in every inn and workshop in the realm". Dr Lucas ends his book with the delightful statement that "democracy can flourish only in a land of pubs".[11]

To me it is sad that many Christians become contaminated by the mood of alienation. "To be sure," they agree, "the quest for social justice is our concern and we cannot escape this fact. But the obstacles are immense. Not only are the issues complex (we claim no expertise), but society is pluralistic (we claim no monopoly of power or privilege), and the forces of reaction dominate (we have no influence). The receding tide of Christian faith in the community has left us high and dry. In addition, human beings are selfish and society is rotten. It is entirely unrealistic to hope for social change."

The witness of history

The first antidote to this mixture of secular alienation and Christian pessimism is history. In the first chapter I showed how Christian influence could change a society from one which was brutal and ungodly to one where both evangelism and social justice had made a huge impact. But the social influence of Christianity has been worldwide. K. S. Latourette sums it up at the conclusion of his seven-volume *History of the Expansion of Christianity*. He refers in glowing terms to the effects of the life of Christ through his followers.

> No life ever lived on this planet has been so influential in the affairs of men ... From that brief life and its apparent frustration has flowed a more powerful force for the triumphal waging of man's long battle than any other ever known by the human race ... Through it hundreds of millions have been lifted from illiteracy and ignorance, and have been placed upon the road of growing intellectual freedom and of control over their physical environment. It has done more to allay the physical ills of disease and famine than any other impulse known to man. It has emancipated millions from chattel slavery and millions of others from thraldom to vice. It has protected tens of millions from exploitation by their fellows. It has been the most fruitful source of movements to lessen the horrors of war and to put the relations of men and nations on the basis of justice and peace.[12]

The witness of the Bible

So Christian pessimism is historically unfounded. It is also theologically inept. We have seen that the Christian mind holds together the biblical events of the creation, the fall, the redemption and the consummation. Christian pessimists concentrate on the fall ("human beings are incorrigible") and the consummation ("Christ is coming to put things right"), and imagine that these truths justify social despair. But they overlook the creation and the redemption. The divine image in human beings has not been obliterated. Though evil, they can still do good, as Jesus plainly taught (Matthew 7:11). The evidence of our eyes confirms it. Many people who are not Christians have good marriages, are good parents, professionals with high standards and activists concerned about the world in which we live. This is partly because the truth of God's law is written on all human hearts, and partly because the values of the kingdom of God, when embodied in the Christian community, are often recognized and to some extent imitated by people outside it. In this way the gospel has borne fruit in Western society over many generations.

In addition, Jesus Christ redeems people and makes them new. Are we saying that regenerated and renewed people can do nothing to restrain or reform society? Such an opinion is monstrous. This is the thrust of Charles Colson's book *Kingdoms in Conflict*. The radical values of the kingdom of God, which was inaugurated by Jesus Christ, confront, challenge and change the kingdoms of men, especially through the agency of what Edmund Burke in the eighteenth century called "little platoons". Charles Colson has in mind small voluntary associations of people who love God and their neighbour, exhibit transcendence in the midst of secularism, refuse to acquiesce in evil, oppose injustice, and spread mercy and reconciliation in the world.[13]

The combined witness of history and Scripture is that Christian people have had an enormous influence on society. We are not powerless. Things can be different. Nikolai Berdyaev summed the situation up admirably in these words: "The sinfulness of human nature does not mean that social reforms and improvements are impossible. It only means that there can be no perfect and absolute social order ... before the transfiguration of the world."[14]

THE NATURE OF CHRISTIAN INFLUENCE

From history and Scripture I turn to the expectation which Jesus had for his followers. He expressed it most vividly in the Sermon on the Mount by his use of the salt and light metaphors:

You are the salt of the earth. But if the salt loses its saltiness, how can it be made salty again? It is no longer good for anything, except to be thrown out and trampled by men.

You are the light of the world. A city on a hill cannot be hidden. Neither do people light a lamp and put it under a bowl. Instead they put it on its stand, and it gives light to everyone in the house. In the same way, let your light shine before men, that they may see your good deeds and praise your Father in heaven.

MATTHEW 5:13–16

Everybody is familiar with salt and light. They are found in virtually every household in the world. Jesus himself, as a boy in the Nazareth home, must often have watched his mother, Mary, use salt as a preservative in the kitchen and light the lamps when the sun went down. He knew their practical usefulness.

So these were the images which Jesus later used to illustrate the influence he expected his disciples to exert in human society. At that time they were very few in number, the initial nucleus of his new society; yet they were to be salt and light to the whole earth. What did he mean? Two truths cannot be missed.

Christians should be distinctive

Firstly, Christians should be fundamentally different from those who are not Christians. Both images set the two communities apart. The world is dark, Jesus implied, but you are to be its light. The world is decaying, but you are to be its salt and hinder its decay. In English idiom we might say they are as different as "chalk from cheese" or "oil from water". This is a major theme of the whole Bible. God is calling out from the world a people for himself, and the vocation of this people is to be "holy" or "different". "Be holy," he says to them again and again, "because I am holy."

So Christians must retain their Christian distinctness. If salt does not retain its saltiness, it is good for nothing. If light does not retain its brightness, it becomes ineffective. So we who claim to be Christ's followers have to fulfil two conditions if we are to do any good for him. On the one hand, we are to immerse ourselves in the life of the world. On the other hand, while doing so, we have to avoid becoming assimilated to the world. We must retain our Christian convictions, values, standards and lifestyle. We are back with the "double identity" of the church ("holiness" and "worldliness") which I mentioned in chapter 2.

If it be asked what the "saltiness" and "brightness" of Christian holiness are, the rest of the Sermon on the Mount gives us the answer. In it Jesus tells us not to be like others around us: "Do not be like them" (Matthew 6:8). Instead, he calls us to a greater righteousness (of the heart), a wider love (even of enemies), a deeper devotion (of children coming to their Father) and a nobler ambition (seeking first God's rule and righteousness.[15] It is only as we choose and follow his way that our salt will retain its saltiness and our light will shine, that we shall be his effective witnesses and servants and exert a wholesome influence on society.

Christians should be influential

Secondly, Christians must permeate society. Although Christians are (or should be) morally and spiritually distinct from non-Christians, they are not to be socially segregated. On the contrary, their light is to shine into the darkness, and their salt is to soak into the decaying meat.

Christians can influence society even when it strongly rejects the Christian faith. Before the days of refrigeration, salt was the best known preservative. Either it was rubbed into fish and meat, or they were left to soak in it. In this way bacterial decay was retarded, though not of course entirely arrested. Light is even more obviously effective: when the light is switched on, the darkness is actually dispelled. Just so, Jesus must have meant, Christians can hinder social decay and dispel the darkness of evil. William Temple wrote of the "pervasive sweetening of life and of all human relationships by those who carry with them something of the mind of Christ".[16]

This prompts the question: Why have Christians not had a far greater influence for good on the non-Christian world? I hope my American friends will forgive me if I take the United States as my example. The published statistics of American Christianity are staggering. According to a 2002 poll, 85% of Americans would describe themselves as "Christian", with 41% describing themselves as "born again or evangelical".[17] In 2005, 45% of American adults attended church in a typical weekend, not including a special event such as a wedding or a funeral.[18]

Why, then, has this great army of Christian soldiers not been more successful in beating back the forces of evil? This is American futurologist Tom Sine's explanation: "We have been remarkably effective at diluting his [Christ's] extremist teaching and truncating his radical gospel. That explains why we ...

make such an embarrassingly little difference in the morality of our society."[19] More important than mere numbers of professing disciples are both the quality of their discipleship (maintaining Christ's standards without compromise) and their strategic deployment (capturing positions of influence for Christ).

Our Christian habit is to bewail the world's deteriorating standards with an air of rather self-righteous dismay. We criticize its violence, dishonesty, immorality, disregard for human life, and materialistic greed. "The world is going down the drain," we say with a shrug. But whose fault is it? Who is to blame? Let me put it like this. If the house is dark when nightfall comes, there is no sense in blaming the house; that is what happens when the sun goes down. The question to ask is, "Where is the light?" Similarly, if the meat goes bad and becomes inedible, there is no sense in blaming the meat; that is what happens when bacteria are left alone to breed. The question to ask is, "Where is the salt?" Just so, if society deteriorates and its standards decline, till it becomes like a dark night or stinking fish, there is no sense in blaming society; that is what happens when fallen men and women are left to themselves, and human selfishness is unchecked. The question to ask is, "Where is the church? Why are the salt and light of Jesus Christ not permeating and changing our society?" It is sheer hypocrisy on our part to raise our eyebrows, shrug our shoulders or wring our hands. The Lord Jesus told us to be the world's salt and light. If darkness and rottenness abound, it is largely our fault and we must accept the blame.

This purpose and expectation of Christ should be enough to overcome our sense of alienation. We may be ostracized by some at work or in our local community. Secular society may do its best to push us to the circumference of its concerns. But, refusing to be marginalized, we should seek to occupy a sphere of influence for Christ. Ambition is the desire to succeed. There is nothing wrong with it if it is genuinely subordinated to the will and glory of God. True, power can corrupt. True also, the power of Christ is best displayed in our weakness. And indeed we shall continue to feel our personal inadequacy. Yet we should determine by his grace to infiltrate some secular segment of society and raise his flag there, maintaining without compromise his standards of love, truth and goodness.

How can we exert some influence for Christ? What does it mean in practice to be the world's salt and light? What can we do for social change? I will try to develop six ways, in three pairs.

PRAYER AND EVANGELISM

Firstly, there is the power of prayer. I beg you not to dismiss this as a pious platitude, a sop to Christian convention. It really is not. We cannot read the Bible without being impressed by its constant emphasis on the efficacy of prayer.

The power of prayer

"The prayer of a righteous man is powerful and effective," wrote James (5:16). "I tell you," said Jesus, "that if two of you on earth agree about anything you ask for, it will be done for you by my Father in heaven" (Matthew 18:19). We do not claim to understand the rationale of intercession, but somehow it enables us to enter the field of spiritual conflict, and to align ourselves with the good purposes of God, so that his power is released and the principalities of evil are held back.

Prayer is an indispensable part of the individual Christian's life. It is also indispensable to the life of the local church. Paul gave it priority. "First of all, then, I urge that supplications, prayers, intercessions, and thanksgivings be made for all men, for kings and all who are in high positions, that we may lead a quiet and peaceable life, godly and respectful in every way. This is good, and it is acceptable in the sight of God our Saviour, who desires all men to be saved and to come to the knowledge of the truth" (1 Timothy 2:1 – 4 RSV). Here is prayer for national leaders, that they may fulfil their responsibility to maintain conditions of peace and order, in which the church is free both to obey God and to preach the gospel.

In theory, we are convinced of this duty to pray. Yet some Christian social activists seldom stop to pray. And some churches hardly seem to take it seriously. If in the community (indeed, in the world) there is more violence than peace, more oppression than justice, more secularism than godliness, is it because Christians and churches are not praying as they should?

We also rejoice over the growth of parachurch movements whose goal is to stimulate the prayers of the people of God (e.g., in the UK the Lydia Fellowship, Crosswinds, and Intercessors for Britain, and in the US Intercessors for America and the AD 2000 movement[20]).

The power of the gospel

Secondly, I turn now from the power of prayer to the power of the gospel, and so to evangelism. This book is about Christian social responsibility, not evangelism. Nevertheless, the two belong together. Although different Christians have received different gifts and callings, and although in some situations it is perfectly proper to concentrate on either evangelism or social action without combining them, nevertheless in general and in theory they cannot be separated. Our love for our neighbours will be fleshed out in a holistic concern for all their needs – for the needs of their bodies, souls and community. That is why, in the ministry of Jesus, words and works went together. As the Grand Rapids Report put it, evangelism and social activity are "like the two blades of a pair of scissors or the two wings of a bird".[21]

There are, however, two particular ways in which evangelism should be seen as a necessary prelude to and foundation of social action.

The gospel changes people

Firstly, the gospel changes people. Every Christian should be able to echo Paul's words with conviction: "I am not ashamed of the gospel, because it is the power of God for the salvation of everyone who believes" (Romans 1:16). We know it in our own lives, and we have seen it in the lives of others. If sin is at root self-centredness, then the transformation from "self" to "unself" is an essential ingredient of salvation. Faith leads to love, and love to service. So social activity, which is the loving service of the needy, should be the inevitable result of saving faith, although we have to confess that this is not always so.

There are other situations in which positive social change is taking place apart from explicit Christian initiatives. So we must not bind evangelism and social change together so indissolubly as to say that the former always issues in the latter and the latter never happens without the former. Nevertheless, these are exceptions which prove the rule. We still insist that evangelism is the major instrument of social change, for the gospel changes people, and changed people can change society. We have seen that society needs salt and light, but only the gospel can create them. This is one way in which we may declare without embarrassment that evangelism takes primacy over social action. Logically speaking, "Christian social responsibility presupposes socially responsible Christians", and it is the gospel which produces them.[22]

When John V. Taylor, who later became the Bishop of Winchester, was still General Secretary of the Church Missionary Society, he described in his CMS Newsletter (May 1972) his reactions to Geoffrey Moorhouse's book Calcutta, and indeed to the apparent hopelessness of that city's problems. "But invariably what tips the balance from despair to faith," he wrote, "is the person who rises above the situation." Such persons are neither "trapped" in the city, nor have they "escaped" from it. "They have transcended the situation ... Salvation is not the same as solution: it precedes it and makes it a possibility ... Personal salvation – salvation in first gear – is still the way in. It is the key to unlock the door of determinism and make possible the 'salvation' of corporate organizations and institutions – salvation in second gear – by providing those who can transcend the situation."

There is another way in which social uplift is facilitated by evangelism. When the gospel is faithfully and widely preached, it not only brings a radical renewal to individuals, but produces what Raymond Johnston once called "an antiseptic atmosphere", in which blasphemy, selfishness, greed, dishonesty, immorality, cruelty and injustice find it harder to flourish. A country which has been permeated by the gospel is not a soil in which these poisonous weeds can easily take root, let alone luxuriate.

The gospel changes cultures

Secondly, the gospel which changes people also changes cultures. One of the greatest hindrances to social change is the conservatism of culture. A country's laws, institutions and customs have taken centuries to develop; they have a built-in resistance to reform. In some cases it is the moral ambiguity of culture which is the hindrance. Every political programme, economic system and development plan depends on values to motivate and sustain it. It cannot operate without honesty and some degree of altruism. So progress is effectively blocked if the national culture (and the religion or ideology which shapes it) connives at corruption and selfishness, and offers no incentive to self-control or self-sacrifice. Then culture stands in the way of development. It is entirely logical, therefore, that Brian Griffiths, in his book on Christian approaches to economic life, concludes by saying,

> Christianity starts with faith in Christ and it finishes with service in the world ... Because of this I believe that evangelism has an indispensable part to play in the establishment of a more just economic order. Obedience to Christ demands change, the world becomes his world, the poor, the weak and the suffering are men, women and children created in his image; injustice is an affront to his creation; despair, indifference and aimlessness are replaced by hope, responsibility and purpose; and above all selfishness is transformed by love.[23]

So the gospel changes both people and cultures. This is not to say that no development is possible without evangelism, but rather that development is hindered without, and greatly facilitated by, the cultural changes which the gospel brings. And the more the gospel spreads, the more hopeful the situation becomes. Even a few Christians in public life can initiate social change, but their influence is likely to be far greater if they have massive grass-roots support, as the nineteenth-century British evangelical reformers had. So Christians in every country should pray for a widespread acceptance of the gospel. As the nineteenth-century American evangelicals clearly saw, revival and reform belong together.

WITNESS AND PROTEST

We have seen that the gospel is God's power for salvation, but in fact all truth is powerful. God's truth is much more mighty than the Devil's crooked lies. We should never be afraid of the truth. Nor do we ever need to be afraid for the truth, as if its survival hung in the balance, for God watches over it and will never allow it to be completely suppressed. As Paul put it, "We cannot do anything against the truth, but only for the truth" (2 Corinthians 13:8). And as John put it, "The light shines in the darkness, and the darkness has not overcome it" (John 1:5, text note). One contemporary Christian thinker who is convinced about this is Solzhenitsyn. His Nobel Speech on Literature (1970) was entitled "One Word of Truth". He confessed that writers lack all material weapons like rockets and tanks. So "what can literature do," he asked, "in the face of the merciless onslaught of open violence?" Firstly, it can refuse "to take part in the lie". Secondly, writers and artists can "vanquish the lie". For "one word of truth outweighs the whole world. And on such a fantastic breach of the law of conservation of mass and energy are based my own activities and my appeal to the writers of the world."[24]

All Christians are called like their Master "to bear witness to the truth". This, John added, was why he had been born and why he had come into the world (John 18:37). The supreme truth to which we testify is, of course, Jesus Christ himself, for he is the truth (John 14:6). But all truth – scientific, biblical, theological, moral – is his, and we are to be fearless in defending, maintaining and arguing it. This is the place for developing an ethical apologetic, as I was urging earlier, and for entering into the public debate of contemporary issues. From the pulpit (still a much more influential "platform" than is commonly realized, especially in the shaping of public opinion), through letters to and articles in national and local newspapers, in discussions at home and work, through opportunities on radio and television, by poetry, drama and popular songs, we are called as Christians to witness to God's law and God's gospel, without fear or apology. Moreover, as with Jesus so with his followers, the true witness (*martyr*) must be prepared to suffer, and even if necessary to die, for his testimony. Such costly testimony is the chief weapon of those who are denied the democratic process because they live under an oppressive regime.

Alongside a positive witness to the truth must go its negative counterpart, protest against folly, deceit and wickedness. Many seem to be disenchanted with the weapon of rational protest, but I think they should not be. Public agitation can be an effective weapon even where it is not ultimately successful. Let me give you two examples, the first illustrating a situation where mass protest was successful, the second where it was unsuccessful in achieving its immediate goals but was nevertheless a powerful expression of public protest.

Firstly, Ukraine's "Orange Revolution" of 2004 – 5 was a series of protests and political events that took place throughout the country in response to allegations of massive corruption, voter intimidation and direct electoral fraud during Ukraine's presidential election of 21 November 2004, in which the main candidates were prime minister Viktor Yanukovych and opposition leader Viktor Yushchenko. Hundreds of thousands of protesters gathered in Independence Square, most wearing orange, the colour of the opposition, to call for new elections. Protests were also organized throughout the Ukraine, as well as general strikes and sit-ins. A new election was called by the Ukrainian Supreme Court under intense international scrutiny, and Viktor Yushchenko was declared to be president. With his inauguration on 23 January 2005 in Kiev, the Orange Revolution reached its successful and peaceful conclusion. Citing this as an example of successful protest does not mean, however, that the government which resulted was free from its own problems of corruption and bad governance. In a subsequent election, the trouble-prone governor was voted out of office and power reverted to those who were sympathetic to communism.

My second example is the mass protest against the second Iraq war. On 15 February 2003 there was a mass protest against Britain going to war against Iraq. The demonstration was the biggest ever held in the UK, with police estimates of 750,000 people and organizers' estimates at up to 2,000,000. The protest was peaceful and consisted of a march followed by a rally with high-profile speakers who called upon the government to resist war and to continue with negotiations. Christian groups joined others in calling for peace and not war (although other Christians, of course, supported the decision to go to war). One of the aims of the protest was to ensure that if the government went to war it could not claim that it had unqualified support. In the end Britain did go to war against Iraq and, therefore, this mass protest was a failure in terms of its specific objectives. But in calling the government to account for its behaviour, it demonstrated that many people were still willing to protest publicly when they felt that they were being drawn into something that was morally wrong and strategically disastrous.

DEMONSTRATION AND ORGANIZATION

Truth is powerful when it is argued; it becomes even more powerful when it is also demonstrated. People need not only to understand the argument, but to see its benefits displayed. One Christian nurse in a hospital, teacher in a school, secretary in an office, assistant in a shop or worker in a factory can have an influence out of all proportion to numbers and percentages. And who can calculate the influence for good on the whole neighbourhood of a single Christian home, in which husband and wife are faithful to and find fulfilment in each other, their children grow up in the disciplined security of love, and the family are not turned in on themselves but outgoing to the community? Christians are marked people both at work and at home; the world is watching us.

More influential even than the example of Christian individuals and families is that of the local church. The church is meant by God to be his new and redeemed community, which embodies the ideals of his kingdom. We must not underestimate, writes Dr John Howard Yoder, "the powerful ... impact on society of the creation of an alternative social group". For "the primary social structure through which the gospel works to change other structures is that of the Christian community."[25]

Small groups of Christian people can be visible embodiments of the gospel. They can also make use of all the means of influencing society which I have mentioned so far. There is power in prayer and in the gospel; there is even more if we pray and evangelize together. There is power in witness and protest; there is even more if we testify and take action together. The group was our Lord's own chosen way. He began with the Twelve. And the long history of the church abounds in examples of the strategic influence of small groups. In sixteenth-century Cambridge the early Reformers met in the White Horse Inn to study

Erasmus's Greek New Testament; in eighteenth-century Oxford the Holy Club, to which the Wesleys and Whitefield belonged, although at first engaged in barren good works, was the background against which the evangelical revival began; and in nineteenth-century south London the Clapham Sect gave their support to Wilberforce in his anti-slavery campaign and to many other social and religious causes. Today one of the most promising features of modern church life is the hunger for the small group experience. Thousands of congregations have divided their membership into small fellowship or home groups. Many churches also encourage the formation of specialist groups – evangelistic visiting teams, missionary prayer groups, music groups, contemporary issue groups, reading groups, social study and action groups – the list is almost endless.

Then there are communities experimenting in new styles of living, sharing and/or working together – for example, the Kairos Community in Buenos Aires (for theological reflection on discipleship in the secular world), the Sojourners Community in Washington, DC (involved in producing the Sojourners' magazine, in promoting its concern for peace and justice, and in serving local black families) and TRACI in New Delhi (The Research And Communication Institute of young Indian thinkers and writers). In Britain there are groups like CARE Trust and CARE Campaigns (Christian Action, Research and Education) which promote moral standards in society, and I might also mention the Institute for Contemporary Christianity in London, whose goals are to stimulate the integration of consistent Christian thought and action in the world.[26]

A widely respected Roman Catholic leader who believed strongly in the potential of small groups was Dom Helder Camara, former Archbishop of Recife in northeast Brazil, who died in 1999. Accused of being subversive, forbidden access to the media, under constant threat of assassination, this "violent peacemaker" (as he was called) was committed to justice and peace. Having travelled half the world for several years, appealing to institutions, he came to put more faith in groups. He encouraged the formation of "Abrahamic minorities" (so-called "because like Abraham we are hoping against hope")[27] in neighbourhoods, universities and unions, within the media, in management, among politicians and in the armed forces. Sharing a common thirst for justice and freedom, they gather information; they try to diagnose the problems relating to housing, unemployment, sweated labour and social structures; they pool experiences and carry out whatever form of "peaceful violence" they deem appropriate. Dom Helder believed that such minority groups have "the power for love and justice which could be likened to nuclear energy locked for millions of years in the smallest atoms and waiting to be released".[28] "All these minorities united could become an irresistible force," he added.[29] Some ridiculed him, but he persevered. "My plan, I am well aware," he wrote, "may call to mind the combat against Goliath. But the hand of God was with the young shepherd, and David conquered the Philistine with his faith, a sling and five small stones."[30] "Keep in mind," he urged elsewhere, "that throughout the centuries humanity has been led by daring minorities."[31]

This contrast between the giant and the boy, the sword and the slingstones, arrogant boasting and humble trust, is characteristic of God's activity in the world. Tom Sine has captured it well in his book *The Mustard Seed Conspiracy*, whose title alludes to the tiny seed out of which a large bush grows. Its subtitle is "You can make a difference in tomorrow's troubled world". He writes:

> Jesus let us in on an astonishing secret. God has chosen to change the world through the lowly, the unassuming and the imperceptible ... That has always been God's strategy – changing the world through the conspiracy of the insignificant. He chose a ragged bunch of Semite slaves to become the insurgents of his new order ... And who would have ever dreamed that God would choose to work through a baby in a cow stall to turn the world right side up! "God chose the foolish things ... the weak things ... the lowly things ... the things that are not" ... It is still God's policy to work through the embarrassingly insignificant to change his world and create his future...[32]

If it is true that God often works through the insignificant and the small to bring about his purposes, then there is no excuse for Christians to feel alienated. Quite the contrary: we should delight that nobody is too insignificant to be used by God to change the world.

NOTES

1 Peter Brierley (ed.), *UK Christian Handbook Religious Trends 5 – 2005/06* (London: Christian Research, 2005), p. 2.23.
2 Ibid., p. 12.5.
3 Richard Gutteridge, *Open Thy Mouth for the Dumb!, The German Evangelical Church and the Jews, 1870 – 1950* (Oxford: Basil Blackwell, 1976).
4 Ibid., p. 128.
5 Ibid., p. 298.
6 Ibid., p. 299.

7 Abraham Lincoln concluded his famous Gettysburg Address (1863) with the resolve "that this nation, under God, shall have a new birth of freedom, and that government of the people, by the people, for the people, shall not perish from the earth". He seems to have borrowed this definition of democracy from the Rev. Theodore Parker, who used it in a speech in Boston in 1850.

8 John R. Lucas, *Democracy and Participation*, p. 166.

9 Ibid., p. 184.

10 Ibid., p. 198.

11 Ibid., p. 264.

12 K. S. Latourette, *History of the Expansion of Christianity*, vol. 7 (London: Eyre & Spottiswoode, 1945), pp. 503 – 4.

13 Charles W. Colson, *Kingdoms in Conflict: An Insider's Challenging View of Politics, Power and the Pulpit* (New York: William Morrow; Grand Rapids: Zondervan, 1987), e.g., pp. 238, 253 – 64, 371. Fran Beckett, in her book *Called to Action* (London: Fount, 1989), emphasizes the responsibility of each church to get to know its local community and to mobilize teams to serve the needs it has discovered.

14 Nikolai Berdyaev, *The Destiny of Man* (London: Geoffrey Bles, 1937), p. 281.

15 Matthew 5 – 7. I try to develop this exposition in *The Message of the Sermon on the Mount, Christian counter-culture* (Leicester: InterVarsity Press, 1978).

16 Temple, *Christianity and the Social Order*, p. 27.

17 Barna Research Online, *www.barna.org*, "American Faith Is Diverse, as Shown Among Five Faith-Based Segments", 29 January 2002. For a discussion on why Europe might be an exception to this, see Grace Davie, *Europe: The Exceptional Case, Parameters of faith in the modern world* (London: Darton, Longman & Todd, 2002).

18 Ibid., *www.barna.org/FlexPage.aspx?Page=Topic&TopicID=10*.

19 Sine, *The Mustard Seed Conspiracy*, p. 113.

20 *www.lydiafellowship.org*; Intercessors for Britain, 14 Orchard Road, Moreton, Wirral, Merseyside L46 8TS; *www.ifapray.org*; *www.ad2000.org*.

21 "Evangelism and Social Responsibility", in Stott (ed.), *Making Christ Known*, p. 182.

22 Ibid., p. 183.

23 Brian Griffiths, *Morality in the Marketplace* (London: Hodder & Stoughton, 1989), pp. 154 – 55.

24 Alexander Solzhenitsyn, *One Word of Truth* (London: Bodley Head, 1972), pp. 22 – 27.

25 John Howard Yoder, *The Politics of Jesus* (Grand Rapids: Eerdmans, 1972), pp. 111, 157.

26 Kairos Community: *www.kairos.org.ar/english.php*; Sojourners: *www.sojo.net/*; TRACI: TRACI House, E-537, Greater Kailash II, New Delhi 110048, India; CARE: *www.care.org.uk*; London Institute of Contemporary Christianity: *www.licc.org.uk*.

27 Dom Helder Camara, *Spiral of Violence* (1970; London: Sheed & Ward, 1971), p. 69.

28 Dom Helder Camara, *The Desert Is Fertile* (London: Sheed & Ward, 1974), p. 3.

29 Camara, *Spiral of Violence*, p. 43.

30 Dom Helder Camara, *Race Against Time* (London: Sheed & Ward, 1971), pp. vii – viii.

31 Ibid., p. 17.

32 Sine, *The Mustard Seed Conspiracy*, pp. 11 – 12.

PART TWO

GLOBAL
ISSUES

War and Peace

4

Of all the global problems which confront us today, none is graver than the threat of the self-destruction of the human race. War is no longer restricted to an engagement between armies. On the one hand, nation states have steadily developed weapons of mass destruction which have the capacity to eradicate whole societies and indeed to destroy human civilization. On the other, we are seeing the growth of terrorist groups, committing powerful and symbolic acts of violence before the eyes of the watching world. At the outset of the twenty-first century we are apprehensive lest the two come together and weapons of mass destruction, whether nuclear, biological or chemical, fall into the hands of terrorists or "rogue states" who will use them to further their own cause with horrific results.

Of course, even primitive weapons can create a sickening bloodbath when wielded by those who are motivated by hatred and bent on genocide. In 1994 more than 800,000 people were killed over 100 days in Rwanda, many of them by machete. One only needs to mention the name Srebrenica, Bosnia, to recall the atrocities which were committed there when thousands of innocent people were slaughtered in the name of "ethnic cleansing".

Perhaps the worst emergency to unfold in Africa in recent decades has been the civil war in the Democratic Republic of Congo (formerly Zaire). It has been estimated that 2,500,000 people were killed either as a direct result of the fighting or due to disease and malnutrition.[1]

So we do not need to focus on weapons of mass destruction to see the suffering that human conflict causes. In 2003 the International Campaign to Ban Land Mines, founded by American Vietnam veterans, estimated that 100,000,000 land mines remained in the ground and that there are 15 – 20,000 new land mine casualties each year. Despite an encouraging reduction in 2002 which was a result of more countries having organized mine-clearing activities as well as cease-fires in countries such as Angola, Sri Lanka and the Sudan,[2] in 2003 the Mines Advisory Group[3] estimated that as a result of the two Gulf wars in 1991 and 2003, two decades of conflict had left between 8,000,000 and 12,000,000 mines. In Kurdish-controlled northern Iraq the casualty rate due to mines or other unexploded ordinance increased by 90% during and after the 2003 hostilities.

Or consider one of the most poignant aspects of human conflict, which is the involvement of children in war. Increasing numbers of children are dying during armed conflict; 300,000 child soldiers are fighting wars and countless others are in support roles; 25,000,000 children have been uprooted from their homes as a result of conflict.[4] Girl children and children with disabilities are especially vulnerable. One child soldier describes the terrible experiences that he went through: "I planted landmines, stopped vehicles, set homes on fire and destroyed crops ... What troubled me the most was when a child got too tired, we captives were ordered to kill them."[5]

But now we also have the power to destroy the total legacy of past civilizations, the present delicate ecological balance of the biosphere and, through radiation, the genetic potential of the future. The very survival of the human race and of our planet is at stake. The Christian mind cannot operate in a vacuum. However strongly we hold fast to God's once-for-all revelation of himself in Christ and Scripture, we have to struggle to relate this to the harsh facts of the present situation. Thus revelation and reality belong together as we seek to discern God's will. There are five issues which I want to consider before coming to the call to Christians to be peacemakers in a troubled world.

THE END OF THE COLD WAR

With the collapse of the Berlin Wall on 9 November 1989, the balance of world power shifted as Communism imploded as an ideology and Soviet military power began to wane. The global superpower that was once the Soviet Union began to change, and in many cases to fall apart, at a rapid rate. This was partly due to the positive vision of Soviet leader Mikhail Gorbachev, represented by his introduction of the concepts of perestroika (restructuring) and glasnost (openness), which were intended to bring about a measure of democratic accountability to the system. But it was also due to the economic poverty, political oppression and industrial backwardness of a Soviet model that had become a bureaucratic nightmare to manage.

In July 1989 the Solidarity movement in Poland, led by Lech Walesa, defeated the communists in free elections. Then Gorbachev announced that countries in the Warsaw Pact were free to decide their own futures. Hungary then opened its border to the West. Czechoslovakia went through its "velvet revolution", making playwright Vaclav Havel president. Then, after some bloodshed, the ruthless reign of President Ceausescu of Romania was brought to an end when he and his wife were executed on Christmas Day.

Despite the new measures, economic decline continued in the Soviet Union. Gorbachev became more unpopular at home, although he remained a hero abroad, winning the Nobel Peace Prize. He became Soviet president rather than leader of the Communist Party like his forebears, taking on new powers and becoming more hard-line. But Russia, in its first elections, chose Boris Yeltsin, Gorbachev's arch-rival, as its president. He outlawed the Communist Party in Russia, forcing Gorbachev to dissolve its Central Committee. In 1991 the four Soviet republics voted for independence. Moscow recognized their sovereign status on 6 September 1991. Other republics, Ukraine, Armenia, Georgia and Moldova, planned to break away. The leaders of Ukraine, Russia and Belarus met on 8 September 1991 near Minsk and agreed to disband the Soviet Union and form the Commonwealth of Independent States (CIS). On 25 December 1991 Gorbachev went on television to announce his resignation as Soviet president. The Soviet flag was taken down from the Kremlin and the Russian flag was raised. The Soviet Union was over. Although this did not prevent a bitter war in 1950 between US and communist forces over the division of Korea, and during the 1960s over Vietnam, the extent of the change is evident from the fact that most of the former communist states of Central and Eastern Europe joined the European Union (EU) on 1 May 2004. Two more countries, Bulgaria and Romania, plan to join in 2007.

With this wave of democratization sweeping the former Soviet Union, the world was expected to be a safer place. Yet a decade later, expectations of peace have proved illusory, and new conflicts have arisen. During the fifty years between 1945 and 1995 there were eighty wars. Yet of these only twenty-eight were "traditional" wars between the regular armies of nation states, while forty-six were civil or guerrilla wars.

What, then, are the causes of this escalation of violence? Professor Samuel P. Huntington of Harvard, in his book *The Clash of Civilizations and the Remaking of World Order*, develops the thesis that, whereas during the Cold War global politics had been "bipolar" (between the two superpowers), after the Cold War it has become "multipolar and multi-civilizational".[6] In particular, "in coping with identity crisis, what counts for people are blood and belief, faith and family. People rally to those with similar ancestry, religion, language, values and institutions, and distance themselves from those with different ones."[7] Thus today the important distinctions between people are not so much ideological and political as cultural. Professor Huntington goes on to divide the world into seven or eight major civilizations, whose prominent distinctives are cultural and which shape "the antagonisms and associations of states".[8]

A global war, involving the core states of the world's major civilizations, Professor Huntington declares, is "highly improbable but not impossible". He even paints a vivid scenario in which the USA, Europe, Russia and India are aligned against China, Japan and most of Islam.[9] This is his concluding sentence: "Clashes of civilizations are the greatest threat to world peace, and an international order based on civilizations is the surest safeguard against world war."[10] Yet we must be careful not to succumb to fatalism, as if this clash were inevitable. After the events of 9/11 some talked of this "clash of civilizations" as if it were already happening – an attitude which can only have had a negative impact on relationships between the West and the world of Islam.

Former UN Secretary-General Perez de Cuellar has said that the current proliferation of civil wars is "the new anarchy". The fact that in 1993 forty-two countries were engulfed in major conflicts, and thirty-seven others in lesser ones, certainly seems to demonstrate "this anarchic trend".[11] "We are not in control," he concludes, and "the idea that a global élite like the UN can engineer reality from above is ... absurd." We live in "an age of localized mini-holocausts".[12]

In the light of the changed world situation since the end of the Cold War, it is not surprising that Western defence specialists have completely revised their strategy. They are no longer preparing for a single large-scale war with the Soviet Union, but rather for multiple regional conflicts. Nevertheless, while weapons of mass destruction exist, so does the fear of their use either in local conflicts or in crazy acts of terrorism. It is to these weapons that we now turn.

WEAPONS OF MASS DESTRUCTION

Nuclear weapons

Seven nations are known to have both nuclear weapons and delivery systems – the United States, Russia, Britain, France, China, India and Pakistan. Israel is almost certainly an eighth member of this deadly club. Recently a Pakistani nuclear physicist disclosed that he had shared nuclear secrets with Libya, Iran and North Korea – countries which are widely regarded as "rogue states" and which are part of US president George W. Bush's "axis of evil".

Many people are tempted to write off nuclear weapons (and, therefore, ethical reasoning about them) as no longer posing a threat, since they equate them with the threat posed by the Cold War, during which time both the US and the Soviet Union had massive overkill in the number of weapons they possessed. Yet this is a temptation to be resisted. In 2006 one of the key concerns in global international relations was the fact that Iran had made enriched uranium from which nuclear bombs could be made. They stated that this was being done to provide nuclear power as a source of energy, but their nuclear programme became a source of global concern. This was especially the case because the newly elected president of Iran, Mahmoud Ahmadinejad, an extreme nationalist, called for Israel to be "wiped off the map" – although it is only fair to mention that he also commented that "a nation which has culture, logic and civilization does not need nuclear weapons".

It is the prospect of such a horrific scenario taking place in the future which means that we must never forget what happened when nuclear weapons were last used or why they should never be used again. Probably nothing can bring home to us the ghastly effects of a nuclear explosion more vividly than the eyewitness accounts of what happened at Hiroshima and Nagasaki. Lord Mountbatten quoted one such account shortly before he was himself killed by an act of senseless violence:

> Suddenly a glaring whitish, pinkish light appeared in the sky accompanied by an unnatural tremor which was followed almost immediately by a wave of suffocating heat and a wind which swept away everything in its path. Within a few seconds the thousands of people in the streets in the centre of the town were scorched by a wave of searing heat. Many were killed instantly, others lay writhing on the ground screaming in agony from the

intolerable pain of their burns. Everything standing upright in the way of the blast ... was annihilated ... Hiroshima had ceased to exist.[13]

That was the result of a single, smallish atomic explosion. What the consequences of a nuclear war would be like it is impossible to predict with accuracy because of the many imponderables, such as the number of warheads used, the distribution of people in the target zone, the degree of civil defence available, and the climatic conditions at the time. But the United States Congress document *The Effects of Nuclear War* (1979) says that "the minimum consequences would be enormous".

During the Cold War many scenarios were examined to analyse what the impact of a nuclear exchange would be between the two superpowers. For instance, a single megaton weapon attack on a single big city like Detroit or Leningrad would mean up to 2,000,000 dead and a further 1,000,000 injured. "A very large attack against a range of military and economic targets", in which the former USSR struck first and the USA retaliated, would mean the death of up to 77% of the American population (or 220,000,000 people) and up to 40% of the Russian population (being more scattered in rural areas). These casualties would be the immediate effects (within the first thirty days) of the heat, blast, wind, firestorm and direct radiation. Many more millions would die of their injuries (since the medical facilities would be completely inadequate) and of epidemics (due to the breakdown of sewerage and the non-availability of clean water), or would starve or freeze to death during the first winter (because of the collapse of services). A pall of sooty toxic smoke over the devastated area would not only poison many survivors but so completely blot out the warmth and light of the sun as to return the earth to ice-age conditions. In the long term cancer would claim many more victims, and both the genetic consequences and ecological devastation would continue for decades and be incalculable.[14]

Biological weapons

Biological warfare is the deliberate spreading of diseases such as anthrax, smallpox, botulism or plague. The 1925 Geneva Protocol prohibits the use of chemical or biological weapons in war and the 1972 Biological and Toxic Weapons Convention (BWC), which came into force in 1975, bans the development, production, acquisition, stockpiling and retention of them. However, many[15] have produced such weapons.[16] Concerns about their possible use grew when

Russian president Boris Yeltsin admitted in 1992 that for twenty years the former Soviet Union had had a biological weapons programme. In 1995 Iraq, a signatory to the BWC, was also found to have a biological weapons programme. It was subsequently found to have used bombs and missiles containing biological agents during the 1991 Gulf War. One of the key issues at the heart of the war with Iraq in 2003 was the suspicion that it had weapons of mass destruction that it was prepared to use. None, in fact, were found.

Although biological weapons can take some time to take effect, depending on the type used, the possibility of an epidemic or pandemic cannot be discounted. The speed of international travel means that a disease could be transmitted to another continent before it has even been discovered at its origin.

One of the attractions of biological weapons to any potential user is that they are cheap compared to other weapons. "In one analysis the comparative cost of civilian (unprotected) casualties is $2,000 per square kilometer with conventional weapons, $800 with nuclear weapons, $600 with nerve gas weapons, and $1 with biological weapons ... Not surprisingly, biological weapons have become known as the poor man's atom bomb."[17]

Biological warfare is also remarkably deadly when compared to other weapons: "In one well-known scenario, a single aircraft leaving a trail of 100 kilograms of anthrax along a line upwind of Washington, DC, could result in 1 to 3 million deaths. In comparison, a one-megaton hydrogen bomb dropped over the US capitol would only cause some 0.5 to 1.9 million deaths."[18]

This led Colin Powell, then Chairman of the US Joint Chiefs of Staff, to say, "The one that scares me to death, perhaps even more so than tactical nuclear weapons, and the one we have less capability against, is biological weapons." They do not need sophisticated delivery systems to make them effective. Terrorists could use a vehicle, small plane or even simply release the agent upwind to make it effective. On one occasion the Aum Shinrikyo cult drove a van containing a fan around the streets of Tokyo and attempted to spread botulinum toxin. On this occasion, however, no one was harmed.[19] Following 9/11 the apprehension that such an attack might happen was not helped by a small amount of expertly prepared anthrax being distributed through the postal system. Nevertheless, many scientists have protested that it is much more difficult to use biological weapons than is commonly supposed. Although things may change at any time, biological warfare has not, to date, been the weapon of choice for terrorist groups such as Al Quaeda.

Chemical weapons

Chemical weapons work through direct contact with the substance causing injury or death. They fall into several types. "Choking agents", such as chlorine or phosgene, work through the respiratory tract through inhalation and were used extensively in World War I. "Blister agents", such as mustard gas, act through inhalation and contact with skin affecting the eyes, respiratory tract and skin, first irritating and then destroying cells. "Blood agents", such as hydrogen cyanide, are distributed via the blood and generally enter the body through inhalation. They are essentially poisons which cause the body to suffocate. Finally, "nerve agents", such as sarin or tabun, block impulses between nerve cells or across synapses. They are divided into several groups with the most well known, CS gas, being used by riot control agents (RCAs) and the most deadly, such as VX gas, only needing a few milligrams to cause death.

In January 1989 representatives of nearly 150 nations met in Paris for a conference on banning chemical weapons, and on 29 April 1997 the Chemical Weapons Convention came into force, with 117 signatories. This was the world's first multilateral disarmament agreement to provide for the elimination of an entire category of weapons of mass destruction within a given time frame. The Organization for the Prohibition of Chemical Weapons (OPCW) was set up to oversee the process.

If this occurs, it will bring to completion a process which has continued since 1675, when France and Germany condemned and prohibited the use of poisoned bullets. The 1875 Brussels conference banned the use of poison gases and arms. The 1899 Hague Convention banned projectiles that could spread "asphyxiating or deleterious gases". But World War I saw chemical weapons used on a massive scale, most notably at the battle of Ypres in Belgium on 22 April 1915. By the war's end some 124,000 tons of chlorine, mustard and other chemical agents had been released and more than 90,000 soldiers had suffered painful deaths because of them.[20]

This was a breach of the 1907 Hague Convention. The 1925 Geneva Protocol bound its signatories (by now nearly every nation) not to be the first to use such weapons. In World War II no signatory nation broke this pledge, although Italy had used chemical weapons in Abyssinia in the 1930s. Stories about "yellow rain", however, have led to the widespread belief that Soviet troops used poison gas in Afghanistan, and that the communist forces used it in Kampuchea and Laos. Iraq has certainly used it both against the Kurds and in their war with Iran.

Yet the use of chemical weapons by nation states is not the only problem we face. In 1995 the Aum Shinrikyo cult released sarin gas in the Tokyo subway, leading to a dozen people being killed and 5,500 people being admitted to hospital. The sarin gas was diluted to 30% of its full strength, to protect those using it. Had it been 70% pure, thousands would have perished. This single event showed that the threat of terrorist groups using biochemical weapons had become a reality, even though no group had used them to effect mass fatalities. Many analysts believe that it is only a matter of time before such an attempt is made.

Meanwhile the public needs to understand that modern nerve gases are to the chemist what nuclear weapons are to the physicist. Gas masks might not offer protection, because some chemical weapons could penetrate the skin. If they were to be dropped from the air, it is reckoned that twenty civilians would be killed to one combatant, because only combatants would be issued with protective clothing.

These three (atomic, biological and chemical) are sometimes referred to as "ABC" weapons. They surely constitute the most gruesome alphabet ever conceived. The invention and refinement of ABC weapons, especially of nuclear devices, have radically changed the context in which one has to think about the morality of war. They challenge the relevance of the "just war" theory. A war could still have a just cause and a just goal. But at least if macro-weapons were used ("strategic" or "tactical"), there would be no reasonable prospect of attaining the goal, since in the case of nuclear wars they are not winnable. The means would not be just, since nuclear weapons are neither proportionate, nor discriminate, nor controlled. Millions of non-combatants would be killed. In a nuclear holocaust much innocent blood would be shed. Therefore, the Christian conscience must declare the use of indiscriminate nuclear weapons, and also chemical and biological weapons, immoral. A nuclear war could never be a just war. As President Reagan and Mr Gorbachev declared in 1985 in Geneva, "A nuclear war cannot be won and must never be fought."

THEOLOGICAL AND MORAL REFLECTIONS

Christians do not fully agree about problems associated with war. Yet it is important not to exaggerate our differences, nor understate our substantial areas of agreement. All Christians affirm that the character of the kingdom of God is righteousness and peace. We believe that the conduct of Jesus was a perfect example of the ideals of the kingdom he proclaimed. We are called as the kingdom community to hunger for righteousness, to pursue peace, to forbear revenge, to love enemies – in other words, to be marked by the cross. We look forward to the consummated kingdom in which "they will beat their swords into ploughshares and their spears into pruning hooks", for "nation will not take up sword against nation, nor will they train for war any more" (Isaiah 2:4).

All this must mean that, as Christians, we are primarily committed to peace and righteousness. This quest for peace with justice is much more costly than appeasement, as many Christian martyrs have found. We also admire the loyalty, self-sacrifice and courage of serving soldiers. Yet we must not glamorize or glorify war in itself, however just we may perceive its cause to be. Some Christians believe that in some circumstances it may be defended as the lesser of two evils, but it should never be regarded by the Christian mind as more than a painful necessity in a fallen world.

Apart from this general biblical background, however, there are three main positions which Christians hold and defend – the just war theory, and either total or relative pacifism.[21]

The "just war" tradition[22]

The concept of the "just war" can be traced back both to the "holy wars" of the Old Testament and to Greek and Roman ethical teaching. In the fourth century it was Christianized by Augustine. In the thirteenth century Thomas Aquinas placed it in a systematic framework, and it was further developed by Francisco de Vitoria in the sixteenth century and endorsed by most of the Reformers. It is held by a majority of Roman Catholics and Protestants today. The just war tradition is usually expressed through seven conditions that have to be met if a war can be just. These are: formal declaration, last resort, just cause, right intention, proportionate means, non-combatant immunity and reasonable expectation. There is some overlap in these seven criteria, however, and I find it more helpful to reduce them to three, relating to the beginning, the conduct and the end of a war.

How, then, can we judge whether a war is "just" or not?

Firstly, *its cause must be righteous.* It must be defensive, not aggressive. Its objectives must be to secure justice or remedy injustice, to protect the innocent or champion human rights. It must be undertaken as a last resort only, after all attempts at negotiation and reconciliation have been exhausted, and then only after a formal declaration (following an ultimatum) by a legitimate authority, not by groups or individuals. Moreover, the intention must be as righteous as the cause. Just causes are not served by unjust motives. So there must be no hatred, no animosity, no thirst for revenge.

Secondly, *its means must be controlled.* There must be no wanton or unnecessary violence. In fact, two key words are used to describe the legitimate use of violence in a just cause. One is "proportionate" and the other "discriminate". "Proportionate" signifies that the war is perceived as the lesser of two evils, that the violence inflicted is proportionately less than that which it is intended to remedy, and that the ultimate gains will outweigh the losses. "Discriminate" means that the war is directed against enemy combatants and military targets, and that civilians are immune. We have to concede that the total immunity of non-combatants is impossible to preserve. But in a "just war" the distinction must be preserved and the intentional killing of civilians outlawed. The principle of non-combatant immunity was implicit in the Hague Conventions (1899 and 1907), became explicit in the Geneva Conventions and their Additional Protocol (1949 and 1977), and has been emphatically reaffirmed by the General Assembly of the United Nations (1970).

Thirdly, *its outcome must be predictable.* That is, like the king in Jesus' little parable who "counted the cost" before going to war (Luke 14:31 – 32), there must be a calculated prospect of victory, and so of achieving the just cause for which the war was begun. However, there may be occasions when a country goes to war on a matter of principle even though it feels that the enemy is more powerful and therefore it is taking a risk. Some might argue that this was the case when Britain went to war in World War II, to fulfil its treaty obligations. Nevertheless, to go to war when there is no reasonable expectation of victory is foolhardy and is in danger of sacrificing the lives of thousands of people with no prospect of establishing the cause for which they died.

To sum up, a "just war" is one fought for a righteous cause, by controlled means, with a reasonable expectation of success.

The "just war" theory is only a tradition, however. Can it be commended from Scripture? Some try to do so on the basis of the wars commanded and directed by Yahweh in the Old Testament. But this is a precarious procedure, since these were expressly sanctioned, and no nation can claim today to enjoy Israel's privileged position as a "holy nation", God's special covenant people, a unique theocracy.

A more secure basis is provided by Paul's teaching about the state in Romans 13:1 – 7, and its context. It is actually embedded in a passage about neighbour-love, since it is preceded by injunctions to love and serve our enemies (12:14 – 21) and followed by statements that love never harms our neighbour (13:8 – 10). We are, therefore, confronted by a difficult exegetical problem. In particular, the end of Romans 12 and the beginning of Romans 13 appear to be in conflict with one another. The first, echoing the Sermon on the Mount, forbids us to repay anybody evil for evil; the second, echoing rather the Old Testament, describes the state as God's agent for the punishment of evil-doers. The first says that evil-doers are to be served; the second that they are to be punished. How can these instructions be reconciled?

The apostle Paul asserts that the governing authorities have been established by God, and that he has delegated his authority to them. Therefore, in submitting to them we are submitting to him and in rebelling against them we are rebelling against him. Further, "the one in authority" (any official of the state) is "God's servant" to reward the good citizen and punish the evil-doer. In fact, three times Paul repeats that the state's "authority" is God's authority and three times that the state's "ministry" is God's ministry (vv. 4a, 4b, 6). It seems clear to me that these are not grudging concessions that God has "assigned a place" to the state, which when using force to punish evil is nevertheless "sinning"; this is a genuine affirmation that God has "established" the state with his authority and that when exercising its authority to punish evil it is doing God's will. This being so, I cannot say that Christian people should remain insulated from public life; they should rather involve themselves in it, knowing that in doing so they are "ministers of God" just as much as pastors to whom the same expression is applied. There is nothing anomalous about Christians serving in the police force or the prison service, as politicians or magistrates or town councillors. Christians worship a God who is just and are, therefore, committed to the quest for justice. The Christian community should not stand aloof from the secular community, but should seek to penetrate it for Christ.

Among those who accept the legitimacy of Christian participation in the work of the secular authority are most pacifists who are not members of the Peace Churches. But, like all other Christians, they regard their participation as critical and conditional. For example, they would refuse to obey the state's call to take up arms.

How, then, should we resolve the apparent discrepancy between Romans 12:17 – 21, with its call for the loving service of enemies, and Romans 13:1 – 7, with its call for the punishment of evil-doers? We shall begin to perceive the answer when we notice that the contrast *between* forgiveness and punishment is not only between these paragraphs but embedded *within* the first. The prohibition "Do not repay anyone evil for evil" is followed by " 'I will repay,' says the Lord", and the prohibition "Do not take revenge, my friends" is followed by "leave room for God's wrath, for it is written: 'It is mine to avenge' " (vv. 17, 19). So the reason why wrath, revenge and retribution are forbidden us is not that they are in themselves wrong reactions to evil, but that they are *God's* prerogative, not ours. Similarly, Jesus himself, when "they hurled insults at him", not only "did not retaliate", but also instead "entrusted himself [and his cause] to him who judges justly" (1 Peter 2:23).

It is better, then, to see the end of Romans 12 and the beginning of Romans 13 as complementary to one another. Members of God's new community can be both private individuals and state officials. In the former role we are never to take personal revenge or repay evil for evil, but rather we are to bless our persecutors (12:14), serve our enemies (12:20) and seek to overcome evil with good (12:21). In the latter role, however, if we are called by God to serve as police or prison officers or judges, we are God's agents in the punishment of evil-doers. True, "vengeance" and "wrath" belong to God, but one way in which he executes his judgement on evil-doers today is through the state. To "leave room for God's wrath" (12:19) means to allow the state to be "an agent of wrath to bring punishment on the wrongdoer" (13:4). This is not to say that the administration of justice should not be tempered with mercy. It should. And state officials should be concerned not only to "punish" evil but to "overcome" it, since retributive and reformative justice should go hand in hand. Nevertheless, what this passage of Scripture emphasizes is that, if evil is to be punished (as it deserves to be), then the punishment must be administered by the state and its officials, and not by individuals who take the law into their own hands.[23]

It should be clear, then, that the state's punishing role is strictly limited and controlled. There is no possible justification in Romans 13:1 – 7 for an oppressive regime to whom the words "law and order" have become a synonym for tyranny. No. The state is God's agent to execute his wrath only on evil-doers – that is, on particular and identifiable people who have done wrong and need to be brought to justice. This implies a threefold restriction on the powers of the state. Firstly, the *people* the state punishes must be limited to evil-doers or law-breakers. Secondly, the *force* used to arrest them must be limited to the minimum necessary to bring them to justice. Thirdly, the *punishment* given must be limited in proportion to the evil which they have done. All three – the people, the force and the punishment – must be carefully controlled.

The same principles have to be applied to soldiers as to the police. Indeed, the distinction between them is a comparatively modern one. The enforcement of law, the maintenance of order and the protection of the innocent, which today are usually the work of the police, were in Paul's day the responsibility of Roman soldiers. Still in our own times there are situations of civil disorder (e.g., during the Mau Mau rebellion in Kenya) in which the army is called in to supplement the police. Whenever this happens, the behaviour of soldiers has to be understood as an extended form of police action and regulated accordingly. The British Ministry of Defence, for example, explains existing law relating to security operations by the useful catchphrase "minimum necessary force": "No more force may be used than is both necessary and reasonable in the circumstances. The degree of force can never be reasonable if it is more than that required to achieve the immediate aim" – the main aims being the prevention of crime and the arrest of criminals.

What, however, if the disturber of the peace is not an individual or group but another nation? The argument now is that, by legitimate extrapolation, the state's God-given authority to administer justice includes the restraint and resistance of evil-doers who are aggressors rather than criminals, and so the protection of its citizens' rights when threatened from outside as well as from inside. True, the analogy is not exact. On the one hand, the state which goes to war is acting as judge in its own cause and not as a third-party arbitrator, while on the other hand, the cool judicial procedures of the law court have no parallel in the declaration and conduct of war. These differences are due to the fact that acceptable international justice (in arbitration, intervention and peace-keeping) is only in its infancy. Nevertheless, the development of the "just war" theory "represented a systematic attempt to interpret acts of war by analogy with acts of civil government", and so to see them as belonging to "the context of the administration of justice" and as subject to "the restraining standards of executive justice".[24]

Executive justice, however, whether in relation to crime or civil disorder or international warfare, must always be both *discriminate* action (limiting the people involved to evil-doers who have to be brought to justice) and *controlled* action (limiting the force used to the minimum necessary to secure this end).

A commitment to pacifism[25]

In an age where nuclear weapons and other weapons of mass destruction are in existence, pacifism can be either total or relative (sometimes referred to as nuclear pacifism). I will deal with total pacifism first.

Total pacifism

Pacifists tend to begin with the Sermon on the Mount. At least it is from this part of the teaching of Jesus that many develop their commitment to non-violence. We are not to resist an evil person, Jesus said. Instead, if he strikes us on the right cheek, we are to turn to him the other also. We are to love our enemies, do good to those who hate us and pray for those who persecute us. Only so can we qualify as children of our heavenly Father, for his love is indiscriminate, and he gives the blessings of rain and sunshine to the evil and the good alike. To hate those who love us is the Devil's way. To love those who love us and hate those who hate us is the way of the world. If we would follow Jesus, however, and accept the standards of his kingdom, we must love those who hate us (Matthew 5:38 – 48; Luke 6:27 – 36).

Moreover, Jesus practised what he preached. He exemplified his call to non-resistance. He resisted neither betrayal nor arrest, neither trial nor sentence, neither torture nor crucifixion. When he was insulted, he did not retaliate. He was the innocent, suffering Servant of the Lord. "He was led like a lamb to the slaughter, and as a sheep before her shearers is silent, so he did not open his mouth" (Isaiah 53:7). He loved those who despised and rejected him. He even prayed for the forgiveness of those who nailed him to the cross.

Thus, pacifists conclude, the teaching and example of Jesus together commit us to the way of non-resistance and non-violence. This is the way of the cross, and Jesus calls us to take up our cross and follow him. Moreover, it seems to be historically proven that for two centuries, until the conversion of Constantine, the great majority of Christians refused to serve as soldiers. There is clear evidence that their refusal related to the idolatrous practices associated with life in the Roman army. Pacifists argue that they also perceived war to be incompatible with their Christian obedience. This is not certain.

The pacifist position was adopted by the so-called "Radical Reformers" of the sixteenth century (the various Anabaptist groups), is preserved by the Peace Churches today (Quakers, Mennonites, United Brethren, etc.), and is also held by considerable minorities in the "historic" Reformation churches.

Relative or nuclear pacifism[26]

The invention of weapons of mass destruction brought an entirely new dimension to the debate about war. The old categories of conventional wisdom seemed to become as obsolete as the old weapons of conventional warfare. Both scientists and theologians began to call for new and bold thinking. As the Roman Catholic bishops said at the Second Vatican Council, the church has "to undertake a completely fresh appraisal of war".[27] For everybody knows that where weapons of mass destruction are used, the casualties resulting from their use could be numbered in millions or even hundreds of millions and could not be limited (as they largely have been in the past, though indeed less in the twentieth century) to armies confronting one another.

The relevant biblical principle, which we need to evoke and apply, seems to be the great evil of "shedding innocent blood". The importance of "blood" in Scripture is that it is the carrier and so the symbol of life (e.g., Genesis 9:4; Leviticus 17:11; Deuteronomy 12:23). To "shed blood" is, therefore, to take life by violent means, in other words to kill. But human life, being the life of human beings made in the image of God, is sacrosanct. In the Old Testament the shedding of human blood was strictly forbidden except by specific divine sanction; i.e., in the execution of a murderer and in wars explicitly authorized by God. It is true that in the Mosaic law a small number of other serious offences (e.g., kidnapping, cursing parents, sorcery, bestiality, idolatry and blasphemy, see Exodus 21, 22 and Leviticus 24) were punishable by death. But this does not override the principle: "Whoever sheds the blood of man, by man shall his blood be shed; for in the image of God has God made man" (Genesis 9:6). That is, the bloodshedding of murder deserves the bloodshedding of capital punishment, for in the latter case it is the blood of the guilty which is shed. In all other cases, the sin of "shedding innocent blood" has been committed. Hence Abigail's thankfulness that, because David did not avenge himself against Nabal, he did not have "on his conscience the staggering burden of needless bloodshed" (1 Samuel 25:31).

This understanding was enshrined in the Old Testament provision of six "cities of refuge", three on each side of the River Jordan, carefully sited to cover the whole country. It was based on the distinction between murder (intentional killing) and manslaughter (unintentional), and was designed to protect the manslayer from the "avenger of blood" and so prevent the shedding of innocent blood (Numbers 35:9 – 34; Joshua 20:1 – 9).

A distinction was made in Old Testament times not only between murder and manslaughter, but also between blood shed in war (which was permissible) and blood shed in peace (which was not). Thus when Joab killed both Abner and Amasa, the two commanders of Israel's army, David condemned him for "avenging in time of peace blood which had been shed in war", and so bringing upon David's house the guilt of shedding "innocent blood" (1 Kings 2:5, 31 – 4 RSV).

Against this background of Old Testament law, the prophets uttered fierce denunciations against Israel. Jeremiah warned them of God's coming judgement because they had forsaken him and profaned Jerusalem. How? They had "burned sacrifices in it" to other gods and "filled this place with the blood of the innocent" (Jeremiah 19:4). Thus idolatry and bloodshed were bracketed. No sin against God was worse than worshipping idols. No sin against man was worse than shedding innocent blood. Similarly, Ezekiel described Jerusalem as bringing doom upon herself "by shedding blood in her midst" and "by making idols" (Ezekial 22:1 – 4; cf. 36:18). Both these prophets coupled worshipping idols and killing the innocent as the two paramount sins.

The same horror over the shedding of innocent blood continues in the New Testament. Judas confessed that he had "betrayed innocent blood" (Matthew 27:4), and when Pilate claimed to be "innocent of this man's blood", the people recklessly responded, "Let his blood be on us and on our children" (Matthew 27:24 – 5).

The biblical evidence on this matter is an impressively united testimony from the time of the patriarchs through the law and the prophets to the New Testament. Human blood is sacrosanct because it is the life of godlike human beings. To shed the blood of the innocent is, therefore, the gravest social sin, whether committed personally in murder or judicially by an oppressive regime. God's judgement fell on Israel in the seventh century BC because they were guilty of shedding much innocent blood, and in the first century AD because they shed the innocent blood of Jesus Christ. "Hands that shed innocent blood" are among the things which Yahweh is said to hate (Proverbs 6:16 – 17).

This biblical message must not be evaded. The judicial authority God has given the state, including the use of "the sword" (Romans 13:4), is strictly limited. In the case of the police it is to be used only to arrest criminals and bring them to justice, in the case of the army only to engage in a just war by just means for a just end. In both cases the immunity of the innocent is to be ensured – of law-abiding citizens in peacetime and of non-combatants in wartime. Therefore, any unlimited, uncontrolled or indiscriminate use of force is forbidden. In particular, a distinction has always been recognized in war between combatants and non-combatants, between the army and the civilian population. It is true that the army consists of human beings made in God's image, who may have been conscripted against their will, and who may be entirely innocent of the crimes committed by their government. Nevertheless, if it is legitimate to resist an aggressor nation, it is legitimate to regard its army as its agent in a way that its civilian population are not. This distinction is endorsed both by international law ("the protection of civilian persons in time of war") and by biblical teaching (the prohibition of the shedding of innocent blood). It applies in two ways.

Firstly, the principle of non-combatant immunity condemns the indiscriminate use of "conventional" (i.e., non-nuclear) weapons. For example, the Christian conscience rebels against the "obliteration" or "saturation" bombing of Hamburg, Cologne and Berlin in 1942 and 1943, and especially of Dresden in 1945. British and American leaders (notably Churchill and Roosevelt) had previously denounced the Nazi bombings of cities as odious and shocking, and the British government publicly announced that it was no part of its policy to bomb non-military targets, whatever the Nazis might do. But the Allies went back on their word, as they had reserved the right to do if Germany did not observe the same restrictions. Allied bombs on Hamburg in 1943 and on Dresden in 1945 created a "firestorm" of unimaginable horror. It was reckoned that about 135,000 people died in two days of raids on Dresden in February 1945 (considerably more than the immediate deaths caused by the atomic bombs dropped on both Hiroshima and Nagasaki); they included thousands of refugees who were fleeing before the Russian advance. I, for one, am thankful that Bishop George Bell of Chichester had the courage to protest in the House of Lords against this policy. Obliteration bombing "is not a justifiable act of war", he said, and "to justify methods inhumane in themselves by arguments of expediency smacks of the Nazi philosophy that Might is Right". The report of a Church of England commission *The Church and the Atom* (1948) concurred with his judgement, describing the raids on Dresden as "inconsistent with the limited ends of a just war: it violates the principles of discrimination".[28]

Secondly, the principle of non-combatant immunity condemns the use of all indiscriminate weapons. I have already considered earlier in this chapter the development of nuclear, biological and chemical weapons which are indiscriminate in their impact. A Christian consensus on this issue seems to be growing steadily. The Second Vatican Council said, "Any act of war aimed indiscriminately at the destruction of entire cities or of extensive areas along with their population is a crime against God and man himself. It merits unequivocal and unhesitating condemnation."[29] The British Council of Churches, at its November 1980 assembly, said of nuclear weapons that "to make use of the weapons would be directly contrary to the requirements of the so-called just war".[30]

Evangelical Christians have been slow to catch up with the biblical perspectives of other sections of the church. In 1980, however, an ecumenical group (with strong evangelical participation) met in the United States, saw a parallel between the nineteenth-century movement to abolish slavery and the need for a twentieth-century movement to abolish nuclear weapons, and issued "The New Abolitionist Covenant". It includes these sentences: "Unlimited in their violence, indiscriminate in their victims, uncontrollable in their devastation, nuclear weapons have brought humanity to an historical crossroads. More than at any previous time in history, the alternatives are peace or destruction. In nuclear war there are no winners."[31] What these Christian statements affirm about nuclear weapons is equally applicable to chemical and biological weapons, for all three, being indiscriminate in their effects, are indefensible in their use.

Christians everywhere, together with all those who want peace, should therefore campaign for the abolition of weapons of mass destruction. There has been considerable progress especially in the relationship between America and the former Soviet Union in reducing nuclear weapons, but countries such as India and Pakistan have nuclear weapons and are in conflict over issues related to Kashmir. This means that although some of our most terrifying and apocalyptic fears which we experienced during the Cold War may be reduced, the threat of nuclear weapons in our world is a very real one. This is also true of biological and chemical warfare. As biotechnology becomes an increasingly important part of our lives, new technologies whose major relevance is to heal the body may also provide more efficient ways of destroying the body. It is difficult to see how this paradox can be resolved, for in discovering more about the workings of the human body we are dependent on the goodwill of those who are making the discoveries to put them to a benevolent use rather than using them to create more efficient forms of warfare. There has never been a time when it has been more important for the world to act in concert to bring about peace.

QUESTIONS AND QUALIFICATIONS

Yet I can think of four issues which we have to address if we are to grapple with the real world.

The distinction between combatants and non-combatants

Is the distinction between combatants and non-combatants not obsolete? That is, modern war is total war, and there are no non-combatants any longer. The nation's whole population is sucked into the war effort. Every taxpayer is helping to finance it. Even people in civilian jobs are thereby releasing others for military service. Therefore, since everybody is involved, the use of indiscriminate weapons is legitimate.

In reply, we agree that the old clear-cut distinction between a country and its small professional army no longer applies, and that certainly everybody engaged in the manufacture, deployment or use of weapons may be regarded as a combatant. Nevertheless, there are still some categories like elderly people, little children and the physically and mentally sick who should be guaranteed non-combatant immunity, for to kill such people would clearly be to shed innocent blood.

It will not do to quote Old Testament examples of universal slaughter, since in such cases we are specifically told that the guilt was universal too. They were, therefore, not "indiscriminate" judgements. Before the flood, "The LORD saw how great man's wickedness on the earth had become, and that every inclination of the thoughts of his heart was only evil all the time" (Genesis 6:5). Sodom and Gomorrah would have been spared if only ten righteous people could have been found there (Genesis 18:32), while the Canaanites' practices were so depraved and detestable that the land itself is said to have "vomited out its inhabitants" (e.g., Leviticus 18:25).

If the universal judgements of the Old Testament supply no precedent for indiscriminate warfare, what about the Old Testament principle of corporate solidarity or responsibility? God described himself as "punishing the children for the sins of the fathers to the third and fourth generations" of those who hated him (Exodus 20:5), and the humiliated survivors of the destruction of Jerusalem complained: "Our fathers sinned ... and we bear their punishment" (Lamentations 5:7). Does this divine action, it is asked, not justify the slaughter of the innocent with the guilty in war? No. The principle was exemplified in God's dealings with his people as a nation; it was not transferred to the law courts, where guilt had to be established. If, therefore, we are right that a moral defence of the "just war" is possible only if it can be seen as an extension of the administration of justice, then the distinction between the innocent and the guilty must somehow be preserved.

It is also important but disturbing to note that even in local and civil wars the distinction between combatants and non-combatants is frequently not adhered to. The Campaign Against Arms Trade (CAAT) has stated: "Tens of millions of people have been killed in wars since 1945. By the end of the 1990s nearly 90% of war-victims were non-combatants and at least half of these were children."[32]

Although we may feel far removed from the theatre of war, the slaughter of the innocent should stimulate in us a righteous outrage. It will not do to pass off such actions as inevitable in war. We have to recover a sense of what it means for those who are innocent to fear for their lives or to be tortured for no reason at all. Compared to the power of such evil, our own protestations seem weak. Yet, being stirred to action, we will surely feel that doing something is better than doing nothing. Drawing the attention of the media to such situations by letter-writing, or calling upon your constituency MP to raise the issues in parliament, or joining a human rights association that actively promotes enhanced human rights for the innocent in these countries may all go some way to resolving the issue. It is also the case that where war threatens to break out, mediation can be effective in preventing it from happening. Christian peacemakers are therefore needed to mediate where such a conflagration is threatened. But as well as all these things, Christians are called to pray: to pray because we believe that prayer changes the world and because it is an act of solidarity with the purposes of God, who is the God of justice, who cares about championing the cause of the innocent.

The distinction between discriminate and non-discriminate weapons

Some point out that not all ABC weapons are indiscriminate. Chemical weapons, for instance, can be used on the battlefield in reasonably controlled ways. It is even suggested that nuclear weapons have become so sophisticated that they could home in on precise targets with incredible accuracy. The enhanced radiation weapon, or "neutron bomb", can immobilize a single tank by killing its crew. So, as the processes of miniaturization and precision targeting continue, nuclear weapons will become increasingly discriminate in their effects, and their use cannot be given a blanket condemnation. That is the argument.

There is plainly some cogency in this reasoning. The less indiscriminate weapons become, the less unacceptable they are. There might conceivably, therefore, be a situation in which it would be morally permissible to use a very limited nuclear weapon, even though there would be some degree of radioactive fallout, and therefore some non-combatants would probably be killed. It would have to be a situation of the utmost urgency, in which the only alternative would be the worse evil of surrender to a godless regime.

In the Cold War scenario, two superpowers faced each other, each having nuclear weapons. The question was whether any use of nuclear weapons would lead to escalation. However, it is conceivable that with the collapse of the Soviet Union it is unlikely that two powers will face each other with comparable stocks of nuclear weapons. The fear is rather that with nuclear technology becoming more widespread, a rogue state will use a nuclear weapon to destabilize an area or attack an enemy and that this enemy may or may not have the ability to respond with nuclear weapons. If Iran does make a nuclear weapon, the potential for the destabilization of the Middle East is alarming, especially if Israel does also possess nuclear weapons. Even the use of a limited nuclear weapon could prove disastrous in the tinderbox of the Middle East. The weapon may well be called limited in terms of its physical power, but it would be naïve to suggest that such a weapon would be limited in its political and social consequences. Certainly it is highly unlikely that once a nuclear exchange of any kind had been entered into, its progress could be predictable and controlled.

The distinction between use and possession of weapons

If the use of ABC weapons would be evil, must their retention as a deterrent not be declared equally evil? Supposing we agree that the use of weapons of mass destruction would be immoral, and the situation too fragile even to use micro-weapons, does that not mean that all Christians should be committed to unilateral nuclear disarmament? No, not all relative (or nuclear) pacifists are unilateralists. For there is a moral distinction between possession, threat and use.[33] It is probably true that if an action is immoral, then the active threat to perform it is immoral too. But possession is more a conditional warning than an aggressive threat. Indeed, since the intention behind possession is not to encourage use but to deter it, possession cannot be pronounced as immoral as use.

Shall we then renounce use but defend possession? This seems to be the conclusion to which we are coming. Of course, we can immediately see its logical inconsistency. The effectiveness of a deterrent depends on the skill (technical) and the will (moral and political) to use it if necessary, and on the belief of the enemy that we intend to do so. A deterrent lacks credibility if the enemy knows we would never use it, and if it lacks credibility it loses its power to deter. So "retaining possession, renouncing use", though morally defensible, seems practically self-defeating. We are caught between the ineffective and the immoral, or rather between a moral stance which is ineffective and an effective deterrent which (if used) would be immoral, and so between principle and prudence, between what is right and what is realistic. Professor Wolfhart Pannenberg has put his finger on this tension. He writes about "the conflict ... between two different ethical attitudes: an ethics of conviction that adheres to the purity of moral principles, and an ethics of responsibility that feels obliged to consider the consequences that might follow from the decision embraced".[34]

Speaking for myself, however, I am not willing to be forced to choose between Christian idealism and Christian realism, if I may use these terms loosely. Relative pacifists are certainly idealists, who perceive clearly and refuse to compromise the principle that the use of weapons of mass destruction would be immoral. But in clinging to this ideal, we must also face the realities of evil in our fallen world and of the current situation which reflects it. How, then, can we reconcile the ideal and the reality? Is there any escape from the dilemma which I have expressed as "immoral to use, prudent to keep"? Certainly there are five issues which we need to bear in mind when considering this.

The balance between deterrence and disarmament

I accept the argument that immediate unilateral disarmament might well, in the case of nuclear weapons particularly, make nuclear war more rather than less likely. It might tempt an enemy to exploit our self-imposed weakness. They might either bully us into surrender by using nuclear missiles without fear of retaliation (in which case we have precipitated use by others through forswearing use ourselves), or blackmail us by threatening to use them (in which case our renunciation will have encouraged an enemy takeover). The question is how to prevent the use of nuclear weapons by *both* sides, and at the same time preserve our freedom. It seems to be safer, therefore, and more consistent with both ideal and reality, to retain a nuclear deterrent while developing the search for a disarmament which is mutual, progressive and verifiable.

Deterrence as a temporary step towards disarmament

The retention of a deterrent whose weapons it would be immoral to use can be morally justified only as a temporary expedient. As Pope John Paul II said in June 1982 to the UN Second Special Session on Disarmament, the nuclear deterrent "may still be judged morally acceptable", but only if it is seen "certainly not as an end in itself, but as a step on the way towards a progressive disarmament".[35] This should increase the urgency with which the quest for effective disarmament proposals is pursued.

"Audacious gestures of peace"

Within the framework of bilateral disarmament there is a place for imaginative unilateral initiatives, which Pope John Paul II has called "audacious gestures of peace". Some were earlier taken by the West without being reciprocated (e.g., the American removal from Europe in 1979 of 1,000 nuclear warheads, although, to be sure, they had long been obsolete). Yet more could surely have been taken without undue danger. Whoever the perceived enemy may be, we should have the courage to declare a "no first use" commitment.

Sufficient not superior

Whether or not our conscience can accept a distinction between limited and unlimited weapons, we should be able to agree that the latter should be renounced and abolished as soon as possible. Professor Keith Ward, for example, who on the moral principle that we may "commit an evil act (one causing harm) in order to prevent a much greater evil" thinks that the use of a limited nuclear weapon might in an extreme situation be the lesser of two evils, nevertheless declares that "all-out nuclear war must ... stand unequivocally condemned ... It is morally unjustifiable." "It is therefore imperative," he adds, "to dismantle the apparatus which makes all-out war possible,"[36] and to retain only "a limited nuclear deterrent", indeed the minimum necessary to deter. Nuclear "superiority" is entirely unnecessary; nuclear "sufficiency" is enough. Moreover, because of the enormous "overkill" of the superpowers' arsenals, to reduce them further would not appear to entail unacceptable risk. And such a reduction might well be the impetus which is needed to accelerate the downward spiral of disarmament on both sides.

Credible yet uncertain

Meanwhile, the deterrent must somehow remain credible. If the use of nuclear weapons would be immoral, we cannot threaten their use. Yet if we want the deterrent to deter, we cannot bluff either. The only alternative seems to be to cultivate uncertainty. We might say to a perceived enemy, "We believe that the use of weapons of indiscriminate destruction would be both crazy and immoral. We are determined not to use them. We are sure you do not want to use them either. Yet if you attack us, you may provoke us to act against both our reason and our conscience. We beg you not to put us in that position."

The distinction between subjugation and annihilation

Would an enemy takeover not be a greater evil even than nuclear war? The scenario which is frequently envisaged and greatly feared is that we and our allies, threatened with defeat by an invading army equipped with superior conventional weapons, would be tempted in self-defence to resort to nuclear weapons, and so would plunge the world into nuclear war. "Would that not be justified?" we are asked. Can we seriously envisage the possibility that we would allow our country to be overrun and subjugated? For, if we anticipate the worst that might happen, then the freedom we have come to accept as indispensable to our quality of life would be brutally suppressed. Would such an evil not be literally "intolerable", worse even than the evil of nuclear war? True, the evil of subjugation would be perpetrated by the atheistic aggressor, not by us. Yet if it could be avoided by some moral action on our part, and we do not take action, we would become accomplices in the evil. If something could be done, then to do nothing is to do evil. On the other hand, if the "something" which could be done to prevent a takeover is a resort to nuclear war, we are back with the original question: Which is the greater evil?

Relative pacifists, however, are concerned about moral principle, not prudential balance. Our position is this: To start (or share in starting) a nuclear war would be a moral evil of such magnitude that no situation could ever justify it, not even the fear that we ourselves would otherwise be subjugated or destroyed. How can we hope to preserve our values by violating them? Would it not be better to live under an oppressive regime, with all the suffering and slavery that would involve, than be responsible for destroying the whole of human civilization? It would be appalling indeed to allow millions of people to be deprived of liberty; but would we be prepared to incinerate millions in order to prevent it happening? Would it not be better to suffer injustice ourselves than inflict it on others?

In the end, then, we have to decide which blessing we value the more: social freedom, though at the cost of losing our moral integrity by starting a nuclear war; or moral integrity as a nation, though at the cost of losing our social freedom by allowing our country to be overrun. If this might one day be the option before us, I hope we should know which to choose. It would be better to suffer physical defeat than moral defeat; better to lose freedom of speech, of assembly, even of religion, than freedom of conscience before God. In his sight integrity is yet more valuable than liberty.

THE RISE OF TERRORISM

In my argument so far I have said a lot about nuclear war and indeed, by association, about all weapons of mass destruction. But, it could be argued, the human conflict with which we are grappling at the outset of the twenty-first century is not the threat of nuclear exchange between nation states, but the rise of terrorism. Over the last ten years the growth of terrorism has reached epic proportions. Many countries, including the USA, Kenya, Spain, Peru, Indonesia, Israel, Palestine, Northern Ireland and Britain have seen horrific violence perpetrated by terrorists from one background or another.

If the collapse of the Berlin Wall in 1989 signalled the beginning of new freedoms for those who were used to oppression, the collapse of the Twin Towers in New York on 11 September 2001 signalled a new sense of oppression for those who were used to freedom. Certainly, America will never again feel that it is invincible within its own borders. When those two passenger jets deliberately crashed into the World Trade Center, and another narrowly missed its target in Washington, DC, the profile of terrorism increased. Suddenly terrorists had a global audience. On 7 July 2005, London was also the target of suicide bombers when three bombs exploded within fifty seconds of each other on three London Underground trains. A fourth exploded on a bus. Fifty-six people were killed and seven hundred injured. The incident on 9/11 was the most serious act of terrorism on Americans since the bombing of Pan Am flight 103 in 1988, when

270 people were killed. The train bombings were the deadliest in London since World War II.

There are many acts of violence conducted throughout the world, but we, through the news media, are the ones who label some of them acts of terrorism. Mark Juergensmeyer, in his book *Terror in the Mind of God: The Global Rise of Religious Violence*,[37] says that they are "public acts of destruction, committed without a clear military objective, that arouse a widespread sense of fear".

The word terrorism comes from the Latin word *terrere*, which means "to cause to tremble". So our response is part of the meaning of the term. In other words, the meaning of terrorism is provided by the trembling it produces in those who are affected by it or witnesses to it, not solely by the party committing the act. Terrorism is notoriously difficult to define, but all definitions have in common the fact that it is characterized first and foremost by the use of violence. Yet the purpose for which this violence is used and the motivation behind it are often not clear. It is often separated from criminal activity by giving it some political legitimacy, but even then many terrorists cannot even define their own aims in terms that are coherent.

It is often the case, however, that acts of terrorism claim many victims who are innocent in that they are caught up in the violence by accident. This means that many people have little sympathy with their actions. Occasionally this may lead terrorists to realize that their acts of violence are disaffecting public or international opinion. This may lead them to return to political and diplomatic means by which they attempt to achieve their goals. The Irish Republican Army (IRA) could perhaps be seen as a terrorist group who appear to be in the process of laying down their arms in favour of political engagement. It remains to be seen whether this will be a permanent state of affairs. At the time of writing, Hamas, known as a Palestinian terrorist organization which refuses to recognize the state of Israel, has won an overwhelming victory in the elections in Palestine. This places the international community in a dilemma, since Palestine is dependent on international aid for its economy to function. Yet few of those international bodies and nation states that fund Palestine are happy recognizing a Palestinian state governed by Hamas if they have not renounced violence or recognized the state of Israel. It remains to be seen how this scenario will be resolved.

In recent years the growth of terrorism has had horrific consequences. In particular, Al Quaeda has moved from being a movement which was unknown in the West to being a terrorist network synonymous with the worst excesses of violence. Yet there is a difficulty inherent in the response of the nation state to acts of terrorism in that this is a very different form of violence and it is difficult to combat according to the conventional rules of war. It is, therefore, possible for a nation state with exceptional military power to respond in a disproportionate way to a very real terrorist threat. The response of America and Britain among others to the events of 9/11 brought about a debate on such a response. There was no doubt that such acts of horror and violence had to be combated and those who perpetrated them brought to justice, yet in calling the response to the events of 9/11 a "war on terror", George W. Bush signalled the start of an ethical debate which should always accompany a declaration of war by the state on whatever kind of violence.

There was grave concern when the focus of activity shifted from searching for Osama bin Laden and Al Quaeda in Afghanistan to going to war with Iraq. Having used the existence of weapons of mass destruction as one of the key reasons for going to war, it was found that no such weapons appeared to exist. The weapons inspectors had not finished their scrutiny of those sites where such weaponry may have been found. Also, the action was not legitimated by the United Nations, but both America and Britain, along with their other partners, acted pre-emptively in going to war. This raised queries in the minds of some of those who were antagonistic to the war as to whether it had been declared by legitimate authorities and whether a pre-emptive action could be justified according to the principles of the just war.

However, at the time of writing this book, Iraq has held elections for its first parliament and is attempting to form a government. Are those who support military action right in saying that these democratic elections would never have taken place were it not for the military intervention of the West? Yet others still maintain that diplomacy might have deposed Saddam Hussein and his corrupt regime without such loss of life. We shall never know. Many people in Iraq see themselves as having been liberated from oppression. Others see the actions of countries such as America and Britain as resulting in them becoming occupying forces with ulterior motives. This has led to an insurgence not only by some Iraqis but also by terrorists from other countries. The jury is still out on the consequences of the military action, but we must still hope that peace will come to Iraq and that the government which results will govern with justice and with a constitution that guarantees freedom and human rights for its people.

Terrorism can have several roots, but there are three in particular. Firstly, the West sees modernization and the spread of democracy as not only inevitable but desirable. Yet others may see the spread of Western secular materialism as a threat to their own cultural identity. Smaller groups can feel swamped by the impact of globalization on their local culture and at the extremes such groups can resort to violent means in order to preserve their own culture. Secondly, economic explanations are also important. As globalization increases the expectations of a higher standard of living, those who see a widening gap between such possibilities and their own poverty may react against "the system" because they can see that those expectations will not be realized in their own lives. In this case, then, it could be said that terrorist violence is an attack on the inequalities of the global system. Those who take this view would point out that the two terrorist attacks on the World Trade Center in 1993 and 2001 could be interpreted as attacks on a capitalist icon. Ironically, the power and efficiency of global financial systems are frequently used by terrorist groups in planning and funding their campaigns. Yet thirdly, what is sometimes called the "new terrorism" is religious in origin. This has also been called "postmodern terrorism". It is difficult to use force to defeat this kind of terrorism, for how can one come with force against somebody who regards dying for their cause as leading to the rewards of martyrdom which exist beyond death? It would seem that the language of religion and acts associated with religion are part of the mix of terrorism being used to achieve other political objectives.[38]

Religiously violent groups grew during the last decades of the twentieth century. Juergensmeyer says that in 1980 the US State Department's list of international terrorist groups contained scarcely a single religious organization. In 1998 US Secretary of State Madeleine Albright listed thirty of the world's most dangerous groups; over half were religious. Other analysts have added to those figures, leading former US Secretary of State Warren Christopher to comment that terrorist acts in the name of religion and ethnic identity had become "one of the biggest security challenges we face in the wake of the Cold War".

In the light of this it is vital that we do not demonize other world religions because of the violent acts of terrorists who claim to be inspired by that religion or to have a mandate derived from that religion. Islamophobia is not an option for Christians, as it sets up stereotypes of Islam which are distorted and can only serve to damage good relations between Christians and Muslims. However, as Vinoth Ramachandra points out in his book *Faiths in Conflict: Christian Integrity in a Multicultural World*, this challenge is mutual. Religions and cultures can demonize one another and become defensive and fearful of the impact the other may have on them. Many cultures in the Middle East are sharply critical of Western values, including what they see as the imposition of Western values cloaked in the language of human rights. Yet Islam must also avoid a militant "Westo-phobia" and what has been called a "Christophobia", which is the distorted stereotyping of Christians and the Christian faith. Ramachandra comments:

> "Islamophobia", "Westo-phobia", "Christophobia" – these are ugly words but they draw our attention, however unsatisfactorily, to ugly realities. All phobias are the result of ignorance and the inability to look critically at oneself and one's own community. Good relations can be established between Christians and Muslims in the West only if Christians are forthright in exposing and condemning all expressions of anti-Muslim bigotry in the West, and if Muslim leaders condemn, with equal fervour, similar bigotry and discrimination by their own ranks both in the West and in what they regard as the *dar-ul-Islam*.[39]

We also need to remember that religiously inspired violence has appeared in all the world's religions, including the violence exhibited between Protestants and Catholics in Northern Ireland. Whether it is Hindu extremists or Jewish fundamentalists, violence is not confined to one religion.

The growth of religiously inspired violence is also one of the signs that religion is increasing in influence in the twenty-first century. From the standpoint of twenty-first-century Europe, we have been misled into thinking that religion is no longer a player on the world scene. Nothing could be further from the truth. Religious identity is becoming increasingly important throughout the world and in many sources of conflict it has been the defining characteristic that has identified the fault-line between those peoples who are in conflict. This was true, for instance, in Bosnia, where religion was as important as ethnicity or any political allegiance in determining the nature of the conflict.

One of the things that seems to be necessary for terrorism to take root in the imagination is the belief that the world is already violent and that one is in some sense in a state of war. This is necessary if someone is to see his or her own perpetration of an act of violence as justified. The existence of a violent world gives the terrorist a moral justification for engaging in violence. Also, if the state is seen as weak or compromised and unable to right wrongs, then violence may fill the void. It is sometimes the case that when Christians mistakenly cite their religion as a reason for terrorist acts they see the end results of their actions as more just or righteous than if the status quo were allowed to continue. This was the case in the bombing of abortion clinics in the US. Those who did it said that they wanted to bring about a Christian society by ridding the world of its evils. Instead, they themselves perpetrated evil as well as bringing shame and dishonour on the very faith that they purported to espouse.

Many of these acts do not seem to be done to achieve a specific goal, but to make a symbolic statement. Here Juergensmeyer says, "By calling acts of religious terrorism 'symbolic' I mean that they are intended to illustrate or refer to something beyond their immediate target: a grander conquest, for instance, or a struggle more awesome than meets the eye." [40]

It is important to be cautious about the use of religiously inspired violence, because it may be the case that it is being used cynically by those in authority to serve political ends, whereas those who are committed enough to be "martyrs" see it as an end in itself. Such a political goal might be the desire by some to bring about an Islamist state. Yet it is also the case that religious violence can have a symbolism which is important and with which we must engage.

There is an even deeper and grander context in which religiously inspired violence must be placed. In many cases religious violence is placed in the context of a divine struggle, a "cosmic" war, which is taking place invisibly around us. This means that religious violence can be seen as being about a much deeper spiritual confrontation. One of the potent symbols of this is that Islamic suicide bombers believe that by killing the enemies of Islam they will be received into paradise, with greater reward because of their acts. As I have already said, it is difficult enough to defeat a suicide bomber because of the strategies they employ, but it is much harder to engage with the imagination of a suicide bomber who believes that by committing such an atrocity he or she will be received into paradise. In the minds of these people, such a belief seems to justify any action they may be about to take, whether it be in a packed restaurant or a crowded bus, even when there may be children present.

Such a distorted view of the nature of religion can, however, provide opportunities for peacemaking for those who are committed to non-violence and who see such a commitment as powerful, if not more powerful than the ends attained by violence itself. The revulsion felt by all those who desire peace can unite people across many cultural and religious divides in a desire to foster community, respect and understanding. As Christians called to hope, based on the possibility of personal transformation and social justice, we believe that people can be turned away from violence and can embrace peacemaking as a vocation. To this end we should not give up the struggle to wage peace in a violent world.[41]

It is true that Christianity speaks of cosmic war. The apostle Paul in his letter to the Ephesians says that we are fighting not just flesh and blood but also "principalities and powers". He advises the Christians in Ephesus to clothe themselves with what he calls "the whole armour of God", but this armour consists of the characteristics of Christian virtue and Christian mission. One element of the armour, for instance, is described as the gospel of peace, another is truth and yet another is faith. The idea of the armour is the very opposite of the concept of a viciously fought campaign of religious violence. In a world of falsehood, Paul is saying, truth and honesty are the only weapons; in a world of violence, peacemaking is the only effective resistance. Religiously inspired violence can only end through the rediscovery of the true Christian faith.

A CALL TO CHRISTIAN PEACEMAKING

Jesus spoke of both war and peace. On the one hand, he warned us of "wars and rumours of wars"; on the other, he included in his characterization of the citizens of God's kingdom the active role of peacemaking. He pronounced his peacemaking followers blessed by both God and the children of God (Matthew 5:9). Peacemaking is a divine activity. God has made peace with us and between us through Christ. We cannot claim to be his authentic children unless we engage in peacemaking too.

What practical peacemaking initiatives is it possible for us to take?

Christian peacemakers must recover their morale

There are two tendencies in today's church which undermine Christian morale. Both must be firmly repudiated.

The first is the tendency to trivialization. We prefer the passivity of being entertained to the challenge of becoming engaged. It is easy to ignore the troubles of the world by reducing the world to our own agenda. But nothing could be more urgent than the threat of self-destruction, the suffering of millions or the destruction of our way of life.

The second tendency which undermines morale is to be so pessimistic about the future as to acquiesce in the general mood of helplessness. But both indifference and pessimism are inappropriate in the followers of Jesus. We are called to engage with our contemporary culture rather than be indifferent to it, and to be an example of hope in a culture of despair where people have become cynical about any possibility of change for the better. It is important for the voice of the Christian church to be heard not only locally but nationally and internationally, and this means making our points clearly in the media and by lobbying the government when change is necessary. The world needs militant peacemakers.

Christian peacemakers must pray

Please do not reject this exhortation as a piece of pietistic irrelevance. For Christian believers it is nothing of the sort. Irrespective of the rationale and the efficacy of praying, we have been commanded to do it. Jesus our Lord specifically told us to pray for our enemies. Paul affirmed that our first duty when we assemble as a worshipping congregation is to pray for our national leaders, so that "we may live peaceful and quiet lives in all godliness and holiness" (1 Timothy 2:2). Yet today "often the pastoral prayer in public worship is brief and perfunctory; the petitions are so unimaginative and stale as to border on 'vain repetitions'; and the people doze and dream instead of praying".[42] There is a great need to take seriously the period of intercession in public worship, and to pray for rulers and governments, peace and justice, friends and enemies, freedom and stability, and for deliverance from the spectre of war. The living God hears and answers the sincere prayers of his people.

Christian peacemakers must set an example as a community of peace

God's call to us is not only to "preach peace" and to "make peace" but also to embody it. His purpose, through the work of his Son and his Spirit, is to create a new reconciled society in which no curtains, walls or barriers are tolerated, and in which the divisive influences of race, nationality, rank and sex have been destroyed. He means his church to be a sign of his kingdom – that is, a model of what human community looks like when it comes under his rule of righteousness and peace. An authentic kingdom community will then challenge the value system of the secular community and offer a viable alternative.

We can hardly call the world to peace while the church falls short of being the reconciled community God intends it to be. If charity begins at home, so does reconciliation. We need to banish all malice, anger and bitterness from both church and home, and make them instead communities of love, joy and peace. The influence for peace of communities of peace is inestimable.

Christian peacemakers must contribute to confidence building

There is no reason why the concept of "confidence building measures" (CBMs) should be restricted to specifically military matters. In every situation in which people feel threatened, our Christian response should be to seek to remove fear and build confidence. I have already talked about the need for "audacious gestures of peace" and these need to be followed by CBMs. Whether it is setting up joint schools for Protestant and Roman Catholic children, or bringing together Palestinian and Israeli families to share their culture, CBMs are vital to peace. Personal contacts break down caricatures and help people to discover one another as human beings. It is even more important for Christians to travel, to serve and to share, so that they may find one another as brothers and sisters in Christ.

Christian peacemakers must promote public debate

Peace movements will contribute to peacemaking only if they succeed in stimulating informed discussion. There is always need for a fresh debate with fresh questions. Why do we need arsenals of weapons of mass destruction? Is "moral possession, immoral use" a viable stance or totally self-contradictory? Are there what are sometimes called "alternative defence policies"?[43] Would the build-up of "conventional" armies make it safer for weapons of mass destruction to be reduced, or can both be reduced simultaneously? Would it ever be justifiable to buy national defence at the cost of millions of civilian lives? Which is the more important in the end: national integrity or national security? Such questions – and many more – need to be raised and debated.

Every Christian is called to be a peacemaker. The Beatitudes are not a set of eight options, so that some may choose to be meek, others to be merciful, and yet others to make peace. Together they are Christ's description of the members of his kingdom. True, we shall not succeed in establishing Utopia on earth, nor will Christ's kingdom of righteousness and peace become universal within history. Not until he returns will swords be beaten into ploughshares and spears into pruning hooks. Yet this fact gives no possible warrant for the proliferation of factories for the manufacture of swords and spears. Does Christ's prediction of famine inhibit us from seeking a more equitable distribution of food? No more can his prediction of wars inhibit our pursuit of peace. God is a peacemaker. Jesus Christ is a peacemaker. So, if we want to be God's children and Christ's disciples, we must be peacemakers too.

NOTES

1 In May 2001, a US refugee agency estimated this figure killed since August 1998. See *http://news.bbc.co.uk/1/hi/world/africa/1072684.stm*.

2 Land Mine Monitor Report, 2003; cf. *www.icbl.org/lm/2003/findings.html*.

3 MAG, "Iraq Fact Sheet – An Overview", ReliefWeb, 20 January 2003.

4 Child Soldiers Global Report 2001, Campaign to Stop the Use of Child Soldiers. Protecting Refugees, UN Refugee Service (UNHCR), *www.unhcr.org*.

5 O. Robinson, in *World Vision News* (December 1999), pp. 10 – 11.

6 Samuel P. Huntington, *The Clash of Civilizations and the Remaking of World Order* (New York: Simon & Schuster, 1997), p. 21.

7 Ibid., p. 126.

8 Ibid., p. 29.

9 Ibid., pp. 312 – 16.

10 Ibid., p. 321.

11 Cited in Robert Kaplan, *The Ends of the Earth: A Journey at the Dawn of the Twenty-First Century* (New York: Random House Inc., 1996), pp. 8 – 9.

12 Ibid., p. 436.

13 From Earl Mountbatten's "The Final Abyss?" speech, May 1979, published in *Apocalypse Now?* (Nottingham: Spokesman Books, 1980), p. 11.

14 See also *The Long-Term Consequences of Nuclear War* (1983), the report of an international conference sponsored by thirty-one groups. Two imaginative scenarios, written by military men, were published in 1978. *World War 3, A military projection founded on today's facts,* edited by Brigadier Shelford Bidwell (London: Hamlyn, 1978), predicted that in 1983 the third world war would start "as a result of some intolerable provocation" (p. xiii); e.g., the invasion of West Germany by Soviet tanks to prevent her becoming a nuclear power. The last chapter is entitled "Doomsday" and describes the final, total devastation. *The Third World War* by General Sir John Hackett, assisted by top-ranking American and German generals (London: Sidgwick & Jackson, 1978), calls itself "A future history". It also describes an invasion of West Germany by Soviet tanks, though in 1985, which steadily escalates until first Birmingham and then in retaliation Minsk are obliterated by nuclear missiles. This time, however, the final

holocaust is averted by the uprising against the Soviet Union of her satellites. The ghastly consequences of a nuclear explosion are factually described by Donald B. Kraybill in *Facing Nuclear War* (Scottdale, Penn.: Herald Press, 1982) and in *Common Security* (The Palme Commission Report, 1982), pp. 49–70.

15 USA, Libya, Israel, Syria, Iraq, Iran, Russia, China, Taiwan, North Korea and South Korea are thought to have biochemical weapons capabilities.

16 Graham S. Pearson, *Biological Weapons Proliferation: Reasons for Concern, Courses of Action* (Henry L. Stimson Centre Report No. 24, January 1998). This can also be found at *www.brad.ac.uk/acad/sbtwc/other/disease.htm* as "The Threat of Deliberate Disease in the 21st Century".

17 Julian Perry Robinson with Carl-Goran Hedan and Hans von Screeb, *The Problem of Chemical and Biological Warfare: CB Weapons Today,* vol. II (New York: Stockholm International Peace Research Institute, 1973), p. 135; cited in Pearson, *Biological Weapons Proliferation.*

18 US Congress, Office of Technology Assessment, *Proliferation of Weapons of Mass Destruction: Assessing the Risks,* OTAISC 559 (Washington, DC: Government Printing Office, August 1993), pp. 52–55; United Nations, *Report of the Secretary General, Chemical and Bacteriological (Biological) Weapons and the Effects of their Possible Use,* Document A/7575/Rev.1, S/9292/Rev. 1, 1969; Stephen Fetter, "Ballistic Missiles and Weapons of Mass Destruction: What Is the Threat? What Should be Done?", *International Security* 16, no. 1 (Summer 1991), pp. 5–42.

19 Pearson, *Biological Weapons Proliferation.*

20 "The Chemical Weapons Convention and the OPCW – How They Came About", OPCW Fact Sheet 1, *www.opcw.org.*

21 For a debate between eight Christian thinkers who assess the arguments for and against these three positions, see Oliver R. Barclay (ed.), *Pacifism and War, When Christians disagree* (Leicester: InterVarsity Press, 1984). Similar ground is covered in Robert G. Clouse (ed.), *War: Four Christian Views* (Downers Grove: InterVarsity Press, 1981). See also J. Andrew Kirk (ed.), *Handling Problems of Peace and War* (London: Marshall Pickering, 1988).

22 The theory of the "just war" is carefully argued in two books by Paul Ramsey: *War and the Christian Conscience* (Durham, N.C.: Duke Univ. Press, 1961) and *The Just War* (New York: Scribner's, 1968). For more recent statements of the "just war" position, see Arthur F. Holmes in Clouse (ed.), *War: Four Christian Views,* pp. 120–21; *The Church and the Bomb* (London: Hodder & Stoughton, 1982), pp. 81–98; and *The Challenge of Peace: God's Promise and Our Response,* the US Bishops' Pastoral Letter (London: CTS/SPCK, 1983), pp. 24–32. For a similar position based on the justice of God, see Jerram Barrs, *Peace and Justice in the Nuclear Age* (Chicago: Garamond Press, 1983).

23 It needs to be added that in some emergency situations when no policeman is present, it may be right for a citizen to intervene in a fight, protect an innocent person against assault or arrest a burglar. But in such cases, the citizen is temporarily constituting himself an arm of the law; he is not acting as a private individual, nor is he justified in feeling personal animosity or taking personal revenge.

24 Oliver O'Donovan, *In Pursuit of a Christian View of War*, Grove Booklet on Ethics no. 15 (Cambridge: Grove Books, 1977), pp. 13 – 14. This booklet is a valuable enquiry into the legitimacy of the analogy between domestic justice and warfare.

25 For information on pacifism, the following Mennonite website contains some resources: *http://peace.mennolink.org.* Cf. also Jean Lasserre, *War and the Gospel* (Cambridge: E. T. James Clarke, 1962); Ronald J. Sider, *Christ and Violence* (Scottdale, Penn.: Herald Press, 1979); Ronald J. Sider and Richard K. Taylor, *Nuclear Holocaust and Christian Hope* (Downers Grove: InterVarsity Press, 1982); Myron Augsburger, *Christian Pacifism* (Downers Grove, InterVarsity Press, 2001).

26 Dana Mills-Powell (ed.), *Decide for Peace, Evangelicals against the bomb*, is a symposium of sixteen contributions by both nuclear and total pacifists (London: Marshall Pickering, 1986).

27 *Pastoral Constitution*, para. 80.

28 *The Church and the Atom*, the report of a Church of England commission (1948), p. 43. For a factual account of the bombing of German and Japanese cities, see Brigadier Peter Young (ed.), *The Almanac of World War II* (London: Hamlyn, 1981). Bishop Bell's speech in the House of Lords is recorded in *Hansard* (9 February 1944), vol. 130, pp. 738 – 46. It is also referred to in Ronald C. D. Jasper, *George Bell, Bishop of Chichester* (Oxford: Oxford Univ. Press, 1967), pp. 276 – 77.

29 *Gaudium et Spes* ("The Church in the Modern World"), 1965, para. 80, in W. M. Abbott and J. Gallagher, *The Documents of Vatican II* (London: Geoffrey Chapman, 1966).

30 British Council of Churches resolution.

31 "The New Abolitionist Covenant" is printed in Jim Wallis (ed.), *Waging Peace: A Handbook for the Struggle to Abolish Nuclear Weapons* (San Francisco: Harper & Row, 1982), pp. 17 – 21. See also Jim Wallis (ed.), *Peace-Makers: Christian Voices from the New Abolitionist Movement* (San Francisco: Harper & Row, 1983).

32 CAAT, "The Arms Trade: An Introductory Briefing", *www.caat.org.uk.*

33 See, e.g., Walter Stein (ed.), *Nuclear Weapons and Christian Conscience* (London: Merlin Press, 1961 and 1980); Geoffrey Goodwin (ed.), *Ethics and Nuclear Deterrence* (London: Croom Helm, 1982). See also Richard Harries, "The Strange Mercy of Deterrence", in John Gladwin (ed.), *Dropping the Bomb* (London: Hodder & Stoughton, 1985), pp. 64 – 73; Richard Harries, *Christianity and War in a Nuclear Age* (Oxford: Mowbray, 1986), especially pp. 134 – 44.

34 Ernest Lefever and Stephen Hunt (eds.), *The Apocalyptic Premise: Nuclear Arms Debated* (Washington, DC: Ethics and Public Policy Center, 1982), pp. 351 – 59. See also Anthony Kenny, *The Logic of Deterrence* (London: Firethorn Press, 1985).

35 Quoted in US Bishops' Pastoral Letter, *The Challenge of Peace*. The bishops elaborated the pope's statement, declaring that they had "arrived at a strictly conditional, moral acceptance of deterrence".

36 Francis Bridger (ed.), *The Cross and the Bomb, Christian ethics and nuclear debate* (Oxford: Mowbray, 1983), pp. 50, 60, 64 – 5.

37 Mark Juergensmeyer, *Terror in the Mind of God: The Global Rise of Religious Violence* (Berkeley: Univ. of California Press, 2000), p. 5.

38 James D. Kiras, "Terrorism and Globalization", in John Baylis and Steve Smith (eds.), *The Globalization of World Politics* (Oxford: Oxford Univ. Press, 2005), pp. 479 – 97.

39 Vinoth Ramachandra, *Faiths in Conflict, Christian integrity in a multicultural world* (Leicester: InterVarsity Press, 1999), p. 44. *Dar-ul-Islam* literally means "household of Islam", and there is a myth associated with it, that within the household of Islam, there is both unity and equality of all Muslims.

40 Juergensmeyer, *Terror in the Mind of God*, p. 123.

41 R. Scott Appleby, *The Ambivalence of the Sacred: Religion, Violence, and Reconciliation* (Lanham, Md.: Rowman & Littlefield, 2000).

42 "Evangelism and Social Responsibility", in Stott (ed.), *Making Christ Known*, p. 200.

43 See, e.g., *Defence without the Bomb: The report of the Alternative Defence Commission* (London: Taylor and Francis, 1983).

Caring for Creation

In September 2002 world leaders, with the notable exception of President George W. Bush, assembled in Johannesburg for the follow-up conference to the first United Nations Conference on Environment and Development which had been held in Rio de Janeiro in June 1992. Popularly known as the "Earth Summit", this original gathering of more than 100 heads of state with representatives of other governments, of the scientific community and of special interest groups is thought to have been the largest conference ever held. A decade later, the Johannesburg conference seemed to many to reveal the intractable difficulties we currently face in trying to address problems that had only intensified since 1992. The 2002 agenda focused on sustainable development, biodiversity, resource depletion, pollution and climate change, but all, with the possible exception of water conservation, were discussed in an atmosphere of growing controversy and disappointment that led to few definite proposals. Even the conventions initiated at Rio ten years earlier had subsequently been ratified by few national governments. Despite this, there was perhaps a more positive development as a result of the growing awareness that earlier, more confrontational approaches were giving place to new alliances between economic and social development and environmental concerns, and that in this creative process ways forward might be more easily found. Mark Malloch Brown, administrator of the United Nations Development Program (UNDP), said, "The old environmental movement had a reputation of elitism. The key now is to put people first and the environment second, but to remember that when you exhaust resources, you destroy people." For Brown, as for many others, sustainable development became the watchword of the new decade.

Meanwhile, the scientific community entered into vehement debate following the publication of statistician Bjorn Lomberg's *The Skeptical Environmentalist* in 2002, in which he challenged many of the more pessimistic scenarios of environmental groups and non-governmental organizations (NGOs). The violence of the argument revealed the central role that ideology and economic theory continue to play in the discussion of environmental issues, even when the subject is apparently restricted to data and its interpretation. A sad result has been the wariness of the Christian community in the wealthier world to face the urgent questions that impact the daily life of the poor, and the well-being of the wider creation.

Even so, in wider society, it is remarkable how quickly a dedicated, campaigning minority succeeded in the last decades of the twentieth century in alerting the general public to green concerns. Significant numbers of people in the wealthier world nowadays seem to be apprehensive about the destruction of the tropical rainforest, the depletion of the ozone layer, climate change and the imminent disappearance of a number of spectacular large mammals such as the Siberian tiger. The key is to translate these concerns into lifestyle changes and political action. Previously indifferent politicians have become obliged to add green issues to their agendas. Corporations have departments specializing in the ecological aspects of their businesses. Most petrol-engine cars on the road use lead-free petrol, and emissions laws are being tightened. In addition, householders are becoming "green consumers", using more products that are environmentally friendly, eating more "natural" or "organic" foods and encouraging the recycling of paper, glass and metals.[1]

There seem to be five[2] main areas of widespread environmental concern which help to explain this rise in public awareness. They should be seen in relation to one another.

REASONS FOR ENVIRONMENTAL CONCERN

Population growth

The first is population growth. It has been known for centuries that the world population is growing. Only since World War II, however, has the accelerating growth rate been clearly perceived and the potential for disaster in the aftermath of an unchecked population explosion predicted. It is said that in the year AD 1800 there were about 1,000,000,000 people on earth. By 1900 this had doubled to 2,000,000,000, and by 1974 it had doubled again to 4,000,000,000. It is estimated that we currently rely on the equivalent of 1.2 planets to supply our annual needs, and yet despite a decelerating growth rate, world population is still increasing such that the current 6,100,000,000 will grow to a probable 11,000,000,000 by the middle of this century according to UN figures.

Out of 4,000,000,000 people in the 1980s, one fifth of them (800,000,000) were destitute, and it is being anxiously asked how more than 7,000,000,000 people can possibly be fed thirty-five years later. This is a special problem in the developing world where 90% of population growth is taking place. The earth cannot sustain a larger population which, owing to poverty and even starvation, is forced to use its resources with only short-term gain in mind, often making long-term destruction inevitable. But this is not just a Majority World problem. In Britain, for example, the population is growing at the comparatively slow rate of 116,000 people per year. However, each new Briton uses more than thirty times the amount of fossil fuel consumed by the average Bangladeshi. Thus it takes a population growth of 3,390,000 Bangladeshis to equal the environmental impact of just over 100,000 Britons.[3] The wealthy consume too much and are wasteful, while the poor are preoccupied with their immediate survival, rather than with the long-term care of the planet. Worldwide, sickness through crowded urban conditions and rural land degradation are pushing millions to the brink of starvation.

There are varying opinions even among Christians about the extent of the population problem and what should be done in response to it. In his Grove booklet entitled *Population Growth and Christian Ethics*, Roy McCloughry argues that the population problem is primarily neither economic nor environmental but moral, because it is basically about relationships. He pleads for "a positive vision for human life", in which (1) human beings are seen to have an intrinsic value because they are made in God's image; (2) access to education, especially by women and children, enables them to develop their full potential and to enjoy a quality of life compatible with their human dignity; and (3) the limiting and spacing of children is determined not by coercive governments but by the free decision of the parents.[4] Any discussion of population must begin by reaffirming the dignity of all human life, and the rights of human beings to live out their full potential. As Professor John Guillebaud has argued, if the vicious spiral of poverty and population is not to continue – where poverty leads to families having more children in order to increase family income and yet they find they are unable to cope with the numbers – then both planned parenting and social justice will be needed. The former enables them to take responsible decisions about family size; the latter enables poor people to climb out of their poverty.[5]

It is this concern that people should be able to live out their full potential which causes us great concern when we consider the impact of AIDS on so many countries. In some a generation has been so affected that every area of society has suffered. I consider this in more detail in the next chapter.

Resource depletion

The second cause for concern is resource depletion. It was the so-called "Club of Rome" which in 1972 drew the world's attention to the finite nature of the earth's resources. Until then Western leaders had confidently been predicting an annual growth rate of 4%. Now continuous growth and finite resources were seen to be incompatible. It was E. F. Schumacher who in 1973 popularized the unpalatable truth in his famous book *Small Is Beautiful*, subtitled "A study of economics as if people mattered". He wrote of "the failure to distinguish between income and capital where this distinction matters most ... namely the irreplaceable capital which man has not made, but simply found". His first example of this "natural capital" was fossil fuels: "Fossil fuels are not made by men; they cannot be recycled. Once they are gone they are gone for ever." In 2003 the Association of Peak Oil (ASPO) predicted that world demand for oil would outstrip the ability of the world's oilfields to produce economically before 2015. This is not an issue of how much oil there is in the ground, but the increasingly limited rate at which it can be extracted. Much of the "easy oil" has been produced.[6]

Schumacher's other example was "living nature" (the plankton of the oceans, the green surface of the earth, clean air, etc.), much of which was being destroyed by pollution. "If we squander our fossil fuels, we threaten civilization," he wrote, "but if we squander the capital represented by living nature around us, we threaten life itself." The folly of "the modern industrial system", he continued, is that it "consumes the very basis on which it has been erected. To use the language of the economist, it lives on irreplaceable capital, which it cheerfully treats as income."[7]

One of the scarce resources which is a focus of concern is water. It has long been said that water will be even more important than oil as a threatened scarce resource in the next fifty years. Some have even predicted that violence between nation states will take place over access to water and rights to rivers which cross boundaries betweeen countries. Access to clean water and adequate sanitation were declared to be a "human right" in 2002. The United Nations Committee on Economic, Cultural and Social Rights stated in a "general comment" that "water is fundamental for life and health. The human right to water is indispensable for leading a healthy life in human dignity. It is a prerequisite to the realization of all other human rights".[8]

Two other aspects of environmental degradation are extremely important and could have their own sections. The first is deforestation and the second is land degradation.

Deforestation has been happening for many years, but not at the current rate, and its impact is now global rather than local. If the current rate continues, the world's rainforests are predicted to disappear within 100 years, causing an incalculable impact on climate and on plant and animal species. Much clearing is done for agricultural purposes such as grazing cattle and planting crops by poor farmers in the process called "slash and burn". But in the case of intensive agriculture many square miles can be deforested at a time, to graze cattle. Commercial logging can also cut hundreds of square miles of trees. The causes of deforestation and its impact are very complex. As the need for products grows in a consumer-orientated world, more wood is needed to meet the demand. In other cases forests are cut down to build towns, and the construction of dams causes areas of forest to be flooded. The impact on the climate is due to the fact that forests are "the lungs of the planet". According to the earth observatory at NASA, the plants and soil of tropical forests hold 460 – 575,000,000,000 metric tons of carbon worldwide, with each acre of tropical forest storing about 180 metric tons of carbon. When a forest is cut and burned to establish cropland and pastures, the carbon that was stored in the tree trunks (wood is about 50% carbon) joins with oxygen and is released into the atmosphere as CO_2. The destruction of tropical rainforests also has the potential for making many millions of species of flora and fauna extinct.[9]

Vast areas of America, Africa and Asia, once fertile agricultural land, are now through misuse irrevocable deserts or dustbowls. Worldwide, deserts have increased by 150% during the past 100 years, so that almost 50% of the earth's land surface is now desert or semi-desert. The Aral Sea, once the most productive fishing site in central Asia and the fourth largest inland sea in the world, is now at half its volume of thirty years ago. A poorly conceived irrigation scheme to channel water away from the rivers that feed the sea resulted in its virtual drying out. In some places the coast has moved thirty miles, replaced by a desert of sand and salt deposits.[10] Deforestation leads to severe soil erosion. It is estimated that 25,000,000,000 tons of topsoil are lost each year. Soil has been so abused in parts of the world that 11% of the world's vegetated soil is now beyond recovery. This is an area the size of China and India.[11] Some of this destruction of the environment undoubtedly happens as a result of human ignorance (e.g., the early dust bowls). Nevertheless, the Church of England's Board for Social Responsibility were not exaggerating when they said that "despoiling the earth is a blasphemy, and not just an error of judgement, a mistake".[12] It is a sin against God as well as humankind.

Reduction in biodiversity

Biodiversity is a term that, according to Sir Ghillean Prance, Director of the Royal Botanic Gardens at Kew, London, encapsulates "the diversity of species of living organisms on earth, the genes or genetic information which they contain and the complex ecosystems in which they live".[13] Estimates for the number of different living species on earth range from 5,000,000 to 50,000,000, with conservative estimates generally around the 10,000,000 mark.[14] Each species contains a unique genetic code and lives in a certain habitat, often requiring very specific conditions for life. Extinction is a daily part of normal life in a world where species exist in a surprising amount of flux. The concern in the biodiversity discussion, however, is not simply with the natural extinction of species, but with the rate at which human intervention in the natural environment has accelerated those extinctions since humans have been the main cause of extinction. Habitat loss, introduced species and overexploitation are the main threats, with human-induced climate change becoming an increasingly important problem. According to the World Conservation Union (IUCN), the largest and most prestigious conservation network, current extinction rates are at least 100 – 1,000 times higher than background or "natural" rates.[15]

The reason why scientists are worried about the loss of biodiversity is not only that individual species become extinct, but that when they do, the delicate balance of their ecosystem is disturbed. And when a so-called "keystone" species becomes extinct, large-scale problems are quickly encountered. A well-known example is the near extinction of sea otters off the west coast of the United States. Stephen Schneider, a professor in biological sciences at Stanford University, describes what happened. "After their decline, a major disturbance propagated through the offshore marine community. Sea urchins, normally a principal food for otters, multiplied rapidly and in turn decimated the kelp forests leading to biologically impoverished, desert-like stretches of sea floor known as sea-urchin barrens. Only after controversial political pressures to restore the otter were successful did the urchin populations decline, the kelp grow back, and a new community of fish, squid, and lesser organisms reestablish themselves."[16]

According to the 2004 IUCN Red List of Threatened Species, a total of 15,589 species face extinction. One in three amphibians and almost half of all freshwater turtles are threatened, on top of the one in eight birds and one in four mammals known to be in jeopardy falling into the Critically Endangered, Endangered or Vulnerable categories.[17] This lineup has now been joined by one in three amphibians (32%) and almost half (42%) of turtles and tortoises. With amphibians relying on fresh water, their catastrophic decline is a warning about the state of the planet's water resources. Even though the situation in freshwater habitats is less well known than for terrestrial habitats, early signs show it is equally serious. More than half (53%) of Madagascar's freshwater fish are threatened with extinction. The vast ocean depths are providing little refuge to many marine species which are being overexploited to the point of extinction. Nearly one in five (18%) of assessed sharks and rays are threatened. Many plants have also been assessed, but only conifers and cycads have been completely evaluated, with 25% and 52% threatened respectively. There is good news with a quarter of threatened bird species benefiting from conservation measures, but the number of species threatened with extinction is an underestimate as so few have been assessed.

Waste disposal

A third reason for concern is waste disposal. An increasing population brings an increasing problem of how to dispose safely of the undesirable by-products of production, packaging and consumption. The average person in the UK throws out his or her body weight in rubbish every three months. The average American's waste output has nearly doubled in the last forty years, and although the US recycles more than a third of its waste, this still represents more than most other countries' total waste output. In the mid-1990s OECD (Organization for Economic Cooperation and Development) countries were producing almost two tons in household and industrial waste per person each year. Although Africans generate less, more than two thirds of their rubbish is not formally disposed of at all, but up to 96% of a typical family's waste in poor countries is made up of food and biodegradable products.[18] Most of the rubbish from wealthy economies could be reprocessed, but instead it is sent to incinerators or landfill sites.[19] A glaring example of the problem occurred in 1987 when the so-called "garbage barge" left Long Island, New York, and spent six months searching for a port that would take its 3,000-plus tons of garbage. Having been declined entry to numerous ports in the US and elsewhere, the barge eventually returned to New York where the problem had begun.

In January 1994 the British government published an extensive report entitled *Sustainable Development: The UK Strategy*. It recommended a four-fold "hierarchy of waste management", namely "reduction", "reuse", "recovery (including recycling and energy recovery)" and "disposal without energy recovery by incinerator or landfill". The last of these options, although the commonest, is the least environmentally friendly. It is still unavoidable, however, whenever "the environmental costs of recycling waste, in terms of energy consumption and emissions, are higher than for disposal". Clearly the best option in the hierarchy is to reduce the waste which we produce and so have less to dispose of. The implications of poor waste disposal can be disastrous for natural resources. Calvin B. DeWitt cites an example of the presence of DDT in the fatty tissue of penguins in Antarctica as well as the presence of pesticides in a remote lake on Isle Royale in Lake Superior which are far removed from the places where these chemicals were used.[20]

Climate change

A fourth major environmental concern, which has been at the forefront of discussion since the 1980s, is our damaged atmosphere, owing to a combination of ozone depletion and climate change.

The depletion of the protective ozone layer exposes us to ultraviolet radiation, which causes skin cancers and upsets our immune system. In consequence, the discovery in 1985 of a continent-sized hole in the ozone over the Antarctic caused widespread public alarm. By 1991 this hole had reached a record size, extending over 21,000,000 square kilometres, and by 1993 the concentration of Antarctic ozone was the lowest ever registered. The neighbouring countries of Argentina and Chile, Australia and New Zealand have been reporting damage to animals and vegetation as well as to humans, and by the mid-1990s serious ozone depletion was recorded in the more temperate regions of the Northern Hemisphere as well.[21] In the spring of 2005, the ozone depletion in the Northern Hemisphere was the most severe so far recorded.

Soon after the discovery of the Antarctic ozone hole, its cause was traced to chlorofluorocarbons (CFCs), chemicals which are used in aerosol propellants, air conditioners and refrigerators. Recognizing the gravity of the crisis, the United Nations Environmental Programme took action. The Montreal Protocol (1987) called for the halving of CFC use by 1999, while several amendments in the 1990s resolved that industrialized nations should phase out CFCs completely by 1996 and non-industrialized nations by 2006. By 2006, when asked whether the Montreal Protocol had been successful in reducing ozone-depleting gases in the atmosphere, the National Oceanic and Atmospheric Administration (NOAA), a branch of the US Department of Commerce, could state:

> Yes, as a result of the Montreal Protocol, the total abundance of ozone-depleting gases in the atmosphere has begun to decrease in recent years. If the nations of the world continue to follow the provisions of the Montreal Protocol the decrease will continue throughout the 21st century. Some individual gases such as halons and hydrochlorofluorocarbons (HCFS) are still increasing in the atmosphere, but will begin to decrease in the next decades if compliance with the Protocol continues. By mid-century, the effective abundance of ozone-depleting gases should fall to values present before the Antarctic "ozone hole" began to form in the early 1980s.[22]

The issue of climate change is a different, though related, problem.[23] The warmth of the earth's surface (which is essential for the planet's survival) is maintained by a combination of the radiation it absorbs from the sun and the infrared radiation it emits into space. This is the so-called "greenhouse effect". Atmospheric pollution by "greenhouse gases", methane, nitrous oxide and especially carbon dioxide, results in reducing the infrared emission and so increasing the earth's surface temperature.

With some notable exceptions, there is widespread agreement among scientists about the seriousness of the human contribution to the greenhouse effect. Nor is the public's reaction uniform. It ranges from the fear of an imminent catastrophe to a dismissal of the threat as a fiction. There is general agreement, however, that by the year 2100 the average global temperature is likely to rise between 2° and 6° centigrade.[24] The Arctic is warming at twice the global average and nearly all mountain glaciers are shrinking. Mount Kilimanjaro will lose its ice cap over the next twenty years, having survived all climate fluctuations experienced over the last 9,000 years. The long-term effects could include substantial climatic changes, including further thermal expansion of the oceans, the flooding of many islands, port cities and low-lying countries like Bangladesh, the drying out of previously fertile regions, and the regional extinction of plants which cannot adjust to the changes.

The year 2005 saw hurricanes added to the list of indications that climate change was taking place. "This hurricane season shattered records that have stood for decades – most named storms, most hurricanes and most category five storms. Arguably, it was the most devastating hurricane season the country has experienced in modern times," said Conrad C. Lautenbacher Jr, NOAA administrator.[25] Hurricane Katrina, which devastated the town of New Orleans, is likely to be the costliest US hurricane on record, and the final tally for damage is likely to be the greatest in US history, breaking a record set only the previous year. Katrina was also the deadliest US hurricane since 1928, claiming at least 1,200 lives. Examination of such extraordinary weather conditions shows that there is at least a case to answer as to whether such hurricanes are here to stay as a consequence of climate change and not just, as some have suggested, an aberration which will eventually go away.

Ocean acidification is also a serious problem. According to a report from the Royal Society,[26] oceans are absorbing carbon dioxide at an unsustainable rate. They help stave off climate change and over the past 200 years have absorbed about half of the carbon dioxide produced by humans, primarily through the burning of fossil fuels. They are currently taking up one ton of this carbon dioxide for each person on the planet every year, but with acidity rising their ability to do this will decrease and the finely balanced and complex mechanisms which sustain ocean life are being affected. This is yet another reason for reducing emissions of greenhouse gases into the atmosphere and particularly carbon dioxide.

We need to reduce greenhouse gas emissions globally at an incremental rate to 60% below year 2000 levels by 2050.[27] To achieve 60% reduction, multilateral action by the global community will have to deliver significant reductions by 2025.[28] However, to date there is a reticence about being held to targets.

In December 1997 negotiators from all over the world met in Kyoto, Japan, to discuss setting limits and reducing greenhouse gas output. After eleven days of intense debate and multiple compromise by all sides, those attending reached a tentative agreement. Thirty-eight industrialized nations, including the USA, the EU, Russia and Japan, all agreed to reduce emissions to 6–8% below 1990 levels by 2008–2012. Developing countries are not required to meet these same requirements, but have been given the option to comply and receive technological and material aid in return. As part of reaching their individual reduction goals the industrialized nations are able to "trade" emissions between themselves. Thus if the EU, having pledged to reduce emissions to 8% below 1990 levels, were to achieve a 12% reduction, they could then sell the surplus reduction to another country that had been unable to reach its own goal. The country buying the surplus would then be able to apply it towards its own reduction goal. In this way, a potential for economic incentive was worked into the reduction process.

The Kyoto Protocol became a legally binding treaty on 16 February 2005, having fulfilled two conditions. Firstly, it was ratified by at least fifty-five countries. Secondly, it had been ratified by nations accounting for at least 55% of emissions from "Annex 1" countries, plus thirty-eight industrialized countries given targets for reducing emissions, plus Belarus, Turkey and now Kazakhstan. However, Australia and the USA did not ratify the treaty and in 2001 the US, which is responsible for about a quarter of the world's emissions, pulled out with President George W. Bush saying that implementing it would gravely damage the US economy. His administration said that the treaty was "fatally flawed" because it does not require developing countries to commit to emissions reductions and the rapidly developing economies of China and India fall into this category. However, President Bush did say that he backed emissions reductions by voluntary action and new energy technologies. China and India, however, have ratified the protocol. Environmental groups commented that at the world summit of the G8 in 2005 the agreement on climate change was weakened by the decision to opt for consensus between the eight nations, when in fact only seven had ratified the protocol. One indication of this is that a draft of the communiqué used the word "threat" of climate change, but the official version talked of a "serious long-term challenge". Dialogue with the United States and broad consensus across all nations came at the price of definitive targets and a united stance on the urgency of the problem.

These five major reasons for concern – population growth, resource depletion, loss of biodiversity, waste disposal and climate change – are integrally related to one another and together constitute a single "interlocking global crisis". This expression was used in *Our Common Future*, the official report of the 1987 UN World Commission on Environment and Development. The central notion of the report was that the various environmental, development and energy problems which plague the world are all aspects of the same crisis, the solution to which lies in "sustainable development". This was reaffirmed at the 1992 Earth Summit in Rio, and given sweeping endorsement in *Agenda 21: A blueprint for action for global sustainable development into the 21st century*. One of the official papers to come out of Rio, *Agenda 21* is a wide-ranging document which has been adopted by 178 governments. It sets environmental, development and economic goals covering a whole spectrum of human and national activities. It does not have the power of a fully legal document, but it has been called "international soft law", meaning that it carries moral authority and that all nations should adhere to it to the best of their ability. Although the term "sustainable development" has been variously interpreted, it was defined in *Our Common Future* as development which "meets the needs of the present without compromising the ability of future generations to meet their own needs".[29] Indeed, the intergenerational responsibility implicit in the word "sustainable" has been captured in the popular expression "not cheating on our kids".

THE BIBLICAL PERSPECTIVE

The biblical approach to the environmental issue is to ask this basic question: "To whom does the earth belong?" It is deceptively elementary. How shall we reply? The first answer is straightforward. It is given in Psalm 24:1: "The earth is the LORD's, and everything in it." God is its Creator, and so by right of creation is also its owner. But this is only a partial answer. Here is Psalm 115:16: "The highest heavens belong to the LORD, but the earth he has given to man." So then, the balanced biblical answer to our question is that the earth belongs to both God and man – to God because he made it, to us because he has given it to us. Not, of course, that he has handed it over to us so completely as to retain neither rights nor control over it, but he has given it to us to rule on his behalf. Our possession of the earth is leasehold, therefore, not freehold. We are only tenants; God himself remains (in the most literal sense) the "landlord", the Lord of all the land.

This double truth (that the earth is both his and ours) is spelled out more fully in Genesis 1 and 2. In several verses of Genesis 1 (RSV) the word "earth" occurs:

Verse 10:   God called the dry ground "earth".

Verses 11, 12: Then God said, "Let the earth produce vegetation" ... And it was so. The earth produced vegetation.

Verse 24:   And God said, "Let the earth produce living creatures" ... And it was so.

Verse 26:   Then God said, "Let us make man in our image ... and let them rule ... over all the earth."

Verse 28:   God blessed them and said to them, "Fill the earth and subdue it."

We may legitimately make three affirmations from this biblical material.

Dominion over the earth

Firstly, God has given us dominion over the earth. We note the two divine resolves of verse 26, "Let us make man in our image" and "let them have dominion over the earth" (RSV). We note also the two divine actions in which his resolves were expressed: "So God created man in his own image" and "God ... said to them, '...fill the earth and subdue it'" (vv. 27 – 28). Thus from the beginning human beings have been endowed with a double uniqueness: we bear the image of God (consisting of rational, moral, social and spiritual qualities which make it possible for us to know God) and we wield dominion over the earth and its creatures.

Indeed, our unique dominion over the earth is due to our unique relation with God. God arranged an order, even a hierarchy, of creation. He set human beings midway between himself as Creator and the rest of the creation, animate and inanimate. In some ways we are one with the rest of nature, being a part of it and having the status of creatures. In other ways we are distinct from nature, having been created in God's image and given dominion. Biologically, we are like the animals. For example, we breathe like them ("a living being", Genesis 1:21, 24; 2:7), eat like them (1:29 – 30) and reproduce like them ("be fruitful and increase", 1:22, 28). But we also enjoy a higher level of experience, in which we are unlike the animals and like God: we are able to think, choose, create, love, pray and exercise dominion. This is our intermediate position between God and nature, between the Creator and the rest of his creation. We combine dependence on God with dominion over the earth. Gerhard von Rad comments: "Just as powerful earthly kings, to indicate their claim to dominion, erect an image of themselves in the provinces of their empire, where they do not generally appear, so man is placed upon earth in God's image as God's sovereign emblem."[30]

Generally speaking, human beings have obeyed God's command to fill the earth and subdue it. At first progress was slow as they graduated from food-gathering to farming. They learned to cultivate the soil, to protect cultivated areas from marauding animals and to use the earth's produce to feed, clothe and house themselves and their families. Next they learned to domesticate animals and harness them to their service, in order to make their labour lighter and to bring them pleasure as well. Then they learned the secrets of power which God had locked up inside the created world – the power of fire and water, later that of steam, coal, gas and oil, and now that of uranium, the atom and the mighty silicon chip.

In all this, in human research, discovery and invention, in biology, chemistry, physics and other spheres, and in all the triumphs of technology, human beings have been obeying God and exercising their God-given dominion. There is no question (at least in principle) of their having behaved like Prometheus, who stole fire from the gods. In their progressive control of the earth, they have not been invading God's private sphere and wresting power from him, still less imagining that they have stopped up the gaps in which God used to lurk, so that they can now dispense with him. It is foolish to draw these deductions. Human beings may not have known it, or humbly acknowledged it, but in all their research and resourcefulness, far from usurping God's prerogatives or power, they have been exercising the dominion God gave them. Developing tools and technology, farming the land, digging for minerals, extracting fuels, damming rivers for hydroelectric power, harnessing atomic energy – all are fulfilments of God's primeval command. God has provided in the earth all the resources of food, water, clothing, shelter, energy and warmth which we need, and he has given us dominion over the earth in which these resources have been stored.

Cooperation with the earth

Secondly, our dominion is a cooperative dominion. In exercising our God-given dominion, we are not creating the processes of nature, but cooperating with them. It is clear from Genesis 1 that the earth was made fruitful before man was told to fill and subdue it. It is true that we can make the earth more fruitful. We can clear, plough, irrigate and enrich the soil. We can put plants under glass to catch more of the sun. We can manage the soil by rotating our crops. We can improve our stock by selective breeding. We can produce hybrid grains with a fantastic yield. We can mechanize our reaping and threshing by using huge combine harvesters. But in all these activities we are merely cooperating with the laws of fruitfulness which God has already established. Moreover, the "painful toil" which we experience in agriculture, because of God's "curse" upon the ground (Genesis 3:17), only modifies and does not override our continuing care of the soil under God's "blessing" (Psalm 65:9ff.).

True again, we are controlling and even accelerating things artificially. But it is an artificial control of essentially natural processes. It is humans cooperating with God. It is a recognition that what God gives is "nature", whereas what we do with it is "culture" or "cultivation".

It is also true that God has humbled himself to need our cooperation (that is, he needs us to subdue the earth and till the soil). But we too must humble ourselves to acknowledge that our dominion over nature would be entirely fruitless if God had not made the earth fruitful, and if he did not continue to "give the increase".

This combination of nature and culture, of human helplessness and human prowess, of resources and labour, of faith and work, throws light on the recent fashion of declaring that "man has now come of age" and that (in our newly acquired adulthood) we can dispense with God. The truth is that humankind has come of age technologically. We have developed extraordinary expertise in taming, controlling and using nature. In this respect we are lords, as God meant and told us to be. But we are also children in our ultimate dependence on the fatherly providence of God, who gives us sunshine, rain and fruitful seasons. E. F. Schumacher quotes Tom Dale and Vernon Gill Carter in this respect: "Man, whether civilized or savage, is a child of nature – he is not the master of nature. He must conform his actions to certain natural laws if he is to maintain his dominance over his environment."[31]

Entrusted with the earth

Thirdly, our dominion is a delegated and, therefore, a responsible dominion. That is, the dominion we exercise over the earth does not belong to us by right, but only by favour. The earth "belongs" to us not because we made or own it, but because its Maker has entrusted its care to us.

This has important consequences. If we think of the earth as a kingdom, then we are not kings ruling our own territory, but viceroys ruling it on the king's behalf, since the king has not abdicated his throne. Or if we think of the earth as a country estate, then we are not the landowners, but the bailiffs who manage and farm it on the owner's behalf. God makes us, in the most literal sense, "caretakers" of his property.

God's continuing ownership and caring supervision of the earth (indeed of the universe) is asserted many times in Scripture. We have already considered the assertion of Psalm 24:1 that "the earth is the LORD's". This includes all living things which inhabit the earth: "Every animal of the forest is mine, and the cattle on a thousand hills. I know every bird in the mountains, and the creatures of the field are mine" (Psalm 50:10 – 11). In the Sermon on the Mount Jesus extended the divine dominion further – from the largest to the smallest of creatures. On the one hand, God makes "his sun" to rise (it belongs to him), and on the other, he feeds the birds and he clothes the lilies and the grass of the field (Matthew 5:45; 6:26, 28, 30). He thus sustains the whole of his creation; in committing it to us, he has not renounced responsibility for it.

This must be the reason why even Canaan, "the land of Israel", did not belong to Israel. True, it was "the Promised Land" because God had promised to give it to Abraham's descendants, and did in fact do so. Yet individuals owned land only as representatives of their tribe. No one was allowed to transfer land outside the tribe (Numbers 36:5ff.), nor to sell it to anyone in perpetuity. Every fifty years, in the Year of Jubilee, all land was to revert to its original owner. God was teaching that the land was still his, and that no human being had freehold rights. True, property rights were acknowledged, so that not only theft but also covetousness were forbidden in the law. Nevertheless, the proprietors were to remember two fundamental truths.

Firstly, they were only temporary residents: "The land must not be sold permanently, because the land is mine and you are but aliens and my tenants" (Leviticus 25:23).

Secondly, they must not keep all the produce of the land for themselves, but must provide for their needy neighbour out of it. As Professor Martin Hengel has put it, "The right to property was in principle subordinated to the obligation to care for the weaker members of society."[32] It is interesting that Pope John Paul II summed up the Christian tradition on this matter in similar terms. In his encyclical "Human Work" he distanced himself from both Marxist "collectivism" and liberal "capitalism". In the latter case, he explained, the question is how "the right to ownership or property is understood". He continued: "Christian tradition has never upheld this right as absolute and untouchable. On the contrary, it has always understood this right within the broader context of the right common to all to use the goods of the whole creation: the right to private property is subordinated to the right to common use, to the fact that goods are meant for everyone."[33]

If, therefore, our dominion over the earth has been delegated to us by God, with a view to our cooperating with him and sharing its produce with others, then we are accountable to him for our stewardship. We have no liberty to do what we like with our natural environment; it is not ours to treat as we please. "Dominion" is not a synonym for "domination", let alone "destruction". Since we hold it in trust, we have to manage it responsibly and productively for the sake of both our own and subsequent generations.

THE CONSERVATION DEBATE

Trusteeship includes conservation. The greatest threat to humankind may prove in the end to be not a wartime but a peacetime peril, namely the spoliation of the earth's natural resources by human folly or greed. All life on earth is dependent on the biosphere, the narrow layer of water, soil and air in which we live. Yet our record in conserving it, especially during the twentieth century, is not good.

At the same time, not all Christians have accepted the responsibility which Scripture lays upon us; some have even used the Genesis story to excuse their irresponsibility. Gavin Maxwell, author of books on otters, especially *Ring of Bright Water*, once wrote how he lost two lovely otter cubs he had brought back from Nigeria: "A minister of the Church of Scotland, walking along the foreshore with a shotgun, found them at play by the tide's edge and shot them. One was killed outright, the other died of her wounds in the water. The minister expressed regret, but reminded a journalist that 'the Lord gave man control over the beasts of the field.'"[34] As Professor C. F. D. Moule rightly comments, "A crime against sense and sensibility cannot be defended by the appeal to mere texts".[35]

To be sure, the biblical texts have been variously interpreted. In the Middle Ages, for example, Thomas Aquinas taught that animals exist entirely for human pleasure and profit, whereas Francis of Assisi treated them as his equals, his brothers and sisters. It was Jeremy Bentham, however, at the end of the eighteenth century, who first maintained that animals have rights, because they are sentient creatures which feel pain. In our day Dr Peter Singer, professor of bioethics at Princeton University, has gone much further. In his controversial book *Animal Liberation*,[36] although he concedes that there are differences between humans and animals, he yet argues for the extension of the "basic principle of equality" to animals (or rather to "non-human animals", as he calls them). He rejects what he calls "species-ism" as vigorously as he rejects racism and sexism. He defines it as "a prejudice or attitude of bias in favour of the interests of members of one's own species and against those of members of other species".[37] In consequence, the presupposition that "the human animal" has the right to rule "over other animals" is in his opinion "now obsolete".[38]

This is an extreme overreaction, however. We cannot possibly surrender the fundamental truth that human beings alone of all God's creatures are made in his image and are given a responsible dominion over the earth and its creatures. It is more meaningful, therefore, to speak of our responsibilities to and for animals than of rights possessed by animals themselves. Since God created them (Genesis 1), since he shows his concern for them by giving them life, food and shelter (Psalm 104), and since Jesus spoke of their intrinsic "value" (Matthew 10:31; 12:12), we too must be committed to their welfare. The Bible is quite clear on this point. According to the law, the benefits of the Sabbath rest were to be enjoyed by animals as well as humans (Exodus 20:10). According to the Wisdom Literature, "A righteous man cares for the needs of his animal" (Proverbs 12:10).

Anxious public debate continues, not least among Christians, about the application of these biblical principles to such practices as vivisection, intensive farming, the shipping and slaughter of animals for food, their domestication for work and play and the keeping of pets. Christians should protest against all perceived cruelty to animals, and campaign for their humane treatment in all circumstances, asking ourselves whether each practice is consonant with their value (as God's creatures) and with our responsibility (as God's stewards).[39]

What about the Genesis texts, however? Are we sure that we have interpreted them correctly? Or are the critics of Christianity right in saying that these verses are to blame for contemporary ecological irresponsibility? For example, the American historian Lynn White, of the University of California, Berkeley, has written: "Christianity ... not only established a dualism of man and nature, but also insisted that it is God's will that man exploit nature for his proper ends ... Christianity bears a huge burden of guilt." [40] More outspoken still is Ian L. McHarg. He is a Scot, who spent his childhood between the ugliness of Glasgow and the beauty of the Firth of Clyde and the Western Highlands and Islands. He became a town planner, an ecologist and the founder and chairman of the Department of Landscape Architecture and Regional Planning at the University of Pennsylvania. In 1969 he wrote that the Genesis story, "in its insistence upon dominion and subjugation of nature, encourages the most exploitative and destructive instincts in man rather than those that are deferential and creative. Indeed, if one seeks license for those who would increase radioactivity, create canals and harbors with atomic bombs, employ poisons without constraint, or give consent to the bulldozer mentality, there could be no better injunction than this text" (i.e., Genesis 1:26, 28). "When this is understood," he continues, "the conquest, the depredations and the despoliation are comprehensible." [41] God's affirmation about man's dominion was "also a declaration of war on nature". He concludes with these words: "Dominion and subjugation must be expunged as the biblical injunction of man's relation to nature." [42]

In his Dunning Trust lectures in 1972 – 73, Ian McHarg further extended his assault. He traced Western man's attitude to the natural world to "three horrifying lines" in Genesis 1 about the dominion which God gave to man. "Dominion is a non-negotiating relationship," he said. "If you want to find one text of compounded horror which will guarantee that the relationship of man to nature can only be destruction, which will atrophy any creative skill ... which will explain all of the destruction and all of the despoliation accomplished by Western man for at least these 2,000 years, then you do not have to look any further than this ghastly, calamitous text." [43]

Ian McHarg uses very intemperate language to state his case. Some misguided people (e.g., Gavin Maxwell's minister) may have tried to defend their irresponsible use of Genesis 1. But it is absurd to call this text "horrifying", "ghastly" and "calamitous", and then attribute to it two millennia of Western man's exploitation of the environment.

A much more temperate judgement is supplied by Keith Thomas, the Oxford University social historian. In his *Man and the Natural World*, he provides meticulously thorough documentation for changing attitudes towards nature in England between 1500 and 1800. [44] His theme is that at the beginning of this period, "human ascendancy" was taken for granted. People accepted "the long-established view ... that the world had been created for man's sake and that other species were meant to be subordinate to his wishes and needs".[45] Gradually, however, this "breathtakingly anthropocentric" interpretation of the early chapters of Genesis was discarded.[46] It is true that some Christians did use the grant of "dominion" over the creatures as a mandate even for such cruel sports as bear-baiting and cock-fighting.[47] But Dr Thomas also writes that Genesis 1 cannot be blamed for ecological problems, since (a) they exist in "parts of the world where the Judaeo-Christian tradition has had no influence", (b) Genesis also contains a "distinctive doctrine of human stewardship and responsibility for God's creatures", and (c) other parts of the Old Testament clearly inculcate care for the animal creation.[48] In fact he concedes that "the modern idea of the balance of nature ... had a theological basis before it gained a scientific one. It was belief in the perfection of God's design which preceded and underpinned the concept of the ecological chain, any link of which it would be dangerous to move."[49] So let us look at the Genesis text again.

It is true that the two Hebrew words used in Genesis 1:26 and 28 are forceful. The verb translated "have dominion" (RSV) means to "tread" or "trample" on, so that the paraphrase in Psalm 8 is "you put everything under his feet". It is often used in the Old Testament of the rule of kings. The other verb, "subdue", was used of subduing enemies in warfare and of bringing people into subjection or bondage as slaves. So man was commanded to rule the creatures of the sea, sky and earth (v. 26) and to enslave the earth, bringing it into subjection (v. 28). Ian McHarg is right, then? No, he is not. It is an elementary principle of biblical interpretation that one must not establish the meaning of words by their etymology alone, but also and especially by the way they are used in their context. What I have written earlier about this biblical instruction is germane to the interpretation of these texts. We have seen that the dominion God has given us is delegated, responsible and cooperative; that it is intended to express the same sustaining care of the environment as its Creator's; and that, far from exploiting the earth and its creatures, we are to use them in such a way as to be accountable to God and to serve others. We have no liberty to do what Ian McHarg did in one of his lectures, namely to set Genesis 1 and 2 in opposition to each other as if Genesis 2 taught "cultivation" and Genesis 1 "destruction". On the contrary, the two passages interpret each other. The dominion God has given humankind is a conscientious and caring stewardship which involves the husbanding of the earth's resources. It would be ludicrous to suppose that God first created the earth and then handed it over to us to destroy it.

CONTEMPORARY AWARENESS

Certainly our generation is taking environmental responsibility more seriously than our immediate predecessors did. Scientists are emphasizing the delicate balance of nature. God has established in nature almost unbelievable powers of recuperation and regeneration, and in particular a cycle for the renewal of energy (from sun to plants to animals to bacteria to earth, and back to plants again). It is an example of what Barbara Ward called "the most majestic unity" of our planet. It is due to natural laws which produce a "dynamic equilibrium of biological forces held in position by checks and balances of a most delicate sort".[50] "They are so intricate," commented Dr John Klotz, the American conservationist, "that they could not have developed by chance."[51] But if we despoil the green surface of the earth, or destroy the plankton of the oceans, we will quickly reach the point of no return in the recycling process. Our immense modern scientific knowledge teaches us "one thing above all", wrote Barbara Ward, namely the "need for extreme caution, a sense of the appalling vastness and complexity of the forces that can be unleashed, and of the eggshell delicacy of the agents that can be upset".[52]

There have been a number of encouragements in recent years. The environment has, once again, become an important agenda item at world summits. Yet it is easier to sign treaties than to live lives that are consistent with good trusteeship of God's world.

Have Christians a distinctive contribution to make to the ecological debate? Yes, we believe both that God created the earth, entrusting its care to us, and that he will one day recreate it, when he makes "the new heaven and the new earth". For "the whole creation has been groaning as in the pains of childbirth right up to the present time". Its groans are due to its "bondage to decay" and its consequent "frustration". In the end, however, it will come to share in "the glorious freedom of the children of God". That is, its bondage will give place to freedom, its decay to glory, and its pain to the joy of a new world being born (Romans 8:19 – 22). These two doctrines, regarding the beginning and the end of history, the creation and the consummation, have a profound effect on our perspective. They give us an appropriate respect for the earth, indeed for the whole material creation, since God both made it and will remake it.

In consequence, we must learn to think and act ecologically. We repent of extravagance, pollution and wanton destruction. We recognize that human beings find it easier to subdue the earth than they do to subdue themselves. Ronald Higgins' book *The Seventh Enemy* is significant in this respect. The first six "enemies" are the population explosion, the food crisis, the scarcity of resources, environmental degradation, nuclear abuse and scientific technology. The seventh enemy, however, is ourselves, our personal blindness and political inertia in the face of today's ecological challenge. That is why the subtitle of Ronald Higgins' book is "The human factor in the global crisis". The human race needs a new self-awareness, and fresh vision, a reawakening of its moral and religious capabilities.[53] But is this possible? Yes, Christians are convinced it is.

One of the particular merits of the late Professor Klaus Bockmuhl's booklet *Conservation and Lifestyle* is that he goes beyond the "Christian criteria" for environmental responsibility to the "Christian motives". In his conclusion he presses the challenge home: "What is sought from Christians is the motivation for selfless service, which once distinguished the Christian heritage. We should be pioneers in the care of mankind ... We should show whence the power and perspective for such a contribution come. We are charged to give an example." We have to "reawaken the heart of the gospel ethic".[54] We may be thankful that there are now a number of Christian organizations working specifically in the area of care for creation. Among them are the John Ray Institute, the International Evangelical Environmental Network, A Rocha and the Au Sable Institute. At the root of the ecological crisis is human greed, what has been called "economic gain by environmental loss". Often it is a question of competing commercial interests (though some multinational corporations have an environmental department). It is only logical that the consumer should pay the cost of production without pollution, whether in increased prices or (through a government subsidy to the manufacturer) in increased taxes. Christians should not grudge this, if it is the cost of responsible, ecological stewardship.

Those who want to live responsibly in the light of the biblical vision for the environment and the current crises which are besetting it will find many practical suggestions in Ruth Valerio's recent book *L Is for Lifestyle*, which is subtitled "Christian living that doesn't cost the earth".[55] The book goes through the alphabet and looks at particular issues we are facing and offers indications of how we could change our lifestyle or be better informed about that particular issue. So, A is for activists, B is for bananas, H is for HIV, R is for recycling, S is for simplicity, T is for tourism and so on. The book is a combination of practical suggestions and thoughtful meditations on issues such as globalization and simplicity. It also contains suggestions of where to go for further information and help.

As Majority World countries struggle to raise their standards of living, the environment is often given less priority than the more immediate problems of undernourishment, disease and poverty. This is understandable, and these deeper issues must be addressed if we are ever to make headway in preserving and enhancing the natural environment. Furthermore, to insist on the protection of tropical forests in the Majority World, if we are unwilling to reduce CO_2 output in our own countries, is rank hypocrisy. We must also be willing both to share technologies which can help curb natural destruction and to create economic benefits for environmentally safe business practices. While the vast disparity between wealth and poverty remains, Christians are bound to have an uneasy conscience. We should strenuously avoid all wastefulness and greed, not only out of solidarity with the poor but also out of respect for the living environment.

NOTES

1 Many "green" consumer guides are available in most bookshops.

2 Calvin B. DeWitt divides the "degradations of creation" into seven categories: (1) alteration of earth's energy exchange with the sun; (2) land degradation; (3) deforestation; (4) species extinction; (5) water-quality degradation; (6) waste generation and global toxification; (7) human and cultural degradation. See Calvin B. DeWitt, "Creation's Environmental Challenge to Evangelical Christianity", in R. J. Berry (ed.), *The Care of Creation: Focusing Concern and Action* (Leicester: InterVarsity Press, 2000), pp. 61 – 62.

3 Ghillean Prance, *The Earth Under Threat* (Glasgow: Wild Goose Publications, 1996), p. 31.

4 Roy McCloughry, *Population Growth and Christian Ethics*, Grove Ethical Studies no. 98 (Cambridge: Grove Books, 1995).

5 John Guillebaud, "Population Numbers and Environmental Degradation", in Berry (ed.), *The Care of Creation*, pp. 155 – 60.

6 On this, see *www.peakoil.net/TheLamp/TheLamp.html*.

7 E. F. Schumacher, *Small Is Beautiful* (1973; London: Abacus, 1974), pp. 11 – 16. The vision of unlimited growth has been pertinently criticized by Bishop Lesslie Newbigin in *Foolishness to the Greeks* (London: SPCK, 1986). "Growth ... for the sake of growth", he writes, which "is not determined by an overarching social purpose", is "an exact account of the phenomenon which, when it occurs in the human body, is called cancer" (p. 114).

8 *www.unhchr.ch/htm/menu2/6/gc15.doc*

9 *http://earthobservatory.nasa.gov/Library/Deforestation/*

10 Jessica Tuchman Matthews, "Nations and Nature: A New View of Security", in Gwyn Prins and Hylke Tromp (eds.), *Threats without Enemies* (London: Earthscan Publications, 1993), p. 36.

11 Ibid., pp. 48 – 49.

12 *Man in His Living Environment: An Ethical Assessment*, a report from the Board for Social Responsibility (London: Church Information Office, 1970), p. 61. See also *Our Responsibility for the Living Environment*, a report from the Board for Social Responsibility's Environmental Issues Reference Panel (London: Church House Publishing, 1986).

13 Prance, *The Earth Under Threat*, p. 45.

14 Ibid.

15 *www.iucn.org*.

16 Stephen Schneider, *Laboratory Earth: The Planetary Gamble We Can't Afford to Lose* (New York: Basic Books, 1998), p. 107.

17 *www.iucn.org/themes/ssc/red_list_2004/English/newsrelease_EN.htm*

18 *http://news.bbc.co.uk/hi/english/static/in_depth/world/2002/disposable_planet/*

19 *www.foe.co.uk/campaigns/waste/issues/what_a_mess/index.html*

20 Calvin B. DeWitt, "Creation's Environmental Challenge to Evangelical Christianity", in Berry, *The Care of Creation*, p. 62, endnote 9.

21 Prance, *The Earth Under Threat*, p. 41.

22 *www.al.noaa.gov/assessments/2002/Q&As16.pdf*.

23 See Sir John Houghton (Chairman of the Royal Commission on Environmental Pollution), *Global Warming: The Complete Briefing* (Oxford: Lion, 1994).

24 *Climate Change 2001: The Scientific Basis* (London: Intergovernmental Panel on Climate Change, 2001). Text can be found at *www.grida.no/climate/ipcc_tar/wg1/*.

25 *www.noaanews.noaa.gov/stories2005/s2540.htm*.

26 Royal Society, *Ocean Acidification Due to Increasing Atmospheric Carbon Dioxide* (London: Royal Society, 2005). Text can be found at *www.royalsoc.ac.uk/displaypagedoc.asp?id=13249*.

27 Royal Commission on Environmental Pollution Report 21. In 2003 the UK government adopted this target at the core of its energy policy.

28 According to the IEA, world energy demand is projected to *increase* between 2002 and 2030, and 85% of the increase will come from fossil fuels. Two thirds of the increase in energy demand will come from the Majority World, which by 2030 will constitute 50%. Figures from *World Energy Outlook 2004* (Paris: International Energy Agency, 2004).

29 World Commission on Environment and Development, *Our Common Future* (Oxford: Oxford Univ. Press, 1987), pp. 8, 43.

30 Gerhard von Rad, *Genesis* (1956; London: SCM, 1963), p. 58.

31 Tom Dale and Vernon Gill Carter, *Topsoil and Civilization* (Norman, Okla.: Univ. of Oklahoma Press, 1955), quoted in Schumacher, *Small Is Beautiful*, p. 84.

32 Martin Hengel, *Property and Riches in the Early Church* (1973; Minneapolis: Fortress, and London: SCM, 1974), p. 12.

33 *Laborem Exercens*, Pope John Paul II's Encyclical Letter "Human Work" (London: Catholic Truth Society, 1981), pp. 50–51.

34 Gavin Maxwell's article appeared in the *Observer*, 13 October 1963.

35 C. F. D. Moule, *Man and Nature in the New Testament, Some reflections on biblical ecology* (London: Athlone, 1964; Minneapolis: Fortress, 1967), p. 1. See also Andrew Linzey, *Christianity and the Rights of Animals* (London: SPCK, 1988).

36 Peter Singer, *Animal Liberation* (1990; 2nd ed., London: Pimlico Books, 1995). See also his more recent work, *Rethinking Life and Death, The collapse of our traditional ethics* (Oxford: Oxford Univ. Press, 1995), in which he attempts to narrow the difference between humans and animals.

37 Ibid., p. 6.

38 Ibid., p. 185.

39 For a good discussion of animal rights, see *Green Cross*, Winter 1996, vol. 2, no. 1. This issue is devoted to the discussion of Christian responsibility for animals. See also Richard Griffiths, *The Human Use of Animals* (Cambridge: Grove Booklets, 1982); Tony Sargent, *Animal Rights and Wrongs, A biblical perspective* (London: Hodder & Stoughton, 1996).

40 From an address to the American Association for the Advancement of Science, which was published as "The Historical Roots of our Ecological Crisis", in *Science* 155 (1967), pp. 1203–7, and was reprinted as chapter 5 of his *Machina ex Deo: Essays in the Dynamism of Western Culture* (Cambridge, Mass., and London: MIT Press, 1968).

41 Ian L. McHarg, *Design with Nature* (New York: Doubleday, 1969), p. 26.

42 Ibid., p. 197.

43 These extracts from Ian McHarg's Dunning Trust lectures were quoted in the *Ontario Naturalist*, March 1973.

44 Keith Thomas, *Man and the Natural World* (1983; Harmondsworth: Penguin, 1984). See also Edward Echlin, *The Christian Green Heritage, World as creation*, Grove Ethical Studies no. 74 (Cambridge: Grove Books, 1989); Colin A. Russell, *The Earth, Humanity and God* (London: UCL Press, 1994), especially pp. 86–93.

45 Thomas, *Man and the Natural World*, p. 17.

46 Ibid., p. 18.

47 Ibid., p. 22.

48 Ibid., p. 24; cf. p. 151.

49 Ibid., p. 278.

50 Barbara Ward and Rene Dubos, *Only One Earth, The care and maintenance of a small planet* (London: Penguin, 1972), p. 83.

51 Ibid., p. 45.

52 Ibid., p. 85.

53 Ronald Higgins, *The Seventh Enemy* (London: Hodder & Stoughton, 1978).

54 Klaus Bockmuehl, *Conservation and Lifestyle* (1975, translated by Bruce N. Kaye; Cambridge: Grove Books, 1977), pp. 23–24. For a more recent Christian evaluation of environmental issues, see Ron Elsdon, *Greenhouse Theology* (London: Monarch, 1992); Stan LeQuire (ed.), *The Best Preaching on Earth: A Collection of Sermons on Care for Creation* (Valley Forge, Penn.: Judson Press, 1996); Colin A. Russell, *The Earth, Humanity*

and God (London: UCL Press, 1994). See also the quarterly magazine *Green Cross*, a publication of the Christian Society of the Green Cross, a ministry of Evangelicals for Social Action – Green Cross, 10 East Lancaster Avenue, Wynnewood, PA 19096-3495, USA.

55 Ruth Valerio, *L Is for Lifestyle* (Leicester: InterVarsity Press, 2004).

Living with Global Poverty

6

President Roosevelt famously articulated the values for which the Allies fought World War II: "We look forward to a world founded upon four essential human freedoms. The first is freedom of speech and expression. The second is freedom of every person to worship God in his own way. The third is freedom from want ... the fourth is freedom from fear." From the efforts of the Marshall Plan to rebuild Europe after the devastation of war, when Europe was a continent of refugees and food shortages, came a new vision for a response to the needs of the poor – the Third World, as it was then popularly known, but which should perhaps more accurately be called the Majority World.[1]

Serious political attention began to be given to the issue of global poverty. The first UNCTAD (United Nations Conference on Trade and Development) in 1964 saw the beginnings of political organization by the developing countries. But it was the publication of the Brandt Commission report *North-South: A Programme for Survival* in 1980 that moved the debate into a new phase, emphasizing the urgent need for action and arguing that it was in the interests of the rich as well as the poor to solve the problem of global poverty. The "principle of mutuality of interest has been at the centre of our discussions", they wrote.[2] That is, "North and South depend on each other in a single world economy", and now that they are "increasingly aware of the interdependence, they need to revitalize the dialogue to achieve specific goals, in a spirit of partnership and mutual interest rather than of inequality and charity".[3]

Part of the response to world need was the establishment of charitable institutions such as Oxfam (1942), which was followed by Christian Aid (1953). Tearfund was formally launched by the Evangelical Alliance in 1968, with an explicit aim of "removing the alibi" by which evangelical Christians escaped

161

the challenge of relief and development by leaving it to others. It was no coincidence that the launch of Tearfund, under the leadership of George Hoffman and with the slogan "They Can't Eat Prayer", was accompanied by the first television pictures of famine, originating from Biafra, the breakaway state in a civil war in Nigeria.

In October 1984, famine struck Ethiopia and people all over the world were exposed to graphic images of people starving to death. Television journalist Michael Buerk referred to it as a famine of "biblical proportions"; rock singer Bob Geldof, moved by the plight of the poor and angry with the lack of response in the West, brought together other musicians to raise money through Band Aid and the Live Aid concert in 1985.

A whole generation was touched by a unique moment of awareness and responded generously. But the following decade was characterized by a dramatic explosion of economic growth among the world's richest nations and a complete failure to share the wealth that was generated, with the result that levels of aid actually fell during the 1990s,[4] and the gap between rich and poor widened inexorably. The result was that although some countries, particularly in Asia, took advantage of the opportunities for economic growth generated by what became known as globalization, some countries were left behind, including most of sub-Saharan Africa.

So as the new millennium began, it was clear that global poverty was more complex than a simple North-South divide. Some countries seem to lack any prospects for economic growth that will have significant impact on the levels of poverty in their communities. At the same time there are countries, most notably China and India (accounting for almost one third of the world's total population), that are producing rapid economic growth but at the same time seeing high proportions of their people still trapped in poverty. Although some countries are becoming richer with respect to the rest of the world, some of them are seeing the opening up of vast disparities within their own societies.

Thus our world, God's world, is still marked by a widening gap between rich and poor both within and between countries. The statistics are sometimes almost too much to take in, given the numbers of people involved. An estimated 1,100,000,000 people live in a condition of extreme poverty, defined as living on an income of less than a dollar a day; 2,800,000,000, nearly half the world's population, live on less than two dollars a day; 1,100,000,000 live without access to a clean and safe drinking water supply; 2,400,000,000 have no access to basic sanitation.[5]

The Chronic Poverty Report 2004–2005 talks of "chronic poverty" being distinguished by duration and says,

> Between 300 and 420 million people are trapped in chronic poverty. They experience deprivation over many years, often over their entire lives, and commonly pass poverty on to their children. Many chronically poor people die prematurely from health problems that are easily preventable. For them poverty is not simply about having a low income: it is about multidimensional deprivation – hunger, under-nutrition, dirty drinking water, illiteracy, having no access to health services, social isolation and exploitation. Such deprivation and suffering exists in a world that has the knowledge and resources to eradicate it.[6]

THE MILLENNIUM DEVELOPMENT GOALS

It is against this background that we can also say that we are living at a unique moment in world history. At the turn of the millennium the largest ever gathering of world leaders debated what could be done about issues related to global poverty. The Millennium Development Goals and targets come from the resulting Millennium Declaration signed by 189 countries, including 147 heads of state, in September 2000. The goals are matched by a series of detailed targets (not outlined here) which represent the indicators of whether the goals are being met. They represent a determination, as the declaration states, "to create an environment – at the national and global levels alike – which is conducive to development and the elimination of poverty".[7]

The declaration outlined ways in which nations could join together to fight problems such as environmental degradation, war and poverty. World leaders agreed a plan which, among other things, set out to halve the proportion of the world's population living in poverty by 2015. The Millennium Development Goals (MDGs) became the focus of attention and a measure by which progress could be judged.[8] What made them significant was that there were signs that some politicians and leaders were willing to take them as serious intentions rather than as a statement of idealistic vision. The twentieth century closed not only with a unique global consensus for action, but also in a unique political atmosphere created by the election of a number of world leaders[9] sensitized to issues of global poverty.

The Millennium Development Goals[10]

1 Eradicate extreme poverty and hunger.
2 Achieve universal primary education.
3 Promote gender equality and empower women.
4 Reduce child mortality.
5 Improve maternal health.
6 Combat HIV/AIDS, malaria and other diseases.
7 Ensure environmental sustainability.
8 Develop a global partnership for development.

Of course it is easy to be cynical about the signing of such documents. Dozens of such pledges have been signed by world leaders but have never been attained. Will the MDGs be met? The picture is mixed. The *Global Monitoring Report 2005*, the document which monitors the progress of the MDGs, sees signs of hope. With respect to the first target of halving income poverty from 1990 to 2015, it says,

> Globally, prospects are promising for halving income poverty between 1990 and 2015 – the first MDG. China and India, the two countries with the highest numbers of poor people, have achieved strong, sustained growth and made major, rapid progress in reducing poverty. Due largely to their efforts, East Asia has already achieved the poverty MDG, and South Asia is on target.[11]

A particularly striking example is Vietnam, a low-income country that reduced poverty from 51% in 1990 to 14% in 2002. Yet in other countries the situation is dire. Sub-Saharan Africa, in particular, is in difficulties with respect to all the goals.

The difficulties associated with reaching the MDGs in this region led Gordon Brown, then the UK Chancellor of the Exchequer, to say at the launch of the Commission on Africa Report in March 2005:

> At best on present progress in sub-Saharan Africa the millennium development promise – free primary education for all – will not be met on time in 2015. Indeed will not be met on present rates of progress until 2130. The promise to halve poverty will not be met in 2015 but in 2150. The promise to cut by two-thirds avoidable infant and maternal mortality not by 2015 as promised but by 2165. Africans have long known the virtues of patience but the whole world should now know that 150 years is too long to ask

peoples to wait for justice. And the question we must ask is "if not now, then when; if not us, then who?"[12]

Gordon Brown's words show us again that words without deeds are worse than useless. If the issue is the absence of political will on behalf of those nations who are rich, then we are falling short of the biblical demands of justice for the poor.

The Monterrey Consensus – the outcome of a meeting on financing development in 2002 – discussed what needed to be done for the MDGs to be met. It reaffirmed the need for developed and developing countries to see themselves as interdependent, as Brandt had done in 1980. It also issued a call to developing countries to put sound policies in place, enable good governance, fight corruption and enforce private property rights and the rule of law within a democratic framework.[13] In other words, developing countries had to construct sound policies and institutions which they owned and on which the international community could rely.

AID, TRADE AND DEBT

When looking at global poverty, three issues are always on the agenda – aid, trade and the indebtedness of poor nations.

Aid

The year 2005 marked thirty-five years since this target was first affirmed by UN member states in a 1970 General Assembly resolution.

> In recognition of the special importance of the role which can be fulfilled only by official development assistance, a major part of financial resource transfers to the developing countries should be provided in the form of official development assistance. Each economically advanced country will progressively increase its official development assistance to the developing countries and will exert its best efforts to reach a minimum net amount of 0.7% of GNP at market prices by the middle of the decade.[14]

Rich countries committed themselves to this again at the Earth Summit in Rio in 1992. Monterrey also finished with a call to rich nations to recommit themselves to providing 0.7% of GNP as official development assistance. Yet few countries have ever come near this target. A handful of countries, notably Norway, Denmark, Sweden, Luxembourg and the Netherlands, do. But although the US contribution is the highest in volume terms, it is the lowest when measured as a proportion of GNP (0.14% in 2003). Overall the share of financial aid as a proportion of the GNP of wealthy countries actually fell from 0.3% to 0.2% during the 1990s.[15] Yet recently Gordon Brown has called for a doubling of aid if the MDGs are to be met.[16]

Recently Africa has seen the birth of NEPAD (The New Partnership for Africa's Development) initiated by five African heads of state (Algeria, Egypt, Nigeria, Senegal and South Africa). This framework for Africa's renewal states that Africa's development is Africa's responsibility. It takes as its task the development of Africa into a continent which can participate effectively in world markets and the fostering of health, peace, transparency and meeting those other conditions necessary for stable societies.

Aid has a vital place to play in helping Majority World countries to grow and develop, as well as providing the urgent relief with which we are all too familiar when tragedy strikes through disasters such as tsunami or famine. As I shall show later, it is part of the way in which we work out the biblical principle of equality.

Trade

Justice in international trade is of the utmost importance if there is to be equality of opportunity for all countries. Development aid is important, but it is not an end in itself. Surely the aim of aid must be to prepare a healthy and stable country to be able to trade on equal terms with the rest of the world. As Christians we cannot remain bystanders to an international trading system which has injustice enshrined within it. We should therefore welcome every attempt by Christian agencies and churches to draw attention to trade injustice in such a way that governments, multinational corporations and intergovernmental organizations feel they cannot ignore public opinion. In 2005 the Global Campaign for Action Against Poverty, utilizing the slogan "Make Poverty History", called people to focus again on the need to support trade justice, cancel debt and foster efficiently delivered, quality aid for Majority World countries. Even though it is difficult and maybe impossible to achieve equality, it is surely possible to reduce inequality. We neglect this at our peril, not only politically and economically, but also morally and spiritually.

Many Majority World countries are up against the protectionism of rich countries when they try and trade on world markets. When Ghana developed a tomato industry, Italy dumped surplus tomatoes in Ghana to kill it off.[17] Mozambique produces 200,000 tons of sugar a year, but because of quotas can only sell a fraction of this to Europe and the US, who also subsidize sugar beet production. Consequently, Mozambique loses out.[18] Such examples could be multiplied endlessly, with famous examples of bananas, textiles and coffee being among those products which are unfairly traded. As Christians we should support fair trade wherever we can.

Debt

So there are still vast structural inequities in the world today which perpetuate global poverty and which we must challenge. For instance, people in the Majority World have to pay £30,000,000 every day to the rich world in debt repayments while millions are in poverty. In 1998, fifty-two countries owed a total of $375,000,000,000. The G8 countries agreed to cancel (or "forgive") $100,000,000,000 of this. As of April 2005 only $48,000,000,000 had actually been cancelled.[19] At a meeting of the powerful "G7" nations in February 2005 (they are known as "G8" when Russia is included), Canada, Germany, France, Japan, Italy, the US and the UK agreed that some countries, notably the forty-two Heavily Indebted Poor Countries (HIPC), needed 100% debt relief.

Many countries carry a heavy debt burden due to massive lending in the 1970s. Although, of course, in principle all contracts should be kept and debts repaid, one wonders if the present situation does not fall under the Old Testament condemnation of usury. It certainly gives the appearance of the exploitation of the poor through extortionate money-lending by the rich. Zambia's debt repayments to the IMF (International Monetary Fund) alone cost $25,000,000, more than the country's education expenses, despite 40% of rural women being unable to read and write. Malawi spends more on servicing its debt than on health, despite nearly one in five Malawians being HIV positive. Despite being the second country to be granted debt cancellation (after Uganda), Bolivia still spends more on debt servicing than on health, even though its infant mortality rate is ten times that of the UK.[20]

The debt crisis cannot be attributed in a simplistic way to mismanagement and extravagance by unscrupulous governments and their elite supporters. It is mainly due to factors over which the country's leaders have little if any control:

the worldwide recession of the early 1980s, rising interest rates in the lending countries, crippling inflation in the borrowing countries, and the instability – in some cases collapse – of commodity prices. So in many cases the debts have increased even while the ability to repay them has decreased.

Of course unscrupulous governments can squander resources, and those cancelling debts have often imposed conditions on countries as to how they should restructure their economy and reform their civil society before debts can be cancelled. Sometimes this is warranted, but often it is another burden for a country which is already under intolerable pressure. It is true that Majority World countries must take responsibility for their policies and for good governance, but at the same time, in rescheduling and cancellation arrangements it is morally wrong for rich countries to compel debtor governments to reduce their public expenditure on social programmes like education, health and employment, since it is the poor who suffer most from such cuts. Critics claim that this is often what happens under the Structural Adjustment Programmes initiated by the World Bank and the IMF's stabilization policies, both of which are aimed at long-term structural change of unproductive economic practices.

Debt cancellation makes a real difference to a country. The Jubilee Debt Campaign gives four examples of this. In Benin, 54% of the money saved through debt relief has been spent on health, including on rural primary health care and HIV programmes. In Tanzania, debt relief enabled the government to abolish primary school fees, leading to a 66% increase in attendance. After Mozambique was granted debt relief, it was able to offer all children free immunization. In Uganda, debt relief led to 2,200,000 people gaining access to water.

Much of the focus on debt relief came about through the work of the Jubilee 2000 campaign, supported by a broad coalition of Christian and non-Christian agencies. The work of retired diplomat Bill Peters and academic Martin Dent (Keele University) was linked to the visionary and inspiring leadership of Ann Pettifor, who had been working for the Debt Network that coordinated the activity of charities on the debt issue. A number of evangelical Christians were prominent. Mark Greene, then at London Bible College, helped to create what many, including Bob Geldof, saw as an impossibility – a popular campaign on an abstruse economic issue. Tearfund played a key role in getting it off the ground, with Stephen Rand playing a particularly prominent role; Christian Aid and CAFOD were vital in spreading the campaign through the breadth of churches in the UK, and the Catholic Church, significantly augmented by the Mothers' Union, spearheaded the internationalization of the campaign. More than 24,000,000 people signed the Jubilee 2000 debt campaign petition. It was a powerful tool in the success of the campaign. It has been estimated that for each signature more than £4,000 of debt was cancelled. Social spending across all Highly Indebted Poor Countries is estimated to have risen by about 20%.[21]

A sense of injustice and moral outrage fuelled the desire for change and provided the energy to take action. This was articulated in the application of the principles of the Jubilee teachings of Old Testament law. It was not a close exegesis of the biblical passages, but more an expression of aspiration that resonated with biblical values, so much so that economist Will Hutton wrote in the *Observer*, "At the end of the twentieth century it is the words of Leviticus rather than the teachings of Karl Marx that have proved the inspiration for a significant change in world affairs." Gordon Brown, speaking at a Jubilee 2000 rally in December 2000, commented: "The success of Jubilee 2000 can be attributed to the idealism and tireless strength of our churches. We are assembled here to rededicate ourselves to what we have to do together. In the words of Isaiah 'to undo the heavy burdens and let the oppressed go free.'"[22]

THE IMPACT OF AIDS

Many parts of the Majority World have been further impoverished by the advent of AIDS, which has devastated their society. In Zambia, for instance, life expectancy has been reduced to forty years or below. AIDS (the Acquired Immune Deficiency Syndrome) was identified and described for the first time in 1981 in the United States.[23] It is caused by HIV (the Human Immunodeficiency Virus), which may lie dormant and unsuspected in its human host for as long as ten years. But in time it will manifest itself by attacking and damaging the body's immune and nervous systems, eventually rendering it defenceless against certain fatal diseases. HIV can be transmitted by several means, including blood transfusion, intravenous drug use via shared or contaminated needles, sexual contact or mother-to-child transmission.[24] At present, though there are anti-retroviral drugs which can slow its development, it is always fatal.

When the West first became aware of AIDS, it was thought of as an illness that was mainly confined to the gay community. In its early years it was known of as the "gay plague" because of the number of gay men affected by it, the number of sexual partners they had and the "high-risk" sexual practices in which they indulged. However, we now know that AIDS can affect anybody, whether men, women or children, heterosexual or homosexual. Indeed, women and girls will soon outnumber men and boys infected with HIV. In sub-Saharan Africa young women aged between fifteen and twenty-four are three times more vulnerable to HIV than their male peers. They are physically more susceptible, often lack control over their own lives and are more open to abuse and exploitation.

Although AIDS exists throughout the world, it is most often associated with the Majority World. Although epidemics are growing in countries such as India, China and throughout Eastern Europe, AIDS has become associated with the African continent. It is here that the greatest tragedy is being played out. Over the next twenty years, if nothing is done, nearly 90,000,000 Africans could be infected by HIV – 10% of the continent's population. Yet many of these deaths are preventable, especially if aid increases and health, agriculture and education are improved. More generally, in 2005, the global figure for people living with HIV/AIDS was 40,300,000.[25] People newly infected with HIV in 2005 totalled 4,900,000,[26] while 3,170,000 people with AIDS died.[27] In some countries it is difficult to get accurate figures or to reach vulnerable people because of the stigma of drug addiction or of being a man who has sex with men in a culture in which this behaviour is hidden.

The link between poverty and AIDS is a circular one. Poor health causes poverty and poverty contributes to poor health.[28] Poverty makes treatment unaffordable, access to health care inadequate and nutrition often poor. It means surviving in the short term rather than investing for longer-term benefits. AIDS reduces a family's ability to farm the land, deflects funds into medicine and reduces savings. In his book *The End of Poverty*, Jeffrey Sachs says the following:

> Africa is losing its teachers and doctors, its civil servants and farmers, its mothers and fathers. There are already more than 10 million orphaned children. Business costs have soared because of disarray from massive medical costs for workers, relentless absenteeism, and an avalanche of worker deaths. Foreign investors are deterred from stepping into Africa's AIDS morass and millions of households are battling the illness of the head of household, resulting in an incredible toll in time and expense, to say nothing of the emotional trauma for the family.[29]

Yet in Uganda, HIV prevalence peaked at around 15% in 1991 and fell to 5% by 2001. This cause for hope was examined in a paper written by Edward Green and four others who are experienced analysts of AIDS in Africa.[30] They found that although the situation was complex, the leadership of President Museveni, who spoke out publicly about AIDS, was crucial. Priority was given to education about HIV/AIDS in schools, local gatherings and in religious institutions. Leaders of faith communities were encouraged to overcome their reticence about getting involved. Community leaders were trained and utilized. Voluntary Counselling and Testing (VCT) was also important.

However, perhaps the most important determinant of the reduction in HIV/AIDS in Uganda was a decrease in multiple sexual partnerships. In comparison with men from Kenya, Zambia and Malawi, Ugandan men in 1995 aged between fifteen and nineteen were less likely to have ever had sex, more likely to be married and to be loyal to their partner, and less likely to have multiple partners, particularly if never married.

Uganda's president and his wife often talked of the "ABC approach" to AIDS[31] – in other words that people should *abstain* from sex, *be* faithful to their partner and, if they could do neither of these, use *condoms*. The emphasis on the first two brought about a change in behaviour which could not have come about solely through the use of condoms. According to Stoneburner, one of the authors of the report, "The effect of HIV prevention interventions in Uganda (particularly partner reduction) during the past decade appears to have had a similar impact as a potential medical vaccine of 80 percent efficacy."[32] This approach was not without its critics. On the one hand, some of those who supported abstinence and faithfulness criticized those who focused solely on condom usage as encouraging sexual promiscuity, whereas those who felt that encouraging the use of condoms was the most important strategic approach saw the call to abstinence and faithfulness as unrealistic and inadequate. They had very different approaches. One group was trying to change the sexual choices people made, while the other was trying to respect the sexual choices people made without changing them.

Christians should not be surprised at the impact of abstinence and faithfulness in this situation. God's call on our lives includes a joyful celebration of sexual intercourse within marriage and of celibacy outside it. When this call on our lives is ignored or rejected, the results can be tragic and in some cases catastrophic. Nor can these dangers be avoided merely by the use of a condom, which can be an unreliable contraceptive. Dr Patrick Dixon, founder of ACET

(AIDS Care, Education and Training) sums the matter up succinctly: "Condoms do not make sex safe, they simply make it safer. Safe sex is sex between two partners who are not infected! This means a lifelong, faithful partnership between two people who were virgins and who now remain faithful to each other for life".[33] Or, to quote the United States Catholic Conference, "Abstinence outside of marriage and fidelity within marriage, as well as the avoidance of intravenous drug abuse, are the only morally correct and medically sure ways to prevent the spread of AIDS."[34]

What is our Christian response to this desperate situation?

A theological response

Firstly, it must be theological. Of course, many people throughout the world who are living with HIV/AIDS do so through no fault of their own. They may have been the faithful wives of men who are infected, children infected through their mother's milk, or simply those who have been given a contaminated blood transfusion. As Christians, our first response to people must be compassion. This does not mean that we should avoid the issue which has often been raised of whether AIDS is God's judgement on those who are acting immorally. The apostle Paul wrote: "Do not deceive yourselves; no one makes a fool of God. People will reap exactly what they sow" (Galatians 6:7 GNB). The fact that we reap what we sow or that evil actions bring evil consequences seems to have been written by God into the ordering of his moral world. Christians cannot regard it as an accident, for example, that promiscuity exposes people to STDs (sexually transmitted diseases), that heavy smoking can lead to lung cancer, excessive consumption of alcohol to liver disorders and overeating to heart conditions. Moreover, this cause-and-effect mechanism is viewed in Scripture as one of the ways in which "God's wrath" – that is, his just judgement on evil – is revealed (Romans 1:18 – 32). Before the day of judgement arrives, Jesus taught, a process of judgement is already taking place (John 3:18 – 21; 5:24 – 29). AIDS may rightly be seen, then, as "part of God's judgement on society". "It is calling the bluff of the permissive society that there is any such thing as sexual liberation in promiscuity."[35]

A prophetic response

Secondly, it must be prophetic. As Christians, we are called to hold the authorities to account for their actions, and in this case it is important and urgent that we do so. Christians must monitor the behaviour of governments and other institutions to ensure that their response to the AIDS crisis throughout the world is not only adequate but efficient. Millions of lives could be saved were there the international political will to commit resources to fighting AIDS. We need to be those who are willing to ask awkward questions about what is being done to help those who are suffering but who are also powerless. Wealthy countries may think that they have problems of their own, but compared to the issues faced by those living in countries decimated by AIDS, few of us can complain about the situation in which we live. As Jeffrey Sachs points out, 3,000 people died needlessly and tragically at the World Trade Center on 11 September 2001, yet 10,000 Africans die needlessly and tragically every day and have died every single day since 11 September – of AIDS, TB and malaria. Many of those deaths are preventable.[36]

A pastoral response

Thirdly, it must be pastoral. Even if people have AIDS as a result of their own actions, this provides us with no justification for shunning or neglecting them. As the American Roman Catholic bishops have put it, "Stories of persons with AIDS must not become occasions for stereotyping or prejudice, for anger or recrimination, for rejection or isolation, for injustice or condemnation." Instead, "They provide us with an opportunity to walk with those who are suffering, to be compassionate towards those we might otherwise fear, to bring strength and courage both to those who face the prospect of dying as well as to their loved ones."[37] Thankfully many churches both in the Majority World and in the West are involved with helping those who have HIV/AIDS, both practically and in terms of emotional support for them and for their families.

An educational response

Fourthly, it must be educational. Given the extent of the AIDS crisis, education may be thought to be an inadequate response compared to the development of drugs and other medical interventions. But education is a powerful force for good in our world where so much poverty and powerlessness results from ignorance. All three aspects of the ABC approach to the prevention of AIDS rely on education and information. In many countries Voluntary Counselling and Testing (VCT) has been important in preventing the spread of HIV/AIDS. Certainly in the West we are aware of the need constantly to keep the issues alive, as successive generations can become complacent or indifferent to the dangers of promiscuous behaviour or intravenous drug use. Churches should have a major role in this. We must not fail, but rather challenge society to sexual self-control and faithfulness and point to Jesus as the source of forgiveness and power.

HOLISTIC DEVELOPMENT

Important fresh thinking in the development debate was contributed by the UN's World Commission on Environment and Development (chaired by Mrs Gro Harlem Brundtland, at that time prime minister of Norway), whose report *Our Common Future* was published in 1987. Characterized by the same urgent tone as the Brandt reports, it called for the integration of the world's environmental and developmental problems (since economics and ecology are insepa-rable) and for the cooperation of all nations in solving them. It popularized the notion of "sustainable development", defining it as "development that meets the needs of the present (in particular, the essential needs of the poor) without compromising the ability of future generations to meet their own needs".[38] The definition combines "two key concepts" – meeting needs and setting limits. It thus promotes development and protects the environment simultaneously. Sustainable development became the hallmark of the 1992 United Nations Con-ference on the Environment and Development in Rio de Janeiro, where details of the interplay between the environment and development were more thor-oughly worked out. Yet from the perspective of the 2002 Johannesburg Sum-mit on Sustainable Development, progress over the previous decade had been extremely disappointing. I have talked more about the importance of environ-mental issues elsewhere in this book.

The decade of the 1990s was marked by a continuous questioning and reformulating of the basic ideas of development. This resulted in much broader concerns being addressed than those with a purely economic focus.[39] In particular, the "three core values of development" are defined as (1) "suste-nance", or the ability to meet one's basic needs (i.e., food, health and shelter), (2) "self-esteem", or the ability to be a person (with the dignity that comes from education and employment), and (3) "freedom from servitude", or the abil-ity to make choices (economic, social and political).[40] In recent years, poverty has increasingly been measured not just in economic terms but holistically in terms of the quality of life measured by indicators such as life expectancy, literacy and "standard of living", measured by real per capita income adjusted by cost of living and other factors that differ between countries. The Human Development Index (HDI) was created to analyse the extent to which people were impoverished in this wider sense. More recently, some have focused on a "rights-based" approach to development, emphasizing that when people are granted their human rights they will be able to participate fully in a healthy democratic society.[41]

Women, especially, can be affected by poverty in all its dimensions and are often denied their human rights. They can have less access to economic resources and private property rights, where they exist, are often not available to women but only to men. Many women cannot afford the medical care that they need and in many countries the education of women and girls is secondary to that of boys. Indeed, in some parts of Asia the perceived costs of giving birth to a girl child means that some people will have the fetus scanned and, if a girl child is found, may abort the fetus in a private or sometimes backstreet clinic. Some researchers have therefore talked about the "feminization of poverty".[42] Since men and women are both made in the image of God, development should become more gender sensitive, and it is gratifying to see in recent years that there has been an increased emphasis on the access of women to those resources necessary for a higher quality of life and on women's rights.

Yet it is sad that at some conferences which focus on the needs of women internationally, there has been an undue place given to what is sometimes called "reproductive health", ostensibly an important part of women's health needs but a phrase which is all too often used to denote a demand for increased access to abortion facilities. It is true that women need access to a much higher quality of medical care at every stage of their lives and that, tragically, many women in the Majority World die because of "unsafe abortions". It is also true that population growth and issues related to demographic change are important priorities to consider when looking at global poverty or environmental challenges. But Western countries can seek to manipulate debates on these issues and impose their worldview on other cultures. This took place at the United Nations Conference on Human Settlements (known as Habitat II) in Istanbul in June 1996. Designed to address issues of sustainable urban development in the Majority World, it descended into a battle over "reproductive health". Majority World countries resisted the political agenda of the European and North American pro-abortion lobby. As a result of their stubbornness, a courageous speech by John Gummer (then British Secretary of State for the Environment), and the support of pro-life non-governmental organizations present, the Majority World majority radically modified the pro-abortion vocabulary of some conference resolutions, reaffirmed the family as a cornerstone of society, and left no room for universal abortion on demand. Such debates also took place at the UN Conference on Population and Development in Cairo in 1994, the Beijing Conference on Women in 1995 and the Beijing + 5 Conference in 2000.

THE TRANSFORMATION OF CULTURE

So if a country's prospects are to be transformed from being impoverished to flourishing, much more is at stake than economics. We need to look at the influence of culture and indeed the way in which people view themselves, since true development cannot be imposed from above but must start with the people themselves. Professor Brian Griffiths (now Lord Griffiths), a well-known Christian economist, banker and policy adviser, reminds us that the causes of Majority World poverty concern people and their political, economic and cultural behaviour.[43] The political factors include mismanagement, the expulsion of racial minorities, extravagance and corruption on the part of governments and their leaders. Then there is the economic system which they choose and operate. But above all there is the cultural factor – that is, the profound effect of people's cultural background on their motives, thoughts, aspirations and actions.

Brian Griffiths rightly seized on Willy Brandt's own assertion, on behalf of the Brandt Commission, "We take it for granted that all cultures deserve equal respect, protection and promotion." [44] "While all cultures deserve respect," Brian Griffiths responded, "they do not all deserve equal protection and promotion." On the contrary, how can we wish to "protect and promote" cultures which actively hinder development, for example by inculcating a spirit of fatalism and apathy? He continues:

> If we really wish to understand the origins of poverty in Majority World countries, I believe we are driven back to an examination of the culture of different countries and to asking basic questions. Why is it that in some societies individual human beings have the views of the physical world, of the importance of work, and the sense of self-discipline which they do? Why is it that in other societies they do not? ... Personally, I find it impossible to answer these questions satisfactorily in purely economic terms. It

is at this point that economic analysis needs a religious dimension ... To the extent that any culture contains Judaeo-Christian values, then surely those facets of that culture deserve especial protection and promotion.[45]

So from a Christian perspective we must also include humanity's need to be transformed spiritually, and this cannot be separated from those other goals which are at the heart of more traditional views on development. This concept is outlined in a book by Bryant Myers entitled *Walking with the Poor: Principles and Practices of Transformational Development*.[46] For Bryant Myers, transformation is a continuous process which includes people's spiritual well-being and self-esteem as well as their social and economic resources. Although he uses the word "development", he adds the caveat that it is often associated with Westernization or modernization. The poor and the non-poor have different challenges.

> The poor suffer from marred identities and the belief that they have no meaningful vocation other than serving the powerful. The non-poor, and sometimes development facilitators, suffer from the temptation to play God in the lives of the poor, and believe that what they have in terms of money, knowledge and position is the result of their own cleverness or the right of their group. Both the poor and the non-poor need to recover their true identity and their true vocation.[47]

He then goes on to bring together biblical insight and development practice to argue that true transformational development comes from poor people understanding what it means to be made in the image of God and the fact that they have gifts that can be used to further a fruitful vocation. It also results from the non-poor realizing that their resources and gifts are gifts from God, given to be utilized in the service of the poor.

This concept is an appropriate partner for "integral mission". This idea is at the heart of the Micah Network, Christian development agencies committed to working together on behalf of the poor.[48] The Micah Declaration on Integral Mission arose out of a consultation in Oxford in September 2001. It enshrined the concept outlined elsewhere in this book that evangelism and social involvement are interdependent. It called the church back to the centrality of Jesus Christ and to the grace of God as the heartbeat of integral mission and talked of treating the poor with respect, enabling them to be architects of change themselves. It saw the church among the poor as being in the unique position to restore their God-given dignity, which should be at the heart of all true transformation. It is called Micah, of course, because the prophet Micah said, "What does the LORD require of you but to do justice, and to love kindness, and to walk humbly with your God?" (Micah 6:8 RSV).

This has been expressed in the launch of the Micah Challenge, a global campaign aiming to encourage Christians to build on the impetus of Jubilee 2000 and focused on challenging world leaders to meet the Millennium Development Goals. It has begun by encouraging individuals and churches to sign up to the "Micah call", which affirms the centrality and urgency of integral mission at the heart of the gospel and the requirement to live as Christians in today's world.[49]

Not being an economist or development expert,[50] I lack the expertise to comment on the technical issues and policies which lie at the heart of the development issues outlined here. What I do feel able to do, however, is to offer some biblical thoughts as justification for continuing to seek global economic and environmental cooperation. It is another case of struggling to clarify the principles involved, while leaving the framing of policies to those who have the necessary training, knowledge and influence. It seems to me that two fundamental biblical principles apply to this issue.

THE PRINCIPLE OF UNITY

The first is the principle of unity, namely that the earth is one, and the human race is also one. Yet this double unity does not control our behaviour. Instead, the basic human predicament is that "the Earth is one but the world is not".[51] So nothing is more important than that the two unities God has created should permeate our consciousness. This is a clear biblical vision. "The earth is the LORD's, and everything in it, the world, and all who live in it" (Psalm 24:1). I have already quoted this verse in reference to the environment: the earth belongs to God. Now we take note that those who live in it belong to him too. God has created a single people (the human race) and placed us in a single habitat (the planet Earth). We are one people inhabiting one planet. Moreover, these two unities (planet and people) are closely related to one another. God said, "Be fruitful and increase in number; fill the earth and subdue it" (Genesis 1:28). Thus the one people were to populate and tame the one earth, in order to harness its resources to their service. There was no hint at the beginning of the partitioning of the earth or of rivalry between nations. No, the whole earth was to be developed by the whole people for the common good. All were to share in its God-given riches. This principle of "distributive justice" still applies today.

But this divine purpose has been frustrated by the rise of competitive nations who have carved up the earth's surface and now jealously guard its mineral deposits and fossil fuels for themselves. Of course the Bible (realistic book that it is) recognizes the existence of nations, indicates that their developing histories and territorial frontiers are ultimately under God's sovereign control, welcomes the cultural diversity (though not all the cultural practices) they have created, and warns us that "nation will rise against nation" till the end. But it does not acquiesce in this international rivalry. On the contrary, it tells us that the multiplicity of mutually hostile nations with mutually incomprehensible languages is a consequence of God's judgement on man's disobedience and pride (Genesis 11).

The Bible also indicates that one of God's major purposes in redemption will be to overcome the enmity which separates nations and to reunite the human race in Christ. So, immediately after the Tower of Babel episode, God promised through Abraham's posterity to bless all the peoples of the earth (Genesis 12:1 – 3); he predicted through the prophets that all nations would one day "flow" like rivers to Jerusalem (e.g., Isaiah 2:2); the risen Jesus told his followers to go and make disciples of all the nations (Matthew 28:19); the Holy Spirit came upon "all people", the nineteen national groups Luke mentions representing the known world (Acts 2:5 – 11, 17); Paul describes the accomplishment of Christ's cross in terms both of the abolition of the dividing wall of hostility between Jew and Gentile and of the creation out of the two of "one new man" or a single new humanity (Ephesians 2:14 – 15); and the vision of the redeemed before God's throne is of a countless multitude "from every nation, tribe, people and language" (Revelation 7:9). It would be impossible to miss this strand of internationalism which appears right through the biblical revelation.

So then, we cannot evade our responsibility to the world's poor people on the ground that they belong to other nations and are no concern of ours. The main point of the parable of the Good Samaritan is its racial twist. It is not just that neighbour-love ignores racial and national barriers, but that in Jesus' story a Samaritan did for a Jew what no Jew would ever have dreamed of doing for a Samaritan.

Patriotism is a legitimate love for the country to which we belong. But Sir Alfred Duff Cooper was wrong when he remarked (I think in the early 1950s) that "the love of one's country should be like all true love – blind, prejudiced and passionate". I hope he had his tongue in his cheek, for what he was describing was not "patriotism" but "nationalism", namely a blinkered and exaggerated loyalty to "my country right or wrong". It is nationalism, not patriotism, which leads to the framing of trade policies which benefit us at the expense of developing nations. Nationalism is incompatible with the perspective of the Bible and the mind of Christ. Instead, we Christians should seek to become more committed internationalists, symbolizing our resolve to affirm the biblical principle of unity (one planet, one people), to develop a global perspective, and to recognize everybody's unavoidable interdependence.

THE PRINCIPLE OF EQUALITY

I move now from the first biblical principle (unity) to the second (equality). Consider the following teaching of the apostle Paul in 2 Corinthians 8:8 – 15:

Verse 8	I am not commanding you, but I want to test the sincerity of your love by comparing it with the earnestness of others.
Verse 9	For you know the grace of our Lord Jesus Christ, that though he was rich, yet for your sakes he became poor, so that you through his poverty might become rich.
Verse 10	And here is my advice about what is best for you in this matter: Last year you were the first not only to give but also to have the desire to do so.
Verse 11	Now finish the work, so that your eager willingness to do it may be matched by your completion of it, according to your means.
Verse 12	For if the willingness is there, the gift is acceptable according to what one has, not according to what he does not have.
Verse 13	Our desire is not that others might be relieved while you are hard pressed, but that there might be *equality*.
Verse 14	At the present time your plenty will supply what they need, so that in turn their plenty will supply what you need. Then there will be *equality*,
Verse 15	as it is written: "He who gathered much did not have too much, and he who gathered little did not have too little."

The two references to the goal of equality have been italicized in the text, so that we do not overlook them. Yet we need to see them in the whole context of Paul's instruction about the collection for the poor Judean Christians which he is organizing in the Greek churches. He begins by assuring them that his teaching is not a command but a test; he is seeking evidence of the genuineness of their love (v. 8). So their giving is to be voluntary – not in the sense that it is optional (because they are under obligation to share with their more needy Christian brothers and sisters), but in the sense that it is spontaneous and free (an expression of their love for the poor, rather than mere obedience to the apostle).

That leads Paul straight to Christ, and to a sublime statement of his spontaneous grace (v. 9). He grounds his mundane appeal for the disadvantaged on the theology of the incarnation, and the gracious renunciation which it entailed. He makes two references to wealth and two to poverty. Christ had been rich, but he became poor; not as a meaningless gesture of asceticism, but "for your sakes", namely that through his poverty you might become rich. That is to say, because of our poverty he renounced his riches, so that through his poverty we might share them. It was a renunciation with a view to a certain equalization. Moreover, both his concern to end our poverty and his decision to renounce his riches were expressions of his "grace" (v. 9), as similar action on our part will be of our "love" (v. 8). Grace is free, undeserved love.

To his exhortation that they should prove their love Paul adds some practical advice as to how to do so. They should now complete what a year previously they desired and began to do. Desiring and doing must go together, according to their means (vv. 10 – 12). Christian giving is proportionate giving, and is acceptable according to what one has, provided that the willingness is there. Paul is not wanting them to relieve the needs of others by putting themselves in want, for that would be merely to reverse the situation, solving one problem by creating another. No, his desire is rather "that there might be equality" (v. 13). He puts the affluence of some alongside the want of others, and then calls for an adjustment – that is, an easing of want by affluence (v. 14). Twice he says that this is with a view to *isotēs*, which normally means "equality", but can also mean "fairness" or "justice". Finally (v. 15), he appeals to an Old Testament quotation about manna. God provided enough for everybody. Larger families gathered a lot, but not too much, for they had nothing over; smaller families gathered only a little, but not too little, for they had no lack. Each family had enough, because they collected according to need, not greed.

Let me try to sum up these instructions, in the reverse order, applying them to the world situation today. (1) God has provided enough for everybody's need

(adequate resources in sun and rain, earth, air and water); (2) any great disparity between affluence and want, wealth and poverty, is unacceptable to him;
(3) when a situation of serious disparity arises, it ought to be corrected by an
adjustment, in order to secure "equality" or "justice"; (4) the Christian motive
for desiring such "justice" is "grace", loving generosity, as in the case of Jesus
Christ who, though rich, became poor, so that through his poverty we might
become rich; (5) we are to follow his example in this, and so prove the genuineness of our love. Just how a worldwide equalization could or should be effected
is another question. Economists differ. Whatever the method, however, the
motivation for seeking equality or fairness is love.

It may be objected by some that Paul's instructions related to an equalization within the household of God, Gentile Christians from Greece coming to
the aid of Jewish Christians in Judea, and that we have no liberty to extend its
application from the church to the world. But I cannot accept this limitation.
The "poor" for whose sake the rich Christ impoverished himself were unbelieving sinners like us. Besides, the principle that grave disparity should be
evened out sounds like a universal truth. And when Paul wrote, "As we have
opportunity, let us do good to all people, especially to those who belong to the
family of believers" (Galatians 6:10), the purpose of his "especially" was not
to exclude unbelievers, but to remind us that our first responsibility is to our
Christian brothers and sisters.

I need now to interpret Paul's teaching with an important qualification:
the "equality" he sets before us as a goal is relative rather than absolute. He is
not recommending a total "egalitarianism", by which all people become precisely the same, receiving an identical income, living in an identical home with
identical furniture, wearing identical clothes and developing an identical lifestyle. The living God is not the Lord of drab uniformity but of colourful diversity. True, he made us equal in dignity and worth (for we all share his life and
bear his likeness). True also, he gives the blessings of sunshine and rain to all
humankind indiscriminately (Matthew 5:45). But he has not made us equal in
ability. On the contrary, by creation we differ from one another – intellectually
(we have different IQs), psychologically (our temperaments vary) and physically (some are handsome, others plain, some are strong, others weak). And
the new creation extends this disparity. For although we are "all one in Jesus
Christ" (Galatians 3:28), equally God's children, justified by his grace through
faith, and although we have all received the same Holy Spirit to indwell us, yet

Christ by his Spirit bestows on us different spiritual gifts, whose value differs according to the degree to which they build up the church.[52]

PERSONAL AND ECONOMIC REPERCUSSIONS

How, then, can we put together what we find in the Bible – this unity and diversity, this equality and inequality? Two answers may be given. Firstly, there is the question of our personal economic lifestyle. Is there any criterion by which to decide at what level we should choose to live and how much difference we should permit between ourselves and others in our neighbourhood? It is a question which all missionaries have to face, especially when they go from an affluent situation to a developing country. The Willowbank Report was helpful on this topic: "We do not believe that we should 'go native', principally because a foreigner's attempt to do this may not be seen as authentic but as play-acting. But neither do we think there should be a conspicuous disparity between our lifestyle and that of the people around us. In between these extremes, we see the possibility of developing a standard of living which expresses the kind of love which cares and shares, and which finds it natural to exchange hospitality with others on a basis of reciprocity, without embarrassment."[53] This strikes me as a very practical rule of thumb. The moment I am embarrassed either to visit other people in their home or to invite them into mine, because of the disparity between our lifestyles, something is wrong. The inequality has broken the fellowship. There needs to be an equalization in one or other direction, or both. In 1967 Julius Nyerere, then president of Tanzania, applied this challenge to the building of a Tanzanian state in which "no man is ashamed of his poverty in the light of another's affluence, and no man has to be ashamed of his affluence in the light of another's poverty".[54]

Secondly, this principle can help us in our thinking about North-South economic inequality. Since we all have equal worth (despite our unequal capacity), it must be right to secure equal opportunity for each person to develop his or her God-given potential for the common good. We cannot abolish all inequalities, nor even (because of the diversity of creation) attempt to. It is inequality of privilege we should seek to abolish, in order to create equality of opportunity. Millions of people are unable to develop their human potential. This Christians see to be the real scandal. It is an offence not only to human beings, since they are frustrated and unfulfilled, but also to their Creator, who bestowed his gifts on them to be developed and used in service, not to be wasted. I have already discussed the vital importance of justice in trade, the forgiving of debt, the need for effective aid and the urgent need to fight AIDS. But there are two further areas where equality of opportunity is also of real importance. They are education and participation.

Education

Education must surely come first. One in four adults in the Majority World is illiterate; 130,000,000 of the world's children aged between six and eleven are not in school; of these, 90,000,000 are girls; one in four girls who start primary school drop out within four years.[55] We should therefore support every programme which seeks equality of educational opportunity. Universal education is probably the shortest route to social justice, for it develops people's social awareness and thus gives them the understanding and the courage to take hold of their own destiny. The child of a Zambian mother with primary school education has a 25% higher chance of survival than the child of a mother with no education. In the Philippines, a mother's primary education reduces by half the risk of child mortality.

Participation

Secondly, the developing nations should be given equality in international participation. The International Monetary Fund, the World Bank and the General Agreement on Trade and Tariffs (now WTO) were all set up as a result of the Bretton Woods conference in 1944, more than twenty years before the first meeting of UNCTAD at which for the first time representatives of Majority World countries had a forum of their own. It would seem to be elementary justice that developing countries should be given a greater say in these international institutions which control so much of their economic life. Those affected by decisions made should have a share in the decision-making. There are some positive signs: the GATT had twenty-three signatories when it came into effect in January 1948. As of January 2000, the WTO has 135 members with an additional thirty-one in the process of accession. Yet the influence of Majority World countries is still far too small for them to overcome the injustices done to them by rich and powerful countries.

It is perhaps equality of opportunity in these areas (education and participation) as well as action in the other vital areas I have discussed which would ensure, more than anything else, a fairer distribution of the world's wealth.

The present situation of North-South inequality ("a gap so wide that at the extremes people seem to live in different worlds") is not God's fault (for he has provided ample resources in earth and sea), nor is it the fault of the poor (since they were mostly born into it, though some government leaders are to blame for corruption and for incompetence), nor is it necessarily our fault (although our colonial forefathers may have had a share in creating it). We become personally culpable only if we acquiesce in its continuance. In Jesus' story of the rich man and Lazarus there is no hint that the rich man was responsible for the poor man's plight. The rich man was guilty, however, because he ignored the beggar at his gate, did nothing about his destitution, failed to use his affluence to relieve the poor man's need and acquiesced in a situation of gross economic inequality which had dehumanized Lazarus and which he could have remedied. The pariah dogs who licked the poor man's wounds showed more compassion towards him than the rich man. The rich man went to hell not because he had exploited Lazarus, but because of his scandalous indifference and apathy (Luke 16:19 – 21).

Our temptation is to use the complexity of macro-economics as an excuse to do nothing. We need to pray that God will call more of his people to develop new international economic policies, work for political solutions and give their lives in the field of Majority World development, practical philanthropy and evangelism. But these are the callings of only some.

All of us, however, can feel what Jesus felt: the pangs of the hungry, the alienation of the poor and the indignities of the "wretched of the earth". Ultimately, the inequalities between North and South are neither political nor economic but moral problems. Until we feel moral indignation over worldwide social injustice, and compassion for worldwide human suffering, we are not likely to act. What action can we take? We can begin by informing ourselves. As Lazarus lay at the rich man's gate, so the Majority World lies at ours. The rich man could not plead ignorance; nor can we. We should ensure that our daily paper has adequate Majority World coverage, and perhaps subscribe to a magazine devoted to Majority World needs and/or join an organization dedicated to transforming the lives of poor people. We could make friends with somebody from a developing country and perhaps offer for short-term service in a Majority World situation. Self-education of this kind may lead to political agitation. It will also undoubtedly affect our pocket. Those who read this book will all be comparatively rich; they could not afford to buy it otherwise. We should be thankful for the good things God has given us, but also remember the biblical principles of unity and equality. Then we shall give generously to both world development and world evangelization. Our personal commitment to a simpler lifestyle will not, of course, solve the world's economic problems. But it will be an important symbol of Christian obedience, of solidarity with the poor and of our share in the grace of Jesus Christ which induced him to empty himself and take the form of a servant.

NOTES

1 I am indebted to Rev Dr Christopher Wright for pointing out to me that this phrase is not only more accurate but does not contain any connotations of inferiority which may be attached to the idea of some countries being "third" rather than "first". It is also a salutary reminder that we who live in relative wealth are a minority in the world.

2 *North-South: A Programme for Survival*, The Report of the Independent Commission on International Development Issues (1980), p. 64.

3 Ibid., p. 30.

4 More precisely, levels of aid as a percentage of donors' gross national income fell during the 1990s. When ODA (Official Development Assistance) is the aid definition, the percentage of ODA fell during the 1990s, but not the absolute levels, except in 1997. See *www.oecd.org*.

5 The WHO and UNICEF Joint Monitoring Programme for Water Supply and Sanitation (JMP), *Global Water Supply and Sanitation Assessment 2000 Report*.

6 "Chronic Proverty Report 2004 – 05", *www.chronicpoverty.org/resources/cprc_report_2004-2005.html*.

7 United Nations, *Millennium Declaration*, A/RES/55/2, New York, 18 September 2000.

8 More information on the MDGs can be found on the relevant UN website: *www. un.org/millenniumgoals/*.

9 Most notably, Blair, Brown and Clinton, with Schröder in Germany. Their election was a significant shift from the conservative politics and neo-liberal economics of Thatcher and Reagan.

10 United Nations, *The Human Development Report 2004*, p. 129, 135 – 36.

11 *Global Monitoring Report 2005: Millennium Development Goals from Consensus to Momentum* (Washington, DC: World Bank, 2005), p. 2.

12 Remarks by the Rt Hon. Gordon Brown MP, UK Chancellor of the Exchequer, at the launch of the Commission for Africa report at the British Museum, 11 March 2005. See *www.hm-treasury.gov.uk/newsroom_and_speeches/press/2005/press_26_05.cfm*.

13 See the Monterrey Consensus on *www.un.org/esa/ffd/monterrey-consensus-excepts-aconf-198_11.pdf*.

14 *www.unmillenniumproject.org/reports/costs_benefits2.htm*. This first deadline passed. Having fallen from 0.51% as a share of donor GNP in 1960 to 0.33% in 1970, official development assistance reached 0.35% in 1980. By 1990 it was at 0.34% and then fell to

0.23% by 2002, the same year that the 0.7% target was reconfirmed by all countries in the Monterrey Consensus.

15 OECD: *www.oecd.org.*

16 Lack of space precludes consideration of other developments such as the Millennium Challenge Account and the International Finance Facility, although these are also important to the process of realizing the MDGs.

17 Brian Griffiths, "Trade, Aid and Domestic Reform", in Peter Heslam (ed.), *Globalisation and the Good* (London: SPCK, 2004), p. 22.

18 Ibid.

19 See Jubilee Debt Campaign, *www.jubilee2000uk.org/.*

20 Ibid.

21 *www.micahchallenge.org/home/default.asp*

22 4 December 2000, *www.cafod.org.uk.*

23 *www.avert.org*

24 It is not possible to go into the many important questions about HIV/AIDS and its impact in the space available here. Frequently asked questions and answers can be found on the UNAIDS website at *www.unaids.org/en/.*

25 Adults 38,000,000; children under fifteen years 2,300,000.

26 Adults 4,300,000, children under fifteen years 700,000.

27 Adults 2,600,000, children under fifteen years 570,000.

28 Jeffrey Sachs, *The End of Poverty, How we can make it happen in our lifetime* (London: Penguin Books, 2005), p. 204.

29 Ibid., p. 201.

30 Janice A. Hogle (ed.), with contributors: Edward Green, Vinand Nantulya, Rand Stoneburner, John Stover, *What Happened in Uganda?: Declining HIV Prevalence, Behavior Change and National Response* (Washington, DC: USAID, 2002), p. 11. The paper can be found at *www.usaid.gov/our_work/global_health/aids/Countries/africa/uganda_report.pdf.*

31 For a discussion of the importance of ABC STD prevention initiatives, see S. K. Genuis, "Primary Prevention of Sexually Transmitted Disease: Applying the ABC Strategy", *http://pmj.bmjjournals.com.*

32 Hogle (ed.), *What Happened in Uganda?*, p. 11.

33 Patrick Dixon, *The Truth About AIDS* (Eastbourne: Kingsway Communications, 1994), p. 113. See also p. 88 and the whole chapter entitled "Condoms are Unsafe", pp. 110–22.

34 *The Many Faces of AIDS: A Gospel Response* (United States Catholic Conference, 1987), p. 18.

35 Roy McCloughry and Carol Bebawi, *AIDS, A Christian response* (Nottingham: Grove Books, 1987), no. 64, pp. 4, 18. See the theological discussion, "Is AIDS the Judgement of God?", pp. 12–19.

36 Sachs, *The End of Poverty*, p. 215.

37 *The Many Faces of AIDS*, p. 6.

38 World Commission on Environment and Development, *Our Common Future*, pp. 8, 43.

39 See M. P. Todaro, *Economic Development in the Third World* (7th ed., London: Pearson Education, 2000), p. 69.

40 Ibid., pp. 7–19.

41 See Roy McCloughry, *Rights or Wrong, Christian reflections on a human rights approach to development* (Milton Keynes: World Vision, 2003).

42 For example, "Poverty has become feminized to a significant degree", *Christian Faith and the World Economy Today*, a 1992 study document from the World Council of Churches, p. 26.

43 Brian Griffiths, *Morality and the Market Place* (London: Hodder & Stoughton, 1980), p. 127.

44 Ibid., p. 25.

45 Ibid., p. 143.

46 Bryant Myers, *Walking with the Poor: Principles and Practices of Transformational Development* (New York: Orbis Books/World Vision, 2000).

47 Ibid., pp. 14–15.

48 *www.micahchallenge.org/home/intro.asp*

49 Tim Chester (ed.), *Justice, Mercy, and Humility: Integral Mission and the Poor* (Carlisle, Penn.: Paternoster, 2002).

50 I have read that there are at least "five major and often competing development theories". See Todaro, *Economic Development*, pp. 69–95.

51 World Commission on Environment and Development, *Our Common Future*, p. 27.

52 For the same Spirit, see e.g., Romans 8:9; 1 Corinthians 12:13. For different spiritual gifts, see e.g., Romans 12:3–8 and 1 Corinthians 12:4–31.

53 "Gospel and Culture, the Willowbank Report", in Stott (ed.), *Making Christ Known*, pp. 77–113.

54 From a 1967 speech on the Arusha Declaration, published in *Freedom and Socialism, uhuru na ujamaa: A selection from the writings and speeches of Julius Nyerere 1965–1967* (Dar-es-Salaam: Oxford Univ. Press, 1968), p. 326.

55 *www.literacytrust.org.uk/Database/stats/keystatsadult.html*

Human Rights

A lthough the idea that people have value and should be treated with dignity and respect has been with us for thousands of years, it was the twentieth century that used the language of human rights to express this. Human rights describe the kind of life a human being should be able to expect by virtue of being human, rather than rights which people may have by virtue of being citizens of a country or having signed a contract for sale, which are special human rights.

There are many kinds of human rights, but the difference between the two principal groups of rights is illustrated by the situation Mary Robinson found when she became the UN High Commissioner for Human Rights in January 2002. She found that the human rights agenda was a source of disagreement and wrote:

> Listening carefully I discerned two different strands of these complaints. The first alleged that the agenda of human rights amounted to finger-pointing by Western countries, largely at developing countries, for their failure to uphold all civil liberties, and that this was done selectively. The second strand concerned the narrow emphasis of this finger-pointing exercise. Human rights was seen to be largely confined to civil liberties such as fair trial, freedom of expression, association, and religion, and the absence of torture – and ignored economic and social and cultural rights, such as the right to food, to education and to basic health care.[1]

It is important to consider both elements of human rights. Broadly speaking we can say that civil rights are rights to have something not happen to us, such as torture and violence. Economic rights, sometimes called welfare rights, describe a right to have something, such as education or food. The Bible, however, is concerned with poverty *and* oppression, as both are insults to God's intentions for humanity.

FLAGRANT BREACHES OF HUMAN RIGHTS

It is no coincidence that it was in the twentieth century that the idea of human rights came to the fore and found its most potent expression in the signing of the Universal Declaration of Human Rights in 1948. The century had been characterized by extreme violence which had sickened and horrified the world. Two world wars had taken the lives of 60,000,000 people and destroyed the hopes of millions. The world community had witnessed genocide on more than one occasion, with 6,000,000 Jews exterminated in the concentration camps and gas chambers of World War II. The names of Stalin, Idi Amin, Milton Obote, Saddam Hussein or Pol Pot all conjure up sickening pictures of the murder of innocent people.

In many societies, such as Argentina or Iraq, people just "disappeared" never to be seen again. The mass graves of Bosnia or Iraq bear witness to the brutal suppression of human rights in those countries. There are many "forgotten" conflicts which have taken their toll on human rights and human lives. In the Democratic Republic of Congo over the five years to 2003, Amnesty International estimated that 3,000,000 people had lost their lives. Yet the list of places where human rights abuses continue is all too long. Despite its universal condemnation, torture continues to be used in many parts of the world which, as Dr Emilio Castro has written, "kills the human in the torturer, and crushes the personality of the one tortured".[2]

In 1989 the Berlin Wall came down and many in the West thought we were witnessing the dawn of an era of freedom and security for people around the world. There was a wave of democratization as countries which had formerly belonged to the Soviet Union opted for democracy and some became members of the EU. Little did we imagine that in spite of some improvements, the world was about to embark on a decade of widespread human rights abuses, massive continued exploitation of women and children, the re-emergence of blatant genocide, and a growing persecution of Christians.

In Central Africa we have seen ethnic and tribal disputes erupt into what has been described as the "systematic planned and condoned" killing of 500,000 Tutsis in Rwanda in 1994 alone.[3] Moreover, a majority of the Rwandan killings were carried out with clubs or machetes against unarmed citizens, many of whom had gathered together in churches for protection.[4] The story is much the same in the Balkans, where "ethnic cleansing" (a horrible expression) led to severe repression, death and "disappearance". Two top Bosnian Serb leaders, Radovan Karadzic and Ratko Mladic, are accused of having personally seen to the executions of 8,000 Muslims in Serbian territory.

Christians too have been increasingly oppressed in certain parts of the world and are killed each year by governments or mobs because of their faith. They are especially persecuted in Egypt, Sudan, Iran, Indonesia and China, where kidnapping into slavery, torture and church burning are reported to have taken place. In China in 2004, more than 100 Protestant house church leaders were beginning a two-week retreat at Kaifeng City in Henan (central eastern China) when over 200 Public Security Bureau officers appeared. They did not show any arrest warrants or official identification papers, but took the leaders into custody, including some of the children present. This mass arrest was the third of its kind within three months, and although most are usually released, Christian leaders can still face long prison sentences.

In Somalia, being openly Christian can lead to death. Somalia has a long history of hostility towards Christianity. Following independence, church institutions were nationalized and all missionary activity was ended. Severe persecution broke out when the state collapsed after the fall of Siad Barre in 1991. Entire congregations were massacred as the country was increasingly influenced by militant Islamists. In April 2004, Sheikh Nur Barud, vice-chairman of the influential Somali Islamist group Kulanka Culimda, said in an interview with Reuters, "All Somali Christians must be killed according to Islamic law. Such people do not have a place in Somalia and we will never recognize their existence and we will slaughter them."[5]

Faced with such a list of atrocities, we run the risk of selective indignation, as if human rights violations are being perpetrated only by militant ethnic groups, corrupt police and evil dictators. We British need, therefore, to remember with shame that in 1978 the European Court of Human Rights in Strasbourg ruled that the interrogation methods used briefly in 1971 on fourteen IRA terrorist suspects by the Royal Ulster Constabulary violated Article 3 of the European Convention on Human Rights. Although the court cleared Britain of Irish government charges that these techniques amounted to "torture", it nevertheless described them as "inhuman and degrading treatment". The

British government accepted the court's ruling, set up a review committee and implemented the committee's recommendations.

In 2004, speculation that the American and British forces in Iraq were abusing the human rights of the indigenous population became a reality when the conditions in which prisoners were being held at Abu Ghraib prison near Baghdad were exposed. Stories began to circulate of torture, humiliation and the abuse of religious customs of those Muslims in custody. Photographs had been taken of these abuses taking place, and these became available to the general public and were published in newspapers and shown on television and on the internet. Following an enquiry into what happened, it was concluded that there had been a widespread abuse of human rights and some of the participants were court-martialled as a result.

At the same time, there was widespread protest against the conditions in which people were being held in the prison facility at Guantanamo Bay in Cuba. This facility was run by the American government and contained men who had been imprisoned on suspicion that they may have been terrorists and who were arrested during the time of the American involvement in Afghanistan. The protests arose from the fact that those incarcerated at Guantanamo Bay did not have access to due process and some who were released not only said that they were never told what they were being held for, but also alleged that the conditions in which they were held were poor and that interrogation methods were inconsistent with the Geneva Convention.

EMERGENCE OF HUMAN RIGHTS

The concept of human rights has a very long history. Plato and Aristotle wrestled with the notions of freedom and justice, while Thomas Aquinas and other medieval theologians Christianized the thought of the Greeks in terms of "natural rights". Britain looks back gratefully to Magna Carta, which King John was induced to sign in 1215, and which King Henry III reissued ten years later. Among its provisions were the guarantees of freedom for the church and of fair trial by one's peers. Another milestone in British history was the Bill of Rights (1688 – 9) which made the crown subject to parliament.

America and France look back to their revolutions towards the end of the eighteenth century as the time when constitutional rights were secured for their citizens. The American Declaration of Independence (1776), drafted by

Thomas Jefferson, affirmed as "self-evident" that "all men are created equal" and that they "are endowed by their Creator with certain inalienable rights", especially the rights to "life, liberty and the pursuit of happiness". Similar language was used in France's Declaration of the Rights of Man and of Citizens, which was promulgated by its National Assembly in 1789. It speaks of man's "natural, imprescriptible and unalienable rights", or "the natural, inalienable and sacred rights of man". This Declaration was eloquently defended by Thomas Paine in his celebrated book *The Rights of Man* (1791). I shall quote from it presently.

Yet it was World War II, with the horrors of Hitler's savagery and of Japan's brutality, which brought human rights to the top of the world's agenda. In June 1941 President Roosevelt made his famous "State of the Union" speech, in which he looked forward to the emergence of "a world founded upon four essential freedoms" – freedom of speech and expression, the freedom of every person to worship God in his or her own way, freedom from want, and freedom from fear – after each of which he added the words "everywhere in the world".[6]

The United Nations organization was established in 1945. The preamble to its charter reads: "We, the people of the United Nations", are determined "to reaffirm faith in fundamental human rights, in the dignity and worth of the human person, the equal rights of men and women and of nations large and small..." Article 1 speaks of international cooperation "in promoting and encouraging respect for human rights and for fundamental freedoms for all without distinction as to race, sex, language or religion". Article 55 goes further and says that the United Nations shall promote "universal respect for, and observance of, human rights and fundamental freedoms for all without distinction as to race, sex, language or religion".

The following year the United Nations established the Human Rights Commission, under the chairmanship of President Roosevelt's widow Eleanor, charged with the task of preparing a Universal Declaration of Human Rights as the first element in the international Bill of Rights which it had been commissioned to produce. Its preamble affirms that "recognition of the inherent dignity, of the equal and inalienable rights, of all members of the human family, is the foundation of freedom, justice and peace in the world". Article 1 declares that "all human beings are born free and equal in dignity and rights". Article 2 adds that "everyone is entitled to all the rights and freedoms set forth in the Declaration, without distinction of any kind, such as race, colour, sex, language, religion, political or other opinion, national or social origin, property, birth or other status". The first part of the Declaration covers political and civil rights, and the second part economic, social and cultural rights. It was adopted by the UN General Assembly in Paris on 10 December 1948, though not all nations ratified it.

Writing of the late 1940s, while the draft Declaration was being prepared, the late Dr Charles H. Malik, who belonged to the Christian community of Lebanon and was later to become President of the UN General Assembly, wrote: "We believed that nothing was more needful in a world that had just emerged from a most devastating war – devastating not only physically, economically, politically, but above all morally, spiritually, humanly – than to recapture and reaffirm the full integrity of man."[7]

There are now hundreds of covenants, treaties and other documents which protect human rights, whether they are moral, legal or economic in scope.[8] Usually some mechanism is set up to ensure compliance, but in some cases a country may sign up to a convention and yet neglect its responsibilities in practice. However, there is a growing body of international law through which countries, companies and other agencies can be called to account with respect to international human rights. Although signing up to human rights treaties means that a government accepts that how it treats its own people is now a matter of international concern, it is important to hold governments accountable for what they have agreed to. People only enjoy their rights when they are implemented, not when they are promised, and it is, therefore, important that human rights are protected and that they are fully implemented and monitored. If this is not done, the hundreds of documents and dozens of conferences and summit meetings on human rights may add only to a scepticism that what is being agreed will be shelved and ignored or be a matter of empty rhetoric. It is, however, extraordinary that every country in the world has ratified at least one treaty protecting human rights.[9]

THE BIBLICAL FOUNDATIONS OF HUMAN RIGHTS

It is important for Christians to ask whether they have anything distinctive to add to this debate. Some Christians have denied the whole concept of human rights, believing that we only have responsibilities and duties towards one another. Others are concerned that the notion of human rights is becoming so dominant that human responsibilities are diminishing. Yet others believe that the modern notion of human rights contains within it an essential Christian component which it is the duty of the church to preserve and the mission of the church to propagate. In assessing this debate we need to ask some fundamental questions. Where do human rights come from? What do they consist of? If Christians have anything distinctive to contribute, what is it?

It may be good to begin our answers with Thomas Paine. Although he was a deist and, therefore, far from being an orthodox Christian, his father was a Quaker and his mother an Anglican, so that he was still Christian enough in his outlook to know that the rights of man go back to the creation of man. He wrote in 1791:

> The error of those who reason by precedents drawn from antiquity, respecting the rights of man, is that they do not go far enough into antiquity. They do not go the whole way. They stop in some of the intermediate stages of an hundred or a thousand years ... But if we proceed on, we shall at last come out right; we shall come to the time when man came from the hand of his Maker. What was he then? Man. Man was his high and only title, and a higher cannot be given him.[10]

Thomas Paine was correct. The origin of human rights is creation. Human beings have never "acquired" them, nor has any government or other authority conferred them. We have had them from the beginning. We received them with our life from the hand of our Maker. They are inherent in our creation. They have been bestowed on us by our Creator.

This is an important principle to understand, as the relativistic, secular worldview of our postmodern era threatens to leave the traditional human rights community with little ground to stand on in its support of human rights. Gary Haugen, former director of the United Nations' genocide investigation in Rwanda and one-time president of the International Justice Mission, sums up the problem by saying that the human rights movement is rooted in the Judeo-Christian worldview and its commitment to ethical absolutes. With the advent of postmodernity and cultural relativism, this commitment is now adrift. He comments:

> Since World War II, the traditional human rights community has taken a courageous stand for justice out of a passionate moral intuition that is rooted, consciously or not, in the Judeo-Christian commitment to ethical absolutes. The human rights activists of the nineties, however, are the children of a secular philosophy of moral relativism, multiculturalism,

and radical pluralism. Consequently, when push comes to shove in the new disorderly world of the next century, the international human rights movement may find it increasingly difficult to navigate its way without a moral compass, to avoid moral confusion, or to avoid being captured by the political fashion of the day.[11]

Michael Ignatieff, Carr Professor of Human Rights at Harvard University, concurs with this: "Human rights has become the major article of faith of a secular culture that fears it believes in nothing else. It has become the lingua franca of modern thought, as English has become the lingua franca of the global economy."[12]

Ignatieff is concerned that in the absence of moral absolutes, human rights might become a kind of secular religion, the ultimate frame of reference for moral problems globally. At the outset of an article on human rights as idolatry, he comments:

> Human rights is misunderstood, I shall argue, if it is seen as a secular religion. It is not a creed; it is not a metaphysics. To make it so is to turn it into a species of idolatry: humanism worshipping itself. Elevating the moral and metaphysical claims made on behalf of human rights may be intended to increase its universal appeal. In fact, it has the opposite effect, raising doubts among religious and non-Western groups who do not happen to be in need of Western secular creeds.[13]

So those people who have a religious faith will look to their fundamental religious teachings for their views on human rights, whether those teachings are found in the Koran or the Bible, for instance. This is one of the reasons why Muslims have sometimes had problems with the Universal Declaration of Human Rights. For some of them there is nothing universal about the language of the Declaration. It is rooted in the language and philosophy of the West and its emphasis on individualism and human autonomy. Indeed, when the Universal Declaration was drafted in 1947 the Saudi Arabian delegation raised particular objection to Article 16 on free marriage choice and Article 18 relating to freedom of religion. Such criticisms are still encountered from time to time in the relationship between Islam and Western human rights.

Wanting to be protected from abuse or have access to legal redress or education does not imply that you need to become Western in your dress, language or attitude. Michael Ignatieff says of this:

The women in Kabul who come to Western human rights agencies seeking their protection from the Taliban militias do not want to cease being Muslim wives and mothers; they want to combine respect for their traditions with an education and professional health care provided by a woman. They hope the agencies will defend them against being beaten and persecuted for claiming such rights.[14]

It is important, then, to be cross-cultural in our discussion over human rights. On the one hand, we cannot succumb to cultural relativism which may allow a nation to escape its human rights commitments because of its claim to have a different culture. But, on the other hand, we cannot impose the values of our own Western culture on the rest of the world. What the West thinks of as universal, the rest of the world may think of as Western and should feel quite free to be critical of it.

Human rights language is a moral language in that it is an attempt to describe the right and the good. But it is also a political language. Appealing to human rights does not end a debate. More often than not it starts a debate. Human rights do not represent a moral trump card. There is a need for some moral framework beyond human rights from which they can derive their authority and which provides their foundation. Without that framework they exist in a moral vacuum and are in danger of becoming self-referential.

The nature of human rights depends on our concept of what it means to be human. Why should people not be tortured? Why are we concerned that people be fed and educated? What is it about being human that demands our attention whenever others live in misery? Yet, in the twenty-first century, human rights do not only come into sharp focus when people are threatened or denied the means to live with an adequate quality of life. They are also essential to understand when we propose to create human life. For this reason, human rights are also at the heart of the debates on cloning and genetic engineering. Since the Bible focuses on the divine purpose for human beings, it has much to say on this topic. Three words seem to summarize it: "dignity", "equality" and "responsibility".

Human dignity

The dignity of human beings is asserted in three successive sentences in Genesis 1:27 – 28, which we have already examined in relation to the environment.

Firstly, "God created man in his own image." Secondly, "Male and female he created them." Thirdly, "God blessed them and said to them, '...fill the earth and subdue it.'" Human dignity is here seen to consist of three unique relationships which God established for us by creation, which together constitute a large part of our humanness, and which the fall distorted but did not destroy.

The first is our relationship to God. Human beings are godlike beings, created by God's will in his image. The divine image includes those rational, moral and spiritual qualities which express something of who God is. In consequence, we can learn about him from evangelists or teachers (it is a basic human right to hear the gospel); come to know, love and serve him; live in conscious, humble dependence upon him; understand his will and obey his commands. So then, all those human rights we call the freedom to profess, practise and propagate religion, the freedom of worship, of conscience, of thought and of speech, come under this first rubric of our relationship to God. It is striking that even the deistic leaders of the American and French Revolutions knew this instinctively. As we saw earlier, the American Declaration of Independence (1776) famously proclaimed: "We hold these truths to be self-evident: that all men are created equal, that they are endowed by their Creator with certain inalienable rights, that among these are life, liberty and the pursuit of happiness."[15]

The second unique capacity of human beings concerns our relationship to one another. The God who made humankind is himself a social being, one God comprising three eternally distinct modes of personhood. He said, "Let us make man in our image," and "It is not good for the man to be alone." So God made man male and female, and told them to procreate. Sexuality is his creation, marriage his institution and human companionship his purpose. So then, all those human freedoms which we call the sanctity of sex, marriage and family, the right of peaceful assembly, and the right to receive respect, whatever our age, sex, race or rank, come under this second rubric of our relationship to each other.

Our third distinctive quality as human beings is our relationship to the earth and its creatures. God has given us dominion, with instructions to subdue and cultivate the fruitful earth and to rule its creatures. So then, all those human rights we call the right to work and the right to rest, the right to share in the earth's resources, the right to food, clothing and shelter, the right to life and health and to their preservation, together with freedom from poverty, hunger and disease, come under this third rubric of our relationship to the earth.

In spite of the oversimplification, we may sum up what is meant by human dignity in these three ways: our relationship to God (or the right and responsibility of worship), our relationship to each other (or the right and responsibility of fellowship), and our relationship to the earth (or the right and responsibility of stewardship) – together, of course, with the opportunity which our education, income and health provide to develop this unique human potential.

Thus all human rights are at base the right to be human, and so to enjoy the dignity of having been created in God's image and of possessing in consequence unique relationships to God himself, to our fellow human beings and to the material world. Christians have something important to add to this, namely that our Creator has also redeemed or re-created us, at great personal cost, through the incarnation and atonement of his Son. And the costliness of God's redeeming work reinforces the sense of human worth which his creation has already given us. William Temple expressed this truth with his customary clarity:

> There can be no Rights of Man except on the basis of faith in God. But if God is real, and all men are his sons, that is the true worth of every one of them. My worth is what I am worth to God; and that is a marvellous great deal, for Christ died for me. Thus, incidentally, what gives to each of us his highest worth gives the same worth to everyone; in all that matters most we are all equal.[16]

Our value depends, then, on God's view of us and relationship to us. As a result of this, human rights are not unlimited rights, as if we were free to be and do absolutely anything we like. They are limited to what is compatible with being the human person God made us and meant us to be. As one writer has commented, "If God has not given something as a right, then it cannot be claimed as a right and it is this that may cause Christians to be at odds with those who root human rights in the Western ideal of the autonomous individual who has freedom to choose their own goals."[17] True freedom is found in being our true selves as authentic human beings, not in contradicting ourselves. That is why it has been essential to define "human being" before defining "human rights". This principle is important in considering "women's rights" and "gay rights". The question these demands pose is how far feminism and homosexual practices are compatible with the humanness God has created and intends to safeguard, and these topics are discussed in chapters 12 and 16.

There is no situation in which it is permissible to forget the dignity of human beings by creation, and their consequent right to respect. Convicted criminals may justly be deprived of their freedom during a period of imprisonment, but the right to incarcerate does not imply the right to inflict solitary confinement on prisoners, or to treat them inhumanly in other ways. I am thankful for the work of Prison Fellowship International, founded by Charles Colson after his personal experience of the brutalizing effects of incarceration. Prison Fellowship now has more than 100,000 volunteers working in over seventy-five countries with inmates who have been deprived of liberty by a court, but may not be deprived of other rights. "I was in prison," Jesus said, "and you visited me."

Before moving on to human equality, it is important to note that although we may be committed to human dignity as foundational to the notion of human rights, it is sometimes the case that we imperfectly discern the practices and traditions which constitute dignity. Michael Ignatieff is aware of this problem; he points to the way in which different cultures express the idea of dignity and the way in which this is itself culturally relative. Although he affirms the notion of "ultimate respect", he says:

> While I concede this point, I still have a difficulty about dignity. There are many forms and expressions of human dignity and some of them strike me as profoundly inhumane. Rituals of sexual initiation, like genital cutting, for example, are linked to an idea of womanly dignity and worth. Likewise, ultra-Orthodox Judaism imposes a role on women that secular women find oppressive but that religious women find both fulfilling and respectful of their dignity. So ideas of dignity that are supposed to unite different cultures in some shared attachment to human rights actually divide us. There is no easy way round the culturally specific and relative character of the idea of dignity.[18]

So we cannot accept the practices of others' cultures (or our own) unconditionally. In affirming the importance of human dignity, we must be careful to have the highest standards and ensure that nothing we do in any way dehumanizes those with whom we live and work. In saying this, Christians must be aware that in many centuries it was the church that on the one hand claimed to portray the gospel, but on the other sanctioned practices which dehumanized people and even tortured them in the name of the Christian faith. Our desire to promote human dignity in all aspects of human life must begin at our own front door.

Human equality

It is a tragedy that "human rights" have not always meant "equal rights". The good gifts of the Creator are spoiled by human selfishness. The rights God gave to all human beings equally, easily degenerate into "my rights" on which I insist, irrespective of the rights of others or of the common good. So the history of the world has been the story of conflict between my rights and yours, between the good of each and the good of all, between the individual and the community. Indeed, it is when human rights are in conflict with one another that we are presented with a difficult ethical dilemma. It may be the tension between an individual landowner's right to property and peace on the one hand, and the community's need for a new motorway or airport on the other; or between the freedom of speech and assembly which a civil rights group claims for its demonstration and the freedom which the local inhabitants claim not to have their quiet disturbed or their patience exhausted.

The conflict of rights regularly envisaged in the Bible, however, takes a rather different form. Its emphasis is that no powerful individuals may impose their will on the community, and that no community may violate the rights of an individual or minority. The weak and vulnerable were carefully protected by the Mosaic law. Far from exploiting them, God's people were to be the voice of the voiceless and the champion of the powerless, including their enemies. Paul Oestreicher has put it well:

> When the electrodes are turned on, the torture victim suffers equally when the "security" think they are saving free enterprise from the revolution or the revolution from reaction ... My own commitment is neither to liberalism nor to Marxism, but to a curious idea put about by a carpenter turned dissident preacher in Palestine that the test of our humanity is to be found in how we treat our enemies ... A society's maturity and humanity will be measured by the degree of dignity it affords to the disaffected and the powerless.[19]

The equality of human beings is clearly expressed when the Authorized Version of the Bible says that God is "no respecter of persons". It is a misleading phrase, because of course persons must at all costs be respected. But what the original Greek expression means literally is "no acceptance of faces". In other words, we must show "no partiality" in our attitude to other people, and give no special deference to some because they are rich, famous or influential. The biblical authors attach real importance to this. Moses declared, for example: "The LORD your God is God of gods and Lord of lords, the great God, mighty and awesome, who shows no partiality..." Therefore Israelite judges were to show no partiality either, but rather give justice "to small and great alike" (Deuteronomy 10:17; 1:16 – 17; cf. 16:18 – 19).

The same emphasis occurs in the New Testament. God is the impartial Judge. He does not regard external appearances or circumstances. He shows no favouritism, whatever our racial or social background may be (e.g., Acts 10:34; Romans 2:11; 1 Peter 1:17). Jesus was once described (perhaps in flattery, but still with accuracy) in these terms: "Teacher, we know you are a man of integrity. You aren't swayed by men, because you pay no attention to who they are" (Mark 12:14). That is, he neither deferred to the rich and powerful, nor despised the poor and weak, but gave equal respect to all, whatever their social status. We must do the same.[20]

I rather think the best illustration of this principle is to be found in the book of Job. It is Job's final appeal for justice, after his three comforters have at last stopped their unfair, unkind, untrue accusations. Job clings to his innocence, while at the same time acknowledging that God is a just judge. If he has broken God's laws (by immorality, idolatry or oppression), then indeed let God's judgement fall upon him. He continues:

> If I have denied justice to my menservants and maidservants
>> when they had a grievance against me,
> what will I do when God confronts me?
>> What will I answer when called to account?
> Did not he who made me in the womb make them?
> Did not the same one form us both within our mothers?

JOB 31:13 – 15

Job continues in a similar vein with reference to the poor and needy, widows and orphans. We have equal rights because we have the same Creator. Both the dignity and the equality of human beings are traced in Scripture to our creation.

This principle should be even more obvious in the New Testament community, since we have the same Saviour also. Paul regulates the behaviour of masters and slaves to each other by reminding both that they have the same heavenly master, and that "there is no favouritism with him" (Ephesians 6:9;

cf. Colossians 3:25). James seeks to banish class distinctions from public worship by urging that there must be no "favouritism" between rich and poor among believers in Jesus Christ (James 2:1 – 9). Yet the same truth is self-evident among unbelievers. Our common humanity is enough to abolish favouritism and privilege, and to establish equal status and rights. All human rights violations contradict the equality we enjoy by creation. "He who oppresses the poor shows contempt for their Maker" (Proverbs 14:31). If God shows, and if we should show, a "bias to the poor" (as is now often claimed, and as we considered in chapter 6), and if such bias is not an infringement of the "no favouritism" rule, it must be justified either because society as a whole is biased against them, or because they have no one else to champion them.

The fact that "there is no favouritism with God" is the foundation of the biblical tradition of prophetic protest. The prophets were courageous in denouncing tyranny in leaders, especially in the kings of Israel and Judah. The fact that they were monarchs, and even "the Lord's anointed", did not make them immune to criticism and rebuke. To be sure, due respect was to be shown to rulers because of their office, but any attempts on their part to convert authority into tyranny or rule into despotism were to be strenuously resisted. David was the best known of all the kings of Israel, but that gave him no warrant to kill Uriah and steal his wife Bathsheba; God sent the prophet Nathan to rebuke him. When Ahab was king in Samaria, his wife Jezebel thought his power was absolute. "Do you not govern Israel?" she asked contemptuously, when she found him sulking because Naboth had refused to sell him his vineyard. God sent Elijah to denounce Ahab's later murder of Naboth and seizure of his property. Jehoiakim was king of Judah in the seventh century BC, yet he had no right to build himself a luxurious palace by forced labour. "Woe to you," cried Jeremiah. "Does it make you a king to have more and more cedar?" The prophet then reminded him of his father Josiah. "He did what was right and just, so all went well with him. He defended the cause of the poor and needy, and so all went well ... But your eyes and your heart are set only on dishonest gain, on shedding innocent blood and on oppression and extortion." No one would lament him when he died, Jeremiah added; he would have the burial of a donkey and would be dragged away and thrown outside the gates of Jerusalem.[21]

In our day dictators try to defend arbitrary arrest and detention, and even imprisonment or execution without public trial, on the ground of "national security". One wonders how a biblical prophet would react. Protest or denunciation within the country concerned would doubtless cost the prophet his life. Yet history has many examples of people who stood up against injustice and suffered the consequences as a result, which in some cases included torture and martyrdom. Today we are not only fortunate in the growth of a consensus as to what is acceptable behaviour in terms of international law, but several organizations now have as their main aim the scrutiny of the behaviour of governments, corporations and other agencies with reference to human rights. Here I am thinking of organizations such as Amnesty International, Human Rights Watch, Christian Solidarity Worldwide, International Justice Mission[22] and Barnabas Fund[23] which, although they may have different agendas, give a high profile to abuses of human rights throughout the world.[24] Such work is consistent with biblical precedent and with the recognition that with God "there is no favouritism".[25] Human rights are both universal and equal.

Human responsibility

Christians often have problems with the concept of human rights. It seems to suggest conflict, as one person is asserting his or her rights against another. It seems also to encourage selfishness. It overlooks the fact that human beings have duties and responsibilities as well as rights. In 1989 Solzhenitsyn called for this balance to be redressed. "During these 300 years of Western Civilization, there has been a sweeping away of duties and an expansion of rights. But we have two lungs. You can't breathe with just one lung and not with the other. We must avail ourselves of rights and duties in equal measure."[26] Let me try, then, to clarify the relationship between rights and responsibilities.

The Bible says much about defending other people's rights, but little about defending our own. On the contrary, when it addresses us, it emphasizes our responsibilities, not our rights. We are to love God and to love our neighbour. These primary requirements comprise our whole duty, for "all the Law and the Prophets hang on these two commandments," Jesus said (Matthew 22:40).

The link between seeing others as our neighbour and taking action on their behalf is clear within Scripture. What is also clear is that such action is not always a matter of our generosity but of their human rights. Nicholas Wolterstorff says, "Our concern with poverty is not an issue of generosity but of rights. If a rich man knows of someone who is starving and has the power to help that person but chooses not to do so, then he violates the starving person's rights as surely and reprehensibly as if he had physically assaulted the sufferer."[27]

In fact, what the Bible contains, as Dr Christopher Wright has written, is a "Universal Declaration of Human Responsibilities" (especially in terms of loving God and neighbour), not of human rights.[28] As he further comments, "It is not so much the case that I am under obligation *to* my fellow human beings as that I am under obligation to God *for* my fellow human beings."[29] Within a Christian worldview, people have rights because God requires others to do certain things for them. Not to do them is to perpetrate injustice and to disobey God. It goes far beyond secular concepts of human rights, bringing together love and justice with responsibility to God and realizing that the consequences of this are not restricted to the behaviour of governments but will have personal consequences as well.[30]

The Bible is radical in this respect. It emphasizes that our responsibility is to secure the other person's rights. We must even forgo our own rights in order to do so. Of this responsible renunciation of rights, Jesus Christ is the supreme model. Although eternally "in very nature God", he "did not consider equality with God something to be grasped, but made himself nothing, taking the very nature of a servant, being made in human likeness" (Philippians 2:6 – 7). Throughout his life he was a victim of abuses of human rights. He became a refugee baby in Egypt, a prophet without honour in his own country and the Messiah rejected by the religious establishment of his own people to whom he had come. He became a prisoner of conscience, refusing to compromise in order to secure his release. He was falsely accused, unjustly condemned, brutally tortured and finally crucified. And throughout his ordeal he declined to defend or demand his rights, in order that by his self-sacrifice he might serve ours.

"Let this mind be in you, which was also in Christ Jesus," wrote Paul (Philippians 2:5 AV). And Paul practised what he preached. He had rights as an apostle (the right to marry, the right to receive financial support), but he renounced them for the sake of the gospel, in order to become everybody's slave and so serve their rights (see, e.g., 1 Corinthians 9).

The renunciation of rights, however unnatural and idealistic it may seem, is an essential characteristic of God's new society. In the world outside people assert their own rights and exercise authority. "Not so with you," Jesus said. On the contrary, in his community those aspiring after greatness must become servants, the leader the slave, and the first last. Love "is not self-seeking", Paul wrote. This fundamental stance, learned from Jesus, applies in every situation. For example, believers should not prosecute one another, especially in an unbelieving court. Christian litigation was a scandal in Corinth; it still is in India, Pakistan, Sri Lanka and other countries. Christians should at the very least settle their own disputes. Better still, "Why not rather be wronged? Why not rather be cheated?" Is this not the way of Christ? Another first-century application was to Christian slaves with cruel masters. What if they were unjustly beaten? They must bear it patiently, following in the footsteps of Jesus, who did not retaliate, but entrusted himself and his cause to the just Judge of all.[31] This last point, that the non-retaliation of Jesus was accompanied by a commitment of himself to God, is an important addition. To renounce rights is not to acquiesce in wrongs. The reason we do not judge is that this is God's prerogative, not ours (Romans 12:19). Besides, Christ is coming back, and then all evil will be judged, and justice finally and publicly vindicated.

Here, then, is a Christian perspective on human rights. Firstly, we affirm human dignity. Because human beings are created in God's image to know him, serve one another and be stewards of the earth; therefore, they must be respected. Secondly, we affirm human equality. Because human beings have all been made in the same image by the same Creator; therefore, we must not be obsequious to some and scornful to others, but behave without partiality to all. Thirdly, we affirm human responsibility. Because God has laid it upon us to love and serve our neighbours; therefore, we must fight for their rights, while being ready to renounce our own in order to do so.[32]

Two main conclusions follow. Firstly, we have to accept that other people's rights are our responsibility. We are our brother's keeper, because God has put us in the same human family and so made us related to and responsible for one another. The law and the prophets, Jesus and his apostles, all lay on us a particular duty to serve the poor and defend the powerless. We cannot escape this by saying they are not our responsibility. To quote Solzhenitsyn again, "There are no internal affairs left on this globe of ours. Mankind can be saved only if everybody takes an interest in everybody else's affairs."[33] We need, then, to feel the pain of those who suffer oppression. "Remember those in prison as if you were their fellow-prisoners, and those who are mistreated as if you yourselves were suffering" (Hebrews 13:3). In order to do this, we may need to inform ourselves more thoroughly about contemporary violations of human rights.[34] Then whatever action we may believe it right to take, we need to ensure that the methods we use do not infringe the very human rights we are seeking to champion.

Secondly, we have to take more seriously Christ's intention that the Christian community should set an example to other communities. I am not thinking only of our Christian conduct at home and work, in which as husbands and wives, parents or children, employers or employees we are to be submissive to one another out of reverence for Christ (Ephesians 5:21). I am thinking particularly of the life of the local church, which is meant to be a sign of God's rule. The church should be the one community in the world in which human dignity and equality are invariably recognized, and people's responsibility for one another is accepted; in which the rights of others are sought and never violated, while our own are often renounced; in which there is no partiality, favouritism or discrimination; in which the poor and the weak are defended, and human beings are free to be human as God made them and meant them to be.

An exciting new initiative in the United States gives an excellent example of how Christians can become involved in defending the rights of others. In November 1994 a study was commissioned to examine the need for "a specialized Christian ministry that could help people overseas who suffer injustice and abuse in circumstances where local authorities cannot be relied upon for relief".[35]

Eighteen months of extensive research and consultation provided overwhelming evidence that overseas Christian workers all over the world were regularly observing human rights abuses in situations where the local authorities could not be counted on to provide relief. It also showed that the existence of a faith-based ministry with the professional expertise to document human rights abuses and to intervene on behalf of victims without putting missionaries and their agencies in compromising positions was not only a welcome idea but an absolute need. It was in response to this that the International Justice Mission was founded and has begun to work with overseas ministries to support the rights of all people, Christian and non-Christian, in the face of abuse and oppression. Most recently, the IJM's attention has been drawn to cases of child sexual exploitation in Asia, land expropriations in Latin America and detentions without charge or trial in Africa. In such cases, the IJM is seeking to bring to bear professional expertise in documenting the abuses and securing appropriate relief for the victims. Initiatives like this indicate to the world that Christians take seriously our commitment to the needs and rights of others.

CAMPAIGNING FOR HUMAN RIGHTS

It is important, then, that Christians are not only aware of abuses of human rights but actively campaign against them. Slavery is rife today in many forms, whether it is the sexual trafficking of women, forced or bonded labour, child labour or forced marriage. There are three, often powerless, groups for whom we have a special concern, which are children, women and people with disabilities. In each case we are not talking about a group having rights which are only applicable to them. We are talking about each group being denied fundamental human rights which should be universal.

Children's rights

When we look at the global picture of children's rights, we see hundreds of thousands of children having their rights abused on a daily basis. I have talked about child soldiers, for instance, in chapter 4. But many children are not even safe in their own homes. In Latin America, for instance, there are 185,000,000 children and adolescents in the region. No fewer than 6,000,000 are subjected to severe aggression, while another 80,000 are killed every year in the "safety" of their own homes. In fact, of the top ten countries with the highest child murder rates, seven are in Latin America.[36] In Brazil, according to World Vision International, it is estimated that 3% of children under the age of eighteen sell themselves for sex (approximately 2,000,000 in any given year). One third of the 50,000 prostitutes in Cambodia are under eighteen years old. The problem of AIDS worldwide becomes especially poignant when one realizes that 1,000,000 children work in the Asian sex trade. Yet such exploitation is not only present in the developing world. It is estimated that nearly 4,000 children work as prostitutes in Australia.[37] And 10,000,000 children in the world work as domestic servants.

Recently, the use of child labour in factories making luxury goods for the Western market has been highlighted by Western investigative journalism. Child labour is a pressing problem throughout the world. Anti-Slavery International estimates that the worst forms of child labour place 179,000,000 children in work that is harmful to their health and welfare. Children are most vulnerable when families or communities are living in poverty with a need for income. If they cannot find work in a sector which is monitored, then they may slip from sight into exploitative labour. It is these kinds of issues which must spur the church on to include effective advocacy on behalf of child rights as a priority.

It was this that led to the drafting of the UN Convention on the Rights of the Child (CRC), the most rapidly accepted human rights convention. Some Christians see this convention as being anti-family and overempowering of children, but the convention places the well-being of children at the heart of family life, saying that a happy family environment is essential for the child's "full and harmonious development". It also clearly affirms the rights of parents. As we have seen, the flagrant disregard of children's rights makes it essential that there are universal norms to which governments and other agencies can be held to account for their treatment of children. For the first time the CRC gives special attention to the needs of refugee children (Article 22); children with disabilities (Article 23); ethnic minority children or children of indigenous origin (Article 30); working children (Article 32); children who are victims of sexual, physical or other forms of abuse (Articles 34 and 36); children in war and armed conflicts (Article 39); and children in conflict with the law (Articles 37 and 40).[38] Yet it is also essential that such a convention is based on a biblical understanding of the nature of humanity, the family, and the value of children in our world.

Women's rights

One of the slogans of the 1990s was "Women's rights are human rights". If human rights are not universal then they are not human, yet for many thousands of years women have not enjoyed their rights and at the outset of the twenty-first century it is still the case that millions of women are abused and oppressed throughout the world. This contravenes the twin principles of equality and non-discrimination which are at the heart of human rights.

It was as long ago as 1792 that Mary Wollstonecraft published *A Vindication of the Rights of Woman*, arguing that it is not charity that is needed for women, but justice.[39] Since then many countries around the world have changed their policies in order to increase the equality between men and women. However, a substantial amount of discrimination still remains, and this led the UN to adopt the Convention on the Elimination of Discrimination Against Women (CEDAW) in 1979, which came into force in 1981. The 165 states which ratified CEDAW undertook to eliminate discrimination against women in all fields, to take affirmative action and to suppress all forms of traffic in women. It also affirmed their right to vote and their eligibility for election, and affirmed the importance of their participation in government policy and in holding public office. In many parts of the world women are a low priority when it comes to expenditure on education, employment and health care, but CEDAW addresses these issues, calling its signatories to bring gender equity in these areas. Lastly it covers civil and family rights, providing for equality before the law and elimination of discrimination in all matters relating to marriage and family relations. As in other human rights conventions, nation states have four duties: to respect, protect, promote and to ensure realization.[40] In other words, they are to place the dignity and value of women at the heart of their policies and to do everything in their power to protect and promote their human rights.

Disability rights

It is estimated that there are approximately 600,000,000 people with disabilities in the world today.[41] If all those people with disabilities lived in one country it would be the poorest in the world, because they are the poorest of the poor, the world's most powerless people, with women and children with disabilities being the most powerless. The vast majority of them, around 80%, live in developing countries where few have access to the necessary rehabilitation services. When their careers and families are also taken into account, disability affects a large number of people throughout the world. Disability is not just about impaired bodies – it is also about the need for empowerment, advocacy and human rights.[42] One of the key issues over recent decades has been a shift in the perception of disabled people by the community and the transformation of disabled people's view of themselves. All too often disabled people are seen as passive, dependent and non-contributors to the community. They are consumers of the community's resources rather than contributors to its life. Yet gradually this has changed. As Abdul Rahman Sahak from the Free Welfare Society for Afghan Disabled has said, "Disability is not inability, charity is not the solution to our problems. We need equality, and our rights as human beings in all sectors of life. Disabled people have much to contribute." [43]

The emphasis of what has come to be known as the "disability movement" is on organizations run by disabled people for disabled people as well as on disability rights. One of their popular slogans is "Nothing about us without us". Rather than seeing disability primarily as a medical issue, they see it as a social issue. It is society that needs to adjust to the needs of disabled people, rather than disabled people who need to be adjusted to live in a non-disabled society. The "disability rights movement" campaigns for changes in access to buildings, health care, political priorities and even language. Their agenda is controversial and their anger often palpable, but they are seeking to draw attention to the fact that all too often they have been denied their human rights and in some cultures and periods of history even denied their humanity.

In this area, as in many others, we need to remind ourselves that we cannot just accept the secular arguments of those who believe in human rights. We need to bring each idea to Scripture and ensure that it is consistent with Christian thinking. It is only by doing this that Christians can maintain their distinctiveness. The Christian vision of dignity, equality and responsibility means that we should surely put our weight behind such campaigns where they seek to highlight the value of each person made in the image of God. The church is rightly concerned about ending poverty and oppression wherever it is found, and empowering those who are poor and powerless to live as God intended.

NOTES

1 Mary Robinson, "Ethics, Human Rights and Ethical Globalisation", Second Global Ethic Lecture, the Global Ethic Foundation (University of Tübingen, Germany), 21 January 2002.

2 From the editorial by Emilio Castro in *International Review of Mission*, vol. LXVI, no. 263, devoted to "Human Rights" (July 1977), p. 218.

3 Amnesty International Annual Report 1995, p. 249.

4 Gary Haugen, "Rwanda's Carnage", in *Christianity Today*, 6 February 1995, pp. 52 – 54.

5 *Response*, October 2004, issue 131, pp. 4 – 5 (China) and p. 13 (Somalia). *Response* is the magazine of Christian Solidarity Worldwide – *www.csw.org.uk*.

6 The most handy collection of these texts is Ian Brownie (ed.), *Basic Documents on Human Rights* (2nd ed., Oxford: Clarendon, 1981).

7 From Dr Malik's introduction to O. Frederick Nolde, *Free and Equal: Human Rights in Ecumenical Perspective* (Geneva: WCC, 1968), p. 7.

8 For a description of the main treaties and covenants which cover international human rights, go to *www.un.org*.

9 Robert McCorquodale, "Contemporary Human Rights and Christianity", a paper delivered to the Shaping the Christian Mind Conference, Sydney, Australia, in July 1996.

10 Thomas Paine, *The Rights of Man* (1791), 8th ed., pp. 47 – 48.

11 From personal communication to the author.

12 Michael Ignatieff, *Human Rights as Politics and Idolatry* (Princeton, N. J.: Princeton Univ. Press, 2001), p. 53.

13 Ibid.
14 Michael Ignatieff, *The Warrior's Honour, Ethnic war and the modern conscience* (London: Vintage, 1995), pp. 55 – 69.
15 *www.constitution.org/usdeclar.htm*
16 William Temple, *Citizen and Churchman* (London: Eyre & Spottiswoode, 1941), pp. 74 – 75.
17 McCloughry, *Rights or Wrong*, p. 9.
18 Ignatieff, *Human Rights as Politics and Idolatry*, p. 164.
19 Paul Oestreicher, *Thirty Years of Human Rights* (The British Churches' Advisory Forum on Human Rights, 1980).
20 In contemporary discussions of human rights, the phrase "non-discrimination" is often used, and equality and non-discrimination are often seen as essential to any notion of human rights worth the name.
21 The prophetic protest against these three kings is found in 2 Samuel 11 – 12 (Nathan and David); 1 Kings 21 (Elijah and Ahab); and Jeremiah 22:13 – 19 (Jeremiah and Jehoiakim).
22 *www.ijm.org*
23 *www.barnabasfund.org*
24 Websites for the other three organizations mentioned here are: *www.amnesty.org*; *www.hrw.org/*; *www.csw.org.uk/*.
25 However, Christians are sometimes uncomfortable with the agenda of human rights organizations. I am thinking specifically of gay rights in this context and will deal with this in the chapter on same-sex relationships.
26 From an interview published in *TIME* magazine, 24 July 1989.
27 Nicholas Wolterstorff, *Until Justice and Peace Embrace* (Grand Rapids: Eerdmans, 1983), p. 82, quoted in McCorquodale, "Contemporary Human Rights and Christianity", p. 11.
28 Christopher J. H. Wright, *Human Rights: A Study in Biblical Themes*, Grove Booklet on Ethics no. 31 (Cambridge: Grove Books, 1979), p. 16.
29 Christopher J. H. Wright, *Walking in the Ways of the Lord, The ethical authority of the Old Testament* (Leicester: Apollos, 1995), p. 251.
30 McCloughry, *Rights or Wrong*.
31 For this renunciation of rights, see Mark 10:42 – 45 ("not so with you"); 1 Corinthians 13:5 (love); 1 Corinthians 6:1 – 8 (litigation); and 1 Peter 2:18 – 25 (slaves).
32 Christians will, of course, wish to assert their right to come together for worship and not be persecuted. However, the existence of persecution does not stop churches from meeting and taking the consequences of doing so, as I have already discussed with respect to the church in China and similar countries.
33 Nobel Prize speech, 1970.
34 For information about human rights violations in general, and about imprisonment and torture in general, write to Amnesty International, 1 Easton Street, London WC1X 8DJ, UK, or visit their website at *www.amnesty.org*.
35 "A Christian Witness for Justice, a Needs Assessment and Operational Outline" (November 1996, p. 1), conducted by the International Justice Mission, PO Box 58147, Washington, DC, 20037-8147, USA; or on the internet at *www.ijm.org*.

36 Figures from UNICEF, "Stop Violence against Women and Girls", 1999. Cited in World Vision, *Faces of Violence in Latin America and the Caribbean* (Monrovia, Calif.: World Vision International, 2002), p. 10.

37 World Vision International, *Protecting Children: A Biblical Perspective on Child Rights* (Monrovia, Calif.: World Vision International, 2002), pp. 20, 22.

38 *Here We Stand, World vision and child rights* (Milton Keynes: World Vision UK, 2002).

39 Cf. *Human Development Report 2000* (New York: United Nations Publications, 2000), p. 32, box 2.1, "The Long Struggle for Women's Rights".

40 Julia Häusermann, *Rights and Humanity, A human rights approach to development* (London: Rights and Humanity, 1998), pp. 76 – 79.

41 It is only recently that attempts to measure disability worldwide have become more rigorous, since it is difficult to aggregate statistics from different countries which may have diverging definitions of disability. Estimates vary from 550,000,000 to 650,000,000 people. Cf. *www.un.org* and *www.who.int/en/*.

42 Roy McCloughry and Wayne Morris, *Making a World of Difference: Christian Reflections on Disability* (London: SPCK, 2002), p. 1.

43 Quoted in Ibid., p. 2.

PART THREE

SOCIAL
ISSUES

The World of Work

Work occupies such a significant place in most people's lives, that as Christians we must learn how to think Christianly about it.[1] We need to learn to celebrate it as a gift from God, protest against unjust and oppressive practices where they exist and call people to work with integrity, in a working world which is often compromised. In some parts of the world there is little prospect of productive paid employment, since the country is on the rack of civil war, famine or other forms of abject poverty. Where paid employment is available, it comes in many forms. The shoeshine boy on the streets of Nairobi, the call-centre worker in Bangalore, the oil worker in Siberia, the child labourer in Beijing, the exploitative entrepreneur in Kiev, the barrister in London and the teacher in Memphis are all working in some sense. Some are oppressed by what they are doing, others are the source of oppression; still others are contributing creatively to the community by using the gifts they have been given, however modest. Such diverse experience causes us to ask, what did God originally intend work to be, and what should it be today?

Now please let me say it before you think it: a clergyman is the last person in the world to write about work. For, as everybody knows, he has not done an honest day's work in his life. As the old saying goes, he is "six days invisible and one day incomprehensible"! Some years ago I was travelling by train in South Wales when a rather drunk communist miner entered my compartment. When he discovered that I was a pastor, he treated me to a lecture on work: "It's time you became productive, man; you're a parasite on the body politic."

He knew that I was in employment, but did not think that it was "real work". It is also important, however, to point out the opposite, which is that not all work is employment. Many people are rightly sensitive when the impression

217

is given that if a person is not being paid for their efforts then their activities do not constitute work. Nothing could be further from the truth. Many people work in the home, and contribute to voluntary work and to the care of children and other dependents. Such work can be arduous yet go unnoticed. Many people who are "retired" work just as hard in voluntary work as they once did when in paid employment. Indeed, the work of those who are not paid is such a contribution to society that we depend on people being willing to do it just as much as we depend on people being willing to work in paid employment. Certainly the work of the church depends, overwhelmingly, on the willingness of people to give their time voluntarily in the service of God.

Thinking about work is especially important now, as the way we work is being changed by the advent of new technologies and people are attempting to renegotiate the work-life balance. In contemporary society not everybody wants to sacrifice everything in the pursuit of work-orientated goals. The encouragement to "get a life" is often said to people who are "workaholics" and who develop few interests or strong relationships outside the world of work. The persistence of the old joke that nobody wants to have written on their gravestone "I wish I'd spent more time at the office" is an indication that, although work is an important part of life, it is not its totality. Nevertheless, work is one of the main ways through which we express what it means to be human.

So, with the exception of those who shirk the work which is available, we are all workers. In consequence, we need a philosophy of work which will determine our attitude to it.

THE PURPOSE OF WORK

What is the purpose of work? Those who are trying to develop a Christian mind on work look first to creation. The fall turned some labour into drudgery (the ground was cursed, and cultivation became possible only by toil and sweat), but work itself is a consequence of our creation in God's image. God himself is represented in Genesis 1 as a worker. Day by day, or stage by stage, his creative plan unfolded. Moreover, when he saw what he had made, he pronounced it "good". He enjoyed perfect job satisfaction. His final act of creation, before resting on the seventh day, was to create human beings, and in doing so to make them workers too. He gave them some of his own dominion over the earth and told them to exercise their creative gifts in subduing it. So from the beginning men and women have been privileged stewards of God, commissioned to guard and develop the environment in his name.

Then in the second account of creation, which concentrates on the human perspective, we read: "Now the LORD God had planted a garden ... The LORD God took the man and put him in the Garden of Eden to work it and take care of it" (Genesis 2:8, 15). Thus God planted the garden and God created the man. Then he put the man he had made into the garden he had planted, and told him to cultivate and protect it. As he had put the earth in general into man's charge, now in particular he committed the garden to him. Later (Genesis 4:17ff.) Adam's descendants are pictured as building cities, raising livestock, making and playing musical instruments and forging tools of bronze and iron. It seems, in fact, to be the Middle Stone Age which is being described.

Here, then, is God the worker, together with man the worker, who shares God's image and dominion. And (Christians will want to add) there is Jesus the worker, demonstrating at the carpenter's bench the dignity of manual labour. In the light of these revealed truths about God, Christ and human beings, what is the Christian understanding of work? In particular, what is the biblical paradigm through which we understand God's original intentions for work and in comparison with which we can understand our contemporary experience of work, both positive and negative?

Fulfilment for the worker

Work is intended for the fulfilment of the worker. That is, an important part of our self-fulfilment as human beings is to be found, according to God's purpose, in our work. We can affirm this with confidence in view of the very first instruction which God addressed to man and woman: "Be fruitful and increase in number; fill the earth and subdue it" (Genesis 1:28). Here are three successive commands, each leading logically to the next. They could not subdue the earth without first filling it, and they could not fill it without first reproducing themselves. This original and composite commandment expresses, then, a basic aspect of our vocation as human beings.

We have already seen, when thinking in chapter 5 about our responsibility for the environment, that our dominion over nature is due to our likeness to God. Or, to express the same truth in different terms, our potential for creative work is an essential part of our godlikeness. Our Creator has made us creative creatures. Dorothy Sayers was right in her epigram: "Work is not primarily a thing one does to live, but the thing one lives to do."[2] Since the Creator has given us gifts, he intends them to be used. He wants us to be fulfilled, not frustrated.

Pope John Paul II was clear and outspoken about the fundamental place of work in human life. In his encyclical "Human Work" entitled *Laborem Exercens*, he wrote: "Work is one of the characteristics that distinguish man from the rest of creatures, whose activity for sustaining their lives cannot be called work."[3] From the early chapters of Genesis, "the Church is convinced that work is a fundamental dimension of man's existence on earth".[4] For this reason, he continues, "human work is a key, probably the essential key, to the whole social question". If the latter is "making life more human", as the Second Vatican Council said it was, "then the key, namely human work, acquires fundamental and decisive importance".[5] So then, "work is a good thing for man", not only because through work he transforms nature to serve his needs, but because through it "he also achieves fulfilment as a human being, and indeed, in a sense, becomes 'more a human being'".[6]

It would be an exaggeration, however, to affirm that work is actually "indispensable" to our humanness, for the climax of Genesis 1 is not the creation of man, male and female, to subdue the earth, but the institution of the Sabbath. We human beings are at our most human not so much when we work, as when we lay aside our work in order to worship. Thus the Sabbath "relativizes the works of mankind, the contents of the six working days. It protects mankind from total absorption by the task of subduing the earth, it anticipates the distortion which makes work the sum and purpose of human life".[7] We cannot be fulfilled through work alone, since we need the act of worship to realize our full humanity.

Nevertheless, we must say that if we are idle (instead of active) or destructive (instead of creative), we are denying a basic aspect of our humanity, contradicting God's purpose for our lives, and so forfeiting a part of our own fulfilment. This does not mean, of course, that a child, a hospital patient or a retired person is not a human being because he or she cannot work. A child wants to grow up, and a sick person to get well, in order to be able to serve. Similarly, retired people are wise to seek an active retirement, in which they have opportunities for constructive service, even if it is unpaid.[8] I shall discuss unemployment later in this chapter. Pessimistic as the preacher in Ecclesiastes was regarding the meaninglessness of life lived without God, and about "toilsome labour under the sun", he was able to be positive about our daily work: "A man can do nothing better than to eat and drink and find satisfaction in his work." Again, "There is nothing better for a man than to enjoy his work" (Ecclesiastes 2:20, 24; 3:22).

E. F. Schumacher did not exaggerate when he wrote about monotonous work: "Mechanical, artificial, divorced from nature, utilizing only the smallest part of man's potential capacities, it sentences the great majority of workers to spending their working lives in a way which contains no worthy challenge, no stimulus to self-perfection, no chance of development, no element of Beauty, Truth or Goodness."[9] He drives home the anomaly of this by pointing out that "the modern world takes a lot of care that the worker's body should not accidentally or otherwise be damaged" and, if it is damaged, provides compensation. But what about "his soul and his spirit"? "If his work damages him, by reducing him to a robot – that is just too bad."[10] He then quotes Ananda Coomaraswamy, who says that "industry without art is brutality". Why? Because it damages the worker's soul and spirit.[11] Schumacher's solution is in the "small is beautiful" concept with which his name will always be associated.

So when human life is work-centred rather than worship-centred, we are missing an essential part of our human calling. When work displaces rest, we discover that we cannot operate as human beings. In an increasingly globalized world, economic values are dominating personal and community values. While this enhances the profile of technological efficiency, it illuminates the fact that human beings are made for lives which are productive and fruitful but are not meant to be under the tyranny of any values which are not God-centred. The pattern of six days work and one day rest and worship has, therefore, become a prophetic standard through which the church should call the world back to patterns of work which enhance human life rather than demean it.

Benefit to the community

Work is intended not only for the fulfilment of the worker, but also for the benefit of the community. Adam did not cultivate the garden of Eden merely for his own enjoyment, but to feed and clothe his family. Throughout the Bible the productivity of the soil is related to the needs of society. Thus God gave Israel a "land flowing with milk and honey", and at the same time issued instructions that the harvest was to be shared with the poor, the alien, the widow and the orphan. Similarly in the New Testament, the converted thief is told to stop stealing and to start working with his own hands, so that "he may have something to share with those in need" (Ephesians 4:28).

The knowledge that our work is beneficial and appreciated adds considerably to our sense of job satisfaction. I understand that Henri de Man's studies in Germany between the wars, and the Hawthorne experiments which were conducted at the same time at the Chicago plant of the Western Electric Company, were the first pieces of scientific research into this now well-accepted fact. The Hawthorne studies in particular showed "that workers would increase their output even when the lights were dimmed to the strength of moonlight, if they thought that their labours were considered by other people to be important and significant".[12]

Certainly the Bible regards work as a community project, undertaken by the community for the community. All work needs to be seen as being, at least to some degree, public service. I will discuss the relationship between the profit motive and the role of business in the community in chapter 9. It is easy to suggest that businesses are only honourable if they serve the community, but it must also be taken into account that, for instance, businesses listed on the stock exchange also serve their shareholders, and the relationship between the two is important when looking at the role of business. But it is important here to reiterate that work is a contribution to the community and not a detraction from it. We shall see below that all work involves compromise and that because of this some people have problems when attempting to see their work as a positive contribution to the community. Even if the only contribution made is to feed the family of the worker and to sustain their life and enable them to maintain their interest in community life, then that work is worthwhile.

Glory to God

More important even than the service of the community is the service of God, though the two cannot be separated. Christians believe that the third and highest function of work is that through it God should be glorified – that is, his purpose should be revealed and fulfilled. God has deliberately arranged life in such a way that he needs the cooperation of human beings for the fulfilment of his purposes. He did not create the planet earth to be productive on its own; human beings had to subdue and develop it. He did not plant a garden whose flowers would blossom and fruit ripen on their own; he appointed a gardener to cultivate the soil. We call this the "cultural mandate" which God gave to humankind. "Nature" is what God gives us; "culture" is what we do with it. Without a human cultivator, every garden or field quickly degenerates into a wilderness.

God does indeed provide soil, seed, sunshine and rain, but we have to do the ploughing, sowing and reaping. God provides the fruit trees, but we have to prune the trees and pick the fruit. As Luther once said in a lecture on Genesis, "For God will be working all things through you, he will be milking the cows through you and will be performing the most menial duties through you, and all duties, from the greatest to the least, will be pleasing to him." Of what use to us would be God's provision of an udder full of milk, if we were not there to milk it?

So there is cooperation, in which indeed we depend on God, but in which (we add reverently) he also depends on us. God is the Creator; man is the cultivator. Each needs the other. In God's good purpose, creation and cultivation, nature and nurture and raw materials and human craftsmanship go together.

This concept of divine-human collaboration is applicable to all honourable work. God has humbled himself and honoured us by making himself dependent on our cooperation. Take the human baby, perhaps the most helpless of all God's creatures. Children are indeed a "gift of the Lord", although procreation is itself a form of cooperation. After the birth it is as if God drops the newborn child into the mother's arms and says, "Now you take over." He commits to human beings the upbringing of each child. In the early days the baby remains almost a part of the mother, so close are they to each other. And for years children depend on their parents and teachers.

Even in adult life, although we depend on God for life itself, we depend on each other for the necessities of life. These include not only the basic needs of physical life (food, clothing, shelter, warmth, safety and health care), but also everything which makes up the richness of human life (education, recreation, sport, travel, culture, music, literature and the arts), not to mention spiritual nurturing. So whatever our job – in one of the professions (teaching, medicine, the law, the social services, architecture or construction), in national or local politics or the civil service, in industry, commerce, farming or the media, in research, management, the services or the arts, or in the home – we need to see it as being cooperation with God. The words of Ambroise Paré, the sixteenth-century French surgeon sometimes described as "the founder of modern surgery", are inscribed on a wall of the École de Médicine in Paris: "I dressed the wound; God healed him."

The story is told of a man who, while taking a walk down a country lane, came across a stone quarry in which a number of men were working. He questioned several of them about what they were doing. The first replied irritably, "Can't you see? I'm hewing stone." The second answered without looking up, "I'm earning £200 a week." But when the same question was put to the third man, he stopped, put his pick down, stood up and said with obvious pride, "If you want to know what I'm doing, I'm building a cathedral." So it is a matter of how far we can see. The first man could not see beyond his pick, and the second beyond his Friday pay packet. But the third man looked beyond his tools and his wages to the ultimate end he was serving. He was cooperating with the architect. However small his particular contribution, he was helping to construct a building for the worship of God.

So *laborare est orare*, "work is worship", provided that we can see how our job contributes, in however small and indirect a way, to the forwarding of God's purpose for humankind. Then whatever we do can be done for the glory of God (1 Corinthians 10:31).

Dr Miroslav Volf, however, in his book *Work in the Spirit*, has challenged this view not as inaccurate but as inadequate. Careful in argument and lucid in style, he has developed a comprehensive theology of work. In essence he bids us look not so much back to the original creation as on to the new creation, whose fullness is yet to come. As there will be a fundamental continuity between our present body and our future resurrection body, so we are looking forward not to the destruction of the world, but to its transformation. It is this expectation which gives human work its significance, since "through it human beings contribute in their modest and broken way to God's new creation".[13]

Dr Volf also rejects Luther's teaching on our different "vocations" in favour of Paul's teaching on our different "charisms" (charismata, "gifts of the Spirit"). These, he maintains, include daily mundane work, even that performed by non-Christians, for "all human work … is made possible by the operation of the Spirit of God in the working person".[14] I am left with some uneasy questions, however. Although indeed the Holy Spirit is at work in the world, and although the nations will bring their "splendour" into the New Jerusalem (Revelation 21:24, 26), does Paul's vision of the charismata really embrace the work of non-Christians? And can humans really cooperate with God in the eschatological transformation of the world? Is the kingdom of God, both in its present reality and in its future perfection, not a gift of God, rather than a human achievement? Nevertheless, as we look to the future regeneration of the world, we are authorized to say that our present "labour in the Lord is not in vain" (1 Corinthians 15:58).

In the light of the three purposes for work which we have been considering, we are ready to attempt a definition:

> Work is the expenditure of energy (manual or mental or both) in the service of others, which brings fulfilment to the worker, benefit to the community and glory to God.

Fulfilment, service and worship (or cooperation with God's purpose) all intertwine, as indeed our duties to God, others and self nearly always do. Certainly self-fulfilment cannot be isolated from service. Job satisfaction is not primarily attained by a fair wage, decent conditions, security and a measure of participation in profits, important as these are. It arises from the job itself, and especially from that elusive thing, "significance". Moreover, the main component of significance in relation to our job is not even the combination of skill, effort and achievement, but the sense that through it we are contributing to the service of the community and of God himself. It is service which brings satisfaction, discovering ourselves in ministering to others. We need not only to develop this perspective on our own work, but, if we are employers or managers, to do our utmost to develop it in our workforce.

Some years ago I was shown around the Handicrafts Centre in Dacca, Bangladesh, which was operated by HEED (the Health, Education and Economic Development project). Here young people from refugee camps were being taught a skilled trade, carpet making or tapestry, weaving or straw art. What impressed me most was the degree of their concentration on what they were doing. They hardly noticed us, and did not even look up as we walked by. They were absorbed in their craft. Their work had given them dignity, significance, a sense of self-worth through service.

In a survey conducted by the Work Foundation in July 2004, many people said that they feel positive about their work and enjoy doing it. Two thirds of UK workers were satisfied or very satisfied with their work or job. The survey found that pay is less important to people than the content of their job and fulfilling personal ambitions. Interestingly, 42.2% of people believed that their most important relationships are at work. So whoever we are and wherever we live, work is an intrinsic part of who we are as human beings. It is not something we do; it is a reflection of who we are made to be, as a reflection of God the worker. Yet as we shall see, work sometimes goes wrong and can be the means through which people suffer or cause suffering to others.

WHEN WORK GOES WRONG

The world of work can become a negative area of our lives for many reasons. These can be related to our attitude to work, our dissatisfaction with work, the impact of work stress on us or the absence of work, and it is to these that I now turn.

Attitudes to work

Attitudes to work are changing all the time – whether it is because new technology means that a person can work from home, or a dual-career household starts a family and finds the new pressures difficult to manage, or changes are being made which increase job stress, or achievement of goals leads to promotion and recognition. Yet underneath these changes in our daily working lives there are important undercurrents which determine our attitude to work in general. It is these that we shall examine now.

I shall come in a moment to the impact of stressful work on people's lives, but some have positive and others negative attitudes to work. Some people wish to avoid work at all costs and would rather be on a perpetual holiday, only being prevented from doing so by having no money to spend on such a holiday unless they work. Yet others see work as essentially a tedious nuisance. They complain about their work and see the worst elements in it, ignoring the positive aspects of it and the fulfilment it could bring for them if their attitude were different. Work is, of course, a means to an end, in that it provides food, shelter and other resources for individuals and their families, yet work is an end in itself and Christians should see work and worship as inextricably intertwined with one another.

In the Work Foundation survey conducted in July 2004, over 4,000,000 workers in the UK (15%) were found to be dissatisfied or very dissatisfied with their jobs. Those suffering most are the unemployed and economically inactive, whose well-being has been affected by their experience of working life. Nearly 500,000 workers earn less than £16,000 a year for working more than sixty hours a week. Nearly 40% of people agree that they work long hours for fear of losing their job, and this is especially true of women.

Stressful work

Until fairly recently the negative impact of work was focused on those occupations which by nature were destructive of the human body and oppressive to the human spirit. Those who worked in the mines worked under the most appalling conditions and often had shortened life spans as a result. Some who worked in factories on production lines were reduced to automatons in work that was oppressive. Across the world, we are also acutely aware of the many places of work where men, women and children work for a pittance and often do so to serve Western interests. In recent years there have been scandals associated with some of the biggest brand names of sportswear and fashion goods in the West, who have been found to use child labour and have their goods made in conditions far below those which any worker should have by right. When talking about work, then, we need to have a global perspective and realize that we are not just talking about well-remunerated work: as workers we must look to the interests of others and understand that globalization connects us as consumers to producers across the world. How few of us look at our possessions and wonder about the circumstances in which those goods were made.

Yet without detracting from this focus on working patterns which are destructive and demeaning, one of the increasing trends in the last fifty years and particularly recently has been the sharp increase in work-related stress among people whose jobs would traditionally have been seen as a creative expression of their gifts and as an important contribution to the community. According to a United Nations report, workers are having record levels of stress and these levels of anxiety, burnout and depression are spiralling out of control. The problem is costing employers billions in sick leave and lost working time and is leaving anxious employees with psychological and emotional fragility for some time afterwards. This study, which focused on the UK, US, Germany, Finland and Poland, found that in all five countries as many as one in ten workers was affected and that depression in the workplace is the second most disabling illness for workers after heart disease. In the UK in 2004/5, around 13 million working days were lost due to work-related stress, depression and anxiety, and this affected half a million people who on average took thirty days off[15] at a cost to UK employers of an estimated £3.7 billion.[16] This also, of course, has knock-on effects on the National Health Service and Social Services. For this reason, a great deal more attention is being paid to reducing stress in the workplace.

This has a huge impact on industry, since globalization is speeding up the working world and increased communications are leading to increased expectations. The International Labour Organization blames unrealistic deadlines, poor management and inadequate childcare arrangements. In Finland stress has led to high suicide rates, with 7% of Finnish workers being "severely burnt out". In Germany 7% of workers opt for early retirement because they are stressed and depressed. In Poland workers are prone to anxiety as unemployment increases due to the collapse of communism. The World Federation for Mental Health has warned that by 2020 stress and mental disorders will overtake road accidents, AIDS and violence as the primary cause of lost working time.[17]

Work is a gift from God. It is meant to bring us fulfilment, yet we know that the Bible tells us in Genesis 3 that since the fall the environment we work in can be hostile and work can be a struggle.

The absence of employment

When we have grasped how central a place work occupies in God's purpose for men and women, we see at once how serious an assault on our humanity unemployment is. Referring to unemployed people in the North of England during the Depression years, William Temple wrote: "The gravest and bitterest injury of their state is not the animal (physical) grievance of hunger or discomfort, nor even the mental grievance of vacuity and boredom; it is the spiritual grievance of being allowed no opportunity of contributing to the general life and welfare of the community."[18] It is a shocking experience to be declared "redundant", and many people live in fear of it happening to them.

In 1982 unemployment was running at 13% of the workforce in the UK, an extraordinarily high figure, but by 2004 the UK economy was near full employment and 4.8% of the workforce were still unemployed.[19] Across the EU in 2003 rates of unemployment varied widely, from 3.8% in Luxembourg and 11.4% in Spain to 20% in Poland. In some countries unemployment was increasing, in others declining, but overall unemployment rates were stable across the EU. In Japan the rate was 4.6% and in the US 5.6%.[20] However, when this is broken down into different groups, a striking picture emerges. "The unemployment rates for the major worker groups – adult men (5.0%), adult women (5.0%), teenagers (16.8%), whites (5.0%), blacks (10.1%), and Hispanics or Latinos (6.7%) ... the unemployment rate for Asians was 5.0% ..."[21] The picture is similar in Europe and there are persistently high youth unemployment rates throughout the world.[22] British disabled people are half as likely to be in employment as non-disabled people.

Moreover, the future is unpredictable and the worldwide problem may well get worse. Although the deregulation and increasing globalization of markets have many advantages, they often make a negative impact on the labour market. Companies are able to search anywhere for cheap labour, which often means lost jobs in the industrialized world, while those who in turn receive new jobs in the developing world do not gain ample benefits from them. Most of the new jobs created in the 1990s have been part-time and, although meeting real needs, often do not bring in sufficient income for a family.

Unemployment is not just a problem of statistics, however, but of people. In the Majority World, where no wage-related unemployment benefit is available, it is often a question of actual survival. Even in the West, where some form of job-seeker's allowance or unemployment benefit is paid, the quality of life lived is often quite low and associated with factors such as poor housing, diet and health. But the suffering is also psychological. It is a poignant personal and social tragedy. Of course, becoming unemployed in a booming economy where jobs may be plentiful is different from becoming unemployed at a time when there are few jobs available, yet even so, the impact of unemployment can be considerable. Psychologists have likened unemployment to bereavement, the loss of one's job being in some respects similar to the loss of a relative or friend.

They describe three stages of trauma. The first is shock. A young unemployed man in our congregation spoke of his "humiliation", and an unemployed woman of her "disbelief", since she had been given assurances that her job was safe. On hearing that they have been sacked or made redundant, some people are angry, others feel rejected and demeaned. At this stage, however, they are still optimistic about the future. The second stage is depression and pessimism. Their savings, if they had any to start with, are exhausted and their prospects look increasingly bleak. So they lapse into inertia. As one man summed it up, "I stagnate." Then the third stage is fatalism. After remaining unemployed for several months and being repeatedly disappointed in their applications for jobs, their struggle and hope decline, their spirit becomes bitter and broken, and they are thoroughly demoralized and dehumanized. The church should be a place where such people feel accepted and loved as well as being helped practically in their search for work.

THE ROLE OF THE CHURCH

In addressing the issues that arise in the world of work, it is important for the church to affirm the importance of work, to understand the needs of those who are stressed at work and to support those who are unemployed.

Affirming the importance of work

Many people say that they have never heard a sermon on work, even though they may have been a member of their church for many years. Yet the congregations of our churches are composed of people who are workers, either in paid employment or in some other context. Many of their deepest challenges emotionally, ethically and spiritually will be faced in the context of work. It is essential, then, that churches show that work is important by bringing it into the teaching of the church and by praying for those in the church as workers, and not simply as family members or for what they are doing in the church.

Church leaders also need to listen to the concerns of those in their communities and congregations regarding the world of work. It is difficult to reach out to people pastorally or in mission if this vital area of life is neglected. A whole new perspective can open up on a person's life when they are visited in their work setting rather than at home. In other words, if work is important in the society then it should be important in the church.

On one occasion a church wanted to do more work in the community and called in somebody from outside to see what new projects could be undertaken. He found that the members of the congregation were heavily involved in the community, either professionally, as doctors, teachers, social workers, etc., or voluntarily as debt counsellors, scout leaders or workers with refugees. They were willing to serve their church, but did not feel they could do any more. He therefore recommended that the church formally recognize what it was already doing by making it visible through prayer, support in fellowship groups and in sharing information. Suddenly it seemed that the church's involvement in the community had increased tenfold. People now felt as though what they had been doing all along, which they previously felt had been ignored by the church, was of real importance to God.

Laypeople need to know that their daily work is important to God. Indeed, it is essential to furthering God's purposes for the world. They are not in a waiting room designed for those who are not doing "Christian work", nor are they in some second league because they do not preach every weekend. What they do they are called to do "as unto the Lord", because it is service for him. Every church needs to know what its members do, whether paid or not, because they *are* the church and they need to be supported in all that God has called them to do and be.

Understanding stress at work

It is very easy for the church to offer simple answers to complex problems. Yet those who suffer from inordinate stress at work often do so because they are in situations where the stress is being generated by the systems in which they work, the expectations placed on them, the pace of change around them, or the work practices of colleagues. A doctor recently said that he could not keep up with the pace of change in his world. The paperwork he was required to fill in was not only voluminous but was constantly changing. The resources he had at his disposal were also always changing. He found it difficult to cope however many hours he worked. Similarly, an architect for one of the world's largest hotel chains talked of how the expectations on him were such that no one person could possibly fulfil them. He felt that he had been "set up to fail". On yet another occasion, a newly qualified childcare social worker had double the number of cases that she should have had, was poorly supervised and felt that it was only a matter of time before she made a mistake with potentially horrific consequences. She was not sleeping well at night.

These are important issues and it is essential that stress at work is not seen as personal failure or spiritual defeat, but instead is understood. On some occasions a person may have to be supported while they change their job. On other occasions a person may have to take sick leave and be cared for so that they can return to work. However, it is also important to mention that some people do exploit the system and take days off ("sickies") citing stress when there is little, if anything, wrong with them.

Supporting job seekers

Faith-based initiatives are frequently referred to by all sides of the political debate as being important to the social health of the UK.[23] The same is true of America, where churches are often deeply involved in the life of the community, especially as the idea of the welfare state is not as prevalent as it is in Europe and the need for the voluntary sector's involvement is, therefore, even more pressing. However, while it is good to see government endorsing the importance of faith-based initiatives, it is essential that this is never done so that governments can avoid their own responsibilities to provide for those in need. As Archbishop of Canterbury Rowan Williams put it in his recent Hinton Lecture:

> There is also a strong and not unfounded suspicion that government is always eager to contract its business out to volunteers, to save money and administrative time – in a way that can leave essential services vulnerable to the ups and downs of volunteer enthusiasm, local interest or capacity for fundraising and other unplannable factors.[24]

Enabling job seekers to find work cannot be a task delegated to the voluntary sector, yet the church can do a lot to help. Job seekers have different needs depending on their background, skills and abilities. The needs of somebody who was born in the UK and is a graduate are very different from those of someone who has recently entered the country as an asylum seeker. The needs of such a person will seldom be restricted to finding a job. They will often need help to find housing, to ensure they are getting the right benefits and that they are enrolled in English classes, should that be required. In other cases people will need help in filling out application forms or being given interview practice. Some people will need advice on setting up their own business. The church has a great deal to offer in all these areas and, indeed, many churches now have schemes which aim to meet many of these needs. Many church buildings have been adapted and new church buildings designed to be multifunctional so that community groups, luncheon clubs and debt-counselling sessions can be based there.

Then there is the whole sphere of community service, through the local church or a voluntary organization or on one's own initiative: visiting the sick, the elderly or prison inmates; redecorating an old person's home; working with mentally or physically handicapped people; baby-sitting; collecting other people's children from school; teaching children with learning disabilities, or ethnic families for whom English is a second language, to read and write; helping in the local hospital, school, club or church.

Humankind by creation is creative; we cannot discover ourselves without serving God and our neighbour; we must have an outlet for our creative energies. So if people without employment have no facilities for the range of activities I have mentioned, and they are not available elsewhere in the community, should the church not provide them? Is it impossible for the church to make available a workshop (and tools), a garage or studio, in which people can both learn and practise new skills? And could most local churches not develop a much broader programme of service to the local community? Increasing numbers of unemployed, semi-employed and retired people will need to be encouraged to use their leisure time creatively. As a result of automation, as Marshall McLuhan wrote in 1964, "we are suddenly threatened with a liberation that taxes our inner resources of self-employment and imaginative participation in society".[25]

WORKING IT OUT

Work is a personal issue

Firstly, as I have already discussed, work is a personal issue in the attitudes we have to our work, the involvement we have with our work and the outcomes from our work. Work is one of the key ways in which we express our Christian character. It is evident from how we do our work whether we are honest, efficient and trustworthy, and we must strive to be people who have the highest standards. Work often provides people with ethical problems which are difficult to resolve. It is important that we grapple with such issues as Christians rather than succumbing to the status quo, and this might mean that we have to bear the cost of being people of integrity in the world of work. However, in the majority of cases employers want people on whom they can rely, and businesses which are transparent and reliable often find that they prosper as their reputation grows. We must never forget that work is an expression of Christian character and we should never give people cause to be sarcastic about the Christian faith because there is a gulf between what we claim and what we do.

Secondly, one of the reactions to the advent of automation is an increased trend towards the personalization of work. We live in the age of flexible working and of the portfolio worker who seeks to be in control of what they are doing at all costs. Here we are dealing with the ultimate expression of personal work and we must remember that work is not only a moral expression but also an emotional issue. Those who work at home, for instance, may quickly find that they miss the company of others, because we are social beings and we are not made to be isolated individuals. When working alone it can also be difficult to maintain the balance between working too hard and not being disciplined enough. So in evaluating work we need to be aware of the impact of work on people, not only in terms of new technology, but also in terms of potentially isolating working conditions. In whatever setting we work, we need to encourage one another to work with integrity, contribute to the well-being of others and do all to the glory of God.

Work is a relational issue

One of the key problems facing people today is work-life balance.[26] It provides a challenge to employers in keeping their workforce motivated and positive rather than succumbing to stress. It is also a challenge to workers who want to have time for family, friends and other interests outside work.

Outside the workplace

Firstly, good work allows for a high quality of relationship *outside* the workplace. We know from Genesis 1 and 2 that human identity depends on several relationships – with God, with each other, with the environment and with our work. I have also discussed the importance of the Sabbath as the context in which we work. All of these things are necessary if we are to be able to place work in its right perspective.

When materialism grips a culture, work can become synonymous with its material rewards. The importance of these other relationships can fade. In particular people lose their relationship with God, and with it their sense of identity and purpose. Relationships with other people also come under pressure. Time becomes the new scarce resource as people find little time to relax with husbands, wives, children and friends.

Within the workplace

Secondly, good work allows for a high quality of relationship *within* the workplace. If we take the basic insight into human identity from Genesis 2, which is that it is founded on relationships and not individualism, then the more relational work is, the more expressive of human identity it will become. One of the reasons why there was so much unrest amongst production line workers in the 1960s and 70s was that not only were workers stressed by having to work at repetitive tasks under pressure, but there was little time to relate to those around them, let alone work cooperatively and collaboratively on joint projects. The car industry was an example of how long production lines began to change into team-based car construction, so that a group of workers would work on a car together before moving on to the next car. Not only did production go up, but the level of unrest and complaint went down, because people felt that they were working together towards a common goal. In his book *God in Work*, Christian Schumacher talks about "six team-building dispositions" – six behavioural traits which, if acquired and practised regularly, will result in productive team working.

- A resolve always to value one's own skills and those of others.
- A willingness to listen and to communicate honestly and purposefully with one another.
- A commitment to help and encourage one another.
- A readiness to extend trust to one's leader who earns this trust by striving to maximize the team's welfare and performance.
- A feeling of responsibility for the team as a whole as it works for the completion of a worthwhile task.
- A willingness to contribute one's own creative inputs and allow them to be transformed into other better team outputs.

Schumacher points out that these principles or behavioural traits are expressive of key Christian insights, although they are not exclusively drawn from a Christian worldview. The values of encouragement, honesty, trust, responsibility and transformation are at the heart of all human interaction which is positive and fruitful. It is one thing to work in a purely functional way together; it is quite another to work in a context of mutual respect and mutual encouragement which seeks not individual self-interest but the rewards which can come to the good of the group.[27]

When we look at work in the light of these principles, we can see that for many people work falls short of the ideal. They work in organizations which are so large that they are alienating; they do not share in the work holistically, but only ever see a very small part of what their company is attempting to do; they are organized functionally with an emphasis on only using a small part of their gifting, rather than being respected as human beings with a great deal to offer; they may not be able to contribute to the vision of the organization in which they work, but have to receive and carry out the vision of others, which may be distorted; there may be lack of communication and a division of cultures at work between the powerful and the powerless; and they may be expected to do either too much or too little in terms of their actual capabilities and also in terms of the health of their other relationships outside the world of work. It is the neglect of these basic principles that underlie all healthy human relationships and endeavours which leads work to become dysfunctional and in some cases evil.

Work is a communal issue

Work is not only personal – it is also communal. It is communal in terms of the culture of the workplace. What environment do we create when we work together? Is it a culture of mutual respect and encouragement towards excellence? Sadly, this is not always the case. There have been several high-profile cases of sexual harassment in the UK in recent years which have shown the extent to which even women who are at the top of their profession can receive destructive and humiliating treatment, leading either to their resignation or to their unfair dismissal. Others suffer racial abuse or are the victims of disablism. Older people can find themselves edged out or overlooked for promotion because a younger team is more desirable. The culture of the workplace may be cutthroat and even dishonest in its pursuit of ever-higher profits. Working in such an environment means that either one has to delude oneself about the fact that these things are happening, or one has to collude with them.

It is not only Christians who need to ask themselves how long they can put up with such working practices. Many people work in circumstances they wish were otherwise, but do not see themselves as having any alternative, given their need to make a living. But all of us need to draw a line over which we will not step, because we are spiritual and moral human beings who can be destroyed through bad work, even as we are built up through good work.

Work is also communal in terms of where we live. It may well be that we live in an area which is dominated by one particular industry, as was the case in previous decades in the mining villages or in the towns dominated by the steel industry. In these circumstances the difference between good work and bad work can be marked for whole communities. Where work depresses and demeans the human spirit, communities may suffer. In such settings the church may find that it needs not only to bring a message of the love of God and of the worth of each human being, but also to protest lucidly and persistently that conditions should change for the better.

Work is a global issue

In a globalized world, of course, we are aware that we are linked not only to the conditions of the workers who live next door, but to the workers whose goods we buy and who may be working thousands of miles away in Asia or Africa. We are now more aware than ever of the importance of ethical consumption and there is a great deal of guidance available on how to be an ethical consumer and, indeed, how to be an ethical tourist, written from a Christian perspective.[28] Certain well-known supermarkets use their commitment to ethical products as part of their marketing profile. Buying products with the Fair Trade logo is one way of ensuring that producers in the Majority World receive a higher income from their product than might otherwise be the case.

Globalization presents us, therefore, with three major concerns about the world of work: firstly, the identity of the worker; secondly, the quality of the conditions; thirdly, the adequacy of the pay. Firstly, then, we are concerned about whether people are vulnerable because of their identity. The primary example of this is child labour, where children who should be at school or enjoying the leisure of childhood in some other way are working in poor conditions and being exploited in ways which are outrageous. We are fortunate that good investigative journalism has recently begun to expose the practices of Western companies who have used child labour, but globally child labour, and indeed child slavery (for that is what it often amounts to), is all too common.

Women can also be vulnerable in the labour market because they have a lower status in their society and may not feel able to protest. In this case, advocacy is required to enable women who are powerless to have a voice. One of the most important developments in recent years in the international community has been a new focus on advocacy and particularly self-advocacy, which means empowering people to change their own lives for the better.

Many people feel that where people are exploited because of their identity and are rendered powerless because of this, the products of these companies should be boycotted, protests should be made at their shareholders' meetings and they should be given a thoroughly bad press, exposing these practices to the public gaze, until they change their minds and begin to act ethically.

Secondly, we are concerned with the conditions in which people work. Many people still work in sweatshops. These still exist, to some extent, in Western countries, yet are not as prevalent there as they are in the Majority World. Fortunately some companies in the West now go and inspect the factories which make products for them at low cost in places like Asia and Africa. If the conditions in those factories do not fulfil certain criteria, then the contract may be taken away and placed with someone else. In some places the idea of an employment contract is non-existent. People work long hours and the conditions may be unhygienic, cramped or even unsafe. In some cases, such as in the mining or chemical industries, conditions have been life threatening, since the workers have been valued so little that their lives are regarded as cheap, relative to the profits that are being made out of them. In other situations the conditions are emotionally or psychologically distressing, as when those in management or ownership are cruel to those who work for them or hold the power of instant dismissal over them, thus keeping them working in fear that if they do not work they will be sacked and left without sufficient income for their families to survive.

Thirdly, we should be concerned about remuneration. Of course we do not expect those who live in countries with much lower standards and costs of living to be paid the same wage as in countries with much higher standards and costs of living. What we are concerned about is that the wage should be sufficient to provide people with an adequate standard of living, so that they can live without being impoverished. Work should be the way out of impoverishment, not the cause of entrapment within it. One of the reasons why there has been such a sense of outrage about the extraordinarily high payments and bonuses given to senior managers in large Western corporations has been the vast differential between those at the top of the organization and those at the bottom, who may be working in a factory in Asia with inadequate remuneration and poor conditions, but who are providing the very means through which the company gains its profits.

When we look at these three issues – the identity of the worker, the quality of the conditions and the adequacy of the remuneration – we are dealing with issues of justice. Globalization has brought the faces of exploited workers onto our television screens, and we are faced with the old biblical question: How should we then live? People may respond to this question in different ways. Some will make a priority out of being an ethical consumer. Others will set up or support church initiatives. Many will join campaigning organizations which lobby government, and some shareholders will wish to raise these issues at shareholders' meetings, calling the management to account ethically. We cannot ignore the fact that we live in a world of work which is troubled. God intended the world of work to be a place where people could express and celebrate the fact that they are made in the image of God the Creator. When we look at the current state of the world of work and compare it to God's original intentions, we must be saddened that work is sometimes used to dehumanize people to such an extent that those responsible must face the judgement of the God of justice.

In the next chapter we shall see that business has an important role to play in making our world more pleasing to God. If people are to climb out of poverty, it will often be because they have been enabled to start their own small business or have been given opportunities to achieve their potential by working for someone else. Whatever our calling and place in the world, Christians need to hold fast to a high view of work, which is given to us all to express what it means to be truly human, since we are made in the image of God the worker.

NOTES

1 I would like to commend the work of Mark Greene, currently director of the London Institute for Contemporary Christianity, in this area. He has written a great deal on this subject and his books include *Thank God It's Monday* (London: Scripture Union Publishing, 2001) and *Supporting Christians at Work* (London: Administry and LICC, 2001). LICC has developed a number of resources, courses and other events focused on the area of work. They can be found at *www.licc.org.uk*.

2 Quoted from Dorothy Sayers, *Creed or Chaos?*, in Ted W. Engstrom and Alec Mackenzie, *Managing Your Time* (Grand Rapids: Zondervan, 1967), pp. 21 – 23.

3 Pope John Paul II, *Laborem Exercens* (London: Catholic Truth Society, 1981), p. 4.

4 Ibid., p. 13.

5 Ibid., p. 12.

6 Ibid., p. 33.

7 Henri Blocher, *In The Beginning, The opening chapters of Genesis* (Leicester: InterVarsity Press, 1984), p. 57.

8 The future of retirement is discussed helpfully in Michael Moynagh and Richard Worsley, *The Opportunity of a Lifetime: Reshaping Retirement* (The Tomorrow Project with the Chartered Institute of Personnel and Development, 2004). Copies of the full report can be obtained through *www.tomorrowproject.net*.

9 E. F. Schumacher, *Good Work* (London: Abacus, 1980), p. 27.

10 Ibid., pp. 119 – 20.

11 Ibid., p. 121.

12 From Henri de Man, *Joy in Work* (1929), quoted in Sherwood E. Wirt, *The Social Conscience of the Evangelical* (London: Scripture Union, 1968), p. 38.

13 Miroslav Volf, *Work in the Spirit* (Oxford: Oxford Univ. Press, 1991), p. 92.

14 Ibid., p. 114.

15 *www.hse.org.gov.uk/stress/*

16 *www. cbi.org.uk*

17 *Mental Health in the Workplace: Introduction*, prepared by Phyllis Gabriel and Marjo-Riitta Liinatainen (Geneva: International Labour Office, October 2000).

18 Quoted in F. A. Iremonger, *William Temple* (Oxford: Oxford Univ. Press, 1948), p. 440. See also chapter 1, "The Unemployment Experience", in Michael Moynagh, *Making Unemployment Work* (Oxford: Lion, 1985); and Ann Warren, *Living with Unemployment* (London: Hodder & Stoughton, 1986).

19 Figure for June 2004 (Office for National Statistics).

20 Figures for June 2004 (Statistics Bureau: Labour Force Survey, Japan; United States Department of Labor, Employment Situation Summary).

21 United States Department of Labor, Employment Situation Summary. Figures not seasonally adjusted.

22 International Labour Organization, *Global Employment Trends*, 2004.

23 For recent research on the role of faith-based communities in urban regeneration, see Richard Farnell et al., *"Faith" in Urban Regeneration? Engaging Faith Communities in Urban Regeneration* (London: Policy Press, 2003).

24 The Nicholas Hinton Lecture, given at the AGM of the National Council for Voluntary Organizations, 17 November 2004; see *www.archbishopofcanterbury.org/sermons_speeches/2004041117.html*.

25 Marshall McLuhan, *Understanding Media* (1964; London: Abacus, 1973), p. 381.

26 Care for the Family, among many others, has done work on work-life balance issues. Their division entitled Letsdolife works with industry to find a sustainable and healthy work-life balance for their employees. They can be found at *www.careforthefamily.org.uk* and *www.letsdolife.com*.

27 Christian Schumacher, *God in Work* (Oxford: Lion Publishing, 1998), p. 203.

28 See, for instance, Valerio, *L Is for Lifestyle*. On ethical tourism, see Tearfund's literature, such as *Tourism: Don't Forget Your Ethics!* This and a campaign pack for churches can be obtained from *www.tearfund.org*.

Business Relationships

A t the outset of the twenty-first century, the world is a vast network of inter-connected global and local markets. At the heart of those markets are businesses dealing in goods and services which they then sell to consumers throughout the world. In the past it has often been the case that Christians have ignored the role of business in the world or have assumed that to be involved in business life is, in some mysterious way, to compromise what it means to be a Christian. Yet the role of business in the world today is so important that it is essential that Christians become not only involved, but also influential throughout business life. We also need to use our Christian minds to assess its impact within a biblical framework.

We have talked about our attitudes to work in chapter 8. Here it is important to look at relationships within business culture and at the impact of business on culture in general. As we shall see, business relationships depend on both love and justice if they are to be truly Christian.

Whatever we think of business, one thing is certain: it has played a key role in God's plan for humanity's development. Something which contributes to so many important aspects of human life, not least producing enough food and clothing for the whole planet (if we would only share it properly), cannot be low down on God's list of priorities. When we think of business in a global perspective, we often think of big business, and in this chapter I reflect on the role of multinationals and on the impact of business on culture. But it is also important to remember the strategic importance of the very small business. Anybody who has travelled to Majority World countries, as I have done, cannot fail to be amazed by the hundreds of thousands of one-person businesses and the way in which they provide resources for families sometimes composed of many people. Whether it is the sweet-maker in Bombay or the shoe-repairer in Nairobi or the rug-weaver in Kabul, these are all businesspeople who use scarce resources to make money using their own talents, techniques and creativity. Indeed, many churches have set up agencies which make small interest-free loans to people to enable them to set up their own businesses. In many cases, these loans enable people to start a business, which though small, can be something they are proud of and which has the potential to grow, employ others and provide for their families. It is encouraging to see groups of Christians with business experince who are passionately committed to helping those in poverty by enabling them to start up and run their own businesses, believing that productive employment and business investments are the best way for people to retain their dignity, use their gifts and achieve independence. However, in what follows, I reflect on businesses of somewhat larger size.

The business world can be a powerful place, where innovation, rigour, vision and constant change shape our world. It also has its dangers, as any area of power must do: greed, pride and pitilessness are as much part of the mix as courage, strength and vision. Four aspects of the successful business environment are particularly notable, however.

Firstly, businesses are *practical*. The essential question at the heart of any course of action is: will it do the job? This is one of the great strengths of business – it makes things work and is capable of being very honest about whether it can achieve its goals with the limited resources it has at its disposal. This can create a vigorous environment where failure and success can be clearly identified and are often rewarded (or punished) directly.

Secondly, they are *accountable*. There is normally a direct line of responsibility and accountability in place which ensures that someone has the task of doing the job, and it is in his (or her) hands whether it is a success or failure. This accountability again creates a vigorous atmosphere. You know what you have to achieve, and it is your job to do it. The absence of accountability can lead to poor business relationships or even fraudulent activity, which can end up in business failure or court action.

Thirdly, they are *profitable*. Profit is one of the measures of how good a company is at managing its resources – and in fact of its ability to make good judgements with existing resources to make more. Successful companies are normally those which get it right most of the time. No company which persists in making a loss will survive. A company can, of course, be profitable but behave unethically, treat its workers harshly or have a destructive impact on the environment. Making a profit is essential for the long-term success of a business, but there may be so many costs to the community and to the environment that it would be better if the business did not exist or changed radically.

Fourthly, they are *pressured*. That pressure can come from throughout the commercial environment, internally or externally: from shareholders, industry stakeholders or customers, or from the top down, or from other sections of the business. That pressure has to be managed, and this forms the day-to-day activities of the business. Successful business practice consists of the use of resources to deal with that pressure and carry out the tasks which need to be done. It is when those resources are inadequate – too few people, too little machinery, too little time – that the pressure builds up and can become intolerable. It is the management's aim to reach a point of balance, where the resources or power at their disposal match the requirements of the task. This is one of the key goals of business, to have all you need to do the job well. Unfortunately, many businesspeople seem to spend much of their time short of the power they need and so do their best under excessive pressure, enduring the sense of powerlessness and frustration which that brings with it. Inadequate power produces pressure, which over time becomes strain and then stress and finally, if uncorrected, breakdown.

MUTUALITY IN BUSINESS RELATIONSHIPS

In such an environment, what are the desirable characteristics of the business community? Any community needs to be characterized by both love and justice if it is to reflect the character of God, and this is no less true of the business community than of any other. In what follows I want to look at some of the biblical principles that apply to the character of the business community, before coming on to the way in which the principle of justice can be helpfully applied to difficult business decisions, and then finally looking at the role of powerful multinational corporations in our globalized world.

In any community we should seek to develop right relationships. Business communities can often be characterized by conflict and compromise, and in these situations having a clear vision for what it means to be a healthy community is essential. Conflict and competition can, of course, lead to great good as they contribute to the pursuit of excellence and the rejection of the inferior. However, it is also the case that where power exists, powerlessness also is present, and it is one of the prime concerns of the Christian to uphold the cause of those who have been disenfranchised, who have been the victims of injustice, or who have been treated as inferiors within any community. Christians must not only have a concern to pursue excellence in business life and, therefore, to be successful in their achievements, but must also be concerned for reconciliation where there is conflict and for justice to be present for all parties.

John V. Taylor, formerly Bishop of Winchester, has justly called God's kingdom "the kingdom of right relationships".[1] Reconciliation is at the top of the Christian agenda, because it lies at the heart of the gospel. Sin disrupts relationships; salvation rebuilds them. Jesus came on a mission of reconciliation. He is the supreme peacemaker; he tells his followers to be peacemakers too.

I invite you, therefore, to reflect on the situation in Israel after King Solomon died. I recognize that an industry or business is not a kingdom, and that any analogy between them is bound to be only partial. Yet there are some significant parallels. The early united monarchy (under Saul, David and Solomon) had not been uniformly absolutist. At times there had been a reasonable degree of consultation, as when David "conferred with" his officers, and then with the whole assembly, about bringing the ark to Jerusalem. He did not wish to make a unilateral decision, but to take action only "if it seems good to you and if it is the will of the LORD our God". Then, after consultation, we are told, "the whole assembly agreed to do this, because it seemed right to all the people" (1 Chronicles 13:1 – 4).

David's son and successor Solomon, however, despite all his wisdom and greatness, was a despot. His ambitious building programme was completed only by the use of forced labour. Industrial relations (if I may use this term) were at an all-time low. When he died, the people described his oppressive regime as a "heavy yoke" and appealed to his son Rehoboam to lighten it. When Rehoboam consulted his father's elder statesmen, they advised him, "If . . . you will be a servant to these people and serve them . . . they will always be your servants" (1 Kings 12:7). This splendid principle was rejected by Rehoboam, and in consequence the kingdom split into two. But it remains the essential basis of every constitutional monarchy (the motto of the Prince of Wales since the fourteenth century has been *Ich dien*, "I serve") and, indeed, of every democratic institution, in at least two ways.

Firstly, it embodies the principle of mutual service: "If you will serve them, they will serve you." Jesus himself went beyond a prudential arrangement (we serve in order to be served) and affirmed that true leadership must be interpreted in terms of service ("whoever wants to become great among you must be your servant"). Later Paul stated it clearly ("Each of you should look not only to your own interests, but also to the interests of others"), and went on to illustrate it from the incarnation and death of Jesus (Mark 10:43; Philippians 2:4, 5 – 8).

Secondly, it is mutual service based on mutual respect. One might say it is service based on justice and not on expediency alone. To be sure, expediency enters into it ("You serve them and they will serve you"), but the principle's real foundation is justice, namely that the other party is a group of human beings with human rights, created in God's image as we have been, and, therefore, deserving our respect, as we deserve theirs. To oppress the poor is to insult their Maker; to serve them is to honour him (see Proverbs 14:31; 17:5; 22:2). It was this truth which lay behind the many detailed social instructions of the Old Testament – for example, the commandment to pay servants their wages the same day, to care for the deaf and the blind, to have compassion on the widow and the orphan, to leave the gleanings of the harvest to the poor and the alien and to administer justice impartially in the courts. The same principle also lay behind the New Testament instructions to masters and servants to respect each other, for they served the same Lord and were responsible to the same Judge.

Turning from biblical principle to contemporary reality, the contrast is stark. Wherever there is conflict in business life, for instance between workers and management, the fault is seldom if ever limited to one side. Just as we need to look at the positions of all concerned to see the demands of justice, so we also need to overcome our own myopic self-centredness to see the opportunities for reconciliation. Otherwise we see everything from our own perspective. We seek our own interests rather than the other's. It is a situation of conflict born of suspicion and rivalry, instead of a situation of mutual service born of respect and trust. Such a state of affairs, one need hardly say, is wholly incompatible with the mind and spirit of Jesus Christ, and in his name we should set ourselves resolutely against it. This commitment is all the more necessary in a world where it can be weakened by the existence of the corporate shareholder. The days when all shareholders were interested in the culture of the company and its long-term well-being are long gone. Many shareholders are large, corporate entities such as investment trusts and pension funds, whom Sir Fred Catherwood calls "absentee landlords".[2] As Will Hutton has commented, companies can be tempted to adopt short-term policies which may threaten the long-term health and growth of the enterprise. The power of the corporate shareholder, whose interests are to achieve high short-term dividends, puts the business under pressure and may make healthy relationships a low priority. As we have seen in recent years, scandals such as those at Enron expose the fact that the pressure on the company had led to serious fraud which had permeated many of the relationships within the corporation and, indeed, relationships with those who were its consultants and advisers.

When it comes to creating a workforce who feel that they are valued and who have dignity, both love and justice are important. In the case of American industrialist Wayne Alderson, mutual respect transformed a company. Wayne's father would return from the coalpit saying, "If only they'd value me as much as they value the mule" (it was easier to replace a miner than a well-trained mule). In the early 1970s Wayne Alderson became vice-president of operations in the Pitron Corporation, which had a steel foundry near Pittsburgh. It was struggling to survive after a bitter and long strike, and it was at this time that he placed the importance of human value at the heart of a plan to rescue the company by ending the old management style of confrontation in favour of cooperation. He got to know the men by name, walked daily round the foundry, enquired after their families, visited them when they were sick and treated them like human beings. He also started a small Bible study group which grew into a chapel service in a storage facility underneath the furnace. Such was the mutual confidence which developed that the workplace was transformed, with absenteeism and grievances disappearing and productivity and profits rising substantially. He became well known for his "value of the person" vision, with its three key ingredients of love (a positive "I'm for you" attitude), dignity (people count) and respect (appreciation instead of criticism). He once said, "Christ is at the centre of the Value of the Person approach. But even an atheist can accept the worth of the person."[3]

THE NEED TO ABOLISH DISCRIMINATION

No Christian vision for business life can be sustainable if it sanctions discrimination. Both the realities and the symbols, which together perpetuate an unwholesome "them – us" confrontation, need to be abolished.

It is still the case in many parts of the business world that management enjoy perks and bonuses that other workers do not. In recent days some of the extraordinary bonuses paid to company directors have come under fire, especially as in some cases they have been paid even when the business was in decline. Other examples include lavish corporate entertainment, first-class air travel, private health care, "top hat" pension schemes and free theatre tickets. What Christians should oppose is the inequality of privilege, and what we should seek to ensure is that all differentials are due to merit, not privilege. In fact, it is a healthy and confidence-building arrangement when discrimination is both open and limited to pay and does not extend to hidden perquisites for senior management. In recent years many companies have put an end to such offensive distinctions, but many have not.

"We know there are 'untouchables' on other continents," commented Jock Gilmour, a shop steward in the car industry. "What we haven't recognized is that our own industrialized society can have its untouchables too." I know, of course, that my examples may be seen by some as trivial or even justifiable, but they are status symbols which appear deliberately to give self-respect to some and deny it to others. Besides, behind the symbols of discrimination there lies the reality of social injustice, namely the excessive disparity between the high paid and the low paid. Yet we need to recognize, as I suggested in chapter 6, that total egalitarianism should not be the Christian goal, for God himself has not made us identical in either our natural or our spiritual endowments.

Human beings have a built-in sense of fair play, so that in all industrial conflicts there are appeals to "fairness" and complaints of "unfair practices". This concept is the central focus of the book *Social Values and Industrial Relations*, subtitled "A study of fairness and inequality".[4] Already in 1881 Engels had described the expression "a fair day's wage for a fair day's work" as "the old time-honoured watchword of British industrial relations".[5] One of the expressions of this, in 1999, was the introduction in the UK of a minimum wage.

The UK minimum wage currently stands at £5.35 per hour.[6] The CBI (Confederation of British Industry) estimates that the minimum wage has made a real difference to the income of 1,200,000 employees.[7] While the minimum wage is to be welcomed, what about the ridiculously high salary increases which some top directors regularly vote themselves? An example was the CEO of the WorldCom Corporation, before it filed for bankruptcy in 2002, who received more than $142,000,000 in 1999 and in all was loaned $408,000,000.[8] This may be an extreme example, but Joseph Stiglitz, former Chief Economist of the World Bank, reports that during 2000 it was common for American CEOs to be paid more than 500 times the wages of the average employee, up from eighty-five times at the beginning of the decade, and forty-two times two decades earlier.[9]

The Greenbury Committee was set up in 1995 in response to public anger over executive pay, and the Cadbury Committee (set up in 1991) had examined the financial aspects of corporate governance in general. The recommendations of both committees, which are included in what is now called the Combined Code, advise that companies should not pay more than is necessary to attract directors needed to run the company successfully.[10] In 2002, the Directors' Remuneration Report Regulations were introduced. Following these, quoted companies must now publish an annual report on directors' pay, which includes individual pay packages and justifications for them. This remuneration report is then subject to an advisory shareholder vote at each AGM.[11] These changes to the law are to be applauded. We must not forget the principle, summed up well by John Monks, former General Secretary of the TUC (Trades Union Congress), that "all staff in a company contribute to its performance, and while roles clearly differ, interdependence is at the heart of all good working relationships".[12]

I confess that I have admired the Scott Bader Commonwealth ever since I first read about it in E. F. Schumacher's *Small Is Beautiful* (1973) and subsequently corresponded with Mr Ernest Bader. Mr Bader, a Quaker, who died in 1982 at the age of ninety-one, came to England from Switzerland before World War I. The company he founded became a leading producer of plastics, and in 1951 was converted into a "Commonwealth" in which "there are no owners or employees" because they are "all co-owners and co-employees". In 2006 the company is still owned by its employees, and it is proud of its tradition as a socially responsible company.

In 1979 the celebrated economist and writer E. F. Schumacher (who was a director of Bader's company) wrote: "We have settled the maximum spread between the highest paid and the lowest paid; that is, before tax. It may shock many people [egalitarians, he must mean] that, in spite of a lot of goodwill from all concerned, that spread is still one to seven. There is no pressure from the community that it should be narrowed, because it is understood that this spread is necessary. But of course this includes everybody, the lowest paid juvenile compared with the highest paid senior employee." The scale is reviewed and fixed by "a sort of parliament of workers".[13] In 2006 the Community Council at Scott Bader still determines the ratio between the highest paid and the lowest paid worker.[14]

There must be differentials. But unwarranted discrimination in pay, conditions or promotion – "unwarranted" because based on privilege, not merit –

must be abjured. It is incompatible with social justice and with the Christian ideal of mutual respect.

A final important issue to discuss under this heading is discrimination against women's pay.

Although the gender pay gap has fallen in the last twenty years, average hourly earnings for women working full-time in the UK are still 18% lower than for men, and for women working part-time are 40% lower than for men.[15] In fact, the UK has the widest gender pay gap in the EU, when both full-time and part-time workers are included.[16] Interestingly, the widest gap is found in financial intermediation.[17] *The Economist* magazine reported in 2004 that in the City of London, opaque pay structures involving large bonuses make it easier to discriminate against women, with one senior executive reporting that women's salaries tend to be 25% lower than those of men doing the same job.[18] But the situation appears to be improving. A 2004 survey by the *Financial Times* found that 20% of City fund managers, traditionally a male-dominated profession, are now women.[19] American firms seem to be leading the charge against sexual discrimination, with all of the big American-owned investment banks now having diversity programmes.[20] Research shows that less discrimination against women will lead to improved business performance. Professor Welbourne from the University of Michigan, using a sample of 535 IPO businesses, found that having a mix of men and women in key management positions was a significant determinant of short-term and long-term share price performance.[21]

THE NEED TO INCREASE PARTICIPATION

It seems to be increasingly recognized that the workers in any enterprise, on whose skill and labour its success largely depends, should have a share in both decision-making and profits. Although some directors and managers resist this, and naturally feel threatened by it, the principle accords with natural justice. I want to concentrate on the concept of decision-making, since the Christian mind discerns in it a basic component of humanness.

Participation in decision-making

However we define the "godlikeness" of humankind, it will surely include the capacity to make choices and decisions. Adam in the Genesis story is certainly regarded, and therefore treated, by God as a morally responsible person. True, the first command addressed to him was identical with that addressed to the living creatures of the sea, namely "be fruitful and increase in number" (Genesis 1:22, 28), and the injunction to the fish did not denote that they had freedom of choice. Yet what animals do by instinct, humans do by free decision. The divine mandate to subdue the earth clearly implies responsibility, and a higher degree still is implicit in the words, "You are free to eat from any tree in the garden; but you must not eat from the tree of the knowledge of good and evil" (Genesis 2:17). Here side by side are a liberal permission and a single prohibition. It was assumed that Adam was able both to distinguish between "you may" and "you may not", and to choose between them. Moreover, God held him responsible for his choice.

Christian tradition has always taught this biblical truth, that moral freedom is an essential ingredient in the dignity of human personhood. "For the supreme mark of a person," wrote William Temple, "is that he orders his life by his own deliberate choice."[22] In consequence, he added, "Society must be so arranged as to give to every citizen the maximum opportunity for making deliberate choices and the best possible training for the use of that opportunity. In other words, one of our first considerations will be the widest possible extension of personal responsibility; it is the responsible exercise of deliberate choice which most fully expresses personality and best deserves the great name of freedom."[23] Intuitively people know this. They want to be treated as adults with freedom to decide things for themselves; they know that if decision-making is taken away from them, their humanness will be demeaned. They will be reduced either to a child instead of an adult, or to a robot instead of a person.

The essential difference between a "community" and an "institution" is that in the former members retain their freedom to choose, while in the latter it is to some degree taken away from them. Erving Goffman's interesting book *Asylums* is, strictly speaking, an investigation into "the social situation of mental patients and other inmates".[24] But he begins with some general observations. What he calls a "total institution" is a place of residence or work where people "lead an enclosed, formally administered round of life".[25] This includes hospitals, orphanages, homes for the elderly, prisons, army barracks, boarding schools, monasteries, and (I would have thought, although they are non-residential) many businesses, and in particular, rigidly controlled environments such as some (though not all) factories. In such places, the day's activities are "tightly scheduled" and "imposed from above by a system of explicit formal rulings and a body of officials".[26] The key factor is the bureaucratic control, and the existence of a "basic split between a large managed group, conveniently called 'inmates', and a small supervisory staff".[27] "Characteristically, the inmate is excluded from knowledge of the decisions taken regarding his fate."[28] Therefore, in "total institutions" an inmate ceases to be "a person with adult self-determination, autonomy and freedom of action".[29] Decision-making is a basic right of human beings, an essential component of our human dignity.

The cry for industrial democracy, in order to facilitate a greater participation of workers in their own enterprise, does not make factories a special case, but is the expression within industry of the universal cry for the humanization of society. In the West we now take political democracy for granted and are grateful to those who struggled long to secure universal suffrage, so that ordinary citizens might share in governing their country and in making the laws they are then required to obey. Is the propriety of industrial democracy not equally self-evident? Already more than fifty years ago William Temple wrote, "The cause of freedom will not be established till political freedom is fulfilled in economic freedom."[30] He looked back with feelings of horror to the oppressive beginnings of the Industrial Revolution: "The pioneers showed little respect for the personality of those who earned their living by working in factories and mills. They were often called 'hands', and a hand is by nature a 'living tool', which is the classical definition of a slave."[31] Indeed, in a historic letter to the *Leeds Mercury* in 1830, Richard Oastler, a Christian landowner in Yorkshire, had the courage to draw this very analogy, three years before Wilberforce and his friends had secured the abolition of slavery in the British colonies. "Thousands of our fellow creatures and fellow subjects, both male and female, are at this moment existing in a state of slavery more horrid than the victims of that hellish system of colonial slavery." He went on to refer particularly to little children from seven to fourteen years of age, who were working thirteen hours a day in the factories, with only a half-hour break.[32] This is tragically still the case in many countries, for example in India, where young children are in effect bonded into slavery as they crouch for many hours in poor light, making *beedis*, a local cigarette, and in other Asian countries, where they make clothes for export to the West.[33]

While we have come a long way in 170 years, yet we still have some way to go. William Temple continued: "The worst horrors of the early factories have been abolished, but ... the 'workers' usually have no voice in the control of the industry whose requirements determine so large a part of their lives."[34] He states the principle in these clear terms: "Every citizen should have a voice in the conduct of the business or industry which is carried on by means of his labour."[35] The analogy with slavery, though very inexact, is yet instructive at this point. Christians opposed slavery because human beings are dehumanized by being owned by someone else. Christians now should oppose all forms of labour in which human beings are used by someone else. True, the evil is much smaller, because the work is undertaken voluntarily and is regulated by a contract. Yet it is a contract which diminishes humanness if it involves the relinquishing of personal responsibility and the undertaking to obey without consultation.

Christians will agree that at the very least there should be a procedure of consultation, and, more important, that this should not be a piece of window-dressing but a genuine discussion early in the planning process which is reflected in the final decision. After all, production is a team process, in which the workers' contribution is indispensable; should decision-making not be a team process too, in which the workers' contribution is equally indispensable? Self-interest undoubtedly lies at the root of each side's viewpoint. Managers tend to begin their thinking with profit, on which the company's survival depends, whereas workers tend to begin with rising costs and, therefore, wages, on which their personal survival depends. Their different starting points are understandable. But in discussion each side comes to understand the other's legitimate concerns, and then to see that the two, far from being incompatible, are in fact interdependent.

The TUC Partnership Institute, launched in 2001, acknowledges this interdependence. It aims to provide expertise and advice to unions and employers on developing successful workplace partnerships. One of the key beliefs underlying this institute is that "trade unions must be involved in the decision-making process and individual employees must have more control over the day-to-day decisions that affect them".

Once the principle of worker participation has been conceded, there can be a legitimate difference of opinion about the best ways and means to ensure it. The CBI welcomes the idea of partnerships between employers and employees, but does not think that this must necessarily include trade unions. Indeed, it is afraid that these partnerships may lead to an unwanted build-up of union influence by the backdoor.[36]

An important element of partnership is giving information to employees about the business and, moreover, consulting them about it. A variety of structures has been advocated and tried, ranging from thorough consultation at all levels to the election of worker-directors.[37] The 2002 EU directive on Information and Consultation, which is currently in the process of being implemented into UK law,[38] will give workers in firms with over fifty employees improved rights. Workers will be able to vote for the setting up of an Information and Consultation Committee, made up of elected worker representatives, which will be informed and consulted about, amongst other things, any probable developments of the organization's activities and the effects of this on employment.[39] Brendan Barber, General Secretary of the TUC, commented, "These new rights could lead to the biggest change in workplace relations for a generation."[40] Announcing the draft implementation regulations for this directive in 2003, then Trade and Industry Secretary Patricia Hewitt said, "I want these changes to lead to a 'no surprises' culture at work where employers and employees discuss common ground and find solutions to mutual problems."[41]

I doubt if any Christian would disagree with what Robin Woods, at that time Bishop of Worcester and Chairman of the Church of England's Board for Social Responsibility, wrote in a letter to *The Times*: "It is consistent with Christian vision that society should develop in such a way that each person can exercise his God-given ability to make choices, to take responsibility, and to share in shaping his own environment."[42]

Trade unions are concerned that workers are sometimes not given the choice about the 1998 EU Working Time Directive,[43] which limits European workers to an average working week of forty-eight hours. While automatic exclusions, for example for young doctors, are contained in the provisions of the directive, the UK government allows any worker to opt out should they so wish. Due to the number of people taking this opt-out, the number of long-hours worked was only reduced by 3% and still nearly 4,000,000 people work more than forty-eight hours per week.[44] Indeed, UK full-time workers work the longest hours in the EU.[45] The TUC argues that workers should not be permitted to opt out of health and safety laws. They also claim that many workers are pressurized into taking this opt-out, and a 2003 poll found that 25% of those who signed an opt-out were not given a choice.[46] While the CBI says that such claims are exaggerated,[47] it is very important that workers are not coerced into signing any such opt-out.

Participation in profit-sharing

The second kind of participation is profit-sharing. Another clear biblical principle seems to be involved, namely that "the worker deserves his wages" (1 Timothy 5:18). Presumably, then, there should be some correlation between work and wage. If a company prospers, shared power (responsibility) should bring shared profit. If shareholders benefit from profit, so should workers, whether in bonuses of company stock or deferred benefits (e.g., pensions).

One example of where the trend is going the other way is the closure of so many final salary pension schemes, thereby transferring the risk of stock market downturns away from the employer and onto the employee.

The world pioneer in this area of profit-sharing appears to have been Karl Zeiss of Jena, Germany, who in 1896 transferred the ownership of his firm to the workforce. In the United States it was Sears Roebuck, who in 1916 decided to use 10% of his firm's annual pre-tax profits to enable employees to buy its shares in the open market. In Britain, however, the credit for being first in the profit-sharing field seems to belong to the John Lewis Partnership in Oxford Street, London. John Lewis was twenty-eight years old when he opened a small drapery shop there in 1864. By the turn of the century his son Spedan had become troubled in conscience that he, his father and his brother as shareholders were jointly drawing from the business substantially more than all their employees put together. So he determined to devise a more equitable division of the rewards of industry, and in 1920 the first distribution of "Partnership Benefit" was made, representing an extra seven weeks of pay. Spedan Lewis later made two irrevocable settlements in trust for the benefit of the workers. From 1928 to 1970 the "Partnership Bonus" (as it is now called) was made in the form of stock, but since 1970 it has been wholly in cash. The company's policy is stated thus: "After paying preference dividends and interest, and providing for amenities, pensions and proper reserves, the remainder of the profits in any year is distributed to the members of the Partnership in proportion to their pay. In this way the profits are shared among all who work in the business." In 2004 John Lewis gave 59% of its profit as the Partnership staff bonus.[48]

Such an arrangement was innovative in the 1920s. Today similar profit-sharing arrangements or profit-linked share plans are multiplying in Britain and continental Europe, though unfortunately much more among management than across all workers. As we will see later when we look at multinational corporations, profit-sharing arrangements also have their disadvantages, but overall they are to be welcomed, and the wider they reach into all levels of a firm's hierarchy, the better.

Both aspects of participation (decision-making and profit-sharing) appeal to the Christian mind on the ground not only of expediency (increased industrial peace and productivity) but also of justice (workers have a right to share in power and profits).

It is to the demands of justice that I now turn. I have already said that both love and justice are important characteristics of business life from a Christian perspective, and the principles of mutuality, participation and the abolition of discrimination have both elements of love and justice within them. Indeed, love and justice, although they are distinctive, are interdependent. As I have said elsewhere, "What love desires, justice demands." Yet there are many situations in business life in which love appears to be an inappropriate response or even an inadequate guide to both manager and worker. What is the role of justice in these difficult decisions which need to be made in the business environment?

JUSTICE IN DECISION-MAKING

If we accept that our calling should take us beyond personal evangelism or even personal integrity (though they are essential) to influencing the structures within which we operate, what values and virtues can we look to in order to guide us as Christians? Since being part of business life is also about living in community, some have seen that Jesus' commandment to love one another (John 15:12) is the primary calling of Christians in business life. As we shall see in what follows, love is necessary, it is even essential, but it is not sufficient.

Something more is required than the simple ethic of loving one another if hard decisions and ethical conflicts are to be handled well and in a Christian way. The alternative is for Christians to avoid all situations where there is no obvious way forward. However, this will simply create vast tracts of business operations where no Christian dares to go. Surely it is in these most difficult areas that Christian witness and influence are needed most! Therefore, we must have another approach which is strong enough to handle these situations positively and powerfully, and according to the values God himself lays down. How can we do this? I think another instruction is required: "He has showed you, O man, what is good. And what does the LORD require of you? To act justly and to love mercy and to walk humbly with your God" (Micah 6:8). It is not just to act with kindness that is required of us, but to *seek justice*. This changes the whole approach of what it means to be a Christian in business.

Although business communities can claim no exemption from the demands of love, in a corporate realm where power, conflict and self-interest often prevail, it is difficult to see how one can attempt to "love" a large, powerful multinational.

Perhaps this can give us the ethic which will unlock those difficult moral situations Christians find themselves having to deal with in the business world. Love is an expression towards the business *community*, but justice is the response to the business *structure*. The role of Christians in the corporate world is to use whatever power is at their disposal to *achieve* justice. Christians acting within the business community will realize that both love and justice are important and interdependent, but in any situation the one may have a higher priority or be a more appropriate response, whether the issue is relationships, disciplinary hearings, environmental impact or structural change. Understanding when one is more important than the other releases Christians to carry out the functions of their God-given calling with strength and confidence.

The role of a Christian seeking to establish justice must be to use the power available to balance the demands of their company (and so fulfil the responsibilities placed upon them by their role) against the wider situation of their competitors. When dealing with equals (or bigger companies), presumably it is defending the just position for one's own company which would be required. However, when dealing with smaller or weaker parties, the situation changes. Here the temptation may either be to bully and exploit, or else to be unduly lenient, making unnecessary allowances. Notice the "unduly", for surely there is nothing wrong in being generous where possible; but being free and easy with your company's resources is not what is required. Justice demands that *all* parties receive their due, not just the one to which we might feel more sympathetic, or the one in the strongest position.

We can explore a few examples to consider how this might work in practice. So for example, what about a call-centre operator having to deal with a persistently poor payer, who is now about to have his or her phone or electricity supply disconnected? Employing the pure ethic of loving-kindness may let the debtor off the hook – but it betrays the trust placed in the operator by the company, which has dutifully provided the debtor with its carefully won resources and is now out of pocket. The argument that the company can afford it does carry some weight if the ethic of love is employed – but this is hardly just for both sides. Bringing justice demands that the legitimate requirements of all sides are recognized. There may be some leniency which is appropriate, for example in the length of time given to pay, but employing the right ethic allows Christians in this difficult situation to act according to one of God's most fundamental qualities – justice – while fulfilling their responsibilities for both company and debtor. It also stops them getting fired for not doing the job they were employed to do.

What other situations might benefit from employing this ethic? One difficulty often faced by team managers is how to deal with poorly performing staff. When a team has a task to carry out with a given number of people, how is the Christian manager to deal with one member of staff who, maybe due to serious personal problems, is underperforming? What principle should be employed to manage the situation correctly?

Again, we may intuitively feel that our approach should be one of compassion, citing Jesus' instruction to make allowances, forgive "seventy times seven" times, and provide all means necessary to help the individual. Yet we need to recognize that pursuing this path also has a cost associated with it, first for the team who have to work extra hard to carry the struggling member, and second for the company as it continues to pay for an underperforming staff member. On the other hand, no one would consider it just for a company to get rid of its staff at the first sign of a problem. So we have two extremes: at one end, the individual's needs take priority over the business's, regardless of cost; and at the other end, the business's priorities take complete precedence over the individual, and all underperforming staff are dismissed as a matter of course.

Supporting the individual at the expense of the others in the equation would result in the individual being satisfied, but with resentment in the team and the manager's career on the line for failing to be strong and perhaps failing to deliver the team's targets. Ultimately, this kind of behaviour can bring a business down if it gets out of hand. But what happens if we see justice as the priority? Here, the other factors in the situation come into play, and it becomes a matter of balancing the different forces in the equation to come to a correct solution. So the needs of the distressed individual must be balanced against team needs and company objectives. The pressure factors then need to be weighed. What has to be done and what resources are available to do them? Where is there slack in the system, or resources available from outside the situation to be applied where they are now needed? Finally, the role of conflict needs to be factored in. What needs challenging, and what will be the effect of that? The manager is then in a position to make a just decision and manage through the consequences. This might include formally disciplining the team member concerned, or challenging his or her manager or company ethos.

Recognizing that justice may be the priority in business decisions brings a new dynamic to the situation. This is particularly the case when the role of conflict is understood as being a natural and often essential part of the process of bringing justice into a situation. It is easy to shy away from confrontation, when in fact it is a healthy part of our role and something we should expect and for which we should be fully prepared.

Exposing and challenging evil, in the power of God, is surely one of the key tasks of the Christian in any situation. The problem many Christians have in confronting evil is that the surety and directness that this confrontation requires is undermined by a fear that acting assertively is somehow ungodly. In fact, of course, the opposite is true. *Real* love is not shy of confronting evil forcibly, as Jesus' example of driving out the money-changers in the temple courts demonstrates; and of course the Old Testament is full of instances of God bringing destructive judgement against evil to purify Israel. Using the ideal of justice as the benchmark for Christian behaviour in business clarifies what is required in this kind of situation.

It is the challenge of living out the Christian life in a powerful and effective way which attracts many Christians. Surrounded by "non-Christians" on a daily basis, faced regularly with difficult decisions which will involve employing huge financial resources and are likely to affect the well-being of many thousands of people, the business environment is highly stimulating and demands a deep level of practical faith. Some areas in particular (usually where angels fear to tread!), often viewed as the "dirty" areas of work where it is expected that moral compromise is inevitable – sales, advertising, journalism, negotiating – are of course those most in need of Christian involvement. It is in these demanding areas that high standards of integrity and courage can be the most successful and can make the greatest difference to the day-to-day lives of people right across the world. There is a long and honourable tradition of Christians shaping the business environment, and through that directly affecting other powerful spheres of influence, including the political world.

However, one failing for some Christian-run organizations seems to be excessive tolerance of poor performance and badly run operations. On many occasions this has arisen because the ethic of loving kindness has been put into place, when in fact the ethic of justice is required. The moral act of hiring someone who would not be employed by a mainstream operation needs to be balanced against the (correct) expectations of the organization's clients that its business will be carried out in a professional manner. Incompetence, laxity, late delivery or rudeness from staff should not be tolerated in a Christian company any more than in a secular one. Indeed, as a representation of the kingdom of God, any Christian organization should be a pleasure to do business with.

It is understandable but sad that there is still a debate about whether it is a good thing to be ethical in business. After all, how is one measuring the outcome? The fact is that it is important to be ethical whatever the outcome. Yet all boards of directors will face this question from time to time, as we have seen. *The Economist* puts at the top of its ten-point checklist of necessary qualities for successful leadership "a sound ethical compass".[49] Joseph Reitz, who is co-director of the International Centre for Ethics in Business at the University of Kansas, has found that while there is much evidence that companies insisting on doing business in the right way may suffer in the short term, in the long run they perform well.[50] That the motive for ethical behaviour comes in part from financial advantage is demonstrated by this quote from Clive Mather, chairman of Shell: "We are not embracing a commitment to sustainable development out of the goodness of our heart. Shell sees sustainable development as making good business sense in helping to differentiate us from our competitors and providing competitive business advantage."[51]

However, Amar Bhide and Howard Stevenson, writing in the *Harvard Business Review*, argue that unethical business behaviour, in particular breaking trust, does not in general have long-term financial penalties.[52] They acknowledge that there is undoubtedly some value in being honest in business and goodwill does help carry a company through bad times. But, on the whole, the future costs of breaking trust are outweighed by the immediate benefits of breaking inconvenient agreements. They argue that the fact people in business do seem to keep their word most of the time is more down to social and moral behaviour than financial incentive. They write, "People keep promises because they believe it is right to do so, not because it is good business."[53]

Whether it pays to be ethical in business or not, on a society-wide level it is vital that there is an undergirding of integrity and honesty in business. As Dr Sissela Bok wrote in her book *Lying: Moral Choice in Public and Private Life*,[54] the continuance of society itself depends on the acceptance by members of that society of the rule "Do not lie". Francis Fukuyama, in his influential 1996 book *Trust: The Social Virtues and the Creation of Prosperity*, comments how trust has economic value in and of itself. Indeed, trust is at the heart of any healthy society.

This leads me lastly to a brief discussion of the role and influence of multinational corporations (MNCs). It is, I think, true to say that they are widely distrusted by many people in the world today. On the one hand, they wield a great deal of power, but on the other hand, it is sometimes unclear who benefits from the exercise of that power.

MULTINATIONAL CORPORATIONS

MNCs exert a massive influence on the world's economy. They now account for about 25% of world production and 70% of world trade, while their sales are equivalent to almost 50% of world GDP.[55] Today they employ twice as many people as they did in 1990.[56] Their growth has been facilitated by many factors, particularly the deregulation of capital markets and rapid advances in communication and information technology.

There are very mixed reactions to the rise in MNCs and two main criticisms are levied at them. The first is that they are overly powerful. The second is that they are overly self-interested. These two implicit traits have led to numerous examples in recent decades of selfish and irresponsible behaviour. Some of the following cases have been identified by Richard Higginson in his 2002 book *Questions of Business Life*.[57]

- The explosion at the Union Carbide factory in Bhopal, India, in 1984, with the deaths of hundreds of people and damaged health of thousands. The cause was culpable corporate negligence.
- Nestlé's selling of powdered baby milk to mothers in countries where water hygiene made it dangerous to use. Indeed, this is still an ongoing criticism of Nestlé.[58]
- Meagre wages paid by sports shoe manufacturers to workers. Nike allegedly paid the US basketball supremo Michael Jordan $20,000,000 in 1992 in sponsorship. This exceeded the entire annual payroll of the Indonesian factories that made the shoes he was employed to advertise.
- Advertising tactics of tobacco manufacturers like Philip Morris to persuade people in the South to take up smoking.

- Southern farmers being exploited by Northern agribusiness which learns and then patents their indigenous knowledge. Vandana Shiva, author of the 1997 book *Biopiracy*, wrote: "The knowledge of the poor is being converted into the property of global corporations, creating a situation where the poor will have to pay for the seeds and medicines they have evolved and have used to meet their own needs for nutrition and healthcare."
- Concentration of research by pharmaceutical companies on medical ailments of the North, to the detriment of diseases plaguing southern countries. For example, tropical diseases such as malaria that cause around 50% of the world's illnesses attract only 3% of the research money.
- The distribution of sponsored teaching packs to schools. In the view of the US Consumer's Union, nearly 80% contained "biased or incomplete information, promoting a viewpoint that favours consumption of the sponsor's product or service".[59]

We now move on to the second criticism of MNCs: that they have too much power. The following is a *Guardian* newspaper headline quoted in *Future Perfect*, a book about globalization: "What is the difference between Tanzania and Goldman Sachs? One is an African country that makes $2.2 billion a year and shares it among 25 million people. The other is an investment bank that makes $2.6 billion and shares it between 161 people."[60]

One of the fiercest proponents of the notion that MNCs have too much power is George Monbiot. This is a quote from his recent book, *Captive State*: "Corporations, the contraptions we invented to serve us, are overthrowing us. They are seizing powers previously invested in government, and using them to distort public life to suit their own ends."[61]

It is clear that MNCs are tremendously wealthy. They constitute fifty of the world's 100 largest economies.[62] And money brings power. Two important ways in which MNCs exert their power are over suppliers and over governments. We begin by briefly examining suppliers. Take, for example, supermarkets, which exert a phenomenal influence in the UK market – the largest five firms between them control nearly 80% of the grocery market.[63] This market power gives them a large influence over suppliers, which need to sell to supermarkets to gain access to the majority of the market. Monbiot gives examples of unsatisfactory practices. One is ordering far more food from suppliers than

they require, in order to keep the price low, and then finding excuses for rejecting large segments of the order and paying nothing for the produce they turn
away.[64] Another is that sometimes when supermarkets are asked to make a
donation to charity, they will ask one of their suppliers to pay the money to the
charity in the superstore's name.[65] If true, such dishonest practices should be
prevented.

MNCs also exert their influence on governments. Joseph Stiglitz, who
served as a senior adviser to Bill Clinton, gave the following insight:

> We in the Clinton administration did not have a vision of a new post-Cold
> War international order, but the business and financial community did:
> they saw new opportunities for profits. To them, there was a role for gov-
> ernment: helping them gain access to markets. The policy framework that
> we pushed abroad was the one that would help our businesses do well
> abroad.[66]

One of the main mechanisms used by companies to influence governments
apart from direct political lobbying is to threaten to disinvest in a country. In
a competitive marketplace it is understandable that companies should seek
to reduce costs in line with their competitors, and firms have sought to do
this in the last decade by outsourcing to other countries. It is predicted that
the global outsourcing market will grow from £33,000,000,000 in 2001 to
£214,000,000,000 by 2008.[67] In 2002 the management consultancy firm Accen-
ture caused much alarm when it predicted that more than 65,000 British call-
centre jobs might be transferred to India by insurance companies.[68] The main
reason why firms choose to outsource abroad is cost. US domestic IT staff have
an average cost of $960 per day, and they are being replaced by suitably quali-
fied and motivated personnel at an expense of only $200 per day.[69]

While it is understandable that firms should wish to reduce costs, there are
disadvantages inherent in an ever-increasing drive to find the cheapest source
of labour. Monbiot argues:

> Corporations have learnt that by threatening to move elsewhere, precipi-
> tating the loss of thousands of jobs, they can ensure not only that the regu-
> lations they dislike are removed, but also that governments will pay vast
> amounts of money to persuade them to stay. By playing nations or regions
> off against each other, the companies can effectively auction their services,
> securing hundreds of millions of pounds . . .[70]

If Monbiot's analysis is correct, then business in general and large companies in particular do indeed exert much power over governments, perhaps too much.

We also need to remember the extent to which the power of advertising and marketing can affect people's view of themselves and of the ideal life which they should be living. Not only can this be a problem for people in terms of the creation of discontent on which Western consumption depends, but it can go so far as to affect and distort the view we have of our own bodies, such as when young girls suffer from anorexia in part because of repeated images of ideal women as being slim. It is also the case that in some cultures Western images are portrayed which are unsuitable for the moral climate of the culture, and sex is used to sell advertising which is offensive to those who are viewing it. Added to this are the areas of product safety and quality, where goods are sold which are dangerous to use; the impact of production on the environment or the ethics of insider trading, mergers and acquisitions, which affect the daily lives of millions of people without their awareness of what has gone on. Such a list only begins to delineate the areas within which business ethics is debated and within which action needs to be taken. It is easy to make simplistic accusations of wrongdoing, but these are complex problems and, just as with the other issues studied in this book, we need informed Christian businessmen and women to guide us through these debates.[71]

However, in all this we need to remember that those who wield power can wield it for the good. It is easy to demonize multinational corporations because the mistakes they have made and the wrongs they have perpetrated have attained a high profile. Throughout this chapter I have drawn attention to several examples of businesses where human values were paramount and business ethics were important. It is just as important to give a high profile to good practice in business as it is to expose evil and unethical behaviour where it exists.

It is frequently assumed that because multinational corporations are powerful, they are invulnerable and those of us who are critical of their behaviour and who wish to bring about transformation are, therefore, powerless to do anything about it. We should remember, however, that in the fight between David and Goliath, it was David who won. There are several ways in which multinational corporations, indeed any businesses, are open to question. The first is through the activity of pressure groups and NGOs who are monitoring the area within which the business is working. The biotechnology company

Monsanto came under intense pressure from groups such as Greenpeace when it announced field trials of its genetically modified wheat called "Roundup Ready". In May 2004 it withdrew this wheat under concerted global rejection of its plans. This is one example of the way in which monitoring by NGOs as well as direct action can place such pressure on a company that it has to change its plans.

The second vulnerability is investigative journalism. In October 2000 the BBC documentary programme *Panorama* screened an investigation into the conditions in which products branded by Nike were being made in countries such as Cambodia. Despite the fact that the company had an ethical code, it transpired that children under fifteen were working in the factories, under poor conditions. The programme placed Nike on the defensive and a great deal of unwelcome publicity meant that their share price was hit and court action was taken against them. It took until April 2005 for their response to be made, which was to publish a thorough audit of 569 of 830 factories worldwide where Nike products are made. The report was frank in listing a number of contraventions of labour standards, such as long working weeks, mistaken wage calculations, verbal abuse and curbs on toilet visits. A total of 650,000 workers were potentially at risk, most of them women aged between nineteen and twenty-five. Nike's response was unusual both in its frankness and in its openness, as it was willing to publish its audit on its own website. One of the reasons for this was given by Dusty Kidd, vice-president of compliance, when he said, "I would have been a lot more worried . . . three or four years ago, but now I'm not because we collaborate more with the non-governmental organizations."[72]

It is becoming evident that consumers are growing more ethically aware, not only in conventional areas such as fair-trade coffee, but also in asking difficult questions about working conditions in the factories where products are made, trading practices of supermarkets and the impact of unjust subsidies and protectionist policies.

Lastly, publicly quoted corporations are sensitive to questions being asked at their shareholders' meetings. It is the right of anybody who owns shares in a corporation to attend a shareholders' meeting and to ask questions. In recent years, large corporations have been embarrassed by the anger expressed in shareholders' meetings about payments made to directors in the company and also about practices which were considered to be unethical. Yet again, such pressure results in unwelcome media attention which could reflect negatively on market share, profits or the share price.

It is important, then, for Christians, along with others who are concerned about justice in business life, to realize that however powerful a business may be, it is open to question. Even if the motivation to behave ethically does not come from within the business itself, the fact that it depends on others buying its products means that if they become sensitive ethically, then the business must either respond or be confronted by the stark reality of a declining market.

Businesses are not only enterprises which exist to achieve goals by the use of scarce resources. They are also communities of people, made in the image of God, who need dignity and respect. It is important, therefore, when we look at the role of business from a Christian perspective, to see that both love and justice are needed if business life is to be honouring to God. When both come together, reconciliation, cooperation and participation will be the by-products. As globalization proceeds, it is to be hoped that we will become more sensitive to the needs of the world's poor, more concerned about the working conditions of the world's workers and more active in calling companies to account for their behaviour. There is evidence that such a movement is underway and that at least a few of the world's largest corporations are finding it beneficial to raise their ethical standards and the quality of life of those who work for them. When business life is placed in this context, we can see that Christians in business have a high calling, as they are not only fulfilling the mandate to be good stewards of the world's resources, but they have a direct impact on the lives of many other people.

NOTES

1 John V. Taylor, *Enough Is Enough* (London: SCM, 1975), p. 102. For the central importance of relationships, see Michael Schluter and David Lee, *The R Factor* (London: Hodder & Stoughton, 1993).

2 Sir Fred Catherwood, *Jobs and Justice, Homes and Hope* (London: Hodder & Stoughton, 1997), pp. 77–79.

3 From a news report in *Christianity Today* in 1979, a tape-recorded conference address, and especially R. C. Sproul's book *Stronger than Steel: The Wayne Alderson Story* (New York: Harper and Row, 1980).

4 Richard Hyman and Ian Brough, *Social Values and Industrial Relations, A study of fairness and inequality* (Oxford: Blackwell, 1975).

5 Ibid., p. 11.

6 *www.dti.gov.uk/er/nmw/*. For workers aged twenty-two or over, the rate is £5.35 per hour. For workers aged eighteen to twenty-one inclusive, the rate is £4.45 per hour.

7 *www.cbi.org.uk*, under the section on Minimum Wage as of 28 June 2004.

8 Joseph Stiglitz, *The Roaring Nineties – Seeds of Destruction* (London: Allen Lane, Penguin, 2003), p. 166.

9 Ibid., p. 124.

10 "Executive Pay", *www.guardian.co.uk*.

11 "Rewards for Failure", Directors' Remuneration – Contracts, Performance and Severance, DTI Company Law Consultative Document, June 2003; also "Executive Pay", *www. guardian.co.uk*.

12 TUC press release, 20 December 1996.

13 Schumacher, *Good Work*, p. 79.

14 *www.scottbader.com/*

15 ONS (2003), New Earnings Survey 2003. For trends over time, see *Kingsmill Review*, 2001, p. 23.

16 "1995 Structure of Earnings Survey", in *Kingsmill Review*, p. 21. Note that this statistic pre-dates the 2004 EU enlargement.

17 2000 Labour Force Survey, in *Kingsmill Review*, pp. 25 – 26.

18 "Sexism and the City", *The Economist*, 12 June 2004, p. 29.

19 As reported in *The Economist*, 12 June 2004, pp. 29 – 30.

20 Ibid., p. 30.

21 Prof. T. Welbourne, "Wall Street Likes Its Women", CAHRS, Cornell University, Working Paper 99-07, Ithaca, New York, p. 11, in *Kingsmill Review*, p. 40.

22 Temple, *Christianity and the Social Order*, p. 87.

23 Ibid., p. 61.

24 Erving Goffman, *Asylums:Essays on the Social Situation of Mental Patients and Other Inmates* (New York: Anchor Books, Doubleday, 1961).

25 Ibid., p. xiii.

26 Ibid., p. 6.

27 Ibid., p. 7.

28 Ibid., p. 9.

29 Ibid., p. 43.

30 Temple, *Christianity and the Social Order*, p. 96.

31 Ibid.

32 Quoted in David Bleakley, *In Place of Work, The sufficient society* (London: SCM, 1981), pp. 16–17.

33 Richard Higginson, *Questions of Business Life* (Carlisle: Authentic Lifestyle, 2002), p. 43.

34 Temple, *Christianity and the Social Order*, p. 87.

35 Ibid., p. 99.

36 CBI press release, 23 June 1999, "CBI President raises fears about trade union partnerships", *www.cbi.org.uk*.

37 The principle of "co-determination", first developed in the 1930s, was put into practice in West Germany after World War II. In essence it advocated (1) a "works council", which represented the workers, (2) a "supervisory board" (two thirds of whose members were

owners and one third workers' representatives), which appointed (3) the executive board, which ran the company. West Germany's post-war economic progress and good record of labour relations are thought by many to be at least partly due to this arrangement. See H. F. R. Catherwood, *A Better Way, The case for a Christian social order* (Leicester: InterVarsity Press, 1975), p. 121.

38 Implementation will take place between March 2005 and March 2008 depending on the size of the organization.

39 "High Performance Workplaces – Informing and Consulting Employees", DTI Consultation Document, July 2003, pp. 6 – 10, *www.dti.gov.uk.*

40 *www.partnership-at-work.com*

41 Ibid.

42 Bishop Robin Woods of Worcester, letter to *The Times,* 16 February 1977.

43 The Labour government signed up to the EU Social Chapter of the Maastricht Treaty in 1997. The Social Chapter empowers the European Community to issue "directives" for the implementation of its policies. One such is the 1998 Working Time Directive.

44 Also, more than 500,000 UK employees work in excess of sixty hours a week. See TUC, Working Time Directive Review 2003: The Use and Abuse of the "Opt-Out" in the UK, p. 1, *www.tuc.org.uk.*

45 TUC, Working Time Directive Review 2003, p. 2.

46 Ibid., p. 7.

47 CBI press release, "CBI Chief Urges Ministers to Fight 'Nanny State' Limit on UK Working Hours", 25 June 2003, p. 2, *www.cbi.org.uk.*

48 2004 John Lewis Annual Report. Partnership bonus was £87,300,000. Profit after tax was £148,800,000.

49 "How to run a company well", *The Economist,* 23 October 2003.

50 "Integrity on a global scale", *The Economist Global Executive,* 10 February 2003.

51 Heslam (ed.), *Globalisation and the Good,* p. 33.

52 Amar Bhide and Howard H. Stevenson, "Why Be Honest if Honesty Doesn't Pay?", *Harvard Business Review* (September – October 1990), pp. 121 – 29, in Scott B. Rae and Kenman L. Wong, *Beyond Integrity: A Judeo-Christian Approach to Business Ethics* (Grand Rapids: Zondervan, 1996), pp. 70 – 78.

53 Ibid., p. 77.

54 Sissela Bok, *Lying: Moral Choice in Public and Private Life* (New York: Random House, 1978).

55 David Held, in Heslam (ed.), *Globalisation and the Good,* p. 5.

56 Ibid., p. 4.

57 Higginson, *Questions of Business Life,* p. 33.

58 See, e.g., *www.babymilkaction.org.*

59 This last criticism of MNCs comes from George Monbiot, *Captive State* (1st ed., London: Macmillan, 2000; 2nd ed., London: Pan Books, 2001), p. 332.

60 In Charles Handy, *The Elephant and the Flea: Looking backwards towards the future* (London: Arrow, 2002), p. 148.

61 Monbiot, *Captive State,* p. 4.

62 T. Gorringe, in Heslam (ed.), *Globalisation and the Good*, p. 81. The statistic uses Trans-National Corporations, which are the same as MNCs.

63 *www.arthurrankcentre.org.uk*. The five firms are Tesco, Sainsbury's, Asda, Safeway and Somerfield.

64 Monbiot, *Captive State*, p. 182.

65 Ibid., p. 184.

66 Stiglitz, *The Roaring Nineties*, pp. 23 – 24.

67 This estimation comes from McKinsey, a large consultancy firm. See Steve Crabb, "East India Companies", *People Management* magazine, 20 February 2003.

68 Ibid. The total current estimate for call-centre staff in the UK is 400,000.

69 Dushyant Shahrawat, "How Offshore Outsourcing Will Hit Home", *Securities Industry News*, 16 June 2003, vol. 15, issue 24.

70 Monbiot, *Captive State*, pp. 348 – 49.

71 One of the books which is a very helpful resource on business ethics is Rae and Wong, *Beyond Integrity: A Judeo-Christian Approach to Business Ethics*.

72 See, for instance, the section on "workers and factories" on the Nike website at *www.nike.com/nikebiz/nikebiz.jhtml?page=25*. The full report can be downloaded from *www.nike.com/nikebiz/nikebiz.jhtml?page=29&item=fy04*.

Celebrating Ethnic Diversity 10

On 28 August 1963 Martin Luther King, who was committed equally to non-discrimination and non-violence, in other words to justice and peace, led a march of 250,000 people, three quarters of whom were African-American,[1] to Washington, DC. There he shared his dream of a multi-ethnic America:

> I have a dream that one day on the red hills of Georgia the sons of former slaves and the sons of former slave-owners will be able to sit down together at the table of brotherhood.

> I have a dream that one day even the state of Mississippi, a state sweltering with the heat of injustice ... and oppression, will be transformed into an oasis of freedom and justice.

> I have a dream that one day in Alabama, with its vicious racists ... little black boys and black girls will be able to join hands with little white boys and white girls as sisters and brothers...

> With this faith we will be able to transform the jangling discords of our nation into a beautiful symphony of brotherhood.

> With this faith we will be able to work together, to stand up for freedom together, knowing that we will be free one day...[2]

We are still waiting for the fulfilment of his dream. Yet it is a Christian dream. God has given us in Scripture a vision of the redeemed as "a great multitude that no one could count, from every nation, tribe, people and language, standing before the throne" (Revelation 7:9). That dream, we know, will come true. Meanwhile, inspired by it, we should seek at least an approximation to it on earth, namely a society characterized by justice (no discrimination) and harmony (no conflict) for all ethnic groups. We are looking for a fully integrated society which continues to celebrate diversity. When he was Home Secretary, Roy Jenkins said, "I define integration not as a flattening process of assimilation, but as equal opportunity, accompanied by cultural diversity, in an atmosphere of mutual tolerance."[3]

Before considering some biblical teaching about ethnicity, it may be helpful to define racism and institutional racism. These definitions come from the report on the death of Stephen Lawrence, who was killed in a racist attack at the age of eighteen, which I will come to later in this chapter. The report defines racism in the following way:

> Racism in general terms consists of conduct or words or practices which disadvantage or advantage people because of their colour, culture, or ethnic origin. In its more subtle form it is as damaging as in its overt form.[4]

The report defined institutional racism as:

> The collective failure of an organization to provide an appropriate and professional service to people because of their colour, culture or ethnic origin. It can be seen or detected in processes, attitudes and behaviour, which amount to discrimination through unwitting prejudice, ignorance, thoughtlessness and racist stereotyping which disadvantage minority ethnic people.[5]

In what follows I will look at some examples of racism, both historical and contemporary, describing the false foundations on which it is built. I begin with the history of slavery.

SLAVERY IN AMERICA

It is not possible to jump straight to contemporary examples of racism in Europe and America, and ignore the evils of slavery and of the slave trade out of which it has largely sprung. No sensitive American can confront issues arising from ethnicity in the US today without looking back beyond the Civil War to the cruelty and degradation of life on the plantations.

It is generally accepted that "the slave has three defining characteristics: his person is the property of another man, his will is subject to his owner's authority, and his labour or services are obtained through coercion".[6] Being regarded as nothing but property, slaves were normally deprived of elementary human rights; e.g., the right to marry or to own or bequeath possessions or to witness in a court of law. Although slavery of different kinds and degrees was universal in the ancient world, it is inexcusable that the professedly Christian nations of Europe (Spain and Portugal, Holland, France and Britain) should have used this inhuman practice to meet the labour needs of their New World colonies. Worse still, practising Christians developed an elaborate but false defence of slavery on several grounds.

- Social and economic necessity, since there was no other source of labour in the colonies to provide raw materials for the Industrial Revolution in Europe.
- Ethnic superiority, since negroes deserved no better treatment.
- Biblical permission, since Scripture regulates but nowhere condemns slavery.
- Humanitarian benefit, since the trade transferred slaves from African savagery to American civilization.
- Missionary opportunity, since African "infidels" would be introduced to Christianity in the New World.

The blatant rationalizations of slave-owners make one blush with embarrassment today.

The slave as property

The inherent evil of slavery (which in principle is the evil of racism also) is that it denies the godlike dignity of human beings. Being the property of their owners, slaves were advertised for sale alongside livestock, corn and plantation tools. Having first been captured, chained and branded in West Africa, they were shipped across the Atlantic in such overcrowded and unhygienic conditions that about half of them died during the passage. On arrival they were auctioned, forced to work, often separated from wife and children, if recalcitrant flogged, if escaped pursued by bloodhounds, and if caught killed.

The slave as animal

Some writers argued that the reason why they were property was that they were animals. In *The History of Jamaica* (1774) Edward Long developed the outrageous argument that in the Creator's "series or progression from a lump of dirt to a perfect man", African negroes were inferior to human beings. "When we reflect on ... their dissimilarity to the rest of mankind, must we not conclude that they are a different species of the same genus?"[7] The French author J. H. Guenebault went even further in his *Natural History of the Negro Race* (1837). He wrote: "It is then impossible to deny that they form not only a race, but truly a species, distinct from all other races of men known on the globe." They belong to "the ape genus", he declared, and placed them somewhere between orangutangs and white human beings.[8]

The slave as child

A third inferiority theory, popularized by Ulrich B. Phillips in his *American Negro Slavery* (1918), is that negroes were neither property nor animals, but children. Stanley M. Elkins, in his book *Slavery* (1959), examines the familiar image of the plantation slave as "Sambo". He was "docile but irresponsible, loyal but lazy, humble but chronically given to lying and stealing ... his relationship with his master was one of utter dependence and childlike attachment: it was indeed the childlike quality that was the very key to his being."[9] The Sambo stereotype was of "the perpetual child incapable of maturity".[10]

The horror of eighteenth-century slavery, then, was that it regarded adult men and women as tools, animals or children. Each of these reflected the belief that they were inferior. Christian opponents of slavery found it necessary, therefore, to demonstrate that negro slaves were human beings who were in no way inferior.

Racists may reluctantly concede the humanity of those ethnic groups whom they seek to oppress, but still believe that they are inferior. They may defend their position as "scientific", or merely cherish "vague notions about a unilinear evolution 'from monkey to man'". This encourages them to believe that such people are "lower" in the "scale" of evolution than themselves and that therefore there is "a hierarchy of 'races'".[11] Yet this concept of race is not derived from science, but from bigotry, and is a stratagem invented to justify discrimination.

Institutional racism has often restricted African-Americans to certain areas and certain roles, and given inferior education, housing and employment. The most obvious example of white supremacism was the appearance of the Ku Klux Klan from 1866 to 1869, after the end of the Civil War, and its subsequent re-emergence in 1915, with shameful support from white racist Christians whose churches were segregated and silent, despite the fact that there were riots and lynchings.

In 1957, despite large parts of the church being mute and ineffective, the Southern Christian Leadership Conference was formed following the bus boycotts in Montgomery, Alabama, during 1955 and 1956. Under the leadership of Martin Luther King, it supported non-violent direct action and protest. In Birmingham, Alabama, in 1963 an anti-segregation march including teenagers and children was met with violent resistance by the police. When televised, this led to support for the civil rights movement and on 28 August 1963, 250,000 people gathered in Washington to support civil rights and to hear King give his speech, "I have a dream..." In 1965 a protest march in Alabama was met with violence from the police, sending seventy people to hospital. Yet again, televised scenes of the violence shocked the nation and created support for the Voting Rights Act of 1965.

Even this was only a beginning. In 1968 the National Advisory Commission on Civil Disorders, which had been appointed by President Lyndon B. Johnson, delivered its report (known as the Kerner Report). Here is its conclusion: "Our nation is moving toward two societies, one black, one white – separate and unequal." Further, "Segregation and poverty have created in the racial ghetto a destructive environment totally unknown to most white Americans ... White institutions created it, white institutions maintain it, and white society condones it." However, we may be thankful that many Christians heeded God's call to change this situation in obedience to Jesus Christ, the God of justice.

GERMAN ANTI-SEMITISM AND SOUTH AFRICAN APARTHEID

Anti-Semitism in Germany and apartheid in South Africa seem at first sight so different from one another as to be entirely unsuitable for comparison. In particular, the unspeakable outrage of the Holocaust has had no parallel in South Africa. Nevertheless, although it will shock some readers to learn this, the theory of "race" on which both systems were built is almost identical. So is the sense which many Germans and South Africans have expressed that they are "destined to rule" and must at all costs preserve their "racial purity".

In *Mein Kampf*, published eight years before he came to power, Hitler extolled the splendour of the Aryan race. "Every manifestation of human culture, every product of art, science and technical skill, which we see before our

eyes today, is almost exclusively the product of the Aryan creative power ...
it was the Aryan alone who founded a superior type of humanity ... he is the
Prometheus of mankind, from whose shining brow the divine spark of genius
has at all times flashed forth..."[12]

Borrowing his ideas from Wagner's dream of Germanic greatness,
Nietzsche's notion of a "daring ruler race" and Darwin's concept of the ruthless struggle needed for survival, Hitler developed both his illusions of Aryan
destiny and his insane phobia of the Jews, who, he declared, were economically,
politically, culturally, religiously and morally destroying civilization.[13] The
insulting and irrational language he used of them is unrepeatable. He dared
even to claim that in dealing with them he would be acting on behalf of the
Almighty Creator.[14] In this he was able to quote Christian scholars who had
developed a "creation theology" to justify racism. Paul Althaus, for example,
recognizing marriage, family, race and *Volk* as God's order of creation, wrote:
"We champion the cause of the preservation of the purity of the Volk and of
our Race."[15] Hitler himself knew, it seems, that this racial theory of Aryan *Her-
renvolk* ("master race") had no scientific basis. In private he conceded this. Yet
he continued to use it because he needed it as a politician: "With the conception of race, National Socialism will carry its revolution abroad and recast the
world."[16]

The origins of the Afrikaners' sense of divine destiny are bound up with
their history. When the Dutch first arrived at the Cape of Good Hope (1652),
they saw themselves as the heirs and bearers of European Christian civilization. They saw a parallel between themselves and the exodus of the Old Testament people of God, destined for a new promised land. The Africans were their
equivalent to the Amalekites and the Philistines. After they defeated the Zulus
at the Battle of Blood River, they entered into a solemn covenant with God, and
henceforth thought of the Transvaal and the Orange Free State as the promised
land to which God had brought them. "Afrikanerdom is not the work of men,"
said Dr D. F. Malan, the Nationalist leader who became prime minister in 1948,
"but the creation of God."[17] Thus Afrikaners believed that they had a messianic
vocation, that they were born to rule, and that God had called them to preserve
Christian civilization in Africa.

Added to their history (which gave them this sense of destiny) was their
theology (which gave them their theory of race). It was this combination which
undergirded their determination to ensure their distinct survival by means of
apartheid. For, said the Dutch Reformed Church (until 1989, see below), "the

Scriptures ... teach and uphold the ethnic diversity of the human race" and regard it as a "positive proposition" to be preserved. Consequently, "a political system based on the autogenous or separate development of various population groups can be justified from the Bible".[18] But keeping South Africa white could only be achieved through white domination.

In *Mein Kampf* Hitler wrote that sexual relationships between different racial groups were to be opposed with the utmost vigour, in order to preserve the purity of Aryan stock. Intermarriage, he declared, invariably causes physical and mental degeneration. It is "a sin against the will of the Eternal Creator".[19] In South Africa the Prohibition of Mixed Marriages Act became law in 1949. It made marriage between "Europeans and non-Europeans" (i.e., between "whites" and "non-whites") illegal, while an Act of 1968 extended this law to include South African male citizens domiciled outside the country. Professor Dupreez tried to give this legislation a theological basis. "Is it God's will," he asked, implying that it is not, "that all the nations he has created in such rich diversity should now be equalized and assimilated, through intermarriage, to a uniform and mixed race?"[20]

Yet humanity as a race is fundamentally hybrid. "Not one of the major human groups is unmixed, nor is any one of its ethnic groups pure; all are, indeed, much mixed and of exceedingly complex descent."[21] "Pure British blood", for example, is a figment of the imagination. At the very least we are a mixture of Jute, Celt, Goth, Saxon, Roman and Norman. We have to ask, therefore, where are these "pure" ethnic groups which fear hybridity?

CHANGE IN SOUTH AFRICA

During the second half of the 1980s in South Africa, a number of Christian statements were issued and a number of events took place which gave ground for hope that the whole apartheid structure would be completely destroyed. These took place against a background of increasing global concern about the injustice of the situation in South Africa, with boycotts of companies trading in South Africa, campaigns such as the one to release Nelson Mandela, and sanctions such as the US Comprehensive Anti-Apartheid Act of 1986. The Act prohibited US trade and other economic relations with South Africa.

In September 1985 Michael Cassidy and nearly 400 other Christian leaders from a variety of ethnic backgrounds and denominations launched the National Initiative for Reconciliation. Describing the church as "a community of hope", its statement affirmed the sovereignty of God, called for humility, repentance, prayer and fasting before the cross, espoused non-violence even at the cost of suffering, and urged President Botha to end the state of emergency, release detainees and begin talks with representative leaders with a view to eliminating discrimination.

A few weeks later a group of about 150 black theologians issued the Kairos Document.[22] Passionate in concern, it sought to relate liberation theology to the *kairos*, the contemporary South African crisis, and outlined the three options. The first it called the "State Theology" of the Afrikaner churches, which justified the racist status quo by an appeal to Romans 13, the need for "law and order" and the threat of communism. This theology, it declared, "is not only heretical, it is blasphemous". Secondly, there was the "Church Theology" of the English-speaking churches which, though cautiously critical of apartheid, sought reconciliation without repentance and peace without justice. This too was rejected. The third option, which was ardently commended, was a "Prophetic Theology". Claiming to return to the Bible and its prophetic tradition, it identified the Nationalist government as so oppressive that it had forfeited its legitimacy. The right stance to adopt towards such a regime, therefore, was not negotiation but confrontation. The document ended with a "challenge to action" through the church's solidarity with the oppressed and through campaigns and protests, civil disobedience and participation in the armed struggle for liberation.

In July 1986, 130 black evangelicals published their hard-hitting *Evangelical Witness in South Africa*. Here were black evangelicals deliberately identifying with their white fellow evangelicals in order to condemn the whole evangelical constituency for its Greek dualism (being concerned for people's "spiritual", as opposed to their "material", welfare). They also repudiated its Western capitalistic conservatism, its pursuit of reconciliation without repentance, its misuse of Romans 13 to defend the status quo, the patronizing attitude of "white" people (even many missionaries) to "black" people, ulterior motives in evangelism (especially to secure the subservience of black converts to an unjust regime), and gospel preaching which was silent about the brutalities of the apartheid system. Alongside these criticisms, *Evangelical Witness* called for true repentance. That is, it made a radical and comprehensive demand for change.

Then in October 1986 the Dutch Reformed Church issued *Church and Society*, which was a "Testimony" approved by its synod. It was a thorough exposition of "Basic Scriptural Principles" and "Practical Implications", in the course of which the following astonishing statements were made: "Racism is a grievous sin which no person or church may defend or practise ... As a moral aberration, it deprives a human being of his dignity, his obligations and his rights. It must be rejected and opposed in all its manifestations" (para. 112). Again, "Apartheid ... a forced separation and division of peoples, cannot be considered a biblical imperative. The attempt to justify such a prescription as derived from the Bible must be recognized as an error and be denounced" (para. 305), for it "contravenes the very essence of neighbourly love and righteousness, and inevitably the human dignity of all involved" (para. 306). This was an extraordinary volte-face for a church which previously had supported and defended apartheid.

It seems to be of great significance that in 1985 and 1986 these four Christian documents, in spite of the distinction between so-called "state", "church" and "prophetic" theologies, should all have condemned apartheid as an indefensible system and have committed themselves to its abolition. Their united witness and protest must have had a significant influence on the government.

During this same period some important events, in the state rather than the church, also took place. In 1986 the hated Pass Laws, which for forty years had required so-called "non-whites" to carry their pass books and decreed where they might live and work, were abolished. Then in March 1989 a judicial commission called (1) for the total dismantling of apartheid, (2) for the repeal of two of its main legal pillars, the Group Areas Act (which forbade residential integration) and the Population Registration Act (which made classification by race compulsory), both passed in 1950, and (3) for a universal franchise which would inevitably lead to black majority rule. The same year Mr F. W. de Klerk replaced Mr P. W. Botha as president and immediately signalled the direction in which he intended to move by releasing some long-imprisoned leaders of the African National Congress (though not at first intending to release its acknowledged senior leader, Nelson Mandela), and by turning a blind eye to the ANC marches and rallies which followed.

During the 1990s, with almost bewildering speed, the structures of apartheid were dismantled and a democratic South Africa was born. In 1990 Nelson Mandela was released from prison after twenty-six years, talks began between the Nationalist Party and the African National Congress, the state of emergency was lifted, and the ANC agreed to cease their armed struggle. At the same time violence continued, much of it between the ANC and the Zulu Inkatha movement, fuelled by white police.

In 1991 Nelson Mandela was elected ANC president without opposition, and a significant turning point was reached when official multi-party talks began at the Convention for a Democratic South Africa (CODESA). In 1992 the National Party's referendum resulted in a 69% vote for a continuation of the reform process initiated by President F. W. de Klerk. By the end of the year official negotiations culminated in plans for a five-year power-sharing "Government of National Unity". It was fitting that the 1993 Nobel Peace Prize was awarded jointly to Nelson Mandela and F. W. de Klerk. The general election of 27 April 1994 won the ANC 252 of the parliament's 400 seats, brought Nelson Mandela to the presidency and paved the way for a new constitution.

The Truth and Reconciliation Commission was brought into being in 1995, with Archbishop Desmond Tutu as its chairman. It has been a remarkable initiative inspired by Christian principles, and based on the final clause of the Interim Constitution, which reads:

> This Constitution provides a historic bridge between the past of a deeply divided society characterized by strife, conflict, untold suffering and injustice, and a future founded on the recognition of human rights, democracy, peaceful co-existence and development opportunities for all South Africans, irrespective of colour, race, class, belief or sex.

The Commission rightly brackets "truth" and "reconciliation", since its primary brief has been to investigate, discover and publish the truth about human rights violations, as the only basis on which the perpetrators could be forgiven and their victims (or their relatives) could receive both limited reparation and the restoration of honour and dignity. Reconciliation is offered to those (1) who have offended against human rights between 1960 and 1995, (2) whose offence was politically motivated, (3) who make a full disclosure of all the relevant facts, and (4) who apply for amnesty.

BRITISH ATTITUDES AND TENSIONS

British colonial rule brought some positive good to the countries colonized, not so much in material terms (e.g., roads and railways) as in education, health care and standards of public justice. Yet these benefits have tended to be eclipsed by the offensive attitude of superiority implicit in "the British Raj mentality".

Sometimes, I regret to say, this was expressed in racist terms ominously reminiscent of the German and South African outlook we have just considered. Cecil Rhodes, for example, spoke of "the predominance of the Anglo-Saxon race" and the need to preserve it. Successive British secretaries of state for the colonies talked similarly, even using the language of "destiny", although fortunately such an illusion was never embodied in official policy.

For Jomo Kenyatta, the quest for the independence of Kenya was "not just a question of Africans ruling themselves, though that was the first thing", but also "an end to the colour bar, to the racist slang of the settler clubs, to the white man's patronizing attitudes of half a century and more".[23] At a political rally at Wundanyi in January 1962, Kenyatta said about his attitude to Europeans: "I am not against anyone. I am only against *ubwana*, the boss mentality."[24]

This British boss mentality was perhaps even more obvious in India. It would be hard to resist Arnold Toynbee's verdict that "the English Protestant rulers of India ... distinguished themselves from all other contemporary Western rulers over non-Western peoples by the rigidity with which they held aloof from their subjects".[25]

The British colonial record is a necessary background to understanding the racial tensions in Britain. I will now consider these under the headings of immigration, race relations and institutional racism.

Immigration

British immigration has to be seen against the background of global patterns of migration. One in thirty-five persons worldwide is an international migrant. The total number is estimated at 175,000,000 (2.9% of the world's population) in 2000, up from 105,000,000 in 1985.[26] There are also vast numbers of people who flee but do not cross a border to become refugees or asylum seekers. There are an estimated 25,000,000 internally displaced people (IDPs) worldwide, outnumbering refugees by two to one.[27] Refugees make up 9% of the global migrant total and most of these are in developing countries, with only 3,000,000 in developed countries. It is in the developing countries that the ratio of refugees to local population is extremely high. In Liberia the ratio of refugees per 1,000 of the local population is 87, in Georgia it is 51, but in the UK it is only estimated to be 3.2.[28] Such a low figure does not warrant the demonization of refugees and asylum seekers which has been a part of British mythology for far too long.

Migrant workers are needed across Europe. The UN's Population Division reports that low birth rates mean that the EU will need to import 1,600,000 migrants a year simply to keep its working-age population stable between now and 2050.[29] The population of the EU is predicted to fall from 482,000,000 in 2003 to 454,000,000 in 2050 – a decline of 6%.[30]

It must also be remembered that migration can have positive effects on the societies and economies of the host countries. The majority of legal migrants to the industrialized world are educated – 88% of migrants to the OECD have a secondary education and two thirds of those also have a tertiary education.[31] In many areas of the British economy, such people are badly needed. According to the Greater London Authority, 23% of doctors and 47% of nurses working within the NHS were born outside the UK.[32] These people are not taking jobs away from the indigenous population, as is commonly feared by those who would discriminate against migrants. They are in fact answering a need by filling gaps in the labour market. A recent Home Office study found that migrants made a net contribution of approx £2,500,000,000 to income tax in 1999 – 2000.[33]

In Britain, legislation and policy on immigration and asylum have frequently been a reaction to social attitudes about race relations. Despite being a hybrid nation, too many people in Britain have a tendency towards xenophobia. About half the people in the UK think that immigration of minority ethnic groups has led to a decline in their quality of life.[34] Negative attitudes towards race relations have led to increasingly restrictive immigration and asylum policies.

Although the British Nationality Act of 1948 defined a British citizen as anybody who had been born in Britain or in a British colony and gave citizens freedom of entry and settlement, the law from that point became increasingly restrictive and racially motivated. In 1962 the automatic right to enter and settle was removed.[35] In 1968 entry by refugee Asians from East Africa was regulated.[36] In 1971 the right of entry was restricted to those with at least one grandparent who had been born in the UK.

In 1981 a sweeping reform established three distinct citizenship categories. "British citizenship" was granted only to those whose parents were British or "settled" (with unrestricted stay). The other two categories were "British Dependent Territory citizens" and "British Overseas citizens", who would have no right of abode. Despite lobbying by the churches, this Act failed to express the true, multi-ethnic character of British society.[37] Controls were further tightened in 1988 and 1990, with the 1991 Asylum Bill limiting entry by asylum seekers. The Immigration and Asylum Act of 1999 was followed by the Immigration and Asylum Act of 2002 and the Asylum and Immigration Bill of 2003. By 2004, the focus was on asylum seekers rather than general immigration.

By 1997, the mood of the country was so negative and the media coverage so persistent that issues related to asylum seekers were a high priority for the government. By 2003, applications for asylum had fallen dramatically as a result of the tough measures introduced by the government. Among those measures were the tougher policing of the border with France, as well as the denial of access by asylum seekers to the British benefit system. This was replaced by a specialist service called the National Asylum Support Service. A list of "safe countries" was drawn up, from which asylum seekers would not be received, and the emphasis of the policy became control and repatriation rather than support. As a result of such policies, applications for asylum fell signficantly. In 2003 as a whole, following a surge in applications before tougher benefit rules came into force, applications fell by 41% – four times as much as the average across the rest of the EU.[38]

At several points during this long process, church leaders have complained about the impact of the increasingly restrictive policies regarding immigration and asylum. In recent years, for example, they have protested that too many asylum seekers are living on the streets, with little or no financial support. Even when they do have housing, one in five of the places where they live is unfit for human habitation.[39] In some cases this has had a devastating impact on family life. In other cases people have been deported, even though there was evidence to suggest that they might face persecution in their country of origin. Some have even been killed in racist attacks. In 2003 the Churches' Commission for Racial Justice published the book *Asylum Voices*, which consisted of interviews with asylum seekers throughout the UK. Although some asylum seekers had received a welcome in this country and had been granted their human rights with dignity, many others had faced hostility, abrogation of human rights, and had been stereotyped as "bogus", "scroungers", or even as potential terrorists, especially following the events of 11 September 2001 in New York. It is important that a church which has a passion for justice should stand up against any culture or system which overlooks injustice, especially when it refers to the weaker members of society. Yet such injustice goes further:

it denies the very roots of the creation story as affirming each person as made in the image of God and worthy of dignity and respect.

Race relations

Over the last forty years, two trends could be observed within legislation covering these areas. On the one hand, immigration and asylum policy seems to have reflected a negative attitude to minority ethnic groups, while on the other hand, race relations policy seems to have attempted to promote a multi-ethnic society. This should not surprise us, since both positive and negative attitudes are present together throughout British society.

The negative strand within British society was, in 1967, focused in the formation of the National Front, which was formed out of a coalition of extreme right-wing groups and was blatantly fascist in its origins and values. It found its supporters in those who were hostile to immigrants and members of minority ethnic groups. Their commitment to racial purity and racial superiority mirrored Nazi doctrines, and it should come as no surprise to know that some of their leaders admired Adolf Hitler and had been involved in Nazi activities.

In 1982 the National Front gave way to the British National Party (BNP), which was larger and at first glance seemed to be more moderate, working in part through the electoral system and putting up fifty candidates for the 1997 election. In 2005 the BNP contested 119 seats and took 192,850 votes in total, compared with 47,129 at the 2001 election. Its overall vote share rose by 0.55%.

Yet closer inspection still reveals the racist rhetoric which, with an arrogant insolence, draws on the xenophobia that still exists in Britain today. The party's leader, Nick Griffin, appears as a semi-respectable and rational leader, yet he calls the Holocaust "the hoax of the twentieth century", refers to the "mythical gas chambers of Auschwitz", and prefers to control the streets rather than the ballot box. In the 1990s, after a brief success in Millwall in the East End of London, he commented: "The electors of Millwall did not back a Post-Modernist Rightist Party, but what they perceived to be a strong, disciplined organization with the ability to back up its slogan 'Defend Rights for Whites' with well-directed boots and fists. When the crunch comes, power is the product of force and will, not of rational debate." [40]

It is hardly surprising that on occasions racial violence has broken out in the UK. Already in 1976 and 1979 there were clashes in Southall (West London) fuelled by the National Front. More serious street riots occurred between 1980 and 1983 in Bristol, Brixton (South London), Toxteth (Liverpool), Manchester, Nottingham, Leeds and other cities. In 1985 a riot broke out in Handsworth (Birmingham) in which two shopkeepers died in a fire, and this was followed by a riot in Broadwater Farm in London in which a policeman was murdered. In 2001 there were riots in Oldham, Burnley and Bradford, areas which were heavily influenced by the BNP. Although the source and cause of each of these acts of violence was different, they all grew out of the fertile ground provided by hostility towards minority ethnic groups, as well as the poor conditions in which they lived and worked and the nature of the policing in that area. In 1981 Lord Scarman, who had been commissioned by the Home Secretary to investigate the cause of the riots in the early 1980s, concluded that "there was a strong racial element in the disorders".[41]

However, there were and still are today many people who wish to celebrate ethnic diversity, who see immigration as a strength and who welcome people who seek asylum because they are fleeing from persecution. One of the positive moves was the creation of the Commission for Racial Equality as a result of the 1976 Race Relations Act. This was given some teeth to enforce and monitor the law, which made it unlawful to discriminate on the basis of race in such areas as employment and education, made "incitement to racial hatred" a criminal offence, and gave local authorities the responsibility to eliminate discrimination and to promote equal opportunities. Nonetheless, perhaps the most intractable form of racism was institutional, which, although Lord Scarman claimed in his report did not exist in Britain, was found to be a persistent problem throughout organizational structures and cultures. It is to this that we now turn.

Institutional racism

One of the issues that dominated the conduct of race relations in the 1990s in Britain was the murder of Stephen Lawrence, aged eighteen, on 22 April 1993. He had been waiting for a bus, and he died in an unprovoked racist attack by five white youths. The fact that no one was convicted for his murder and the unprofessional manner in which the tragedy was handled by the police led his parents to campaign for justice.[42] In July 1997 the Home Secretary set up a public enquiry to investigate the matters arising from his death. Of the report's seventy recommendations, sixty-six were concerned with the "openness, accountability and the restoration of confidence" in the police service and "to increase trust and confidence in policing amongst minority ethnic communities". The enquiry found that the police were guilty of institutional racism.

In order to explain the nature of institutional rascism, I will give two examples.

Police and the criminal justice system

The Stephen Lawrence enquiry highlighted an issue which had also arisen in the context of the Scarman Report, namely the hostility of some minority ethnic groups towards the police. The Scarman Report had been widely applauded, but its agenda had been largely ignored. So the Lawrence enquiry highlighted the need for action and accountability as well as the monitoring of the relationship between minority ethnic groups and the police.

One of the key issues was the use and abuse of the powers of "stop and search" by the police. In 2004 the Home Office's own report on progress which had arisen after the Stephen Lawrence enquiry stated its concern about trends in this area. Stop and search amongst the black population was double that of the Asian population, and year on year from 1999 to 2002 there was a percentage increase of minority ethnic people being stopped and searched. More specifically, the report stated that "the 2001/02 figures showed that black people were eight times more likely to be stopped and searched than white people". This was a rise from five times more likely in 1999/2000 and seven times more likely in 2000/01.

The situation changed even further following the Terrorism Act of 2000 and an increased sensitivity to the possible presence of Al Quaeda activists. The most notable statistic was that the number of people from Asian backgrounds stopped and searched by the police had increased by 300% since the Terrorism Act came into force. In 2003 the total number of stop and searches rose by 22% from the year before and was the highest ever, yet the percentage resulting in arrests remained at 13% for the second year and an even smaller percentage led to convictions. Part of this is, of course, due to the need for police to respond to the very obvious threat of terrorism in the West and should not be put down to any institutional racism. However, even the Home Office has commented that this level of stop and search for people from ethnic minorities is unacceptable. One commentator noted, "Once black people are arrested and charged, it becomes increasingly difficult for them to demonstrate their innocence. Many say it feels as if it is for them to prove their innocence rather than for the police to prove their guilt." [43]

This problem is not confined to Britain. In November 2000 it was reported that US police used racial profiling in their pursuit of those who might be carrying drugs. They stopped motorists on a main road into New York City – and 80% of those stopped were black. The police just assumed that black people and drugs went together, but 70% of those black people who were stopped were not carrying any drugs. New Jersey's Attorney General said that from a social policy point of view, this was a disaster and the policy was scrapped. [44]

There are further aspects of institutional racism in the justice system which are extremely disturbing. Far too few police officers in the UK come from ethnic minorities. In 1999 Jack Straw, then Home Secretary, set the target of 6,000 more police from minority ethnic groups by 2009. In 2002, however, out of a police force of approximately 130,000, only 3,300 came from minority ethnic groups, constituting 2.6% of the police force, making such a target a distant reality. [45] There are also too few black judges and magistrates. The White Paper "Justice for All", published in July 2002, recognized that there was little evidence of major improvements in the experience of people from minority ethnic communities. Other issues relate to impartiality in dealing with complaints, unexplained deaths in police custody and miscarriages of justice.

However, there is cause for encouragement. There is much greater awareness of racial injustice and reports of racial violence have increased by 100%, showing that people from minority groups are more willing to come forward. The police are more willing to prosecute than they were, and pilot projects on stop and search show that stops can be reduced while the proportion of arrests increases.

Employment practices

In 1997 Prime Minister Tony Blair pointed out that there were just two Asian and black people in Whitehall's top four grades and a mere fifty-eight among its three thousand senior policy makers. This highlighted the fact that institutional racism was by no means confined to the criminal justice system but was endemic throughout society, including health care, housing and social security as well as the private sector. Unemployment is another area in which racism is institutional as well as personal, as it is considerably higher among ethnic minority communities.

John Monks, former General Secretary of the TUC, was not exaggerating when he called the level of racial discrimination in the jobs market "intolerable".[46] The Churches' Commission for Racial Justice is rightly encouraging companies to adopt the so-called "Wood-Sheppard Principles on Race Equality in Employment".[47] Named after Bishop Wilfred Wood of Croydon, the Church of England's first black bishop, and Bishop David Sheppard, formerly Bishop of Liverpool, these principles call for "positive action" to redress the current inequalities.

Following the Stephen Lawrence enquiry, the Church of England set up an enquiry into its own practices. Several reports, books and parish resources followed which highlighted the need for the church to repent of its own institutional racism to become the church Christ intended it to be.[48] Racial Justice Sunday was established on the second Sunday of September, and the Ecumenical Racial Justice Fund was instituted.

In sum, racism can be both personal and institutional. It also has two origins. One is a pseudo-scientific myth, and the other is pure prejudice. The myth, which is foundational to Hitler's anti-Semitism, South Africa's apartheid and Britain's National Front, was defined by UNESCO (United Nations Educational, Scientific and Cultural Organization) in 1967 as a "false claim that there is a scientific basis for arranging groups hierarchically in terms of psychological and cultural characteristics that are immutable and innate". The popular prejudice is not based on any particular theory, but is a psychological reaction to people of other ethnic groups arising usually from resentment, fear or pride.

What is needed is an equally powerful conviction that racism is an affront to the unique dignity of human beings. Nothing I have read has helped me to understand better the damage which racism does to people than *The Autobiography of Malcolm X*. His red-hot anger was due in part to "the world's most monstrous crime" of slavery, in part to the black American's economic dependence on white America, but above all to the humiliation caused by the white man's "malignant superiority complex".[49] The problem, he writes, is not "civil rights" but "human rights": "Human rights! Respect as human beings! That's what the American black masses want. That's the true problem. The black masses want not to be shrunk from as though they are plague ridden. They want not to be walled up in slums, in the ghettoes, like animals. They want to live in an open, free society where they can walk with their heads up, like men and women."[50]

BIBLICAL FOUNDATIONS FOR ETHNIC DIVERSITY

We turn from mythology, prejudice and tension present in the contemporary world to the biblical vision of a multi-ethnic society. It was thoroughly developed by the apostle Paul in his famous sermon to the Athenian philosophers (Acts 17:22 – 31). Ancient Athens was a centre of ethnic, cultural and religious pluralism. From the fifth century BC it had been the foremost Greek city-state, and when it was incorporated into the Roman Empire it became one of the leading cosmopolitan cities in the world. As for religions, it is easy to understand Paul's comment that the Athenians were "very religious", for according to a Roman satirist, it was "easier to find a god there than a man". The city was crammed with innumerable temples, shrines, altars, images and statues.

What, then, was Paul's attitude to this multi-ethnic, multicultural and multireligious situation? He made four proclamations.

God is the God of creation

Firstly, he proclaimed the unity of the human race, or the God of creation. God is the Creator and Lord of the world and everything in it, he said. He gives to all human beings their life and breath and everything else. From one man he made every nation, that they should inhabit the whole earth, so that human beings would seek and find him, though he is not far from any of us. For "in him we live and move and have our being", and "we are his offspring". From this portrayal of the living God as Creator, Sustainer and Father of all humankind, the apostle deduces the folly and evil of idolatry. He could equally well have deduced from it the folly and evil of racism, for if he is the God of all human beings, this will affect our attitude to them as well as to him.

Although in terms of an intimate personal relationship God is the Father of those he adopts into his family by his sheer grace, and our brothers and sisters are fellow members of his family, nevertheless in more general terms God is the Father of all humankind, since all are his "offspring" by creation, and every human being is our brother or sister. Being equally created by him and like him, we are equal in his sight in worth and dignity, and, therefore, have an equal right to respect and justice. Paul also traces our human origin to Adam, the "one man" from whom God made us all. Some scientists now believe that there is evidence to suggest that humanity has the same remote ancestry, and they base this on evidence drawn from anatomy, palaeontology, serology and genetics. Yet however strong the scientific evidence is for this, the Bible affirms that humanity is a unity created by God.

God is the God of history

Secondly, Paul proclaimed the importance of ethnic and cultural diversity, affirming that God is the God of history. The living God not only made every nation from one man, that they should inhabit the earth, but he also "determined the times set for them and the exact places where they should live" (Acts 17:26; cf. Deuteronomy 32:8). Thus the times and the places of the nations are in the hands of God. We may not use this fact to justify the conquest and annexation of foreign territory, although even these historical developments are not beyond God's sovereign control. Probably Paul is alluding to the primeval command to multiply and fill the earth. Such dispersal under God's blessing inevitably resulted in the development of distinctive cultures, quite apart from the later confusing of languages and the scattering under his judgement at Babel.

Now culture is the complement of nature. What is "natural" is God-given and inherited; what is "cultural" is man-made and learned. Culture is an amalgam of beliefs, values, customs and institutions developed by each society and transmitted to the next generation. Human cultures are ambiguous because human beings are ambiguous. "Because man is God's creature, some of his culture is rich in beauty and goodness. Because he is fallen, all of it is tainted with sin and some of it is demonic." [51]

Scripture celebrates the colourful mosaic of human cultures. It even declares that the New Jerusalem will be enriched by them, since "the kings of the earth will bring their splendour into it", and "the glory and honour of the nations will be brought into it" (Revelation 21:24, 26). If they will enrich human life and community in the end, they can begin to do so now. Paul was a product of three cultures. By descent and upbringing a "Hebrew of the Hebrews", he also possessed Roman citizenship and had absorbed Greek language and concepts. We too can enhance our human life by learning other languages and experiencing other cultures. We need to ensure, therefore, that a multi-ethnic society is not a monocultural society. We must simultaneously assert both the unity of the human race and the diversity of ethnic cultures.

God is the God of revelation

Thirdly, Paul proclaimed the finality of Jesus Christ, or the God of revelation. He concluded his sermon with God's call to universal repentance because of the coming universal judgement, for which God had both fixed the day and appointed the judge (Acts 17:30 – 31). Paul refused to acquiesce in the religious pluralism of Athens or applaud it as a living museum of religious faiths. Instead, the city's idolatry provoked him (v. 16) – probably to jealousy for the honour of the living and true God. So he called on the city's people to turn in repentance from their idols to God.

We learn, then, that a respectful acceptance of the diversity of cultures does not imply an equal acceptance of the diversity of religions. The richness of each particular culture should be appreciated, but not the idolatry which may lie at its heart. We cannot tolerate any rivals to Jesus Christ, believing as we do that God has spoken fully and finally through him, and that he is the only Saviour, who died and rose again and will one day come to be the world's Judge. Nevertheless, we should never allow any person, whatever his or her religion, to be discriminated against as has happened to so many Muslims in the West following the events of 9/11. We must fight for justice for all, even as we proclaim the uniqueness of Christ.

God is the God of redemption

Fourthly, Paul proclaimed the glory of the Christian church, or the God of redemption. It is clearer in some of the apostle's letters than it is in Luke's record of this sermon that Jesus died and rose to create a new and reconciled community, his church. Thus the flow of history is being reversed. The Old Testament is the story of human scattering, of nations spreading abroad, falling apart, fighting. But the New Testament is the story of the divine ingathering of nations into a single international society. It is hinted at here in verse 34, in which we are told that a few men believed, one of whom was named Dionysius, and a woman named Damaris, and a number of others. So here was the nucleus of the new community, in which men and women of all ages, and of all racial, cultural and social origins, find their oneness in Christ.

Since God has made all nations and determines their times and places, it is clearly right for each of us to be conscious of our nationality and grateful for it. But since God has also brought us into his new society, he is thereby calling us into a new internationalism. Every Christian knows this tension, and nobody more keenly than Paul, who was at the same time a patriotic Jew and the apostle to the Gentiles. Christian "internationalism" does not mean that our membership of Christ and his church obliterates our nationality, any more than it does our masculinity or femininity. It means rather that, while our ethnic, national, social and sexual distinctions remain, they no longer divide us. They have been transcended in the unity of the family of God (Galatians 3:28). Raymond Johnston was right to say that "a proper understanding of nationhood calls attention to the human need for roots, a security and an identity mediated by the community, on the basis of which each individual knows that he 'belongs'".[52] Yet it needs to be added that in Christ we have found even deeper roots, and an even stronger security and identity, for through him God has called us into a new and wider unity.

The church must, therefore, exhibit its multi-ethnic, multinational and multicultural nature. There has been considerable debate in recent years whether a local church could or should ever be culturally homogeneous. A consultation on this issue concluded that no church should ever acquiesce in such a condition: "All of us are agreed that in many situations a homogeneous unit church can be a legitimate and authentic church. Yet we are also agreed that it can never be complete in itself. Indeed, if it remains in isolation, it cannot reflect the universality and diversity of the Body of Christ. Nor can it grow to maturity. Therefore every homogeneous unit church must take active steps to broaden its fellowship in order to demonstrate visibly the unity and the variety of Christ's Church."[53] The statement goes on to suggest how this might be done.

In his well-researched book on race and theology entitled *From Every People and Nation: A Biblical Theology of Race*,[54] J. Daniel Hays talks of the necessity of going beyond talking to action, within the church. He shows the extent to which the Bible story "constantly includes individuals and groups from a wide spectrum of ethnicity".[55] In particular he says, "Within the context of the Black-White racial problem in the United States, it is significant to note that Black Africans from Cush/Ethiopia play an important part throughout scripture".[56] The Bible is not peopled with "white Anglo-Americans"! In a strongly worded concluson he states that "the continuance of racially divided churches in the United States points only to the fact that a large majority of Christians in that country are probably identifying themselves more with their racial background, with all its cultural baggage, than they do with Christ and his gospel".[57] This is a challenge which all Christians must heed, whatever country they live in.

Yet there are many stories of reconciliation, indeed healing, around the world. Michael Duffey has chronicled several case studies from Northern Ireland, South Africa, Poland, East Germany, the Philippines, the Balkans, the Middle East and America which show that it is possible to break through divisions based on ethnicity and be reconciled to one another.[58]

Combating racism must start in the way we raise our children. Even at an early age they can be taught an appreciation of our multi-ethnic society. Schools now have programmes and curricula which emphasize the importance of mutual respect between different ethnic groups, and yet this teaching needs to be re-emphasized in our homes, churches and community groups. It is all too easy, especially in responding to the behaviour of young adults, to let racial stereotyping and violence become endemic in the culture. Churches must be at the forefront of condemning racism and not seeing it as a subject on which an occasional talk might be given if there is sufficient interest. The true church includes people from every background and offers them hospitality and a welcoming community. If that is not the case, then the church must consider whether it exemplifies the good news of the gospel.

Only a true theology, the biblical revelation of God, can deliver us from racism. Because he is the God of creation, we affirm the unity of the human race. Because he is the God of history, we affirm the diversity of ethnic cultures. Because he is the God of revelation, we affirm the finality of Jesus Christ. And because he is the God of redemption, we affirm the glory of the Christian church. Whatever policies for ethnic integration may be developed, we should try to ensure that they will reflect these doctrines. Because of the unity of humankind, we demand equal rights and equal respect for ethnic minorities. Because of the diversity of ethnic groups, we renounce cultural imperialism and seek to preserve all those riches of culture which are compatible with Christ's lordship. Because of the finality of Christ, we affirm that religious freedom includes the right to propagate the gospel. Because of the glory of the church, we must seek to rid ourselves of any lingering racism and strive to make it a model of harmony, in which the multi-ethnic dream comes true.

NOTES

1 In this chapter, the language used is in transition and some words and phrases used are changing. The recognition that there is only one human race means that words such as "ethnic" and "ethnicity" are sometimes preferred to "race" and "racial". So "multi-ethnic" is often preferred to "multiracial". However, in the work of the Commission for Racial Equality, for instance, the words "racial" and "race" are still used. I have tried to use such words as seem appropriate in their context. It is not, of course, possible to change the use of words in quotations. The word "racism" continues to be important, as no other word, as yet, conjures up the horrors associated with the injustice and pain associated with its practice. Changes have also come about in the use of the word "black" when referring to people. It has, of course, been used as a derogatory term in some cultures. But many people of African descent use it of themselves as a mark and indeed a celebration of their ethnicity. I have tried to be sensitive in the way I have used such words throughout this chapter. It is also important to acknowledge that discrimination affects many ethnic groups, including, for instance, the Asian community, those from the Balkan states and, particularly since 9/11, those from the Middle East.

2 Martin Luther King's "I Have a Dream" speech is recorded in Coretta Scott King, *My Life with Martin Luther King Jr* (London: Hodder & Stoughton, 1969), p. 249.

3 From an address by Roy Jenkins, then Home Secretary, in May 1966, to a meeting of Voluntary Liaison Committees.

4 The Stephen Lawrence Enquiry Report, p. 20, para 6.4.

5 Ibid.

6 David Brion Davies, *The Problem of Slavery in Western Cultures* (Ithaca, N. Y.: Cornell Univ. Press, 1966), p. 31.

7 Edward Long, *The History of Jamaica* (London: Lowndes, 1774), pp. 351 – 56.

8 J. H. Guenebault, *The Natural History of the Negro Race* (English translation, Charleston, S.C.: Dowling, 1837), pp. 1 – 19. See also the references to this book in Wilson Armistead, *A Tribute for the Negro* (Manchester and London: W. Irwin, 1848), e.g., p. 36.

9 Stanley M. Elkins, *Slavery: A Problem in American Institutional and Intellectual Life* (1959; 2nd ed., Chicago: Univ. of Chicago Press, 1968), p. 82.

10 Ibid., p. 84.

11 M. F. Ashley Montagu, *Man's Most Dangerous Myth, the fallacy of race* (1942; 5th ed., revised and enlarged, Oxford: Oxford Univ. Press, 1974), p. 101.

12 Adolf Hitler, *Mein Kampf* (1925; translated by James Murphy; London: Hutchinson, 1940), p. 150.

13 Ibid., p. 284.

14 Gutteridge, *Open Thy Mouth for the Dumb!*, p. 69.

15 Ibid., p. 48.

16 Quoted in Montagu, *Man's Most Dangerous Myth*, p. 50.

17 Quoted in John W. de Gruchy, *The Church Struggle in South Africa* (Grand Rapids: Eerdmans, 1979), pp. 30 – 31. For recent assessments of Christian attitudes to racism in South Africa, see Zolile Mbali, *The Churches and Racism, A black South African perspective* (London: SCM, 1987); and Cassidy, *The Passing Summer.*

18 *Human Relations and the South African Scene in the Light of Scripture,* a 1974 report of the Dutch Reformed Church (Dutch Reformed Publishers, 1976), pp. 14, 32, 71.
19 Hitler, *Mein Kampf,* p. 248.
20 Professor Dr A. B. Dupreez, *Inside the South African Crucible* (Kapstaad-Pretoria, South Africa: HAUM, 1959), p. 63.
21 Montagu, *Man's Most Dangerous Myth,* p. 10.
22 In this case, the use of the word "black" is important, since it is not a term imposed on the group by the apartheid regime but a term that connotes a sense of their shared cultural identity in carrying out this task.
23 Jeremy Murray-Brown, *Kenyatta* (London: George Allen & Unwin, 1972), p. 306.
24 Mzee Jomo Kenyatta, *Suffering without Bitterness* (Nairobi: East African Publishing House, 1968), p. 166. For similar African reactions to French colonial rule, see Frantz Fanon, *Black Skin, White Masks* (1952).
25 Arnold Toynbee, *A Study of History,* vol. 1, p. 213, quoted by Archbishop Cyril Garbett in *World Problems of Today* (London: Hodder & Stoughton, 1955), p. 135.
26 *www.iom.int/DOCUMENTS/PUBLICATION/EN/MPI_series_No_2_eng.PDF*
27 *www.oxfam.org.uk/what_we_do/issues/conflict_disasters/downloads/migration_development.pdf, p. 12.*
28 Ibid., p. 4.
29 *www.cre.gov.uk*
30 *www.oxfam.org.uk,* p. 4.
31 Ibid., p. 9.
32 *www.cre.org.uk*
33 *www.cre.gov.uk,* "The Migrant Population in the UK: Fiscal Effects" (Home Office occasional paper 77).
34 *www.mmu.ac.uk*
35 The Commonwealth Immigrants Act (1962) – from that point immigrants needed an employment voucher to get in.
36 The Commonwealth Immigrants Act (1968) – the right to enter and settle was given to some East African Asians during the Kenyan government's programme of Africanization.
37 See Anne Owers, *Sheep and Goats, British nationality law and its effects* and *Families Divided, Immigration control and family life* (London: CIO, 1984).
38 Home Office press release, 24 February 2004, ref: 070/2004.
39 Commission for Racial Equality, *www.cre.gov.uk.*
40 This statement was originally published in *Rune* magazine (an anti-Semitic quarterly published by the Croydon BNP). For this and other information regarding Nick Griffin and the BNP, see the BBC website's *Panorama* pages: *news.bbc.co.uk/hi/english/static/in_depth/programmes/2001/bnp_special/the_leader/beliefs.stm.*
41 Lord Scarman, *The Scarman Report: The Brixton Disorders 10 – 12 April 1981* (Harmondsworth: Penguin, 1981), pp. 77 – 78.
42 For an excellent analysis of the church's response to institutional racism, and indeed of institutional racism in general, see Glynne Gordon-Carter, *An Amazing Journey, The Church of England's response to institutional racism* (London: Church House Publishing, 2003).

43 David Haslam, *Race for the Millennium, A challenge to church and society* (London: Church House Publishing, 1996).

44 "Stephen Lawrence – What Next?", speech given by Lord Dholakia, 22 March 2001, at the Criminal Justice Conference held at Pendley Manor.

45 *www.statistics.gov.uk/STATBASE/ssdataset.asp?vlnk=6377,* Police officer strength: by sex, minority, ethnic group, and rank, 2002: Social Trends 33.

46 TUC news release, April 1997.

47 A copy of the principles, revised in 2003, can be found at *www.industrialmission.org/ reep/reep1.html.*

48 Cf. *Called to Lead, A challenge to include minority ethnic people, report by the Stephen Lawrence Follow-up Staff Group* (London: Church House Publishing, 2000); Report of an independent inquiry into institutional racism within the structures of the Diocese of Southwark (March 2000); Glynne Gordon Carter, *An Amazing Journey, The Church of England's response to institutional racism* (London: Church House Publishing, 2003).

49 Malcolm X, *The Autobiography of Malcolm X* (New York: Grove Press, 1964), pp. 175, 275.

50 Ibid., pp. 179, 272.

51 "The Lausanne Covenant", para. 10, "Evangelism and Culture", in Stott (ed.), *Making Christ Known*, pp. 39 – 42.

52 O. R. Johnston, *Nationhood, Towards a Christian perspective* (Oxford: Latimer Studies, no. 7, 1980), p. 14.

53 "The Pasadena Statement on the Homogeneous Unit Principle", in Stott (ed.), *Making Christ Known*, p. 64. For an Asian Christian's experience of living in Britain, see Philip Mohabir, *Building Bridges* (London: Hodder & Stoughton, 1988). Also recommended is the "Study Pack for Christians in a Multi-Racial Society", entitled *New Humanity* and produced by Evangelical Christians for Racial Justice, 109 Homerton High Street, London, E9 6DL, UK.

54 J. Daniel Hays, *From Every People and Nation, A Biblical theology of race* (Leicester: InterVarsity Press, Apollos imprint, 2003).

55 Ibid., p. 201.

56 Ibid.

57 Ibid., p. 205.

58 Michael K. Duffey, *Sowing Justice, Reaping Peace: Case Studies of Racial, Religious, and Ethnic Healing around the World* (Franklin, Wis.: Sheed and Ward, 2001).

Simplicity, Generosity and Contentment

It is no wonder that we in the West are so frequently described as being materialistic, superficial and selfish. Our drive to possess and consume, as well as our tendency to believe that worth can be measured by wealth, are hallmarks of a society that has lost its way. One only needs to travel in the Majority World, meeting people who live in the barriadas and favelas of Latin America or the slums and ghettoes of India and Africa, to realize that there is something fundamentally wrong, and indeed inexcusable, about such attitudes.

Although North America and Europe are characterized as being wealthy, poverty has not been eliminated from them by any means. In the United States in 2003 there were 35,900,000 people living below the poverty line, or 12.5% of the population.[1] In Britain, according to government statistics, approximately one in four of the population is living below the poverty line.[2] According to Oxfam, recent surveys have shown that about 6,500,000 adults in the UK go without essential clothing, such as a warm waterproof coat, because of lack of money. Over 10,500,000 people live in financial insecurity: they cannot afford to save, insure their house contents or spend even small amounts on themselves. About 9,500,000 cannot afford adequate housing – heated, free from damp and in a decent state of decoration. The crucial factor about these findings is that they are based on a survey of what the general population sees as necessities.[3]

In 1982, Church Action on Poverty (CAP) was launched as an ecumenical charity dedicated to tackling poverty in the UK. It sees its calling as standing alongside those for whom poverty is their daily living experience, and it defines poverty as an amalgam of different issues: a battle of invisibility, a lack of resources, exclusion, powerlessness, and being blamed for society's problems.[4]

In 1985, the report of the Archbishop of Canterbury's Commission on Urban Priority Areas entitled *Faith in the City* was published. "Chapter after chapter of our Report," its conclusion begins, "tells the same story: that a growing number of people are excluded by poverty or powerlessness from sharing in the common life of our nation. A substantial minority – perhaps as many as one person in every four or five across the nation, and a much higher proportion in the urban priority areas – are forced to live on the margins of poverty or below the threshold of an acceptable standard of living."[5] Such was the impact of *Faith in the City* that in 2003 the Commission on Urban Life and Faith was established to report on the changes which had taken place in the twenty years since it was published.[6]

The truth is that a grave disparity between wealth and poverty is to be found not only between nations, but within most nations as well. In the UK and the US, the richest 10% earn about 30% of the income and the poorest 10% earn only 2%, and if wealth rather than income is measured, the situation is even more unequal and seems to be widening.[7] What the Latin American Roman Catholic bishops said at Puebla in 1979 still resonates today: "The cruel contrast between luxurious wealth and extreme poverty, which is so visible throughout our continent and which is further aggravated by the corruption that often invades public and professional life, shows the great extent to which our nations are dominated by the idol of wealth."[8]

THREE APPROACHES TO POVERTY

How should Christians approach the harsh fact of poverty in the contemporary world?

An empirical analysis of poverty

Firstly, we need to approach the problem rationally, with cool statistical detachment. In chapter 6 I have looked at the issues surrounding international development and discussed issues relating to poverty in detail. Here I would like to focus on child poverty, a pressing claim on anybody who is concerned about social justice. Every year, 4,000,000 babies die during the first month of life; 70% of avoidable newborn deaths could be averted through interventions delivered through medical health services.[9]

Even when children survive the traumas of birth and the early months of life, they can still suffer from the impact of poverty. In an authoritative report sponsored by UNICEF, it was found that over 1,000,000,000 children suffer the severe effects of poverty.[10]

- One child of every three lives in a dwelling with more than five people per room, or with a mud floor.
- Nearly 20% of the world's children do not have safe water sources or have more than a fifteen-minute walk to water.
- Over 15% of children under five in the developing world are severely malnourished. In South Asia alone, more than 90,000,000 children go hungry every day.
- 134,000,000 children between the ages of seven and eighteen have never been to school.
- Girls are more likely to go without schooling than boys. In the Middle East and North Africa, in particular, girls are three times more likely than boys never to have attended school.

In the case of the UK, many children are still living in poverty, although it has become a key target of the UK government to reduce child poverty.

- There are 3,600,000 children living in poverty – 31%.[11]
- 2,000,000 British children go without at least two things they need (such as three meals a day, toys or adequate clothes).[12]
- A UNICEF report found that in a league table of twenty-three industrialized nations Britain was fourth worst in terms of the proportion of children living in "relative" poverty and sixth worst in terms of children living in "absolute" poverty. In Britain 30% of children live in "absolute" poverty, while in Sweden it is less than 5%.[13]
- The UK has the second highest child poverty rate in the EU.[14]

Therefore, child poverty is also high on the British government's agenda. In 1999 an annual report was launched, *Opportunity for All – Tackling Poverty and Social Exclusion*, which describes the government's strategy and progress in addressing these problems.[15] One of its key targets was to reduce child poverty by a quarter between 1998 and 2004. The Joseph Rowntree Foundation, one of the UK's largest independent social policy research organizations, reports that the government seems to have met this objective.[16] But, in order to halve child poverty, the poorest families require an extra £10 per week, per child.[17] Child poverty in the UK may not be as stark as that in areas of the Majority World, but it is an ever-present reality which needs to be addressed by both church and government.

An emotional reaction to poverty

Secondly, we could approach the phenomenon of poverty emotionally, with the hot-blooded indignation aroused by the sights, sounds and smells of human need. When I visited Calcutta airport, the sun had already set. Over the whole city hung a pall of acrid smoke from the burning of cow-dung on myriad fires. Outside the airport an emaciated woman clutching an emaciated baby stretched out an emaciated hand for baksheesh. A man whose legs had both been amputated above the knee dragged himself along the pavement with his hands. I later learned that over 250,000 homeless people sleep on the streets at night, and during the day hang their blanket – often their only possession – on some convenient railing. My most poignant experience was to see men and women scavenging in the city garbage dumps like dogs. Extreme poverty is demeaning; it reduces human beings to the level of animals. To be sure, Christians should be provoked by the idolatry of a Hindu city, as Paul was by the idols in Athens, and moved to evangelism. But, like Jesus when he saw the hungry crowds, we should also be moved with compassion to feed them (compare Acts 17:16f. with, e.g., Mark 8:1 – 3).

It is not only the absolute poverty of Majority World slums which should arouse our emotions, however, but also the relative (though real) poverty of the decayed and deprived inner-city areas of the West, which the affluent seldom if ever see. This was the emphasis which David Sheppard, Bishop of Liverpool until 1997, made in his Richard Dimbleby Lecture broadcast in 1984. He urged "Comfortable Britain" to stand in the shoes of the "Other Britain". He spoke with deep feeling of youth and long-term unemployment, neglected housing, poor opportunities in schooling, and the sense of alienation, even desertion. He felt indignant, indeed angry, because poverty "imprisons the spirit", spawns "sick human relationships" and wastes God-given talent.[18]

A biblical response to poverty

The third way, which should stimulate both our reason and our emotion simultaneously, is to approach the problem of poverty biblically. As we turn again to that book in which God has revealed himself and his will, we ask: How according to Scripture should we think about wealth and poverty? Is God on the side of the poor? Should we be? What does Scripture say? Moreover, as we ask these questions, we have to resolve to listen attentively to God's Word, and not manipulate it. We have no liberty either to avoid its uncomfortable challenge, in order to retain our prejudices, or to acquiesce uncritically in the latest popular interpretations.

Psalm 113 seems a good place to begin. It is an invitation to Yahweh's servants, indeed to all people "from the rising of the sun to the place where it sets", to praise his name, since he "is exalted over all the nations, his glory above the heavens". It continues:

> Who is like the LORD our God,
>   the One who sits enthroned on high,
> who stoops down to look
>   on the heavens and the earth?
> He raises the poor from the dust
>   and lifts the needy from the ash heap;
> he seats them with princes,
>   with the princes of their people.
> He settles the barren woman in her home
>   as a happy mother of children.

vv. 5 – 9

The psalmist is affirming something distinctive – indeed unique – about Yahweh, which enables him to ask the rhetorical question, "Who is like the LORD our God?" It is not just that he reigns on high, exalted above both the nations and the sky; nor only that from these lofty heights he condescends to look far below to the heavens and the earth; nor even that on the distant earth he regards with compassion the depths of human misery, the poor discarded on the scrapheaps of life and trampled in the dust by their oppressors. It is more than all these things. It is that he actually exalts the wretched of the earth; he lifts them from the depths to the heights: "He raises the poor from the dust and ... seats them with princes." For example, he takes pity on the barren woman (whose childlessness was regarded as a disgrace) and makes her a joyful mother. That is the kind of God he is. No other god is like him. It is not primarily the wealthy and the famous with whom he delights to fraternize.

What is characteristic of him is to champion the poor, to rescue them from their misery and to transform paupers into princes.

This affirmation is many times repeated and exemplified in Scripture, usually with its corollary that the God who lifts up the humble also puts down the proud. This was the essence of Hannah's song when, after years of childlessness, her son Samuel was born:

> He raises the poor from the dust
> and lifts the needy from the ash heap;
> he seats them with princes
> and has them inherit a throne of honour.
>
> 1 SAMUEL 2:8

This too was the theme of the Magnificat, which the Virgin Mary sang after learning that she (and not some famous, noble or wealthy woman) had been chosen to be the mother of God's Messiah. God had looked upon her lowly state, she said; the Mighty One had done great things for her, for which she gave him thanks and praise:

> He has performed mighty deeds with his arm;
> he has scattered those who are proud in their inmost thoughts.
> He has brought down rulers from their thrones
> but has lifted up the humble.
> He has filled the hungry with good things
> but has sent the rich away empty.
>
> LUKE 1:51 – 52

In Psalm 113, and in the experiences of Hannah and Mary, the same stark contrast is painted, although the vocabulary varies. The proud are abased and the humble exalted; the rich are impoverished and the poor enriched; the well fed are sent away empty and the hungry filled with good things; powerful rulers are toppled from their thrones, while the powerless and the oppressed are caused to reign like princes. "Who is like the LORD our God?" His thoughts and ways are not ours. He is a topsy-turvy God. He turns the standards and values of the world upside down.

Jesus himself is the greatest example of this. One of his favourite epigrams seems to have been that "everyone who exalts himself will be humbled, and he who humbles himself will be exalted" (e.g., Luke 18:14). He did not only enunciate this principle, however; he personally exhibited it. Having emptied himself of his glory, he humbled himself to serve, and his obedience took him even to the depths of the cross. "Therefore God exalted him to the highest place..." (Philippians 2:5 – 11).

It is this principle, which pledges the reversal of human fortunes, which alone can bring hope to the poor. But who are the "poor" whom God is said to "raise"? And what does he do when he "raises" them? These words demand definition.

WHO ARE THE POOR? THE PARADOX OF POVERTY

A number of studies of the biblical material have been made and published.[19] They focus on the Old Testament, in which a cluster of words for poverty, deriving from six main Hebrew roots, occurs more than two hundred times. These may be classified in a variety of ways, but the principal division seems to be fourfold. Firstly, and economically speaking, there are the indigent poor, who are deprived of the basic necessities of life. Secondly, and behaviourally speaking, there are the indolent poor, who are responsible for becoming impoverished because of their own behaviour. Thirdly, and sociologically speaking, there are the powerless poor, who are oppressed victims of human injustice. Fourthly, and spiritually speaking, there are the humble poor, who acknowledge their helplessness and look to God alone for salvation. In each case God is represented as coming to them and making their cause his own, in keeping with his characteristic that "he raises the poor from the dust".

The indigent poor

The first group, the indigent poor, are economically deprived. They may lack food or clothing or shelter, or all three. As we have seen, many millions of people in the world today are in this position. The Old Testament focuses its attention on poverty as an involuntary social evil to be abolished, not tolerated, and represents the poor (who included widows, orphans and aliens) as people to be succoured, not blamed. They are regarded not as sinners but as "the sinned against" – an expression popularized at the 1980 Melbourne Conference by Raymond Fung, a Baptist minister who had spent eleven years serving factory workers in Hong Kong.[20]

In the Law, God's people were commanded not to harden their hearts or close their hands against their poor brother or sister, but to be generous in maintaining those who could not maintain themselves, by taking them into their home and feeding them without charge. Their regular tithes were also to be used to support the Levites, the aliens, the orphans and the widows (Deuteronomy 15:7ff.; Leviticus 25:35ff.; Deuteronomy 14:29; Leviticus 26:12). If an Israelite lent money to somebody in need, he was not to charge interest on it. If he took a pledge (collateral) to secure his loan, he was not to go into the house to fetch it, but was to stand respectfully outside and wait for it to be brought out to him. If he took as a pledge his neighbour's cloak, he was to return it before sunset because the poor person would need it as a blanket to sleep in (Exodus 22:25; Leviticus 25:36f.; Deuteronomy 24:10f.; Exodus 22:26ff.; Deuteronomy 24:12). In particular, the support and the relief of the poor were the obligations of the extended family towards its own members.

Employers were to pay their workers' wages promptly, the same day that they were earned. Farmers were not to reap their fields "to the very edges", nor to go back to pick up a dropped or forgotten sheaf, nor to gather the gleanings after harvesting, nor to strip their vineyard bare, nor to gather fallen grapes, nor to go over the branches of their olive trees a second time. The borders, the gleanings and the fallen fruit were all to be left for the poor, the alien, the widow and the orphan. They too must be allowed to share in the harvest celebrations. Every third year a tenth of the agricultural produce was to be given to the poor. Every seventh year fields were to lie fallow, and vineyards and olive groves were to be unharvested, for the benefit of the poor who could help themselves to the fruit (Leviticus 19:13; Deuteronomy 24:14ff.; Leviticus 19:9f.; 23:22; Deuteronomy 16:9ff.; 24:19ff.; 14:28ff.; 26:12ff.; Exodus 23:10ff.; Leviticus 25:1ff.).

The Old Testament Wisdom Literature confirmed this teaching. One of the characteristics of a righteous man is that he "cares about justice for the poor"; "he is generous and lends freely", and "has scattered abroad his gifts to the poor"; whereas "if a man shuts his ears to the cry of the poor, he too will cry out and not be answered" (Psalm 111:1 – 9; Proverbs 21:13; 29:7; cf. 14:20ff.; 19:7; 31:20; Job 31:16ff.; Ezekiel 16:49). The wise teachers of Israel also grounded these duties on doctrine, namely that behind the poor Yahweh himself was standing, their Creator and Lord, so that people's attitude to him would be reflected in their attitudes to the poor. On the one hand, "He who mocks the poor shows contempt for their Maker"; on the other, "He who is kind to the poor lends to the LORD" (Proverbs 17:5; 19:17).

Jesus himself inherited this rich Old Testament legacy of care for the poor, and put it into practice. He made friends with the needy and fed the hungry. He told his disciples to sell their possessions and give alms to the poor, and when they gave a party to remember to invite the poor, the crippled, the lame and the blind, who would probably be in no position to invite them back. He also promised that in feeding the hungry, clothing the naked, welcoming the homeless and visiting the sick, they would thereby be ministering to him (Luke 12:33; 14:12ff.; Matthew 25:35 – 40).

The indolent poor

The second group, the indolent poor, can become poor because of the consequences of their own behaviour, whether it is laziness, extravagance or gluttony. Hopefully this situation is not applicable to many people and we must be careful not to suggest that the vast majority of people who are impoverished in the world are poor because of their own sin. However, in some cultures, perhaps particularly in the West, we are encouraged to overconsume. In some cases this leads people to get into debt, particularly credit card debt, because they prefer to consume rather than to save. It is, of course, true that many people work excessively hard and are stressed as a result, but it is also true that some people think life owes them a living. The book of Proverbs has much to say about this. The sluggard is exhorted to study the ways of the ant, in order to learn wisdom. Ants gather and store food during the summer, while sluggards stay in bed: "A little sleep, a little slumber, a little folding of the hands to rest – and poverty will come on you like a bandit and scarcity like an armed man" (Proverbs 6:6 – 11; cf. 24:30 – 34). Similarly, "Lazy hands make a man poor, but diligent hands bring wealth" (10:4; cf. 19:15; 20:13; 28:19). Closely linked to laziness, as causing poverty, are greed and drunkenness: "Drunkards and gluttons become poor, and drowsiness clothes them in rags" (Proverbs 23:20ff.; cf. 21:17). Not only did these particular sins bring individual poverty, however. National poverty also was due to sin. During the theocracy, when God ruled over his people in Israel, he promised to bless their obedience with fruitfulness of field and orchard, and to curse their disobedience with barrenness (see, e.g., Leviticus 26; Deuteronomy 8 and 28; Isaiah 1:19ff. and 5:8ff. for national blessing and curses).

The powerless poor

The third group, the powerless poor, are socially or politically oppressed. It was clearly recognized in the Old Testament that poverty does not normally just happen. Although sometimes it was due to personal sin or national disobedience, and to God's judgement on them, it was usually due to the sins of others – that is, to a situation of social injustice, which easily deteriorated because the poor were not in a position to change it. We do not understand the Old Testament teaching on this subject unless we see how frequently poverty and powerlessness were bracketed. At the same time, although the poor often had no human helper, they knew that God was their champion. "He stands at the right hand of the needy one." Again, "I know that the LORD secures justice for the poor and upholds the cause of the needy" (Psalm 109:31; 140:12).

Moses' law laid emphasis on the need for impartial justice in the courts, in particular for the poor and powerless. "Do not deny justice to your poor people in their lawsuits ... Do not accept a bribe, for a bribe blinds those who see and twists the words of the righteous." "Do not pervert justice; do not show partiality to the poor or favouritism to the great, but judge your neighbour fairly." "Do not deprive the alien or the fatherless of justice." Moreover, the reason repeatedly given was that they themselves had been oppressed in Egypt, and the Lord had liberated them (Exodus 23:6, 8; Leviticus 19:15; Deuteronomy 24:17; 27:19; 15:15).

The Wisdom books were as explicit as the Law books in demanding justice for the helpless. In Psalm 82 the judges were instructed to "defend the cause of the weak and fatherless" and "maintain the rights of the poor and oppressed". In Proverbs 31 King Lemuel was exhorted by his mother to "speak up for those who cannot speak for themselves, for the rights of all who are destitute", to "speak up and judge fairly" and "defend the rights of the poor and needy" (Psalm 82:1 – 3; Proverbs 31:8 – 9; cf. Job 29:11ff.; Proverbs 22:22ff.; 29:7, 14).

It is well known that the prophets were even more outspoken. They not only urged the people and their leaders to "seek justice, encourage the oppressed, defend the cause of the fatherless, plead the case of the widow", and conversely forbade them to "oppress the widow or the fatherless, the alien or the poor", but were also fierce in their condemnation of all injustice. Elijah rebuked King Ahab for murdering Naboth and stealing his vineyard. Amos fulminated against the rulers of Israel because in return for bribes they trampled on the heads of the poor, crushed the needy and denied justice to the oppressed, instead of letting "justice roll on like a river, and righteousness like a never-failing stream". Jeremiah denounced King Jehoiakim for using forced labour to build his luxurious palace. Other examples could be given. The national life of Israel and Judah was constantly tarnished by the exploitation of the poor. And James in the New Testament, sounding just like an Old Testament prophet, also inveighs against the rich. It is not their wealth in itself which he condemns, nor even primarily their self-indulgent luxury, but in particular their fraudulent withholding of wages from their workforce and their violent oppression of the innocent (Isaiah 1:17; Zechariah 7:8ff.; 1 Kings 21; Amos 2:6f.; 4:1ff.; 5:11ff.; 8:4ff.; 5:24; Jeremiah 22:13ff. Other examples of the prophetic stress on justice are Isaiah 3:13ff.; 5:7ff.; 10:1f.; Jeremiah 5:28ff.; Ezekiel 18:10ff.; James 5:1ff.).

In contrast to this dark tradition of the prophets' diatribe against injustice, their predictions of the Messiah's righteous reign shine the more brightly: "With righteousness he will judge the needy, with justice he will give decisions for the poor of the earth" (Isaiah 11:1 – 5).

It is abundantly clear from this evidence that the biblical writers saw the poor not only as destitute people, whose condition must be relieved, but as the victims of social injustice, whose cause must be championed. The biblical perspective is not "the survival of the fittest" but "the protection of the weakest". Since God himself speaks up for them and comes to their aid, his people must also be the voice of the voiceless and the defender of the defenceless.

The humble poor

The fourth group, the humble poor, are spiritually meek and dependent on God. Since God succours the destitute and defends the powerless, these truths inevitably affect their attitude to him. They look to him for mercy. Oppressed by human beings and helpless to liberate themselves, they put their trust in God. It is in this way that "the poor" came to be synonymous with "the pious", and their social condition became a symbol of their spiritual dependence. Zephaniah describes them as "the meek and humble, who trust in the name of the LORD", and Isaiah calls them the "humble and contrite in spirit" who tremble at God's Word (Zephaniah 2:3; 3:12; Isaiah 66:2; cf. 49:13).

It is particularly in the Psalms, however, that the otherwise rather blurred portrait of the humble poor comes into sharp focus. The Psalter is the hymnbook of the helpless (see, e.g., Psalms 22, 25, 37, 40, 69, 74, 149). It is here that we listen to their expressions of dependence upon God, and to God's promises to come to their aid. They are "the lonely and afflicted" who cry to him to be gracious to them; they commit their way to the Lord, are quiet before him, and wait patiently for him to act. They are given the assurance that "the poor will eat and be satisfied", that "the meek will inherit the land" and that "he crowns the humble with salvation" (Psalm 25:16; 37:5, 7; 40:1; 22:26; 37:11; 149:4).

More striking even than these references to the poor and meek as a group, however, are the individual testimonies to Yahweh's salvation. There is Psalm 34, for example: "This poor man called, and the LORD heard him; he saved him out of all his troubles." As a result, he determines to "boast in the LORD" and is confident that others who are "afflicted" like him will hear and rejoice with him, and will in their turn call upon Yahweh. For, he goes on to affirm, "The LORD is close to the broken-hearted and saves those who are crushed in spirit" (Psalm 34:1 – 6, 15 – 18). Another example occurs in Psalm 86. The psalmist describes himself as savagely assaulted by arrogant, godless and ruthless men. His only hope is in God. "Hear, O LORD, and answer me," he cries, "for I am poor and needy. Guard my life, for I am devoted to you. You are my God; save your servant who trusts in you." And he goes on to express his confidence that God will rescue him, because he is "a compassionate and gracious God, slow to anger, abounding in love and faithfulness" (Psalm 86:1 – 4, 14 – 17).

All this biblical teaching enables us to affirm that although God challenges the indolent poor, he succours the indigent poor, champions the powerless poor and exalts the humble poor. In each of these three cases "he raises the poor from the dust", whether it be the dust of penury or of oppression or of helplessness.

GOOD NEWS FOR THE POOR

At the risk of oversimplification, however, it will be helpful (especially if we are to grasp what the Christian attitude to poverty should be) if we reduce these three categories to two, namely the material poverty of the destitute and powerless, and the spiritual poverty of the humble and meek. God concerns himself with both. In both cases "he raises the poor from the dust", but the way he does it is different, for the first kind of poverty is a social evil which God opposes, while the second is a spiritual virtue which he approves. Moreover, there is only one human community in which the two are combined, namely the kingdom community, the new and redeemed society in which God rules through Christ by his Spirit.

This is clear from the Old Testament expectation of the kingdom of God. God promised the coming of his ideal king, who would both judge the poor with justice and give the blessing of his rule to the humble and lowly. We meet such people in the first two chapters of Luke's Gospel. Zechariah and Elizabeth, Joseph and Mary, Simeon and Anna were humble, poor believers. They were looking and waiting for the kingdom of God, in which God would throw down the mighty from their thrones and exalt the humble and meek.

Clearer still was the fulfilment through Jesus Christ. Who are the "poor" he spoke about, those to whom he had been anointed to preach the good news of the kingdom and to whom the kingdom would be given (Luke 4:18ff.; Matthew 11:5; cf. Luke 7:22; Matthew 5:3; cf. Luke 6:20)? They surely cannot be either just the materially poor (for Christ's salvation is not limited to the proletariat) or just the spiritually poor (for this overlooks his ministry to the needy). He must have been referring to both in combination. The "poor" are those to whom the kingdom comes as great good news, partly because it is a free and unmerited gift of salvation to sinners, and partly because it promises a new society characterized by freedom and justice.

The church should exemplify both these truths. On the one hand, it consists of the spiritually poor, the "poor in spirit", who acknowledge their bankruptcy before God. They have no righteousness to offer, no merit to plead, no power to save themselves. They know that the only way to enter God's kingdom is to humble themselves like little children and receive it as a gift. So they come as beggars, with nothing in their hands, and on their lips the publican's prayer, "God be merciful to me, a sinner." To such Jesus says, "Blessed are the poor in spirit, for theirs is the kingdom of heaven." By contrast, the rich or self-satisfied, who imagine they have something to offer, are sent away empty.

On the other hand, the church must proclaim the good news of the kingdom to the materially poor, welcome them into the fellowship and share in their struggles. Indeed, the special concern for the poor shown by the biblical authors, and more particularly by Jesus himself, has led some contemporary thinkers to speak of God's "bias" in their favour. Bishop David Sheppard's 1983 book was entitled *Bias to the Poor*. "I believe that there is a divine bias to the disadvantaged," he writes, "and that the church needs to be much more faithful in reflecting it."[21] He concludes his analysis of deprivation in Liverpool with these words: "If we can put ourselves in the shoes of the poor and disadvantaged, we may see how matters appear to their consciousness . . . They are to do with the righteousness of God which has a persistent tendency to favour those at a disadvantage. They are to do with God taking flesh in the person of Jesus, living out his life in a special relation to the poor."[22]

I confess that I am uncomfortable with the word "bias", since its commonest meaning is "prejudice", and I do not think God is "biased" in that sense. Less misleading is the language of the Latin American bishops. At their Second General Conference at Medellín in 1970, they spoke of a "preference for, and solidarity with, the poor". At their Third General Conference ten years later at Puebla in Mexico, they affirmed "the need for conversion on the part of the whole church to a preferential option for the poor".[23] It is because of Jesus' ministry to the poor that "the poor merit preferential attention".[24] "Preferential" does not mean "exclusive", however, for the next chapter of the conference's report is entitled "A Preferential Option for Young People". Nevertheless, the option for the poor is "demanded by the scandalous reality of economic imbalances in Latin America".[25]

The 1980 Melbourne Conference quoted the Puebla conclusions, and then echoed them in asserting that "God has a preference for the poor".[26] It seems to me, however, that better than the vocabulary of personal "bias" or "preference" is the language of mission priority. Because of God's own care for the poor, and because of their exploitation by the unscrupulous and their neglect by the church, they should now receive a "positive" or "reverse" discrimination. The church should concentrate its mission where the need is greatest, and move from the centre out "towards the periphery",[27] to the "sinned against" – in other words, to the poor and the oppressed.

Moreover, the church should not tolerate material poverty in its own fellowship. When Jesus said, "The poor you will always have with you" (Mark 14:7), he was not acquiescing in the permanence of poverty. He was echoing the Old Testament statement, "There will always be poor people in the land" (Deuteronomy 15:11). Yet this was intended not as an excuse for complacency but as an incentive to generosity, as a result of which "there should be no poor among you" (Deuteronomy 15:4). If there is one community in the world in which justice is secured for the oppressed, the poor are freed from the indignities of poverty, and physical need is abolished by the voluntary sharing of resources, that community is the new society of Jesus the Messiah. It happened in Jerusalem after Pentecost, when "there were no needy persons among them", as Luke is at pains to show, and it can (and should) happen again today. How can we allow our own brothers and sisters in God's family to suffer want?

The church, then, as the community which is called to exemplify the ideals of the kingdom of God, should bear witness to the biblical paradox of poverty, by opposing one kind and encouraging the other. We should set ourselves both to eradicate the evil of material poverty and to cultivate the good of spiritual poverty. We should hate injustice and love humility. It is in these two complementary ways that the gospel may be said to be "good news for the poor", and God may be described as on their side.

Not that our Christian concern should be confined to those poor who are church members. Although we have a special responsibility to "the family of believers" (or, in older versions of the Bible, "the household of faith"), we are also required to "do good to all people" (Galatians 6:10). How will this express itself to the poor? Certainly in terms of personal philanthropy, as we seek to help needy individuals and families in our neighbourhood and further afield. But we cannot allow our duty to stop there. The Bible itself indicates, as we have seen, that most poverty is the fault rather of society than of the poor themselves. We, therefore, have a social as well as a personal responsibility towards them, and this will begin with a painful appraisal of the causes of poverty. I call it "painful" because the tendency of the affluent is to blame the poor, or to find some other scapegoat, whereas the problem may lie in the very structure of society in which we ourselves are implicated.

This is the thesis of Robert Holman's carefully researched, well-written and overtly Christian book *Poverty: Explanations of Social Deprivation.*[28] He rejects as incomplete three common scapegoat explanations – "individual" (genetic, economic or psychological inadequacies in the poor themselves), "cultural" ("the transmission of poverty from one generation to the next"[29]), and "the deficient agent" (the inefficiency of teachers, social workers and bureaucrats). Instead, he traces the cause of most poverty (at least in Britain) to the stratified structure of society itself, in which resources (especially income, wealth and power) are unequally divided. "Poverty exists," he writes, "in order to support or uphold these social divisions."[30] It is tolerated, even justified, because it (and, therefore, its affluent opposite) is made to appear merited, and because it provides a useful pool of workers who have no choice but to undertake the most unattractive occupations.

Bob Holman's approach is sociological. In consequence, he avoids the polarized economic debate between those who blame poverty on capitalism, on the ground that it is inherently covetous and therefore exploits the poor, and those who blame socialism, on the ground that it perpetuates the dependency of the poor and undermines the enterprise of wealth creators. Neither position has a monopoly of truth. Christians should oppose in both systems what they perceive to be incompatible with biblical faith.

THREE OPTIONS FOR RICH CHRISTIANS

Conscientious Christians have further questions to ask. It is one thing to discern what our attitude to the poor should be; it is another to define our attitude to poverty itself. Involuntary material poverty is a scandal, as we have seen; but what about voluntary poverty? And what is an authentically Christian attitude to money and property? What should rich Christians do?

In the context of Western affluence, there are three options before us. The first is to become poor, the second to stay rich, and the third to cultivate generosity, simplicity and contentment.

Should we become poor?

Firstly, should we become poor? Paul wrote, "For you know the grace of our Lord Jesus Christ, that though he was rich, yet for your sakes he became poor, so that you through his poverty might become rich" (2 Corinthians 8:9). This voluntary self-impoverishment of Jesus was the theological ground on which the apostle based his appeal to the Christians of Greece to contribute to the relief of the Christians of Judea. Did he intend them to divest themselves of all their possessions for the sake of their Jewish brothers and sisters? Does he mean us to do the same? At first sight it seems so, and arguments have been advanced for this from the example, teaching and early church of Jesus.

The example of Jesus

Renouncing the wealth of heaven, Jesus was certainly born into a poor home. When Joseph and Mary came to the temple to present their child to the Lord, they availed themselves of the law's provision for poor people and brought as their sacrifice a pair of doves instead of a lamb and a dove. During his public ministry as an itinerant preacher, Jesus had no home and few possessions. To an applicant for discipleship he once said, "Foxes have holes and birds of the air have nests, but the Son of Man has nowhere to lay his head." He taught from a borrowed boat, rode into Jerusalem on a borrowed donkey, spent his last evening in a borrowed room and was buried in a borrowed tomb. He and his apostles shared a common purse and depended for their support on a group of women who sometimes accompanied them (Luke 2:2ff.; cf. Leviticus 12:6ff.; Luke 9:57ff.; Mark 4:1; 11:1ff.; 14:12ff.; 15:42ff.; John 12:6; Luke 8:1ff.). The poverty of Jesus seems to be beyond question.

Yet he was a carpenter by trade, which means that he belonged to the craftsman class. Professor Martin Hengel writes, "Jesus himself did not come from the proletariat of day-labourers and landless tenants, but from the middle class of Galilee, the skilled workers. Like his father, he was an artisan, a *tektôn*, a Greek word which means mason, carpenter, cartwright and joiner all rolled into one ... As far as we can tell, the disciples whom he called to follow him came from a similar social milieu."[31] Moreover, the women who supported him evidently "cared for his needs" adequately (Mark 15:41). So he was not destitute.

The teaching of Jesus

To would-be followers Jesus said, "Any of you who does not give up everything he has cannot be my disciple." The twelve apostles did this literally. Simon and Andrew "left their nets and followed him"; James and John "left their father Zebedee in the boat with the hired men and followed him"; and Levi-Matthew "got up and followed him", abandoning his tax-collector's booth and work. Similarly, Jesus told the rich young ruler to sell all his possessions, give the proceeds to the poor and then follow him. It was this which prompted Peter to blurt out, "We have left everything to follow you!" (Luke 14:33; Mark 1:16ff.; 2:13ff.; 10:21, 28)

Does Jesus then expect all his followers to give up everything in order to follow him? The apostles did it. And the rich young man was challenged to do it. But is it a universal rule? In reply, we must be careful not to whittle down the radical summons of Jesus by a little prudential exegesis. He did say that we should store our treasure in heaven not on earth; that we must put devotion to God's rule and righteousness above material things; that we must beware of covetousness; and that it is impossible to serve God and money simultaneously (Matthew 6:19ff.; cf. Luke 12:33ff.; Matthew 6:33; Luke 12:15; Matthew 6:24). But he did not tell all his followers to get rid of all their possessions. Joseph of Arimathea is described both as "a rich man" and as "a disciple of Jesus". So these two were evidently not incompatible. Zacchaeus the wealthy tax-collector promised both to pay back to people he had cheated four times what he had taken, and to give half of his possessions to the poor, which presumably means that he kept the other half, apart from what he paid back to his victims. Yet Jesus said that salvation had been given to him (Matthew 27:57; Luke 19:8ff.). So then, when he said that no one could be his disciple unless he both "renounced" all his possessions and "hated" his parents and other relatives, we shall need to understand both these verbs as dramatic figures of speech. We are not to hate our parents literally, nor to renounce all our possessions literally. What we are summoned to do is to put Jesus Christ first, above even our family and our property.

The early church of Jesus

Luke writes of the first Christian community in Jerusalem that they "had everything in common", that "no one claimed that any of his possessions was his own", that "they shared everything they had" and "gave to anyone as he had need" and that in consequence "there were no needy persons among them" (Acts 2:44f.; 4:32ff.). Is Luke setting their common life before us as an example for every church to copy? In the sense that the early Spirit-filled believers loved and cared for one another, and eliminated poverty within their fellowship, yes. But is he also advocating the common ownership of goods? Among the Essene groups, especially in their central community of Qumran, this was obligatory, and every novice entering the order had to hand over his property.[32] But it is plain from Luke's narrative that the Christians' selling and sharing were neither universal nor compulsory. Some believers still had houses in which they met. The sin of Ananias and Sapphira was not that they were selfish to withhold some of their property, but that they were deceitful to pretend they had given it all. Peter said to Ananias, "Didn't it belong to you before it was sold? And after it was sold, wasn't the money at your disposal?" (Acts 5:4) Thus the Christian's right to property is affirmed, together with the voluntary nature of Christian giving.

The example, teaching and early church of Jesus all challenge us to renounce covetousness, materialism and luxury, and to care sacrificially for the poor. But they do not establish the case that all Christians must actually become poor.

Should we stay rich?

If the first option for affluent Christians is to become poor, the second and opposite option is to stay rich. Some seek to defend this stance by an appeal to biblical arguments. Human beings were commanded in the beginning (they rightly say) to subdue and develop the earth – that is, to extract its animal, vegetable and mineral wealth and to harness it for their use. Wealth, moreover, is a sign of God's blessing, and they intend to claim and enjoy it. "The LORD will send a blessing on your barns and on everything you put your hand to. The LORD your God will bless you in the land he is giving you ... You will lend to many nations but will borrow from none" (Deuteronomy 28:8, 12). "What could be clearer than that?" they ask.

The most shameless example of this reasoning which I have come across was in the literature of a certain Pentecostal evangelist. He was appealing for funds to enable him to send Christian materials to the Majority World. "There's no better way to ensure your own financial security," he argued, all in capital letters, "than to plant some seed-money in God's work. His law of sowing and reaping guarantees you a harvest of much more than you sow ... Have you limited God to your present income, business, house or car? There's no limit to God's plenty! ... Write on the enclosed slip what you need from God – the salvation of a loved one, healing, a raise in pay, a better job, newer car or home, sale or purchase of property, guidance in business or investment ... whatever you need ... Enclose your slip with your seed-money ... Expect God's material blessings in return."

Our first response to this is to deny vigorously what such Christians are affirming and to repudiate strenuously their false "prosperity" or "health and wealth" gospel. When God's people were a nation, he did indeed promise to reward their obedience with material blessings, but in Christ he has blessed us "with every spiritual blessing" (Ephesians 1:3). Our second response is to draw attention to what they are omitting. There are other biblical principles which they have overlooked. The earth was to be developed for the common good, and its riches shared with all humankind. The Old Testament economy which promised wealth also commanded the care of the poor. And the rich man in the parable of Jesus found himself in hell, not because of his wealth, but because of his neglect of the beggar at his gate. That is, Dives indulged himself at the very time when Lazarus was starving.

In the light of these additional biblical truths, and of the contemporary destitution of millions, it is not possible for affluent Christians to "stay rich", in the sense of accepting no modification of economic lifestyle. We cannot maintain a "good life" (of extravagance) and a "good conscience" simultaneously. One or other has to be sacrificed. Either we keep our conscience and reduce our affluence, or we keep our affluence and smother our conscience. We have to choose between God and mammon.

Consider Paul's instruction to Timothy regarding rich people:

Command those who are rich in this present world not to be arrogant nor to put their hope in wealth, which is so uncertain, but to put their hope in God, who richly provides us with everything for our enjoyment. Command them to do good, to be rich in good deeds, and to be generous and willing to share. In this way they will lay up treasure for themselves as a firm foundation for the coming age, so that they may take hold of the life that is truly life.

1 TIMOTHY 6:17 – 19

We observe at once that the apostle does not tell "those who are rich in this present world" to "become poor". But he does not allow them to "stay rich" either. Instead, he first warns them of the spiritual dangers of wealth (as Jesus said, it is not impossible for the rich to enter God's kingdom, but it is hard) and then tells them to be generous with their wealth, which will inevitably result in a lowering of their own standard of living.

Wealth and pride

The first danger of wealth is pride: "Command those who are rich ... not to be arrogant." Wealth makes people feel self-important and so "contemptuous of others" (J. B. Phillips). Rich people are tempted to boast of their home, car, possessions and gadgets. It is easy for wealthy people to become snobs, to emphasize their social "class" and despise others. James pictures the situation when a rich man enters a Christian assembly wearing fine clothes, and then a poor man in rags comes in. If we behave obsequiously to the rich person and show him to one of the best seats, while rudely telling the poor person to stand on one side or sit on the floor, we have been guilty of class discrimination and so have disrupted the fellowship. It is not difficult to tell whether our affluence has alienated us from our less well-to-do brothers and sisters. If it has, we find ourselves embarrassed in each other's company.

Wealth and materialism

If wealth's first peril is pride, its second is materialism: "Command those who are rich ... not to put their hope in wealth which is so uncertain, but to put their hope in God." "Materialism" is not the mere possession of material things, but an unhealthy obsession with them. It is but a short step from wealth to materialism, from having riches to putting our trust in them, and many take it. But it is foolish. There is no security in wealth. It is not for nothing that Paul writes of "uncertain riches". Burglars, pests, rust and inflation all take their toll. Many have gone to bed rich and woken up poor, or, like the rich fool in Jesus' parable, have not woken up at all.

Trust in wealth is not only foolish, it is also unworthy of human beings, since our trust should not be in a thing but in a Person, not in money but in God, "who richly provides us with everything for our enjoyment". This is an important addition. The Christian antidote to materialism is not asceticism; austerity for its own sake is a rejection of the good gifts of the Creator.

Here, then, are the two main dangers to which rich people are exposed – pride (looking down on the poor) and materialism (enjoying the gift and forgetting the Giver). Wealth can spoil our two noblest relationships. It can make us forget God and despise our fellow human beings. These negative warnings prepare us for the positive instruction which follows.

Simplicity, generosity and contentment

After considering and rejecting the opposite options of becoming poor and staying rich, we come to the third, which is to be generous and contented. The apostle summons Christian believers to be both. I am not, of course, claiming that this approach by itself will solve the problem of world poverty, but at least it is an appropriate expression of solidarity with the poor.

Take generosity. The skeleton of 1 Timothy 6:17 – 18 is striking: "Command those who are rich ... to be rich." More precisely, "Command those who are rich in this present world ... to be rich in good deeds." In other words, let them add one kind of wealth to another. Tell them "to do good, to be rich in good deeds, and to be generous and willing to share". Then they will be imitating our generous God, "who richly provides us with everything for our enjoyment". They will also store up treasure in heaven (v. 19), as Jesus urged us to do.

It would be impossible, however, to describe as "generous" the voluntary giving to charity of those of us who live in the North of the world, although in the US there is greater charitable giving than in the UK.[33] According to the Charities Aid Foundation (CAF), in 2004 only 23% of people in the UK gave regularly to charity. Overall, the average UK household gives £1.70 per week. This compares to £5 spent on tobacco, £6 on alcohol and £30 on eating out, and represents a fall of 25% as a proportion of GDP over the last decade.[34]

Next, contentment needs to be added to generosity. It would be anomalous if generous giving to others resulted in discontent with what we had left. Paul extols contentment in 1 Timothy 6:6 – 10, as follows:

> But godliness with contentment is great gain. For we brought nothing into the world, and we can take nothing out of it. But if we have food and clothing, we will be content with that. People who want to get rich fall into temptation and a trap and into many foolish and harmful desires that plunge men into ruin and destruction. For the love of money is a root of all kinds of evil. Some people, eager for money, have wandered from the faith and pierced themselves with many griefs.

We notice that, whereas the other paragraph in 1 Timothy 6 which we considered relates to "those who are rich" (v. 17), this one is addressed to "people who want to get rich" (v. 9), that is, the covetous. Paul sets covetousness and contentment in contrast to one another. Covetousness is a self-destructive passion, a craving which is never satisfied, even when what has been craved is now possessed. As Schopenhauer said, "Gold is like sea water – the more one drinks of it, the thirstier one becomes."[35] "Beware of all covetousness," warned Jesus. "Covetousness ... is idolatry," added Paul (Luke 12:15 RSV; Colossians 3:15 RSV; cf. Ephesians 5:5). It seduces the heart from love of God and imprisons it in love for money. It brings much pain and many sorrows, for "the love of money is a root of all kinds of evil" (1 Timothy 6:10).

Contentment, on the other hand, is the secret of inward peace. It remembers the stark truth that "we brought nothing into the world, and we can take nothing out of it" (1 Timothy 6:7). Life, in fact, is a pilgrimage between two moments of nakedness, namely birth and burial. So we should travel light, and live simply. Bishop John V. Taylor has put it well: "The word 'poverty' has come to sound so negative and extreme in our ears that I prefer the word 'simplicity', because it puts the emphasis on the right points ... Our enemy is not possessions but excess. Our battle-cry is not 'nothing!' but 'enough!' "[36] Simplicity says that "if we have food and clothing, we will be content with that" (v. 8), for Christian contentment is coupled with godliness, the knowledge of God in Jesus Christ, and "godliness with contentment is great gain" (v. 6).

We have looked at the three options which confront all affluent Christians. Should we become poor? No, not necessarily. Though doubtless Jesus Christ still calls some, like the rich young ruler, to a life of total voluntary poverty, it is not the vocation of all his disciples. Then should we stay rich? No, this is not only unwise (because of the perils of conceit and materialism) but actually impossible (because we are to give generously, which will have the effect of reducing our wealth). Instead of these two, we are to cultivate generosity on the one hand and simplicity with contentment on the other.

At this point the temptation is to lay down rules and regulations, whether for ourselves or others, and so lapse into pharisaism. This makes three "isms" for us to avoid – materialism (an obsession with things), asceticism (an austerity which denies the good gifts of the Creator), and pharisaism (binding one another with rules). Instead, we would be wise to stick to principles.

The principle of simplicity is clear. Its first cousin is contentment. It concentrates on what we need and measures this by what we use. It rejoices in the Creator's gifts, but hates waste, greed and clutter. It says with the book of Proverbs, "Give me neither poverty nor riches, but give me only my daily bread", for to have either too much or too little may lead to disowning or dishonouring God (30:8ff.). It wants to be free of anything and everything which distracts from the loving service of God and others.

One of the most controversial sections of the Lausanne Covenant, adopted at the conclusion of the International Congress on World Evangelization in 1974, relates to the need for simpler living. It goes like this: "All of us are shocked by the poverty of millions and disturbed by the injustices which cause it. Those of us who live in affluent circumstances accept our duty to develop a simple lifestyle, in order to contribute more generously to both relief and evangelism."[37] It was to elucidate the implications of these sentences that an International Consultation on Simple Lifestyle was held in 1980. It issued "An Evangelical Commitment to Simple Lifestyle", whose nine paragraphs deserve careful study. Paragraph 5 is entitled "Personal Lifestyle" and develops the concept of "simplicity". It includes a general resolve to "renounce waste and oppose extravagance in personal living, clothing and housing, travel and church buildings". But it betrays no negative asceticism. On the contrary, it picks up from Dr Ronald Sider's paper "Living More Simply for Evangelism and Justice" a number of important distinctions: "We also accept the distinction between necessities and luxuries, creative hobbies and empty status symbols, modesty and vanity, occasional celebrations and normal routine, and between the service of God and slavery to fashion."[38] The point is that simple living is not incompatible with careful enjoyment.

But simple living is incompatible with living beyond one's means – that is, borrowing in order to purchase what one cannot afford. A BBC news article in October 2004 reported that the "US is living beyond its means", with a private debt burden now of $9,700,000,000,000.[39] In the UK, total personal debt reached £1,000,000,000,000 in July 2004, up from £500,000,000,000 in 1997.[40] Average UK household debt, excluding mortgages, is now £7,000,[41] but this average masks the extreme cases. Calls to the Consumer Credit Counselling Service rose by more than a third to 90,000 in the first six months of 2004, and these callers have an average debt of £25,000 (excluding mortgages). In 2004, the UK National Consumer Council reported that 20% of people were borrowing money just to pay household bills, and 25% were struggling to meet bills and credit repayments.[42] If this is the situation with interest rates at historically low levels,[43] any future rate rises will bring further hardship, especially for the 28% of households in Britain who have no savings.[44] The Jubilee Centre Research Paper "Families in Debt" highlights three major biblical principles which "provide a coherent and highly reasonable foundation for policy initiatives" covering the prevention and cure of debt problems, namely "justice" (taking seriously the responsibilities of both lenders and borrowers), "mercy" (lenders giving good advice and being lenient with defaulters), and "hope" (the prospect of ultimate rescue from the debt trap).[45] The charity Credit Action provides, through its advocacy and advice, a needed Christian response to the problems of debt in our society.[46]

If the principle of simplicity is clear, so is the principle of generosity. John expresses it in these terms: "If anyone has material possessions and sees his brother in need but has no pity on him, how can the love of God be in him?" (1 John 3:17). Our God is a generous God. If his love indwells us, we shall relate what we "have" (possessions) to what we "see" (others' needs) and take action.

May God help us to simplify our lifestyle, grow in generosity and live in contentment!

NOTES

1 US Census Bureau, "Income, Poverty & Health Insurance Coverage in the United States: 2003", published August 2004, p. 9. A set of money income thresholds that vary by family size and composition is used to determine who is in poverty. For example, the threshold for one person is $9,393, two people $12,015 and four people $18,810, p. 39.

2 www.oxfamgb.org/ukpp/poverty/thefacts.htm#fn1. Poverty is measured here as below 60% of contemporary median net disposable income in 2000/01. This is the "poverty line" which has been accepted recently across the EU to measure the extent of poverty

in member states; it is not the same as a comprehensive definition of poverty, which includes many other dimensions. These figures look at incomes in Great Britain, after housing costs have been paid, and include the self-employed.

3 D. Gordon et al., *Poverty and Social Exclusion in Britain* (York: Joseph Rowntree Foundation, 2000); the figures refer to a survey carried out in 1999, based on asking the general population what they saw as necessities for people living in Britain today and whether they could afford them.

4 CAP National Poverty Hearing, 1996.

5 *Faith in the City: A call for action by church and nation* (London: Church House Publishing, 1985), p. 359.

6 For further details, see *cofe.anglican.org/info/socialpublic/urbanaffairs.html*.

7 Human Development Report 2004, p. 188. US survey year was 2000; UK survey year was 1999. In terms of wealth, in the UK in 2001, the most wealthy 1% owned 23% of the wealth (17% in 1991), whereas the least wealthy 50% owned only 5% of the wealth (8% in 1991). See *Social Trends* 34: 2004 edition (London: HMSO, 2004), Table 5.26, p. 89; also at *www.statistics.gov.uk/socialtrends/*.

8 Puebla, "Evangelization at Present and in the Future of Latin America", *Conclusions of the Third General Conference of Latin American Bishops* (Manila: St Paul Publications, 1980), p. 107, para. 494.

9 *Developments*, issue 24, 4th quarter 2003, p. 29.

10 David Gordon et al., *Child Poverty in the Developing World* (Bristol: The Policy Press, 2003).

11 Department of Work and Pensions, *Second Report on Child Poverty*, 31 March 2004, *www. publications.parliament.uk/pa/cm200304/cmselect/cmworpen/85/8502.htm*.

12 Joseph Rowntree Foundation, Findings Ref. 930, "Poverty and social exclusion in Britain", September 2000.

13 "League Table of Child Poverty in Rich Nations", Innocenti Research Centre, UNICEF, June 2000.

14 Koen Vleminckx and Timothy M. Smeeding (eds.), *Child Well-Being, Child Poverty and Child Policy in Modern Nations, What do we know?* (Bristol: The Policy Press, February 2001).

15 For further details, *see www.dwp.gov.uk/ofa/*.

16 M. Brewer and A. Shephard, *Has Labour Made Work Pay?* (York: Joseph Rowntree Foundation/Institute of Fiscal Studies, November 2004), p. 40.

17 *www.publications.parliament.uk/pa/cm200304/cmselect/cmworpen/85/8503.htm*

18 Bishop David Sheppard's Richard Dimbleby Lecture, "The Poverty that Imprisons the Spirit", was published in *The Listener* (19 April 1984). See also Paul Harrison, *Inside the Inner City* (Harmondsworth: Penguin, 1983).

19 See, e.g., Albert Gelin, *The Poor of Yahweh* (1964; English translation, Collegeville, Minn.: Liturgical Press); Julio de Santa Ana, *Good News to the Poor* (Geneva: WCC, 1977); Julio de Santa Ana (ed.), *Towards a Church of the Poor* (New York: Orbis, 1979); Conrad Boerma, *Rich Man, Poor Man and the Bible* (1978; London: SCM, 1979); Atholl Gill, *Christians and the Poor* (Canberra: Zadok Centre Series, no. 9, undated); *Christian*

Witness to the Urban Poor (Lausanne Occasional Paper, no. 22, 1980), a group report from the Consultation on World Evangelization at Pattaya, Thailand, which incorporates as an appendix, Jim Punton's analysis of the nine Hebrew words for the poor; *Your Kingdom Come* (Geneva: WCC, 1980), the report of the World Conference on Mission and Evangelism, held in Melbourne in 1980; Vinay Samuel and Chris Sugden, *Evangelism and the Poor* (Bangalore: Partnership in Mission, Asia, revised ed. 1983); Redmond Mullin, *The Wealth of Christians* (Carlisle, Penn.: Paternoster, 1983); Peter Lee, *Poor Man, Rich Man: The priorities of Jesus and the agenda of the church* (London: Hodder & Stoughton, 1986).

20 Raymond Fung's speech, "Good News to the Poor", is published in *Your Kingdom Come*, pp. 83 – 92.

21 David Sheppard, *Bias to the Poor* (London: Hodder & Stoughton, 1983), p. 16.

22 Ibid., p. 225.

23 Puebla, p. 178, para. 1134.

24 Ibid., p. 179, paras. 1141 – 2.

25 Ibid., p. 180, para. 1154.

26 *Your Kingdom Come*, p. 171.

27 This was Professor Kosuke Koyama's expression at Melbourne, see *Your Kingdom Come*, p. 161.

28 Robert Holman, *Poverty, Explanations of social deprivation* (London: Martin Robertson, 1978).

29 Ibid., p. 134.

30 Ibid., p. 88.

31 Martin Hengel, *Property and Riches in the Early Church* (Minneapolis: Fortress, 1974), pp. 26 – 27.

32 Ibid., pp. 32 – 33.

33 *The Economist* reports that Americans give away 1.8% of GDP, compared to the British who give 0.8% of GDP (2002 figures). "Charitable lot, the rich", *The Economist*, 6 May 2004.

34 C. Pharoah, CAF Research Briefing, "Fitting charity into household budgets", October 2004, *www.cafonline.org*. Figures have been rounded.

35 Quoted by Bishop Otto Dibelius in his autobiography, *In the Service of the Lord* (New York: Holt, Reinhart & Winston, 1964), p. 31.

36 Taylor, *Enough Is Enough*, pp. 81 – 82.

37 See "The Lausanne Covenant: An Exposition and Commentary", in Stott (ed.), *Making Christ Known*.

38 "An Evangelical Commitment to Simple Lifestyle", in Stott (ed.), *Making Christ Known*, pp. 139 – 53. See also the papers prepared for the International Consultation on Simple Lifestyle, published in Ronald J. Sider (ed.), *Lifestyle in the Eighties* (Carlisle, Penn.: Paternoster, 1982), pp. 16, 35 – 36.

39 J. Madslien, "US economy: The challenges ahead", 31 October 2004, *news.bbc.co.uk/go/pr/fr/-/1/hi/business/3959867.stm*. The article also reported US government debts rising to $7,400,000,000,000.

40 Creditaction – debt facts and figures – 4 November 2004, *www.creditaction.org.uk*. Of this 2004 figure, 83% is secured lending on homes and 17% is consumer credit lending.

41 Ibid. Average personal debt including mortgages is £45,000 per household.

42 See *www.ncc.org.uk/moneymatters/index.htm*, accessed in November 2004.

43 For historical trends, see *www.federalreserve.gov/releases/h15/data.htm* and *www. bankofengland.co.uk/index.htm*.

44 2001/02 figures as reported by *Social Trends* 34: 2004 edition, p. 69.

45 Andrew Hartropp (ed.), *Families in Debt, The nature, causes and effects of debt problems, and policy proposals for their alleviation* (Cambridge: Jubilee Centre Publications, no. 7, 1987); Michael Schluter and David Lee, *Credit and Debit, Sorting it out* (London: Marshall Pickering, 1989).

46 Credit Action is now the largest debt-counselling agency in the UK. It has two websites which have many resources for those who have debt problems: *www.creditaction.org.uk* and *www.moneybasics.co.uk*. In the US, a similar organization exists, which is Crown Financial Ministries, *www.crown.org*. Keith Tondeur, the director of Credit Action, recommends two books for those who wish to take the issues further. They are Neil Hood, *God's Wealth, Whose Money Is It Anyway?* (Carlisle, Penn.: Authentic Media, 2004); and Randy Alcorn, *Money, Possessions, and Eternity* (Carol Stream, Ill.: Tyndale, 2003).

PART FOUR
PERSONAL
ISSUES

Women, Men and God

The record of the oppression of women has been so long-standing and wide-spread that there is a need for reparation by a male-dominated society. In my own thinking on this subject I have been challenged by what women, from all perspectives and ideological convictions, are saying. I have tried to understand their hurts, frustration and even rage. I have also tried to listen to Scripture and have found this double listening painful. But it should save us both from denying the teaching of Scripture in a determination at all costs to be relevant and from affirming it in a way that ignores such challenges and is insensitive to the people most deeply affected by them.

During the twentieth century the status of women changed, especially in the West. There are still many parts of the world where this fundamental shift has not happened and where women are still treated as property, not consulted about their own destiny or abused. I have written more about these issues in the chapters on Human Rights and on Global Poverty. But in the West things have changed, or at least they have begun to change. It is remarkable to think that it was as recently as 1918 that women won the right to vote in the UK, thanks to the courageous campaigns of the suffragettes.

Changes in cultural, legal, economic and political norms accelerated in the 1960s. The women's revolution resulted in several key thinkers challenging the status quo as being unnecessarily patriarchal and unjust from a woman's perspective. Writers such as Germaine Greer, despite her tendency to extremes and vulgarity of expression, came to prominence and her book *The Female Eunuch* (1970) stated that women were "the truly oppressed majority".[1] Their identity was defined by men in the most demeaning way, especially when women were seen by men as sexual objects. In America, Kate Millett's book *Sexual Politics*[2] added fuel to an already heated debate about the distribution of power between men and women. Carol Gilligan's book *In a Different Voice: Psychological Theory and Women's Development* became essential reading for those who wanted to find new ways of understanding male and female psychology.[3]

In 1970 the top managers of major American corporations were 99% male. A young woman joining a corporation then had every right to believe that by the time she had achieved seniority, that percentage would have changed in her favour. It did. Twenty-five years later, only 95% of top managers of major corporations were men. At this rate, it will be the year 2270 before women and men are equally likely to be top managers of major corporations. In the US Congress, women were 6% of elected representatives in the mid-1990s, a tripling of the 2% they were in 1950. At this rate, the Congress will achieve equality between men and women by the year 2500.[4] Yet despite this, Margaret Thatcher, Benazir Bhutto, Golda Meir, Indira Gandhi, Mary Robinson and Edith Cresson, among others, all became leaders in their respective countries.

By the 1970s, changes in legislation were coming about which did begin to change the status of women in society. In the UK the Equal Pay Act was passed in 1970, and the Sex Discrimination Act in December 1975 made it illegal to discriminate against women in education, recruitment or advertising. The Employment Protection Act (1975) made it illegal to sack a woman because she was pregnant.

Since the 1960s, society has increasingly opened up to women so that they can explore their gifts and callings alongside men. Yet in reality many women would still point to areas where equality does not exist, whether of opportunity, income or treatment in the labour market, and where further reform is needed. The "glass ceiling" which prevents women's advancement unjustly, exploitative part-time work done by poor women in poor conditions, sexual harrassment at work and domestic violence in the home are still pervasive throughout our "sophisticated" societies, to our shame.

As far as feminist writer Janet Radcliffe Richards was concerned, feminism had arisen from the conviction that "women suffer from systematic social injustice because of their sex". Therefore, it was "a movement for the elimination of sex-based injustice".[5] This cry for justice should be enough to make every Christian sit up and take notice, for justice is concerned with God-given rights.

It would be a mistake, however, to regard feminism as a largely non-Christian movement. Elaine Storkey corrects this error in her fine, largely historical and sociological survey entitled *What's Right with Feminism*.[6] Analysing the three main streams of secular feminism – liberal, Marxist and radical – and acknowledging their positive insights, she rejects them as inadequate, due in part to their Enlightenment view of persons as autonomous. Yet some Christian responses to feminism are also inadequate. Some reject it out of hand as unchristian, while others go to the opposite extreme, either seeing feminism as essential to salvation or adopting a post-Christian stance by attempting to redefine it as a woman-centred religion. Elaine Storkey ends with "A Third Way", which traces biblical feminism back to the Reformation and lays down its theological foundations. In the last paragraph of the book she states that "a Christian feminist programme would clearly be no piece of cake":[7]

> Throughout it all the underlying critique is of contemporary humanism and *a humanism in which men define the norms.* Instead the desire is to recover a Christian definition: to discern how women are to be treated in God's terms and to move our society from being one which debases and devalues them to one in which they have dignity, equality and freedom to be really human. God created people as male and female, and this difference will always be there. What need not be there are the penalties women pay for their sex in so many areas of life. Following the tradition from which they come, Christian feminists will not be working and praying on their own account and from their own self-concerns but to really help those to liberation who need it most. The programme might be a daunting one. But the alternatives are less than human.[8]

It is clear, then, that feminism in all its forms – whether non-Christian, Christian or post-Christian – presents the church with an urgent challenge. Feminism cannot be dismissed out of hand. It is about creation and redemption, love and justice, humanity and ministry. It obliges us to ask ourselves some searching questions. What does "justice" mean in reference to both men and women? What does God intend our relationships and roles to be? What is the meaning of our masculinity or femininity? How are we to discover our true identity and dignity? In endeavouring to summarize and synthesize the biblical teaching on these sensitive topics, I shall focus on four crucial words – equality, complementarity, responsibility and ministry.[9]

EQUALITY BETWEEN MEN AND WOMEN

It is essential to begin at the beginning, namely with the first chapter of Genesis.

Equality is based on creation

> Then God said, "Let us make man in our image, in our likeness, and let them rule over the fish of the sea and the birds of the air, over the livestock, over all the earth, and over all the creatures that move along the ground."
>
> > So God created man
> > in his own image,
> > in the image of God
> > he created him;
> > male and female
> > he created them.
>
> God blessed them and said to them, "Be fruitful and increase in number; fill the earth and subdue it. Rule over the fish of the sea and the birds of the air and over every living creature that moves on the ground."
>
> GENESIS 1:26–28

If we put together the divine resolve ("Let us make man ... and let them rule ..."), the divine creation ("So God created ...") and the divine blessing ("Be fruitful ... fill the earth and subdue it ..."), we see that the emphasis seems to be on three fundamental truths about human beings, namely that God made (and makes) them in his own image, that he made (and makes) them male and female, giving them the joyful task of reproducing and that he gave (and gives) them dominion over the earth and its creatures. Thus from the beginning humanity was "male and female", and men and women were equal beneficiaries both of the divine image and of the earthly rule. There is no suggestion in the text that either sex is more like God than the other, or that either sex is more responsible for the earth than the other. No. Their resemblance to God and their stewardship of his earth (which must not be confused, although they are closely related) were from the beginning shared equally, since both sexes were equally created by God and like God.

Moreover, the threefold affirmation of God's creation in verse 27 is not just poetic parallelism. There is surely a deliberate emphasis here, which we are intended to grasp. Twice it is asserted that God created man in his own image, and the third time the reference to the divine image is replaced by the words "male and female". We must be careful not to speculate beyond what the text warrants. Yet, if both sexes bear the image of God (as is forcefully asserted), then this seems to include not only our humanity (authentic humanness reflecting divinity), but our plurality (our relationships of love reflecting those which unite the persons of the Trinity) and even, at least in the broadest sense, our sexuality. Is it too much to say that since God, when he made humanity in his own image, made them male and female, there must be within the being of God himself something which corresponds to the "feminine" as well as the "masculine" in humankind?

So we should not, in the name of eradicating male bias in Scripture, create an androgynous language to refer to God. What we should do is give full weight to those passages of Scripture which speak of God in feminine – and especially maternal – terms, for these texts help to illumine the nature and quality of his "fatherhood". For example, according to the Song of Moses, Yahweh was not only "the Rock who fathered you" but also "the God who gave you birth". This is a remarkable statement that he was simultaneously Israel's Father and Mother. In consequence, Israel could be sure of God's preserving faithfulness – for though a human mother might "forget the baby at her breast and have no compassion on the child she has borne", yet, Yahweh promised, "I will not forget you!" Instead, he would unfailingly love and console his people: "As a mother comforts her child, so will I comfort you." Moreover, if Yahweh in these texts revealed himself as the mother of his people Israel, the individual Israelite felt at liberty to enter into this relationship. The psalmist dared even to liken his quiet confidence in God to the humble trustfulness of a breast-fed child. Then Jesus himself on occasion used feminine imagery, likening God to a woman who had lost a coin, as well as to a father who had lost a son, and likening himself in his anguish over impenitent Jerusalem to a hen wanting to gather her chicks under her wings (Deuteronomy 32:18; cf. Isaiah 42:14; Isaiah 49:15; 66:13; Psalm 131:1ff.; Luke 15:8ff.; Matthew 23:37).

So then, returning to the creation story, it is clear that from the first chapter of the Bible onwards, the fundamental equality of the sexes is affirmed. Whatever is essentially human in both male and female reflects the divine image which we equally bear. And we are equally called to rule the earth, to cooperate with the Creator in the development of its resources for the common good.

Equality is distorted by the fall

This primeval sexual equality was, however, distorted by the fall. Part of God's judgement on our disobedient progenitors was his word to the woman: "Your desire will be for your husband, and he will rule over you." Thus the sexes would experience a measure of alienation from one another. In place of the equality of the one with the other, and of the complementarity of the one to the other (which we have yet to consider), there would come the rule of the one over the other. The domination of woman by man is due to the fall, not to the creation.

Moreover, men have misused this judgement of God as an excuse to maltreat and subjugate women in ways God never intended. Examples could be given from many cultures and historical periods. I will give four. Firstly, from Gandhi's autobiography: "A Hindu husband regards himself as lord and master of his wife, who must ever dance attendance upon him."[10] Next, consider Sura 4 of the Koran, entitled "Women": "Men have authority over women because Allah has made the one superior to the other ... As for those from whom you fear disobedience, admonish them and send them to beds apart and beat them..."[11] My third example comes from the Eskimos. Raymond de Coccola spent twelve years among the "Krangmalit" in the Canadian Arctic as a Roman Catholic missionary and got to know them well. He was shocked when an Eskimo hunter used a word of a woman which was also applied to a she-wolf or a bitch. "Trained to do all manner of mean tasks," he reflected, "the Eskimo woman is used to enduring the weaknesses and appetites of men. But I still could not get used to what appeared to be a master-and-slave relationship between the hunter and his wife."[12] As my fourth example I choose pornography, a major symbol of Western decadence, in which women are made the objects of male abuse and violence.

These are examples of the exploitation of women. In the Old Testament the husband was certainly the patriarch and *ba'al* (lord or ruler) of his clan. Yet his womenfolk were not despised or ill-treated. They were regarded as an integral part of the covenant community, so that "men, women and children" were together assembled to listen to the public reading of the Torah and to share in the worship (e.g., Deuteronomy 31:12). Marriage was held in high honour, modelled on Yahweh's covenant love to Israel, the beauty of sexual love was celebrated (as in the Song of Songs), the capabilities of a good wife were praised (e.g., Proverbs 31), godly and enterprising women like Hannah, Abigail, Naomi, Ruth and Esther were held up for admiration, and it was constantly emphasized that widows must be cared for.

Yet the prophets looked forward to the days of the new covenant in which the original equality of the sexes would be reaffirmed. For God would pour out his Spirit on all flesh, including sons and daughters, menservants and maid-servants. There would be no disqualification on account of sex.

Equality is affirmed by Jesus

When Jesus came, he was born of a woman (Galatians 4:4). Although Protestants are anxious to avoid the exaggerated veneration of the Virgin Mary accorded to her in the Roman Catholic and Orthodox Churches, we should also avoid the opposite extreme of failing to honour her. If the angel Gabriel addressed her as "highly favoured", and if her cousin Elizabeth called her "blessed ... among women", we should not be shy to think and speak of her in the same terms, because of the greatness of her Son (Luke 1:28, 42).

It was not only his birth of a woman, however, which restored to women that measure of dignity lost by the fall, but also his attitude to them. In addition to his apostles, who were all men, Jesus was accompanied on his travels by a group of women, whom he had healed and who then provided for him out of their means. Next, Jesus had a theological discussion with someone at Jacob's Well despite the fact that she was a woman, a Samaritan and a sinner, which gave him three reasons to ignore her. It was similar with the woman who had been caught in the act of adultery; he was gentle with her and refused to condemn her. Then he allowed a prostitute to come behind him as he reclined at table, to wet his feet with her tears, wipe them with her hair and cover them with kisses. He accepted her love, which he interpreted as gratitude for her forgiveness. In doing so, he risked his reputation and ignored the silent indignation of his host. He was probably the first man to treat this woman with respect; previously men had only used her (Luke 8:1ff.; Mark 15:41; John 8:1ff.; Luke 7:36ff.).

Here were three occasions on which he received a sinful woman in public. A Jewish male was forbidden to talk to a woman on the street, even if she were his wife, daughter or sister. It was also regarded as impious to teach a woman the law; it would be better for the words of the law to be burned, said the Talmud, than that they should be entrusted to a woman. But Jesus broke these rules of tradition and convention. When Mary of Bethany sat at his feet listening to his teaching, he commended her as doing the one thing that was needed, and he honoured another Mary as the very first witness of the resurrection.[13] All this was unprecedented. Without any fuss or publicity, Jesus terminated the curse of the fall, reinvested woman with her partially lost nobility and reclaimed for his new kingdom community the original creation blessing of sexual equality.

Equality is celebrated by Paul

That the apostle Paul had grasped this is plain from his great charter statement of Christian freedom: "There is neither Jew nor Greek, slave nor free, male nor female, for you are all one in Christ Jesus" (Galatians 3:28). This does not mean that Jews and Greeks lost their physical differences, or even their cultural distinctives, for they still spoke, dressed and ate differently; nor that slaves and free people lost their social differences, for most slaves remained slaves and free people free; nor that men lost their maleness and women their femaleness. It means rather that as regards our standing before God, because we are "in Christ" and enjoy a common relationship to him, racial, national, social and sexual distinctions are irrelevant. People of all races and classes, and of both sexes, are equal before him. The context is one of justification by grace alone through faith alone. It affirms that all who by faith are in Christ are equally accepted, equally God's children, without any distinction, discrimination or favouritism according to race, sex or class. So whatever may need to be said later about sexual roles, there can be no question of one sex being superior or inferior to the other. Before God and in Christ "there is neither male nor female". We are equal.

Sexual equality, then, established by creation but perverted by the fall, was recovered by the redemption that is in Christ. What redemption remedies is the fall; what it recovers and re-establishes is the creation. Thus men and women are absolutely equal in worth before God – equally created by God like God, equally justified by grace through faith, equally regenerated by the outpoured Spirit. In other words, in the new community of Jesus we are not only equally sharers of God's image, but also equally heirs of his grace in Christ (1 Peter 3:7) and equally indwelt by his Spirit. There is nothing which can destroy this Trinitarian equality (our common participation in Father, Son and Holy Spirit). Christians and churches in different cultures have denied it, but it is an indestructible fact of the gospel.

THE COMPLEMENTARITY OF MEN AND WOMEN

Although men and women are equal, they are not the same. Equality and identity are not to be confused. We are different from one another, and we complement one another in the distinctive qualities of our own sexuality, psychological as well as physiological. This fact influences our different and appropriate roles in society. As J. H. Yoder has written, "Equality of worth is not identity of role."[14]

When we investigate male and female roles, however, we must be careful not to acquiesce uncritically in the stereotypes which our particular culture may have developed, let alone imagine that Moses brought them down from Mount Sinai along with the Ten Commandments. This would be a serious confusion of Scripture and convention.

Feminists are understandably rebelling against the expectation that women must fit into a predetermined role. For who fixed the mould but men? This is what the American author Betty Friedan meant by "the feminine mystique" in her book of that title (1963). It is an image which has been imposed on them by a male-dominated society. "It is my thesis", she wrote, "that the core of the problem for women today is not sexual but a problem of identity – a stunting or evasion of growth that is perpetuated by the feminine mystique... Our culture does not permit women to accept or gratify their basic need to grow and fulfil their potentialities as human beings..."[15] Motherhood is indeed a divine vocation and calls for great sacrifices. But it is not woman's only vocation. There are other equally serious and equally unselfish forms of service to society which she may be called to give.

There is nothing in Scripture to suggest, for example, that women may not pursue their own careers or earn their own living; or that married women must do all the shopping, cooking and cleaning, while their husbands remain non-contributing beneficiaries of their labour; or that baby-rearing is an exclusively feminine preserve into which men may not trespass. The German saying which restricts the province of women to *Kinder, Küche und Kirche* ("children, kitchen and church") is an example of blatant male chauvinism. Scripture is silent about this kind of division of labour. Does it then say anything about sexual roles and relationships?

It is without doubt by a deliberate providence of God that we have been given two distinct creation stories, Genesis 2 supplementing and enriching Genesis 1:

> The LORD God said, "It is not good for the man to be alone. I will make a helper suitable for him."
>
> Now the LORD God had formed out of the ground all the beasts of the field and all the birds of the air. He brought them to the man to see what he would name them; and whatever the man called each living creature,

that was its name. So the man gave names to all the livestock, the birds of the air and all the beasts of the field.

But for Adam no suitable helper was found. So the LORD God caused the man to fall into a deep sleep; and while he was sleeping, he took one of the man's ribs and closed up the place with flesh. Then the LORD God made a woman from the rib he had taken out of the man, and he brought her to the man.

GENESIS 2:18 – 22

What is revealed in this second story of creation is that, although God made male and female equal, he also made them different. In Genesis 1 masculinity and femininity are related to God's image, while in Genesis 2 they are related to each other, Eve being taken out of Adam and brought to him. Genesis 1 declares the equality of the sexes; Genesis 2 clarifies that "equality" means not "identity" but "complementarity". It is this "equal but different" state which we find hard to preserve. Yet they are not incompatible; they belong to each other as essential aspects of the biblical revelation.

Because men and women are equal (by creation and in Christ), there can be no question of the inferiority of either to the other. But because they are complementary, there can be no question of the identity of one with the other. Further, this double truth throws light on male-female relationships and roles. Because they have been created by God with equal dignity, men and women must respect, love, serve and not despise one another. Because they have been created complementary to each other, men and women must recognize their differences and not try to eliminate them or usurp one another's distinctives.

Commenting on the special creation of Eve, Matthew Henry wrote with quaint profundity more than three hundred years ago that she was "not made out of his head to top him, nor out of his feet to be trampled upon by him, but out of his side to be equal with him, under his arm to be protected, and near his heart to be loved". Perhaps he got this idea from Peter Lombard, who in about AD 1157, just before becoming Bishop of Paris, wrote in his *Book of Sentences*: "Eve was not taken from the feet of Adam to be his slave, nor from his head to be his lord, but from his side to be his partner."[16]

It is when we try to elaborate the meaning of complementarity, to explain in what ways the two sexes complement each other and to define the distinctives of men and women, that we find ourselves in difficulties. Feminists become uncomfortable. They are suspicious of attempts to define femininity, partly because the definitions are usually made by men, who have (or at least may have) vested interests in securing a definition congenial to them, and partly because many sexual distinctives, as we have seen, are not intrinsic but established by social pressures. As Janet Radcliffe Richards has put it, feminists consider that it is "not by nature that women are so different from men, but by contrivance".[17]

Perhaps it is because of this identity confusion that people will opt for prescriptive books and programmes which purport to solve their problems. Dr John Gray's book *Men Are from Mars, Women Are from Venus* has been a phenomenal success. To him the differences between the sexes are so profound that men and women seem to have come from different planets. "Martians" (men) value power and achievement, "Venusians" (women) value love and relationships. Dr Gray illustrates the differences from the way people communicate. When a woman is hurting, "she wants empathy, but he thinks she wants solutions".[18] They differ too in how they cope with stress. "Martians go to their caves to solve their problems alone", whereas "Venusians get together and openly talk about their problems".[19] Men are empowered "when they feel needed", women "when they feel cherished".[20] Christians find the book's generalizations somewhat naïve and note that its author is descriptive, not evaluative. He does not recommend that we try to change one another, only that we understand and accept one another. But at least he urges us to remember that we are "supposed to be different".[21]

There has been a lot of discussion of the implications of this for men and many books have been written recently about the crisis in masculinity.[22] Some argue that men should be more like women in learning to be more intimate, open and expressive. Others, such as the Promise Keepers movement in the US, argue that men have lost something which is their essential masculinity, on which is based leadership both in the home and in the church. Men should therefore recover the distinctiveness of masculinity and focus on the difference between men and women. Of course, there is no one style of personality which exemplifies Christian masculinity. Jesus respected John the Baptist, yet also loved John the Beloved. These men were very different from one another, yet both were respected and loved by Jesus.

In her book *Fathers and Sons: The Search for a New Masculinity*, psychologist Mary Stewart van Leeuwen talks of the need for both personal and structural change to take place if "a more just and creationally healthy model for gender and family relations" is to be achieved.[23] The traditional assumption has been that it is women who must adjust if marriage, childrearing and employment are to be balanced. But, she argues, it is only when men, both individually and corporately, are willing to risk changes in their worldview and patterns of behaviour that things will change for both men and women. She comments, "In particular, Christian men must be ready to substitute biblical notions of responsibility and service for the dubious ideals of the male code of honour that keeps reinventing itself, Hydra-like, in every generation."[24] Part of the problem in a consumer society is the tacit acceptance by men that in a society characterized by economic growth there should be no limits to men's ambitions. The honour code of the warrior has been replaced by the language of the successful career into which men pour their energy. But, she points out, there is another image for men to consider and that is the steward who guards God's resources and is more vigilant even than the warrior. His job, shared with that of women, is "to guard *shalom*". Here we come back to the complementarity of men and women as well as to their equality, for it is only when we recover the fact that the creation and cultural mandate is given to both, and when men reject the concept of unlimited economic growth, that we will create the space for the gifts of women, the importance of family life and the rightful place of the gifts of God to the world in *shalom*. Perhaps, she points out, things would be better if we stopped thinking of men and women as "opposite sexes", as if they are in competition with one another, and thought of them instead as "neighbouring sexes", which brings a spirit of cooperation to the complementarity between them.

THE ROLE OF RESPONSIBILITY

All students of Genesis agree that chapter 1 teaches sexual equality and chapter 2 sexual complementarity. To these concepts, however, the apostle Paul adds the idea of "masculine headship". He writes both that "the husband is the head of the wife" (Ephesians 5:23) and, more generally, that "the head of every man is Christ, and the head of the woman is man, and the head of Christ is God" (1 Corinthians 11:3). But what does this mean? How can it possibly be reconciled with sexual equality and complementarity? These questions still seem to me to lie at the heart of the debate about male-female relationships and about the ordination and ministry of women.

Three attempts to resolve the paradox between sexual equality and masculine headship have been made. Some affirm headship so strongly as to contradict equality (or so it seems). Others deny headship because they see it as incompatible with equality. The third group seeks to interpret headship and to affirm it in such a way as to harmonize with, and not contradict, equality.

Authoritarian headship

The first of these options could perhaps be called "traditionalist" and even "hard-line". It assumes that "headship" equals "lordship", since the husband is said to be head of his wife as Christ is head of the church. This view understands Paul's prohibition of women speaking in church or teaching men, and his requirement of female submission and silence, as literal, permanent and universal injunctions. It therefore deduces that, although women do have ministries, leadership and decision-making in both the church and the home are male prerogatives. One of the most outspoken and persuasive expositions of this viewpoint is David Pawson's *Leadership Is Male*. He defines "the paradox of gender" in terms of "vertical equality" (equal in relation to God) and "horizontal inequality" (unequal in relation to each other). But "inequality" (even when restricted to the horizontal plane) is a misleading term ("complementarity" is better) and seems impossible to reconcile with that full equality of the sexes which has been established by creation, redemption and Pentecost.[25]

The denial of headship

Secondly, there are those who go to the opposite extreme. They deny any and every concept of masculine headship as being irreconcilable with the unity of the sexes in Christ. They declare Paul's teaching to be inapplicable on one or other of four grounds; namely, that it is mistaken, confusing, culture-bound or purely situational.

Is Paul's teaching wrong?

Perhaps, as Dr Paul Jewett states in his otherwise admirable book *Man as Male and Female*,[26] Paul had two views which were impossible to harmonize. On the one hand he affirmed equality (Galatians 3:28), while on the other hand he favoured women's subjection (1 Corinthians 11:13). This reflects the dialectic between the hierarchical Old Testament and the Jesus who treated men and women as equals.[27] "These two perspectives," Dr Jewett continues, "are incompatible, there is no satisfying way to harmonize ... them."[28] Indeed, "female subordination" is "incompatible with (a) the biblical narratives of man's creation, (b) the revelation which is given us in the life of Jesus, and (c) Paul's fundamental statement of Christian liberty" (i.e., Galatians 3:28).[29] This incongruity, he concludes, is due to the fact that Scripture is human as well as divine, and that Paul's "insight" has "historical limitations".[30] In other words, Paul was mistaken. He did not grasp the full implications of his own assertion that in Christ there is neither male nor female. He did not know his own mind. We are, therefore, free to choose between the apostle of Christian liberty and the unreformed rabbi, and, says Dr Jewett, we greatly prefer the former.

Now there is much in Dr Jewett's book which is excellent, especially his exposition of the attitudes and teaching of Jesus. But to abandon the task of harmonization and declare the apostle Paul to be double minded and mistaken is a counsel of despair. It is better to give him credit for consistency of thought. The truth is that submission does not imply inferiority and that distinct sexual identities and roles are not incompatible with equality of worth.

Is Paul's teaching confused?

The second way of rejecting the concept of headship is to declare Paul's teaching to be too confusing to be helpful. This is the position adopted by Gretchen Gaebelein Hull in her book *Equal to Serve*. Her study of Pauline "hard passages" led her to the discovery that "there is no scholarly consensus on the meaning or interpretation of these passages".[31] In consequence, she decided to put them aside as peripheral and to focus instead on "the larger truth of women's equal redemption and equal inheritance rights",[32] and their "equal opportunity to serve God".[33] "That all believers are equally redeemed," she writes, "and therefore equally eligible to serve, forms the basis for any philosophy of Christian life and service. God makes no distinction based on race, class or gender."[34] I enjoyed reading Mrs Hull's book, and particularly appreciated her repeated emphasis on the sacrificial and suffering servanthood to which all Christ's people are called.[35] Yet I do not myself feel able, in the face of difficult texts, to surrender the tasks of interpretation and harmonization. Nor do I think it logical to argue that our equal redemption necessarily implies equal service.

Is Paul's teaching culture-bound?

If Paul's teaching was neither mistaken nor too confusing to understand, then was it culture-bound? That is to say, can we argue that his position on masculine headship was valid for his own day, and so for first-century churches in the Graeco-Roman world, but that it is not binding on us in today's world? My immediate response to these questions must be to draw attention to the danger inherent in the argument. If we may reject Paul's teaching on men and women on the ground that it is culture-bound, may we not on the same ground also reject his teaching on marriage, divorce and homosexual relationships, indeed on God, Christ and salvation?[36] If the teaching of the apostles was binding only on their own generation, then none of it has any necessary relevance to us or authority over us. But we have no liberty to engage in cultural rejection (i.e., repudiating God's revelation because of its first-century cultural clothing); our task is rather that of cultural transposition (i.e., guarding God's essential revelation and translating it into an appropriate modern idiom).

The attempt is sometimes made to strengthen the cultural argument by a reference to slavery. If Paul told wives to submit to their husbands, he also told slaves to submit to their masters. Since slaves have long ago been liberated, is it not high time that women were liberated too? The argument is flawed, however. The analogy between women and slaves is extremely inexact on two counts. Firstly, women were not chattel property, bought and sold in the marketplace, as slaves were. And secondly, though Paul sought to regulate the behaviour of slaves and masters, he nowhere appealed to Scripture in defence of slavery, whereas he did base his teaching about masculine headship on the biblical doctrine of creation. He drew his readers' attention to the priority of creation ("Adam was formed first, then Eve", 1 Timothy 2:13), the mode of creation ("man did not come from woman, but woman from man", 1 Corinthians 11:8), and the purpose of creation ("neither was man created for woman, but woman for man", 11:9). Thus, according to Scripture, although "man is born of woman" and the sexes are interdependent (11:11f.), yet woman was made after man, out of man and for man. One cannot dismiss these three arguments (as some writers try to) as "tortuous rabbinic exegesis". On the contrary, as Dr James B. Hurley demonstrates in his *Man and Woman in Biblical Perspective*, they are exegetically well founded. For (a) by right of primogeniture "the firstborn inherited command of resources and the responsibility of leadership", (b) when Eve was taken out of Adam and brought to him, he named her "woman" and "the power to assign … a name was connected with control", and (c) she was made for him neither as an afterthought, nor as a plaything, but as his companion and fellow worker, to share with him "in the service of God and in the custodial ruling of the earth".[37]

It is essential to note that Paul's three arguments are taken from Genesis 2, not Genesis 3. That is to say, they are based on the creation, not the fall. And, reflecting the facts of our human creation, they are not affected by the fashions of a passing culture. What creation has established, no culture is able to destroy. The wearing of a veil or of a particular hairstyle was indeed a cultural expression of submission to masculine headship,[38] and may be replaced by other symbols more appropriate to the twenty-first century, but the headship itself is creational, not cultural.

Is Paul's teaching situational?

If we may not reject Paul's teaching on masculine headship on the grounds that it is mistaken, unclear or culture-bound, may we do so because it was situational – that is, because it was addressed to highly specific situations which no longer exist today? This argument is similar to the previous one, but differs from it in one important respect. To declare Paul's teaching "culture-bound" is a judgement which we form, namely that it seems to us dated and, therefore, irrelevant; to call it "culture-specific" is to recognize the particularity of the apostle's instruction, and to argue that he himself did not regard it as applicable to all times and places.

This suggestion is often made with regard to Paul's requirement that "women should remain silent in the churches" and should be "not allowed to speak" (1 Corinthians 14:34 – 35). Again, "I do not permit a woman to teach or to have authority over a man; she must be silent" (1 Timothy 2:12). The scholarly attempt to restrict these prohibitions to particular situations in Corinth and Ephesus is associated with the names of Richard and Catherine Clark Kroeger, who have addressed these issues in a series of scholarly articles and books.[39] In one article entitled "Pandemonium and Silence in Corinth"[40] they pointed out that ancient Corinth was a well-known centre of the worship of Bacchus (identified by the Greeks with Dionysus), which included frenzied shouting, especially by women. They, therefore, suggest that Paul was urging self-control in worship, in place of wild ecstasies, and that the *lalein* he was forbidding (an onomatopoeic word) was either the mindless ritual shouting of "alala" or the babbling of idle gossip.

The Kroegers also suggest in a subsequent article that a different kind of feminist movement had developed in Ephesus, where Timothy was superintending the churches, and where Diana (Artemis) the great mother goddess reigned, served by her numerous fertility priestesses. They point out that there is a strong emphasis in the Pastoral Epistles on the need to "silence" heretics (e.g., 1 Timothy 1:3; Titus 1:10); that the prohibition of women teaching may well refer to their teaching of heresy; and that the heresy which Paul combats in the Pastorals may have been an incipient Gnosticism, whose later developments "based their *gnosis* on a special revelation given to a woman", notably Eve. She was the first to eat from the tree of knowledge (*gnosis*), had also (some taught) enjoyed a prior existence and was even Adam's creator. She was, therefore, well qualified to instruct Adam. If such a heresy was already current in Ephesus, then Paul's insistence that Adam was created first and Eve deceived – not enlightened – first (1 Timothy 2:13 – 14) would certainly take on an extra significance.[41]

As for the verb *authenteô*, whose only New Testament occurrence is in 1 Timothy 2:12, meaning to "domineer", it is argued that it sometimes had sexual overtones. Some scholars have therefore suggested that what Paul was forbidding was the seduction of men which was doubtless common in Ephesian temple prostitution. Catherine Clark Kroeger, however, prefers to translate it "to proclaim oneself the author or originator of something" and to understand it as prohibiting the Gnostic mythology that "Eve pre-dated Adam and was his creator".[42]

These theories have been developed with considerable learning and ingenuity. They remain speculations, however. Not only is it anachronistic to refer to "Gnosticism" as if it were already a recognizable system by the 60s of the first century AD, but also there is nothing in the text of either 1 Corinthians 14:3 – 5 or 1 Timothy 2:11 – 12 to indicate that Paul was alluding to specific feminist movements in Corinth and Ephesus. On the contrary, the command to "silence" in both passages would seem a strangely roundabout way to prohibit the beliefs and practices which these scholars have described. Besides, Paul gives directions about "a woman" and "women"; his references are generic, not specific. Finally, even if this apostolic instruction can be proved to have been situational, it remains applicable to similar situations today. After all, every New Testament epistle is an occasional document, which addresses particular problems in particular churches; the epistles nevertheless continue to speak to our condition today.

Harmonizing equality and headship

So far we have looked at the two opposite viewpoints on relationships between men and women. On the one hand, there are those who affirm masculine headship (rightly, in my view), but do it so strongly as to seem to deny the full equality of the sexes. On the other hand, there are those who deny headship, in order to affirm (rightly, in my view) the equality of the sexes. But, as I have tried to show, all attempts to get rid of Paul's teaching on headship (on the grounds that it is mistaken, confusing, culture-bound or culture-specific) must be pronounced unsuccessful. It remains stubbornly there. It is rooted in divine revelation, not human opinion, and in divine creation, not human culture. In essence, therefore, it must be preserved as having permanent and universal authority.

Is there, then, no way to resolve the paradox between sexual equality and masculine headship, except by denying one of them? Can they not both be affirmed? Many believe that they can, since Scripture itself does so. The right way forward seems to be to ask two questions. Firstly, what does "headship" mean? Can it be understood in such a way as to be compatible with equality, while at the same time not manipulating it or evacuating it of meaning? Secondly, once headship has been defined, what does it prohibit? What ministries (if any) does it render inappropriate for women? Thus, the meaning and the application of "headship" are crucial to the ongoing debate.

The meaning of headship

How, then, can we interpret the meaning of headship with care and integrity, and allow Scripture to reform our traditions in this respect? We certainly have to reject the whole emotive language of hierarchy, as if headship means patriarchy or patronizing paternalism, autocracy or domination, and as if submission to it means subordination, subjection or subjugation. We must develop a biblical understanding of masculine headship which is fully consistent with the created equality of Genesis 1, the outpouring of the Spirit on both sexes at Pentecost (Acts 2:17ff.) and their unity in Christ and in his new community (Galatians 3:28).

Headship as "source"

Two interpretations of headship are being proposed. The first is that *kephalē* ("head") means not "chief" or "ruler" but rather "source" or "beginning", and that Paul was describing man as woman's "origin", referring to the priority of his creation. This view goes back to an article by Stephen Bedale entitled "The Meaning of *Kephalē* in the Pauline Epistles", which appeared in the *Journal of Theological Studies* in 1954. It was taken up and endorsed in 1971 by Professors F. F. Bruce and C. K. Barrett in their respective commentaries on 1 Corinthians, and has been quoted by many authors since then. In 1977, however, Dr Wayne

Grudem published his computerized survey of 2,336 uses of *kephalē* in ancient Greek literature, drawn from thirty-six authors from the eighth century BC to the fourth century AD. In his article he rejects Bedale's argument that *kephalē* means "source"; he provides evidence that instead it means "authority over".[43] In its turn Dr Grudem's thesis has been both criticized and reaffirmed.[44] So what *Christianity Today* has called "the battle of the lexicons" continues.[45]

Headship as "authority"

I find myself wondering, however, if this lexical controversy is not to some extent a false trail. To be sure, it is important to determine how *kephalē* was used outside the New Testament. Yet much more important is its meaning in the New Testament, and this is determined less by its etymology than by its use in each context. "Headship" seems clearly to imply some kind of "authority", to which "submission" is appropriate, as when "God placed all things under his [Christ's] feet and appointed him to be head over everything for the church" (Ephesians 1:22). But we must be careful not to overpress this. It is true that the same requirement of "submission" is made of wives to husbands, children to parents, slaves to masters and citizens to the state. There must, therefore, be a common denominator between these attitudes. Yet I cannot believe that anybody conceives the wife's submission to her husband to be identical with the obedience expected of children, slaves or citizens. A very different relationship is in mind. Besides, the word "authority" is never used in the New Testament to describe the husband's role, nor "obedience" the wife's. Nor does "subordination" seem to me to be the right word to describe her submission. Although it would be a formally correct translation of the Greek *hupotagç*, it has in modern parlance unfortunate overtones of inferiority, even of military rank and discipline.[46]

Headship as "responsibility"

How, then, shall we understand *kephalē*, "head", and what kind of masculine headship does Paul envisage? It is unfortunate that the lexical debate confines us to the choice between "source of" and "authority over". There is a third option which contains an element of both. On the one hand, headship must be compatible with equality. If "the head of the woman is man" as "the head of Christ is God", then man and woman must be equal as the Father and the Son are equal. On the other hand, headship implies some degree of leadership, which, however, is best expressed in terms not of "authority" but of "responsibility". The choice of this word is not arbitrary. It is based on the way in which *kephalē* is understood in Ephesians 5,[47] and on the two models Paul develops to illustrate the head's attitude to the body. The first is Christ's attitude to his body, the church, and the second is the personal concern which we human beings all have for the welfare of our own bodies.

The responsibility to love sacrificially

Firstly, "The husband is the head of the wife as Christ is the head of the church, his body, of which he is the Saviour" (v. 23). Those last words are revealing. Christ is "head" of the church in the sense that he is its "Saviour". Changing the metaphor, he loved the church as his bride, "and gave himself up for her, to make her holy … and to present her to himself … holy and blameless" (vv. 25 – 27). Thus the very essence of his headship of the church is his sacrificial love for her.

The responsibility to care selflessly

Secondly, "Husbands ought to love their wives as their own bodies. He who loves his wife loves himself. After all, no one ever hated his own body, but he feeds and cares for it [RSV "nourishes and cherishes it"], just as Christ does the church – for we are members of his body" (vv. 28 – 30). The ancient world did not think of the head's relationship to the body in modern neurological terms, for they did not know about the central nervous system. They thought rather of the head's integration and nurture of the body. So Paul wrote elsewhere of Christ as head of the church, by whom the whole body is "joined and held together" and through whom it "grows" (Ephesians 4:16; Colossians 2:19).

The husband's headship of his wife, therefore, is a liberating mix of care and responsibility rather than control and authority. This distinction is of far-reaching importance. It takes our vision of the husband's role away from questions of domination and decision-making into the sphere of service and nurture. I am glad that John Piper and Wayne Grudem, in their massive symposium *Recovering Biblical Manhood and Womanhood*, have opted for the word "responsibility": "At the heart of mature masculinity is a sense of benevolent responsibility to lead, provide for and protect women …"[48] All of this takes place within the sphere of self-giving love.

At the risk of causing offence, I think it is necessary for us to face the apostle Peter's description of women as "the weaker sex" (1 Peter 3:7). Women can, of course, be physically extremely strong and in many countries perform arduous manual labour. The fact that in some sense women are "weaker" than men is embarrassing because this is not something which is regarded as a quality to be admired in the twenty-first century. We have absorbed (unconsciously, no doubt) something of the power philosophy of Nietzsche. In consequence we tend to despise weakness, whereas Peter tells us that it is to be honoured. It is also not incompatible with Peter's other statement in the same verse, that she and her husband are equally "heirs ... of the gracious gift of [eternal] life". Although women have many different personality traits, the characteristics of femininity have always focused on words such as "gentle", "sensitive", "tender" and "patient". In a world obsessed with power, such virtues deserve respect and promotion, for they can easily be disregarded or abused. In 1 Peter 3:7, therefore, Peter says that husbands are to treat their wives with respect and honour for two reasons: the first is that, in some sense, they are the "weaker" partner, and the second is that they are equal sharers in the gracious gift of life.

The resolute desire of women to know, be and develop themselves, and to use their gifts in the service of the world, is so obviously God's will for them that to deny or frustrate it is an extremely serious oppression. It is a woman's basic right and responsibility to discover herself, her identity and her vocation. The fundamental question is, in what relationship with men will women find and be themselves? Certainly not in a subordination which implies inferiority to men and engenders low self-esteem. Only the biblical ideal of headship, which because it is selflessly loving may justly be called "Christlike", can convince them that it will facilitate, not destroy, their true identity.

Does this truth apply only to married women, whose caring head is their husband? What about single women? Perhaps the reason why this question is not directly addressed in Scripture is that in those days unmarried women were under their father's protective care, as married women were under their husband's. Today, however, at least in the West, it is usual for unmarried women to leave their parents and set up their own home independently. I see no reason to resist this. But I think it would be unnatural for such women to isolate themselves from men altogether, as it would be for single men to isolate themselves from women. Men and women both need to experience the respectful and supportive care of one another.

THE IMPLICATIONS OF HEADSHIP FOR MINISTRY

That women are called by God to ministry hardly needs any demonstration. "Ministry" is "service" (*diakonia*), and every Christian, male and female, young and old, is called to follow in the footsteps of him who said he had not come to be served, but to serve (Mark 10:45). The only question is what form women's ministry should take, whether any limits should be placed on it, and in particular whether women should be ordained. As deaconesses and as pioneer missionaries, of course, women already have an outstanding record of dedicated service.

The Roman Catholic and Eastern Orthodox Churches have no women priests; they set themselves firmly against this development. Many Lutheran Churches now have them, for example in Scandinavia, although disagreement on the issue continues. The French Reformed Church accepted women ministers in 1965 and the Church of Scotland in 1966. Among the British Free Churches, the Congregationalists have had female ministers since 1917, while Methodists and Baptists have followed suit more recently. In the Anglican Church the pattern is uneven. Bishop R. O. Hall of Hong Kong was the first to ordain a woman priest (that is, presbyter) in 1944. In 1968 the Lambeth Conference of Anglican bishops declared that "the theological arguments as at present presented for and against the ordination of women to the priesthood are inconclusive".

In 1975, however, the Church of England's General Synod expressed the view that there are "no fundamental objections to the ordination of women to the priesthood". Nevertheless, no women were yet ordained. Then, at the 1978 Lambeth Conference, the bishops recognized that some Anglican provinces now had women clergy and agreed to respect each other's discipline in this matter. (It should be noted that eleven female bishops from various areas of the Anglican Communion attended this conference.) The first women priests of the Church of England were ordained in Bristol cathedral in March 1994, but in 2000 there remained about 1,000 congregations in the Church of England who refused to accept the authority of women priests.[49] Yet a deep division remains, which is partly theological and partly ecumenical, about the impact of women's ordination on Anglican relationships with the Roman Catholic and Orthodox Churches. Some parishes which refuse to recognize the ordination of women have taken the option of being cared for by a "flying bishop" rather than their own diocesan bishop. He serves congregations upon request, either in addition to or as an alternative to the diocesan bishop. This is a radical departure from Anglican tradition, which has always recognized the authority of a single bishop within each diocese.

Some Christians, anxious to think and act biblically, will immediately say that the ordination of women is inadmissible. Not only were all the apostles and the presbyters of New Testament times men, but the specific instructions that women must be "silent in the churches" and "not teach or have authority over a man" (1 Corinthians 14:34; 1 Timothy 2:12) settle the matter.

That is only one side of the argument, however. On the other side, a strong prima facie biblical case can be made for active female leadership in the church, including a teaching ministry. In the Old Testament there were prophetesses as well as prophets, who were called and sent by God to be bearers of his word, women like Huldah, in the time of King Josiah. Before her Miriam, Moses' sister, was described as a "prophetess", while Deborah was more – she also "judged" Israel for a number of years, settling their disputes, and actually led them into battle against the Canaanites (2 Kings 22:11ff.; cf. 2 Chronicles 34:19ff.; Exodus 15:20; Judges 4 and 5). In the New Testament, although indeed Jesus had no women apostles, it was to women that he first revealed himself after the resurrection and entrusted the good news of his victory (John 20:10ff.; Matthew 28:8ff.). In addition, the Acts and the Epistles contain many references to women speakers and women workers. Philip the evangelist's four unmarried daughters all had the gift of prophecy, and Paul refers to women who prayed and prophesied in the Corinthian church. He seems to have stayed on several occasions with Aquila and Priscilla ("my fellow workers in Christ", he called them), and Priscilla was evidently active for Christ in their married partnership, for twice she is named before her husband, and it was together that they invited Apollos into their home and "explained to him the way of God more adequately" (Acts 21:9; 1 Corinthians 11:5; cf. Joel 2:28; Acts 2:17; Acts 18:26).

Paul also seems to have had women helpers in his entourage, as Jesus had in his. It is impressive to see the number of women he mentions in his letters. Euodia and Syntyche in Philippi he describes as "fellow workers" (a word he also applied to men like Timothy and Titus), who had "contended" at his side "in the cause of the gospel". In Romans 16 he refers appreciatively to eight women. He begins by commending "our sister Phoebe, a servant [or perhaps "deacon"] of the church in Cenchrea", who had been "a great help to many people", including Paul himself, and then sends greetings (among others) to Mary, Tryphena, Tryphosa and Persis, all of whom, he says, have worked "hard" or "very hard" in the Lord's service (Philippians 4:2ff.; Romans 16:1ff.). Then in verse 7 he greets "Andronicus and Junias" and describes them as "outstanding among the apostles". It seems clear (and was assumed by all the early church fathers) that Junias (or Junia) was a woman.[50] But was she an apostle? She may have been an "apostle of the churches" (2 Corinthians 8:23) – that is, a kind of mission-ary – but, since she is otherwise completely unknown, it is extremely unlikely that she belonged to that small and authoritative group, the "apostles of Christ". Paul could equally well have meant that she was well known among (that is, to) the apostles.

It is true that all the biblical examples in the preceding paragraph are of women's ministries which were either "charismatic" rather than "institutional" (i.e., appointed directly by God, like the prophetesses, not by the church, like presbyters), or informal and private (like Priscilla teaching Apollos in her home) rather than official and public (like teaching during Sunday worship). Nevertheless, if God saw no impediment to calling women into a teaching role, the burden of proof lies with the church to show why it should not appoint women to similar responsibilities.

There is, however, another argument in favour of women's ministry (including leadership and teaching) which is more general than these specific references. It is that on the day of Pentecost, in fulfilment of prophecy, God poured out his Spirit on "all people", including "sons and daughters" and his "servants, both men and women". If the gift of the Spirit was bestowed on all believers of both sexes, so were his gifts. There is no evidence, or even hint, that the charismata in general were restricted to men, although apostleship does seem to have been. On the contrary, the Spirit's gifts were distributed to all for the common good, making possible what is often called an "every-member ministry of the body of Christ" (Acts 2:17ff.; 1 Corinthians 12:44ff.). We must conclude, therefore, not only that Christ gives charismata (including the teaching gifts) to women, but that alongside his gifts he issues his call to develop and exercise them in his service and in the service of others, for the building up of his body.

This much is clear. But now we return to the double command to women to be silent in the public assembly. How shall we handle these texts? In 1 Corinthians 14 Paul is preoccupied with the building up of the church (vv. 3 – 5, 26) and with the "fitting and orderly" conduct of public worship (v. 40). Perhaps, then, his command to silence is addressed more to loquacious women in the congre-gation than to all women. It certainly was not absolute, since he assumed that some women would pray and prophesy publicly (1 Corinthians 11:5). Rather, just as tongue-speakers should "keep quiet in the church" if there is no inter-preter (v. 28), and a prophet should stop talking if a revelation is given to some-body else (v. 30), so too talkative women should "remain silent in the churches" and, if they have questions, put them to their husbands when they get home (v. 34f.). For (and this is the principle which seems to govern all public behaviour in church) "God is not a God of disorder but of peace" (v. 33). It can hardly be a prohibition of all talking by women in church, since Paul has not only referred earlier to prophetesses (v. 5) but here allows "everyone" to contribute "a hymn, or a word of instruction, a revelation, a tongue or an interpretation" (v. 26), without explicitly restricting these to men.

What about 1 Timothy 2:11 – 15?[51] The attempt to limit these verses to particular, heretical, feminist movements has not succeeded in gaining widespread acceptance. The apostle is giving directions about public worship and about the respective roles in it of men (v. 8) and women (vv. 9ff.). His instruction sounds quite general: "A woman should learn in quietness and full submission. I do not permit a woman to teach or to have authority over a man; she must be silent." What strikes me about these sentences (and about 1 Corinthians 14:34), which has not been sufficiently considered by commentators, is that Paul expresses two antitheses, the first between to "learn in quietness" or "be silent" and "to teach", and the second between "full submission" and "authority". The latter is the substantial point, confirms Paul's constant teaching about female submission to male headship and is firmly rooted in the biblical account of creation ("for Adam was formed first, then Eve"). But the other instruction (the requirement of silence and the prohibition of teaching), in spite of the controversial reference to the fact that Eve was "deceived", not Adam, seems to be an expression of the authority – submission syndrome, rather than an addition to it. There does not appear to be anything inherent in our distinctive sexualities which makes it universally inappropriate for women to teach men. So is it possible (I ask myself) that, although the requirement of "submission" is of permanent and universal validity, because grounded in creation, the requirement of "silence", like that of head-covering in 1 Corinthians 11, was a first-century cultural application of it? Is it further possible, then, that the demand for female silence was not an absolute prohibition of women teaching men, but rather a prohibition of every kind of teaching by women which attempts to reverse sexual roles and even domineer over men?

My tentative answer to my own two questions is in the affirmative. I believe that there are situations in which it is entirely proper for women to teach, and to teach men, provided that in so doing they are not usurping any improper authority over them. For this to be so, three conditions need to be fulfilled, relating to the content, context and style of their teaching.

The content of women's teaching

Firstly, the content. Jesus chose, appointed and inspired his apostles as the infallible teachers of his church. They were all men, presumably because their foundational teaching required a high degree of authority. The situation today is entirely different, however. The canon of Scripture has long ago been completed, and there are no living apostles of Christ comparable to the Twelve or Paul. Instead, the primary function of Christian teachers is to "guard the deposit" of apostolic doctrine in the New Testament and to expound it. They do not therefore claim authority for themselves, but put themselves and their teaching under the authority of Scripture. This being so, women may surely be numbered among them. Moreover, if the reference to Eve being deceived (1 Timothy 2:14) is intended to mean that women are vulnerable to deception, then their determination to teach only from the Bible should be an adequate safeguard against it.

The context for women's teaching

Secondly, there is the context of teaching, which should be a team ministry in the local church. Whether directly or indirectly, Paul appointed "elders" (plural) in every church (e.g., Acts 14:23; 20:17; Philippians 1:1; Titus 1:5). Many local churches in our day are repenting of an unbiblical one-man ministry and returning to the healthy New Testament pattern of a plural pastoral oversight. Members of a team can capitalize on the sum total of their gifts, and in it there should surely be a woman or women. Some go further. In keeping with what they regard as biblical teaching on masculine headship, they still think that (ideally at least) the team leader should be a man. Others have regard to the broad sweep of Scripture on men and women in leadership positions and emphasize the value of team leadership but do not insist on a single male leader. The debate continues. The team concept should also take care of the problem of ecclesiastical discipline. Discipline involves authority, it is rightly said, and should, therefore, not be exercised by a woman. But then it should not be exercised by a man on his own either. Discipline (especially in its extreme form of excommunication) should ideally be administered by the whole local church membership and before the ultimate is reached by a team of leaders or elders together (e.g., Matthew 18:17; 1 Corinthians 5:4 – 5; Hebrews 13:17).

The style of women's teaching

The third condition of acceptable teaching by women concerns its style. Christian teachers should never be swashbucklers, whether they are men or women. The humility of Christian teachers is to be seen both in their submission to the authority of Scripture and in their spirit of personal modesty. Jesus warned his apostles against imitating either the vainglorious authoritarianism of the Pharisees or the power-hungry bossiness of secular rulers (Matthew 23:1ff.; Mark 10:42ff.). The apostle Peter, sensitive to the temptation to pride which all Christian leaders face, urged his fellow elders to put on the apron of humility, not lording it over those entrusted to their pastoral care, but rather being examples to Christ's flock (1 Peter 5:1ff.).

It seems, then, to be biblically permissible for women to teach men, provided that the content of their teaching is biblical, its context a team and its style humble (yet these are also important for men). In such a situation they would be exercising their gift without claiming a responsible "headship" which is not theirs. Does this mean, then, that women could and should be ordained presbyter and consecrated bishop? The difficulty I have in giving a straight answer to this question is due to the layers of muddle which have been wrapped round it. But if ordination publicly recognizes God's call and gifts, and authorizes the person concerned to exercise the kind of ministry described above, there is no a priori reason why women should not be ordained or consecrated.

The fact that in recent years in the Anglican Communion some women have been appointed rectors or vicars and that, at the time of writing, fourteen have become bishops (eight diocesan and six suffragan), has not changed my mind about the ideal arrangement. Now that we have been overtaken by events, however, how should we respond? We should surely avoid the two extreme reactions. We should neither make an unprincipled surrender to cultural pressure, nor give up and secede from the church. What then? We should continue the dialogue, refusing to regard the issue as settled. Meanwhile, we should encourage ordained women to exercise their ministry voluntarily in ways which recognize masculine headship, for example in team situations.

Does the principle of masculine headship apply in the world as well as in the church? Although this question is not directly addressed in Scripture, something needs to be said about it. To begin with, many women have been richly endowed by creation and should be encouraged (as should men) to develop their God-given potential and should not be hindered from going to the top of their professions, whether law, education, politics, medicine, business, industry or any other. But Scripture also warns us against becoming isolated, according to the French proverb *qui s'éleve s'isole* (the one who elevates himself isolates himself). Women in leadership are wise to accept a measure of accountability, as are men. The queen is restrained by the constitution, the prime minister by the cabinet, CEOs by their board of directors, and professionals by their professional bodies. The team concept is healthy here too.

THE CALL TO SERVANT LEADERSHIP

Those who begin with the Catholic view of the priest as an icon of Christ (who was male), representing God to us and us to God, conclude that it is impossible for a woman to fulfil this role.[52]

Those who begin instead with the Reformed view of the presbyter as a dominant figure, responsible for the teaching and discipline of the church, conclude that it would be inappropriate for a woman to fulfil such an inherently authoritative role.

Supposing, however, that the church oversight envisaged by the New Testament is neither priestly in the Catholic sense but pastoral, nor presbyteral in the fixed Reformed sense but more fluid, modest and varied, offering different kinds and degrees of ministry? Supposing that we begin instead with the teaching of Jesus Christ about the servant-leader? True, pastors are said to be "over" the congregation in the Lord, and the people are to "obey" their leaders (1 Thessalonians 5:12; Hebrews 13:17). But this was not Jesus' main emphasis. He described two communities, secular and godly, each with its distinctive leadership style. In the world "rulers of the Gentiles lord it over them, and their high officials exercise authority over them". But, he added immediately, "not so with you". "Instead, whoever wants to become great among you must be your servant", for he himself had come not to be served, but to serve (Mark 10:42 – 45). Thus Jesus introduced into the world an altogether new style of leadership.

If, then, our fundamental vision of church leadership is not the priest of Catholic tradition, nor the presbyter of Reformed tradition nor the prelate of medieval tradition, but the servant described by Jesus, why should women be disqualified? If the essence of pastoral care is love, and its style is humility, then no biblical principle is infringed if women are welcomed to share in it. The fundamental issue is neither "ordination" nor "priesthood", but the degree of authority which necessarily inheres in the presbyterate. It may be difficult for us to envisage presbyters (even rectors and bishops) whose whole lifestyle exemplifies the humble servanthood of the kingdom of God, for church history illustrates the constant tendency towards autocracy and prelacy, and we know the pride of our own hearts. But this is the reality we should be seeking, namely a ministry characterized by humility, not authority. For men it will mean expressing their God-appointed headship in self-sacrificial service. For women it will mean submitting to this headship and not attempting to discard or usurp it. Then men will remain men, and women women, and an unbiblical confusion will be avoided.

Our Christian struggle, in the midst of and indeed against the prevailing secularism, is to bear witness to the twin biblical principles of sexual equality and male headship, in church and society as well as in the home, even as we continue to debate how this can best and most appropriately be done. Dr J. I. Packer has expressed this tension well. Scripture continues to convince him, he writes, "that the man-woman relationship is intrinsically non-reversible ... This is part of the reality of creation, a given fact that nothing will change. Certainly, redemption will not change it, for grace restores nature, not abolishes it". We need, therefore, to "theologize reciprocity, spiritual equality, freedom for ministry, and mutual submission and respect between men and women within this framework of non-reversibility ... It is important that the cause of not imposing on women restrictions that Scripture does not impose should not be confused with the quite different goals of minimizing the distinctness of the sexes as created and of diminishing the male's inalienable responsibilities in man-woman relationships as such."[53]

What is forbidden women is not leadership but domineering over men (1 Timothy 2:12), for this not only undermines the created complementarity of sexual roles, but is also incompatible with the fundamental humility of the kingdom of God. The central issue is not what *offices* are open to women (presbyter, rector, bishop), but whether their leadership *style* is consistent with Jesus' teaching on servanthood. The image of the prelate lingers and must be abolished.

I conclude with some central simplicities. If God endows women with spiritual gifts (which he does), and thereby calls them to exercise their gifts for the common good (which he does), then the church must recognize God's gifts and calling, must make appropriate spheres of service available to women, and should "ordain" (that is, commission and authorize) them to exercise their

God-given ministry, at least in team situations. Our Christian doctrines of creation and redemption tell us that God wants his gifted people to be fulfilled not frustrated, and his church to be enriched by their service.

NOTES

1 Germaine Greer, *The Female Eunuch* (London: Paladin, 1971), pp. 12, 18, 22. In her more recent book *Sex and Destiny, The politics of human fertility* (London: Secker & Warburg, 1984), while retaining her power to startle and shock by her unconventional opinions, Germaine Greer is much more positive towards the human family. Indeed, she almost romanticizes the parent-child relationships which are traditional in Asia and Africa, in contrast to the tendency of the Western nuclear family which (in her view) despises and neglects children.
2 Kate Millett, *Sexual Politics* (London: Virago, 1977).
3 Carol Gilligan, *In a Different Voice: Psychological Theory and Women's Development* (Cambridge, Mass.: Harvard Univ. Press, 1982).
4 Pamela McCorduck and Nancy Ramsey, *The Futures of Women: Scenarios for the 21st Century* (New York: Warner Books, 1997).
5 Janet Radcliffe Richards, *The Sceptical Feminist* (Harmondsworth: Penguin, 1982), pp. 13–14, 16.
6 Elaine Storkey, *What's Right with Feminism* (London: SPCK/Third Way Books, 1985). See also Mary Stewart van Leeuwen, *Gender and Grace* (Downers Grove: InterVarsity Press, 1990).
7 Storkey, *What's Right with Feminism*, p. 178.
8 Ibid.
9 A recommended symposium which opens up the issues fairly is Shirley Lees (ed.), *The Role of Women* (Leicester: InterVarsity Press, 1984), in which eight prominent Christians debate with one another. Its American equivalent is Bonnidell Clouse and Robert G. Clouse, *Women in Ministry: Four Views* (Downers Grove: InterVarsity Press, 1989).
10 Mahatma Gandhi, *An Autobiography* (1949; London: Jonathan Cape, 1966), p. 155.
11 *The Koran*, translated by N. J. Dawood (London: Penguin, 1956), pp. 360ff.
12 Raymond de Coccola, *Ayorama* (1955; Ontario: Paper Jacks, 1973), p. 212.
13 Luke 10:38ff.; John 20:10ff. John Wenham argues cogently in *Easter Enigma* (Carlisle, Penn.: Paternoster, 1984) that "Mary of Bethany" was in fact Mary Magdalene (pp. 22–33).
14 Yoder, *The Politics of Jesus*, p. 177, footnote 23.
15 Betty Friedan, *The Feminine Mystique* (Harmondsworth: Pelican, 1963), p. 68. In her subsequent book, *The Second Stage* (1981; London: Abacus, 1983), Betty Friedan declares the first stage of the feminist battle to be over. Women have been liberated from feminine role stereotypes into equality with men. The second stage will transcend the male-female polarization and involve a restructuring of society, especially of the family. The feminine mystique has been overcome; now the feminist mystique must be renounced, which denied the need for the nurturing environment of the family.

16 Leslie F. Church (ed.), *Matthew Henry's Commentary* (1708; London: Marshall, Morgan & Scott, 1960), p. 7.

17 Richards, *The Sceptical Feminist*, p. 65.

18 John Gray, *Men Are from Mars, Women Are from Venus* (London: HarperCollins, 1992), pp. 15–18.

19 Ibid., p. 31.

20 Ibid., p. 43.

21 Ibid., pp. 10, 286.

22 See, for instance, Anthony Clare, *On Men, Masculinity in crisis* (London: Chatto & Windus, 2000); Roy McCloughry, *Hearing Men's Voices, Men in search of their soul* (London: Hodder & Stoughton, 1999).

23 Mary Stewart van Leeuwen, *Fathers and Son, The search for a new masculinity* (Leicester: InterVarsity Press, 2002), p. 247.

24 Ibid.

25 David Pawson, *Leadership Is Male, A challenge to Christian feminism* (Godalming: Highland Books, 1988), pp. 17–18, 57–58.

26 Paul Jewett, *Man as Male and Female* (Grand Rapids: Eerdmans, 1975).

27 Ibid., p. 86.

28 Ibid., p. 112.

29 Ibid., p. 134.

30 Ibid., p. 138.

31 Gretchen Gaebelein Hull, *Equal to Serve: Women and Men in the Church and Home* (Grand Rapids: Revell, 1987), p. 65.

32 Ibid., p. 229.

33 Ibid., p. 210.

34 Ibid., pp. 73–74.

35 Ibid., pp. 55–56, 128, 210, 240, 244.

36 On this, see also William J. Webb, *Slaves, Women and Homosexuals: Exploring the Hermeneutics of Cultural Analysis* (Downers Grove: InterVarsity Press, 2001). In seeking to develop consistent hermeneutical tools to analyse these three issues, William Webb concludes that the homosexual texts are transcultural and the women and slavery texts are cultural and, therefore, there are consistent ways of separating out these different issues.

37 James B. Hurley, *Man and Woman in Biblical Perspective, A study in role relationships and authority* (Leicester: InterVarsity Press, 1981), pp. 206–14.

38 James B. Hurley gives us a thorough treatment of "veils". He points out that the Old Testament contains no law about wearing a veil, and that the Hebrew and Graeco-Roman custom was for women to be normally unveiled. In both cultures, too, it was usual for women to put their hair up: loose or hanging hair was a sign either of mourning or of separation from the community (e.g., because of leprosy, Nazirite vows or being suspected of adultery). Dr Hurley argues, therefore, that the "covering" and "uncovering" Paul mentions refers to the putting up and letting down of the hair. The NIV margin also adopts this interpretation (Ibid., pp. 45–47, 66–68, 162–71, 178–79, 254–71).

39 Richard Kroeger and Catherine Clark Kroeger, *I Suffer Now a Woman: Rethinking 1 Timothy 2:11 – 15 in the Light of Ancient Evidence* (Grand Rapids: Baker Academic, 1998). See my appreciative critique of this book in *The Message of 1 Timothy and Titus* (Leicester: InterVarsity Press, 1996), pp. 76 – 77.

40 *The Reformed Journal*, vol. 28, no. 6, June 1978.

41 "May Women Teach? Heresy in the Pastoral Epistles", in *The Reformed Journal*, vol. 30, no. 10, October 1980. See also Catherine Clark Kroeger, "1 Timothy 2:12 – A Classicist's View", in Alvera Mickelson (ed.), *Women, Authority and the Bible* (1986; London: Marshall Pickering, 1987), pp. 225 – 44.

42 Mickelson (ed.), *Women, Authority and the Bible*, pp. 229 – 32. See also C. C. Kroeger, "Ancient Heresies and a Strange Greek Verb", in *The Reformed Journal*, vol. 29, no. 3, March 1979.

43 "Does *kephalē* (head) mean 'source' or 'authority over' in Greek literature? A survey of 2,336 examples", first published in 1977, reprinted in *Trinity Journal*, no. 6, 1985.

44 See, e.g., Berkeley and Alvera Mickelson, "What does *kephalē* mean in the New Testament?", in Mickelson (ed.), *Women, Authority and the Bible*, pp. 97 – 110; and especially Philip Barton Payne in his response to their paper, Ibid., pp. 118 – 32. See also Gilbert Bilezikian, *Beyond Sex Roles* (Grand Rapids: Baker, 1985); and C. C. Kroeger, "The Classical Concept of Head as 'Source' ", appendix III of Hull, *Equal to Serve*, although in these works neither author betrays any knowledge of Dr Grudem's survey. Dr Bilezikian directly challenged Dr Grudem's thesis, however, at a meeting of the Evangelical Theological Society in Atlanta in November 1986. See also Dr Grudem's paper, "The Meaning of *Kephalē* ('Head'): A Response to Recent Studies", published as appendix I in John Piper and Wayne Grudem, *Recovering Biblical Manhood and Womanhood* (Wheaton: Crossway Books, 1991), pp. 425 – 68.

45 16 January 1987.

46 Stephen B. Clark opts for this word in his magisterial survey *Man and Woman in Christ: An Examination of the Roles of Men and Women in the Light of Scripture and the Social Sciences* (Ann Arbor: Servant Books, 1980), pp. 23 – 45. Despite his distinctions between "coercive", "mercenary" and "voluntary" subordination, I remain uncomfortable with the word and have written further about "authority" and "submission" (1 Timothy 2:11 – 15) in *The Message of 1 Timothy and Titus*, pp. 73 – 88.

47 For a fuller exposition of Ephesians 5:21 – 33, and of its implications for marriage, see my *Message of Ephesians*, in the "Bible Speaks Today" series (Leicester: InterVarsity Press, 1979), pp. 213 – 36.

48 Piper and Grudem, *Recovering Biblical Manhood and Womanhood*, pp. 36 – 45.

49 Stephen Bates, "Church of England Takes Cautious Step towards Female Bishops: England's Anglican branch has resisted the trend toward women bishops accepted in the US, Canada, and New Zealand", *Guardian Unlimited*, 10 July 2000.

50 See, e.g., C. E. B. Cranfield, *Commentary on Romans* (Edinburgh: T. & T. Clark, 1979), vol. II, p. 788.

51 See my fuller exposition of these crucial verses in *The Message of 1 Timothy and Titus*, pp. 73 – 88.

52 For a thorough defence of the Catholic doctrine of priesthood, see Manfred Hauke, *Women in the Priesthood? A Systematic Analysis in the Light of the Order of Creation and Redemption* (first published in German 1986; English translation, San Francisco: Ignatius, 1988).

53 Mickelson (ed.), *Women, Authority and the Bible*, p. 299.

Marriage, Cohabitation and Divorce

13

M arriage is in all societies a recognized and regulated human institution. But it is not a human invention. Christian teaching on this topic begins with the joyful affirmation that marriage is God's idea, not ours. As the Preface to the 1662 Book of Common Prayer Marriage Service says, it was "instituted by God himself in the time of man's innocency"; it was "adorned and beautified" by Christ's presence when he attended the wedding at Cana; and it symbolizes "the mystical union betwixt Christ and his church". In these ways God has shaped, endorsed and ennobled marriage. True, he calls some people to forgo it and remain single in this life (Matthew 19:11ff.; 1 Corinthians 7:7), and in the next world after the resurrection it will be abolished (Mark 12:25). Nevertheless, while the present order lasts, marriage is to be "honoured by all"; those who "forbid people to marry" are false teachers who have been misled by deceiving spirits (Hebrews 13:4; 1 Timothy 4:1ff.). Moreover, because it is a "creation ordinance", preceding the fall, it is to be regarded as God's gracious gift to all humankind.

THE PURPOSE OF MARRIAGE[1]

Classical theology has followed the biblical revelation in identifying three main purposes for which God ordained marriage. It has also usually listed them in the order in which they are mentioned in Genesis 1 and 2, while adding that priority of order does not necessarily signify priority of importance. Firstly, the man and woman were commanded to "be fruitful and increase in number" (Genesis 1:28). So the procreation of children has normally headed the list, together with their upbringing within the love and discipline of the family. Secondly, God said, "It is not good for the man to be alone. I will make a helper suitable for him" (Genesis 2:18). Thus God intended marriage (to quote the 1662 Book of Common Prayer again) for "the mutual society, help and comfort that the one ought to have of the other both in prosperity and adversity". Thirdly, marriage is intended to be that reciprocal commitment of self-giving love which finds its natural expression in sexual union, or becoming "one flesh" (Genesis 2:24).

These three needs have been strengthened by the fall. The loving discipline of family life has become all the more necessary because of the waywardness of children, mutual support because of the sorrows of a broken world, and sexual union because of temptation to immorality. But all three purposes existed before the fall and must be seen as part of God's loving provision in the institution of marriage.

The higher our concept of God's original purpose for marriage and the family, the more devastating the experience of divorce is bound to be. Marital breakdown is always a tragedy. It contradicts God's will, frustrates his purpose, brings to husband and wife the acute pains of alienation, disillusion, recrimination and guilt, and precipitates in any children a crisis of bewilderment, insecurity and often anger.[2]

The nearest the Bible comes to a definition of marriage is Genesis 2:24, which Jesus himself was later to quote as a word of God, when asked about permissible grounds for divorce (Matthew 19:4–5). Immediately after Eve has been created and brought to Adam, and Adam has recognized her (in an outburst of love poetry) as his God-given spouse, the narrator comments: "For this reason a man will leave his father and mother and be united to his wife, and they will become one flesh."

From this we may deduce that a marriage exists in God's sight when a man leaves his parents, with a view not merely to living apart from them but to "cleaving" to his wife and becoming one flesh with her. The "leaving" and the "cleaving" belong together and should take place in that order. They denote the replacement of one human relationship (child – parent) by another (husband – wife). There are some similarities between these relationships, for both are complex and contain several elements. These are physical (in one case conception, birth and nurture; in the other sexual intercourse), emotional ("growing up" being the process of growing out of the dependence of childhood into the maturity of partnership), and social (children inheriting an already existent family unit, parents creating a new one). Yet there is an essential dissimilarity between them too, for the biblical expression "one flesh" clearly indicates that the physical, emotional and social unity of husband and wife is more profoundly and mysteriously personal than the relationship of children to parents.

So Genesis 2:24 implies that the marriage union is an exclusive man – woman relationship ("a man ... his wife..."), which is publicly acknowledged at some social event ("leaves his parents"), permanent ("cleaves to his wife"), and consummated by sexual intercourse ("they will become one flesh"). A biblical definition of marriage might then be as follows: "Marriage is an exclusive heterosexual covenant between one man and one woman, ordained and sealed by God, preceded by a public leaving of parents, consummated in sexual union, issuing in a permanent mutually supportive partnership, and normally crowned by the gift of children."

CHANGING ATTITUDES

Yet the number of divorces continues to be high. In 2001 in the US the marriage rate per thousand population was 8.4, with the divorce rate being 4.0.[3] At the latter end of the twentieth century getting married was delayed for longer, marriages lasted for a shorter duration than earlier in the century and the possibility of divorce increased. One in every two of first marriages now ends in divorce.[4]

In England and Wales in 2002 there were 254,400 marriages, 59% of which were first marriages for both people. Remarriages for both parties accounted for 18%.[5] There were 160,000 divorces, the highest number of divorces since 1997 but still fewer than the peak of 180,000 seen in 1993. This falling divorce rate has been attributed to fewer marriages and the fact that people are choosing to marry later in life. By 2002, 8.4% of the adult population were divorced, which is thirteen people per thousand married people.[6]

Divorce can be correlated with many factors including income, education and religiosity, but among the reasons one must include the fact that women can now often support themselves financially and so are not dependent on their husbands; the stress that many dual-career marriages go through from pressure of work; pressure from unemployment and financial anxiety; and the more liberal attitude to divorce within society including the availability of "no-fault divorce". But undoubtedly the greatest single reason is the decline of Christian faith in the West, together with the loss of commitment to a Christian understanding of the sanctity and permanence of marriage, and the growing non-Christian assault on traditional concepts of sex, marriage and family. A clear indication of secularization in this area is the fact that, whereas in 1850 only 4% of British marriages took place in a registry office (as opposed to a church, chapel or synagogue), by 2002, 66% of all weddings were civil ceremonies. This was a large increase even when compared to 1991, when less than half of all marriages were solemnized in a civil ceremony.[7]

Not only is the Christian view of marriage as a lifelong commitment or contract now a minority view in the West, but the church is in danger of giving in to the world. Among Christian people, too, marriages are no longer as stable as they used to be, and divorces are becoming almost commonplace. Even some Christian leaders divorce their spouses and remarry, while retaining their position of Christian leadership. The Christian mind is showing signs of capitulating to secularism. The dominant worldview seems to be one of selfish individualism.[8]

My concern in this chapter is limited to the Christian understanding of marriage as set forth in Scripture, together with the personal and pastoral issues arising from it. But of primary importance for the Christian mind are the biblical questions. Even the painful trauma of a failed marriage cannot be made an excuse for avoiding these. What has God revealed to be his will in regard to marriage and the possibility of divorce and remarriage? How can we frame our policies and practice in accordance with biblical principles? There are no easy answers. In particular, the church feels the tension between its prophetic responsibility to bear witness to God's revealed standards and its pastoral responsibility to show compassion to those who have been unable to maintain his standards. John Williams is right to bid us remember that "the same God who said through Malachi 'I hate divorce' (2:16) also said through Hosea (whose partner had been blatantly immoral) 'I will heal their waywardness and love them freely, for my anger has turned away from them' (14:4)".[9]

COHABITATION

With the definition of marriage given above in our minds, we are in a position to evaluate cohabitation – that is, the practice of living together as man and wife without being married. This has become an increasingly popular lifestyle. The report of a Church of England working party entitled *Something to Celebrate* and subtitled "Valuing families in church and society" included a ten-page section on this topic.[10] It is a great pity that the media seized on the statement that the church should "abandon the phrase 'living in sin' ", but failed to appreciate the reason for the recommendation, namely that the issues were complex and could not be reduced to a single pejorative phrase. The working party deserved better treatment, and in my view was right to listen open-mindedly, even sympathetically, to those who are unwilling to condemn cohabitation out of hand.

People may decide to cohabit for what they regard as the best of reasons. For instance, they may not wish to replicate the mistakes of their married parents, succumb to the materialism of expensive weddings or reduce their relationship to a marriage licence. It is certainly true that if a man and a woman find themselves marooned on a desert island, they can enter into a valid marriage in the sight of God, even though all the trappings of a traditional wedding are unavailable to them. What constitutes marriage before God is neither a legal document, nor a church service, nor an elaborate reception, nor a shower of gifts, but a reciprocal covenant pledging lifelong fidelity and consummated in sexual union.

In the light of this, some cohabitation may almost be regarded as marriage by another name, since the essence of marriage (a covenant commitment) is there. Nevertheless, two essential elements are usually missing. The first is the promise of a lifetime commitment. Too much cohabitation is an open-ended arrangement, a kind of trial marriage, in which permanent commitment has been replaced by a temporary experiment. This cannot be called marriage; moreover, its provisional nature is bound to destabilize the relationship.

Cohabitation is unstable

Firstly, the period of cohabitation tends to be short-lived. According to an authoritative report published in the US in 2002, unmarried cohabitations overall are less stable than marriages. The probability of a first marriage ending in separation or divorce within five years is 20%, but the probability of a premarital cohabitation breaking up within five years is 49%. After ten years the probability of a first marriage ending is 33%, compared with 66% for cohabitations.[11]

Secondly, for all women the probability of a first premarital cohabitation leading to marriage is 58% after three years of cohabitation and 70% after five years of cohabitation.[12] These figures, however, are different when work status, educational background and ethnicity are included. In the UK around three in five cohabitations lead to marriage.

Thirdly, the claim that a trial period will make a later marriage more stable is not borne out by the facts. "Those couples marrying in the 1980s, having first cohabited, were 50% more likely to have divorced within five years of marrying than those who did not previously cohabit."[13]

Fourthly, there is a greater likelihood within cohabitation that a partner, particularly a man, will have more than one sexual relationship.[14] No relationship can be comparable to marriage which does not include the intention to be faithful to one another for life. "What God has joined together," Jesus said, "let nobody separate" (Matthew 19:6).

Fifthly, cohabitation is related to a series of dysfunctional indicators when compared to marriage. A study carried out in the US shows that the lifetime prevalence of alcoholism, depression and general mental illness is much higher for those who cohabit than for those who have an intact marriage.[15]

Cohabitation is informal

The second missing element in cohabitation is the public context in which marriage is undertaken. We have seen that the biblical definition of marriage (Genesis 2:24) includes the leaving of parents. In the culture of those days such a departure will not have been private, let alone clandestine, but public. In our day it cannot be applied to a casual leaving of home, as when a single student goes up to university. This is a public and symbolic move from dependence to independence, from the old to the new and from the home of one's parents to the establishment of one's own home. A public relationship like this (a man and a woman living together as partners) needs to have a public beginning. This would, of course, be impossible on a desert island, but in society family and friends have a right to know what kind of relationship exists, so that they can adjust to it. They would naturally also desire an opportunity to say goodbye, to celebrate and to promise support in the future. It is neither fair nor kind to leave families in the dark and in the cold.

It is not parents only, however, nor only a wider circle of family and friends, who have a right to know about and share in the new relationship, but also society as a whole. Sexual intimacy is, of course, essentially private, but not the relationship within which it takes place. Yet cohabitees do not make this distinction, and make the mistake of regarding their whole relationship as an entirely private affair. Marriage, however, is public – both the event which initiates it and the relationship to which it leads. Although its due recognition by the law is not essential to the marriage itself (desert island marriages being registered in heaven but not on earth), its legal enactment is certainly advantageous. A solemn pledge can hardly be regarded as "binding" without the sanctions of law. Moreover, a couple who commit themselves to each other need the protection which the law gives them. The public context for marriage is important, as the community witnesses to the promises that the man and the woman make. They are understood to agree both to the definition of marriage and to the purpose of marriage. Each gives their consent freely in the eyes of the public. They are not coerced, they are accountable to one another, and this is witnessed by the community.

In the case of cohabitation, the relationship is ambiguous and the degrees of commitment between the two people may be unequal. Neither person has any public commitment to engender security.[16] In a previous age, sexual intercourse had an iconic status and denoted lifelong, public, exclusive loyalty. Sex was far from casual and if a man made a woman pregnant, the local community regarded them as effectively married. Christopher Ash insists that "either cohabitants accept the obligations of faithfulness or their relationship is immoral; they cannot be at the same time moral and uncommitted to faithfulness".[17] He continues:

> When a man and a woman wish to live morally together they owe each other exclusive life-long faithfulness; this is the only moral context for sexual relations. God calls them to faithfulness, whether or not they recognize this. The one who walks out of a cohabiting relationship is not exempt from God's condemnation simply because they never promised to stay. The public pledges are not an extra degree of commendable commitment volunteered by particularly virtuous couples, thus moving their relationship up to a higher ethical level. The public pledges admit and recognize the moral obligation that God has already laid on them by virtue of their existing relationship.[18]

Cohabitation is inadequate

A church service is no more essential to a marriage in God's sight than the corresponding secular formalities. Neither church nor registry office is to be found on a desert island. Nevertheless, since lifelong vows are solemn and should if possible be made publicly, a church service is most appropriate, especially for Christian believers, for it sets the reciprocal pledges in the presence of God and his people. Although marriage is not a "sacrament" in the sense that baptism is, yet both include a public commitment, which should be made in the presence of chosen witnesses.

To sum up, we should be able to agree that a couple could marry validly in the sight of God on a desert island, provided that they make lifelong vows to one another, even though no representatives of family, law or church are present to witness them. But in the real world in which we live, a couple's commitment needs to be public as well as permanent, and the role of the family, the law and the church make the difference between marriage and cohabitation.

In my view, therefore, *Something to Celebrate* was unwise to take a "both-and" approach, and to recommend Christians "both to hold fast to the centrality of marriage and at the same time to accept that cohabitation is, for many people, a step along the way towards that fuller and more complete commitment".[19] In their laudable desire to be sympathetic and non-judgemental, the authors of the report have blurred the distinction between marriage and cohabitation. It is more accurate and more helpful to speak of cohabitation as falling short of marriage than as a stepping-stone towards it. Our imaginary visit to a desert island should have helped us to clarify theologically what the essence of marriage is in the sight of God. But our responsibility is to stay in the real world and to maintain without compromise the biblical definition of marriage, including its public and permanent nature.

Then we can affirm what Dr George Carey, then Archbishop of Canterbury, said during the General Synod debate on *Something to Celebrate*: "Cohabitation is not, and cannot be, marriage in all but name. Marriage is public and formal, whereas . . . cohabiting relationships . . . remain private and provisional in status . . . Marriage, not cohabitation, is the institution which is at the heart of the good society, and let us not be reluctant to say so. I do not say this in condemnation, I say it as an invitation to a better way. . ."[20]

THE TEACHING OF THE OLD TESTAMENT

In the Old Testament teaching about marriage and divorce, Deuteronomy 24:1 – 4 is of particular importance because it is the only Old Testament passage which refers to grounds or procedures for divorce.

If a man marries a woman who becomes displeasing to him because he finds something indecent about her, and he writes her a certificate of divorce, gives it to her and sends her from his house, and if after she leaves his house she becomes the wife of another man, and her second husband dislikes her and writes her a certificate of divorce, gives it to her and sends her from his house, or if he dies, then her first husband, who divorced her, is not allowed to marry her again after she has been defiled. That would be detestable in the eyes of the LORD. Do not bring sin upon the land the LORD your God is giving you as an inheritance.

Three particular points need to be clarified about this legislation.

Remarrying a former spouse

Firstly, what is the thrust and purpose of the passage? It neither requires, nor recommends, nor even sanctions divorce. Its primary concern is not with divorce at all, nor even with certificates of divorce. Its object is to forbid a man to remarry his former spouse, since this would be "detestable in the eyes of the LORD". It is thought that the ruling was intended to protect the woman from a capricious and perhaps cruel former husband. At all events, the first three verses are all the protasis or conditional part of the sentence; the apodosis or consequence does not begin until verse 4. The law is not approving divorce; what it says is that if a man divorces his wife, and if he gives her a certificate of divorce after which she remarries, they cannot marry again if her second husband dislikes and divorces her or dies.

Divorcing because of indecency

Secondly, although divorce is not encouraged, if it happens, the grounds on which it takes place is that the husband finds "something shameful" (NEB, RSV) or "something indecent" in his wife. This cannot refer to adultery on her part, for this was punishable by death, not divorce (Deuteronomy 22:20ff.; cf. Leviticus 20:10). So what was it? During the first century BC the rival Pharisaic parties led by Rabbi Shammai and Rabbi Hillel debated this. Shammai was strict and understood "something indecent" (whose Hebrew root alludes to "nakedness" or "exposure") as a sexual offence of some kind which, though left undefined, fell short of adultery or promiscuity. Rabbi Hillel, by contrast, was lax. He picked on the phrases which said that the wife "becomes displeasing" to her first husband (v. 1) or that her second husband "dislikes" her (v. 3), and interpreted them as including even the most trivial misdemeanours, for example if she spoiled the food she was cooking for him, or was quarrelsome, or if he came across a woman more beautiful than she, and so lost interest in her.[21] In fact, according to Hillel, "anything which caused annoyance or embarrassment to a husband was a legitimate ground for a divorce suit".[22]

The woman's freedom to remarry

Thirdly, if divorce was allowed, so evidently was remarriage. The text presupposes that, once the woman had been divorced, she was free to remarry, even though she was the guilty party, having done "something indecent". In fact, so far as is known, the cultures of the ancient world all understood that divorce carried with it the permission to remarry. Dr James B. Hurley summarizes the marriage and divorce laws of the Code of Hammurabi, who was king of Babylon in the early eighteenth century BC when Abraham left Ur, and also the harsher Assyrian laws at the time of Israel's exodus from Egypt.[23] Dr Gordon Wenham has added information from the fifth-century BC papyri at Elephantine, a small Jewish garrison town in southern Egypt, as well as from Philo, Josephus and the Greek and Roman world.[24] All these cultures supply evidence for divorce by the husband, and in some cases by the wife as well, with liberty to remarry. Usually the divorced wife had her dowry returned to her, and received some divorce money as well. If divorce was comparatively infrequent in the ancient world, it was because the termination of one marriage and the arrangement of a second would have been financially crippling.

THE TEACHING OF JESUS

Our Lord's instruction on marriage and divorce was given in response to a question from the Pharisees. Mark says they posed their question in order to "test" him (Mark 10:2), and Matthew elaborates what the test question was: "Is it lawful for a man to divorce his wife for any and every reason?" (Matthew 19:3). Perhaps behind their question was the public scandal of Herodias, who had left her husband Philip in order to marry King Herod Antipas. John the Baptist had courageously denounced their union as "unlawful" (Mark 6:17ff.), and had been imprisoned as a result. Would Jesus be equally outspoken, especially when, as seems probable, he was at the time within the jurisdiction of Herod

(Mark 10:1)? Certainly the Pharisees wanted to embroil him in the Shammai – Hillel debate, already mentioned. Hence, the emphasis in their question on the "reasons" or "causes" which justify divorce.

> Some Pharisees came to him to test him. They asked, "Is it lawful for a man to divorce his wife for any and every reason?"
>
> "Haven't you read," he replied, "that at the beginning the Creator 'made them male and female', and said, 'For this reason a man will leave his father and mother and be united to his wife, and the two will become one flesh'? So they are no longer two, but one. Therefore what God has joined together, let man not separate."
>
> "Why then," they asked, "did Moses command that a man give his wife a certificate of divorce and send her away?"
>
> Jesus replied, "Moses permitted you to divorce your wives because your hearts were hard. But it was not this way from the beginning. I tell you that anyone who divorces his wife, except for marital unfaithfulness, and marries another woman commits adultery."
>
> The disciples said to him, "If this is the situation between a husband and wife, it is better not to marry."
>
> Jesus replied, "Not everyone can accept this word, but only those to whom it has been given. For some are eunuchs because they were born that way; others were made that way by men; and others have renounced marriage because of the kingdom of heaven. The one who can accept this should accept it."
>
> MATTHEW 19:3 – 12

It is clear that Jesus dissociated himself from the laxity of Rabbi Hillel. He had already done so in the Sermon on the Mount. His teaching on divorce in that passage was given as one of his six antitheses, introduced by the formula, "You have heard that it was said … but I tell you …" What he was opposing in these antitheses was not Scripture ("it has been written") but tradition ("it has been said"), not the revelation of God but the perverse interpretations of the scribes. The object of their distortions was to reduce the demands of the law and make them more comfortable. In the divorce antithesis the scribal quotation "It has been said, 'Anyone who divorces his wife must give her a certificate of divorce' " appears to be a deliberately misleading abbreviation of the Deuteronomy 24 passage. It gives the impression that divorce was readily permissible, even for trivial reasons (as Hillel taught), provided only that a certificate was given. Jesus categorically rejected this. What did he teach?

The permanence of marriage

Firstly, Jesus endorsed the permanence of marriage. It is significant that he did not give the Pharisees a direct answer to their question about divorce. Instead, he spoke to them about marriage. He referred them back to Genesis 1 and 2 and asked incredulously if they had not read these chapters. He drew their attention to the two facts that human sexuality was a divine creation and that human marriage was a divine ordinance. He bracketed two texts (Genesis 1:27 and 2:24) and made God the author of both, for the same Creator who "at the beginning . . . 'made them male and female'" also said (in the biblical text), "For this reason a man will leave his father and mother and be united to his wife, and the two will become one flesh." "So," Jesus went on, adding his own explanatory assertion, "they are no longer two, but one." And, "Therefore," he said, adding his own prohibition, "what God has joined together [literally "yoked together"], let man not separate."

The teaching is unambiguous. The marriage bond is more than a human contract: it is a divine yoke. The way in which God lays this yoke upon a married couple is not by creating a kind of mystical union, but by declaring his purpose in his Word. Marital breakdown, even the so-called "death" of a relationship, cannot then be regarded as being in itself a ground for dissolution. The basis of the union is not fluctuating human experience ("I love you, I love you not"), but the divine will and Word (they "become one flesh").

The concession of divorce

Secondly, Jesus declared the Mosaic provision of divorce to be a concession to human sinfulness. The Pharisees responded to his quotations from Genesis by asking a second question: "Why then did Moses command that a man give his wife a certificate of divorce and send her away?" To this Jesus replied, "Moses permitted you to divorce your wives because your hearts were hard. But it was not this way from the beginning." Thus what they had termed a "command" Jesus called a "permission", and a reluctant permission at that, due to human stubbornness rather than divine intention.[25]

Since Jesus referred to the Mosaic provision as a concession to human sin, which was also intended to limit its evil effects, it cannot possibly be taken as indicating God's approval of divorce. To be sure, it was a divine concession, for according to Jesus whatever Moses said, God said. Yet the divine concession of divorce was contrary to the divine institution of marriage "from the beginning". The rabbis' error lay in ignoring the distinction between God's will (Genesis 1 and 2) and his legal provision for human sinfulness (Deuteronomy 24). "Human conduct which falls short of the absolute command of God is sin and stands under the divine judgement. The provisions which God's mercy has designed for the limitation of the consequences of man's sin must not be interpreted as divine approval for sinning."[26]

Remarriage as adultery

Thirdly, Jesus called remarriage after divorce "adultery". Putting together his teaching from the Synoptic Gospels and leaving aside for the moment the exceptive clause, we may summarize it as follows: a man who divorces his wife, and then remarries, both commits adultery himself (Matthew 19:9; Mark 10:11; Luke 16:18) and, because it is assumed that his divorced wife will also remarry, causes her to commit adultery as well (Matthew 5:32). A woman who divorces her husband and remarries similarly commits adultery (Mark 10:12). Further, a man (and presumably a woman too) who marries a divorcee commits adultery (Matthew 5:32; Luke 16:18). These are hard sayings. They expose with candour the logical consequences of sin. If a divorce and remarriage take place, which have no sanction from God, then any new union which follows, being unlawful, is adulterous.

DIVORCE ON THE GROUNDS OF IMMORALITY

Jesus permitted divorce and remarriage on the sole ground of immorality (*porneia*). It is well known that Matthew 5:32 and 19:9 both contain an "exceptive clause", whose purpose is to exempt one category of divorce and remarriage from being branded "adultery". Much controversy has raged round this clause. I do not think I can do more than indicate three conclusions which I have reached about it.

It is an authentic utterance

Firstly, the exceptive clause should be accepted as an authentic utterance of Jesus. Because it does not occur in the parallel sayings in Mark and Luke, many scholars have been too ready to dismiss it. Some suggest that it was an early scribal interpolation and no part of Matthew's original text. But there is no manuscript evidence that it was a gloss; even the alternative reading of Codex

Vaticanus, retained in the RSV margin, does not omit the clause. Other scholars attribute the clause to Matthew himself, and/or to the church in which he was writing, but deny that Jesus ever spoke it. But its omission by Mark and Luke is not in itself a sufficient ground for rejecting it as an editorial invention or interpretation by the first evangelist. It is perfectly possible to suppose that Matthew included it for his Jewish readership who were very concerned about the permissible grounds for divorce, whereas Mark and Luke, writing for Gentile readers, did not have the same concern. Their silence is not necessarily due to their ignorance: it may equally well be that they took the clause for granted. Pagan cultures regarded adultery as a ground for divorce. So did both the Jewish schools of Hillel and Shammai, in spite of their disagreements on other points. This was not in dispute.

It needs appropriate definition

The word *porneia* means sexual immorality. In deciding how to translate *porneia*, we need to avoid both extremes of laxity and rigidity.

Several "rigid" views have been held, which identify *porneia* as one particular sexual sin – either "fornication" in the sense of the discovery of premarital immorality, or a marriage within prohibited familial relationships, or post-marriage adultery. The main reason for rejecting any of these translations is that, although *porneia* could mean all of them, it would not be understood as referring to any one of them if there were no further qualification. *Porneia* was, in fact, a generic word for sexual infidelity or "marital unfaithfulness", and included "every kind of unlawful sexual intercourse" (Arndt-Gingrich).

The "lax" view is that *porneia* includes offences which may be regarded as broadly "sexual" in psychological rather than physical terms and so embraces even a basic temperamental incompatibility. It may be possible to use other arguments for the legitimacy of divorce on such grounds as these, but it is not possible to do so from the meaning of the word *porneia*. *Porneia* means physical sexual immorality; the reason why Jesus made it the sole permissible ground for divorce must be that it violates the "one flesh" principle which is foundational to marriage as divinely ordained and biblically defined.

It is allowed but not encouraged

Divorce for immorality is permissible, not mandatory. Jesus did not teach that the innocent party must divorce an unfaithful partner, still less that sexual unfaithfulness ipso facto dissolves the marriage. He did not even encourage or recommend divorce for unfaithfulness. On the contrary, his whole emphasis was on the permanence of marriage in God's purpose and on the inadmissibility of divorce and remarriage. His reason for adding the exceptive clause was to clarify that the only remarriage after divorce which is not tantamount to adultery is that of an innocent person whose partner has been sexually unfaithful, for in this case the infidelity has already been committed by the guilty partner. Jesus' purpose was emphatically not to encourage divorce for this reason, but rather to forbid it for all other reasons. As John Murray wrote: "It is the one exception that gives prominence to the illegitimacy of every other reason. Preoccupation with the one exception should never be permitted to obscure the force of the negation of all others."[27]

After this long excursus on the meaning of the exceptive clause and the permissible ground for divorce, it is important to come back to where we began. Although Jesus knew the realities of the fall and of the hardness of human hearts, he recalled his contemporaries to the norm of the creation and the unchanging purpose of God. He stressed reconciliation not separation, marriage not divorce. We must never move out of earshot of his ringing cry: "What God has joined together, let no one separate."

THE TEACHING OF PAUL

The teaching of Paul which we have to consider occurs in 1 Corinthians 7:10 – 16, and concerns in particular the so-called "Pauline privilege":

> To the married I give this command (not I, but the Lord): A wife must not separate from her husband. But if she does, she must remain unmarried or else be reconciled to her husband. And a husband must not divorce his wife.
>
> To the rest I say this (I, not the Lord): If any brother has a wife who is not a believer and she is willing to live with him, he must not divorce her. And if a woman has a husband who is not a believer and he is willing to live with her, she must not divorce him. For the unbelieving husband has been sanctified through his wife, and the unbelieving wife has been sanctified through her believing husband. Otherwise your children would be unclean, but as it is, they are holy.
>
> But if the unbeliever leaves, let him do so. A believing man or woman is not bound in such circumstances; God has called us to live in peace.

How do you know, wife, whether you will save your husband? Or, how do you know, husband, whether you will save your wife?

Paul teaches with authority

We need to observe, firstly, that Paul is giving authoritative, apostolic instruction. The antithesis he makes between verse 10 – "I give this command (not I, but the Lord)" – and verse 12 – "To the rest I say this (I, not the Lord)" – has been much misunderstood. It is quite mistaken to imagine that he is setting Christ's teaching and his own in opposition to each other, with the further implication that Christ's has authority, whereas his has not. No, his contrast is not between divine, infallible teaching (Christ's) and human, fallible teaching (his own), but between two forms of divine and infallible teaching, the one dominical (the Lord's) and the other apostolic (his own). There can be no doubt that this is correct, for Paul continues to use the authoritative apostolic *ego* "I" in this chapter, in verse 17 ("This is the rule I lay down in all the churches"), verse 25 ("I have no command from the Lord", i.e., no recorded saying of Jesus, "but I give a judgement as one who by the Lord's mercy is trustworthy") and verse 40 ("I think that I too have the Spirit of God"). Later and similarly, he puts his authority above that of prophets and declares his instruction to be the Lord's command: "If anybody thinks he is a prophet or spiritually gifted, let him acknowledge that what I am writing to you is the Lord's command" (14:37).

Paul affirms Jesus' teaching

Secondly, Paul echoes and confirms Jesus' prohibition of divorce. In verses 10 and 11, as in his teaching in Romans 7:1 – 3, and as in the Lord's teaching recorded by Mark and Luke, the prohibition of divorce is stated in absolute terms. "A wife must not separate from her husband ... And a husband must not divorce his wife." This is because he is expressing the general principle. It is not necessary to suppose that he knew nothing of the Lord's exceptive clause.

In verse 11 he adds an important parenthesis to the effect that if a wife does "separate" from her husband, "she must remain unmarried or else be reconciled to her husband". Now the verb Paul uses for separate (*chôrizô*) could refer to divorce and was so used both in marriage contracts in the papyri and by some early church fathers (Arndt-Gingrich). But the context suggests that Paul is not referring to divorce. He seems rather to be envisaging a situation in which the husband has not been sexually unfaithful and the wife is, therefore, not at liberty to divorce him. Some other reason (unstated) has prompted her to "separate" from him. So Paul emphasizes that in this case she is not free to remarry. Her Christian calling is either to remain single or to be reconciled to her husband, but not to remarry.

The case of desertion

Thirdly, Paul permits divorce after a believer has been deserted by an unbelieving partner. He addresses three successive paragraphs "to the unmarried and the widows" (vv. 8 – 9), "to the married" (vv. 10 – 11) and "to the rest" (vv. 12 – 16). The context reveals that by "the rest" he has in mind a particular kind of mixed marriage. He gives no liberty to a Christian to marry a non-Christian, for a Christian woman "is free to marry anyone she wishes, but he must belong to the Lord" (v. 39). The converse is equally true of Christian men (2 Corinthians 6:14ff.). Paul is rather handling the situation which arises when two non-Christians marry, one of whom is subsequently converted. The Corinthians had evidently sent him questions about this. Was the marriage unclean? Should the Christian partner divorce the non-Christian? What was the status of their children? Paul's reply is clear.

If the unbelieving partner "is willing to live with" the believing, then the believer must not resort to divorce. The reason given is that the unbelieving partner "has been sanctified" through his or her believing spouse, and so have the children. The "sanctification" in mind is clearly not a transformation of character into the likeness of Christ. As John Murray puts it, "The sanctification of which Paul speaks ... must be the sanctification of privilege, connection and relationship".[28]

But if, on the other hand, the unbelieving partner is unwilling to stay, and decides to leave, then "let him do so. A believing man or woman is not bound in such circumstances". The reasons given are that God has called us to live in peace, and that the believer cannot guarantee to win the unbeliever by insisting on perpetuating a union which the unbeliever is not willing to continue.[29]

It is important to grasp the situation which the apostle envisages, and not to draw unwarrantable deductions from his teaching. He affirms that, if the unbeliever refuses to stay, the believer "is not bound" – that is, bound to hold on to him or her, indeed, bound to the marriage itself.[30] Several negative points need to be made about the freedom which the believing partner is here given.

It is not due to the believer's conversion

The believer's freedom is not due to his or her conversion, but rather to the partner's non-conversion and unwillingness to remain. Christians sometimes plead for what they call "gospel realism", arguing that because conversion makes all things new, a marriage contracted in pre-conversion days is not necessarily still binding and in its place a new beginning may be made. This is dangerous reasoning, however. Are all pre-conversion contracts cancelled by conversion, including all one's debts? No. Paul's teaching lends no possible support to such a view. Rather, he contradicts it. His teaching is not that after conversion the believing partner is defiled by the unbeliever, and should, therefore, extricate himself or herself from the relationship. It is the opposite, that the unbelieving partner has been "sanctified" by the believer, and that, therefore, the believer should not seek to escape. Further, Paul urges in verses 17 – 24 that Christians should remain in the state in which they were when God called them, and that we are able to do so because now we are there "with God".

It does not result from the believer's initiation

The believer's freedom is not due to any resolve of his or her own to initiate divorce proceedings, but only to a reluctant acquiescence in his or her partner's "desertion" or unwillingness to stay. The initiative must not be the believer's. On the contrary, if the unbelieving partner is willing to remain, "he must not divorce her" and "she must not divorce him" (vv. 12, 13). The furthest Paul goes is to say that if the unbeliever insists on leaving, "let him do so" (v. 15). Perhaps this is the way to reconcile the apparently inconsistent statements that (a) Jesus permitted divorce on one ground only and (b) Paul added another. The first is a case of divorce; the second is an acquiescence in desertion.

It is founded on the pain of rejection

The believer's freedom is not due to "desertion" of any and every kind, nor to desertion for any form of unbelief (e.g., the Roman Catholic Church's view that marriage is not ratum if a partner is unbaptized), but only to the specific unwillingness of an unconverted person on religious grounds to continue living with his or her now-converted partner. The "Pauline privilege" provides no basis, therefore, for divorce on the general grounds of desertion; this is not a Christian option.

Summing up what Scripture teaches in the passages so far considered, we may make the following three affirmations.

* God created humankind male and female in the beginning, and himself instituted marriage. His intention was and is that human sexuality will find fulfilment in marriage, and that marriage will be an exclusive, loving and lifelong union. This is his purpose.
* Divorce is nowhere commanded, and never even encouraged, in Scripture. On the contrary, even if biblically justified, it remains a sad and sinful declension from the divine norm.
* Divorce and remarriage are permissible (not mandatory) on two grounds. Firstly, an innocent person may divorce his or her partner if the latter has been guilty of serious sexual immorality. Secondly, a believer may acquiesce in the desertion of his or her unbelieving partner, if the latter refuses to go on living with him or her. In both cases, however, the permission is given in negative or reluctant terms. Only if a person divorces his or her partner on the ground of marital unfaithfulness is his or her remarriage not adulterous. Only if the unbeliever insists on leaving is the believer "not bound".

IRRETRIEVABLE BREAKDOWN

My position, as defined above, was criticized by Dr David Atkinson in his book *To Have and To Hold* (1979). He called it "legislative" and expressed his uneasiness in the following terms: "The difficulty with this view is that in pastoral practice it can lead to the sort of casuistry which can become negatively legalistic. It concentrates on physical adultery but neglects other 'unfaithfulness', and can mean that the Church's blessing for second marriage is reserved only for those who are fortunate (!) enough to have had their former partner commit adultery against them. It raises the question as to what breaks the marriage bond."[31]

It is, indeed, because of the practical problems which beset us when we insist on a "matrimonial offence" as the only legitimate ground for divorce, that an alternative and more flexible approach has been sought. In the UK, the Church of England report *Putting Asunder* (1966) recommended the concept of "irretrievable breakdown" as an alternative, and the 1969 Divorce Reform Act was based upon it. It nevertheless required that irretrievable breakdown be proved by one of five evidences, three being faults (adultery, desertion and unreasonable behaviour), and two indicating de facto separation (for two years if the couple agree to divorce, and for five years if they do not). Then the Church of England Commission which was presided over by Canon Professor Howard Root, and which reported in *Marriage, Divorce and the Church* (1971), investigated further the concept that some marriages "die" even while both married partners are still alive. A few years later the Commission chaired by Bishop Kenneth Skelton of Lichfield, which reported in *Marriage and the Church's Task* (1978), took a similar line.

Since 1 March 2001, the grounds for divorce are such that couples who wish to divorce must satisfy one of the criteria on jurisdiction that has been standardized throughout the European Community. The grounds for divorce are that the marriage has irretrievably broken down and the person filing for divorce (the petitioner) must prove one of five facts.

- The spouse has committed adultery and the petitioner cannot be expected to continue living together.
- The spouse has exhibited unreasonable behaviour and the petitioner cannot be expected to continue living together.
- The spouse has deserted the petitioner for a period of two years.
- The petitioner and the spouse have been living separately for more than two years and both parties agree to a divorce.
- The petitioner and the spouse have been living separately for more than five years, whether or not the spouse agrees to a divorce.[32]

In practice, however, it is often possible to get around some of these criteria by couples agreeing to cite unreasonable behaviour in order to get a quick divorce. "Quickie" divorces are also available via the internet. Such practices undermine the seriousness of divorce, as well as the period of reflection and the possibility of reconciliation which is owed to a marriage in difficulties.

The 1996 Family Law Act proposed to bring in irretrievable breakdown without the necessity of citing any of the five criteria listed above. This was due to come into effect in 1998. The General Synod debated the issues and approved the proposals, but although some of the Family Law Act 1996 has come into effect, the UK government announced in 2000 that many of its proposals would be delayed for several years.

One can understand the desire to avoid the need to establish culpability. But the arguments against it do not seem to have been adequately considered.

The concept of "irretrievable breakdown" has undesirable consequences. (1) It makes divorce too easy; it virtually opens the door to divorce on demand. (2) It represents marriage in terms of self-fulfilment, instead of self-giving. If it does not deliver what we had expected, then, instead of working at it, we declare that it does not work for us. (3) It gives the impression that marriages break down by themselves. It makes marriage the scapegoat and exonerates the married partners. But if the essence of marriage is a commitment of love and faithfulness, then only a failure in these will threaten it. By adopting the secular approach of no-fault breakdown, Dr Alan Storkey has written, the churches have locked themselves into a contradiction, "affirming ... one view of marriage, while accepting a completely different dynamic behind divorce reform".[33] (4) It is an expression of secular pessimism. If two persons are "incompatible", and a breakdown is "irretrievable", what has become of the grace of God and the gospel of reconciliation?

Here, then, are two different approaches to the vexed question of divorce – "fault" and "no fault", human culpability and irretrievable breakdown. Are we obliged to choose between them? Or is there a third way which embraces the best in both concepts? Perhaps the answer lies in the biblical notion of "covenant" and "covenant faithfulness". It could be described as a third way in the sense that the ground for divorce is neither a breakdown for which nobody accepts responsibility, nor a particular individual fault which has to be proved, but rather a culpable breach of the marriage covenant.

It is clear that Scripture regards marriage as a covenant, indeed – although between two human beings – as a "covenant of God" (Proverbs 2:17, literally), instituted and witnessed by him. In a letter which I received some years ago, Roger Beckwith, warden of Latimer House, Oxford, summarized what he saw to be the five terms of the marriage covenant: (1) love (as in every covenant), but married love involving specific obligations; (2) living together as a single household and family; (3) faithfulness to the marriage bed; (4) provision for the wife by the husband; and (5) submission to the husband by the wife.

In his book *To Have and To Hold*, subtitled "The marriage covenant and the discipline of divorce", David Atkinson develops the covenant idea further. He defines a covenant as "an agreement between parties based on promise, which includes these four elements: first, an undertaking of committed faithfulness made by one party to the other (or by each to the other); secondly, the acceptance of that undertaking by the other party; thirdly, public knowledge of such an undertaking and its acceptance; and fourthly, the growth of a personal relationship based on and expressive of such a commitment".[34] It is not difficult to apply such a definition of "covenant" to marriage, especially because human marriage is used in Scripture as a model of God's covenant with his people, and God's covenant as a model for human marriage.[35] David Atkinson goes on to quote Professor G. R. Dunstan's development of this analogy, in that God's covenant and human marriage both have (1) an initiative of love, inviting a response, and so creating a relationship, (2) a vow of consent, guarding the union against the fitfulness of emotion, (3) obligations of faithfulness, (4) the promise of blessing to those who are faithful to their covenant obligations, and (5) sacrifice, the laying down of life in death, especially in this case death to the old independence and self-centredness.[36]

David Atkinson goes on to argue that "the covenant structure of marriage lends weight to the view ... that marriage is not a metaphysical status which cannot be destroyed; it is rather a moral commitment which should be honoured".[37] Yet a covenant can be broken. "Covenants do not just 'break down', " however, "they are broken; divorce expresses sin as well as tragedy". So then, "from a biblical moral perspective, we cannot dissolve the category of 'matrimonial offence' without remainder into the less personally focused concept of 'irretrievable breakdown' ".[38] Instead, "The covenant model for marriage places the question of divorce in the area of moral responsibility".[39] His conclusion is that "any action which constitutes unfaithfulness to the marriage covenant so persistent and unrepentant that reconciliation becomes impossible may be sufficient to break the bond of marriage and so may release the other partner from their covenant promise".[40]

There is much in the covenant model of marriage which is compelling. To begin with, it is a thoroughly biblical notion. It also emphasizes the great solemnity both of covenant-making and of covenant-breaking – in the former case emphasizing love, commitment, public recognition, exclusive faithfulness and sacrifice, and in the latter the sin of going back on promises and rupturing a relationship of love. I confess, however, that my problem is how to fuse the concepts of covenant loyalty and matrimonial offence. I can understand the reasons for not wanting to build permission to divorce on two offences. But if Scripture regards the marriage covenant as capable of being broken in several ways, how shall we explain the single offence mentioned in our Lord's exceptive clause? Certainly the covenant relationship envisaged in marriage (the "one flesh" union) is far deeper than other covenants, whether a suzerainty treaty, a business deal or even a pact of friendship. May it not be, therefore, that nothing less than a violation (by sexual infidelity) of this fundamental relationship can break the marriage covenant?

God's marriage covenant with "Jerusalem" (personifying his people), described at length in Ezekiel 16, is germane to this issue. God says to her, "I gave you my solemn oath and entered into a covenant with you ... and you became mine" (v. 8). But Jerusalem "played the harlot" (RSV), or rather (because she gave hire rather than receiving it) was a wife guilty of promiscuous adultery (vv. 15 – 34). Therefore, God said he would sentence her to "the punishment of women who commit adultery" (v. 38). Nevertheless, although her behaviour was worse even than her "younger sister Sodom" (vv. 46 – 52), and although she had despised God's oath "by breaking the covenant" (v. 59), yet God said, "I will remember the covenant I made with you in the days of your youth, and I will establish an everlasting covenant with you" (v. 60), bringing forgiveness and penitence.

It seems to me that we must allow these perspectives of God's covenant to shape our understanding of the marriage covenant. The marriage covenant is not an ordinary human contract which, if one party to it reneges, may be renounced by the other. It is more like God's covenant with his people. In this analogy (which Scripture develops), only fundamental sexual unfaithfulness breaks the covenant. And even this does not lead automatically or necessarily to divorce; it may rather be an occasion for reconciliation and forgiveness.

PERSONAL AND PASTORAL REALITIES

This has been a long chapter. Some readers will have been provoked by it, finding it drily academic, or unfeeling towards the profound sufferings of those whose marriages break down, or remote from the realities of the contemporary Western world, or all three. I can understand their reactions. Yet it has been necessary to give the biblical material a thorough examination, for this book is about developing a Christian mind on current issues. Conscientious disciples of Jesus know that Christian action is impossible without Christian thought; they resist the temptation to take short cuts. At the same time, the process of "making up one's mind" means reaching a decision which has practical consequences. What, then, are these likely to be? Because of the great seriousness with which Scripture views both marriage and divorce, I conclude with four urgent pastoral needs.

Firstly, there is the need for thorough biblical teaching about marriage and reconciliation. Pastors must give positive instructions on both these subjects. In sermons, Sunday school and confirmation classes we have to hold before the congregation we serve the divine intention and norm of exclusive, committed, lifelong faithfulness in marriage. We ought also to give clear and practical teaching on the duty and the way of forgiveness, for reconciliation lies at the very heart of Christianity. For some years now I have followed a simple rule, that whenever anybody asks me a question about divorce, I refuse to answer it until I have first talked about two other subjects, namely, marriage and reconciliation. This is a simple attempt to follow Jesus in his own priorities. When the Pharisees asked him about the grounds for divorce, he referred them instead to the original institution of marriage. If we allow ourselves to become preoccupied with divorce and its grounds, rather than with marriage and its essentials, we lapse into pharisaism. God's purpose is marriage not divorce, and his gospel is good news of reconciliation. We need to see Scripture as a whole, and not isolate the topic of divorce.

Secondly, there is the need for preparation for marriage. Couples preparing for marriage usually cherish high ideals for the future, and are ready, even anxious, for help. Yet hard-pressed clergy can often manage to give each couple no more than a single interview, and even then legal and social questions sometimes crowd out the spiritual and moral dimensions of marriage. Some clergy arrange courses for groups of engaged couples or encourage them to attend appropriate weekend conferences. Others give couples a book or a short annotated list of recommended reading.[41] Best of all, perhaps, is the resolve to harness the services of mature lay couples in the congregation, who would be willing to spend several evenings with an engaged couple, meet them again after the wedding, and continue to keep in touch with them during the early days of adjustment.

Thirdly, there is the need for a reconciliation ministry. In the UK during the 1980s, both in-court and out-of-court conciliation services were developed, and there has been a growing desire to see conciliation attempts built into the initial stages of legal proceedings, so that an adversarial approach is avoided. There are also voluntary organizations like RELATE,[42] Marriage Care (formerly the Catholic Marriage Advisory Council),[43] Care for the Family,[44] and Marriage Resource (a network of Christian marriage support groups, which sponsor National Marriage Week).[45] I wish the churches were yet more actively involved in this ministry, especially at the local level. Christians are supposed to be in the reconciliation business. Many more people would seek help, and seek it early when it is most needed, if they knew where they could turn for sympathy, understanding and advice. Sometimes expert marital therapy will be necessary, but at other times a listening ear may be enough.

Fourthly, there is the need for pastoral ministry to the divorced. Because marriage is a "creation ordinance", God's purposes for it do not vary; they are the same for the world as for the church. The non-Christian world will often be unable and unwilling to fulfil them because of the hardness of human hearts, and so is likely to have its own legislation for divorce. It is right, however, to expect higher standards in the new community of Jesus. He repeatedly told his followers not to follow the way of the world. "It shall not be so among you," he said (Mark 10:43 RSV). In marriage, therefore, the church's calling is not to conform to popular trends, but to bear witness to God's purpose of permanence.

Nevertheless, "hardness of heart" is not confined to the non-Christian world. As with the Old Testament people of God, so with the people of the new covenant, some concession to human fallibility and failure will be needed. What institutional arrangements should the church make? Professor Oliver O'Donovan writes: "The primary question is how it may find some arrangement that will give adequate form both to its beliefs about the permanence of marriage and to its belief about the forgiveness of the penitent sinner." [46] It could express this ambivalence either by permitting the remarriage in church (emphasizing the gospel of redemption), while adding some kind of discipline (recognizing God's marriage norm), or by refusing the remarriage in church (emphasizing the norm), while adding some expression of acceptance (recognizing the gospel). I myself incline to the former. But before any church service for the marriage of a divorced person is permitted, the church must surely exemplify its adherence to the revelation of God in two ways. It must satisfy itself, firstly, that the remarriage comes within the range of the biblical permissions, and secondly, that the couple concerned accept the divine intention of marriage permanence.

The sustained policy of the Church of England for several decades has been to refuse to marry in church any person who has a previous spouse still living, while at the same time seeking to offer a ministry of pastoral compassion and care to those who have been divorced. After more than twenty years of debate, however, the Church of England's General Synod gave its blessing to the marriage of divorced people, under exceptional circumstances, on 14 November 2002. Nonetheless, this decision did create problems for local clergy, many of whom felt that a burden had been placed on their shoulders of deciding between couples as to which situations were worthy of remarriage and which were not. They had been told that a primary consideration was whether the marriage would cause hostile public comment, scandal, consecrate a long-standing infidelity or undermine the church's credibility. No vicar would be compelled to conduct a service, yet it was recognized that some remarriages have been quietly taking place while services of blessing after civil ceremonies have also taken place. Out of around 7,500 church marriages a year in the UK, 11% of the total already include at least one divorced partner. Those who opposed this decision felt that such pressure may mean clergy begin to give in to the demand for remarriage and will eventually say "yes" to all applicants. It was also felt that it is extremely important to continue to affirm marriage as a permanent, public and exclusive relationship, while at the same time emphasizing God's forgiveness and the possibility of a fresh start. Jesus and his apostle Paul did allow divorce and remarriage in certain circumstances, and this permission of a new beginning needs what Professor O'Donovan has called "institutional visibility".[47] Whether the current position maintains the necessary faithfulness to Scripture together with the need for pastoral sensitivity remains to be seen.

In this case the church service could not with integrity be identical with a normal marriage ceremony. Some expression of penitence should be included, either in a private preliminary (as suggested by the Root Report in paragraphs 143 – 47), or in the public service itself. Either way would be an acknowledgement that every divorce, even when biblically permissible, is a declension from the divine norm. This is not to stand in judgement on the people concerned in any proud or paternalistic way, but to admit that we, as well as they, are sinners.

In all this we continue to be caught in the tension between law and grace, witness and compassion, prophetic ministry and pastoral care. On the one hand, we need the courage to resist the prevailing winds of permissiveness and to set ourselves to uphold marriage and oppose divorce. The state will continue to frame its own divorce laws, but the church also has its own witness to bear to the teaching of its divine Lord, and must exercise its own discipline. On the other hand, we shall seek to share with deep compassion in the suffering of those whose marriages have failed, and especially of those whom we cannot conscientiously advise to seek an escape by divorce. We may on occasion feel at liberty to advise the legitimacy of a separation without a divorce, or even a divorce without a remarriage, taking 1 Corinthians 7:11 as our warrant. But we have no liberty to go beyond the permissions of our Lord. He knew his Father's will and cared for his disciples' welfare. Wisdom, righteousness and compassion are all found in following him.

NOTES

1 Those wishing to examine the biblical theology surrounding the purpose of marriage will find that Christopher Ash's book *Marriage: Sex in the Service of God* (Leicester: InterVarsity Press, 2003), chapters 6 – 10, looks at this issue in some detail.
2 See Judson J. Swihart and Steven L. Brigham, *Helping Children of Divorce* (Downers Grove: InterVarsity Press, 1982).
3 *www.census.gov/prod/2003pubs/02statab/vitstat.pdf*. It is difficult to put actual figures on the number of divorces as several states do not report their figures. The number of marriages in the US in 2001 was 2,327,000.
4 The rise in the divorce rates in the 1970s and 1980s levelled off in the 1990s. See Rose M. Kreider and Jason M. Fields, *Number, timing and duration of marriages and divorces, 1996* (Household Economic Studies, issued February 2001), at *www.census.gov/prod/2002pubs/p70-80.pdf*.
5 National Statistics, *Marriages in 2002: England and Wales*, *www.statistics.gov.uk*
6 *UK Statistics on Families* (Mothers' Union, March 2004).
7 Not all civil marriages now take place in registry offices, as many venues are licensed as suitable for weddings.
8 For a lyrical meditation on married love and its call to self-giving, see Mike Mason, *The Mystery of Marriage* (London: Triangle, SPCK, 1997). He writes: "Love is an earthquake that relocates the centre of the universe" (p. 26).
9 John Williams, *For Every Cause? A Biblical Study of Divorce* (Carlisle, Penn.: Paternoster, 1981), p. 12.
10 Rosemary Dawson, *Something to Celebrate* (London: Church House Publishing, 1995).
11 Matthew D. Bramlett and William D. Mosher, "Cohabitation, Marriage, Divorce and Remarriage in the United States", *National Survey of Family Growth*, series 23, no. 22, July 2002, *www.cdc.gov/nchs/*.
12 Ibid., p. 12.
13 L. Waite and M. Gallagher, *The Case for Marriage: Why Married People Are Happier, Healthier, and Better Off Financially* (New York: Doubleday, 2000), p. 46. Cited in *www.civitas.org.uk/hwu/cohabitation.php#4*. See also Elaine Storkey, *The Search for Intimacy* (London: Hodder & Stoughton, 1995), p. 173.
14 K. Wellings, J. Field, A. Johnson and J. Wadsworth, "Sexual Behaviour in Britain", *The National Survey of Sexual Attitudes and Lifestyles* (London: Penguin, 1994), p. 116; J. Steinhaiser, "No marriage, no apologies", *New York Times*, 6 July 1995.
15 On alcoholism, see Lee Robbins and Darrel Regier, *Psychiatric Disorders in America: The Epidemiologic Catchment Area Study* (New York: Free Press, 1991), p. 64. On depression, see Ibid., p. 64. On general mental illness, see Ibid., p. 334.
16 Ash, *Marriage: Sex in the Service of God*, p. 222.

17 Ibid., p. 224.

18 Ibid., p. 224.

19 *Something to Celebrate*, pp. 115 – 16.

20 London, 30 November 1995.

21 The details may be found in the tract *Gittin* in the Babylonian Talmud. See also Ecclesiasticus 25:26.

22 William L. Lane, *The Gospel of Mark*, New International Commentary Series (Grand Rapids: Eerdmans, and London: Marshall, Morgan & Scott, 1974), p. 353.

23 Hurley, *Man and Woman in Biblical Perspective*, pp. 22 – 28.

24 "The Biblical View of Marriage and Divorce", three articles published in *Third Way*, October and November 1977 (vol. 1, nos. 20 – 22).

25 It is true that in Mark 10:3ff. Jesus is recorded as having used the verb "command", but there he seems to have been referring either to the Mosaic legislation in general or in particular to the issuing of the divorce certificate.

26 C. E. B. Cranfield, *The Gospel According to Mark*, Cambridge Greek Testament Commentary (Cambridge: Cambridge Univ. Press, 1959), pp. 319 – 20.

27 John Murray, *Divorce* (Committee on Christian Education, Orthodox Presbyterian Church, 1953), p. 21. It is only fair to add that the moderate position developed in these pages, although based on careful exegesis, has not been acceptable to all. Some understand Jesus as having been more lenient than I have suggested, and others as more strict. The more lenient view was expressed by Ken Crispin, an Australian lawyer, in *Divorce: The Forgivable Sin?* (London: Hodder & Stoughton, 1989). Incensed by "callous and irresponsible" church leaders, he interpreted *porneia* so broadly as to include every kind of misconduct which undermines a marriage. The stricter position was presented by William A. Heth and Gordon J. Wenham in *Jesus and Divorce* (London: Hodder & Stoughton, 1984). They argued from Scripture and church history that Jesus placed an absolute ban on divorce and remarriage. Andrew Cornes, in *Divorce and Remarriage* (London: Hodder & Stoughton, 1993), takes a similarly strict position. He concedes that Jesus permitted divorce in the case of a serious sexual offence, and that Paul permitted a Christian to acquiesce if his/her non-Christian partner insists on leaving. But, he urges, Jesus did not permit a remarriage to the divorcee. This is "not because he is divorced but because he is still married. It is because God yoked him and his original partner together. It is because in God's eyes they became, in marriage, no longer two but one" (pp. 307 – 8). Although I am not myself convinced about the total ban on remarriage, Andrew Cornes combines biblical scholarship and pastoral experience, courage and compassion. His book will provoke some furious rethinking; it is indispensable reading for those anxious to develop a Christian mind on these topics. I have not been able to read David Instone-Brewer's scholarly work *Divorce and Remarriage in the Bible* (Grand Rapids: Eerdmans, 2002), but it comes highly recommended by many scholars in the debates as a significant contribution.

28 Murray, *Divorce*, p. 65.

29 RSV and NIV translate "How do you know ... whether you will save your wife/husband?" understanding the question to express doubt, even resignation. It may well be, however, that the apostle is rather expressing hope. The GNB renders the verse: "How can you be sure ... that you will not save your wife/husband?" The NEB is even stronger: "Think of it: as a wife you may be your husband's salvation ..." As F. F. Bruce comments, "A mixed marriage had thus missionary potentialities" (*New Century Bible*, 1971, p. 70). So the Christian partner must do his/her utmost to preserve the marriage.

30 In *The Teaching of the New Testament on Divorce* (London: Williams & Norgate, 1921), R. H. Charles argued that, since in 1 Corinthians 7:39 the opposite of "bound" is "free to marry", therefore in verse 9, "the right of remarriage is here conceded to the believing husband or wife who is deserted by an unbelieving partner" (p. 58).

31 David Atkinson, *To Have and To Hold, The marriage covenant and the discipline of divorce* (London: Collins, 1979), p. 28.

32 In America grounds for divorce vary from state to state. Irretrievable breakdown is commonly accepted and other grounds might include habitual drunkenness, impotence, insanity, intolerable cruelty or adultery.

33 Alan Storkey, *Marriage and Its Modern Crisis* (London: Hodder & Stoughton, 1996), p. 197.

34 Atkinson, *To Have and To Hold*, p. 70.

35 Ibid., p. 71.

36 Ibid., pp. 75 – 76.

37 Ibid., p. 91.

38 Ibid., p. 151.

39 Ibid., p. 152.

40 Ibid., p. 154.

41 I especially recommend a book by Bishop Michael and Mrs Myrtle Baughen, *Your Marriage* (London: Hodder & Stoughton, 1994; US edition entitled *Christian Marriage*, Grand Rapids: Baker, 1994).

42 *www.relate.org.uk/*

43 *www.plymouth-diocese.org.uk/organisations/marr_care.htm*

44 *www.care-for-the-family.org.uk*

45 *www.marriageresource.org.uk*

46 Oliver O'Donovan, *Marriage and Permanence*, Grove Booklet on Ethics no. 26 (Cambridge: Grove Books, 1978), p. 21.

47 Ibid., p. 20.

Abortion and Euthanasia

14

The debates over abortion and euthanasia are admittedly complex. They have medical, legal, theological, ethical, social and personal aspects. They are highly emotional subjects, for they touch on the mysteries of human sexuality and reproduction, life and death. Both often involve acutely painful dilemmas. Yet Christians cannot opt out of personal decision-making or public discussion regarding these topics merely because of their complexity.

THE DOCTRINES OF GOD AND HUMANITY

What is involved in the debates about abortion and euthanasia are nothing less than our Christian doctrines of both God and humanity. All Christian people believe that Almighty God is the only giver, sustainer and taker-away of life. On the one hand, "He himself gives all men life and breath and everything else", and "In him we live and move and have our being". On the other, as the psalmist says to God, "When you take away their breath, they die and return to the dust". Indeed, whenever anybody dies, Christian faith struggles to affirm with Job: "The LORD gave and the LORD has taken away; may the name of the LORD be praised" (Acts 17:25, 28; Psalm 104:29; Job 1:21). To the Christian, then, both life-giving and life-taking are divine prerogatives. And although we cannot interpret "You shall not kill" as an absolute prohibition, since the same law which forbade killing also sanctioned it in some situations (e.g., capital punishment and holy war), yet the taking of human life is a divine prerogative which is permitted to human beings only by specific divine mandate. Without this, to terminate human life is the height of arrogance.

The questions of abortion and euthanasia concern our doctrine of humanity as well as our doctrine of God. However undeveloped the embryo may still

389

be, and however mentally impaired an elderly person may be, everybody agrees that they are living and that the life they possess is human. Yet the decision to terminate a human life involves an implicit judgement that a particular form of human living is not worthy of ultimate respect.

So then, if both divine sovereignty and human dignity are being challenged by the abortion and euthanasia debates, no conscientious Christian can stand aside from them. We will look primarily at abortion and the discussion that surrounds it, returning at the end of the chapter to euthanasia and some of the particular problems which it raises.

THE REVOLUTION IN PUBLIC ATTITUDES

A revolution has recently taken place in public attitudes on these issues. Whether or not doctors have actually subscribed to the ancient Hippocratic Oath (fifth century BC), it has been generally assumed that they took its main undertakings for granted.

> I will follow that method of treatment which, according to my ability and judgement, I consider for the benefit of my patients, and abstain from whatever is deleterious and mischievous. I will give no deadly drug to anyone if asked, nor suggest any such counsel; and in like manner I will not give to a woman a pessary to procure abortion.

Since some other clauses of the oath are decidedly antiquated, the Declaration of Geneva (1948) updated it, while at the same time taking care to include the promise, "I will maintain the utmost respect for human life from the time of conception."

But one's expectations of the situation in the West, the heir of many centuries of Christian tradition, are naturally higher. In Britain abortion remained illegal until the Infant Life (Preservation) Act of 1929, which provided that no action would be punishable "when done in good faith with the intention of saving the life of the mother". David Steel's 1967 Abortion Act appeared to many to be only a cautious extension of this. Two registered medical practitioners were required to express their opinion, "formed in good faith", that the continuance of the pregnancy would involve either (1) risk to the life of the pregnant woman, or (2) and (3) risk of injury to her or her existing children's physical or mental health, "greater than if the pregnancy were terminated", or (4) "substantial risk that if the child were born it would suffer from such physical or mental abnormalities as to be seriously handicapped".

Whatever the intentions were of the Abortion Law Reform Association (who masterminded the Bill), it seems clear that its catastrophic consequences were not foreseen by its parliamentary sponsors. Before the Act became law, the number of legal abortions carried out annually in the hospitals of the NHS in England and Wales had crept up slowly to 6,100 (1966).[1] In 1968, however, the number was already 24,000, in 1973 it was 167,000 and in 1983 over 184,000. In 2000, 185,376 abortions took place.[2] By 2002, over 5,000,000 legal abortions had been performed in the UK since the 1967 Act. Over 98% of abortions are performed for "social" reasons and less than one abortion in a thousand is performed because of a risk to the life of the mother. The total number of legal and illegal abortions throughout the world was estimated in 1968 to be between 30,000,000 and 35,000,000.[3] Today the estimate is that as many as 55,000,000 abortions take place each year,[4] which means that more than one abortion occurs every second.

In addition, many early abortions may not be recorded. In the UK the "morning after pill" (which frequently induces an early abortion by preventing implantation of the fertilized embryo) has been available since 2001 "over the counter", from pharmacists and school nurses. The reality of the current situation in the UK is that abortion is available for most women on request. At present, approximately one in five of all established pregnancies ends in abortion, and more than one in four of all women of childbearing age have had an abortion.

The situation in the United States is equally troubling. In 1970 a Texan woman called Norma McCorvey (who used the pseudonym Jane Roe) became pregnant and decided to fight the anti-abortion legislation of her state. She took Henry Wade, the Dallas district attorney, to court. In January 1973, in the now notorious *Roe v. Wade* case, the US Supreme Court declared by seven votes to two that the Texas law was unconstitutional.[5] Its judgement inhibited all regulation of abortion during the first three months of pregnancy, and during the second and third trimesters regulated it only in relation to the mother's physical or mental health. This ruling implicitly permitted abortion on demand at every stage of pregnancy. The number of legal abortions in the United States in 1969 was less than 20,000. In 1975 it passed the 1,000,000 mark, and in 1980 reached more than 1,500,000. Throughout the 1980s it remained at about this number every year. This means that during this period, for every 1,000 births (natural and induced), there were 300 abortions.

Remarkably, Norma McCorvey became a Christian in 1995 and her true story became public. Norma never had an abortion; her child was adopted. She has become an active voice in opposing the current practice of abortion in the USA and has asked the US Supreme Court to rehear the case.

Meanwhile, the nationwide debate has grown into a deeply held confrontation. Abortion is always a major election issue in the USA, and both pro-life and pro-choice groups have annual marches on Washington.

Any society which can tolerate abortion on this scale has ceased to be civilized. One of the major signs of decadence in the Roman Empire was that its unwanted babies were "exposed" – that is, abandoned and left to die.[6] Can we claim that contemporary Western society is any less decadent because it consigns its unwanted babies to the hospital incinerator instead of the local rubbish dump? Indeed, modern abortion is even worse than ancient exposure because it has been commercialized and has become, at least for some doctors and clinics, an extremely lucrative practice. Yet reverence for human life is an indisputable characteristic of a humane and civilized society.

THE KEY ISSUE[7]

Those who campaign for a lax policy on abortion, and those who campaign for a strict one, begin their argument from opposite positions.

Those in favour of liberal abortion emphasize the rights of the mother, and especially her right to choose; those opposed to abortion emphasize the rights of the unborn child, and especially his or her right to live. The first see abortion as little more than a retroactive contraceptive, the second as little less than prenatal infanticide. The appeal of abortion supporters is often to compassion (though also to the justice of what they see as a woman's right); they cite situations in which the mother or the rest of the existing family would suffer intolerable strain if an unwanted pregnancy were allowed to come to term. The appeal of those opposed to abortion is especially to justice; they stress the need to defend the rights of unborn children who are unable to defend themselves.

Those who oppose a liberal attitude to abortion are not lacking in compassion, however. They recognize the hardships, and even tragedies, which the arrival of an unplanned baby often brings. The psychological distress, financial hardships and impact on other children of an unwanted pregnancy can be devastating. Perhaps the father of the baby is violent or cruel, perhaps an alcoholic or even a psychopath. Perhaps the mother is a schoolgirl or student, and a continued pregnancy would interfere with her education and her career. Or perhaps her pregnancy is due to adultery or incest or rape, and these tragedies are great enough in themselves without adding to them an unplanned, unwanted child. Or perhaps she has contracted rubella during pregnancy and fears that her child will be disabled.

Yet there is growing evidence of the harmful effects of abortion on women, including higher rates of depression, self-harm, psychiatric hospitalization and suicide, as well as a significantly increased incidence of premature labour in subsequent pregnancies.[8]

We have to ask ourselves what principles are involved. Our compassion needs both theological and moral guidelines. If it is expressed at the expense of truth or justice, it ceases to be genuine compassion.

The key issue, then, is a moral and theological one. It concerns the nature of the fetus (*fetus* is Latin for "offspring"). How are we to think of the embryo in the mother's womb? It is our evaluation of the fetus which will largely determine our attitude to abortion.

The fetus as an inanimate object

The first option which is held by some (and which Christians reject as totally false and utterly abhorrent) is that the fetus is merely a lump of jelly or blob of tissue, or a growth in the mother's womb, which may therefore be extracted and destroyed like teeth, tumours or tonsils. For example, K. Hindell and Madelaine Simms (pro-choice campaigners) have written that "medically and legally the embryo and fetus are merely parts of the mother's body, and not yet human".[9] Such people insist that the fetus belongs to the woman who bears it, and that the decision to abort or not to abort rests entirely with the woman. Since it is her body, it is also her choice. Nobody else (and certainly no man, feminists would add) has any say in the matter.

After a mass rally in Hyde Park in London, arranged by the Society for the Protection of Unborn Children in June 1983, we were walking to 10 Downing Street to present a petition to the prime minister, when at the top of Whitehall a group of young women started chanting:

> Not the church, not the state,
> Let the woman decide her fate.

I went over to talk to them and quietly remonstrated that it was not the woman's fate we were concerned about in our rally and march, so much as her unborn child's. Their only reply was to shout unprintable obscenities at me and to make the rather obvious point that I would not be able to give birth to a child in a million years. I am not saying that they were wholly wrong.

I recognize that abortion is more a woman's issue than a man's. It is she who has been made pregnant, perhaps without her consent, who has to bear the pregnancy and who will carry the burden of early childcare. It is all too easy for men to forget these facts. We should also be "pro-choice" in the sense that we recognize a woman's right to decide whether to have a baby or not. But the time for her to exercise her right and make her choice (still assuming that she has not been forced) is before conception, not after. Once she has conceived, her child has independent rights both before and after birth.

Humanization and implantation

A second option focuses on the decisive moment of the embryo's "humanization" at some point between conception and birth. Some opt for implantation when the embryo, six days after fertilization, descends the Fallopian tube and becomes attached to the wall of the uterus. It is true both that implantation is an indispensable stage in the development of the fetus, and that the greatest number of spontaneous abortions (often due to fetal abnormality) take place before this moment. Nevertheless, implantation changes only the environment of the fetus, not its constitution. In former generations "quickening" was regarded by many as the moment of, or at least the evidence for, the "ensoulment" of the embryo, but we now know that this new beginning is not of the child's movement but of the mother's perception of it.

Viability and survival

A third option is "viability", the time when the fetus, if born prematurely, would be able to survive. But advances in medical techniques are constantly bringing this moment forward. When the 1967 Abortion Act was passed in the UK, twenty-eight weeks was taken as the limit of viability. Now it is commonplace for babies to survive at twenty-three or even twenty-two weeks. In the next decade new techniques may allow survival at much earlier stages of pregnancy. Why should the moral status of the fetus be dependent on the state of medical technology?

Birth and welcome

The fourth option is to regard birth itself as the crucial moment. This was the position adopted by Rex Gardner in his *Abortion: The Personal Dilemma* (1972). "My own view," he wrote, "is that while the fetus is to be cherished increasingly as it develops, we should regard its first breath at birth as the moment when God gives it not only life, but the offer of Life." He quoted Genesis 2:7 as biblical evidence, when God breathed into man's nostrils "the breath of life". He appealed also to common human experience: "An audible sigh of relief goes round the delivery room when the baby gives that first gasp."[10] It is certainly true that Scripture usually speaks of "new life" beginning at "new birth". Yet this does not settle the matter, since Scripture also speaks of God "begetting" us and of the implanted "seed" which leads to new birth (see, e.g., James 1:18; 1 Peter 1:23 – 25; 1 John 3:9). In addition, modern scientific understanding is that there is no fundamental difference between the unborn and the newly born: both are dependent on their mother, even if in different ways.

Conception and humanity

The fifth option, which I think should be held by all Christians, although they use different formulations and draw different deductions, looks back to conception or fusion as the decisive moment when a human being begins. This is the official position of the Roman Catholic Church. Pope Pius XII, for example, in his Address to the Italian Catholic Society of Midwives in 1951, said, "The baby, still not born, is a man (that is, a human being) in the same degree and for the same reason as the mother."[11] Similarly, many Protestants, although some find difficulty with the non-recognition of "degree", also affirm that there is no point between conception and death at which we can say, "After that point I was a person, but before it I was not." Certainly the conceptus is alive, and certainly the life it possesses is human life. Indeed, many medical people who make no Christian profession recognize this fact. Thus the First International Conference on Abortion, meeting in 1967 in Washington, DC, declared: "We can find no point in time between the union of sperm and egg and the birth of an infant at which point we can say that this is not a human life."[12]

There is now another option, but this deliberately avoids making a decision about the precise identity of the fetus. It has been persuasively put forward by Professor Ronald Dworkin in his influential book *Life's Dominion*.[13] There is both agreement and disagreement between the liberal and conservative positions, he claims. Both believe in the intrinsic value of human life, but they differ in their understanding of that value. Conservatives tend to regard the fetus as being from conception "a person with rights and interests of its own", whereas liberals affirm "the sanctity of life understood in a more impersonal way".[14]

When Professor Dworkin comes to explain the "value" of human life, however, he seems to be in difficulties. Human lives are intrinsically valuable as great paintings are. Their value is measured by the degree of "investment" contributed to their creation (both natural and human) and by the degree of "waste" involved in their destruction. For example, should a seriously deformed fetus be allowed to be born or be aborted? Either way, there would be a serious "frustration of life". Abortion would mean the destruction of life. Birth "would add, to the sad waste of a deformed human's biological creation, the further heartbreaking waste of personal emotional investment made in that life by others, but principally by the child himself before his inevitable early death".[15] Which is the greater "investment"? Which would be the greater "waste"?

While appreciating Professor Dworkin's emphasis on the "value" of the fetus, Christians will feel very uneasy about the way he develops his thesis. (1) He is much too optimistic in his assessment of the liberals' position. They do not appear to affirm (as he says they do) the "sanctity", let alone the "inviolability", of the life of the unborn. (2) His personification of "nature" (e.g., "not destroying what nature has created"[16]) lacks plausibility. The better and biblical way of explaining the intrinsic value of the human fetus is to acknowledge God as Creator and ourselves as the bearers of his image. It is not "investment" but "creation" which establishes the innate worth of human beings. (3) Professor Dworkin's vocabulary of "investment" and "waste" seem inappropriate in relation to human beings. "Waste" suggests the loss of a commodity, and an "investment" is an outlay with a view to a profit. But it is of the essence of love to give without expecting any return.

THE BIBLICAL BASIS

To me the firmest foundation in Scripture for the fifth view is to be found in Psalm 139, in which the author marvels at God's omniscience and omnipresence, and in the course of his meditation makes important statements about our prenatal existence. To be sure, Psalm 139 makes no claim to be a textbook of embryology. It employs poetic imagery and highly figurative language (e.g.,

v. 15, "I was woven together in the depths of the earth"). Nevertheless, the psalmist is affirming at least three important truths.

Creation

The first concerns his creation. "You created my inmost being; you knit me together in my mother's womb" (v. 13). Two homely metaphors are used to illustrate God's creative skill, namely those of the potter and the weaver. God is like a skilled artisan, who "created" him ("formed" is a better word) as the potter works the clay. The same thought recurs in Job 10:8, where Job affirms that God's hands had "fashioned and made" him (RSV) or "shaped and modelled" him (JB). The other picture is that of the weaver who "knit" him together (v. 13), which the NASB renders "thou didst weave me". Similarly Job asks, "Did you not ... clothe me with skin and flesh, and knit me together with bones and sinews?" (10:10 – 11). In consequence, the psalmist goes on, "For all these mysteries I thank you, for the wonder of myself, for the wonder of your works" (v. 14 JB).

Though not intending to give a scientific account of fetal development, the biblical authors are nevertheless affirming (in the familiar imagery of the ancient Near East) that the process of embryonic growth is neither haphazard nor even automatic, but a divine work of creative skill.

Continuity

The psalmist's second emphasis is on continuity. He is now an adult, but he looks back over his life until before he was born. He refers to himself both before and after birth by the same personal pronouns "I" and "me", for he is aware that during his antenatal and postnatal life he was and is the same person. He surveys his existence in four stages. Firstly (v. 1), "You have searched me" (the past). Secondly (vv. 2 – 3), "You know when I sit and when I rise ... you are familiar with all my ways" (the present). Thirdly (v. 10), "Your hand will guide me, your right hand will hold me fast" (the future). And fourthly (v. 13), "You knit me together in my mother's womb" (the prenatal stage). Yet in all four stages (before birth, from birth to the present, at the present moment and in the future), he refers to himself as "I". He who is thinking and writing as a grown man has the same personal identity as the fetus in the womb. He is aware of no discontinuity between his antenatal and postnatal being. On the contrary, in and out of his mother's womb, before and after his birth, as embryo, baby, youth and adult, he is conscious of being the same person.

Communion

The third truth the psalmist expresses I will term communion, for he is conscious of a very personal and particular communion between God and himself. It is the same God who created him, who now sustains him, knows him and loves him, and who will forever hold him fast. Psalm 139 is perhaps the most radically personal statement in the Old Testament of God's relationship to the individual believer. The "I – you" relationship is expressed in almost every line. Either the pronoun or the possessive in the first person ("I/me/my") comes forty-six times in the psalm, and in the second person ("you/your") thirty-two times. More important than the "I – you" relationship is his awareness of the "you – me" relationship, of God knowing him, surrounding him, holding him (vv. 1 – 6), and of God sticking to him in covenant faithfulness and never leaving him or letting him go (vv. 7 – 12).

Indeed, "communion" may not be the best description of this third awareness, because the word implies a reciprocal relationship, whereas the psalmist is bearing witness to a relationship which God has established and which God sustains. Perhaps, therefore, "covenant" would be a better word, indeed a unilateral covenant, or covenant of "grace" which God initiated and which God maintains. For God our Creator loved us and related himself to us long before we could respond in a conscious relationship to him. What makes us a person, then, is not that we know God, but that he knows us; not that we love God, but that he has set his love upon us. So each of us was already a person in our mother's womb, because already then God knew us and loved us.

It is these three words (creation, continuity and communion or covenant) which give us the essential biblical perspective from which to think. The fetus is neither a growth in the mother's body, nor even a potential human being, but already a human life who, though not yet mature, has the potentiality of growing into the fullness of the individual humanity he or she already possesses.

Other biblical passages express the same sense of personal continuity due to divine grace. Several times in the Wisdom Literature of the Old Testament, the conviction is expressed that it is God who "made me in the womb" (Job 31:15; Psalm 119:73), even though we do not know how (Ecclesiastes 11:5), who "brought me out of the womb", and who, therefore, "from my mother's womb" has been my God (Psalm 22:9 – 10; 71:6). The prophets shared the same belief, whether of the individual like Jeremiah ("before I formed you in the womb I knew you", 1:5), or of "the Servant of the LORD" (whom the Lord both formed and called in the womb, Isaiah 49:1, 5), or by analogy of the nation of Israel (Isaiah 46:3 – 4). The implications of these texts for personal continuity cannot be avoided by analogy with New Testament assertions that God "chose" us in Christ and "gave" us his grace in Christ "before the creation of the world" (e.g., Ephesians 1:4; 2 Timothy 1:9). The argument would then be that, just as we did not exist before the beginning of time except in the mind of God, so we had no personal existence in the womb, although God is said to have "known" us in both cases. The analogy is inexact, however, for the situations are different. In passages which relate to election, the emphasis is on salvation by grace not works, and, therefore, on God's choice of us before we existed or could do any good works. In passages which relate to vocation, however (the calling whether of prophets like Jeremiah or of apostles like Paul – cf. Galatians 1:16), the emphasis is not only on God's gracious choice but on his "forming" or "fashioning" them for their particular service. This was not "before the creation of the world", nor even "before conception", but rather "before birth", before they were yet fully "formed" – that is, while they were still being "fashioned" in the womb. Personal continuity before and after birth is integral to this teaching.

There is only one Old Testament passage which some interpreters have thought devalues the human fetus, namely Exodus 21:22 – 25.[17] The situation envisaged is not in dispute. While two men are fighting, they accidentally hit a pregnant woman with the result that she either miscarries or "gives birth prematurely". The penalty laid down depends on the seriousness of any injury sustained. If the injury is not serious, a fine is to be imposed; if it is serious, there is to be exact retribution, "life for life", etc. Some have argued that the first category (no serious injury) means the death of the child, while the second is serious harm to the mother, and that, therefore, the mere imposition of a fine in the former case indicates that the fetus was regarded as less valuable than the mother. This is a gratuitous interpretation, however. It seems much more probable that the scale of penalty was to correspond to the degree of injury, whether to the mother or to her child, in which case mother and child are valued equally.

Turning to the New Testament, it has often been pointed out that when Mary and Elizabeth met, both being pregnant, Elizabeth's baby (John the Baptist) "leaped in her womb" in salutation of Mary's baby (Jesus), and also that

Luke here uses the same word – *brephos* – of an unborn child (Luke 1:41, 44) as he later uses of the newborn baby (Luke 2:12, 16) and of the little ones whom people brought to Jesus to be blessed by him (Luke 18:15).

It is fully in keeping with all this implied continuity that Christian tradition affirms of Jesus Christ in the Apostles' Creed that he was "conceived by the Holy Spirit, born of the Virgin Mary, suffered under Pontius Pilate, was crucified, dead and buried ... and on the third day he rose again". Throughout these events, from beginning to end, from conception to resurrection, it is the very same person, Jesus Christ, in whom we believe.

Modern medical science appears to confirm this biblical teaching. It was only in the 1960s that the genetic code started to be unravelled. Now we know that the moment the ovum is fertilized by the penetration of the sperm, the twenty-three pairs of chromosomes are complete, the zygote has a unique genotype which is distinct from both parents, and the child's sex, size and shape, colour of skin, hair and eyes, temperament and intelligence are already determined. Each human being begins as a single fertilized cell, while an adult has about 30 million million cells. Between these two points (fusion and maturity) forty-five generations of cell division are necessary, and forty-one of them occur before birth.

Prenatal medical photography has further disclosed the marvels of fetal development. I have in mind particularly the strikingly beautiful pictures in the Swedish photographer Lennart Nilsson's book *A Child Is Born*.[18] At three to three and a half weeks the tiny heart begins to beat. At four weeks, though the fetus is only about a quarter of an inch long, the head and body are distinguishable, as are also the rudimentary eyes, ears and mouth. At six or seven weeks brain function can be detected, and at eight weeks (the time most abortions begin to be performed) all the child's limbs are apparent, including fingers, fingerprints and toes. At nine or ten weeks the baby can use his or her hands to grasp and mouth to swallow, and can even suck his or her thumb. By thirteen weeks, the completion of the first trimester, the embryo is completely organized, and a miniature baby lies in the mother's womb; the baby can alter position, respond to pain, noise and light, and even get a fit of hiccups. From then on the child merely develops in size and strength. By the end of the fifth month and beginning of the sixth (before the second trimester is complete, and while the pregnancy is not yet two thirds complete), the baby has hair, eyelashes, nails and nipples, and can cry, grip, punch and kick (which sometimes happens after an abortion has been performed by hysterotomy, to the extreme distress of the medical team).

Expectant mothers endorse from their own experience their sense of bearing a living child. True, parents sometimes give their little one a humorous nickname, especially if they do not know which sex it will turn out to be. But they also say with pride, "We have a baby on the way." During pregnancy one mother said she "felt herself to be the mother of a person, with certain motherly responsibilities before birth, and others after birth". Another wrote, "My feelings know that this is a person, and thus has his or her own independent rights before God."

A CONTEMPORARY CHRISTIAN DEBATE

It would not be honest to claim that all Christians see eye to eye on this issue, even all Christians who seek to submit to the authority of Scripture. Canon Oliver O'Donovan, Regius Professor of Moral and Pastoral Theology at Oxford University, has argued that the question "Who is a person?" cannot be answered speculatively. Instead, we come to recognize someone as a person "only from a stance of prior moral commitment to treat him or her as a person". Then later we come to know him or her as a person, as he or she is disclosed to us in personal relationships. It is not that personhood is conferred on someone by our resolve to treat him or her as a person, but that personhood is disclosed that way. At the same time, before we commit ourselves to the service of a person, it is right to look for evidence that it is appropriate to do so, either by appearance or (in the case of a fetus) by our scientific knowledge of its unique genotype. There are thus three stages. Firstly, there must be recognition, making it appropriate to engage with a person as a person. Next follows commitment, caring for him or her as a person. And thirdly, there comes encounter: "Those whom we treat as persons when they are yet unborn, become known to us as persons when they are children." These three stages acknowledge the gradualness of development into personal encounter, while affirming the reality of personhood from the moment of conception.[19]

Others have taken issue with this perspective, arguing that in the development of the fetus a critical level of complexity, in particular brain development, is required before the fetus can be regarded as a conscious personal agency. May we then refer to a fertilized ovum as a "potential human being"? Yes, in the sense that it will lead to maturity if gestation proceeds normally, but not if this leads us to attribute to the ovum specific properties of the end product. The value of "potentiality" language is that it emphasizes the importance of beginnings, expectations and resulting obligations; its danger is to imagine that all the attributes and rights of the end product already belong to the beginning. They do not, even if there is a direct line of continuity between the two.

On the one hand, the fertilized ovum is a "physical structure with the richest and most strangely mysterious repertoire known to man", for it can develop into "the embodiment of a new human being in the image of God, loved by God, replete with potentialities of not merely earthly but eternal significance". On the other, to treat it as "a person with the rights of a person" is a conspicuous example of "thin-end-of-the-wedgery".[20]

In summary, some argue that the fetus has "personhood" from the moment of fusion, and that therefore we must commit ourselves to its care, although only later will its personhood be revealed in personal relationships. Others agree that from the moment of fusion the conceptus has biological life and a marvellous repertoire of potentiality, but add that it only becomes a person possessing rights and demanding care when brain development makes self-supervision possible.

The conflict between the two positions sounds irreconcilable. But is this not at base the old tension (with which the New Testament has made us familiar) between the "already" and the "not yet"? Tertullian expressed it as early as the end of the second century: "He also is a man who is about to be one; you have the fruit already in its seed."[21] In our own day, Paul Ramsey has put it like this: "The human individual comes into existence as a minute informational speck ... His subsequent prenatal and postnatal development may be described as a process of becoming what he already is from the moment he was conceived."[22] Lewis Smedes calls the status of a fetus a "deep ontological ambiguity – the ambiguity of not being something yet and at the same time having the makings of what it will be".[23] It is the language of "potentiality" in relation to the embryo which has confused us. Professor Thomas F. Torrance has clarified it by explaining that "the potentiality concerned is not that of becoming something else but of becoming what it essentially is".[24]

This brings me back to Psalm 139 and to the reason for the psalmist's sense of continuity of being, namely God's steadfast love. The sovereign initiative of God in creating and loving is the biblical understanding of grace. Some Christians decline to attribute personhood to the newly conceived embryo because as yet it has no brain to sustain either self-supervision or conscious relationships.

But supposing the vital relationship which confers personhood on the fetus is God's conscious, loving commitment to him or her, rather than his or hers to God? Such a one-sided relationship is seen in parents who love their child, and commit themselves to his or her care and protection, long before that child is able to respond. And a unilateral initiative is what makes grace to be grace. It is, in fact, God's grace which confers on the unborn child, from the moment of its conception, both the unique status which it already enjoys and the unique destiny which it will later inherit. It is grace which holds together this duality of the actual and the potential, the already and the not yet.

TECHNIQUES AND EXCEPTIONS

How will our evaluation of the uniqueness of the human fetus (however we decide to formulate it) affect our thinking and acting, especially in relation to abortion?

To begin with, it will change our attitudes. Since the life of the human fetus is a human life, with the potential of becoming a mature human being, we have to learn to think of mother and unborn child as two human beings at different stages of development. Doctors and nurses have to consider that they have two patients, not one, and must seek the well-being of both. Lawyers and politicians need to think similarly. As the UN's "Declaration of the Rights of the Child" (1959) put it, the child "needs special safeguards and care, including appropriate legal protection, before as well as after birth". Christians would wish to add "extra care before birth", for the Bible has much to say about God's concern for the defenceless, and the most defenceless of all people are unborn children. They are speechless to plead their own cause and helpless to protect their own life. So it is our responsibility to do for them what they cannot do for themselves.

All Christians should therefore be able to agree that the human fetus is in principle inviolable. Lord Ramsey, when as Archbishop of Canterbury he was addressing the Church Assembly in 1967, said, "We have to assert as normative the general inviolability of the fetus ... We shall be right to continue to see as one of Christianity's great gifts to the world the belief that the human fetus is to be reverenced as the embryo of a life capable of coming to reflect the glory of God..."

It is the combination of what the human fetus already is and what it one day could be which makes the realities of abortion so horrific. How can anybody possibly reconcile the reality of abortion with the concept of the abortus as a potential mirror of God's glory?

We need to revise our vocabulary. The popular euphemisms make it easier for us to conceal the truth from ourselves. The occupant of the mother's womb is not a "product of conception" or "gametic material", but an unborn child. Even "pregnancy" tells us no more than that a woman has been "impregnated", whereas the truth in old-fashioned language is that she is "with child". How can we speak of "the termination of a pregnancy" when what is terminated is not just the mother's pregnancy but the child's life? And how can we describe the average abortion today as "therapeutic" (a word originally used only when the mother's life was at stake), when pregnancy is not a disease needing therapy, and what abortion effects nowadays is not a cure but a killing? And how can people think of abortion as no more than a kind of contraceptive, when what it does is not prevent conception but destroy the conceptus? We need to have the courage to use accurate language. Induced abortion is feticide, the deliberate destruction of an unborn child, the shedding of innocent blood.

It is not surprising that abortion may have long-lasting emotional consequences for all concerned. Although severe psychiatric disease is thankfully a rare consequence of abortion, increasingly counsellors are recognizing that many women (and some men) suffer significant but hidden psychological trauma from abortion, trauma which may surface years or decades after the event.

Is abortion, then, never justified? To answer this question in a way that is both faithful and realistic, theologians and doctors need each other. More interdisciplinary consultation is necessary. Doctors are understandably impatient with theologians because they tend to be unpractical, making ivory-tower pronouncements unrelated to painful clinical dilemmas. Theologians, on the other hand, are understandably impatient with doctors because they tend to be pragmatists, making clinical decisions uncontrolled by theological principle. The principle on which we should be able to agree is well expressed as the first aim of the Society for the Protection of Unborn Children, namely "that human life ought not to be taken except in cases of urgent necessity". Professor G. R. Dunstan is probably right that there is an ethic of "justifiable feticide", by analogy with "justifiable homicide".[25] But if we accept the general inviolability of the human fetus, then every exception has to be rigorously and specifically argued. Ever since the Infant Life (Preservation) Act (1929), an abortion to save the mother's life has been legal in England, though not condoned by the Roman

Catholic Church. With the availability of modern obstetric and paediatric practice, however, the necessity of abortion virtually never arises. It is usually possible to allow the pregnancy to continue to a gestational age at which survival of the infant is possible with intensive care. According to Christian tradition, human life may be taken to protect and preserve another life – for example, in self-defence; but we have no liberty to introduce death into a situation in which it is not already present, either as a fact or as a threat.

What about the "substantial risk" of the child to be born being "seriously handicapped", which is dealt with in the fourth clause of the 1967 Abortion Act? Antenatal screening using blood tests, ultrasound and amniocentesis (testing the amniotic fluid) can now reveal abnormalities in the fetus from early on in pregnancy, although some conditions may not be detected until after the twentieth week. Is an abortion then morally justified? Many think so. Dr Glanville Williams has expressed himself forcefully on this issue: "To allow the breeding of defectives is a horrible evil, far worse than any that may be found in abortion."[26] In discussing the tragic predicament of a mother who gives birth to "a viable monster or an idiot child", he even wrote: "An eugenic killing by a mother, exactly paralleled by the bitch that kills her mis-shapen puppies, cannot confidently be pronounced immoral."[27] How should a Christian conscience react to this possibility? Surely with horror.

There are at least three reasons why abortion should be reserved for only the most exceptional cases, such as anencephaly (failure of the brain to develop), in which there is no possibility of survival after birth, and must not be extended to other – even severe – abnormalities.

Sanctity of life

Firstly, it is now frequently said that the issue is not the "sanctity" of life but the "quality" of life, and that the life of a severely handicapped person is not worth living. But who can presume to decide this? At a rally in 1983 for those opposed to abortion, to me the most moving argument was made by Alison Davis, who described herself as "a happy spina bifida adult" and spoke from a wheelchair. "I can think of few concepts more terrifying," she said, "than saying that certain people are better off dead, and may therefore be killed for their own good." One doctor, on hearing her say that she was glad to be alive, "made the incredible observation that no one can judge their own quality of life, and that other people might well consider a life like mine miserable!" On the contrary, she insisted, "Most disabled people are quite contented with the quality of their lives". After all, it is love which gives quality to life and makes it worth living, and it is we – their neighbours – who can choose whether to give love to disabled people or withhold it. The quality of their life is in our hands.

Respect for life

Secondly, once we accept that a disabled child may be destroyed before birth, why should we not do it also after birth? Indeed, the practice of medical infanticide has already begun. Doctors, of course, do not use this word, and some try to persuade themselves that starving babies to death is not intentional killing. The solemn fact is that if society is prepared to kill an unborn child on the sole ground that it will be disabled, there is no logical reason why we should not go on to kill the newborn with a congenital malformation, the comatose victim of a car crash, the mentally impaired and the senile. The disabled become disposable when their lives are judged "worthless" or "unproductive", and we are back in Hitler's horrible Third Reich.

Christians will rather agree with Jean Rostan, the French biologist, who wrote, "For my part I believe that there is no life so degraded, debased, deteriorated or impoverished that it does not deserve respect and is not worth defending with zeal and conviction ... I have the weakness to believe that it is an honour for our society to desire the expensive luxury of sustaining life for its useless, incompetent, and incurably ill members. I would almost measure society's degree of civilization by the amount of effort and vigilance it imposes on itself out of pure respect for life."[28]

Decisions about life

A third reason for not aborting a malformed fetus is that to do so would amount to fallible mortals playing God. We do not have that authority, and those who arrogate it to themselves are bound to make grave mistakes. Maurice Baring used to tell the story of one doctor who asked another: "About the termination of a pregnancy, I want your opinion. The father was syphilitic, the mother tuberculous. Of the four children born the first was blind, the second died, the third was deaf and dumb, and the fourth also tuberculous. What would you have done?" "I would have ended the pregnancy." "Then you would have murdered Beethoven."[29]

In this whole discussion we have to be on our guard against selfish rationalizations. I fear that the real reason why we say that serious disability would be an unbearable burden for a child, if it were allowed to be born, is that it would be an unbearable burden for us. But Christians must remember that the God of the Bible has expressed his special protective care for the vulnerable and the weak.

A CALL TO ACTION

What then shall we do? Firstly, we need to repent. I agree with Raymond Johnston, the late founder director of CARE Trust, when he wrote in a newspaper article: "I personally am convinced that the destruction of the unborn on this massive, deliberate scale is the greatest single offence regularly perpetrated in Britain today, and would be the first thing an Old Testament prophet redivivus would reproach us for." Dr Francis Schaeffer and Dr Everett Koop dedicated their book and film *Whatever Happened to the Human Race?* "to those who were robbed of life, the unborn, the weak, the sick, the old, during the dark ages of madness, selfishness, lust and greed for which the last decades of the twentieth century are remembered". Were they right to condemn our "enlightened" Western civilization as "the dark ages"? At least in this matter I think they were, and I for one am ashamed that we Christians have not been "the light of the world" which Jesus intended us to be. We also need to repent of our tendency to selective campaigning. We lack integrity if we fight for the life of the unborn and care little for the life of the born – for example, of abused or neglected children, battered and abandoned mothers, slum dwellers or refugees. Christians are committed to human life, both to defending its sanctity and to promoting its quality.

Secondly, we need to accept full responsibility for the effects of a more restrictive abortion policy, if it can be secured. To agitate for it without being prepared to bear its costs would be sheer hypocrisy. Our intention is not to create a climate in which illegal "backstreet" abortions become more common. Instead, we shall want to create a social climate in which positive alternatives to abortion are widely promoted and recognized. Every woman who carries an unwanted pregnancy deserves every possible personal, medical, social and financial support. God tells us to "carry each other's burdens, and in this way ... fulfil the law of Christ" (Galatians 6:2). We shall want to ensure that, although some babies are unwanted (and even unloved) by their parents, no baby is unwanted by society in general and by the church in particular.

I thank God for the organizations which have been pioneering a supportive ministry for pregnant women, like Birthright and Heartbeat International in the USA and Canada, and CARE Centres Network, LIFE and SPUC (Society for the Protection of Unborn Children) in Britain.[30] In the USA there are now over 3,000 centres offering counselling and practical support to women with a "crisis" pregnancy, and this movement has grown to over fifteen countries internationally. In different ways the centres, staffed largely by volunteers, are offering a caring service, such as counselling women with an unplanned pregnancy, offering emergency help to those in despair, giving advice on practical problems, finding accommodation for mothers both before and after their child's birth, helping to secure employment for them, granting financial help, and providing counselling for those suffering emotional trauma from a previous abortion. As Louise Summerhill, founder of Birthright, has written, "We help rather than abort, we believe in making a better world for babies to come into, rather than killing them."[31]

Thirdly, we need to support a positive educational and social campaign, not least in schools. Christians must not be shy to teach thoroughly and constantly the biblical understanding of humanness and of the value, indeed the sacredness, of human life. We have to recognize that all abortions are due to unwanted pregnancies, and that all unwanted pregnancies are due to a failure of some kind.

Often it is sexual failure, whether lack of sexual self-control (especially in men, who usually escape the tragic consequences of their action) or lack of a responsible use of contraceptives. The Church of England General Synod's Board for Social Responsibility has called for "a major effort at social education" (and moral education too, we might add), in order "to reduce the number of unwanted pregnancies", "to undermine the habit of mind which leads straight from the recognition of pregnancy to resort to an abortionist", and to move the public "to find a better solution".[32]

Unwanted pregnancies are also often due to social deprivation, to such conditions as poverty, unemployment and overcrowding. So for this reason we also should be working for a better society. Social evils are to be fought; they will not be solved by more abortions.

In less developed countries many people have large families in an attempt to ensure that they have children who will care for them in old age. So paradoxically, the answer to a rapidly growing population is not a liberal abortion policy, but social and medical improvements leading to a significant reduction in infant mortality, improved maternal education and the availability of safe, cheap and effective contraceptives. More important in the end than either education or social action, vital as they both are, is the good news of Jesus Christ. He came to bind up the brokenhearted and support the weak. He calls us to treat all human life with reverence, whether in the unborn, the infant, the disabled or the senile.

I have no desire to stand in personal judgement either on the women who have resorted to an abortion or on the men whose sexual self-indulgence is responsible for most unwanted pregnancies. I want to say to them instead, "There is forgiveness with God" (Psalm 130:4). Christ died for our sins and offers us a new beginning. He rose again and lives, and by his Spirit can give us a new, inward power of self-control. He is also building a new community characterized by love, joy, peace, freedom and justice. A new beginning. A new power. A new community. This is the gospel of Christ.

EUTHANASIA

The obvious parallels between abortion and euthanasia make it appropriate for them to be discussed in the same chapter. Although abortion relates to the beginning of a human life and euthanasia to its end, both are decisions for death. Both, therefore, raise the same urgent question whether it may ever be morally justifiable to terminate life and precipitate death.

The euthanasia debate can be traced back at least to the heyday of Greek philosophy. But a number of factors have combined to bring it to the forefront of public concern in our day – advances in medical technology which prolong life and so are responsible for an ageing population, the AIDS epidemic, some particularly poignant and well-publicized cases which seemed to cry out for euthanasia on compassionate grounds and the persuasive campaigning of EXIT (previously the Voluntary Euthanasia Society) in the UK and the Hemlock Society, its equivalent in the US.

A widely accepted definition of euthanasia is as follows: "Euthanasia is the intentional killing by act or omission of a person whose life is considered not to be worth living."

This is popularly called "mercy killing", and is divided between "voluntary euthanasia" ("assisted suicide", the death occurring at the explicit plea of the patient) and "involuntary euthanasia" (the death occurring by someone else's decision when the patient is incapable of giving consent). It is essential to clarify that euthanasia, whether voluntary or involuntary, is intentional killing. It deliberately introduces death into a situation in which it did not previously exist. But to withhold or withdraw useless treatment from a terminally ill patient is not euthanasia. Nor is the administration of painkillers to a dying patient which may incidentally accelerate death, but the primary intention of which is to relieve pain. In both these cases death is already irreversibly present. To intervene with further treatment would only prolong the process of dying. Although this distinction is not always amenable to precise definition, there is a fundamental difference between causing somebody to die (which is euthanasia) and allowing him or her to die (which is not). During Dr Martyn Lloyd-Jones's final illness in hospital, there came a moment when he refused further treatment, complaining to his doctor, "You are keeping me from the glory!"

There seem to be three basic issues in the euthanasia debate, which I will call "value" (what value has a human life?), "fear" (what are the main fears which euthanasia is intended to relieve?), and "autonomy" (what right do we have over our own life?).

THE QUESTION OF VALUE

Firstly, there is the question of value. Some contemporary non-Christian writers flatly deny that human life has any absolute or intrinsic value. Notable among them is Professor Peter Singer in his book *Rethinking Life and Death*, subtitled "The collapse of our traditional ethics".[33] He is well known for his rejection of "speciesism", namely "discrimination against or exploitation of certain animal species by human beings, based on an assumption of mankind's superiority" (as the Oxford English Dictionary defines it). Accepting both the Darwinian view that "we are animals too" and the corresponding view that the higher animals are "persons" too, he argues that we must "abandon the distinction between humans and non-human animals".[34] Since, then, "neither a newborn human infant nor a fish is a person",[35] we can imagine the logical consequences of such a position for both abortion and euthanasia.

There are other non-Christian scholars, however, who still maintain, albeit not on biblical grounds, that human beings have a unique value. For example, as with abortion so with euthanasia, Professor Dworkin is able to affirm "the intrinsic cosmic importance of human life itself".[36] So far we have seen that, in relation to abortion, he has formulated a person's value in terms of the "investment", both natural and human, which has been made in him or her, adding that the natural investment in a human life is more important than the human. It can therefore be argued that death would frustrate nature's investment and so "cheat nature".[37] Now, however, in relation to euthanasia, Professor Dworkin develops a view of human "value" which is based on our "best interests", distinguishing between "experiential" interests (what causes pleasure or pain) and "critical" interests (what gives life meaning). Only after he has made this distinction is he able to ask the question whether death could ever be in someone's "best interests". Certainly our life's conclusion needs to be consonant with the convictions and commitments which have motivated it throughout, since "none of us wants to end our lives out of character".[38] On the contrary, this would compromise our dignity, our sense of being "someone with critical interests".[39]

These concepts of "investment" and "critical interests" are valiant attempts to construct a secular understanding of human value. They fail to convince, however, and seem too abstract to have popular appeal. The Christian alternative, which we need to defend and promote with increasing determination, is that we have intrinsic value because God has created us in his own image. Human beings are godlike beings, possessing a cluster of unique faculties (rational, moral and social) which distinguish us from animals. In particular, there is our capacity for the relationships of love, since God is love.

But this raises a problem. Is love not an essentially reciprocal relationship? How can we love a person who is unable to respond to our love; for example, a brain-injured person in a "persistent vegetative state" or indeed an unborn fetus? Does their unresponsiveness not disqualify them from being regarded and treated as a human being? No, this is where grace comes in – for grace is precisely love to the unresponsive. Grace is love taking a unilateral initiative. Grace is God's free, spontaneous, unsolicited, even unreturned love, which finds its origin in itself, not in its object. We looked earlier at Psalm 139, in which the psalmist affirms that at every stage of his life (as fetus, baby, youth and adult) he is the same person with the same identity. He is also aware of a special personal relationship to God, which God has initiated and which God sustains. He finds his humanity and dignity not in his knowing and loving God, but in the fundamental truth that God knows and loves him, whether he responds to God or not. This same divine unilateral love binds a mother to her unborn child, and young people to their frail, elderly and perhaps demented relatives. It is not responsiveness which makes people human; it is love – not loving only, but being loved.

THE SPECTRE OF FEAR

Secondly, the spectre of fear haunts the euthanasia debate. One of the strongest incentives of those campaigning for euthanasia is that (understandably) they are afraid of what they see as the only alternative, namely having to endure (or see loved ones endure), the horrors of a lingering, distressing, anguished, messy end. Professor John Wyatt, consultant neonatal paediatrician at University College Hospital, analysed this often inarticulate fear in his 1997 London Lectures in Contemporary Christianity ("Matters of Life and Death"). Firstly, it is fear of uncontrollable and unbearable pain. Secondly, it is fear of indignity, of being subjected to the dehumanizing effect of modern medical technology, "with tubes in every orifice". Thirdly, it is fear of dependence. We want to "write our own script and determine our own exit" and not suffer the ultimate humiliation of total helplessness.

Further, if we are to have a balanced understanding of the place of fear in the euthanasia debate, we need to add a fourth fear, although this is experienced not by those who advocate euthanasia, but by those who oppose it. It is the fear that their doctor might become their killer. A crucial clause in the Hippocratic Oath is the following: "I will use treatment to help the sick according to my judgement and ability, but I will never use it to injure or wrong them." This general promise to heal and not to hurt accounts for the two particular rejections which follow, namely assisted suicide and abortion, although both were very common in the ancient world: "I will not give poison to anyone, even though asked to do so ... I will not give a pessary to a woman to cause abortion." Here is a clear recognition that the vocation of a doctor is to be a healer.

The Hippocratic tradition drew a clear distinction between healing and harming. Margaret Mead, the distinguished anthropologist, commented as follows, "For the first time in the history of humankind there was a complete separation between killing and curing. Throughout the primitive world the doctor and the sorceror tended to be the same person. He with the power to kill had the power to cure ... but with the Greeks the distinction was made clear. One profession was to be dedicated completely to life under all circumstances – the life of a slave, the life of the Emperor, the life of the immigrant, the life of the defective child." [40]

There is therefore a fundamental anomaly about a healer becoming a killer at either end of human life. It undermines the doctor-patient relationship, which is based on trust, not fear. Doctors are the servants of life; they must not become the agents of death. [41]

Reverting to the fears which surround the process of dying, many see euthanasia as the only way to escape this threefold trauma (pain, indignity and dependence). But there is an alternative, which Christians want to promote, namely modern palliative care. One of its Christian pioneers was Dame Cicely Saunders, founder of the St Christopher's Hospice in South London. [42] Another is Dr Robert Twycross, who since 1971 has been a full-time hospice doctor. He says to his patients, "Not only will we enable you to die with dignity, but we will enable you to live before you die." But it appears that large numbers of doctors do not know about this development. It is significant that Dr Nigel Cox, who in 1992 gave a lethal injection to his long-standing patient Lilian Boyes, was rebuked by the General Medical Council for being unaware of the available resources of palliative medicine and was ordered to take a course in this area. Experts in palliative care say that the vast majority of all pain in terminal disease can either be completely controlled or significantly relieved. And Christian people can and should be more actively involved in giving love and support to terminally ill patients at home or in their nearest hospice.

THE RIGHT TO AUTONOMY

The third issue involved in the euthanasia debate is the question of human autonomy or self-determination. The advocates of euthanasia insist, often in strident tones, that all human beings (provided that they are rational and competent) have the right to make their own decisions and dispose of their own life, and that no institution or individual has the authority to deny them that right.

It is certainly a fundamental biblical truth that God has made us rational and volitional beings. That is, we have a God-given mind and will of our own. Consequently, it is an essential aspect of our identity and maturity as human beings that we live by choice and not by coercion, and that we are accountable to God for our decisions. Indeed, this is the meaning of freedom. Freedom presupposes choice, and "freedom is the cardinal absolute requirement of self-respect".[43] While stating in general terms the goodness of choice, however, we need immediately to qualify our assertion in relation to freedom, dependence and life.

Our freedom

The notion of absolute freedom is an illusion. Even God, who is perfect in his freedom, is not free to do absolutely anything. This is not the meaning of his omnipotence. Scripture itself mentions several things God "cannot" (because he will not) do, especially that he cannot deny or contradict himself (2 Timothy 2:13). God's freedom is limited by his nature. He is free to do absolutely anything which it is consistent with his nature to do. The same principle applies to human beings. Human freedom is not unlimited. We find our freedom only in living according to our God-given nature, not in rebellion against it. The notion of total human autonomy is a myth.

Our dependence

Dependence can be good, even though it is the opposite of autonomy. It is highly significant that Jesus chose little children as his model of humility. The "humility" of children is not in their character (which is often self-centred and stubborn) but in their status (dependent on their parents). Just so, we human beings are to acknowledge humbly our dependence on God, not only for the sustaining of our physical existence, but also for our salvation, which is due to his grace, not our achievement. The proclamation of our autonomy in this area, claiming that we can know and reach God by our own effort, is the essence of sin, not of maturity. Dependence is far from being the unmitigated, undignified evil some fear.

Our gratefulness

Life is a gift of God. "I know, O LORD," cried Jeremiah, "that a man's life is not his own" (Jeremiah 10:23). He was right; it is God's. According to a long, consistent, biblical tradition, God is the creator, giver, sustainer and taker-away of life. He said in the Song of Moses: "There is no god besides me. I put to death and I bring to life" (Deuteronomy 32:39; cf. Genesis 39:2; 1 Samuel 2:6; Job 1:21). Similarly, the king of Israel was indignant when the king of Syria wrote to him about Naaman's leprosy: "Am I God? Can I kill and bring back to life?"

(2 Kings 5:7). Moreover, having received this gift from his hands, we are trustees and guardians of it, and he invites us to cooperate with him in fostering it. This includes curing and caring, looking after those who cannot look after themselves, and seeking to restore to health those who are sick. Human beings are not animals, pace Professor Peter Singer and others who reject "speciesism". When necessary, we "put down" or "put to sleep" a favourite pet, but we may not use this vocabulary in relation to the handicapped or the senile, the unborn or the dying. The doctor must not think or behave like a vet.

Yet "there exists in contemporary culture", Pope John Paul II has written, "a certain Promethean attitude which leads people to think that they can control life and death by taking the decisions about them into their own hands."[44] The proper name for this frame of mind is not autonomy but hubris, presumption before God. Although the lines of demarcation between God's responsibility and ours are not always sharp, and although God does call us into a privileged partnership with himself, yet we human beings may not trespass into his territory or assume his prerogatives. Instead, we must let God be God in his unique majesty and power, and humble ourselves before him in worship.

NOTES

1 Report of the Committee on the Working of the Abortion Act 1967, vol. 1 (HMSO, Cmnd, 5579, April 1974), p. 11.

2 National Statistics Office: Abortions in England and Wales (28 September 2001).

3 Quoted from Daniel Callahan, *Abortion: Law, Choice and Morality*, p. 298, in Lewis B. Smedes, *Mere Morality* (Grand Rapids: Eerdmans, 1983), p. 267, footnote 21.

4 See, e.g., Richard Winter, *Choose Life, A Christian perspective on abortion and embryo experimentation* (London: Marshall Pickering, 1988), p. 8.

5 A full description and discussion of the *Roe v. Wade* case may be found in Harold O. J. Brown, *Death Before Birth* (Nashville: Thomas Nelson, 1977), pp. 73–96.

6 For ancient perspectives and practices, see Michael J. Gorman, *Abortion and the Early Church, Christian, Jewish and Pagan attitudes in the Graeco-Roman world* (Leicester: InterVarsity Press, 1982).

7 One of the most thorough treatments of this topic is *Abortion: A Christian Understanding and Response* (Grand Rapids: Baker, 1987). It is an American symposium, edited by James K. Hoffmeier. Fifteen of its contributors are members of the faculty of Wheaton College. See also Nigel M. de S. Cameron, *Is Life Really Sacred?* (Eastbourne: Kingsway, 1990).

8 Cf. "Psychological trauma after abortion", Dominic Beer, *Triple Helix*, Autumn 2002, Christian Medical Fellowship; and "Previous induced abortions and the risk of very

preterm delivery: results of the EPIPAGE study", C. Moreau et al., *British Journal of Obstetrics & Gynaecology*, 2005, 112:430–37.

9 Quoted from Abortion Law Reformed (1971) in R. F. R. Gardner, *Abortion: The Personal Dilemma* (Carlisle, Penn.: Paternoster, 1972), p. 62.

10 Ibid., p. 126.

11 Quoted by John T. Noonan in *The Morality of Abortion* (Cambridge, Mass.: Harvard Univ. Press, 1970), p. 45.

12 Quoted in C. Everett Koop, *The Right to Live; the Right to Die* (Toronto: Life Cycle Books, 1981), pp. 43–44.

13 Ronald Dworkin, *Life's Dominion, An argument about abortion, euthanasia and individual freedom* (London: HarperCollins, 1993).

14 Ibid., p. 39.

15 Ibid., p. 90.

16 Ibid., p. 76.

17 John M. Frame discusses this passage fully, including the meaning of the Hebrew words used, in his chapter in Richard L. Ganz, *Thou Shalt Not Kill, The Christian Case Against Abortion* (New Rochelle, N.Y.: Arlington House, 1978), pp. 50–57.

18 First published by Faber in 1965.

19 For Oliver O'Donovan's position, see his booklet *The Christian and the Unborn Child*, Grove Booklets on Ethics no. 1 (Cambridge: Grove Books, 1973); and his 1983 London Lectures in Contemporary Christianity, *Begotten or Made?, Human procreation and medical technique* (Oxford: Oxford Univ. Press, 1984). See also Paul Fowler, *Abortion: Toward an Evangelical Consensus* (Sisters, Ore.: Multnomah, 1987).

20 Donald MacKay wrote up his position in an essay entitled "The Beginnings of Personal Life", which was published in the Christian Medical Fellowship's magazine *In the Service of Medicine*, no. 30 (2), 1984, pp. 9–13. See also his 1977 London Lectures in Contemporary Christianity, *Human Science and Human Dignity* (London: Hodder & Stoughton, 1979), especially pp. 64–65, 98–102. The two positions represented by Professors O'Donovan and MacKay were given further expression in the Church of England Board for Social Responsibility report *Personal Origins* (CIO, 1985). The minority emphasized the continuity of the individual from the moment of fusion, while the majority stressed consciousness as necessary for personhood and a certain brain structure as necessary for consciousness. Then in 1987 Professor Gareth Jones contributed a full discussion of "personhood" in relation to the fetus in his *Manufacturing Humans, The challenge of the new reproductive technologies* (Leicester: InterVarsity Press), chapter 5, pp. 125–67.

21 Tertullian's *Apology*, chapter ix. Michael J. Gorman gives a popular but thorough account of the unanimous pro-life, anti-abortion stance of the first five centuries of Christianity in his *Abortion and the Early Church*. His references to Tertullian are on pp. 54–58.

22 Paul Ramsey, *Fabricated Man: The Ethics of Genetic Control* (New Haven, Conn.: Yale Univ. Press, 1970), p. 11.

23 Smedes, *Mere Morality*, p. 129.

24 Quoted in the Church of Scotland's Board of Social Responsibility 1985 report to the General Assembly. See Professor Torrance's booklet *Test-tube Babies* (Edinburgh: Scottish Academic Press, 1984).

25 G. R. Dunstan, "The Moral Status of the Embryo: A Tradition Recalled", *Journal of Medical Ethics* 1 (1984):38 – 44. See also Professor G. R. Dunstan's contribution to the article on "Abortion" in Duncan, Dunstan and Welbourn (eds.), *Dictionary of Medical Ethics* (London: Darton, Longman and Todd, 1981).

26 Glanville Williams, *The Sanctity of Life and the Criminal Law* (London: Faber, 1958), p. 212.

27 Ibid., p. 31.

28 Quoted from his book *Humanly Possible*, at the beginning of Koop, *The Right to Live; the Right to Die*.

29 Quoted by Norman St John Stevas in *The Right to Life* (London: Hodder & Stoughton, 1963), p. 20.

30 The addresses of these organizations are as follows. Birthright, 777 Coxwell Avenue, Toronto, Ontario, Canada M4C 3C6. Alternatives to Abortion, International, 2606 1/2 West 8th Street, Los Angeles, California 90057, USA. LIFE, 7 The Parade, Leamington Spa, Warwickshire, UK. SPUC, 7 Tufton Street, London SW1, UK. CARE Trust, 53 Romney Street, London SW1P 3RF, UK. CARENET, 109 Carpenter Dr., Suite 100, Sterling, Virginia 20164, USA.

31 Quoted in Gardner, *Abortion: The Personal Dilemma*, p. 276. See also Louise Summerhill, *The Story of Birthright: The Alternative to Abortion* (Kenosha, Wisc.: Prow Books, 1973).

32 *Abortion: An Ethical Dilemma*, a report of the Board for Social Responsibility (CIO, 1965), p. 57.

33 Peter Singer, *Rethinking Life and Death* (1994; Oxford: Oxford Univ. Press, 1995).

34 Ibid., pp. 176, 180 – 83.

35 Ibid., p. 220.

36 Dworkin, *Life's Dominion*, p. 217.

37 Ibid., p. 214.

38 Ibid., p. 213.

39 Ibid., p. 237.

40 Margaret Mead, quoted in Nigel M. de S. Cameron, *The New Medicine* (London: Hoddert Stoughton, 1991), p. 9.

41 See Nigel M. DeS. Cameron, *The New Medicine: Life and Death after Hippocrates* (Wheaton: Crossway, 1991).

42 See, e.g., her contribution entitled "Euthanasia: The Hospice Alternative", in Nigel M. de S. Cameron (ed.), *Death without Dignity* (Edinburgh: Rutherford House Books, 1990).

43 Dworkin, *Life's Dominion*, p. 239.

44 From the Encyclical *Evangelium Vitae*, March 1995.

The New Biotechnology

by Professor John Wyatt

Historically, the major bioethical issues confronting Christians have concerned the destruction of innocent human life, both at the beginning of life in abortion, and at the end of life in euthanasia. These are dealt with in the previous chapter. Although abortion and euthanasia remain as topics of crucial significance at the beginning of the twenty-first century, a range of new and troubling bioethical dilemmas have arisen over the last twenty years. Instead of the *destruction* of human life, these concern the *creation* and the *manipulation* of human life. This chapter will briefly review the technological advances which lie behind these bioethical dilemmas. This will be followed by an overview of some of the underlying social and philosophical forces, and then by an attempt to develop the outlines of a biblical Christian response.

TECHNOLOGICAL ADVANCES

In vitro fertilization (IVF)

In 1978 the collaboration of embryologist Dr Robert Edwards and gynaecologist Patrick Steptoe led to the birth of Louise Brown, the world's first "test-tube baby", in Oldham District General Hospital in the north of England. One commentator has described this birth as "a singular moment in human evolution".[1] Steptoe and Edwards were the founding fathers of a new science of reproductive technology. From a single birth in a British hospital, the use of

IVF has rapidly expanded worldwide. By 2000 more than fifty countries had established IVF programmes, including many in less developed countries. It is estimated that at the time of writing more than 1,000,000 children have been conceived as a result of IVF worldwide. (Remarkably, most of those children are less than seven years old at the time of writing.) Yet there are probably more than 2,000,000 couples in the USA alone who want to have a child and yet remain infertile, so there is remarkable potential for growth in the use of IVF. There are also substantial commercial profits to be made. In a typical IVF clinic in the USA, a couple may spend from $40,000 to more than $200,000 to achieve a single pregnancy, and surveys have shown that reproductive specialists are amongst the highest-earning doctors in the US.

Not only has IVF offered a means of providing children for infertile couples, it has also offered laboratory access to the human egg and the human embryo, enabling embryo testing, research and manipulation to be carried out. It is not an exaggeration to say that the development of IVF has changed for ever our understanding of human reproduction and parenthood. It is a classic example of how a technological development can lead to a change in our way of thinking about ourselves.

Following the development of IVF, each child can now be regarded as the product of four components: (1) an egg source, (2) a sperm source, (3) a womb or uterus, and (4) one or more caregivers after birth. Another way of looking at this is that any child may have three mothers: a *genetic mother* – the source of the egg, a *carrying mother* – the provider of the uterus and a *social mother* – the one providing care after birth.

The possible permutations and combinations are remarkable. Sperm or egg donation means that one element of the genetic makeup of the embryo is provided by an anonymous donor; alternatively there is embryo donation – where the genetic parents donate the embryo to a carrying mother who then cares for the child. Then there is surrogate pregnancy, where the genetic parents donate an embryo to a carrying mother with the intention that the child should be handed back to them after birth. Embryos, once created, can be frozen indefinitely in liquid nitrogen and thawed for reimplantation more than a decade after freezing. Finally, there is embryo "adoption" in which an "abandoned" embryo is donated to a carrying mother who then passes the child to adoptive parents for care after birth. Embryos can also be used for research or undergo manipulation to create embryonic stem cells intended for therapeutic purposes.

Sex selection

One of the many options which have become available for parents is the use of sophisticated genetic techniques to screen embryos for desired characteristics. This may be used to avoid the implantation of an embryo that carries a serious or fatal disease. But it can also be used to select the sex of the future child. Philosopher John Harris, of Manchester University, has argued neatly that within a liberal secular worldview, parental choice should be paramount. Parents should be able to choose the sex of their child, rather than leave it to chance. "Either the sex of your child is morally significant in which case it's much too important to be left to chance, or it's morally insignificant, in which case it doesn't matter if we let parents choose."

The logic is impeccable. Leaving something as important as the sex of your future child to chance makes no sense at all in a materialistic universe. It only makes sense in a theistic worldview, where a child can be viewed as a mysterious gift and not as a product of human planning and ingenuity. And yet a major public consultation undertaken by the UK Human Fertilization and Embryology Authority in 2003 showed that a majority of the public were strongly opposed to sex selection except on strictly medical grounds, where it may be used to avoid sex-linked diseases. Although there are pragmatic reasons to oppose sex selection, such as a possible shift in the balance of males and females in society, it seems that the main reason for this opposition is a basic human intuition that choosing the sex of one's child is wrong. Yet a number of fertility specialists have argued that sex selection is an essential human right.

In 2001 the American Society for Reproductive Medicine ruled that helping couples to select the sex of their babies for "gender variety" was proper and ethical. In a letter of advice to an infertility specialist, the acting chairman of the society's ethics committee stated that it was acceptable for a couple to choose an embryo of the opposite sex to an older sibling.

Of course, sex selection using pre-implantation diagnosis is a high-tech version of a process which has been going on for thousands of years. There are many people across the world who face intense personal pressure to produce babies of a specific sex. In India pregnant women are often forced by relatives to undergo antenatal tests such as high-resolution ultrasound scanning, or even amniocentesis, to identify the sex of their fetus. If it is found to be female, an abortion is performed. A report in the *British Medical Journal* estimated that at least 50,000 female fetuses per year were aborted in India for this reason.[2] Most of these abortions happen in private abortion clinics and sex determination shops, of which there are 2,000 in Delhi alone. Large profits are made from sex determination tests and, although legislation has been passed in the Indian parliament to outlaw the practice, it is difficult if not impossible for the government to control. It was estimated that 70% of all abortions in Delhi were cases of female feticide. In some Indian regions, the ratio of female babies to males has fallen to below 800 girls for every 1,000 boys. Another recent report estimated that sex selection accounted for approximately 50,000,000 "missing" women in the Indian population as a whole.[3] Girls are seen as an economic burden by parents because they need a dowry for marriage. They are also seen as a potential embarrassment because they are vulnerable to sexual harassment. Not surprisingly, many US and European commentators and ethicists have expressed outrage about these discriminatory practices. It seems that sex selection is ethical, but only if undertaken by those who share Western liberal principles.

Pre-implantation genetic diagnosis and embryo selection

At present pre-implantation genetic diagnosis and selection of embryos is restricted to the detection of childhood diseases – like sickle-cell anaemia or cystic fibrosis – that are regarded as having a severe impact on the quality of life. The rapid increase in the identification of disease-predisposing genes, however, will enable scientists to detect genetic variants that have a less severe impact on a child's life, such as predispositions to obesity, diabetes, heart disease, asthma and various forms of cancer. It seems likely that genetic variations which increase resistance to infective diseases will also be identified. The identification and modification of genes which may predispose to "socially desirable characteristics" is much more speculative and still belongs to the wilder reaches of science fiction. However, the speed of progress in molecular genetics and reproductive technology is enough to dispel complacency.

A distinction is commonly made between *negative* selection against embryos which carry genetic variations likely to cause a disease, and *positive* selection in favour of embryos which are found to carry genetic variations that are socially desirable. In reality the distinction is less clear than it seems at first.

If we choose not to select an embryo with a genotype likely to cause a disease, should we refuse to select an embryo with a genotype likely to be an unaffected carrier of the disease, but who may pass it on to any future offspring? Should one select for a genetic variation which is found to be associated with a *reduced* risk of disease compared with the general population? Of all the embryos available, why not select the ones that have the least risk of disease and the best chance of future well-being?

Many, such as biotechnologist Lee Silver, predict that embryo selection is here to stay, at least in American society, where the majority "hold fast to the overriding importance of personal liberty and personal fortune in guiding what individuals are allowed and able to do". Although embryo selection is currently used by a tiny fraction of prospective parents to screen for a tiny number of disease genotypes, "with each coming year, the power of the technology will expand, and its application will become more efficient. Slowly but surely, embryo selection will be incorporated into American culture, just as other reproductive technologies have been in the past ... Environment and genes stand side by side. Both contribute to a child's chances for achievement and success in life, although neither guarantees it. If we allow money to buy an advantage in one, the claim for stopping the other is hard to make, especially in a society that gives women the right to abort for any reason at all." [4] In other words, if society has accepted that it is legal to destroy an unwanted fetus, on what logical grounds should we refuse to allow selection of embryos with desired characteristics?

In some countries the process of finding an egg or sperm donor is becoming increasingly commercialized. Via the internet, donor profiles can be reviewed and the appropriate ethnic origin, eye colour, stature, educational achievement and interests can be selected. Egg donors are at a particular premium, and it is said that egg donation has become a means for impecunious female students to fund themselves through college.

The selection of donors according to individual preferences may have unexpected results. A lesbian couple with severe deafness deliberately opted to have a deaf child by choosing a friend with familial deafness as a sperm donor. As members of a deaf community, they wished to have a child who would fit easily into their lifestyle. The case sparked discussion over the extent to which personal freedom of choice should govern the application of reproductive technologies.

Saviour siblings

Pre-implantation genetic testing allows the possibility that embryos can be selected to create a child who can act as a matched tissue donor for an existing sibling. In the UK Raj and Shahana Hashmi appealed to the courts in 2003 for permission to create a baby by embryo selection who would be a suitable bone marrow donor for their four-year-old son, Zain, who suffers from beta thalassaemia. After a prolonged legal battle, the Court of Appeal agreed that the procedure could go ahead. In a similar case, another UK family travelled to Chicago for embryo selection to be undertaken to create a baby who could act as a stem cell donor for his older brother, who suffered from the rare condition Diamond Blackfan anaemia. This case illustrated the ease with which international "medical tourism" can overcome national bioethical regulatory frameworks.

Cloning

The creation of Dolly, the cloned sheep, in February 1997 marked a further landmark in biotechnology. Dolly was created using DNA taken from a cell line cultured from a mammary gland cell from an adult sheep. The nuclear material was transferred into an unfertilized egg from which the original nucleus had been removed. The newly created embryo was then inserted into the uterus of another sheep, where it grew into Dolly.

Commentators and ethicists immediately seized on the possibility that the same procedure could be undertaken in humans. It was not a new idea. Aldous Huxley in his novel *Brave New World* had introduced the concept to a mass audience. "Bokanovsky's Process . . . one egg, one embryo, one adult – normality. But a bokanovskified egg will bud, will proliferate, will divide. From eight to ninety-six buds, and every bud will grow into a perfectly formed embryo, and every embryo into a full-sized adult. Making ninety-six human beings grow where only one grew before. Progress."[5] Ira Levin's film *The Boys from Brazil* was based on the use of cloning in a conspiracy aimed at duplicating an army of neo-Nazi thugs.

With these nightmarish ideas in the public consciousness, it is hardly surprising that the response to Dolly's creation was so intense. Many scientists working in the field of mammalian genetics and embryology were dismayed at the unwelcome attention directed at their research. The visions of Huxley and Levin are misleading in that the technology is unlikely to be used in the foreseeable future by totalitarian governments or neo-Nazi dictators. Instead the demand for cloning of human embryos is coming from the medical arena.

It is important to make a distinction between reproductive cloning and so-called "therapeutic" cloning. *Reproductive cloning* involves the creation of an embryo for implantation into a human womb leading to the development of a new individual. *Therapeutic cloning* is the creation of a human embryo which can then be manipulated to produce stem cells for medical purposes. No embryonic development beyond the fourteen-day stage will occur and thus no developed individual will result. Since the creation of Dolly, most legislators and scientists have been vocal in their opposition to reproductive cloning, almost entirely on the basis of the known and unknown risks to the health of the cloned child. But the potential therapeutic benefits of stem cells derived from embryos have been hailed in extravagant terms.

Stem cell therapies

Genetically matched stem cells offer the prospect of remarkable new treatments for a range of medical diseases. Blood, skin, muscle and brain cells could be grown in the laboratory and implanted without the need for anti-rejection treatment because of the identical genetic match with the patient. If we are prepared to accept the generation, manipulation and destruction of human embryos, we may have access to an unparalleled range of new treatments for inherited, degenerative and cancerous diseases. After a prolonged debate, the UK authorities have allowed therapeutic cloning and the creation of stem cell cultures from human embryos under a strict regulatory regime.

Another suggested use of nuclear transfer techniques is to prevent the inheritance of rare disorders (affecting a component of the cell known as the mitochondria) which are passed on in the cytoplasm of the mother's egg. If the nuclear DNA from the mother was inserted into a donor egg from which the nucleus had been removed, followed by IVF, it would be possible for the mother to have a genetically related child without the risk of mitochondrial disease being passed on to the next generation. A third possible scenario is that of the mother who, after giving birth to a baby, receives chemotherapy for cancer which means that she becomes permanently sterile. If her baby were then to die, in a tragic accident for example, cloning from cells taken before or even after the baby's death would enable her to have another child who was still genetically her own.

Cloning might even allow lesbian couples to share biological parentage of a child, and avoid introducing alien genes into their relationship. One member of the couple could provide the donor cell, and the other could provide the unfertilized recipient egg. The newly formed embryo could then be introduced into the uterus of the second woman, allowing the child to be biologically related to both women.

Enhancement technology

The new biotechnology can be used not only to combat serious diseases and disability. It promises to give human beings remarkable powers to change the structure and capabilities of our bodies. In the foreseeable future we will have the power to select children on the basis of a range of desirable characteristics, use gene therapy to manipulate the DNA in different parts of our bodies, enhance muscle strength and endurance, replace or repair body parts with stem cells or artificial substitutes, enhance brain function by the use of psychoactive drugs or direct connection with computers and prolong life expectancy by modification of ageing mechanisms within the cellular machinery. All of these techniques are currently being investigated in animal experiments and many are about to enter the human arena.

THEMES

Behind the bewildering range of issues which are raised by advances in human biotechnology, a number of recurrent themes can be identified.

Biotechnology collapses the distinction between natural and artificial

Historically we have always divided the world into objects which were natural – part of the givens of the natural world, and objects which were artefactual – originating from human purpose and made by human craft. As technology advances, the world of the artefactual expands in importance and the natural diminishes. As Professor Oliver O'Donovan of Oxford University expressed it, "When every activity is understood as making, then every situation is seen as a raw material, waiting to have something made out of it." [6]

Oliver O'Donovan has argued that the relation of human beings to their own bodies is in some ways the last frontier of nature. However much we modify the natural environment and surround ourselves with the products of our invention, we cannot get away from the "givenness" of our own bodies. But now this last frontier of the natural is increasingly being broken. We do not have to accept the limitations of our bodies as they have been given to us. By understanding the molecular and biological mechanisms of which our bodies are constructed, we can learn how to manipulate and improve them. The old technological dream of controlling and improving on nature, which stems from the Enlightenment, can be extended to the design of the human body itself. Our bodies can be regarded as raw material, as potential for modification or enhancement according to our own desires. If the human body is seen as the product of blind random forces over millions of years of evolutionary history, then why should we hesitate to use our evolved intelligence to improve on its design?

Biotechnology changes the nature of parenthood

As reproductive technology develops, it offers new opportunities for parents to exercise control over the process of procreation. We can select the donor of the egg and the sperm that goes to make an embryo. We can test embryos to select the one that has the optimal genetic potential. Some commentators have argued that there is no difference between spending money on education and spending money on ensuring that your child has the optimal genetic potential. Both are ways of improving our children's chances in the lottery of life. And if we can learn how to manipulate an embryo's DNA safely in order to enhance its future potential, then there is no ethical reason why we should not embark on this process, to improve human nature a little at a time.

In fact, some biologists are claiming that the improvement of the genetic makeup of each individual is an essential goal of the human community. These are the words of molecular biologist Lee Silver: "While selfish genes control all other forms of life, master and slave have switched positions in human beings, who now have the power not only to control but to create new genes for themselves. Why not seize this power? Why not control what has been left to chance in the past? Indeed we control all other aspects of our children's lives and identities through powerful social and environmental influences ... On what basis can we reject positive genetic influences on a person's essence when

PART FOUR: PERSONAL ISSUES

we accept the right of parents to benefit their children in every other way?"[7]
And Bentley Glass uses the language of rights to emphasize the role of genetic
technology: "The right of individuals to procreate must give place to a new
paramount right; the right of every child to enter life with an adequate physical
and mental endowment."[8]

In the not-too-distant future, it may be possible to test embryos to determine a wide range of characteristics including aspects of intelligence, physical
strength and size as well as susceptibility to a large number of diseases. For
the first time, couples will be able genuinely to select the child of their choice,
the child who will match with their lifestyle. Perhaps before too long, selecting
the best embryo will be seen as an essential part of responsible parenthood. "I
owe it to myself and to my future child to give him/her the best possible genetic
start in life." Under the guise of middle-class responsibility, the stranglehold of
the god of consumerism will finally have extended to parenthood.

Biotechnology offers the possibility of solutions to the age-old problems of humankind

Since the dawn of civilization, human beings have struggled to come to terms
with the limitations that stem from our physical nature. Every generation has to
learn afresh the human realities of ageing, illness, infertility, disability, frailty,
depression, death. In the face of these realities we struggle to learn wisdom,
insight and acceptance. This is the way we are made – this is the "human condition". But now, for the first time in human history, biotechnology has advanced
to the point where it seems to offer a solution to these age-old problems. We do
not have to face these painful realities with passive acceptance and resignation. We have the technology. We can learn to break free from the limitations
imposed by our physical nature. This is a potent dream for many scientists
and philosophers. The emerging philosophy of transhumanism promotes the
view that human enhancement technologies should be made widely available;
that individuals should have broad discretion over which of these technologies to apply to themselves; and that parents should be free to decide which
reproductive technologies to use when seeking to have children. Many trans-
humanists believe that ultimately enhancement technology may lead to a new
form of "post-human beings", beings who may have indefinite health-spans,
much greater intellectual faculties compared with current human beings, new

types of sensory awareness and enhanced control over their intellectual and emotional functioning.[9]

The possibility of spectacular future therapies trumps ethical concerns in the present

When the first public debates about human embryo research took place in the 1980s, many scientists were eloquent about the dramatic therapeutic advances which would result from this work. Once human embryo research was legalized, it was claimed that infertility would become much rarer, the causes of miscarriages would be unravelled, lethal congenital diseases would be tackled, and abnormal fetal development would become treatable. One newspaper editorial claimed, "In a world with so much suffering, it would be unethical *not* to allow embryo research." More than fifteen years later, therapeutic advances resulting from research on human embryos seem remarkably modest. New techniques for the genetic screening of embryos have certainly resulted, but the promise of wonderful new therapies has not yet been fulfilled. Predicting the likely outcome of medical research is notoriously unreliable, and scientific and medical history is replete with examples of promising avenues of enquiry that came to naught. Yet in public debates about biotechnology, such as those around research into embryonic stem cells, it is the possibility of spectacular future therapies which dominates the discussion and grabs the headlines: spinal cord repair procedures for trauma victims like Christopher Reeves, new hope for victims of Alzheimer's disease, replacement tissues for patients with heart, kidney or liver failure. When the possible future benefits of research are weighed against ethical concerns about the manipulation of embryos in a simplistic utilitarian analysis, it is the prospect of new therapies, however speculative, that will always dominate.

CHRISTIAN RESPONSES

In response to these challenges we need to start by developing an authentic biblical understanding of humanity in the light of God's revelation.

Creation order

A central theme in the creation narrative of Genesis is that God imbues his creation with order. Everything, both animate and inanimate, is assigned a place and a function. In biblical imagery, the sea is often used as an image of disorder, of chaos. However, in creation God imposes limits on the sea itself. As God said to Job, "Who shut up the sea behind doors when it burst forth from the womb … when I fixed limits for it and set its doors and bars in place, when I said, 'This far you may come and no farther…'" (Job 38:8 – 11). God creates the limits beyond which his creation cannot transgress. There is no part of creation, however chaotic, however autonomous, which is not subject to intrinsic limits set by the Creator. God has not only created the physical structures of creation, including the physical structure of our bodies. He has also created a hidden moral order which directs how those structures should be used, in other words how we should behave. It is as though there is a hidden "grain" within all creation. If we live our lives "along" that grain, behaving in a way which is consonant with the created moral order, then our lives will work, we will flourish. This is what the Bible calls the "way of wisdom" (e.g., as in Proverbs 4:10 – 13: "Listen, my son, accept what I say, and the years of your life will be many. I guide you in the way of wisdom and lead you along straight paths. When you walk, your steps will not be hampered; when you run, you will not stumble"). So wisdom, wise living, is living in accordance with the hidden moral order of the universe. God imprints his moral order in the design of his creation and makes his image-bearers rational and morally responsible, capable of both understanding and responding freely to his commands. Human freedom can only operate within the limits set by God. This is the difference between human freedom – freedom within the limits set by our physical design and by the moral order – and godlike freedom – freedom without limits, except those set by God's own unchanging character.

God is the one who imposes order, meaning and purpose on the whole creation. In the biblical narrative both the origin of the human species (Genesis 1 – 2) and the development of the individual fetus within the womb (Psalm 139:13 – 16) are pictured in terms of meticulous and loving design. This is the creation order imposed by the Creator's will.

The image of God

Human beings are unique in all the vast array of creation, because they alone of all the creatures are made in God's image – or, as an alternative translation puts it, they are made as God's image (Genesis 1:27). Human beings are godlike beings. God has chosen no other image-bearer, either animate or inanimate, on planet Earth. In the ancient world it was apparently common for a king to set up a stone or metal image of himself as a physical symbol of his sovereignty over a particular territory. It represented him to his subject peoples. God's image is seen not only in our capacities or attributes, in *what we can do* and in the duties which God gives us, but also in *what we are* by creation, in the stuff of our humanity.

The biblical revelation reminds us that human beings are not self-explanatory. They derive their meaning from outside themselves, from God in whose image they are made. We are not autonomous individuals, creating ourselves constantly by the decisions and choices we make. No, we are images, we are reflections. The dignity of our humanity is derivative; it comes from him whose image we bear. We are dependent beings.

The ethicist Paul Ramsey, speaking of the unborn child, put it in these words: "The dignity of a human being is an overflow from God's dealing with him or her and not primarily an anticipation of anything they will ever be by themselves. The Lord did not put his love upon you because you were intrinsically more than a blob of tissue in the uterus." The theologian Helmut Thielicke put it like this: "The divine likeness rests on the fact that God remembers us." The divine image is like a mirror reflecting God's glory. Like a mirror it goes dark if the source of light is withdrawn. In Thielicke's words, "it possesses only borrowed light".[10]

Within the story of my life, I have a degree of independence, the dignity of genuine choice, the relative freedom of a creature. But it is not simply "my" life to do with as I please. My life can only have meaning in relation to God.

For a society like ours which is penetrated by liberal individualism, this concept is peculiar, nonsensical, even outrageous. Yet the biblical revelation stresses our creaturely dependence. Job expresses this poetically: "Your hands shaped me and made me ... you moulded me like clay ... Did you not pour me out like milk and curdle me like cheese, clothe me with skin and flesh and knit me together with bones and sinews? You gave me life and showed me kindness, and in your providence watched over my spirit" (Job 10:8 – 12). Similarly, Elihu in the book of Job reflects on the dependence of the entire human race on God's continual sustenance: "If it were his intention and he withdrew his spirit and breath, all mankind would perish together and man would return to the dust" (Job 34:14). The same concept is found in the words of Jeremiah: "A man's life is not his own; it is not for man to direct his steps" (Jeremiah 10:23). The biblical revelation reminds us that "we are most ourselves not when we seek to direct and control our destiny, but when we recognize and admit that our life is grounded in and sustained by God".[11]

In biblical thought, each human life has a unique dignity because of the divine image. Hence each life has an incalculable or incommensurable value. In other words, it is not possible to calculate the value of a human life in material terms and it is not possible to compare the ultimate value of one human life with another. Each human being is a unique masterpiece of God's creation. In the literal words of the eighth psalm, each one of us is "lacking a very little of God" (Psalm 8:5).

To many secular thinkers the dignity of personhood depends on your function – on what you can do, on how well your cortex functions, on whether you can choose and exercise personal autonomy. If your level of functioning is critically reduced, then you have less worth. But in Christian thought the dignity of a human being resides not in what you can do, but in what you are, by creation. Human beings do not need to earn the right to be treated as godlike beings. Our dignity is *intrinsic*, in the way we have been made, in how God remembers us and calls us. So biblical ethics, the way we are called to treat one another, is derived from biblical anthropology, the way we are made.

The consequences of the fall

At the heart of the account of the fall in Genesis 3 is a rejection by human beings of the creation order that God has instituted for their enjoyment and well-being. Adam and Eve strike a blow for moral autonomy independent of God. By eating the fruit which had been forbidden, they discover the catastrophic consequences of disobedience.

Although the universe is fractured and broken following the fall, a crucial part of biblical understanding is that the universe still displays the moral order, the hidden grain. Its brokenness is the brokenness of order and not chaos.

As God had warned them, the disobedience of Adam and Eve led directly to the entrance of death into the world: "For when you eat of it you will surely die." In the poetic imagery of the creation narratives, within the garden of Eden Adam and Eve, along with all the other fruit within the garden, had access to the tree of life. They could have chosen to eat the fruit of that tree and live for ever. Instead they chose to disobey God and eat the one fruit of the garden that was forbidden. By giving access to the fruit of the tree of life, God showed that his original intention for human beings was everlasting life. In biblical thought the death of human beings, in all its horror and mystery, is not "natural", it is not part of God's original design. The deep intuition which most of us share, that physical death, especially the death of a child or young person, is an outrage, an alien interruption in the nature of being, and the inexpressible longing we have for eternity, reflect the original creation order. We were not intended to die; we were made to live for ever. That is why death is the "last enemy" (1 Corinthians 15:26). It seems futile to speculate on what would have happened if human beings had not disobeyed. What is clear is that in biblical thought death is not part of God's creation order; it is a mysterious and terrible interruption in the nature of being. And because human beings are "in Adam", we have an organic physical solidarity with him. We too are subject to death and decay.

We may see an echo of this in the biological understanding of human ageing and death. It is interesting that death is not a biological necessity. Every living cell and organism is equipped with the essential machinery to ensure repair and renewal so that life can continue indefinitely. Surprising as it may seem, eternal life is not a biological impossibility! In one sense, although individual cells are destined to die, organisms seem to be designed to live for ever. The ageing process involves active biological mechanisms, as yet poorly understood, which cause the repair and renewal processes to malfunction, leading ultimately to biological decay and death. Perhaps this is a physical counterpart of the biblical truth that through human evil, the creation is "in bondage to decay" (Romans 8:21).

The inevitable accompaniment of death is fear. The blessing of human life is transformed into a slavery of fear, especially fear of death. The terrible, all-pervading fear of death drives human beings to extraordinary and frequently pathetic lengths. Perhaps the most bizarre example is seen in those who arrange for their bodies to be deep-frozen in liquid nitrogen in the forlorn hope that a future generation will discover the elixir of eternal life. But in less obvious ways the fear of death drives both medical research and our desperate attempts to use technology to prolong life.

But there is a better answer to the fear of death. As the writer to the Hebrews states, Christ came to "free those who all their lives were held in slavery by their fear of death" (Hebrews 2:15). For all its terror and mystery, in the biblical worldview death is not an entirely negative concept. It may be, in C. S. Lewis's wonderful phrase, "a severe mercy". At the end of the account of the fall, human beings are banished from the garden of Eden, precisely to prevent them eating from the fruit of the tree of life and living for ever. And to prevent their return and capture of the fruit by force of arms, cherubim and a flaming sword are set to guard the way to the tree of life (Genesis 3:21 – 24). So in God's providential care of his creation, human beings are not meant to live for ever in their degraded fallen state. Human lifespan is limited, not just as a curse, but *out of God's grace.*

Later on in the book of Genesis, because of the escalating wickedness of the human race, human longevity is limited to 120 years (Genesis 6:3). Psalm 90, attributed traditionally to Moses, teaches that because of human sinfulness, "the length of our days is seventy years – or eighty, if we have the strength; yet their span is but trouble and sorrow, for they quickly pass, and we fly away" (v. 10). The psalmist expresses grief and regret at the evanescence of human existence and the need to take this into account. "Teach us to number our days aright, that we may gain a heart of wisdom" (v. 12).

In God's providence, death may be a merciful release from an existence trapped in a fallen and decaying body. Christian attitudes to death should reflect a curious ambivalence. We need to retain, firstly, a sense of outrage at its alien destructive character; secondly, an acceptance that the end of physical life may be evidence of God's grace, a "severe mercy"; and finally, a sense of future hope in the knowledge that ultimately death will be destroyed. Christian health-care professionals are called to struggle against death whilst recognizing the ultimate futility of their struggle and seeking to discern when active life-sustaining treatment may become inappropriate, when the dying process becomes a severe mercy, even a strange form of healing.

The entrance of death into human life condemns our physical existence to an awful futility. Humans are condemned to return to the ground from which they are taken. "Dust you are and to dust you will return" (Genesis 3:19). In the poetic yet bleak words of the Anglican funeral service, the futile cycle of human existence is exposed, "dust to dust, ashes to ashes". So the dust of the ground which is both the origin of our human bodies and the source of their food becomes a symbol of their eventual decay and death.

The reality of death traps human beings in the same cycle of futility as the rest of the animal world. "As for men, God tests them so that they may see that they are like the animals. Man's fate is like that of the animals; the same fate awaits them both: As one dies, so dies the other. All have the same breath; man has no advantage over the animal. Everything is meaningless. All go to the same place; all come from dust, and to dust all return" (Ecclesiastes 3:18 – 20).

The futility and grief of physical ageing, its progressive decay and biological malfunction, are also graphically illustrated by the preacher at the end of the book of Ecclesiastes (12:1 – 8). They are "days of trouble", when you will say, "I find no pleasure in them." To the preacher, ageing brings darkness, physical weakness, fear, disability, apathy and loss of libido – "desire no longer is stirred" – before death brings its inevitable release. The biblical revelation is unsparing in its bleak depiction of the cycle of human life from an earthly perspective.

This biblical perspective helps us to retain a sense of the limitations of medicine and health care. For all our wonderful knowledge and technology, we are unable to redeem our physical bodies from the cycle of death and decay. There can be no technological or biological fix for the ultimate mysteries of the human condition. We cannot overcome ageing and eventual death by medical technology. In God's providential mercy, that route to the tree of life remains blocked by a flashing sword.

In the early chapters of Genesis we see the advent of human artifice and early technology. Jabal was the father of all those who live in tents and raise live-stock. Jubal was the father of all who play the harp and flute. Tubal-Cain forged all kinds of tools out of bronze and iron (Genesis 4:19 – 22). To the author of the narrative it is likely that these characters are living out the creation mandates, subduing the earth and bringing out the wonderfully diverse potential locked in the raw material of the earth.

At Babel we see a darker side to technology. The builders are driven by a twofold desire: to "make a name for ourselves" and to avoid being "scattered over the face of the whole earth". Vinoth Ramachandra suggests that Babel is the marriage of three human dreams, the technological dream (to build a city that would be the envy of gods and nations), the religious dream (to divinize mankind by reaching up into the heavens), and the political dream (to build a totalitarian society based on technology).[12] Babel symbolizes the use of human artefacts and technology to celebrate human autonomy. The words "Come, let us make…" (Genesis 11:3) echo the very words of God in making human beings, "Let us make man in our image…" (Genesis 1:26).

Babel symbolizes the myth of technology which recognizes no limits to human technical possibilities – technology that is used to seize God's rightful place as Creator and to overturn creation order. It is a story of human collective action, a unity which ends in confusion and dispersion. But the confusion created by God is both an act of judgement and, again, an act of mercy. The unfinished tower stands as a monument to the folly of human arrogance and a sign of the mercy of a God who intervenes to prevent a technological dream (or nightmare) coming to fruition.

In the incarnation and resurrection of Christ the created order is vindicated and fulfilled

When God breaks into human history to bring redemption to his fallen people, does he overturn the created order he has previously established to introduce a completely new kind of reality, a radically new creation? No. God reveals himself in the form of an "original model" human being.

In the incarnation, death and resurrection of Christ, the created order is both re-established and fulfilled. Before the resurrection it might have been possible for someone to wonder whether humanity and creation itself were a lost cause. Perhaps the only possible ending for the tragic story of a fallen creation is God's final judgement and destruction of the created order. But when Christ is raised as a *physical human being*, God proclaims his vote of confidence in the created order. The original design of human beings is not abandoned, despised or marginalized; it is affirmed and fulfilled. And in biblical Trinitarian thinking, through the advent of Christ, physical human nature has been assumed in a mysterious way into the Godhead. So Christians should treat the human body, with its strange and idiosyncratic design, with special respect. Why? *Because this is the form in which God became flesh.*

Jesus shares in the stuff of creation. His body is made from dust like ours. The Gospel writers go to great lengths to stress Christ's full humanity. He is tired, angry, hungry, distressed, in agony. And in the resurrection of Christ, the physical creation is not overturned but subsumed, or caught up, into a greater and richer reality. In Jesus, the second Adam, we see both a perfect human being, what the original Adam was meant to be, and the pioneer, the blueprint for a new type of person, the one in whose likeness a new creation will spring, the firstfruits of those who are to come (1 Corinthians 15:20).

Instead of starting afresh with a clean slate, in the resurrection of Christ God declares that for all future time he will sustain, redeem and transform the humanity that was originally made. So Christ's resurrection points backwards to the creation of human beings and forwards to the transformation of human beings at the same time. Our humanity is both vindicated and transformed. In God's mysterious purpose, this is what human beings were always intended to become. This is the ultimate goal of the created order. So Paul writes, "Just as we have borne the likeness of the earthly man, so shall we bear the likeness of the man from heaven" (1 Corinthians 15:49). The image of God inherited from Adam will be transformed and fulfilled into a new and much more glorious image. Yes, we will still be reflections. We do not lose our creaturely dependence. But we will discover the true likeness that we were always intended to bear.

The resurrection is God's final and irrevocable "yes" to humankind. If we take the biblical doctrines of the incarnation and resurrection seriously, we must conclude that the physical structure of our human bodies is not something we are free to change without very careful thought.

However, we must also take seriously the reality of evil in God's world, the all-pervasive distorting and marring effects of the fall. The original masterpiece, created with such love and embodying such artistry, has become flawed, defaced, contaminated, decaying from age. The varnish is cracked and yellowing. The frame is riddled with woodworm. The reflection of God's character is distorted and partially obscured. But through the imperfections we can still see the outlines of the original masterpiece. It still inspires a sense of wonder at the underlying design.

What is the responsibility that we owe to this flawed masterpiece? What is our duty as a human community? If we regard human beings as flawed masterpieces, then our responsibilities are to act as art preservers and restorers. We are called to protect masterpieces from further harm, and attempt to restore them *in line with the original artist's intentions*.

Medical technology as art restoration

Just like doctors, responsible and professional art restorers must act according to a code of ethical practice. It is the *intention of the original creator* or artist which is normative. The restorer must use all the information at his or her disposal – X-ray analysis, historical records, sophisticated chemical tests and so on – to determine the object's original "constitution", to assess what information the object itself embodies about the maker's intention. Only when the original creator's intention is revealed can the restorer decide what form of intervention is appropriate. Unethical restoration is the use of technology to alter, improve or enhance the appearance of the artistic piece.

Of course, art restoration is only an analogy of the role of medical technology and, like all analogies, it has limitations and difficulties. Nonetheless,

I believe the analogy is helpful as we try to assess the mind-boggling possibilities raised by biotechnology. We are called to use technology to preserve and protect the original design, to maintain and preserve the creation order embodied in the structure of the human body. However tempting it may be, however spectacular the consequences which might result, we must not resort to unethical restoration. We are not free to improve on the fundamental design of our humanity.

Within the perspective of medicine as art restoration, what kind of biotechnology is appropriate for "flawed masterpieces"? In my view the use of technology, such as genetic manipulation or stem cell therapy, which is intended to be *restorative*, recreating a damaged length of DNA or replacing damaged tissue with a normal counterpart, seems consistent with ethical practice. The aim is to preserve and restore the original artist's design. There seems to be no fundamental difference between providing artificial thyroid hormone for a patient with congenital hypothyroidism and replacing a segment of DNA, so that the patient is able to synthesize his or her own thyroid hormone. Both actions are aimed at preserving the original design. In the same way, the use of in vitro fertilization to allow a couple to beget a child who is genetically their own can be regarded as restorative. However, therapy which is intended to be *enhancing*, aimed at producing children who have stronger limbs, better growth and quicker brains, seems to me to step over the limits of human responsibility. As biblical Christians we must take creation order seriously. Within ethical art restoration, the intention of the original artist must be normative.

Of course, the distinction between restorative and enhancing therapy is not always clear-cut. What about gene therapy which is intended to lead to an improved resistance to infectious diseases, such as HIV? What about enhancement of cellular repair mechanisms which will prolong human lifespan to 120 or 150 years? What about psychoactive medication which improves concentration, vigilance or memory well above normal levels? Should these be regarded as therapies restoring the original design, or do they represent a fundamental change in the created order?

The new biotechnology is forcing us to reflect more deeply on the natural order given at creation. What does it mean to be human? What are the limits which are laid down by the physical structure and the moral order of our creation?

Parenthood

Similarly, the creation and selection of embryos, in order to determine the required sex or genetic makeup of a child, or reproductive cloning to create a child with a specific genetic structure, seems fraught with problems. In the original creation order, a child can be seen as a gift, a mysterious other who is equal to us in status and significance. But with embryo testing and selection, and also with reproductive cloning, our child becomes a commodity, the one we have chosen, the one who reflects our wishes and desires. To me this seems to change the nature of parenthood. It is to surrender to the controlling spirit of the age. Modern parents are in danger of becoming control freaks. We want to control and design our children to fulfil our deepest desires. Maybe we want to live out our unfulfilled expectations in them. But a biblical perception of parenthood teaches us that we must let go. Although we have a responsibility to protect, nurture and educate, we must *respect* our children as mysterious others, those who are equal to us at a fundamental level. In the words of Gilbert Meilander, "We are very reluctant to let the mystery of personhood – equal in dignity to our own – unfold in the lives of our children." Instead "we need the virtue of humility before the mystery of human personhood and the succession of generations. We need the realization that the children who come after us are not simply a product for us to mould."[13]

What about the selection of embryos to create matched tissue donors for siblings? Here the dilemma is agonizing and poignant. We must empathize with the pain of parents who watch their children suffer from the consequences of a lethal genetic disorder. How can it be wrong to create another child who will not only be loved for him- or herself, but will also be capable of acting as a life-saving donor to a sibling? Yet respect for the integrity and mystery of personhood must make us uneasy about the deliberate creation of saviour siblings. To bring a child into the world for a specific ulterior motive, and to force the child to play a role, however noble, is in some sense manipulative. Of course, the instrumentalization of children is not new in the history of families. Parents have brought children into the world to help with the harvest, to provide support in their old age, to furnish an heir for the family dynasty, to provide a companion in loneliness. But the use of biotechnology to create children with specific desired characteristics is to take this process one step further. It is to subordinate the very being of a child to our will.

In biblical thought we do not create children, we *beget* them. As Oliver O'Donovan pointed out in his London Lectures *Begotten or Made?* there is a profound thought which goes back to the Nicene Creed and the gospel of John. In the words of the creed, the Son of God was "begotten not made". The wording was intended to emphasize that the Son is not part of the creation, a product of God's creative will. Instead he is eternally "of one being with the Father". As beings made in the image of God, we share in the miracle of begetting. Our offspring are human beings who share with us a common human nature. In God's design we do not determine what our offspring are; we receive them as a gift, as beings who are equal with us at a fundamental level, in the same way that the Son is equal in being with the Father. On the other hand, that which we make is *different* from us. It is an artefact, alien from our humanity. It is fundamentally at our disposal, a product of our *will* rather than a product of our *being*. One of the dangers of reproductive technology is that it subtly reflects and contributes to a change in our relationship to our own children. They become a product of our will, a commodity at our disposal.

Does this mean that there is no ethical alternative to the poignant dilemma of children affected by lethal inherited disorders? In public debates about the creation of saviour siblings, it is often implied that the only alternative to the creation of donor siblings is inevitable death for the affected child. Yet in reality there are alternatives, including the creation and use of donor tissue banks, allowing matched adult donors to be identified. This approach has already been highly successful and is likely to become more effective in the future with the tissue-typing of potential donors from communities around the world.

SUMMARY OF CHRISTIAN RESPONSES

In summary, there are no neat solutions or obvious panaceas to the challenges and questions which biotechnology is raising. What is clear is that we need to struggle together as a Christian community to try to understand more clearly the rapid changes which are occurring in our midst and to discern how to respond from a position of Christian faith. Here are some broad outlines of a Christian response.

Firstly, I believe we are called to *empathize* with the deep and hidden pain of childless couples, of families devastated by genetic illness, of individuals facing degenerative conditions such as Alzheimer's disease. It is the reality of this hidden pain, the fear of death and disability, and the quest for technological solutions which drive the research and development in the new biotechnology. Sadly it is often the failure of practical caring in our society which seems to drive a desperate quest for technological fixes to the painful realities of the human condition. The Christian community should be in the vanguard of practical caring for the disabled, the marginalized and the dying.

Secondly, the Christian community is called to *challenge* the reductionist mentality which is starting to pervade modern society and the health-care systems within it. At a social level we need to challenge the economic and political power base which new genetic manipulation and biotechnology is creating and demand democratic accountability, transparency and justice in the actions of those who control the technology.

Thirdly, I believe we have an urgent need to develop a more profound *understanding* of what it means to be a human being, created in God's image, contaminated by evil, yet affirmed and redeemed by the Christ event – the incarnation, death and resurrection of Jesus of Nazareth. We need renewed input from theologians and biblical scholars who can reflect on the nature and implications of the natural created order and our role within it. At the same time we need the insights and practical experience of doctors, geneticists and reproductive scientists who can build a bridge between the biblical world and the world of modern science.

Fourthly, we need to *present* an alternative biblical worldview to our society. A worldview that regards human beings as wonderful but flawed masterpieces, rather than randomly generated, self-replicating organisms. A worldview which encompasses wonder, respect, empathy and protection for the weak and vulnerable in our society. A worldview which respects the givenness of our humanity, supporting and encouraging restorative therapies whilst resisting the abusive possibilities of enhancement biotechnology. A worldview which respects the physical structure of our bodies whilst pointing to a greater reality, a deeper healing, and a hope which transcends the grave.

Finally, we should strive for *global justice* in the application of biotechnology. Every year billions of dollars are spent on sophisticated biotechnology research into the detection and treatment of rare genetic disorders, research into gene therapy and the application of stem cells, research into the slowing of the ageing process. At the same time, hundreds of thousands of children are dying in the poor countries of the world from conditions which are easily treatable with the minimum of medical technology. Children are being permanently blinded for lack of a few cents' worth of vitamin A. Babies are dying of pneumonia which could be treated with a single shot of antibiotics. Mothers are dying in childbirth for lack of basic obstetric care. As we debate the appropriate use of biotechnology, as Christians we cannot ignore the demands of equity and global justice in how limited medical resources should be applied.

NOTES

1 Lee Silver, *Remaking Eden* (New York: Avon, 1997), pp. 224–25.

2 Z. Imam, "India bans female feticide", *British Medical Journal*, 1994, 309: 428.

3 Lee Silver, *Remaking Eden*

4 G. N. Allahbadia, "The 50 million missing women", *Journal of Assisted Reproduction and Genetics*, 2002, 19:411–16.

5 Aldous Huxley, *Brave New World* (London: Chatto & Windus, 1932).

6 O'Donovan, *Begotten or Made?* (Oxford: Oxford Univ. Press, 1984).

7 Silver, *Remaking Eden*.

8 Bentley Glass, "Science, endless horizons or golden age?", *Science*, 1971, 171: 23–29.

9 Nick Bostrom, "Transhumanist values", *Review of Contemporary Philosophy, vol. 4*, 2005, *www.nickbostrom.com/*.

10 O'Donovan, *Begotten or Made?*

11 Gilbert Meilander, *Bioethics: A Primer for Christians* (Carlisle, Penn.: Paternoster, 1997).

12 Vinoth Ramachandra, *Gods That Fail* (Carlisle, Penn.: Paternoster, 1996).

13 Meilander, *Bioethics*.

Same-Sex Relationships

16

F ew subjects have been as explosive as that of homosexuality in recent years. Rapid social change has brought about a degree of acceptance of homosexuality which is unprecedented. This has led to a change in Western perceptions of issues such as the nature of sexuality, the concept of the family, the education of our children and the nature of human rights. It is in this context that the church has to offer leadership by reflecting biblically and responding appropriately to the agenda. It does so at a time when many homosexual campaigners see Christianity as one of the primary sources of resistance to their demands.

As we reflect on the message of the Bible and the demands of our culture, we need to reassert our belief in the authority of Scripture. If we waver in our belief that God has spoken to us in the Scriptures, then we are left with conjecture and opinion. Yet we also need to be sensitive to the fact that we are dealing with people's emotions, their sexual identity and their dreams of finding love and acceptance. We have a mandate to speak the truth, but we are called to speak the truth in love.

We are all human and we are all sexual. If we stereotype and stigmatize one another, then we do not treat each other with the respect that each person deserves. After all, as far as the Bible is concerned, there is no such phenomenon as "a homosexual": there are only people made in the image of God. We all share in the glory and tragedy of being human and we share it in our sexuality as well as other areas of our lives. We may disapprove of homosexual practices; we have no liberty to dehumanize those who engage in them. We are all frail and vulnerable and nobody has been sexually sinless apart from Jesus. Although we must not shy away from making judgements about what is right and wrong in the light of Scripture, we are not to be judgemental. We shall be judged by the standards by which we judge others. Nobody has the right to be morally superior. Besides, sexual sins are not the only sins, nor even necessarily the most sinful; pride and hypocrisy are surely worse.

In what follows, then, I want to explore what the Bible has to say about same-sex relationships from a Christian viewpoint. It may well be that some of those reading this are not Christians, but those who are will surely want to know what light Scripture can throw on this topic. Having discovered this, they will wish to seek God's grace to live in a way which is consistent with his Word, obedient to his will and a witness to his world. Nevertheless, I hope that those who read this who are not Christians may hear the voice of God calling them to discover the liberty of obedience to his will in this area of their lives.

THE INCIDENCE OF HOMOSEXUALITY

Not everybody is exclusively homosexual or heterosexual in inclination. Some people find that they are attracted to people of the same sex, even briefly, during their lives. A major survey in the US, the *National Health and Social Life Survey* published in 1994, found that 2.7% of men reported same-gender sex partners in the last year, 4.1% in the past five years and 4.9% since the age of eighteen. The equivalent figures for women were 1.3%, 2.2% and 4.1%.[1] When asked about "having done anything sexual" with a person of the same sex since puberty, these figures rise to 9.1% for men and 4.3% for women.[2] The figure of 9.1% is higher than any figure reported by similar surveys at the time, but if true implies that around 4% of the men surveyed undertook some form of sexual activity with another man before the age of eighteen, but not after.[3] In examining those people who experienced only same-sex partnerships, the study found that since puberty 0.6% of men have had sex only with other boys or men and never with a female partner. For women, the proportion is 0.2%.

Sexual Behaviour in Britain, a large study published in 1994, found that 3.6% of men (and 1.7% of women) have ever had same-sex genital contact,[4] though this was a one-off isolated act in 50% of these cases.[5] In addition, 1.1% of men had had a homosexual partner during the previous year (0.4% for women), and 1.4% (0.6% for women) in the past five years.[6] Only 0.3% of men (and 0.1% of women) reported having exclusively same-sex partners.[7] A more recent large British study found that the proportion of men aged between sixteen and forty-four years who had ever had a homosexual partner was 5.4%, with those having a homosexual partner in the last five years being 2.6%. The equivalent figures for women were surprisingly high at 4.9% and 2.6%.[8]

These studies suggest that in the Western world, putting aside teenage experimentation, between 3% and 5.5% of men have undertaken a homosexual act in their adult lifetime,[9] between 1.5% and 4% of men have had a homosexual partner in the last five years, and less than 2% of the male population, and less than 1% of the female, are exclusively homosexual in inclination and practice.

ASKING THE KEY QUESTION

Having delineated the context for our discussion, I am ready to ask the question, are same-sex partnerships a Christian option? I phrase my question carefully as it introduces us to three necessary distinctions.

The distinction between sins and crimes

Firstly, at least since the Wolfenden Report of 1957 and the resultant Sexual Offences Act of 1967, we have learned to distinguish between sins and crimes. Adultery has always (according to God's law) been a sin, but in most countries it is not an offence punishable by the state. Rape, by contrast, is both a sin and a crime. The Sexual Offences Act of 1967 declared that a homosexual act performed between consenting adults over the age of twenty-one in private should no longer be a criminal offence. However, there is a difference between decriminalizing an act and legalizing it. Throughout Europe, following a ruling by the Court of Human Rights, laws that criminalize private consensual sex between adult men are now invalid. However, Denmark and the Netherlands, for instance, have given full legal status to same-sex partnerships.

Globally, attitudes are very diverse. In approximately seventy countries around the world homosexual relationships are illegal, and in some of them same-sex relationships are punishable by execution. In other countries jail sentences are long and people are harshly treated. Sometimes this antipathy to homosexuality can threaten the very foundations of our shared humanity. At a session of the United Nations which addressed these issues, President Robert Mugabe of Zimbabwe said that lesbian and gay men are "less than human" and are, therefore, not entitled to human rights.[10] Yet human rights are those

rights which are due to a human being by virtue of him or her being human
and nothing else.

The distinction between preference and practice

Secondly, it is important to note from the outset that what we are concerned
with here is homosexual practice (for which a person is responsible) and not
homosexual orientation or preference (for which he or she is not responsible).
The importance of this distinction goes beyond the attribution of responsibility
to the attribution of guilt. We may not blame people for what they are, though
we may for what they do. In every discussion about homosexuality we must be
rigorous in differentiating between "being" and "doing" – that is, between a
person's identity and activity, sexual preference and sexual practice, constitution and conduct.

Whatever our inclination, we are to bring every thought captive to Christ
and recognize that sexual intercourse is a joyful celebration of the unity
between one man and one woman for life. The person who cannot marry and
who is living a celibate and chaste life, whatever his or her sexual orientation,
is living a life which is pleasing to God.

The distinction between casual and committed

Thirdly, we need to distinguish between casual acts and committed relationships which (it is claimed) are just as expressive of authentic human love as
is heterosexual intercourse in marriage. No responsible homosexual person
(whether Christian or not) is advocating promiscuous "one-night stands".
What some are arguing, however, especially in the Lesbian and Gay Christian
Movement (LGCM), is that a heterosexual marriage and a homosexual partnership are "two equally valid alternatives",[11] being equally tender, mature
and faithful. The Statement of Conviction of the LGCM contains the assertion
that "it is entirely compatible with the Christian faith not only to love another
person of the same sex but also to express that love fully in a personal sexual
relationship".[12]

In 2003 such views were at the heart of a series of events which were very
painful for the Christian church. I shall mention only three. The first occurred
on 28 May 2003, when Michael Ingham, Bishop of the New Westminster diocese
in Canada, announced approval for six Vancouver-area parishes to bless same-
sex unions. This development provoked a storm of protest within the church

worldwide. The Archbishop of Canterbury, Dr Rowan Williams, said that New Westminster was "ignoring the considerable reservations of the church" and was going "significantly further than the teaching of the church or pastoral concern can justify". He continued, "I very much regret the inevitable tension and divisions that will result from this development."[13] J. I. Packer, a highly respected conservative theologian and church leader, was one of those who walked out of the synod which approved the blessing of same-sex unions. For him, it was not legitimate to allow experience to judge Scripture or to mould Scripture in order to provide a basis for the blessing of homosexual relationships.[14] Such a move deviated from biblical teaching, misled people since it did not help them to live a chaste life and deluded people into thinking that God blesses behaviour which he condemns. He simply asked the question, "How could I do it?"

The second issue was the consecration of Rev. Canon Gene Robinson as Bishop of New Hampshire in the USA on 2 November 2003. Canon Robinson had lived in a gay relationship for fifteen years. The impact of this consecration on the global Anglican communion was even greater than the events in New Westminster. Yet again the Archbishop of Canterbury, Rowan Williams, had to respond and recognized in doing so that divisions were being opened up across the world as a consequence of such an event, which he called a "matter of deep regret". The consecration took place despite the fact that thirty-seven archbishops had met the previous month at Lambeth Palace and had warned of the consequences of such a move. His fears were confirmed when primates throughout the world expressed their disquiet and, in some cases, their sense of outrage at this development.

The third issue was the proposed appointment of Rev. Canon Dr Jeffrey John as Bishop of Reading in the UK, which was announced on 21 May 2003 and was proposed by the Bishop of Oxford, Dr Richard Harries. Jeffrey John had been in a gay relationship for more than twenty years but said that, although the relationship continued, it was not now a sexual relationship, nor did he and his friend live together, because of their different ministerial responsibilities. However, he had been extremely critical of previous orthodox teaching on sexuality, especially the teaching which arose from the Lambeth Conference in 1998. Although he stated that he would abide by the teaching and discipline of the church in the area of sexuality were he to be consecrated as a bishop, many felt that there was no real evidence of repentance over his previous lifestyle, nor was there sufficient confidence that he would be able to support orthodox teaching as a bishop, given his own personal views. After a meeting with Archbishop Rowan Williams, he resigned from the appointment, but was later accepted as Dean of St Albans.

These three events were extremely painful for the Church of England, since they exposed the deep divisions which still exist on issues of human sexuality and particularly on same-sex relationships. It is important, therefore, as Bible-believing Christians, to examine the original text of Scripture, to see what light can be thrown on these issues.

The question before us, then, does not relate to homosexual practices of a casual nature, but asks whether homosexual partnerships – lifelong and loving – are a Christian option. Our concern is to subject prevailing attitudes (which range from total revulsion to equally uncritical endorsement) to biblical scrutiny. Is our sexual "preference" purely a matter of personal "taste"? Or has God revealed his will regarding a norm? In particular, can the Bible be shown to sanction homosexual partnerships, or at least not to condemn them? What, in fact, does the Bible condemn?

THE BIBLICAL PROHIBITIONS

There are four main biblical passages which refer (or appear to refer) to the homosexual question negatively: (1) the story of Sodom (Genesis 19:1 – 13), with which it is natural to associate the very similar story of Gibeah (Judges 19); (2) the Levitical texts (Leviticus 18:22; 20:13) which explicitly prohibit "lying with a man as one lies with a woman"; (3) the apostle Paul's portrayal of decadent pagan society in his day (Romans 1:18 – 32); and (4) two Pauline lists of sinners, each of which includes a reference to homosexual practices of some kind (1 Corinthians 6:9 – 10; 1 Timothy 1:8 – 11).

The stories of Sodom and Gibeah

The Genesis narrative makes it clear that "the men of Sodom were wicked and were sinning greatly against the LORD" (Genesis 13:13), and that "the outcry against Sodom and Gomorrah" was "so great and their sin so grievous" that God determined to investigate it (Genesis 18:20 – 21) and in the end "overthrew those cities and the entire plain, including all those living in the cities" (Genesis 19:25) by an act of judgement which was entirely consistent with the justice of "the Judge of all the earth" (Genesis 18:25). There is no controversy about this background to the biblical story. The question is, what was the sin of the people of Sodom (and Gomorrah) which merited their obliteration?

The traditional Christian view has been that they were guilty of homosexual practices, which they attempted (unsuccessfully) to inflict on the two angels whom Lot was entertaining in his home. Hence the word "sodomy". But theologian Sherwin Bailey, in re-evaluating the evidence, challenged this interpretation on two main grounds, and it is important to consider his arguments. Firstly, in his view, the phrase "Bring them out to us, so that we may know them" need not necessarily mean "so that we can have sex with them" (Genesis 19:5). The Hebrew word for "know" (*yada'*) occurs 943 times in the Old Testament, of which only ten occurrences refer to physical intercourse, and even then only to heterosexual intercourse. It would therefore be better to translate the phrase "so that we may get acquainted with them". We can then understand the men's violence as due to their anger that Lot had exceeded his rights as a resident alien, for he had welcomed two strangers into his home "whose intentions might be hostile and whose credentials had not been examined".[15] In this case the sin of Sodom was to invade the privacy of Lot's home and flout the ancient rules of hospitality. Lot begged them to desist because, he said, the two men "have come under the protection of my roof" (v. 8).

However, Robert Gagnon, in what must be the most comprehensive and encyclopaedic treatise on the Bible and homosexuality, entitled *The Bible and Homosexual Practice: Texts and Hermeneutics*, comments that though hospitality may be part of the story, the focus of it is on the demeaning and dehumanizing act of homosexual rape. Commenting on the sins of Sodom, he says of homosexual intercourse itself that it treated a man "as though his masculine identity counted for nothing, as though he were not a man but a woman. To penetrate another man was to treat him like an *assinnu*, like someone whose 'masculinity had been transformed into femininity'. Thus three elements (attempted penetration of males, attempted rape, inhospitality) and perhaps a fourth (unwitting, attempted sex with angels) combined to make this a particularly egregious example of human depravity that justifies God's act of total destruction."[16]

Secondly, Bailey argued that the rest of the Old Testament nowhere suggests that the nature of Sodom's offence was homosexual. Instead, Isaiah implies that it was hypocrisy and social injustice, Jeremiah adultery, deceit and general wickedness and Ezekiel arrogance, greed and indifference to the poor (Isaiah 1:10ff.; Jeremiah 23:14; Ezekiel 16:49ff.; cf. the references in the Apocrypha to pride in Ecclesiasticus 16:8 and to inhospitality in Wisdom 19:8). Then Jesus himself (though Bailey does not mention this) on three separate occasions alluded to the inhabitants of Sodom and Gomorrah, declaring that it would be "more bearable" for them on the day of judgement than for those who reject his gospel (Matthew 10:15; 11:24; Luke 10:12). Yet in all these references there is not even a whiff or rumour of homosexual malpractice. It is only when we reach the Palestinian pseudepigraphical writings of the second century BC that Sodom's sin is identified as unnatural sexual behaviour.[17] This finds a clear echo in the letter of Jude, in which it is said that "Sodom and Gomorrah and the surrounding towns gave themselves up to sexual immorality and perversion" (v. 7), and in the works of Philo and Josephus, Jewish writers who were shocked by the homosexual practices of Greek society.

Sherwin Bailey handled the Gibeah story in the same way, for they are closely parallel. Another resident alien (this time an anonymous "old man") invites two strangers (not angels, but a Levite and his concubine) into his home. Evil men surround the house and make the same demand as the Sodomites, that the visitor be brought out "so that we may know him". The owner of the house first begs them not to be so "vile" to his "guest", and then offers his daughter and the concubine to them instead. The sin of the men of Gibeah, it is again suggested, was not their proposal of homosexual intercourse but their violation of the laws of hospitality.

Although Bailey must have known that his reconstruction of both stories was at most tentative, he yet made the exaggerated claim that "there is not the least reason to believe, as a matter of either historical fact or of revealed truth, that the city of Sodom and its neighbours were destroyed because of their homosexual practices".[18] Instead, the Christian tradition about "sodomy" was derived from late, apocryphal Jewish sources.

But Sherwin Bailey's case is not convincing for a number of reasons:

- The adjectives "wicked", "vile" and "disgraceful" (Genesis 19:7; Judges 19:23) do not seem appropriate to describe a breach of hospitality.
- The offer of women instead "does look as if there is some sexual connotation to the episode".[19]
- Although the verb *yada'* is used only ten times of sexual intercourse, Bailey omits to mention that six of these occurrences are in Genesis and one in the Sodom story itself (about Lot's daughters, who had not "known" a man, v. 8).

- For those of us who take the New Testament documents seriously, Jude's unequivocal reference to the "sexual immorality and perversion" of Sodom and Gomorrah (v. 7) cannot be dismissed as merely an error copied from Jewish pseudepigrapha.

To be sure, homosexual behaviour was not Sodom's only sin, but according to Scripture it was certainly one of its sins, which brought down upon it the fearful judgement of God.

The Leviticus texts

Both texts in Leviticus belong to the "Holiness Code" which is the heart of the book and which challenges the people of God to follow his laws and not copy the practices either of Egypt (where they used to live) or of Canaan (to which he was bringing them). These practices included sexual relations within the prohibited degrees, a variety of sexual deviations, child sacrifice, idolatry and social injustice of different kinds. It is in this context that we must read the following two texts:

> Do not lie with a man as one lies with a woman; that is detestable. (Leviticus 18:22)

> If a man lies with a man as one lies with a woman, both of them have done what is detestable. They must be put to death; their blood will be on their own heads. (Leviticus 20:13)

"It is hardly open to doubt," wrote Bailey, "that both the laws in Leviticus relate to ordinary homosexual acts between men, and not to ritual or other acts performed in the name of religion."[20] Others, however, think differently. They point out that the two texts are embedded in a context preoccupied largely with ritual cleanness, and Peter Coleman adds that the word translated "detestable" or "abomination" in both verses is associated with idolatry. "In English the word expresses disgust or disapproval, but in the Bible its predominant meaning is concerned with religious truth rather than morality or aesthetics."[21] Are these prohibitions merely religious taboos, then? Are they connected with that other prohibition, "No Israelite man or woman is to become a temple prostitute" (Deuteronomy 23:17)? Certainly the Canaanite fertility cult did include ritual prostitution, and therefore provided both male and female "sacred prostitutes" (even if there is no clear evidence that either engaged in homosexual intercourse). The evil kings of Israel and Judah were constantly introducing them into the religion of Yahweh, and the righteous kings were constantly expelling them (see, e.g., 1 Kings 14:22ff.; 15:12; 22:46; 2 Kings 23:7).

The homosexual lobby argues, therefore, that the Levitical texts prohibit religious practices which have long since ceased, and have no relevance to same-sex partnerships today. The burden of proof is with them, however. As William J. Webb points out in his recent work on hermeneutics, the issue here is primarily one of sexual boundaries.[22] The incest laws protect the boundary between parent and child; the bestiality laws protect the boundary between human and animal. Similarly, the homosexual boundaries prohibit intercourse between members of the same sex. These boundaries are not cultural in that they change as Scripture develops, but transcultural, prohibiting such activities in any place at any time.

So the plain, natural interpretation of these two verses is that they prohibit homosexual intercourse of every kind. The requirement of the death penalty (long since abrogated, of course) indicates the extreme seriousness with which homosexual practices were viewed.

Paul's teaching in Romans 1

> Because of this, God gave them over to shameful lusts. Even their women exchanged natural relations for unnatural ones. In the same way the men also abandoned natural relations with women and were inflamed with lust for one another. Men committed indecent acts with other men, and received in themselves the due penalty for their perversion. (Romans 1:26 – 27)

All are agreed that the apostle is describing idolatrous pagans in the Graeco-Roman world of his day. They had a certain knowledge of God through the created universe (vv. 19 – 20) and their own moral sense (v. 32), yet they suppressed the truth they knew in order to practise wickedness. Instead of giving to God the honour due to him, they turned to idols, confusing the Creator with his creatures. In judgement upon them, "God gave them over" to their depraved mind and their decadent practices (vv. 24, 26, 28), including "unnatural" sex. Robert Gagnon says of this: "Quite appropriately, an absurd exchange of God for idols leads to an absurd exchange of heterosexual intercourse for homosexual intercourse. A dishonouring of God leads to a mutual dishonouring of selves. A failure to see fit to acknowledge God leads to an unfit mind and debased conduct."[23]

So the passage seems at first sight to be a definite condemnation of homosexual behaviour. But two arguments are advanced on the other side. Firstly, it is argued, Paul cannot be talking of people of homosexual orientation, since he says that their homosexual acts were "unnatural" and that they had previously had sex with women. But people of homosexual orientation would neither have had sex with the opposite sex, nor would homosexual sex be "unnatural" to them. Secondly, since Paul is evidently portraying the reckless and promiscuous behaviour of people whom God has judicially "given up", what relevance has this to committed, loving homosexual partnerships? These two arguments can be rebutted, however, especially by the apostle's reference to "nature", that is, the created order, as I hope to show later.

The other Pauline texts

> Do you not know that the wicked will not inherit the kingdom of God? Do not be deceived: Neither the sexually immoral nor idolaters nor adulterers nor male prostitutes [*malakoi*] nor homosexual offenders [*arsenokoitai*] nor thieves nor the greedy nor drunkards nor slanderers nor swindlers will inherit the kingdom of God. (1 Corinthians 6:9–10)

> We also know that law is made not for the righteous but for lawbreakers and rebels, the ungodly and sinful, the unholy and irreligious; for those who kill their fathers or mothers, for murderers, for adulterers and perverts [*arsenokoitai*], for slave traders and liars and perjurers – and for whatever else is contrary to the sound doctrine that conforms to the glorious gospel of the blessed God. (1 Timothy 1:9–10)

Here are two ugly lists of sins which Paul affirms to be incompatible in the first place with the kingdom of God and in the second place with either the law or the gospel. It will be observed that one group of offenders are called *malakoi* and the other (in both lists) *arsenokoitai*. What do these words mean? The point is that all ten categories listed in 1 Corinthians 6:9–10 (with the possible exception of "the greedy") denote people who have offended by their actions – for example, idolaters, adulterers and thieves.

The two Greek words *malakoi* and *arsenokoitai* should not be combined, however, since they "have precise meanings. The first is literally 'soft to the touch' and metaphorically, among the Greeks, meant males (not necessarily boys) who played the passive role in homosexual intercourse. The second means literally 'male in a bed', and the Greeks used this expression to describe the one who took the active role."[24] Robert Gagnon translates *malakoi* as "the soft ones" and *arsenokoitai* as "males who take other males to bed".[25] The Jerusalem Bible follows James Moffatt in using the ugly words "catamites and sodomites", while among his conclusions Peter Coleman suggests that "probably Paul had commercial paederasty in mind between older men and post-pubertal boys, the most common pattern of homosexual behaviour in the classical world".[26] If this is so, then once again it can be (and has been) argued that the Pauline condemnations are not relevant to homosexual adults who are both consenting and committed to one another. This is not, however, the conclusion which Peter Coleman himself draws. His summary is as follows: "Taken together, St Paul's writings repudiate homosexual behaviour as a vice of the Gentiles in Romans, as a bar to the Kingdom in Corinthians, and as an offence to be repudiated by the moral law in 1 Timothy."[27]

Reviewing these biblical references to homosexual behaviour, which I have grouped, we have to agree that there are only four of them. Must we then conclude that the topic is marginal to the main thrust of the Bible? Must we further concede that they constitute a rather flimsy basis on which to take a firm stand against a homosexual lifestyle? Are those protagonists right who claim that the biblical prohibitions are "highly specific"[28] – against violations of hospitality (Sodom and Gibeah), against cultic taboos (Leviticus), against shameless orgies (Romans) and against male prostitution or the corruption of the young (1 Corinthians and 1 Timothy), and that none of these passages alludes to, let alone condemns, a loving partnership between people of homosexual orientation?

But no, plausible as it may sound, we cannot handle the biblical material in this way. The Christian rejection of homosexual practices does not rest on "a few isolated and obscure proof texts" (as is sometimes said), whose traditional explanation (it is further claimed) can be overthrown. The negative prohibitions of homosexual practices in Scripture make sense only in the light of its positive teaching in Genesis 1 and 2 about human sexuality and heterosexual marriage.[29] Yet without the wholesome positive teaching of the Bible on sex and marriage, our perspective on the homosexual question is bound to be skewed.

SEXUALITY AND MARRIAGE IN THE BIBLE

The essential place to begin our investigation, it seems to me, is the institution of marriage in Genesis 2. I have devoted a chapter of this book to marriage and readers may wish to refer to that as well. Since members of the Lesbian and Gay Christian Movement deliberately draw a parallel between heterosexual marriages and homosexual partnerships, it is necessary to ask whether this parallel can be justified.

We have seen that in his providence God has given us two distinct accounts of creation. The first (Genesis 1) is general, and affirms the equality of the sexes, since both share in the image of God and the stewardship of the earth. The second (Genesis 2) is particular, and affirms the complementarity of the sexes, which constitutes the basis for heterosexual marriage. In this second account of creation three fundamental truths emerge.

Heterosexual gender: a divine creation

Firstly, the human need for companionship. "It is not good for the man to be alone" (Genesis 2:18). True, this assertion was later qualified when the apostle Paul (surely echoing Genesis) wrote: "It is good for a man not to marry" (1 Corinthians 7:1). That is to say, although marriage is the good institution of God, the call to singleness is also the good vocation of some. Nevertheless, as a general rule, "It is not good for the man to be alone." God has created us social beings. Since he is love, and has made us in his own likeness, he has given us a capacity to love and be loved. He intends us to live in community, not in solitude. In particular, God continued, "I will make a helper suitable for him." Moreover, this "helper" or companion, whom God pronounced "suitable for him", was also to be his sexual partner, with whom he was to become "one flesh", so that they might thereby both consummate their love and procreate their children.

Heterosexual marriage: a divine institution

Having affirmed Adam's need for a partner, the search for a suitable one began. The animals not being suitable as equal partners, a special work of divine creation took place. The sexes became differentiated. Out of the undifferentiated humanity of Adam, male and female emerged. Adam found a reflection of himself, a complement to himself, indeed a very part of himself. Having created the woman out of the man, God brought her to him, much as today the bride's father gives her away. And Adam broke spontaneously into history's first love poem, saying that now at last there stood before him a creature of such beauty in herself and similarity to him that she appeared to be (as indeed she was) "made for him":

> This is now bone of my bones
> and flesh of my flesh;
> she shall be called "woman",
> for she was taken out of man.
>
> GENESIS 2:23

There can be no doubting the emphasis of this story. According to Genesis 1, Eve, like Adam, was created in the image of God. But as to the manner of her creation, according to Genesis 2, she was made neither out of nothing (like the universe), nor out of "the dust of the ground" (like Adam, v. 7), but out of Adam.

Heterosexual fidelity: the divine intention

The third great truth of Genesis 2 concerns the resulting institution of marriage. Adam's love poem is recorded in verse 23. The "therefore" or "for this reason" of verse 24 is the narrator's deduction: "For this reason a man will leave his father and mother and be united to his wife, and they will become one flesh."

Even the inattentive reader will be struck by the three references to "flesh": "This is ... flesh of my flesh ... they will become one flesh". We may be certain that this is deliberate, not accidental. It teaches that heterosexual intercourse in marriage is more than a union; it is a kind of reunion. It is not a union of alien persons who do not belong to one another and cannot appropriately become one flesh. On the contrary, it is the union of two persons who originally were one, were then separated from each other, and now in the sexual encounter of marriage come together again.

Heterosexual intercourse is much more than a union of bodies; it is a blending of complementary personalities through which the rich created oneness of human beings is experienced again. The complementarity of male and female sexual organs is only a symbol at the physical level of a much deeper spiritual complementarity.

In order to become one flesh, however, and experience this sacred mystery, certain preliminaries are necessary, which are constituent parts of marriage. "Therefore" (v. 24),

> "a man" (the singular indicates that marriage is an exclusive union between two individuals)
>
> "shall leave his father and mother" (a public social occasion is in view)
>
> "and cleave to his wife" (marriage is a loving, cleaving commitment or covenant, which is heterosexual and permanent)
>
> "and they will become one flesh" (for marriage must be consummated in sexual intercourse, which is a sign and seal of the marriage covenant, and over which no shadow of shame or embarrassment had yet been cast). (v. 25)

It is of the utmost importance to note that Jesus himself later endorsed this Old Testament definition of marriage. In doing so, he both introduced it with words from Genesis 1:27 (that the Creator "made them male and female") and concluded it with his own comment ("so they are no longer two, but one. Therefore what God has joined together, let man not separate", Matthew 19:6). Here, then, are three truths which Jesus affirmed: (1) heterosexual gender is a divine creation; (2) heterosexual marriage is a divine institution; and (3) heterosexual fidelity is the divine intention. A homosexual liaison is a breach of all three of these divine purposes.

The late Michael Vasey's book *Strangers and Friends*[30] attempts to combine evangelical faith with homosexual advocacy. In doing so he sees Genesis 2:24 as having been used to impose on Scripture the domestic ideals of the nuclear family with its "idolatry" and "self-centredness".[31] Jesus, he says, renounces marriage as part of the present world order in favour of "Christian freedom". With the family denounced as oppressive, the way is open for homosexual partnerships as another, even a better, option.

Yet he has twisted the biblical material to suit his purpose. Neither Jesus' own singleness, nor his teaching that singleness is a divine vocation for some (Matthew 19:11 – 12), may be taken as evidence that he opposed marriage and family, for they belong to the created order. Nor is the family envisaged in Genesis 1 and 2 "nuclear" in a negative or selfish sense. To be sure, Jesus did inaugurate a new order, refer to his new community as his family (Mark 3:34), and warn that if an unavoidable conflict arises between our loyalty to him and our loyalty to our natural family, then our loyalty to him takes precedence (Matthew 10:37; Luke 14:26). But Jesus and his apostles also insisted that Christians have a continuing obligation to their natural family, including reciprocal duties between parents and children, and between husbands and wives (e.g., Mark 7:9 – 13; Ephesians 5:22 – 6:4). The new creation restores and redeems the old; it does not reject or replace it. As for idols, every good gift of God can become an idol, including marriage and family; but in themselves neither is idolatrous or enslaving. A homosexual partnership, however, is essentially incompatible with marriage as the God-ordained context for one-flesh intimacy.

Thus Scripture defines the marriage God instituted in terms of heterosexual monogamy. It is the union of one man with one woman, which must be publicly acknowledged (the leaving of parents), permanently sealed (he will "cleave to his wife") and physically consummated ("one flesh"). And Scripture envisages no other kind of marriage or sexual intercourse, for God provided no alternative.

Christians should not therefore single out homosexual intercourse for special condemnation. The fact is that every kind of sexual relationship and activity which deviates from God's revealed intention is ipso facto displeasing to him and under his judgement. This includes polygamy and polyandry (which infringe the "one man, one woman" principle), cohabitation and clandestine unions (since these have involved no decisive public leaving of parents), casual encounters and temporary liaisons, adultery and many divorces (which conflict with "cleaving" and with Jesus' prohibition "let man not separate"), and homosexual partnerships (which violate the statement that "a man" shall be joined to "his wife").

In sum, the only "one flesh" experience which God intends and Scripture contemplates is the sexual union of a man with his wife, whom he recognizes as "flesh of his flesh". As George Carey, then Archbishop of Canterbury, said in an address at Virginia Theological Seminary on 10 February 1997, "I do not find any justification, from the Bible or from the entire Christian tradition, for sexual activity outside marriage."

CONTEMPORARY ARGUMENTS CONSIDERED

Homosexual Christians are not, however, satisfied with this biblical teaching about human sexuality and the institution of heterosexual marriage. They bring forward a number of objections to it, in order to defend the legitimacy of homosexual partnerships.

The argument about Scripture and culture

Traditionally, it has been assumed that the Bible condemns all homosexual acts. But are the biblical writers reliable guides in this matter? Were their horizons not bounded by their own experience and culture? The cultural argument usually takes one of two forms.

Firstly, the biblical authors were addressing themselves to questions relevant to their own circumstances, but these were very different from ours. In the Sodom and Gibeah stories they were preoccupied either with conventions of hospitality in the ancient Near East which are now obsolete or (if the sin was sexual at all) with the extremely unusual phenomenon of homosexual gang rape. In the Levitical laws the concern was with antiquated fertility rituals, while Paul was addressing himself to the particular sexual preferences of Greek pederasts. It is all so antiquarian. The biblical authors' imprisonment in their own cultures renders their teaching on this topic irrelevant.

The second and complementary culture problem is that the biblical writers were not addressing themselves to our questions. Thus the problem of Scripture is not only with its teaching but also with its silence. Paul (let alone the Old Testament authors) knew nothing of post-Freudian psychology. They had never heard of "homosexual orientation"; they knew only about certain practices. The very notion that two men or two women could fall in love with each other and develop a deeply loving, stable relationship comparable to marriage simply never entered their heads.

If the only biblical teaching on this topic were to be found in the prohibition texts, it might be difficult to answer these objections. But once those texts are seen in relation to the divine institution of marriage, we are in possession of a principle of divine revelation which is universally applicable. It was applicable to the cultural situations of both the ancient Near East and the first-century Graeco-Roman world, and it is equally applicable to modern sexual questions of which the ancients were quite ignorant. The reason for the biblical prohibitions is the same reason why modern loving homosexual partnerships must also be condemned, namely that they are incompatible with God's created order. And since that order (heterosexual monogamy) was established by creation, not culture, its validity is both permanent and universal. There can be no "liberation" from God's created norms; true liberation is found only in accepting them.

This argumentation is the opposite of the "biblical literalism" of which the gay lobby tend to accuse us. It is rather to look beneath the surface of the biblical prohibitions to the essential positives of divine revelation on sexuality and marriage. It is significant that those who are advocating same-sex partnerships usually omit Genesis 1 and 2 from their discussion, even though Jesus our Lord himself endorsed their teaching. It is now important to look at gay relationships and their social context in a little more depth, and to consider the arguments used to support committed gay relationships.

The argument about creation and nature

People sometimes make this kind of statement: "I'm gay because God made me that way. So gay must be good. I cannot believe that God would create people homosexual and then deny them the right to sexual self-expression. I intend, therefore, to affirm, and indeed celebrate, what I am by creation." Or again, "You may say that homosexual practice is against nature and normality; but it's not against my nature, nor is it in the slightest degree abnormal for me." Norman Pittenger was quite outspoken in his use of this argument. A homosexual person, he wrote, is "not an 'abnormal' person with 'unnatural' desires and habits." On the contrary, "A heterosexually oriented person acts 'naturally' when he acts heterosexually, while a homosexually oriented person acts equally 'naturally' when he acts in accordance with his basic, inbuilt homosexual desire and drive."[32]

Others argue that homosexual behaviour is "natural", (a) because in many primitive societies it is fairly acceptable, (b) because in some advanced civilizations (e.g., ancient Greece) it was even idealized, and (c) because it is said to be quite widespread in animals: a matter still the subject of intense debate among zoologists.[33]

In any case, these arguments express an extremely subjective view of what is "natural" and "normal". We should not accept Norman Pittenger's statement that there are "no eternal standards of normality or naturalness".[34] Nor can we agree that animal behaviour sets standards for human behaviour! God has established a norm for sex and marriage by creation. This was already recognized in the Old Testament era. Thus sexual relations with an animal were forbidden, because "that is a perversion" (Leviticus 18:23), in other words a violation or confusion of nature, which indicates an "embryonic sense of natural law".[35] The same verdict is passed on Sodom by the second-century BC Testament of Naphtali: "As the sun and the stars do not change their order, so the tribe of Naphtali are to obey God rather than the disorderliness of idolatry. Recognizing in all created things the Lord who made them, they are not to become as Sodom which changed the order of nature..."[36]

The same concept was clearly in Paul's mind in Romans 1. When he wrote of women who had "exchanged natural relations for unnatural ones", and of men who had "abandoned natural relations", he meant by "nature" (physis) the natural order of things which God has established (as in 2:14, 27; 11:24). What Paul was condemning, therefore, was not the perverted behaviour of heterosexual people who were acting against their nature, as John Boswell argued,[37] but any human behaviour that is against "Nature" – that is, against God's created order. Richard B. Hays has written a thorough rebuttal of John Boswell's exegesis of Romans 1. He provides ample contemporary evidence that the opposition of "natural" (kata physin) and "unnatural" (para physin) was "very frequently used ... as a way of distinguishing between heterosexual and homosexual behaviour".[38]

British commentators on Romans 1 confirm his conclusion. As C. K. Barrett puts it: "In the obscene pleasures to which he [Paul] refers is to be seen precisely that perversion of the created order which may be expected when men put the creation in place of the Creator."[39] Similarly, Charles Cranfield writes that by "natural" and "unnatural", "Paul clearly means 'in accordance with the intention of the Creator' and 'contrary to the intention of the Creator', respectively." Again, "The decisive factor in Paul's use of it [physis, "nature"] is his biblical doctrine of creation. It denotes that order which is manifest in God's creation and which men have no excuse for failing to recognize and respect."[40] Robert Gagnon states that "same-sex intercourse is 'beyond' or 'in excess of' nature in the sense that it transgresses the boundaries for sexuality both established by God and transparent in nature even to Gentiles".[41]

An appeal to the created order should also be our response to another argument. Some point out that the early church distinguished between primary and secondary issues, insisting on agreement about the former but allowing freedom to disagree about the latter. The two examples of Christian liberty which they usually quote are circumcision and idol-meats. They then draw a parallel with homosexual practice, suggesting that it is a second-order issue in which we can give one another freedom. But actually the early church was more subtle than that. The Jerusalem Council (Acts 15) decreed that circumcision was definitely not necessary for salvation (a first-order question), but allowed its continuance as a matter of policy or culture (second-order). The Council also decided that, although of course idolatry was forbidden (first-order), eating idol-meats was not necessarily idolatrous, so that Christians with a strong, educated conscience might eat them (second-order). Thus the second-order issues, in which Christian liberty was allowed, were neither theological nor moral but cultural. This is not the case with homosexual practice.

A second parallel is sometimes drawn. When the debate over women's ordination was at its height, General Synod agreed that the church should not be obliged to choose between the two positions (for and against), declaring one to be right and the other wrong, but should rather preserve unity by recognizing both to have integrity. In consequence, we are living with "the two integrities". Why, it is asked, should we not equally acknowledge "two integrities" in relation to same-sex partnerships, and not force people to choose? The answer should be clear. Even if women's ordination is a second-order issue (which many would deny), homosexual partnerships are not. Gender in relation to marriage is a much more fundamental matter than gender in relation to ministry. Marriage has been recognized as a heterosexual union from the beginning of God's creation and institution; it is basic to human society as God intended it, and its biblical basis is incontrovertible. Dr Wolfhart Pannenberg, professor of theology at Munich University, is outspoken on this subject. Having declared that "the biblical assessments of homosexual practice are unambiguous in their rejection", he concludes that a church which were to recognize homosexual unions as equivalent to marriage "would cease to be the one, holy, catholic and apostolic church".[42]

The argument about quality of relationships

The Lesbian and Gay Christian Movement borrows from Scripture the truth that love is the greatest thing in the world (which it is) and from the "new morality" or "situation ethics" of the 1960s the notion that love is an adequate criterion by which to judge every relationship (which it is not). Yet this view is gaining ground today. One of the first official documents to embrace it was the Friends' Report *Towards a Quaker View of Sex* (1963). It included the statements, "One should no more deplore 'homosexuality' than lefthandedness,"[43] and, "Surely it is the nature and quality of a relationship that matters."[44] Similarly, in 1979 the Methodist Church's Division of Social Responsibility, in its report *A Christian*

Understanding of Human Sexuality, argued that "homosexual activities" are "not intrinsically wrong", since "the quality of any homosexual relationship is ... to be assessed by the same basic criteria which have been applied to heterosexual relationships. For homosexual men and women, permanent relationships characterized by love can be an appropriate Christian way of expressing their sexuality."[45] The same year (1979) an Anglican working party issued the report *Homosexual Relationships, A contribution to discussion*. It was more cautious, judicious and ambivalent than the Quaker and Methodist reports. Its authors did not feel able to repudiate centuries of Christian tradition, yet they "did not think it possible to deny" that in some circumstances individuals may "justifiably choose" a homosexual relationship in their search for companionship and sexual love "similar" to those found in marriage.[46] Surely any relationship characterized by mutual commitment, affection, faithfulness and support should be affirmed as good, not rejected as evil? It rescues people from loneliness, selfishness and promiscuity, and it can be just as rich and responsible, as liberating and fulfilling, as a heterosexual marriage.

In the spring of 1997, in a lecture delivered at St Martin-in-the-Fields in London, Bishop John Austin Baker gave his own version of this argument. Formerly Bishop of Salisbury, chairman of the Church of England's Doctrine Commission, and chairman of the drafting group which produced the moderate report *Issues in Human Sexuality* (1991), he astonished the church by his apparent volte-face. The goal of Christian discipleship, he rightly affirmed, is "Christlikeness" – that is, "a creative living out of the values, priorities and attitudes that marked his humanity", especially of love. Now sex in marriage can be "a true making of love", and "erotic love can and often does have the same beneficial effects in the life of same-sex couples". There are three reasons, however, why this claim for the quality of same-sex love is flawed.

Exclusive relationships are rare

Firstly, the concept of lifelong, quasi-marital fidelity in homosexual partnerships is largely a myth, a theoretical ideal which is contradicted by the facts. The truth is that gay relationships are characterized more by promiscuity than by fidelity. The National Gay Men's Sex Survey 2001, a large UK study of over 14,600 respondents, found that 73% of gay men surveyed had more than one sexual partner during the last year.[47] This compares with 30% of heterosexual men.[48] Thomas Schmidt has commented: "Promiscuity among homosexual men is not a mere stereotype, and it is not merely the majority experience – it is virtually the only experience ... In short, there is practically no comparison possible to heterosexual marriage in terms of either fidelity or longevity. Tragically, lifelong faithfulness is almost non-existent in the homosexual experience."[49] "Non-exclusive relationships are, for many men, simply more fulfilling than monogamous ones," reports SIGMA, a leading research organization examining homosexual practice and AIDS.[50] There seems to be something inherently unstable about homosexual partnerships. The quality of relationships argument does not hold water.

Gay sex can be damaging

I have written at length about AIDS in the chapter about "Global Poverty" (chapter 6), since AIDS is a global phenomenon and frequently associated with poverty. So I will confine my remarks here to the gay community and especially the practices of gay men. It is the sexual practices of gay men which make them an especially high-risk group.

It is difficult to maintain that homosexual partnerships are just as much an expression of love as heterosexual marriages in light of the known damage and danger involved in gay sexual practices. Both the degree of promiscuity and the nature of the practice mean that gay men are at risk of contracting all kinds of STDs and especially AIDS, as well as hepatitis, rectal cancer, non-viral and viral infections and a decrease in life expectancy. It is true that some diseases can also be transmitted by similar activity between heterosexual people, but "these health problems are rampant in the homosexual population because they are easily spread by promiscuity and by most of the practices favoured by homosexuals".[51] If these physical dangers attend common gay sexual activities, can authentic lovers engage in them?

Nor can these dangers be avoided merely by the use of a condom, which is known to be an unreliable contraceptive. Two comments I have already referred to are worth repeating here. Dr Patrick Dixon, founder of ACET (AIDS Care, Education and Training), sums the matter up like this: "Condoms do not make sex safe, they simply make it safer. Safe sex is sex between two partners who are not infected! This means a lifelong, faithful partnership between two people who were virgins and who now remain faithful to each other for life."[52] Or, to quote from the United States Catholic Conference, "Abstinence outside of marriage and fidelity within marriage, as well as the avoidance of intravenous drug abuse, are the only morally correct and medically sure ways to prevent the spread of AIDS."[53]

The gay community has been decimated in some areas by the advent of AIDS. In the early 1980s AIDS was called "the gay plague" precisely because it seemed to hit the gay community hardest. Now we know that AIDS can affect any person, whether male or female, heterosexual or homosexual, adult or child. It is not confined to any one country but is now a global pandemic which Nelson Mandela has called a "global emergency". Transmitted most often by sexual intercourse or by intravenous drug use (with contaminated needles), it is incurable, though modern drugs can delay the onset of death by ten years or more. But eventually, HIV will become full-blown AIDS, manifesting itself by attacking and damaging the body's immune and nervous systems, and so making it defenceless against certain fatal diseases.

The incidence of AIDS remains high in the gay community. According to UNAIDS, "taken world-wide, 5 – 10% of all HIV cases are due to sexual transmission between men. In parts of the world, including North America, parts of Latin America, most of Europe, Australia and New Zealand, sex between men is the main route in the transmission of HIV, being responsible for up to 70% of HIV cases in these areas. Elsewhere, it is a secondary route. In all countries though, the likely extent of male-to-male sex is probably underestimated."[54] The greatest risk comes from the practice of anal sex, due to the fact that tears can occur and small lesions can exist through which the virus has easy access. The presence of other STDs can also magnify the risk of HIV transmission. HIV can be transmitted through other sexual acts, including oral sex, but the incidence is much lower. In many parts of the world sex between men is hidden and difficult to measure, because it is illegal and therefore secretive. Its presence is, therefore, often underestimated.

Within the community of those who study HIV/AIDS, the designation "MSM" has come to be used, which refers to "men who have sex with men". This is a recognition that it is not the sexual identity or inclination of men which is of primary importance in the discussion of AIDS, but the sexual practice itself. It is acknowledged that some MSM may be heterosexual men who either wish to have a casual encounter with another man or cannot "come out" as gay men because of the culture in which they live.

In the US, the estimated number of deaths of persons with AIDS from 1998 to 2002 was 501,669. Of these, half were men who had sex with men.[55] Incidence in this group has been gradually declining not, according to *The American Journal of Public Health*, because of behavioural change, but because of the increased effectiveness of antiretroviral therapy.[56] Approximately 40,000 new

HIV infections occur each year in the US, about 70% among men and 30% among women.[57] Of these newly infected people, half are younger than twenty-five years of age.[58] Of new infections among men in the US, the Centre for Disease Control estimates that approximately 60% of men were infected through homosexual sex.

Our response to HIV/AIDS must be theological, pastoral and educational. I have outlined this response in more detail in chapter 6, so I will make only a few brief (and indeed, similar) points here. Firstly, our response needs to be theological. We need to remind ourselves that we reap what we sow. Though AIDS may not be God's judgement on an individual, Christians cannot regard it as an accident. There is, as I have said in chapter 6, a process of cause and effect at work in our world, both morally and physically, which means that we reap what we sow. If we perpetually reject God's ways, we can, for instance, sear our conscience so that we become less sensitive to its entreaties. Physically we must live with the consequences of our actions. If we are pomiscuous, we risk getting STDs, if we are gluttons, then we risk getting heart disease or diabetes. There are consequences to be faced for our actions. So although we may not be able to say that HIV/AIDS is God's judgement on any particular individual, we can say that if a society tolerates wrongdoing and even celebrates it by calling 'evil good and good evil' then it must face up to the consequences of doing so (Romans 1:18 – 32). Judgement is already at work in this world (John 3:18 – 21; 5:24 – 29).

Secondly, our response must be pastoral. "Don't judge me," an American AIDS patient called Jerome said. "I'm living under my own judgement. What I need is for you to walk with me."[59] Local churches need specially to reach out to AIDS sufferers in their own fellowship and in their wider community. We may be thankful that both the origins of the hospice movement and its extension from terminal cancer patients to those living with AIDS have been due largely, though not solely, to Christian initiatives.[60]

Thirdly, our response must be educational. Christians are likely to prefer a thoroughgoing educational programme as the most human and Christian way to combat ignorance, prejudice, fear and promiscuous behaviour, and so turn back the AIDS tide. Certainly the current complacency and indifference, which are helping to spread the disease, can be overcome only by the relentless force of the facts. In such a preventive education programme the churches should have a major role. Is it not the failure of the churches to teach and exemplify God's standards of sexual morality which, more than anything else, is to blame for the current crisis?[61] We must not fail again, but rather challenge society to sexual self-control and faithfulness, and point to Jesus as the source of forgiveness and power. Several Christian groups have been set up to alert the churches to their responsibilities, to provide educational resources and to encourage support groups.[62]

Above all, "The AIDS crisis challenges us profoundly to be the Church in deed and in truth: to be the Church as a healing community". Indeed, because of our tendency to self-righteousness, "the healing community itself will need to be healed by the forgiveness of Christ".[63]

Love needs the law

If the first reason why Christians cannot accept the quality of love argument is that exclusivity is rare, and the second reason is that gay sex can be damaging, the third is that love needs the law. Christians cannot accept the idea that love is the only absolute, because love needs law to guide it. The moral law has not been abolished. In emphasizing love for God and neighbour as the two great commandments, Jesus and his apostles did not discard all other commandments. On the contrary, Jesus said, "If you love me you will keep my commandments," and Paul wrote, "Love is the fulfilling [not the abrogating] of the law" (John 14:15; Romans 13:8 – 10).

So then, although the loving quality of a relationship is an essential, it is not by itself a sufficient criterion to authenticate it. For example, if love were the only test of authenticity, there would be nothing against polygamy, for a polygamist could certainly enjoy a relationship with several wives. Or let me give you a better illustration, drawn from my own pastoral experience. On several different occasions a married man has told me that he has fallen in love with another woman. When I have gently remonstrated with him, he has responded in words like these: "Yes, I agree, I already have a wife and family. But this new relationship is the real thing. We were made for each other. Our love for each other has a quality and depth we have never known before. It must be right." But no, I have had to say to him, it is not right. No man is justified in breaking his marriage covenant with his wife on the ground that the quality of his love for another woman is richer. Quality of love is not the only yardstick by which to measure what is good or right.

Similarly, we should not deny that homosexual relationships can be loving (although a priori they cannot attain the same richness as the heterosexual complementarity which God has ordained). As the 1994 Ramsey Colloquium put it, "Even a distorted love retains traces of love's grandeur." [64] But the love quality of gay relationships is not sufficient to justify them. Indeed, I have to add that they are incompatible with true love because they are incompatible with God's law. Love is concerned for the highest welfare of the beloved. And our highest human welfare is found in obedience to God's law and purpose, not in revolt against them.

Some leaders of the Lesbian and Gay Christian Movement appear to be following the logic of their own position, for they are saying that even monogamy could be abandoned in the interests of "love". Malcolm Macourt, for example, has written that the Gay Liberationist's vision is of "a wide variety of life patterns", each of which is "held in equal esteem in society". Among them he lists the following alternatives: monogamy and multiple partnerships; partnerships for life and partnerships for a period of mutual growth; same-sex partners and opposite-sex partners; living in community and living in small family units.[65] There seem to be no limits to what some people seek to justify in the name of love.

The argument about justice and rights

If some argue for homosexual partnerships on the basis of the love involved, others do so on the basis of justice. Desmond Tutu, for example, formerly Archbishop of Cape Town and universally admired for his courageous stand against apartheid and for racial equality, has several times said that for him the homosexual question is a simple matter of justice. Others agree. The justice argument runs like this: "Just as we may not discriminate between persons on account of their gender, colour, ethnicity or class, so we may not discriminate between persons on account of their sexual preference. For the God of the Bible is the God of justice, who is described as loving justice and hating injustice. Therefore the quest for justice must be a paramount obligation of the people of God. Now that slaves, women and blacks have been liberated, gay liberation is long overdue. What civil rights activists were in the 1950s and 60s, gay rights activists are today. We should support them in their cause and join them in their struggle."

The vocabulary of oppression, liberation, rights and justice, however, needs careful definition. "Gay liberation" presupposes an oppression from which homosexual people need to be set free, and "gay rights" imply that homosexual people are suffering a wrong which should be righted. But what is this oppression, this wrong, this injustice? If it is that they are being despised and rejected by sections of society on account of their sexual orientation, and are in fact victims of homophobia, then indeed they have a grievance which must be redressed. God opposes such discrimination and requires us to love and respect all human beings without distinction. If, on the other hand, the "wrong" or "injustice" complained of is society's refusal to recognize homosexual partnerships as a legitimate alternative to heterosexual marriages, then talk of "justice" is inappropriate, since human beings may not claim as a "right" what God has not given them.

The analogy between slavery, racism, the oppression of women and homosexuality is inexact and misleading. In each case we need to clarify the Creator's original intention. Thus, in spite of misguided attempts to justify slavery and racism from Scripture, both are fundamentally incompatible with the created equality of human beings. Similarly, the Bible honours womanhood by affirming that men and women share equally in the image of God and the stewardship of the environment, and its teaching on masculine "headship" or responsibility may not be interpreted as contradicting this equality. But sexual intercourse belongs, according to the plain teaching of Scripture, to heterosexual marriage alone. Therefore, homosexual intercourse cannot be regarded as a permissible equivalent, let alone a divine right. True gay liberation (like all authentic liberation) is not freedom from God's revealed purpose in order to construct our own morality; it is rather freedom from our self-willed rebellion in order to love and obey him.

The argument about acceptance and the gospel

"Surely," some people are saying, "it is the duty of heterosexual Christians to accept homosexual Christians. Paul told us to accept – indeed welcome – one another. If God has welcomed somebody, who are we to pass judgement on him (Romans 14:1ff.; 15:7)?" Norman Pittenger says, "The whole point of the Christian gospel is that God loves and accepts us just as we are." [66]

This is a very confused statement of the gospel, however. God does indeed accept us "just as we are", and we do not have to make ourselves good first; indeed we cannot. But his "acceptance" means that he fully and freely forgives all who repent and believe, not that he condones our continuance in sin. Again, it is true that we must accept one another, but only as fellow penitents and fellow pilgrims, not as fellow sinners who are resolved to persist in our sinning.

Michael Vasey makes much of the fact that Jesus was called (and was) "the friend of sinners". His offer of friendship to sinners like us is truly wonderful. But he welcomes us in order to redeem and transform us, not to leave us alone in our sins. No acceptance, either by God or by the church, is promised to us if we harden our hearts against God's Word and will. Only judgement.

FAITH, HOPE AND LOVE

If homosexual practice must be regarded, in the light of the whole biblical revelation, not as a variant within the wide range of accepted normality, but as a deviation from God's norm; and if we should therefore call homosexually inclined people to abstain from homosexual practices and partnerships, what advice and help can we give to encourage them to respond to this call? I would like to take Paul's triad of faith, hope and love, and apply it to homosexually inclined people.

The Christian call to faith

Faith is our human response to divine revelation: it is believing God's Word.

Firstly, faith accepts God's standards. The only alternative to heterosexual marriage is singleness and sexual abstinence. I think I know the implications of this. Nothing has helped me to understand the pain of homosexual celibacy more than Alex Davidson's moving book *The Returns of Love*. He writes of "this incessant tension between law and lust", "this monster that lurks in the depths", this "burning torment".[67]

The secular world says, "Sex is essential to human fulfilment. To expect homosexual people to abstain from homosexual practice is to condemn them to frustration and to drive them to neurosis, despair and even suicide. It's outrageous to ask them to deny themselves what to them is a normal and natural mode of sexual expression. It's 'inhuman and inhumane'.[68] Indeed, it's positively cruel."

But no, the teaching of the Word of God is different. Sexual experience is not essential to human fulfilment. To be sure, it is a good gift of God, but it is not given to all, and it is not indispensable to humanness. People were saying in Paul's day that it was. Their slogan was, "Food for the stomach and the stomach for food; sex for the body and the body for sex" (see 1 Corinthians 6:13). But this is a lie of the Devil. Jesus Christ was single, yet perfect in his humanity.

So it is possible to be single and human at the same time! Besides, God's commands are good and not grievous. The yoke of Christ brings rest, not turmoil; conflict comes only to those who resist it.

At the very centre of Christian discipleship is our participation in the death and resurrection of Jesus Christ. The St Andrew's Day Statement on the homosexuality debate (1995), commissioned by the Church of England Evangelical Council, emphasized this. We are "called to follow in the way of the cross", for "we all are summoned to various forms of self-denial. The struggle against disordered desires, or the misdirection of innocent desire, is part of every Christian's life, consciously undertaken in baptism." But after struggle comes victory, out of death resurrection.[69]

So ultimately it is a crisis of faith: whom shall we believe? God or the world? Shall we submit to the lordship of Jesus, or succumb to the pressures of prevailing culture? The true "orientation" of Christians is not what we are by constitution (hormones), but what we are by choice (heart, mind and will).

Secondly, faith accepts God's grace. Abstinence is not only good, if God calls us to celibacy; it is also possible. Many deny it, however. "You know the imperious strength of our sex drive," they say. "To ask us to control ourselves is just not on." It is "so near to an impossibility", writes Norman Pittenger, "that it's hardly worth talking about".[70]

Really? What, then, are we to make of Paul's statement following his warning to the Corinthians that male prostitutes and homosexual offenders will not inherit God's kingdom? "And that is what some of you were," he cries. "But you were washed, you were sanctified, you were justified in the name of the Lord Jesus Christ and by the Spirit of our God" (1 Corinthians 6:11). And what shall we say to the millions of heterosexual people who are single? To be sure, all unmarried people experience the pain of struggle and loneliness. But how can we call ourselves Christians and declare that chastity is impossible? It is made harder by the sexual obsession of contemporary society. And we make it harder for ourselves if we listen to the world's plausible arguments, or lapse into self-pity, or feed our imagination with pornographic material and so inhabit a fantasy world in which Christ is not Lord, or ignore his command about plucking out our eyes and cutting off our hands and feet – that is, being ruthless with the avenues of temptation. But, whatever our "thorn in the flesh" may be, Christ comes to us as he came to Paul and says, "My grace is sufficient for you, for my power is made perfect in weakness" (2 Corinthians 12:9). To deny this is to portray Christians as the helpless victims of the world, the flesh and the Devil, to demean them into being less than human, and to contradict the gospel of God's grace.

The Christian call to hope

I have said nothing so far about "healing" for homosexual people, understood not now as self-mastery but as the reversal of their sexual orientation. Our expectation of this possibility will depend largely on our understanding of the aetiology of the homosexual condition, and no final agreement on this has yet been reached. Many studies have been conducted, but they have failed to establish a single cause, whether inherited or learned. So scholars have tended to turn to theories of multiple causation, combining a biological predisposition (genetic and hormonal) with cultural and moral influences, childhood environment and experience and repeatedly reinforced personal choices. Dr Jeffrey Satinover concludes his investigation with an appeal to common sense: "One's character traits are in part innate, but are subject to modification by experience and choice." [71] So, if homosexuality is at least partly learned, can it be unlearned?

Just as opinions differ on the causes of homosexuality, so they also differ on the possibilities and the means of "cure". This issue divides people into three categories – those who consider healing unnecessary, and those who consider it either possible or impossible.

Firstly, we have to recognize that many homosexual people categorically reject the language of "cure" and "healing". They see no need, and they have no wish to change. Their position has been summed up in three convictions. Biologically their condition is innate (being inherited), psychologically it is irreversible and sociologically it is normal. [72] They regard it as a great victory that in 1973 the trustees of the American Psychiatric Association removed homosexuality from its official list of mental illnesses. Michael Vasey declares that this decision was not the result of some "liberal" conspiracy. [73] But that is exactly what it was. Seventy years of psychiatric opinion were overthrown not by science (for no fresh evidence was produced) but by politics. [74] At least the Roman Catholic Church was neither impressed nor convinced. The American bishops, in their 1986 Pastoral Letter, continued to describe homosexuality as "intrinsically disordered" (para. 3).

Secondly, there are those who regard "healing", understood as the reversal of sexual orientation, as impossible. "No known method of treatment or punishment," writes D. J. West, "offers hope of making any substantial reduction in the vast army of adults practising homosexuality." It would be "more realistic to find room for them in society". He pleads for "tolerance", though not for "encouragement", of homosexual behaviour.[75]

Are these views, however, not the despairing opinions of the secular mind? They challenge us to articulate the third position, which is to believe that at least some degree of change is possible. Christians know that the homosexual condition, being a deviation from God's norm, is not a sign of created order but of fallen disorder. How, then, can we acquiesce in it or declare it irreversible? We cannot. The only question is when and how we are to expect divine intervention and restoration to take place. The fact is that, though Christian claims of homosexual "healings" are made, either through regeneration or through a subsequent work of the Holy Spirit, it is not easy to substantiate them.[76]

Martin Hallett, who before his conversion was active in the gay scene, has written a very honest account of his experience of what he calls "Christ's way out of homosexuality". He is candid about his continuing vulnerability, his need for safeguards, his yearning for love and his occasional bouts of emotional turmoil. I am glad he entitled his autobiographical sketch *I Am Learning to Love* in the present tense, and subtitled it "A personal journey to wholeness in Christ". His final paragraph begins: "I have learnt; I am learning; I will learn to love God, other people and myself. This healing process will only be complete when I am with Jesus."[77] His most recent book continues the theme, being entitled *Still Learning to Love*.

True Freedom Trust have published a pamphlet entitled *Testimonies*. In it homosexual Christian men and women bear witness to what Christ has done for them. They have found a new identity in him, and have a new sense of personal fulfilment as children of God. They have been delivered from guilt, shame and fear by God's forgiving acceptance and have been set free from thraldom to their former homosexual lifestyle by the indwelling power of the Holy Spirit. But they have not been delivered from their homosexual inclination, and, therefore, some inner pain continues alongside their new joy and peace. Here are two examples. "My prayers were not answered in the way I had hoped for, but the Lord greatly blessed me in giving me two Christian friends who lovingly accepted me for what I was." "After I was prayed over with the laying on of hands a spirit of perversion left me. I praise God for the deliverance I found that afternoon ... I can testify to over three years of freedom from homosexual activity. But I have not changed into a heterosexual in that time."

In the US one prominent organization in this field is Exodus International.[78] Tim Stafford, in the 18 August 1989 edition of *Christianity Today*, describes his investigation into several cases. His conclusion was one of "cautious optimism". What ex-gays were claiming was "not a quick 180-degree reversal of their sexual desires", but rather "a gradual reversal in their spiritual understanding of themselves as men and women in relationship to God". This new self-understanding was "helping them to relearn distorted patterns of thinking and relating. They presented themselves as people in process".

Is there really, then, no hope of a substantial change of inclination? Dr Elizabeth Moberly believes there is. She has been led by her researches to the view that "a homosexual orientation does not depend on a genetic pre-disposition, hormonal imbalance, or abnormal learning process, but on difficulties in the parent-child relationships, especially in the earlier years of life". The "underlying principle", she continues, is "that the homosexual – whether man or woman – has suffered from some deficit in the relationship with the parent of the same sex; and that there is a corresponding drive to make good this deficit through the medium of same-sex or 'homosexual' relationships".[79] The deficit and the drive go together. The reparative drive for same-sex love is not itself pathological, but "quite the opposite – it is the attempt to resolve and heal the pathology". "The homosexual condition does not involve abnormal needs, but normal needs that have, abnormally, been left unmet in the ordinary process of growth." Homosexuality "is essentially a state of incomplete development" or of unmet needs.[80] So the proper solution is "the meeting of same-sex needs without sexual activity", for to eroticize growth deficits is to confuse emotional needs with physiological desires.[81] How, then, can these needs be met? The needs are legitimate, but what are the legitimate means of meeting them? Dr Moberly's answer is that "substitute relationships for parental care are in God's redemptive plan, just as parental relationships are in his creative plan".[82] What is needed is deep, loving, lasting, same-sex but non-sexual relationships, especially in the church. "Love," she concludes, "both in prayer and in relationships, is the basic therapy ... Love is the basic problem, the great need, and the only true solution. If we are willing to seek and to mediate the healing and redeeming love of Christ, then healing for the homosexual will become a great and glorious reality."[83]

Even then, however, complete healing of body, mind and spirit will not take place in this life. Some degree of deficit or disorder remains in each of us. But not for ever. The Christian's horizons are not bounded by this world. Jesus

Christ is coming again; our bodies are going to be redeemed; sin, pain and death are going to be abolished; and both we and the universe are going to be transformed. Then we shall be finally liberated from everything which defiles or distorts our personality. This Christian assurance helps us to bear whatever our present pain may be. For pain there is, in the midst of peace. "We know that the whole creation has been groaning as in the pains of childbirth right up to the present time. Not only so, but we ourselves, who have the firstfruits of the Spirit, groan inwardly as we wait eagerly for our adoption as sons, the redemption of our bodies" (Romans 8:22 – 23). Thus our groans express the birthpangs of the new age. We are convinced that "our present sufferings are not worth comparing with the glory that will be revealed in us" (Romans 8:18). This confident hope sustains us.

Alex Davidson derives comfort in the midst of his homosexuality from his Christian hope. "Isn't it one of the most wretched things about this condition," he writes, "that when you look ahead, the same impossible road seems to continue indefinitely? You're driven to rebellion when you think of there being no point in it and to despair when you think of there being no limit to it. That's why I find a comfort, when I feel desperate, or rebellious, or both, to remind myself of God's promise that one day it will be finished." [84]

The Christian call to love

At present we are living "in between times", between the grace which we grasp by faith and the glory which we anticipate in hope. Between them lies love. Yet love is just what the church has generally failed to show to homosexual people. Jim Cotter complains bitterly about being treated as "objects of scorn and insult, of fear, prejudice and oppression".[85] Norman Pittenger describes the "vituperative" correspondence he has received, in which homosexuals are dismissed even by professing Christians as "filthy creatures", "disgusting perverts", "damnable sinners" and the like.[86] Rictor Norton puts it even more strongly: "The church's record regarding homosexuals is an atrocity from beginning to end: it is not for us to seek forgiveness, but for the church to make atonement."[87] Peter Tatchell, a well-known British campaigner for "gay rights", has said, "The Bible is to gays what *Mein Kampf* is to Jews. It is the theory and practice of Homo Holocaust."[88]

The attitude of personal antipathy towards homosexuals is nowadays termed "homophobia".[89] It is a mixture of irrational fear, hostility and even revulsion. It overlooks the fact that the majority of homosexual people are probably not responsible for their condition (though they are, of course, responsible for their conduct). Since they are not deliberate perverts, they deserve our understanding and compassion (though many find this patronizing), not our rejection. No wonder Richard Lovelace calls for "a double repentance", namely "that gay Christians renounce the active lifestyle" and that "straight Christians renounce homophobia".[90] Dr David Atkinson is right to add, "We are not at liberty to urge the Christian homosexual to celibacy and to a spreading of his relationships, unless support for the former and opportunities for the latter are available in genuine love."[91] I rather think that the very existence of the Lesbian and Gay Christian Movement is a vote of censure on the church.

At the heart of the homosexual condition is a deep loneliness, the natural human hunger for mutual love, a search for identity and a longing for completeness. If homosexual people cannot find these things in the local "church family", we have no business to go on using that expression. The alternative is not between the warm physical relationship of homosexual intercourse and the pain of isolation in the cold. There is a third option, namely a Christian environment of love, understanding, acceptance and support. I do not think there is any need to encourage homosexual people to disclose their sexual inclinations to everybody; this is neither necessary nor helpful. But they do need at least one confidant(e) to whom they can unburden themselves, who will not despise or reject them but will support them with friendship and prayer; probably some professional, private and confidential pastoral counsel; possibly in addition the support of a professionally supervised therapy group; and (like all single people) many warm and affectionate friendships with people of both sexes. Same-sex friendships, like those in the Bible between Ruth and Naomi, David and Jonathan, and Paul and Timothy, are to be encouraged. There is no hint that any of these was homosexual in the erotic sense, yet they were evidently affectionate and (at least in the case of David and Jonathan) even demonstrative (e.g., 1 Samuel 18:1 – 4; 20:41; 2 Samuel 1:26). Of course, sensible safeguards will be important. But in African and Asian cultures it is common to see two men walking down the street hand in hand, without embarrassment. It is sad that our Western culture inhibits the development of rich same-sex friendships by engendering the fear of being ridiculed or rejected as a "queer".

The best contribution of Michael Vasey's book *Strangers and Friends*, in my view, is his emphasis on friendship. "Friendship is not a minor theme of the Christian faith," he writes, "but is integral to its vision of life."[92] He sees society as "a network of friendships held together by bonds of affection". He also points out that Scripture does "not limit the notion of covenant to the institution of marriage".[93] As David and Jonathan made a covenant with each other (1 Samuel 18:3), we too may have special covenanted friendships.

These and other relationships, both same sex and opposite sex, need to be developed within the family of God which, though universal, has its local manifestations. He intends each local church to be a warm, accepting and supportive community. By "accepting" I do not mean "acquiescing"; similarly, by a rejection of "homophobia", I do not mean a rejection of a proper Christian disapproval of homosexual behaviour. No, true love is not incompatible with the maintenance of moral standards. On the contrary, it insists on them, for the good of everybody. There is, therefore, a place for church discipline in the case of members who refuse to repent and wilfully persist in homosexual relationships. But it must be exercised in a spirit of humility and gentleness (Galatians 6:1f.); we must be careful not to discriminate between men and women or between homosexual and heterosexual offences; and necessary discipline in the case of a public scandal is not to be confused with a witch-hunt.

Perplexing and painful as the homosexual Christian's dilemma is, Jesus Christ offers him or her (indeed, all of us) faith, hope and love – the faith to accept both his standards and his grace to maintain them, the hope to look beyond present suffering to future glory and the love to care for and support one another. "But the greatest of these is love" (1 Corinthians 13:13).

NOTES

1 Age range eighteen to fifty-nine. Reported in Edward O. Laumann, John H. Gagnon, Robert T. Michael and Stuart Michaels, *The Social Organization of Sexuality: Sexual Practices in the United States* (Chicago: University of Chicago Press, 1994), pp. 294, 303. This study was "the most comprehensive US sex survey ever" according to *USA Today*. See *www.press.uchicago.edu/cgi-bin/hfs.cgi/00/12747.ct*.

2 Ibid., p. 296.

3 Ibid., p. 296. This high figure of 9.1% caused the authors of the survey to suggest two other explanatory factors: firstly, that this specific question was asked in a private questionnaire rather than face-to-face, and secondly, the broader phrasing of the question about the nature of the sexual activity. A similar question was raised in the *Sexual Behaviour in Britain* study. Respondents were asked about whether they ever had "any kind of sexual experience" with a person of the same sex, also in a private questionnaire. The result showed 6.1% of men and 3.4% of women had such an experience. See K. Wellings, J. Field, A. Johnson and J. Wadsworth, *Sexual Behaviour in Britain* (London: Penguin, 1994), p. 187.

4 Ibid., p. 187. Sample of 18,900 adults aged between sixteen and fifty-nine years. Answers quoted here were made in a confidential self-completed questionnaire.

5 Ibid., p. 213, and as cited in C. Hart, S. Calvert and I. Bainbridge, *Homosexuality and Young People* (Newcastle: The Christian Institute, 1998), p. 32.

6 Wellings et al., *Sexual Behaviour in Britain*, p. 187.

7 Ibid., p. 209.

8 *National Survey of Sexual Attitudes and Lifestyles* (Natsal, 2000), with 11,200 respondents, all aged between sixteen and forty-four years, cited in *The Lancet*, vol. 358, 1 December 2001, p. 1839. It is likely that in keeping the upper band at forty-four years, the survey is overestimating the proportion of homosexual men in the population overall. See, for example, the age breakdown in E. O. Laumann and R. T. Michael (eds.), *Sex, Love and Health in America* (Chicago: University of Chicago Press, 2000), ch. 12, T12.2. In addition, a 1997 National Statistics Office survey of 7,560 adults using an age range of sixteen to sixty-nine years for men found that 3.2% of men in Great Britain had had sex at least once with another man, and 1.7% had only ever had same-sex intercourse. See *Contraception and Sexual Health 1997*, a report on research using the ONS Omnibus Survey produced on behalf of the Department of Health (Office for National Statistics, London, 1999), p. 11, and correspondence with ONS.

9 It is noted, however, that there is higher incidence of homosexuality in the US than in the UK. See, for example, Laumann and Michael, *Sex, Love and Health in America*, pp. 442 – 43, and Hart et al., *Homosexuality and Young People*, p. 49.

10 Cited in Brian Whitaker, "Government Disorientation", April 29, 2003, *Guardian Unlimited*, www.Guardian.co.uk.

11 Malcolm Macourt (ed.), *Towards a Theology of Gay Liberation* (London: SCM Press, 1977), p. 3. The quotation comes from Mr Macourt's own introduction to the book.

12 www.lgcm.org.uk/

13 The full statement can be found at www.archbishopofcanterbury.org/releases/2003/030529.html.

14 J. I. Packer, "Why I Walked", *Christianity Today*, 21 January 2003.

15 Derrick Sherwin Bailey, *Homosexuality and the Western Christian Tradition* (London: Longmans, Green, 1955), p. 4.

16 Robert A. J. Gagnon, *The Bible and Homosexual Practice: Texts and Hermeneutics* (Nashville: Abingdon Press, 2001), pp. 75 – 76.

17 Sherwin Bailey gives references in the Book of Jubilees and the Testaments of the Twelve Patriarchs, in *Homosexuality and the Western Christian Tradition*, pp. 11 – 20. There is an even fuller evaluation of the writings of the intertestamental period in Peter Coleman, *Christian Attitudes to Homosexuality* (London: SPCK, 1980), pp. 58 – 85.

18 Bailey, Ibid., p. 27.

19 See James D. Martin, in Macourt (ed.), *Towards a Theology of Gay Liberation*, p. 53.

20 Bailey, *Homosexuality and the Western Christian Tradition*, p. 30.

21 Coleman, *Christian Attitudes to Homosexuality*, p. 49.

22 William J. Webb, *Slaves, Women and Homosexuals: Exploring the Hermeneutics of Cultural Analysis* (Downers Grove: InterVarsity, 2001), pp. 250 – 51.

23 Gagnon, *The Bible and Homosexual Practice*, p. 253.

24 Coleman, *Christian Attitudes to Homosexuality*, pp. 95 – 96.

25 Gagnon, *The Bible and Homosexual Practice*, p. 306.

26 Coleman, *Christian Attitudes to Homosexuality*, p. 277.

27 Ibid., p. 101.

28 Rictor Norton, in Macourt (ed.), *Towards a Theology of Gay Liberation*, p. 58.

29 Sherwin Bailey's book contains no allusion to these chapters at all. And even Peter Coleman, whose *Christian Attitudes to Homosexuality* is comprehensive, mentions them only in a passing reference to 1 Corinthians 6 where Paul quotes Genesis 2:24.

30 Michael Vasey, *Strangers and Friends* (London: Hodder & Stoughton, 1995), pp. 46, 82 – 83.

31 Ibid., p. 116.

32 Norman Pittenger, *Time for Consent* (London: SCM, 1976), pp. 7, 73.

33 On the evidence that homosexuality is pervasive among animals, see *www.subversions. com/french/pages/science/animals.html*, and the scholarly work by Bruce Bagemihl, *Biological Exuberance: Animal Hospitality and Natural Diversity* (New York: St Martin's Press, 1999).

34 Pittenger, *Time for Consent*, p. 7.

35 Coleman, *Christian Attitudes to Homosexuality*, p. 50.

36 Coleman, Ibid., p. 71, chapter 3.3 – 5.

37 John Boswell, *Christianity, Social Tolerance and Homosexuality* (Chicago: University of Chicago Press, 1981), pp. 107ff.

38 Richard B. Hays, "A Response to John Boswell's Exegesis of Romans 1", *Journal of Religious Ethics*, Spring 1986, p. 192. See also his *The Moral Vision of the New Testament* (Edinburgh: T. & T. Clark, 1996), pp. 383 – 89.

39 C. K. Barrett, *Commentary on the Epistle to the Romans* (London: A. & C. Black, 1962), p. 39.

40 C. E. B. Cranfield, "Commentary on Romans", in the *International Critical Commentary* (Edinburgh: T. & T. Clark, 1975), vol. 1, p. 126. He attributes the same meaning to *physis* in his comment on 1 Corinthians 11:14. What the NIV translates "the very nature of things" Professor Cranfield renders "the very way God has made us".

41 Gagnon, *The Bible and Homosexual Practice*, pp. 299 – 302.

42 *Christianity Today*, 11 November 1996.

43 The Friends' Report, *Towards a Quaker View of Sex* (1963), p. 21.

44 Ibid., p. 36.

45 Methodist Church's Division of Social Responsibility, *A Christian Understanding of Human Sexuality* (1979), chapter 9.

46 See chapter 5 of the report.

47 David Reid et al., "Know the Score: Findings from the National Gay Men's Sex Survey 2001" (London: Sigma Research, September 2002), pp. 12, 24. Wide age range of men surveyed, with average age of thirty-two.

48 Anne M. Johnson et al., "Sexual Behaviour in Britain: Partnerships, practices and HIV risk behaviours", *The Lancet*, vol. 358, 1 December 2001, p. 1838. Men aged sixteen to

forty-four. In the US, the National Health and Social Life Survey found that men with no male partners had an average of five sexual partners in the past five years, as compared to between twelve and twenty-one for men with same-gender partners. See Laumann et al., *The Social Organization of Sexuality*, p. 314.

49 Thomas E. Schmidt, *Straight and Narrow?* (Downer's Grove: InterVarsity Press, 1995), p. 108.

50 F. C. I. Hickson et al., "Maintenance of Open Gay Relationships: Some strategies for protection against HIV", *AIDS Care*, vol. 4, no. 4, 1992, p. 410. Project SIGMA is London-based and under the auspices of the University of Portsmouth. It is openly sympathetic to gay rights. See *http://sigmaresearch.org/*.

51 Thomas E. Schmidt, *Straight and Narrow?, Compassion and clarity in the homosexuality debate* (Leicester: InterVarsity Press, 1995), p. 122.

52 Dixon, *The Truth about AIDS*, p. 113. See also p. 88, and the whole chapter entitled "Condoms Are Unsafe", pp. 110–22.

53 *The Many Faces of AIDS: A Gospel Response* (United States Catholic Conference, 1987), p. 18.

54 *www.unaids.org/en/*

55 CDC Survey Report, vol. 14, Table 7, *www.cdc.gov*.

56 John Karon, L. Fleming, R. Skeketee, Kevin De Cock, "HIV in the United States at the Turn of the Century: An Epidemic in Transition", *The American Journal of Public Health*, vol. 91, July 2001, pp. 1060–68.

57 Centres for Disease Control and Prevention (CDC), *HIV and AIDS – United States 1981–2001, MMWR* 2001, 50:430–34.

58 Centres for Disease Control and Prevention (CDC), *HIV Prevention Strategic Plan through 2005*, January 2001.

59 Quoted in *Christianity Today*, 7 August 1987, p. 17.

60 For example, the London Lighthouse (a twenty-six-bed AIDS hospice), 178 Lancaster Road, London W11 1QU, UK, and the internationally known thirty-two-suite AIDS ward at the Mildmay Mission Hospital, Hackney Road, London E2 7NA, UK. Both hospices also arrange home care. ACACIA (AIDS Care, Compassion in Action) cares for about seventy-five people with HIV/AIDS in their own homes in Manchester, UK.

61 So Gavin Reid rightly argues in his *Beyond AIDS, The real crisis and the only hope* (Eastbourne: Kingsway, 1987).

62 ACET (AIDS Care, Education and Training) has an international network of projects associated with AIDS. Its address is ACET International Alliance Network, 1 Carlton Gardens, Ealing, London, W5 2AN, UK.

63 AIDS, A Report by the Church of England Board for Social Responsibility (GS 795, 1987), p. 29.

64 "The Homosexual Movement: A Response by the Ramsey Colloquium", first published in *First Things*, March 1994.

65 Macourt (ed.), *Towards a Theology of Gay Liberation*, p. 25.

66 Pittinger, *Time for Consent*

67 Alex Davidson, *The Returns of Love* (London: InterVarsity Press, 1970), pp. 12, 16, 49.

68 Norman Pittenger, in Macourt (ed.), *Towards a Theology of Gay Liberation*, p. 87.

69 The St Andrew's Day Statement (published 30 November 1995) begins with three theological "Principles" relating to the incarnate Lord (in whom we come to know both God and ourselves), the Holy Spirit (who enables us to interpret the times), and God the Father (who restores the broken creation in Christ). The statement's second half consists of three "Applications" relating to such questions as our human identity, empirical observations, the reaffirmation of the good news of salvation and the hope of final fulfilment in Christ. Two years later, *The Way Forward?* was published, with the subtitle "Christian voices on homosexuality and the church". This symposium, edited by Tim Bradshaw, consists of thirteen responses to the St Andrew's Day Statement, from a wide range of different viewpoints. One appreciates the call to patient and serious theological reflection. But it is inaccurate to write of "dialogue" and "diatribe" as if they were the only options. Some of us have been listening and reflecting for thirty or forty years! How long must the process continue before we are allowed to reach a conclusion? In spite of claims to the contrary, no fresh evidence has been produced which could overthrow the clear witness of Scripture and the long-standing tradition of the church. The St Andrew's Day Statement says that the church recognizes two vocations (marriage and singleness), and adds that "there is no place for the Church to confer legitimacy upon alternatives to these". Further, the authors of the statement do not consider that "the considerable burden of proof to support a major change in the Church's teaching and practice has been met" by the contributors to the book (p. 3). Yet the book makes a more uncertain sound than the statement. So by all means let there be serious theological reflection, but then let the church make up its mind.

70 Pittenger, *Time for Consent*, p. 7. Contrast *The Courage to be Chaste: An Uncompromising Call to the Biblical Standard of Chastity* (New York: Paulist Press, 1986). Written by Benedict J. Groeschel, a Capuchin friar, the book contains much practical advice.

71 Jeffrey Satinover, *Homosexuality and the Politics of Truth* (Grand Rapids: Baker, 1996), p. 117.

72 Ibid., pp. 18 – 19, 71.

73 Vasey, *Strangers and Friends*, p. 103.

74 See Satinover, *Homosexuality and the Politics of Truth*, pp. 31 – 40.

75 D. J. West, *Homosexuality* (1955; 2nd ed., London: Pelican, 1960; 3rd ed., London: Duckworth, 1968), pp. 266, 273.

76 Nelson Gonzalez's article "Exploding Ex-Gay Myths", in *Regeneration Quarterly*, vol. 1, no. 3, Summer 1995, challenged the aims and claims of the ex-gay movement. In 1991 Charles Socarides founded the National Association for Research and Therapy of Homosexuality (NARTH), which investigates the possibilities for "healing".

77 Martin Hallett, *I Am Learning to Love* (Grand Rapids: Zondervan, 1987), p. 155. Martin Hallett's organization is called True Freedom Trust (TfT), and can be contacted at PO Box 13, Prenton, Wirral, CH43 6BY, UK. It offers an interdenominational teaching and counselling ministry on homosexuality and related problems. The website is *www. truefreedomtrust.co.uk/index.html*. Martin Hallett's new book is available only through TfT.

78 Exodus International can be contacted at PO Box 540119, Orlando, FL 32854, USA, or *http://exodus.to/about_exodus.shtml.*

79 Elizabeth R. Moberly, *Homosexuality: A New Christian Ethic* (Cambridge: James Clarke, 1983), p. 2. See also Lance Pierson, *No-Gay Areas, Pastoral Care of Homosexual Christians*, Grove Pastoral Studies, no. 38 (Cambridge: Grove Books, 1989), which helpfully applies Elizabeth Moberly's teaching.

80 Ibid., p. 28.

81 Ibid., pp. 18 – 20.

82 Ibid., pp. 35 – 36.

83 Ibid., p. 52.

84 Davidson, *The Returns of Love*, p. 51.

85 Macourt (ed.), *Towards a Theology of Gay Liberation*, p. 63.

86 Pittenger, *Time for Consent*, p. 2.

87 Macourt (ed.), *Towards a Theology of Gay Liberation*, p. 45.

88 *www.petertatchell.net*

89 The word seems to have been used first by George Weinberg in *Society and the Healthy Homosexual* (New York: Doubleday, 1973).

90 Richard R. Lovelace, *Homosexuality and the Church* (Grand Rapids: Revell, 1978), p. 129; cf. p. 125.

91 David J. Atkinson, *Homosexuals in the Christian Fellowship* (Oxford: Latimer House, 1979), p. 118. See also Dr Atkinson's more extensive treatment in his *Pastoral Ethics in Practice* (London: Monarch, 1989). Dr Roger Moss concentrates on pastoral questions in his *Christians and Homosexuality* (Carlisle, Penn.: Paternoster, 1977).

92 Vasey, *Strangers and Friends*, p. 122.

93 Ibid., p. 233.

CONCLUSION

A Call for
Christian Leadership

17

There is a serious dearth of leaders in the contemporary world. Massive problems confront us, some of which we have looked at in this book. Globally, there still exist weapons of mass destruction, widespread violations of human rights, environmental and energy crises, climate change and North-South economic inequality. Socially, there are the outbreaks of racial violence, increased drug and alcohol abuse and the continuing trauma of poverty. Morally, Christians are disturbed by the forces which are undermining the stability of marriage and the family, the challenges to sexual standards and the scandal of what is virtually abortion on demand. Spiritually, I might add, there are the spread of materialism and the corresponding loss of any sense of transcendent reality. Many people are warning us that the world is heading for disaster; few are offering us advice on how to avert it. Technical know-how abounds, but wisdom is in short supply. People feel confused, bewildered, alienated. To borrow the metaphors of Jesus, we seem to be like "sheep without a shepherd", while our leaders often appear to be "blind leaders of the blind".

There are many kinds and degrees of leadership. Leadership is not restricted to a small minority of world statesmen or to the national top brass. In every society it takes a variety of forms. Clergy are leaders in the local church and community. Parents are leaders in their home and family. So are teachers in school and lecturers in college. Senior executives in business and industry, judges, doctors, politicians, social workers and union officials all have leadership responsibilities in their respective spheres. So do the opinion-formers who work in the media – authors and playwrights, journalists, sound and vision broadcasters, artists and producers. Student leaders, especially since the 1960s, have been exercising influence beyond their years and their experience. There is a great need in all these situations for more clear-sighted, courageous and dedicated leaders.

Such leaders are both born and bred. As Bennie E. Goodwin, an African-American educationalist, has written: "Although potential leaders are born, effective leaders are made."[1] In Shakespeare's famous lines, "Be not afraid of greatness! Some are born great, some achieve greatness, and some have greatness thrust upon them."[2] Books on management refer to "BNLs" (born natural leaders), men and women endowed with strong intellect, character and personality. And we would want to add with Oswald Sanders that Christian leadership is "a blending of natural and spiritual qualities",[3] or of natural talents and spiritual gifts. Nevertheless, God's gifts have to be cultivated, and leadership potential has to be developed.

What, then, are the marks of leadership in general, and of Christian leadership in particular? How can we give up sitting around, waiting for somebody else to take the initiative, and take it ourselves? What is needed to blaze a trail which others will follow?

Although many different analyses of leadership have been made, I want to suggest that it has five essential ingredients.

VISION

"Where there is no vision, the people perish" is a proverb from the Authorized Version of the Bible, which has passed into common usage. Although it is almost certainly a mistranslation of the Hebrew, it is nonetheless a true statement.[4] Indeed, it has been a characteristic of the post-Pentecost era that "your young men will see visions" and "your old men will dream dreams" (Acts 2:17). Monsignor Ronald Knox of Oxford concluded his critical, though somewhat wistful book *Enthusiasm* with these words: "Men will not live without vision; that moral we do well to carry away with us from contemplating, in so many strange forms, the record of the visionaries. If we are content with the humdrum, the second-best, the hand-over-hand, it will not be forgiven us."[5]

"Dreams" and "visions", dreamers and visionaries sound somewhat unpractical, however, and remote from the harsh realities of life on earth. So more prosaic words tend to be used. Management experts tell us we must set both long-term and short-term goals. Politicians publish election manifestos. Military personnel lay down a campaign strategy. But whether you call it a "goal", a "manifesto" or a "strategy", it is a vision that you are talking about.

So what is vision? It is an act of seeing, of course, an imaginative perception of things, combining insight and foresight. But more particularly, in the sense in which I am using the word, it is compounded of a deep dissatisfaction with what is and a clear grasp of what could be. It begins with indignation over the status quo, and it grows into the earnest quest for an alternative. Both are quite clear in the public ministry of Jesus. He was indignant over disease and death and the hunger of the people, for he perceived these things as alien to the purpose of God. Hence his compassion for their victims. Indignation and compassion form a powerful combination. They are indispensable to vision, and therefore to leadership (see, e.g., John 11:32 – 37).

It will be remembered that Bobby Kennedy was assassinated in 1968 at the age of forty-two. In an appreciation of him which appeared ten years later, David S. Broder wrote that "his distinguishing quality was his capacity for what can only be called moral outrage. 'That is unacceptable,' he said of many conditions that most of us accepted as inevitable . . . Poverty, illiteracy, malnutrition, prejudice, crookedness, conniving – all such accepted evils were a personal affront to him."[6] Apathy is the acceptance of the unacceptable; leadership begins with a decisive refusal of such acceptance. As George F. Will wrote in December 1981, after the declaration of martial law in Poland, "What is outrageous is the absence of outrage." There is a great need today for more righteous indignation, anger and outrage over those evils which are an offence to God. How can we tolerate what he finds intolerable?

But anger is sterile if it does not provoke us to positive action to remedy what has aroused our anger. "One must oppose those things that one believes to be wrong," writes Robert Greenleaf, "but one cannot lead from a predominantly negative posture."[7] Before Robert McNamara retired in 1981 as President of the World Bank after thirteen years, he addressed its annual meeting for the last time, and in his speech he quoted George Bernard Shaw: "You see things as they are and ask 'Why?' But I dream things that never were, and ask 'Why not?' "

History abounds in examples, both biblical and secular. Moses was appalled by the cruel oppression of his fellow Israelites in Egypt, remembered God's covenant with Abraham, Isaac and Jacob, and was sustained throughout his long life by the vision of the "Promised Land". Nehemiah heard in his Persian exile that the wall of the Holy City was in ruins, and its inhabitants in great distress. The news overwhelmed him, until God put into his heart what he could and should do. "Come, let us rebuild the wall of Jerusalem," he said. And the people replied, "Let us start rebuilding" (Nehemiah 2:12, 17 - 18).

Moving on to New Testament times, the early Christians were well aware of the might of Rome and the hostility of Jewry. But Jesus had told them to be his witnesses "to the ends of the earth", and the vision he gave them transformed them. Saul of Tarsus had been brought up to accept as inevitable and unbridgeable the chasm between Jews and Gentiles. But Jesus commissioned him to take the gospel to the Gentile world, and he was "not disobedient to the heavenly vision". Indeed, the vision of a single, new, reconciled humanity so captured his heart and mind, that he laboured, suffered and died in its cause (see, e.g., Acts 26:16 – 20; Ephesians 2:11 – 3:13 for Paul's vision).

In our own generation, US presidents have had noble visions of a "New Deal" and of a "Great Society", and the fact that their expectations did not altogether materialize is no criticism of their vision. Martin Luther King, incensed by the injustices of segregation, had a dream of dignity for all in a free, multiethnic America; he both lived and died that his dream might come true.

There can be little doubt that the phenomenal early success of communists (within fifty years from the Russian Revolution of 1917 they had won over a third of the world) was due to the vision of a better society which they were able to inspire in their followers. This, at least, was the considered opinion of Douglas Hyde, who in March 1948 resigned both from the British Communist Party (after twenty years' membership) and from being news editor of the *Daily Worker*, and became a Roman Catholic. The subtitle he gave to his book *Dedication and Leadership* was "Learning from the Communists", and he wrote it to answer the question "Why are communists so dedicated and successful as leaders, whilst others so often are not?" Here is how he put it: "If you ask me what is the distinguishing mark of the Communist, what is it that Communists most outstandingly have in common ... I would say that beyond any shadow of doubt it is their idealism."[8] They dream, he continued, of a new society in which (quoting from Liu Shao-chi) there will be "no oppressed and exploited people, no darkness, ignorance, backwardness" and "no such irrational things as mutual deception, mutual antagonism, mutual slaughter and war".[9] Marx wrote in his *Theses on Feuerbach* (1888): "The philosophers have only in various ways interpreted the world: the point, however, is to change it." That slogan "change the world", comments Douglas Hyde, "has proved to be one of the most dynamic of the past 120 years ... Marx concluded his Communist Manifesto with the words: 'You have a world to win'."[10] This vision fired the imagination and zeal of young idealistic communists. Because of it, Hyde wrote about the first half of the twentieth century, "The recruit is made to feel that there is a great battle going on all over the world", and "that this includes his own country, his own town, his own neighbourhood, the block of flats in which he lives, the factory or office where he works".[11] "One reason why the Communist is prepared to make his exceptional sacrifices," Douglas Hyde argued, "is that he believes he is taking part in a crusade."[12]

But Jesus Christ is a far greater and more glorious leader than Karl Marx could ever have been, and the Christian good news is a much more radical and liberating message than the Communist Manifesto. The world can be won for Christ by evangelism and made more pleasing to Christ by social action. Why, then, does this prospect not set our hearts on fire? Where are the Christian people today who see the status quo, who do not like what they see (because there are things in it which are unacceptable to God), who, therefore, refuse to come to terms with it, who dream dreams of an alternative society which would be more acceptable to God and who determine to do something about it? "Nothing much happens without a dream. And for something great to happen, there must be a great dream. Behind every great achievement is a dreamer of great dreams."[13]

We see with our mind's eye the 2,000,000,000 people who may never even have heard of Jesus, and the further 2,000,000,000 who have heard but have had no valid opportunity to respond to the gospel;[14] we see the poor, the hungry and the disadvantaged; people crushed by political, economic or ethnic oppression; the millions of babies aborted and incinerated; the serious threat of climate change. We see these things; do we not care? We see what is; do we not see what could be? Things could be different. The unevangelized could be reached with the good news of Jesus; the hungry could be fed, the oppressed liberated, the alienated brought home. We need a vision of the purpose and power of God.

David Bleakley has written about such visionaries, "the people with a 'hunch' alternative, those who believe that it is possible to build a better world". He calls them "Pathfinders", who are "lovers of our planet, who feel a responsibility for God's creation, and wish to give true meaning to the lives of all his people". Indeed, he is confident, as I am, that such "Pathfinders represent a growing ground-swell of change in our society and in societies elsewhere".[15]

INDUSTRY

The world has always been scornful of dreamers. "Here comes that dreamer!" Joseph's older brothers said to one another. "Come now, let's kill him ... Then we'll see what comes of his dreams" (Genesis 37:19ff.). The dreams of the night tend to evaporate in the cold light of the morning.

So dreamers have to become in turn thinkers, planners and workers, and that demands industry or hard labour. People of vision need to become people of action. It was Thomas Carlyle, the nineteenth-century Scottish writer, who said of Frederick the Great that genius means first of all "the transcendent capacity of taking trouble", and it was Thomas Alva Edison, the inventor of electrical devices, who defined genius as "1% inspiration and 99% perspiration". All great leaders, not least great artists, find this to be true. Behind their apparently effortless performance there lies the most rigorous and painstaking self-discipline. A good example is the world-renowned pianist Paderewski. He spent hours in practice every day. It was not unknown for him to repeat a bar or phrase fifty times to perfect it. Queen Victoria once said to him, after she had heard him play, "Mr Paderewski, you are a genius." "That may be, Ma'am," he replied, "but before I was a genius, I was a drudge."[16]

This addition of industry to vision is an evident hallmark of history's great leaders. It was not enough for Moses to dream of the land flowing with milk and honey; he had to organize the Israelite rabble into at least the semblance of a nation and lead them through the dangers and hardships of the desert before they could take possession of the Promised Land. Similarly, Nehemiah was inspired by his vision of the rebuilt Holy City, but first he had to gather materials to reconstruct the wall and weapons to defend it. Winston Churchill loathed the Nazi tyranny and dreamed of Europe's liberation. But he was under no illusions about the cost of the enterprise. On 13 May 1940, in his first speech to the House of Commons as prime minister, he warned members that he had "nothing to offer but blood, toil, tears and sweat", and "many long months of struggle and suffering".

Moreover, the same combination of vision and industry is needed in our more ordinary individual lives. William Morris, who became Lord Nuffield the public benefactor, began his career repairing bicycles. What was the secret of his success? It was "creative imagination wedded to indomitable industry".[17] Thus dream and reality, passion and practicalities must go together. Without the dream the campaign loses its direction and its fire; but without hard work and practical projects the dream vanishes into thin air.

PERSEVERANCE

Thomas Sutcliffe Mort was an early nineteenth-century settler in Sydney, Australia, after whom the "Mort Docks" are named. He was determined to solve the problem of refrigeration, so that meat could be exported from Australia to Britain, and he gave himself three years in which to do it. But it took him twenty-six. He lived long enough to see the first shipment of refrigerated meat leave Sydney but died before learning whether it had reached its destination safely. The house he built in Edgecliffe is now Bishopscourt, the residence of the Anglican Archbishop of Sydney. Painted twenty times round the cornice of the study ceiling are the words "To persevere is to succeed", and engraved in stone outside the front door is the Mort family motto (a play on their Huguenot name) *Fidèle à la Mort*.

Perseverance is certainly an indispensable quality of leadership. It is one thing to dream dreams and see visions. It is another to convert a dream into a plan of action. It is yet a third to persevere with it when opposition comes. For opposition is bound to arise. As soon as the campaign gets under way, the forces of reaction muster, entrenched privilege digs itself in more deeply, commercial interests feel threatened and raise the alarm, the cynical sneer at the folly of "do-gooders", and apathy becomes transmuted into hostility.

But a true work of God thrives on opposition. Its silver is refined and its steel hardened. Of course, those without the vision, who are merely being carried along by the momentum of the campaign, will soon capitulate. So it is that the protesting youth of one decade become the conservative establishment of the next. Young rebels lapse into middle-class, middle-aged, middle-of-the-road mediocrity. Even revolutionaries, once the revolution is over, tend to lose their ideals. But not the real leaders. They have the resilience to take setbacks in their stride, the tenacity to overcome fatigue and discouragement, and the wisdom (in a favourite phrase of John Mott's) to "turn stumbling-blocks into stepping stones".[18] Real leaders add to vision and industry the grace of perseverance.

In the Old Testament Moses is again the outstanding example. On about a dozen distinct occasions the people "murmured" against him, and he had the beginnings of a mutiny on his hands. When Pharaoh's army was threatening them, when the water ran out or was too bitter to drink, when there was no meat to eat, when the scouts brought back a bad report of the strength of the Canaanite fortifications, when small minds became jealous of his position – these were some of the occasions on which the people complained of his leadership and challenged his authority. A lesser man would have given up and abandoned them to their own pettiness. But not Moses. He never forgot that these were God's people by God's covenant, who by God's promise would inherit the land.

In the New Testament the man who came to the end of his life with his ideals intact and his standards uncompromised was the apostle Paul. He too faced bitter and violent opposition. He had to endure severe physical afflictions, for on several occasions he was beaten, stoned and imprisoned. He suffered mentally too, for his footsteps were dogged by false prophets who contradicted his teaching and slandered his name. He also experienced great loneliness. Towards the end of his life he wrote that "everyone in the province of Asia has deserted me" and "at my first defence ... everyone deserted me" (2 Timothy 1:15; 4:16). Yet he never lost his vision of God's new, redeemed society, and he never gave up proclaiming it. In his underground dungeon, from which there was to be no escape but death, he wrote: "I have fought the good fight, I have finished the race, I have kept the faith" (2 Timothy 4:7). He persevered to the end.

In recent centuries perhaps nobody has exemplified perseverance more than William Wilberforce. Sir Reginald Coupland wrote of him that, in order to break the apathy of parliament, a would-be social reformer "must possess, in the first place, the virtues of a fanatic without his vices. He must be palpably single-minded and unself-seeking. He must be strong enough to face opposition and ridicule, staunch enough to endure obstruction and delay."[19] These qualities Wilberforce possessed in abundance.

It was in 1787 that he first decided to put down a motion in the House of Commons about the slave trade. This nefarious traffic had been going on for three centuries, and the West Indian slave-owners were determined to oppose abolition to the end. Besides, Wilberforce was not a very prepossessing man. He was little and somewhat ugly, with poor eyesight and an upturned nose. When Boswell heard him speak, he pronounced him "a perfect shrimp", but then had to concede that "presently the shrimp swelled into a whale".[20] In 1789 in the House of Commons, Wilberforce said of the slave trade: "So enormous, so dreadful, so irremediable did its wickedness appear that my own mind was completely made up for Abolition ... Let the consequences be what they would, I from this time determined that I would never rest until I had affected its Abolition."[21] So Abolition Bills (which related to the trade) and Foreign Slave Bills (which would prohibit the involvement of British ships in it) were debated in the Commons in 1789, 1791, 1792, 1794, 1796 (by which time abolition had become "the grand object of my parliamentary existence"), 1798 and 1799. Yet they all failed. The Foreign Slave Bill was not passed until 1806 and the Abolition of the Slave Trade Bill until 1807. This part of the campaign had taken eighteen years.

Next, soon after the conclusion of the Napoleonic wars, Wilberforce began to direct his energies to the abolition of slavery itself and the emancipation of the slaves. In 1823 the Anti-Slavery Society was formed. Twice that year and twice the following year, Wilberforce pleaded the slaves' cause in the House of Commons. But in 1825 ill-health compelled him to resign as a member of parliament and to continue his campaign from outside. In 1831 he sent a message to the Anti-Slavery Society, in which he said, "Our motto must continue to be perseverance. And ultimately I trust the Almighty will crown our efforts with success."[22] He did. In July 1833 the Abolition of Slavery Bill was passed in both Houses of Parliament, even though it included the undertaking to pay £20,000,000 in compensation to the slave-owners. "Thank God," wrote Wilberforce, "that I have lived to witness a day in which England is willing to give £20,000,000 sterling for the abolition of slavery."[23] Three days later he died. He was buried in Westminster Abbey, in national recognition of his forty-five years of persevering struggle on behalf of African slaves.

Mind you, perseverance is not a synonym for pigheadedness. True leaders are not impervious to criticism. On the contrary, they listen to it and weigh it, and may modify their programme accordingly. But they do not waver in their basic conviction of what God has called them to do. Whatever the opposition aroused or the sacrifice entailed, they persevere.

SERVICE

A note of caution needs to be added at this point. "Leadership" is a concept shared by the church and the world. We must not assume, however, that Christian and non-Christian understandings of it are identical. Nor should we adopt models of secular management without first subjecting them to critical Christian scrutiny. Jesus introduced into the world an altogether new style of leadership. He expressed the difference between the old and the new in these terms:

> You know that those who are regarded as rulers of the Gentiles lord it over them, and their high officials exercise authority over them. Not so with you. Instead, whoever wants to become great among you must be your

servant, and whoever wants to be first must be slave of all. For even the Son of Man did not come to be served, but to serve, and to give his life as a ransom for many.

MARK 10:42–45

Among the followers of Jesus, therefore, leadership is not a synonym for lordship. Our calling is to be servants not bosses, slaves not masters. True, a certain authority attaches to all leaders, and leadership would be impossible without it. The apostles were given authority by Jesus and exercised it in both teaching and disciplining the church. Even Christian pastors today, although they are not apostles and do not possess apostolic authority, are to be "respected" because of their position "over" the congregation (1 Thessalonians 5:12ff.), and even "obeyed" (Hebrews 13:17). Yet the emphasis of Jesus was not on the authority of a ruler-leader but on the humility of a servant-leader. The authority by which the Christian leader leads is not power but love, not force but example, not coercion but reasoned persuasion. Leaders have power, but power is safe only in the hands of those who humble themselves to serve.

What is the reason for Jesus' stress on the leader's service? Partly, no doubt, because the chief occupational hazard of leadership is pride. The Pharisaic model would not do in the new community which Jesus was building. The Pharisees loved deferential titles like "Father", "Teacher", "Rabbi", but this was both an offence against God to whom these titles properly belong, and disruptive of the Christian brotherhood (Matthew 23:1 – 12).

Jesus' main reason for emphasizing the servant role of the leader, however, was surely that the service of others is a tacit recognition of their value. I have been troubled recently to observe that the "service" model of leadership is being borrowed by the world and commended for the wrong reasons. Robert K. Greenleaf, for example, a specialist in the field of management research and education, wrote in 1977 a long book called *Servant Leadership*, to which he gave the intriguing subtitle "A Journey into the nature of legitimate power and greatness". He tells us that the concept of "the servant as leader" came to him from the reading of Hermann Hesse's *Journey to the East*, in which Leo, the menial servant of a group of travellers, turns out in the end to have been their leader. The "moral principle" which Mr Greenleaf draws from this is that "the great leader is seen as the servant first". Or, expressed more fully: "The only authority deserving one's allegiance is that which is freely and knowingly granted by the led to the leader in response to, and in proportion to, the clearly

evident servant stature of the leader. Those who choose to follow this principle
... will freely respond only to individuals who are chosen as leaders because
they are proven and trusted as servants."[24] I do not deny the truth of this, that
leaders have first to win their spurs by service. But the danger of the principle as thus stated is that it regards service as being only a means to another
end (namely, qualifying one as a leader), and is, therefore, commended only
because of its pragmatic usefulness. This is not what Jesus taught, however. To
him service was an end in itself. T. W. Manson expressed the difference beautifully when he wrote: "In the Kingdom of God service is not a stepping-stone to
nobility: it is nobility, the only kind of nobility that is recognized."[25]

Why, then, did Jesus equate greatness with service? Must our answer not
relate to the intrinsic worth of human beings, which was the presupposition
underlying his own ministry of self-giving love, and which is an essential element of the Christian perspective? If human beings are godlike beings, then
they must be served not exploited, respected not manipulated. As Oswald
Sanders has expressed it, "True greatness, true leadership, is achieved not
by reducing men to one's service but in giving oneself in selfless service to
them."[26] Herein also lies the peril of seeing leadership in terms of projects and
programmes. Leadership will inevitably involve the development of these, but
people take precedence over projects. And people must be neither "manipulated" nor even "managed". Though the latter is less demeaning to human
beings than the former, yet both words are derived from *manus*, meaning a
hand, and both express a "handling" of people as if they were commodities
rather than persons.

So Christian leaders serve – indeed, they serve not their own interests but
rather the interests of others (Philippians 2:4). This simple principle should
deliver the leader from excessive individualism, extreme isolation and self-centred empire-building, for those who serve others serve best in a team. Leadership teams are healthier than solo leadership, for several reasons. Firstly,
team members supplement one another, building on one another's strengths
and compensating for one another's weaknesses. No leader has all the gifts,
so no leader should keep all the reins of leadership in his or her own hands.
Secondly, team members encourage one another, identifying each other's gifts
and motivating each other to develop and use them. As Max Warren used
to say, "Christian leadership has nothing whatever to do with self-assertion,
but everything to do with encouraging other people to assert themselves."[27]
Thirdly, team members are accountable to one another. Shared work means

shared responsibility. Then we listen to one another and learn from one another. Both the human family and the divine family (the body of Christ) are contexts of solidarity in which any incipient illusions of grandeur are rapidly dispelled. "The way of a fool seems right to him, but a wise man listens to advice" (Proverbs 12:15).

In all this Christian emphasis on service, the disciple is only seeking to follow and reflect his teacher. Though he was Lord of all, Jesus became the servant of all. Putting on the apron of servitude, he got down on his knees to wash the apostles' feet. Now he tells us to do as he did, to clothe ourselves with humility, and in love to serve one another (John 13:12 – 17; 1 Peter 5:5; Galatians 5:13). No leadership is authentically Christlike which is not marked by the spirit of humble and joyful service.

DISCIPLINE

Every vision has a tendency to fade. Every visionary is prone to discouragement. Hard work begun with zest can easily degenerate into drudgery. Suffering and loneliness take their toll. The leader feels unappreciated and gets tired. The Christian ideal of humble service sounds fine in theory but seems impractical. So leaders may catch themselves soliloquizing: "It is quicker to ride roughshod over other people; you get things done that way. And if the end is good, does it really matter what means we employ to attain it? Even a little prudent compromise can sometimes be justified, can't it?"

It is evident, then, that leaders are made of flesh and blood, not plaster or marble or stained glass. Indeed, as Peter Drucker has written, "Strong people always have strong weaknesses too."[28] Even the great leaders of the biblical story had fatal flaws. They too were fallen and fallible and frail. Righteous Noah got drunk. Faithful Abraham was despicable enough to risk his wife's chastity for the sake of his own safety. Moses lost his temper. David broke all five commandments of the second table of the law, committing adultery, murder, theft, false witness and covetousness, in that single episode of moral rebellion over Bathsheba. Jeremiah's lonely courage was marred by self-pity. John the Baptist, whom Jesus described as the greatest man who had ever lived, was overcome by doubt. And Peter's boastful impetuosity was doubtless a cloak for his deep personal insecurity. If those heroes of Scripture failed, what hope is there for us?

The final mark of Christian leaders is discipline, not only self-discipline in general (in the mastery of their passions, their time and their energies), but in particular the discipline with which they wait on God. They know their weakness. They know the greatness of their task and the strength of the opposition. But they also know the inexhaustible riches of God's grace.

Many biblical examples could be given. Moses sought God, and "the LORD would speak to Moses face to face, as a man speaks with his friend". David looked to God as his shepherd, his light and salvation, his rock, the stronghold of his life, and in times of deep distress "found strength in the LORD his God". The apostle Paul, burdened with a physical or psychological infirmity which he called his "thorn in the flesh", heard Jesus say to him, "My grace is sufficient for you", and learned that only when he was weak was he strong.

Our supreme exemplar, however, is our Lord Jesus himself. It is often said that he was always available to people. This is not true. He was not. There were times when he sent the crowds away. He refused to allow the urgent to displace the important. Regularly he withdrew from the pressures and the glare of his public ministry, in order to seek his Father in solitude and replenish his reserves of strength. Then, when it came to the end, he and his apostles faced the final test together. How is it, I have often asked myself, that they forsook him and fled, while he went to the cross with such serenity? Is the answer not that he prayed while they slept? (For Moses, see Exodus 33:11; Deuteronomy 34:10; for David, Psalm 23:1; 27:1; 1 Samuel 30:6; for Paul, 2 Corinthians 12:7 – 10; for Jesus, Mark 4:36; 6:45; 14:32 – 42, 50.)

It is only God who "gives strength to the weary and increases the power of the weak". For "even youths grow tired and weary, and young men stumble and fall". But those who "hope in the LORD" and wait patiently for him "will renew their strength. They will soar on wings like eagles; they will run and not grow weary, they will walk and not be faint" (Isaiah 40:29 – 31). It is only those who discipline themselves to seek God's face who keep their vision bright. It is only those who live before Christ's cross whose inner fires are constantly rekindled and never go out. Those leaders who think they are strong in their own strength are the most pathetically weak of all people; only those who know and acknowledge their weakness can become strong with the strength of Christ.

I have tried to analyse the concept of Christian leadership. It appears to consist of five main ingredients – clear vision, hard work, dogged perseverance, humble service and iron discipline.

In conclusion, it seems to me that we need to repent of two particularly horrid sins. The first is pessimism, which is dishonouring to God and incompatible with Christian faith. To be sure, we do not forget the fallenness, indeed the depravity, of human beings. We are well aware of the pervasiveness of evil. We are not so foolish as to imagine that society will ever become perfect before Christ comes and establishes the fullness of his rule.[29] Nevertheless, we also believe in the power of God – in the power of God's gospel to change society. We need to renounce both naïve optimism and cynical pessimism and replace them with the sober but confident realism of the Bible.

The second sin of which we need to repent is mediocrity, and the acceptance of it. I find myself wanting to say, especially to young people: "Don't be content with the mediocre! Don't settle for anything less than your full God-given potential! Be ambitious and adventurous for God! God has made you a unique person by your genetic endowment, upbringing and education. He has himself created you and gifted you, and he does not want his work to be wasted. He means you to be fulfilled, not frustrated. His purpose is that everything you have and are should be stretched in his service and in the service of others."

This means that God has a leadership role of some degree and kind for each of us. We need, then, to seek his will with all our hearts, to cry to him to give us a vision of what he is calling us to do with our lives and to pray for grace to be faithful (not necessarily successful) in obedience to the heavenly vision.

Only then can we hope to hear from Christ those most coveted of all words, "Well done, good and faithful servant!"

NOTES

1 Bennie E. Goodwin II, *The Effective Leader: A Basic Guide to Christian Leadership* (Downer's Grove: InterVarsity Press, 1971), p. 8.

2 William Shakespeare, *Twelfth Night*, Act II, scene iv, line 158.

3 J. Oswald Sanders, *Spiritual Leadership* (London: Marshall, Morgan & Scott, 1967; Lakeland ed., 1981), p. 20.

4 Proverbs 29:18. The NIV rendering is, "Where there is no revelation, the people cast off restraint."

5 Ronald A. Knox, *Enthusiasm, A chapter in the history of religion* (Oxford: Oxford Univ. Press, 1950), p. 591.

6 From the *Washington Post*, republished in the *Guardian Weekly*, June 1978.

7 Robert K. Greenleaf, *Servant Leadership: A Journey into the Nature of Legitimate Power and Greatness* (New York: Paulist Press, 1977), p. 236.

8 Douglas Hyde, *Dedication and Leadership: Learning from the Communists* (Chicago: Univ. of Notre Dame Press, 1966), pp. 15 – 16.

9 Ibid., p. 121.

10 Ibid., pp. 30 – 31.

11 Ibid., p. 52.

12 Ibid., p. 59.

13 Greenleaf, *Servant Leadership*, p. 16.

14 See "The Manila Manifesto", 1989, para. 11, in Stott (ed.), *Making Christ Known*, pp. 245 – 46.

15 David Bleakley, *Work: The Shadow and the Substance, A reappraisal of life and labour* (London: SCM, 1983), p. 85.

16 Quoted by William Barclay in his *Spiritual Autobiography, or Testament of Faith* (Oxford: Mowbray, and Grand Rapids: Eerdmans, 1975), p. 112.

17 From a review by Canon R. W. Howard of James Leasor, *Wheels to Fortune, The life and times of Lord Nuffield* (London: J. Lane, 1954).

18 Basil Matthews, John R. Mott, *World Citizen* (London: SCM, 1934), p. 357.

19 Reginald Coupland, *Wilberforce* (London: Collins, 1923; 2nd ed., 1945), p. 77.

20 John C. Pollock, *Wilberforce* (Oxford: Lion, 1977), p. 27. (Sir Reginald Coupland recounts the same incident in different words, *Wilberforce*, p. 9.)

21 Ibid., p. 56.

22 Ibid., p. 304.

23 Ibid., p. 308.

24 Greenleaf, *Servant Leadership*, pp. 7 – 10.

25 T. W. Manson, *The Church's Ministry* (London: Hodder & Stoughton, 1948), p. 27. See also John Stott, *Calling Christian Leaders* (Leicester: InterVarsity Press, 2002).

26 Sanders, *Spiritual Leadership*, p. 13.

27 M. A. C. Warren, *Crowded Canvas* (London: Hodder & Stoughton, 1974), p. 44.

28 Peter F. Drucker, *The Effective Executive* (New York: Harper & Row, 1966), p. 72.

29 See "The Lausanne Covenant", para. 15, in Stott (ed.), *Making Christ Known*, pp. 49 – 53.

STUDY
GUIDE

Study Guide

compiled by Matthew Smith

Before You Begin

This set of questions has been designed primarily for group study, including church groups and school classes, but is also suitable for individual reflection. For effective discussion, it is important that each person within the group has read the relevant chapter beforehand, and that the group leader has not only assimilated the material but given thought to which topics are particularly deserving of discussion in the time available and whether any additional questions would be helpful. The aim of each discussion should be both to understand and to apply the biblical teaching presented, and to this end it is suggested that the discussions start and end with prayer.

Chapter 1: Our Changing World: Is Christian Involvement Necessary?

1 Read Matthew 4:23; 9:35; and Acts 10:38. To what extent do you agree that both evangelism and social action are part of our Christian duty? Is anything gained by emphasizing one over the other?

2 What is your reaction when you hear people saying that the church should steer clear of politics? Given this answer, do you agree that the church should be concerned only with political principles and not policy?

3 Is democracy the only legitimate form of government from a Christian viewpoint?

4 Do you agree that Christians should become involved with society rather than escape from it? In what ways are you in danger of becoming isolated from the world around you? To what extent does your current church commitment prevent you from engaging with wider society?

5 As we look back at slavery and wonder how Christians tolerated it for so long, what issues today will future generations of Christians be critical of us for ignoring?

Chapter 2: Our Complex World: Is Christian Thinking Distinctive?

1 When discussing complex ethical issues, do you think that there can ever be "a Christian view", or only a range of Christian views?

2 Do you believe that God is interested in the "secular" as well as the "sacred"? Do your everyday life attitudes and decisions really reflect the answer you have just given?

3 Read Amos 1:3 – 2:8. Examine the main reason for God's judgement on each of the nations mentioned. Is God's concern for justice any less today than it was then?

4 Take a recent news story and seek to understand it by using the biblical framework of the creation, the fall, the redemption and the consummation.

5 What experience have you had in the past of Christians arguing that the use of the mind is unspiritual? How do such arguments compare with 1 Corinthians 14:20?

Chapter 3: Our Plural World: Is Christian Witness Influential?

1 What is pluralism? What are its dangers? Does it have any advantages?

2 Should Christians attempt to impose their views on a largely non-Christian nation? Can seeking to legislate on some moral issues be counterproductive? What criteria should be used in deciding when to make a sin against God into a crime against the state?

3 To what extent has postmodernism pervaded the thinking of your friends and colleagues? What difficulties have you encountered in persuading them to move away from the postmodern view that there is no absolute truth?

4 "We are called as Christians to witness to God's law and God's gospel without fear or apology." What fears, if any, stop you from speaking out for God's values to be upheld in society, and how can these fears be dealt with?

5 What particular social issue are you really committed to? Is there any group in your church through which you can develop this commitment? If not, would you consider starting up such a group?

Chapter 4: War and Peace

1 With a recent conflict in mind, discuss the legitimacy of this conflict using the principles of the *just war* theory.

2 Read Romans 12:17 – 21, followed by Romans 13:1 – 7. How do you reconcile the apparent discrepancy between the call for loving service of enemies and the call for punishment of evil-doers?

3 Read Genesis 9:6 and Romans 13:4. Does it necessarily follow from these texts that murder deserves capital punishment?

4 Can the indiscriminate use of conventional weapons, for example the "saturation" bombing of Dresden in 1945, ever be justified?

5 Imagine the situation where the UK and the US, threatened with defeat by an invading army equipped with superior conventional weapons, face the decision to resort to nuclear weapons, and so plunge the world into nuclear war. In this scenario, would it not be better to live under an oppressive regime, with all the suffering and slavery that would involve, than be responsible for destroying the whole of human civilization?

Chapter 5: Caring for Creation

1 What is your reaction when you hear horrifying environmental statistics? To what extent are you prepared to change your way of living to help promote environmental sustainability?

2 What do you understand to be the correct biblical interpretation of Genesis 1:26, 28?

3 "Every fifty years, in the Year of Jubilee, all land was to revert to its original owner." What biblical principles underlie the Year of Jubilee and how should those principles be applied today?

4 In terms of environmental stewardship, what debt does a present generation have to a future generation? What is the appropriate response for developed and developing nations to global warming and the Kyoto Protocol?

5 "It is more meaningful to speak of our responsibilities to and for animals than of rights possessed by animals themselves." To what extent does this responsibility cover:

   (a) encouraging production of free-range eggs and organic meat farming?

   (b) outlawing field sports such as fox-hunting, shooting and fishing?

   (c) preventing vivisection for medical (and cosmetic) research?

   (d) eating meat and wearing leather shoes?

Chapter 6: Living with Global Poverty

1 Do you agree that "while all cultures deserve respect, they do not all deserve equal protection and promotion"?

2 Do you accept the principle that as we are prepared to pay taxes in our own country, because we are one nation, so we should be willing to pay an international tax because we are one world?

3 What can you do and what are you prepared to do as an individual to help combat North-South economic inequality?

4 "In 2 Corinthians 8:15 Paul appeals to an Old Testament quotation about manna. God provided enough for everybody. Larger families gathered a lot, but not too much, for they had nothing over; smaller families gathered only a little, but not too little, for they had no lack. Each family had enough, because they collected according to need, not greed." Given the choices made in your current lifestyle, if you were born during this period, would you take sufficient manna or too much?

5 "We Christians should seek to become more committed internationalists" –
   by reading about other countries, visiting them if possible, welcoming overseas visitors into our homes, learning a second language and making friends
   with people of other cultures. Do you agree and if so, is there any action
   which you wish to take in response to this challenge?

6 "When Paul wrote, 'as we have opportunity, let us do good to all people, especially to those who belong to the family of believers' (Galatians 6:10), the
   purpose of his 'especially' was not to exclude unbelievers, but to remind us
   that our first responsibility is to our Christian brothers and sisters." Should
   we as Christians only give to Christian charities? Could your giving, to whatever causes, ever be legitimately described as "sacrificial"?

Chapter 7: Human Rights

1 Do you agree with William Temple when he writes, "There can be no Rights
   of Man except on the basis of faith in God. But if God is real, and all men are
   his sons, that is the true worth of every one of them"?

2 (a) Read Job 31:13 – 15; Proverbs 14:31; and Ephesians 6:9. What do these
       passages tell us about our innate equality as human beings and where
       this stems from?

   (b) "We must show 'no partiality' in our attitude to other people, and
       give no special deference to some because they are rich, famous or
       influential." What steps can we take in order to achieve this?

3 Read Romans 12:19 – 20; 1 Corinthians 6:7; 9:1 – 19; and Philippians 2:6 – 7.
   To what extent should we set aside our own rights in order to secure other
   people's rights? Discuss the difficulties experienced in putting these verses
   into practice.

4 "In our day dictators try to defend arbitrary arrest and detention … on the
   ground of 'national security'. One wonders how a biblical prophet would
   react." What is our reaction when mature democracies undertake seemingly
   similar actions, such as detaining prisoners in Guantanamo Bay in Cuba who
   are later released without charge?

5 It seems that across Western societies, individual rights and freedoms are rising, yet at the same time the rights of Christians to express biblical views are being eroded. How should Christians respond?

6 "The church should be the one community in the world in which human dignity and equality are invariably recognized, and people's responsibility for one another is accepted; in which the rights of others are sought and never violated, while our own are often renounced; in which there is no partiality, favouritism or discrimination; in which the poor and the weak are defended, and human beings are free to be human as God made them and meant them to be." What can you do to help make this more of a reality in your church?

Chapter 8: The World of Work

1 Discuss Genesis 1:28 and Genesis 2:8, 15 concerning the pre-fall commissioning of human beings. Specifically:

(a) Do you view work as a means to an end or an end in itself?

(b) Do you agree that Christians should see work and worship as inextricably intertwined with one another?

(c) In what ways does work (however broadly this is defined) bring fulfilment to yourself, benefit to the community, and glory to God?

2 Does your church affirm you in your work? How does it encourage you to work "as unto the Lord" because it is service for him? How can it support you better?

3 There are many difficulties in working life, for example the prospect of redundancy, a difficult boss, ethical dilemmas. Discuss some of the work difficulties you have faced or are facing at work and what the appropriate Christian response is.

4 Discuss the biblical pattern of six days work and one day rest and worship. In what ways do you treat the Sabbath as special?

5 Has work become so demanding in terms of time and emotions that it has become detrimental to your relationship with family and friends? If so, what is the right response to take?

Chapter 9: Business Relationships

1 Read 1 Chronicles 13:1–4. What does this passage teach us about decision-making, and how can this teaching be practically applied in a business context?

2 Is there such a thing as a "fair" level of pay differential between the salaries of top executives and the average worker? If so, is this fairness best determined by the market, by internal company discussion or by law?

3 Do you welcome the idea of consultation and partnership between employers and employees? Do you think that this partnership must necessarily include trade unions? In your own work environment, how can the helpful ideas of employees be better incorporated into the decision-making process?

4 Using the principles of love and justice as described in this chapter, discuss the "right" way of dealing with an underperforming member of a work team. Should a more lenient approach be taken within the context of a church or Christian organization?

5 Do you agree with George Monbiot's analysis that MNCs exert too much power in the world today? What, if any, should our response be?

Chapter 10: Celebrating Ethnic Diversity

1 Read Acts 17:22–31 and Galatians 3:28. What do these verses teach us about the following?

(a) The origin of every human being and the unity of the human race.

(b) The diversity of nations and cultures, and God's control over them.

(c) The finality of Jesus Christ.

(d) Our relationship to Christians in other nations.

2 (a) When did you last experience a racist attitude from an individual or an organization? What form did it take and how did you seek to challenge it?

(b) If there is a proven threat of terrorism from within particular ethnic groups, is it legitimate for the authorities to "stop and search" a higher percentage of people from these groups? When does such action turn into racism? What safeguards are needed to protect the freedom of the vast majority of people within these groups who are not connnected with terrorism?

3 Are you in the 50% of people (in the UK at least) who reportedly think that immigation of minority ethnic groups has led to a decline in the quality of life for others? What are the reasons for some people reacting against immigrants?

4 How should governments in the West approach immigation and asylum policy? For example:

(a) Should it be completely open?

(b) Should it be based on the ability of the applicant to contribute to the country?

(c) Should the home country of the applicant be relevant?

5 Think of your own culture:

(a) What particular aspects of it are especially tainted by sin?

(b) Read Revelation 21:24, 26, where it declares that the New Jerusalem will be enriched by human cultures. What positive aspects of your own culture can you enjoy and indulge to bring glory to God?

6 In what ways does your church exhibit and emphasize the universality and diversity of the body of Christ? How can you help to improve this?

Chapter 11: Simplicity, Generosity and Contentment

1 What instances of real abject poverty have you experienced or witnessed? What effect has this had on you? How long has this effect lasted?

2 What are the principles behind, and the modern-day equivalents of, the following Old Testament laws, and should these equivalents be practised today?

   (a) Farmers were not to reap their fields "to the very edges".

   (b) Every third year, a tenth of the agricultural produce was to be given to the poor.

   (c) Every seventh year, fields were to lie fallow.

3 In a capitalist economy where the rationale is the "survival of the fittest", how can Christians uphold the biblical perspective of the "protection of the weakest"?

4 Read 1 Samuel 2:8 and Psalm 113:5 – 9. Do you agree that an inherent characteristic of God is to champion the cause of the poor and rescue them from material poverty?

5 Is there any merit in simplifying your own lifestyle (or even living a "simple" lifestyle) out of solidarity with the poor and in order to give more resources to alleviating poverty? Should this be especially so for those involved in Christian leadership?

Chapter 12: Women, Men and God

1 How would you define feminism? With what aspects of it do you agree and disagree?

2 Look at Genesis 1:26 – 8; Deuteronomy 32:18; Isaiah 66:13; and Matthew 23:37. "Is it too much to say that since God, when he made humanity in his own image, made them male and female, there must be within the being of God himself something which corresponds to the 'feminine' as well as the 'masculine' in humankind?"

3 Examine Luke 7:36 – 50; 8:1 – 3; John 4:4 – 30; 8:1 – 11. For each passage, examine the way in which Jesus broke with the prevailing tradition in his attitude towards women.

4 Read 1 Corinthians 11:3 – 12; 14:34 – 35; Galatians 3:28; Ephesians 5:22 – 33; and 1 Timothy 2:11 – 15. How should Paul's writing about "masculine headship" be applied today:

(a) Within marriage?

(b) Within church teaching and leadership?

(c) Within wider society?

5 Think for a moment of how much Christ loved the church. How can husbands in your own church family be encouraged to better love their wives "just as Christ loved the church" (Ephesians 5:25)?

Chapter 13: Marriage, Cohabitation and Divorce

1 Read Matthew 5:31 – 32; 19:3 – 12. Do you think that those people who have been divorced should be able to remarry in church? Does your answer depend on whether the divorce is due to marital unfaithfulness?

2 Read 1 Corinthians 7:10 – 16. How do you respond to the following two allegations?

(a) Verses 10 and 11 have a special authority since they are "from the Lord" not "from Paul".

(b) Jesus permitted divorce on one ground only, and yet Paul added another.

3 (a) Do you agree that "it is more accurate and more helpful to speak of cohabitation as falling short of marriage, than as a stepping stone towards it"?

(b) Should Christians speak about the drawbacks of cohabitation to their friends who are not Christians and who may perceive them as being judgemental?

4 What is the best pastoral approach to take when Christian couples sleep together before marriage?

5 In what ways can your church better encourage and help:

(a) Married people to strengthen their marriage?

(b) Single people – both those who have never married and those who are divorced?

Chapter 14: Abortion and Euthanasia

1 Read the following texts: Psalm 139:13 – 16; Job 31:15; Psalm 119:73; Psalm 22:9 – 10; Jeremiah 1:5; Isaiah 49:1, 5; Luke 1:41, 44.

(a) At what stage from conception to birth do you think a cell or collection of cells becomes a human being?

(b) If you trace back your own history, at what point do you consider that you became "you"? Does Ephesians 1:4 help here?

2 Which of the following two statements do you agree with, and how does the answer reflect your view of the "morning after pill"?

(a) "The fetus has 'personhood' from the moment of fusion, and ... therefore, we must commit ourselves to its care."

(b) "From the moment of fusion the conceptus has biological life and a marvellous repertoire of potentiality, but ... it only becomes a person possessing rights and demanding care when brain development makes self-supervision possible."

3 In 1990 the time limit for abortions in the UK was reduced from twenty-eight weeks to twenty-four. Given that it is now commonplace for babies to survive even when born at twenty-three weeks, should the limit be reduced still further?

4 Is abortion ever justified in the following cases?

(a) The likely endangering of the life of the mother.

(b) To avoid injury to the physical or mental health of the mother or existing children.

(c) The discovery of serious disability.

(d) The pregnancy was the result of rape or incest.

5 Given that reportedly one in four women has had an abortion, what more can be done in churches to support women (and men) who may be suffering in silence?

6 Do you think anybody has the right to order their own death, and if so under what circumstances?

Chapter 15: The New Biotechnology

1 (a) Do you agree that in general, the use of biotechnology for restorative purposes is to be welcomed, whereas the use of biotechnology for enhancement purposes is to go beyond the human responsibility?

(b) In this context:

(i) Do you agree in principle with the practice of IVF as a means of providing children for infertile couples?

(ii) If so, do you agree that embryos should be pre-screened for genetic diseases such as sickle-cell anaemia and cystic fibrosis?

(iii) If so, do you agree that screening should take place for potential carriers as well as potential sufferers of these diseases?

(iv) If so, do you agree that screening should take place for embryos with a reduced risk (rather than a medical certainty) of suffering from serious diseases?

(v) If so, do you think that embryos could be chosen on the basis of the sex or other positive characteristics of the embryo (e.g., stronger limbs, better growth and quicker brains)?

2 Is human stem cell research involving the creation and destruction of human embroys up to fourteen days old consistent with a Christian worldview?

3 Read Genesis 3:21 – 4. Do you agree that in this passage God is protecting human beings from living for ever in their degraded fallen state, and so "human lifespan is limited, not just as a curse, but *out of God's grace*"? If so, to what extent should we seek to extend human life beyond our current average lifespan of seventy to eighty years (Psalm 90)?

4 Consider the situation of "saviour siblings", whereby a child is created for the purpose of acting as a matched tissue donor for an existing sibling with a genetic defect. Should "making" that second child for an ulterior motive, and forcing the child to play a role in the saving of the life of the first child, be considered as compassionate or manipulative?

5 Read Genesis 11:1 – 9. Discuss what implications this passage has for the biotechnology debate. What measures can we take as individuals to prevent bioethical technology in our society becoming a Tower of Babel?

Chapter 16: Same-Sex Relationships

1 Read Genesis 19:1 – 13 and related texts: Isaiah 1:1 – 17; Jeremiah 23:14; Ezekiel 16:49 – 50; Matthew 10:15; 11:24; Jude 7. In the Genesis text, the possible alternative translation of *yada'* allows Bailey's translation "bring them out so that we may get acquainted with them". Given this, do you agree with Bailey that there was no proposal of homosexual intercourse made by the mob outside Lot's house? Alternatively, do you agree that it was homosexual gang rape which was being condemned rather than homosexual intercourse per se?

2 Examine Leviticus 18:22 and 20:13. Do you think the main purpose of these texts are to prohibit ritual homosexual prostitution or to outlaw same-sex intercourse of any kind? What makes these texts binding today when set in the context of other laws such as Leviticus 19:19, "Do not wear clothing woven of two kinds of material"?

3 Read Romans 1:18 – 32; 1 Corinthians 6:9 – 10; and 1 Timothy 1:8 – 11.

   (a) Does Paul's description of homosexual relations as "unnatural" in Romans 1 refer to heterosexual people acting against their own nature (as argued by Boswell), or instead to all homosexual acts, whatever the orientation of the participant?

   (b) Given the meanings of the words translated as "male prostitutes" and "homosexual offenders" in 1 Corinthians 6:9 – 10 and "perverts" in 1 Timothy 1:10, do you think that these two texts refer only to male prostitution and commercial paederasty, or has it a wider implication to all same-sex intercourse?

   (c) Do you agree with Peter Coleman, who writes, "Taken together, St Paul's writings repudiate homosexual behaviour as a vice of the Gentiles in Romans, as a bar to the Kingdom in Corinthians, and as an offence to be repudiated by the moral law in 1 Timothy"?

4 What does Genesis 2:4 – 25 teach us about heterosexual marriage and how is this reinforced by Jesus in Matthew 19:4 – 7? Is there any room within this framework for a biblical endorsement of a lifelong homosexual partnership? Do you agree that since heterosexual monogamy was established by creation, not culture, its validity is both permanent and universal?

5 To what extent should Christians seek to enshrine biblical beliefs on homosexuality in legislation? What do you think of:

(a) Same-sex partnerships being legitimized by the state?

(b) Same-sex marriages being legitimized by the state?

6 Reread Alex Davidson's quote towards the end of the chapter. In what ways can we get alongside and help our Christian friends who struggle with issues of homosexuality? How should Christians react to the charge of homophobia?

Chapter 17: A Call for Christian Leadership

1 What issues in the world are you indignant about?

2 What issue in this book has most captivated you, and how can you become more involved in it?

3 What is your life's vision?

4 "The world can be won for Christ by evangelism, and made more pleasing to Christ by social action." What factors prevent this prospect setting our hearts on fire, and how can we overcome them?

5 Read Mark 4:36; 6:45; 14:32 – 42, 50. How can we learn from Jesus' example to ensure that the urgent does not crowd out the important?

6 "Don't be content with the mediocre! Don't settle for anything less than your full God-given potential! Be ambitious and adventurous for God!" How can we encourage one another to take up this challenge and persevere in it?

Index